Mencius
In
Modern Perspectives

In English and Traditional Chinese

Raymond K. Li

Mencius in Modern Perspectives

Copyright © 2021 Raymond K. Li

Researched and written by Raymond K. Li

All rights reserved. Without limiting the rights under the copyright reserved above, no part of this publication may be reproduced by any means, stored in, or introduced into a retrieval system, or transmitted in any form or by any means (electronic, mechanical, photocopying, recording, or otherwise) without prior written permission of the author.

For permission requests: please contact rayli3312@gmail.com

Printed in US.

Copyright Registration Number: TXu002280781

ISBN: 979-8-9851204-1-7 (paperback)
ISBN: 979-8-9851204-4-8 (ePub)
ISBN: 979-8-9851204-7-9 (mobi)

Library of Congress Control Number: 2021921206

Front Cover: Picture symbolizes that the heart (morality) is more important than money and power.

Other Books by Author:

1. Raymond K. Li, *Confucius Analects, A New Translation with Annotations and Commentaries,* (Bloomington, Indiana, iUniverse, 2020).

2. Raymond K. Li, *Sun Tzu's Military Principles, Applications to Business and Daily Life,* (Amazon Kindle Books, 2020).

3. Raymond K. Li, *Mencius in Modern Perspectives*, appearing in 2021—2022.

4. Raymond K. Li, *Mencius in Modern Perspectives in English and Simplified Chinese*, appearing in 2021—2022.

Table of Contents

PREFACE .... **XVII**

INTRODUCTION **1**
Section 1. Brief Biography of Mencius 1
Section 2. Historical Background 4
Section 3. Chronology of Mencius's Episodes 8
Section 4. Core Concepts of Confucianism 12

HIGHLIGHTS **41**
Constancy 41
Dao 41
Determination 41
Divine Wisdom 41
Fabric of Society 41
Filial Piety 42
Flexibility 42
Flippant Words 42
Forbearance 42
Fortunes vs. Misfortunes 43
Four Virtuous Beginnings 43
Friendship 44
Gift vs. Bribe 45
Governance 45
Good Timing 47
Judging Others 47
Learning 47
Li and Yi 47
Listening Discerningly 48

Magnanimous Spirit and Character	48
Mission of Life	48
Moral Strength	49
Morality	49
Overcoming Adversity	49
Patience	50
Power of Virtues	50
Procrastination	50
Promoting Wickedness	51
Purity	51
Ren	51
Ren and Li	52
Ren and Yi	53
Reputation	53
Sages vs. Fools	54
Self-cultivation	54
Self-examination	55
Self-rectification	55
Setting Good Examples	56
Shame	56
Sharing	56
Sincerity	56
Slander	57
Strong Medicine	57
Support of People	57
Unity	58
Warning	58
Wealth Disparity	58
Wisdom	58
Yi	59

CHAPTER 1: KING HUI OF LIANG (1) 60
Section 1 60
Section 2 64
Section 3 66
Section 4 69
Section 5 71
Section 6 73
Section 7 74

CHAPTER 2: KING HUI OF LIANG (2) 87
Section 1 87
Section 2 90
Section 3 91
Section 4 101
Section 5 104
Section 6 107
Section 7 108
Section 8 110
Section 9 111
Section 10 112
Section 11 113
Section 12 115
Section 13 117
Section 14 118
Section 15 119
Section 16 120

CHAPTER 3: GONG SUN CHOU (1) 123
Section 1 123
Section 2 127

Section 3 155
Section 4 157
Section 5 161
Section 6 162
Section 7 164
Section 8 166
Section 9 168

CHAPTER 4: GONG SUN CHOU (2) 172
Section 1 172
Section 2 174
Section 3 180
Section 4 182
Section 5 184
Section 6 187
Section 7 188
Section 8 190
Section 9 194
Section 10 198
Section 11 201
Section 12 203
Section 13 205
Section 14 206

CHAPTER 5: TENG WEN GONG (1) 208
Section 1 208
Section 2 210
Section 3 214
Section 4 220
Section 5 230

CHAPTER 6: TENG WEN GONG (2) 234
Section 1 234
Section 2 237
Section 3 239
Section 4 242
Section 5 244
Section 6 250
Section 7 251
Section 8 255
Section 9 256
Section 10 261

CHAPTER 7: LI LOU (1) 265
Section 1 265
Section 2 268
Section 3 270
Section 4 270
Section 5 271
Section 6 272
Section 7 274
Section 8 276
Section 9 278
Section 10 280
Section 11 281
Section 12 281
Section 13 282
Section 14 285
Section 15 286
Section 16 287
Section 17 287

Section 18.. 290
Section 19.. 291
Section 20.. 293
Section 21.. 294
Section 22.. 296
Section 23.. 296
Section 24.. 297
Section 25.. 298
Section 26.. 298
Section 27.. 299
Section 28.. 300

CHAPTER 8: LI LIAO (2) 302
Section 1.. 302
Section 2.. 303
Section 3.. 304
Section 4.. 305
Section 5.. 306
Section 6.. 306
Section 7.. 306
Section 8.. 307
Section 9.. 308
Section 10.. 308
Section 11.. 308
Section 12.. 311
Section 13.. 311
Section 14.. 312
Section 15.. 313
Section 16.. 314
Section 17.. 314
Section 18.. 314

Section 19..315
Section 20..317
Section 21..318
Section 22..323
Section 23..324
Section 24..327
Section 25..329
Section 26..331
Section 27..338
Section 28..340
Section 29..342
Section 30..344
Section 31..346
Section 32..348
Section 33..348

CHAPTER 9: WAN ZHANG (1).. **351**
Section 1..351
Section 2..353
Section 3..356
Section 4..360
Section 5..363
Section 6..366
Section 7..370
Section 8..372
Section 9..375

CHAPTER 10: WAN ZHANG (2).. **379**
Section 1..379
Section 2..384

Section 3... 387
Section 4... 389
Section 5... 396
Section 6... 397
Section 7... 401
Section 8... 404
Section 9... 405

CHAPTER 11: GAO ZI (1)... 408
Section 1... 408
Section 2... 410
Section 3... 413
Section 4... 415
Section 5... 418
Section 6... 421
Section 7... 427
Section 8... 430
Section 9... 432
Section 10... 433
Section 11... 436
Section 12... 437
Section 13... 438
Section 14... 438
Section 15... 440
Section 16... 441
Section 17... 443
Section 18... 444
Section 19... 445
Section 20... 445

CHAPTER 12: GAO ZI (2) 447
Section 1 447
Section 2 452
Section 3 455
Section 4 459
Section 5 461
Section 6 463
Section 7 469
Section 8 473
Section 9 475
Section 10 476
Section 11 478
Section 12 479
Section 13 479
Section 14 481
Section 15 482
Section 16 484

CHAPTER 13: UTMOST DEDICATION (1) 487
Section 1 487
Section 2 491
Section 3 492
Section 4 494
Section 5 495
Section 6 496
Section 7 497
Section 8 498
Section 9 500
Section 10 501
Section 11 502

Section 12 503
Section 13 503
Section 14 505
Section 15 506
Section 16 507
Section 17 507
Section 18 508
Section 19 508
Section 20 509
Section 21 510
Section 22 512
Section 23 513
Section 24 514
Section 25 516
Section 26 517
Section 27 518
Section 28 520
Section 29 520
Section 30 521
Section 31 522
Section 32 523
Section 33 524
Section 34 525
Section 35 526
Section 36 527
Section 37 529
Section 38 529
Section 39 530
Section 40 532
Section 41 533
Section 42 534

Section 43 535
Section 44 536
Section 45 537
Section 46 539

CHAPTER 14: UTMOST DEDICATION (2) 541
Section 1 541
Section 2 543
Section 3 544
Section 4 545
Section 5 546
Section 6 547
Section 7 547
Section 8 548
Section 9 548
Section 10 548
Section 11 549
Section 12 550
Section 13 551
Section 14 551
Section 15 556
Section 16 558
Section 17 558
Section 18 559
Section 19 560
Section 20 561
Section 21 562
Section 22 562
Section 23 565
Section 24 567
Section 25 568

Section 26 570
Section 27 571
Section 28 571
Section 29 572
Section 30 573
Section 31 574
Section 32 575
Section 33 576
Section 34 577
Section 35 579
Section 36 580
Section 37 582
Section 38 586

ENDNOTES **588**
1. Story of Yan Ying 588
2. Mo Zi 591
3. Story of Yi Yin 596
4. Story of Bai Li Xi 608
5. Story of Bo Yi and Shu Qi 612
6. Story of Qi Huan Gong and Guan Zhong 614
7. Story of Jiang Zi Ya 618
8. Story of Fu Yue 621
9. Story of Jiao Ge 624
10. Story of Sun Shu Ao 627

REFERENCES **631**

INDEX **632**

Preface

Mencius (also known as Meng Zi 孟子, or Meng Ke 孟轲, circa 372–289 BC) was a philosopher during China's Warring States Period (475–221 BC), a tumultuous and chaotic time. Mencius was the most prominent Confucian after Confucius (孔子, circa 551–479 BC). Confucians revere Mencius as a saint, second to Confucius, because Mencius expounded Confucius's doctrines in great breadth and depth.

The original book, *Mencius*, was written in Chinese by Mencius and his disciples. It documented Mencius's philosophy on self-cultivation, morality, governance, and politics. This philosophy has underpinned China's culture and mindset for millennia. Many salient teachings of Mencius are not only ancient treasures but also gems for modern society.

The objective of this book, *Mencius in Modern Perspectives*, is to expose these gems to English-speaking readers who are unfamiliar with ancient Chinese text. Unlike many translations of this classic, this book is not just a straightforward and verbatim translation of the original text. To facilitate a thorough understanding and deep appreciation of Mencius's philosophy, this book introduces the core concepts and jargon of Confucianism, a brief biography of Mencius, along with a chronology of his life, and the historical background of his era. Annotations, commentaries, and modern perspectives of the subject matter are provided under each section. The annotations contain explanations of the circumstance and location of the narrated episode, as well as the identities, roles, and backgrounds of the characters involved in each episode. Also provided in the commentary are elaborations, analyses, and critiques on the concepts, ideas, and doctrines

Mencius in Modern Perspectives

presented in each section. In the subsection of modern perspectives, the author provides hints about the relevance and applications of the teaching referenced in the section. The Endnotes chapter presents brief synopses of ten stories related to episodes described in earlier chapters. Each story illustrates important moral lessons in Chinese culture.

The author aims to provide an accurate, comprehensible, easy-to-read translation in modern writing style and context while trying to overcome five hurdles. First, the ancient Chinese forms, vocabulary, and sentence structures differ from modern-day Chinese. Hence, a straightforward, word-by-word, phrase-by-phrase translation would be incomprehensible and misleading. Second, writing styles in ancient China were brief and often ambiguous; thus, correctly interpreting the meaning of a sentence or choosing the best interpretation among many alternatives can pose a challenge. Third, ancient objects, social and political background, lifestyle, and concepts also differ from their modern counterparts; hence, it is difficult to find the right modern proxies. Fourth, since some Chinese concepts are abstract, it is difficult to find appropriate English words and phrases to accurately describe these concepts. Fifth, there is a need to cast the translation into a modern Western context so that readers can project ancient ideas into their own environment and lives. The author has tried to overcome these challenges as far as possible so that readers can enjoy reading this book as if Mencius were talking to them vividly in simple and colloquial English, thus enabling them to understand and relate Mencius's ideas to their lives.

In this translation, the names of characters in the original text are transcribed phonetically. Since the same transcribed name in English may refer to two different persons, to avoid confusion, this translation appends the names in Chinese characters to the

Preface

transcribed names. Wherever there is no English word or phrase to capture an abstract Chinese concept, a phonetically transcribed name for this concept is presented. A detailed explanation of the underlying concept of this name is presented in either the annotation sections or the Introduction chapter.

This book includes the ancient text of *Mencius* in traditional Chinese characters. Another version of the same book includes the ancient text of Mencius in simplified Chinese characters. A third version has only the English translation of the ancient text of *Mencius*.

Mencius in Modern Perspectives is neither a fiction nor a typical nonfiction. The primary objective of *Mencius* is to present Mencius's valuable teachings on self-cultivation to common readers. The secondary objective is to expound on the ideology of Mencius regarding political philosophy and public service.

The best way to extract the most benefit for self-cultivation is to read the book slowly, at a pace of a few paragraphs at a time, and then to pause, ponder, and continue with a few more paragraphs later. Upon reading a paragraph, the reader should think critically about the validity and implications of the teaching of the paragraph, internalize the teaching, and then apply it to his or her life, family, friends, work, society, and the world at large. It is important to lift the teachings out of their ancient context and adapt them to modern life. For example, superiors, bosses, authorities, leaders of society, and rulers of governments are substitutes for the notion of "kings" mentioned repeatedly in this book.

I am grateful to Mitchell Hedstrom for his encouragement and suggestions for improvements of this book and Patrick Kwong for his suggestions in editing and formatting the final copy.

Raymond K. Li

Mencius in Modern Perspectives

Introduction

Section 1. Brief Biography of Mencius

Mencius (also known as Meng Zi 孟子, Meng Ke 孟軻, Meng Zi Che 子車, and Meng Zi Ju 子居, circa 372–289 BC) was a native of the state of Zou (鄒國) in China during the Warring States Period (475–221 BC). He was the most prominent Confucian after Confucius (孔子, circa 551–479 BC). Confucians regarded Mencius as a saint second to Confucius.

Mencius was a descendant of a nobleman of the state of Lu (魯國). However, the territory owned by the Meng family was invaded and taken away by the state of Qi (齊) in about 408 BC. Mencius's father was forced to escape to the state of Zou and died when Mencius was just three years old. His mother was then reduced to poverty and needed to make a living by weaving cloth. She was a good mother, and **moved her home three times in search of a better location for her son to grow up. Once upon a time, Mencius played truant. She cut the woven cloth in halves in front of him, reprimanded him, and said, "Education is like weaving a piece of cloth. We must weave the yarn thread by thread. After laborious efforts, the yarn thread can be made into an inch of cloth and then into a foot. We can finally make a long piece of cloth for use. The same is true for education. After a long period of accumulation, you can then be well educated. Otherwise, it is like weaving a piece of cloth halfway, which results in the waste of all previous efforts."

At 15, Mencius became a student of Confucius's grandson, Zi Si (子思). However, the famous historian, Sima Qian (司馬遷, 145–86 BC), wrote in Shi Ji (史記, *Records of the Grand Historian*) that

Mencius learned under the followers of Zi Si. Having learned Confucian philosophy in depth, Mencius became a Confucian scholar and teacher in the state of Zou. He taught 18 excellent disciples, including Gong Sun Chou (公孫丑) and Wan Zhang (萬章).

Hundreds of battles broke out during the tumultuous Warring States Period. Feudal lords often fought against each other to capture more territories and extinguish other states. They were greedy, decadent, and cruel to their people, and the lives of common people were hellish. Morality in society dropped into the abyss. In view of this awful environment, and with the hope of bringing peace and morality to the country, at the age of 40, accompanied by his disciples, Mencius set forth on a tour to many feudal states to preach his doctrine of love, benevolence, righteousness, and propriety to feudal lords. Although he had some success in catching the attention of a couple of feudal lords, he was generally unsuccessful in his endeavor. Most feudal lords rejected Mencius's political philosophy that the people of a country were more important than the king.

On the contrary, the disciples of the School of Strategic Diplomacy (縱橫家), founded by Guiguzi (鬼谷子, also known as the Sage of Ghost Valley, circa 400–320 BC), were employed and highly regarded by feudal lords. For example, Zhang Yi (張儀) became the prime minister of the most powerful state of Qin (秦), while his schoolmate, Su Qin (蘇秦), became the prime minister of the coalition of six hegemons against the state of Qin. The state of Wei hired Pang Juan (龐涓) as the chief commander of its army, and his schoolmate, Sun Bin (孫臏), was appointed the top military strategist for the state of Qi (齊). All these men were contemporaries of Mencius and were successful strategists, diplomats, and statesmen. They all assisted feudal lords in their struggle for more power and conquests. A prominent figure of the Yin-Yang School,

Zou Yan (騶衍), another of Mencius's contemporaries, was also highly regarded by the feudal lords. His reputation and influence among the feudal lords were far above Mencius's. This school applied the mystic theory of Yin and Yang to governance and geopolitics. The apparent sophistication of its theory appealed to feudal lords who believed that its application could help them fulfill their ambition.

In the circle of scholars and philosophers, Mencius also faced two major competing schools of thought. These were respectively led by Yang Zhu (楊朱, circa 440–360 BC), who advocated extreme individualism, and Mo Zi (墨子, circa 470–391 BC, also known as Mo Di, 墨翟), who advocated universal and indiscriminative love. Yang Zhu was popular in the grassroots, while Mo Zi was influential in the state of Song (宋).

Therefore, Mencius was just a lonely voice in the wilderness. His great philosophy was unpopular among feudal lords and people in power. At 65, Mencius retired from politics and retreated to the state of Zou. He focused on teaching disciples and writing the book *Mencius*, which was essentially a memoir of his conversations with feudal lords, scholars, government officials, and his disciples. Some later scholars thought that *Mencius* was co-authored by his top disciple, Wan Zhang, while some other thought that some chapters of the book were appended and compiled by later followers of Mencius.

Zhu Xi (朱熹, 1130–1200 AD), a prominent Confucian in the government of the Song Dynasty (宋), designated the Four Books—*The Book of Great Learning* (大學), *The Book of the Mean* (中庸, also known as *The Doctrine of the Mean*), *The Analects* (論語), and *Mencius* (孟子)—as the required syllabus for the imperial examination for the recruitment to the civil service. In 1330 AD, the emperor of the Yuan Dynasty designated Mencius as the second saint after Confucius.

Section 3 below shows the chronology of episodes of Mencius's journey in life.

Section 2. Historical Background

To have a better understanding and appreciation of the philosophy of Mencius and Confucianism in general, it is necessary to know the history of China. The following summarizes Chinese history up to the Warring States Period.

The Age of Legends

The Chinese civilization began in the Age of Legends. Archeologists are still debating when this period started, with some considering the start as early as 600,000 years ago, while others believe that it was about 10,000 years ago. This period ended about 5000 years ago. This period was subdivided into subperiods—Nu Wa (女媧), Nest Clan (有巢氏), Flint Clan (燧人氏), Fu Xi (伏羲氏), and Shen Nong Clan (神農氏). The society was matrilineal at the beginning of this period but became patriarchal towards the end of the period. According to legends, the leader of Nu Wa was a goddess who mended openings in the sky to protect her clansmen. The Nest Clan learned how to build nests on trees to protect people from wild beasts and floods. The Flint Clan learned how to start a fire with pieces of stone and wood. During the Fu Xi period, the Chinese civilization advanced substantially. The leader, Fu Xi, taught his people husbandry, farming, fishing, and the domestication of horses, dogs, donkeys, pigs, cats, and so on. He also developed the eight trigrams for fortune-telling. The Shen Nong Clan, headed by Emperor Yan (炎帝), further developed agriculture and grew five types of grains for food staples.

Introduction

Period of Five Emperors (circa 3000–2200 BC)

Written language was developed towards the end of the Age of Legends, which led to the production of historical records, albeit scantily. The next period was called the period of Five Emperors: Emperor Yan, Huang Di (黃帝, Yellow Emperor), Yao (堯), Shun (舜), and Yu (禹). Some historians defined the Five Emperors as: Huang Di, Zhuan Xu (顓頊), Ku (嚳), Yao, and Shun. This period started between 5000 and 6000 years ago. The most popular view is that the Yellow Emperor existed 5000 years ago. By this time, the Chinese civilization had developed considerably. The Yellow Emperor invented the compass, discovered silk, and developed weaving, sewing, the science of human biology, internal medicine, the farmers' almanac, the lunar calendar, and simple machinery for farming and hunting. In the eras of Yao (堯, circa 2356–2255 BC) and Shun (舜, circa 2294–2184 BC), Chinese written language was developed further to the extent that even modern scholars can understand or decipher some ancient texts written and inscribed during that time. This was critical to the development of Chinese civilization during the next four millennia. During the period of the Five Emperors, leaders were chosen or elected on their merits, competence, virtue, and track records, and not by force or inheritance. Later scholars, such as Confucians, regarded these leaders as saintly emperors.

Xia Dynasty (circa 2184–1600 BC)

Before Emperor Shun died in approximately 2184 BC, he chose the Great Yu (禹, circa 2237–2139 BC) to be his successor. The Great Yu and his father were civil engineering ministers in charge of flood control, irrigation, and water management. The Great Yu earned immense credit for completing a large-scale water conservancy and flood control project. Before Yu died, he originally wanted to pick a capable minister as his successor. However, other members of his cabinet supported his son, Qi, who was regarded as competent and virtuous as his father. The Great Yu therefore chose Qi as his successor. Emperor Qi then founded the Xia Dynasty (夏朝). From then on, succession to the throne was based on inheritance and family lineage.

Shang Dynasty (circa 1600–1066 BC)

The history of the Xia Dynasty was better documented. The dynasty lasted for about 500 years. After 15 successions to the throne, the empire was ruled by a tyrant, Emperor Jie (桀). In circa 1600, Tang (湯, 1670–1587 BC) overthrew Emperor Jie and founded the Shang Dynasty (商朝), which was also called the Yin Dynasty (殷朝).

Zhou Dynasty (1066–256 BC)

The Shang Dynasty lasted for about 600 years. After 30 successions to the throne, the empire was ruled by a brutal tyrant, Emperor Zhou (紂), also known as Emperor Xin (帝辛). King Wu of Zhou (周武王, died 1043 BC), whose father was King Wen of Zhou (周文王, 1152–1056 BC), overthrew Emperor Zhou and founded the Zhou Dynasty in 1066 BC.

Confucians regarded Yao, Shun, Yu, Tang, King Wen, and King Wu as saintly kings. During their regimes, ancient China had a near utopian society.

From 1066 BC to 770 (or 771) BC, the new dynasty was called the Western Zhou Dynasty (西周) because its capital was located at Hao Jing (鎬京) in the west of China. With the introduction of feudalism, members of the royal family, prominent ministers, and generals were designated into five nobility ranks: duke, marquess, earl, viscount, and baron. Dukes and marquesses were each enfeoffed a territory of one hundred square miles; earls were each enfeoffed a territory of seventy square miles; and viscounts and barons were each enfeoffed a territory of fifty square miles. The feudal lords had autonomy over their enfeoffed territories, which were de facto independent states. The states had their own armies, which must be smaller than that of the central government. The states had to pay taxes and tributes to the central government and respond to summons by the emperor. The states also had the responsibility of defending the central government when it was under foreign attack. After 12 successions of emperors of the Western Zhou Dynasty, nomads from the west invaded the country, pillaged the capital, and killed King You (周幽王) of Zhou in 770 BC. His successor, King Ping (周平王), moved the capital eastward to Luo Yi (雒邑, modern-day Luo Yang 洛陽 in Henan Province 河南). This began the Eastern Zhou Dynasty (東周). During this regime, the emperor of Zhou lost effective control over many feudal states, which only paid a ceremonial homage to the emperor. The feudal states fought among themselves, and small states were conquered, pillaged, destroyed, or annexed by larger states. Historians call this period, which stretched from 771 to 476 BC, the Spring-Autumn period because Confucius wrote the Spring-Autumn Annals, a chronicle of the state of Lu (魯國), between 722 to 479 BC. The political map during the early part of the Spring-Autumn period, from 685 to 591 BC, was dominated by Five Hegemons: the states of Qi (齊), Song (宋), Jin (晉), Qin (秦), and Chu (楚); or alternatively, Qi (齊), Chu (楚), Jin (晉), Wu (吳), and Yue (越). Between 497 to 453 BC, the state of Jin broke up into three states: Han (韓), Zhao (趙), and Wei (魏). Therefore, during the second part of the Spring-Autumn period, from about 592 to 474 BC, there were seven hegemons: the states of Qi (齊), Chu (楚), Yue (越), Han (韓), Zhao (趙), Wei (魏), and Qin (秦).

It was ironic that the Chinese culture and civilization blossomed during a tumultuous time. About a hundred different ideologies were founded by innovative thinkers. Among them, the most famous were the Confucians, Taoists, Yin-Yang, Legalists, Logicians, Mohist, Diplomatic Strategists, Eclectics, and Agriculturists.

Warring States Period (475–221 BC)

The Western Zhou Dynasty lasted for 285 years. Subsequently, the Spring-Autumn period lasted for 295 years and turned into the Warring States Period towards the end of the Eastern Zhou Dynasty. The Warring States Period started in 475 BC and ended in 221 BC. The country was dominated by seven hegemons: Qi (齊), Chu (楚), Yan (燕), Han (韓), Zhao (趙), Wei (魏), and Qin (秦). Many wars broke out during this period as states struggled to gain more territories by conquering and annexing other states. Two battles are relevant to Chapter 1, 2, and 14 below. In the first battle of Gui Ling (桂陵) in 353 BC, the state of Wei (魏), the aggressor, was badly defeated by the state of Qi (齊). In the second battle of Ma Ling (馬陵), the entire army of the state of Wei, once again the aggressor, was annihilated by the state of Qi.

Section 3. Chronology of Mencius's Episodes

The following chronology of episodes during the life of Mencius relates to the conversations and teachings of this book:

Mencius was born in the state of Zou (鄒國) around 372 BC.

When Mencius was 15 years old, he was a student at the Confucian school, led by Zi Si (子思, 483–402 BC), the grandson of Confucius and the author of the *Book of the Mean* (also known as the *Doctrine of the Mean*, 中庸).

After Mencius graduated, he started teaching disciples for over a decade.

At 40, Mencius began meeting feudal lords and preaching his philosophy to them. His first meeting was with Zou Mu Go (鄒穆公, also known as Duke Mu of Zou, 382–330 BC). Their dialogue is shown in Section 12 of Chapter 2 below.

At 41, Mencius moved to the city of Ping Lu (平陸), located on the border of the state of Qi (齊). This event is described in Section 4 of Chapter 4 below.

At 42, Mencius went to the state of Ren (任) and met Ji Ren (季任), the younger brother of the king of the state of Ren and the regent of the state. This episode is shown in Section 5 of Chapter 12 below. He also spoke with Cao Jiao (曹交), a princeling of a small state of Cao (曹) and a spoiled kid. This episode is described in Section 2 of Chapter 12.

At 43, Mencius went to the state of Qi (齊) for the first time. There, he met Prince Dian (王子墊) of Qi. This episode is described in Section 33 of Chapter 13 below.

At 44, Mencius debated with Gao Zi (告子). This episode is described in Sections 1 to 6 of Chapter 11 and Section 3 of Chapter 12. Mencius also spoke with Qi Wa (蚳鼃), an official of the state of Qi.

Mencius also spoke with Kuang Zhang (匡章), a general of the state of Qi. This episode is described in Section 10 of Chapter 6. Mencius then left the state of Qi and traveled to the state of Song (宋).

At 45, Mencius arrived at the state of Song and stayed there.

At 46, still in the state of Song, Mencius met Teng Wen Gong (滕文公), the prince of the state of Teng (滕) at that time. Mencius preached his doctrine to the prince. This episode is described in Section 1 of Chapter 5 below. Mencius also spoke with Song Guo Jian (宋勾踐) about the principles of lobbying. This episode is described in Section 9 of Chapter 13.

At 47, Mencius left the state of Song and returned to the state of Zou.

At 48, Mencius stayed in the state of Zou. Teng Wen Gong (滕文公, also known as Duke Wen of state of Teng (滕), successor to the throne in 326 BC) sent his teacher Ran You (然友) to consult Mencius about the funeral of Teng's father. Mencius subsequently moved to the state of Teng and advised Teng Wen Gong on good governance. The conversation between Mencius and Teng Wen Gong is described in Chapter 5 and 6.

At 49, Mencius debated with Chen Xiang (陳相), an Agriculturist, on the fallacy of the theory of Agriculturists. This episode is described in Section 4 of Chapter 5 below.

At 50, Mencius was asked by Teng Wen Gong about how to deal with the state of Qi, which was fortifying a city wall next to the state of Xue (薛), a neighbor of the state of Teng. This episode is described in Section 14 of Chapter 2 below.

At 52, Mencius visited King Hui of Liang (梁惠王). Their conversation is described in Chapter 1 and 2 below.

At 53, Mencius discussed the duration of a mourning vigil with Gong Sun Chou (公孫丑), his disciple. This episode is described in Section 13 of Chapter 13 below.

At 54, Mencius met King Xiang of Liang (魏襄王), the heir of King Hui of Liang. Mencius considered King Xiang unworthy of being a king. Mencius also met Prince Dian of the state of Qi in the city Fan of Qi. This episode is shown in Section 36 of Chapter 13 below. Later that year, Mencius met King Xuan of Qi (齊宣王, 350–301 BC) and became the top advisor to King Qi. The conversation between Mencius and King Xuan is shown in Section 7 of Chapter 1 and Sections 1 to 11 of Chapter 2 below. Mencius also taught his disciple, Gong Sun Chou, the concepts of magnanimous spirit, great valor, and resolute, undaunted, and incorruptible heart. This lesson is shown in Section 2 of Chapter 3 below.

At 56, Mencius was sent by King Xuan of Qi to attend the funeral of Teng Wen Gong. This episode is described in Section 6 of Chapter 4 below.

At 57, Mencius took a leave of absence from his job in the state of Qi and went to the state of Lu to bury his mother. This episode is described in Section 7 of Chapter 4 below. While Mencius was in the state of Lu, the Duke of the state of Lu, Lu Ping Gong (魯平公, 314–294 BC), wanted to see Mencius but was dissuaded by his eunuch, Zang Can (臧倉). This episode is described in Section 16 of Chapter 2 below. After Mencius returned to the state of Qi, he discussed the thickness of his mother's coffin with his disciple, Chong Yu (充虞). This episode is described in Section 7 of Chapter 4 below. King Xuan of Qi wanted to invade the state of Yan (燕) and consulted Mencius, who advised against the invasion. King Xuan did not take Mencius's advice.

At 60, Mencius told King Xuan that if the king treated his ministers as dirt, they would consider the king to be a robber. This episode is described in Section 3 of Chapter 8 below. Mencius left the state of Qi, frustrated with the behavior of King Xuan of Qi. This episode is described in Sections 10 to 14 of Chapter 4 below. The state of Yan rebelled against the state of Qi. King Xuan of Qi regretted that he did not listen to Mencius. This episode is described in Section 9 of Chapter 4 below. Chun Yu Kun (淳于髡), a minister for King Xuan of Qi, tried to persuade Mencius to stay in the state of Qi. This episode is described in Section 17 of Chapter 7 below.

After Mencius left the state of Qi, he met Song Keng (宋牼), an elderly scholar and lobbyist, at Shi Qiu (石丘). Mencius advised Song Keng against lobbying based on benefits. This episode is described in Section 4 of Chapter 12.

At 65, Mencius retired from his political activities, retreated to the state of Zou, and taught more disciples. He died at the age of 83.

Section 4. Core Concepts of Confucianism

The following core concepts of Confucianism must be explained here to provide an accurate interpretation and understanding of Mencius's thoughts. They are the Four Virtuous Beginnings—Ren, Yi, Li, and Wisdom—together with Dao and Te.

Ren (and Ren virtue, 仁): This Chinese word is translated by some scholars as "benevolence" and "kind-heartedness". Since these English words do not convey the full meaning of Ren under Confucianism, this book adopts the transcription from the Chinese word *Ren* to represent the complex concept and provides detailed explanation of the concept under this transcribed name. This approach will help the reader get a deeper understanding of the Confucian philosophy. The Chinese word (仁) can be analyzed etymologically as a combination of two words—on the left-hand side, there is the word *Man* (亻 or 人), and on the right-hand side, there is the word *Two* (二). Therefore, the combination means "Two Men". The ancient Chinese used this word to symbolize how one person should deal with another person. If the word is re-written as (人人), and the first word (人) is used as a verb and the second word (人) is used as a noun, the combination means how to treat another person as a human being, not as an animal. When social structure and civilization progressed from the pre-historical period to the Yao and Shun dynasties, the concept of Ren became more sophisticated. It evolved from the concept of "treating another person as a human being" to the love and care of dear ones in the family. The concepts of love and care further extended to the love, care and responsibilities to relatives, the clan, the tribe, the country, and finally, to the world. By the Zhou Dynasty, these were explicitly taught, decreed, and mandated in the form of social norms and rituals called the Li (禮) framework.

Confucius further developed the concept of Ren and made it the center of his philosophy. As recorded in the *Analects*, Confucius mentioned Ren over one hundred times, although he did not explicitly define the word. When Confucius was asked by his disciples to describe Ren in brief, he summarized it as thus: "Ren is about people. Ren is about the love of people." When Fan Chi, a disciple of Confucius, asked him about Ren, Confucius replied, "Love people" (see Section 22 of Chapter 12 of *Confucius Analects).* The *Spring-Autumn Annals* (春秋) stated, "Ren is about the love of others, not about the love of myself. Yi (義) is about controlling and correcting myself, not about controlling and correcting others." From the *Analects* and later works by Confucius's followers, Ren was regarded a core moral concept that provided the foundation for many other virtues. For example, filial piety (孝) is an aspect of Ren because it is about the love and care of parents. Fraternity (悌) is an aspect of Ren because it is about the love and care of brothers. Loyalty (忠) is an aspect of Ren because it is about the love of the country, the love of one's boss for his good, and the love of one's company for its good. Honesty and trust (信) are also derived from Ren because the absence of honesty and trust will hurt other people. Forgiveness and leniency (寬) are related to Ren because it is about showing kindness to wrong doers. Generosity (惠) is an aspect of Ren because it concerns kindness to people in need. Respect for ancestors (敬祖) is an aspect of Ren because it is related to the kindness to the dead. Humility (謙) is related to Ren because it promotes friendliness and reduces animosity with people. This list goes on.

The love of people is extended beyond the love of individuals to the love of family, relatives, friends, clan, community, society, country, and the world. Confucius said, "Set yourself on the path to morality, be guided by virtuous principles, act according to Ren, and roam the world with your skills" (see Section 6 of Chapter 7, 述而, of *Confucius Analects*). Confucius also said, "When a person with the Ren virtue sets a goal, he would also help others to set the same. When he desires success in achieving the goal, he would help others to achieve the same. He can find handy occasions and circumstances in daily life to set good examples for people. This is a way to practice the Ren virtue" (see Section 30 of Chapter 6, 雍也, of *Confucius Analects*). Zheng Zi (曾子), the disciple of Confucius, said, "One must persevere in lofty goals because the responsibility is big and the commitment is long. Practicing and fostering the Ren virtue is a big responsibility, isn't it? Upholding this virtue until death is a long commitment, isn't it?" (see Section 7 of Chapter 8, 泰伯, of *Confucius Analects*). The principle of Ren was, therefore, the foundation of the political theory of Confucianism. A chapter in the *Book of Ritual* (also known as *Li Ji*, 禮記：緇衣) quoted Confucius's words: "A sovereign is primarily its people (君以民為本)." Numerous paragraphs of this book mentioned repeatedly Mencius's political philosophy based on Ren principles. For example:

    a) "Sharing one's happiness with people is the true happiness" (Section 2 of Chapter 1).

    b) "Since your people have abundant food, fish, and wood, they do worry about their livelihood and their funerals. This is how a benevolent government should provide for" (Section 3 of Chapter 1).

    c) "Some rich people throw away food for humans to dogs and pigs lavishly and ignore starving people on the street. When they see poor people dying from starvation, they even say, 'It is not my business. It is their fate.' How is this different from killing a person with a sword and saying, 'I did not kill him; the sword killed him'?" (Section 3 of Chapter 1).

d) "Yet many rulers, who are supposed to be protectors and parents of their people, often commit misdeeds, which are equivalent to sending out wild beasts to devour people. They betray their role as protectors and parents of their people. Confucius once said, 'Those who invented the use of figurines as burial artefacts deserved to have no descendants.' This is because even the idea of using of human images as burial artefacts is evil" (Section 4 of Chapter 1).

e) "If your Majesty implements humane and benevolent policies, reduces the severity of punishments and the burden of taxation, promotes farming, and encourages young people to spend their free time to learn and practice the virtues of filial piety, fraternity, loyalty, honor, and trust, so that they will seriously take care of their parents and siblings at home and serve their superiors at work, your country will be strong enough to fight even with cudgels against strong armies of the states of Qin and Chu" (Section 5 of Chapter 1).

f) "Nowadays, there is no ruler who hates killing people. If there is one who hates killing people, everybody in the world will yearn for his advent. People will certainly follow and support him like cascading water. Who can stop them?" (Section 6 of Chapter 1).

g) "This kind heart is already sufficient for you to be a benevolent and magnanimous ruler! Your people know that your Majesty has a kind heart. Your ministers definitely know that you are a compassionate person" (Section 7 of Chapter 1).

h) "Your people are not protected and appeased because you do not want to foster their welfare. Therefore, your Majesty has not implemented a benevolent and magnanimous government and unified the entire dynasty because you do not want to do it, and not because you are unable to do it" (Section 7 of Chapter 1).

i) " 'Be a good model, first to your wife, then to your brothers, and finally, to the country.' It essentially says that you should apply your kindness to others. Therefore, the fostering of kindness can help you protect the whole world. Otherwise, you cannot protect even your wife" (Section 7 of Chapter 1).

j) "If you implement a benevolent governance, all competent and talented people in the entire empire will work for your government, peasants will flock to the fields of your country, merchants will come to your markets to trade, tourists will visit attractions in your country, and all dissidents from other countries will immigrate to your country. If you can accomplish these, who can fight against you?" (Section 7 of Chapter 1).

k) "Suppose that when your Majesty is playing music, your people, hearing the drum-beats and sound of flutes and pipes, say to one another joyfully, 'It is likely that our king has recovered from sickness.

Introduction

That is why he can play music.' Suppose that when your Majesty is hunting, your people, hearing the noise of your carriages and horses and watching glamorous flags of your procession, say to one another joyfully, 'It is likely that our king has recovered from sickness. That is why he can hunt.' Why? It is because you share your happiness with people. Therefore, if you share your happiness with people, you will become a benevolent and magnanimous ruler of the entire empire" (Section 1 of Chapter 2).

l) "If, on the contrary, your Majesty implements a benevolent policy, your people will love you and your officials and will be willing to die for you" (Section 12 of Chapter 2).

On a personal level, Ren occupies the highest place among all virtues. Ren should not be interpreted narrowly as romantic love between two sexes or love that arises from emotion. Ren is a moral concept, and therefore, a virtue. Confucius said, "I have not met a person who is really dedicated to the practice of Ren, and a person who detests others for lack of Ren. Those who are dedicated to Ren are unsurpassable" (see Section 6 of Chapter 6, 里仁, of *Confucius Analects*). The attainment and perfection of the Ren virtue should be a life-long goal for any great man. The requirement of selfless love of others is very demanding. Confucius said, "A hero who is determined to uphold the Ren virtue would not seek to live at the expense of hurting his Ren virtue, but he would sacrifice his life in order to preserve it" (see Chapter 15, 衛靈公, of *Confucius Analects*).

Since Ren occupies the highest place among all virtues,

Confucians consequently consider that Ren is also a fundamental moral yardstick to determine right from wrong.

As a virtue, Ren is an internal quality of one's character and a component of his will. Confucius said, "Is Ren virtue far away? If you desire to have Ren virtue, it is here right now" (see Section 30 of Chapter 7, 述而, of *Confucius Analects*). Ren also affects one's emotions, psychology, and spirit. Mencius advanced the theory that the seed (or root) of Ren virtue is innate, and that people were born with pathos, sympathy, empathy, and compassion (see later chapters). However, such in-born qualities are inadequate and nascent. One must relentlessly learn and listen critically, and gain experience from practicing Ren to develop his Ren virtue. Confucius said, "The love of benevolence and kindness without the quest for learning would lead to the flaw of foolish simplicity" (see Section 8 of Chapter 17, 陽貨, of *Confucius Analects*). Confucius also said, "Reviewing and practicing regularly what you have learned is a pleasure indeed, isn't it?" (see Section 1 of Chapter 1, 學而, of *Confucius Analects*).

Yi (義): This Chinese word is often translated as "righteousness." However, it has a deeper meaning than righteousness. As mentioned above, Ren is a fundamental moral yardstick to determine right from wrong. Ren tells one's heart what needs to be done, whereas Yi tells what must be done by him. Ren is the motivator, and Yi is the implementer. Ren is the internal content, and Yi is the external exercise of that content. Ren is the goal and Yi is the means to achieve the goal. Whereas Ren is about doing good to others, Yi is about the fulfillment of one's mission, self-control, and self-improvement in response to Ren. As a virtue and moral principle, Yi requires one to do what he needs to do and to refrain from doing what he is not supposed to do. The *Spring-Autumn Annals* (春秋)

mentioned that, "Ren is about love of others, not about love of myself. Yi is about controlling and correcting myself, not about controlling and correcting others." One should apply Ren virtue to deal with others but take Yi to direct and control oneself. For example, one should be forgiving on others but strict on oneself.

The Chinese word Yi (義) can, therefore, be analyzed etymologically. It contains two Chinese words: *lamb* (羊) on top of the word *myself* (我). In ancient nomadic times, lamb meat formed a major part of the diet. Over time, a lamb symbolized nourishment, wellness, kindness, graciousness, beauty, purity, and goodness. The arrangement of the word *lamb* on top of the word *myself*, and not by the side of *myself*, means that the principle of goodness, kindness, nourishment, and so on is my master.

As the *Book of Zhong Yong (The Doctrine of the Mean*, 中庸) states, "Yi means appropriateness." This means that the Yi virtue not only motivates one to act righteously in response to Ren, but also appropriately. Hence, this implies flexible and adaptable actions.

Confucius focused on Ren in his teachings, whereas Mencius focused more on Yi and elevated its position next to Ren. Therefore, in Chinese, Ren is often combined with Yi to become Ren Yi (仁義), meaning "the highest virtue." According to Mencius, the Yi virtue also has high idealistic requirements: one must be ready to sacrifice one's benefit, and even his life, for the good of others; one must not expect any reward from doing good; one must have a sense of mission, take responsibility, take risks, and be willing to face negative consequences from his actions to pursue Ren; in the course of doing good, one must have the courage to overcome hardship, hurdles, objections, and economic, social, and political pressures; the beneficiaries of one's good actions may not be related to him, may have lower social status, may be unknown to him or may even be vaguely defined because he is following a righteous principle according to Ren; and the motivation of doing good is spontaneous, and a second-nature. These ideas on Yi are discussed in many chapters of this book.

Mencius considered that the Yi virtue was an internal quality of a person's mind and will, and that it is an integral part of one's personality. The urge and the passion to do good should come naturally from the heart, and not from external requests from others, social expectations, the desire to simply please others and to gain acceptance and fame, submission to pressure, or the need to comply with legal requirements. Confucius said, "Most people nowadays think that filial piety is just about feeding your old parents. Even dogs and horses are fed by people. If you do not respect your parents, how do you differentiate feeding your parents from feeding dogs and horses?" (see Section 7 of Chapter 2, 為政, of *Confucius Analects*). The internalization of the Yi virtue is a key concept of Mencius, who refuted some Confucians of his time, such as Gao Zi. To Mencius, the externalization of the Yi virtue proposed by Gao Zi walked on a slippery slope, which could lead to hypocrisy. Confucius said, "If you use laws and regulations to guide and rule your people, and punishment to enforce their compliance, they will be decadent and shameless because they are solely motivated by their desire for avoidance of punishment. If you foster moral and ethical principles, and regulate your people with Li (禮), they will not only have their sense of shame but will also be compliant" (see Section 3 of Chapter 2, 為政, of *Confucius Analects*). In Section 2 of Chapter 3, the discussion between Mencius and Gong Sun Chou on Gao Zi's approach illustrated this important point.

Mencius also believed that people are born with a seed (or root) of Yi virtue. However, such innate quality is not enough and needs to be cultivated by listening, observation, reasoning, practice, experience, long-term commitment, and courage. The ideal goal is to accumulate a magnanimous and awe-inspiring spirit to attain a resolute, undaunted, and incorruptible heart.

Li (禮): This Chinese word has many meanings in Confucianism and in the Chinese language. In ancient times, it referred to rites, rituals, ceremonies, protocols in courts and government, discipline, regulations, laws and order, social norms and bonding, respect, courtesy, and etiquette in daily life; in modern times, it refers to respect, etiquette, courtesy, presents, and gifts. Nowadays, Li (禮) includes a set of social norms that are motivated by the inner conscience of people and entrenched in the culture, rather than externally imposed by the government through decrees and legislation.

This Chinese word can be analyzed etymologically as a combination of two words. On the left is the word 礻 or 示, which means "To Show". On the right is the word 豊. This word looks rather like an altar with offerings placed on top. In ancient China, worshipping Sky, Earth, and ancestors was of considerable importance. Large vessels such as tripods were used to hold wine and animal sacrifices during such worship rituals. The word 豊 was used to represent such vessels because of its shape. It was later used to mean rituals for worship, and then the respect for gods. When the ancient society developed further, the combination of 礻 and 豊 was then used to mean the showing of respect of people, and then of the family, clan, tribe, and society in general. The meaning of the word 禮 was then further developed into a set of social norms that governed how people were expected to behave in their society. By the early Zhou Dynasty, the Duke of Zhou, also known as Zhou Gong (周公), the brother of King Wu of Zhou (周武王, died 1043 BC) and the first prime minister of the Zhou Dynasty, formalized and further developed the prevailing social norms at that time into a set of official mandates. These mandates were decreed in the Zhou Li (周禮) system. This system was very elaborate and covered many aspects of how a person should behave from birth to death: for example, the paternal lineage of family names, the prohibition of marriages between siblings and close cousins, the prohibition of marriages between two persons with the same family name, inheritance of estate, the definition of relatives within the extended family, how relatives in the extended family should interact with one another, the rituals of celebrations, worship of ancestors, and funerals. More importantly, the Zhou Li system literally defined the political system of the Zhou Dynasty, as well as the roles, power, and entitlement of the Imperial Emperor versus feudal lords. It also defined the protocols in courts and local and central governments. It also specified the rituals and ceremonies for worships of Sky, Earth, ancestors, and other gods. The purpose of this Li system was to maintain an orderly, peaceful, and civilized society at that time. The system of punishment for violations of Li was not fully developed until the Spring-Autumn period. Confucius was an ardent supporter of the Zhou Li system. He objected to the theory of Legalist School, championed by Guan Zhong, the prime minister of the state of Qi before Confucius's time, who implemented strict and harsh laws to maintain social order. Instead, Confucius advanced the concept that the compliance with Li is a moral responsibility. Confucius said, "If you use laws and regulations to guide and rule your people, and punishment to enforce their compliance, they will be decadent and shameless because they are exclusively motivated by their desire for avoidance of punishment. If you foster moral and ethical principles, and regulate your people with Li (禮), they will not only have their sense of shame but will also be compliant" (see Section 3 of Chapter 2, 為政, of *Confucius Analects*). Confucius further internalized Li as a virtue, which was considered next to Ren. A few chapters of the

Book of Li (also known as *Li Ji,* 禮記) were then written by Confucians during the Spring-Autumn period to explain the philosophic and spiritual meaning of Li (禮).

In brief, Ren tells your heart what needs to be done, whereas Yi tells what you must do. Li tells you how to do, and concerns the way and manner to communicate, interact, work, and live with other people, the society, and the world, having determined what must be done by you. Li requires that you behave properly for the good of others so that there is harmony between you and others and in the society. Confucius mentioned that Li is based on both Ren and Yi. He said, "Would a person without the virtue of Ren practice Li?" (see Section 3 of Chapter 3, 八佾, of *Confucius Analects*). He also said, "A Jun Zi regards righteousness and honor as fundamental bases, and acts in line with Li" (see Section 18 of Chapter 15, 衛靈公, of *Confucius Analects*). The three virtues must act together to produce a good result. Confucius also said that "if one becomes an official by his knowledge and academic qualifications but does not maintain such qualities according to Ren principles, he may not be able to keep his position for long. If he becomes an official by his knowledge and academic qualifications, maintains such qualities according to Ren principles, but does not take his responsibilities seriously, his people will not respect him. If he becomes an official by his knowledge and academic qualifications, maintains such qualities according to Ren principles, takes his responsibilities seriously, but acts against Li principles, he is still not faultless" (see Section 33 of Chapter 15, 衛靈公, of *Confucius Analects*). More modern-day examples to explain this point are:

    a) Ren tells you that you need to listen to a sermon. Yi tells you to go to church and attend the sermon. Li tells you that you must listen attentively, show respect to the speaker, and not make noise.

b) You are sitting in a car of a subway train and see a pregnant woman entering the car. Ren tells you to prevent her from falling. Yi tells you to give up your seat and give it to the woman. Li tells you to politely invite the woman to take your seat.
c) You see a weak and elderly person trying to cross the street. Ren tells you to prevent the elderly person from being hit by a car. Yi tells you to hold the arm of the person and help him cross the street safely. Li tells you to politely offer to help such a person by asking, "May I help you?" The act of helping the elderly cross the street is an act of Li.
d) Your subordinate made a mistake and tried to hide it. Ren tells you that you need to rectify him so that he will not make the same mistake again. Yi tells you to teach him a lesson. Li tells you to avoid using harsh, insulting words to reprimand him.
e) You attend a funeral ceremony. Ren tells you to feel sorrowful and appreciative of the past life of the dead. Yi tells you to show your sorrow and appreciation of the dead. Li tells you to say good words about the person in the memorial service.
f) Being in love with your girl or boyfriend is Ren. If, on the Valentine Day, you bought flowers and booked a table for two in a classy restaurant, this is Yi. However, if you are late for the date and send your partner a message, saying, "Darling, I am busy with my work and I may be quite late. Can you wait a while?" then this action shows a lack of Li. The result will frustrate your partner.
g) On Mother's Day, many children take their parents

to restaurants. The love of one's mother is a Ren virtue. Treating the mother with a great dinner is a Yi action. However, if, during the dinner, the child continuously browses his or her smartphone, texting messages to friends and ignoring the presence of the mother, she will be upset. This lack of Li defeats the purpose of showing love and gratitude to the mother.

h) Confucius said, "Most people nowadays think that filial piety is just about feeding your old parents. Even dogs and horses are fed by people. If you do not respect your parents, how do you differentiate feeding your parents from feeding dogs and horses?" (see Section 7 of Chapter 2, 為政, of *Confucius Analects*). The love of one's parents is a Ren matter, while feeding one's elderly parents is a Yi action. However, this action must be taken with respect, which is an aspect of Li. Otherwise, the absence of Li degrades the value of the act of feeding and the parent will be unhappy.

i) Zi Xia once asked about filial piety. Confucius said, "The most difficult behavior is to show respectful, obedient, and amiable manners. If the young person handles chores on behalf of seniors when there is a need, or if seniors are treated with food and wine when available, are such acts enough to show filial piety according to Zheng Zi? [Of course not!]" (see Section 8 of Chapter 2, 為政, of *Confucius Analects*).

There are unlimited examples to illustrate the essence and importance of Li. Every daily activity of a person is related to the Li virtue.

Before Confucius, Li was regarded as an external requirement imposed by the society, tradition, and the government to the individual. Confucius internalized Li as a virtue. External rituals are meaningless and even hypocritic if the heart is not in it. Confucius said, "If my heart is not in the worship, it is equivalent to not worshipping at all" (see Section 12 of Chapter 3, 八佾, of *Confucius Analects*). He also said, "They say it is about Li rituals. They say it is about Li rituals. What is the point of showing off jade and silk in these rituals?" (see Section 11 of Chapter 17, 陽貨, of *Confucius Analects*).

Mencius considered that everybody is born with the seed (or root) of Li. This innate seed enables humans to operate harmoniously in societies and differentiates humans from wild animal species. It is human nature to show some forms of Li to each other without being taught, told, or compelled. For example, most people would feel embarrassed and ashamed to expose themselves naked and make love in public under the sun; moreover, most people would not show disgusting manners while listening to their parents and teachers. Whereas infants smile at their parents and nurses, most people feel an urge to stand up solemnly while the national anthem is sung. However, the seed (or root) of Li virtue is imperfect, inadequate, and nascent, and therefore, requires development to be a Li virtue. Without continual nurturing, this seed and root will rot. People with rotten seeds become sociopaths. On the other hand, the developed Li virtue is an integral part of the personality of a Jun Zi.

Relationship between Ren, Yi, and Li: The above paragraphs have stated that Ren is the foundation of Yi, which is, in turn, a foundation of Li.

However, this relationship is oversimplified. Since Ren, Yi, and Li virtues must be cultivated by relentless nurturing, learning, experiencing, and self-cultivation, the acquisition of these virtues cannot be isolated from the external environment of a person. Among these three virtues, Li is most related to the external world because there are social norms, rules, protocols, rituals, cultures, and laws in the society that a person cannot get away from, and a good person must conform to these norms. In the process of conformance, a wise person knows how to assimilate the essence of Li and internalize the essence into a virtue. The results of this cultivation and learning process then feed the cultivation of the Yi virtue, which is more internal. The results of the cultivation and learning process of Yi, in turn, feed the cultivation of Ren virtue. Therefore, when Yan Yuan asked about the essence of Ren, Confucius replied, "Control yourself so that your words and behavior are in line with the principles of Li (禮). If you can do so in the future, people around the world will emulate you and follow the path to Ren virtue. It is all up to you to have the Ren virtue. Nobody else can help or deter you." When Yan Yuan asked further, "Can you please tell me the key points?" Confucius replied, "Don't look at anything that is against the principles of Li; don't listen to any matter that is against the principles of Li; don't talk about any matter that is against the principles of Li; don't take any action that is against the principles of Li" (see Section 1 of Chapter 12, 顏淵, of *Confucius Analects*). "Control yourself" here referred to the practice of Yi. The rest of Confucius's words related to the practice of Li. Confucius emphasized that the practical path to acquire the Ren virtue is to start practicing Li. This shows the importance of Li in Confucianism.

Wisdom (智): The closest translation of this Chinese word to its original meaning is wisdom. This word can be etymologically analyzed as a combination of three words: 矢, 口, and 日. The first word 矢 means an arrow, the second word means the mouth, and the third word means talking or teaching. In ancient time, the word *arrow* also symbolizes wars. The combination of 矢 and 口 is the word 知, whose modern meaning is knowledge. In ancient China, those who opened their mouths to talk about wars were military strategists, who possessed the essential knowledge of how to protect the country. Therefore, the combination of the word 知 and 曰 into the word 智 represents the ability to talk, teach, and explain important knowledge to people. This ability was later generalized as "wisdom."

Mencius regarded wisdom an important virtue. It is one of the four primary virtues expounded by Mencius. The other primary virtues are Ren, Yi, and Li. The above paragraphs in this section have explained that the Ren, Yi, and Li virtues need to be cultivated through a long process of learning, experiencing, assimilation, and internalization. In this process, a good person must discern right from wrong and draw correct conclusions to accumulate his virtues. This ability is wisdom. Without this virtue, a good person can be misled, deceived, and deluded, and he can go astray.

Mencius mentioned that he was a discerning listener. The ability to discern right from wrong is part of wisdom.

Mencius considered that everyone was born with a seed (or root) of wisdom. For most people, this seed (or root) is inadequate and nascent, and must be cultivated through learning and experience.

Learning (學): The above paragraphs on Ren, Yi, and Li virtues have pointed out the importance of learning because these virtues need to be cultivated. Learning includes not only reading books and listening to teachers, but also practice, experience, observation, and critical thinking. Confucius said that, "Reviewing and practicing regularly what you have learned is a pleasure indeed, isn't it?" (see Section 1 of Chapter 1, 學而, of *Confucius Analects*). He also stated that, "You observe the motivation of a person's behavior and words, the approach and directions he follows, and his mental and emotional conditions. What can he hide? What can he hide?" (see Section 10 of Chapter 2, 為政, of *Confucius Analects*). Further, "Learning from books without critical thinking results in confusion. Thinking vacuously without learning from books is perilous" (see Section 15, Chapter 2, 為政, of *Confucius Analects*), and finally, "I have tried to ponder day and night without eating and sleep. It was useless. It is better to learn" (see Section 31 of Chapter 15, 衛靈公, of *Confucius Analects*).

Confucius also mentioned the importance of learning in the process of cultivation of virtues, and said, "The love of benevolence and kindness without the quest for learning would lead to the flaw of foolish simplicity. The love of knowledge without the quest for learning would lead to the flaw of aimless flirting. The love of sincerity without the quest for learning would lead to the flaw of being credulous. The love of being straightforward without the quest for learning would lead to the flaw of rudeness. The love of boldness without the quest for learning would lead to the flaw of violence. The love of firmness without the quest for learning would lead to the flaw of defiance." (see Section 8 of Chapter 17, 陽貨, of *Confucius Analects*). Confucius's disciple, Zi Xia, said, "Hundreds of mechanics work in factories to accomplish their projects. A Jun Zi learns to attain high moral standards." (see Section 7 of Chapter 19, 子張, of *Confucius Analects*).

Confucius also believed that people were born with an innate seed of virtues. Some people are lucky enough to be born with knowledge and virtue, whereas others are less lucky and need to learn. He said, "Those who are born with knowledge and wisdom are at the top. Those who acquire knowledge through learning are next. Those who learn when in need are further below. Those who do not learn when in need are at the bottom" (see Section 9 of Chapter 16, 季氏, of *Confucius Analects*).

Dao (or Tao, 道): This name has different meanings under Taoism, Buddhism, and Confucianism. It is important to know such distinctions. Otherwise, Confucianist philosophy could be confounded with religious and metaphysical ideas. Owing partly to the lax interpretations of Dao, later Confucians, from the Han Dynasty to the Song Dynasty, have morphed Confucianism into a combination of Confucianism and Taoism. Some modern neo-Confucians even consider Confucianism as a branch of idealism and even mysticism.

Under Taoism, Dao vaguely means something amorphous which is the true self-being (or in the Buddhist term, the svabhava, prakrti, or dharmakaya) of the universe and which existed before the materialization of it. One aspect of Dao is that it has the potential of giving birth to the universe and everything (material and spiritual) in it, while another aspect of Dao is the collection of all rules and laws governing and controlling how the universe and everything in it operates. It is impossible to use human words or concepts to describe it completely. Laozi, the founder of Taoism, wrote in the 25th chapter of his famous book, Dao Te Ching (or Dao Te Jing, 道德經):

"There is something, amorphous and self-complete, that existed before the Sky and Earth. Oh, we cannot hear or see it because it is obscure and immaterial! Its existence does not depend on anything else, and it is there perpetually. It operates everywhere endlessly. I think that it is the mother of the Sky and Earth. I do not know its name. If I must give it a name, I call it Dao. If I must give it a descriptive name, I call it Great."

Furthermore, Laozi wrote the following opening sentence in

Introduction

Chapter 1 of Dao Te Ching:

"The Dao that can be described in language is not the perpetually constant Dao. It can be given a name, but this name cannot be a perpetually constant name. This nameless thing is the origin of the Sky and Earth. Its nameable realization is the mother of everything. Therefore, always be without desires to see its (intrinsic) intricacies, and always have desires to see its (extrinsic) principles and effects. These two aspects are the same thing but have different names. Together, we can refer to them as mystery. This mystery upon mystery is the gateway to all intricacies."

In the above paragraph, the word *two* refers to the nameless thing and its nameable realization. The nameless thing and its nameable realization are two aspects of the Dao. The word *desires* can be interpreted to include deliberate efforts based on pre-conception and assumptions. One must have a pure mind, void of such desires, deliberate efforts, and pre-conception and assumptions to see some intricacies of the nameless thing. On the other hand, one can use deliberate efforts (e.g., vision, senses, instrumentation, measurements, and reasoning) to see some principles of the nameable realization of Dao.

Some scholars interpret the first sentence of Dao Te Ching differently and think that Dao is Null (emptiness, Wu, 無) rather than nameless (無名). They then infer that Null gave birth to the material universe. They further extrapolate Laozi's idea into the theory that the material universe started from the Big Bang and before it, there was nothing. Such interpretation is not only far-fetched but inconsistent with the context of the paragraph in the 25th chapter of Dao Te Ching. Laozi explicitly mentioned that there is something called the Dao that existed before the Sky and Earth. Therefore this "something" cannot be absolutely nothing, otherwise the statement is tautologically wrong. The concept of "Null (emptiness, Wu, 無)" under Taoism should better be interpreted as some immaterial thing which cannot be perceived, defined, and described by human language. This something is called the Dao, Nameless, or Null.

The concept of "giving birth" to the universe can better be interpreted as a logical sequence rather than a chronological sequence of events. This means that the Dao and the universe can co-exist in time, and Dao does not need to precede the universe in time. Under the Big Bang theory, the Dao existed in time before the universe; and therefore, Dao must be different and separate from the universe. For example, under the narrow interpretation of "giving birth", a baby is a separate person from the mother after birth. This inference thus contradicts the statement: "the two are the same thing but have different names." This problem can be avoided by the interpretation of "giving birth" by logical sequence. This means that the material universe is a logical consequence of Dao. The material universe depends on Dao and cannot exist without Dao. At any moment in time, the two, Dao (nameless) and material universe (nameable), can co-exist and are one and the same thing.

An analogy can be borrowed to explain this difficult concept. Consider the concept of "the Music of Beethoven" when Beethoven was alive. When he was alive, Beethoven's mind had the potential of composing many musical pieces. Before a piece of music was written in notes, sung, or played with instruments, the music was already in Beethoven's mind. The music in Beethoven's mind and the music, which were composed by him, and subsequently read, sung, or played, were the same music but exhibited in different forms. Since Beethoven's mind cannot observed directly and perceived clearly by another person and is impossible to define and described in concrete language, it is called "nameless". The latter form of music, which can be read, sung, or played by another person, is perceivable and tangible, and can therefore be called "nameable". The music in Beethoven's mind must exist logically before the explicit form of his music. Without the music in Beethoven's mind, the explicit form of his music which can be read, sung, or played cannot exist. However, at any moment in time, the music in Beethoven's mind can co-exist with the explicit form of music.

To Buddhists in China, Dao means the ways to be liberated from the pain of cycles of reincarnation, to reach the status of nirvana and, ultimately, to become a buddha. The sixth patriarch of the Zen branch (禪宗) of Buddhism in China, Hui Neng (六祖慧能, 638–713 AD), mentioned in the *Podium Sutra of the Sixth Patriarch* (六祖壇經), "If one wants to know the true Dao, it is just about proper behaviors." Buddhists recommend Eight Righteous Ways (or the Noble Eightfold Path) to behave properly. In simple terms, these eight righteous ways are: right view, right resolve, right speech, right conduct, right livelihood, right effort, right mindfulness, and right concentration.

To Confucians, Dao has a more mundane notion. Although Confucius and Mencius mentioned the concept of Dao in the context of Sky and Earth a few times, they considered Dao narrowly as the collection of principles that cultivate a person to be good, virtuous, and ultimately, a saint (i.e., a great man). Dao is also the collection of principles that foster a peaceful society and a benevolent and righteous government. These principles are in line with the Confucian doctrines. The above paragraphs on Ren, Yi, Li and Wisdom have highlighted such a doctrine.

Confucius had the humility of admitting that he did not understand the metaphysical version of Dao as expounded by Laozi. He said, "If one is enlightened with True Way (Dao) in the morning, one is willing to die in the evening" (Section 8 of Chapter 4, 里仁, of *Confucius Analects*). Although he desired to know it, he still could not understand it. However, he did not endorse wasting time in ruminating on supermundane and supernatural matters before more urgent problems in the world are solved. When Zi Lu asked about how to serve and worship gods and spirits, Confucius said, "You still have not served men well. Why do you bother to serve gods and spirits?" Zi Lu then ventured to ask about death and the afterlife. Confucius said, "You don't even know enough about life, why do you bother to know about death?" (Section 11 of Chapter 12, 先進, of *Confucius Analects*). Confucians emphasize pragmatism and discourage the study of supernatural and metaphysical matters. Confucius never talked about myths, violence, revolt, gods, or spirits (Section 21 of Chapter 7, 述而, of *Confucius Analects*). Confucius also said, "If you strive to promote propriety and virtuosity among your people, and if you respect gods and spirits but stay away from them, you have wisdom" (Section 12 of Chapter 6, 雍也, of *Confucius Analects*). Because of this attitude, the Confucian interpretation of Dao is more down-to-earth.

Whenever Mencius made an incidental reference to Dao that bore some resemblance to the Taoist concept of Dao, some scholars immediately extrapolate Mencius's message to the realms of metaphysics and supernatural theory. They further transform Confucianism into a religion. Since this view has little practical value beyond academic interests and is not authentic Confucianism, the author has tried to adhere to Confucius's attitude (i.e., pre-Qin Confucianism, which was not a religion) and refrain from making religious and metaphysical interpretations of Mencius's philosophy. Therefore, this translation tries to avoid words such as *God*, *Creation*, and so on, which have religious connotations.

Te (virtue, 德): This word has different meanings under Taoism, Buddhism and Confucianism. To Taoists, Te is the realization and

Introduction

display of the Taoist version of Dao. Such a realization and display can be material or spiritual.

To Buddhists, Te is the accumulation of good deeds and spiritual achievements in the process of self-cultivation and self-purification on the path to becoming a buddha. There are 12 stages on this path, like grades from kindergarten to Ph.D., and Te is the score card in these grades.

To Confucians, Te is the accumulation of good quality in a person from the practice of following Dao. The words *Dao* and *Te* are often used together, and a Dao Te (道德) means a virtue to Confucians. It is important to know the different meanings of Te under different schools of thoughts. Otherwise, the Confucian philosophy will be distorted.

Tian (Sky, Heaven, God, 天): This term was often mentioned in ancient Chinese classics, especially in Confucian and Taoist literature. Tian is often translated as "Sky," "Heaven," or "God," but none of these English words convey the exact meaning of *Tian* in Chinese philosophic literature. To avoid over-simplification and distortion in translation, this book adopts the transcribed word *Tian* with a parenthesis (Sky). The following paragraphs try to elaborate its comprehensive meaning.

Archeological finds have shown that prehistorical tribes in China worshiped a supreme deity in sky, which governed the climate, natural disasters, harvest or famine, and victory or defeat in wars. During the Yao and Shun period, the concept of a supreme deity in sky was more concrete and it was given the name of Tian, which was also a common word for sky. The concept of this deity became more elaborate during the Xia, Shang (Yan), and Zhou dynasties. Ancient books such as the *Great Oath of Shun, Oath of Tang, the Book of Classic History, Book of Changes,* and *Book of*

Poetry often mentioned Tian as a supreme deity. In brief, people in those dynasties believed that: (1) Tian (Sky) was the creator of Earth, heavenly bodies, and living things on earth; (2) Tian (Sky) regulates natural phenomena; (3) Tian (Sky) was above all emperors, kings, rulers, and gods and spirits; (4) Tian (Sky) was eternal, omnipotent, magnificent, magnanimous, righteous, and omniscient; and (5) Tian (Sky) rewarded good deeds and punishes evil. Therefore, all emperors, rulers, officials, and common people during those eras took part in sophisticated rituals to worship Tian regularly. They prayed to Tian for thanksgiving and to ask for blessings and forgiveness. The procedures and rules of such rituals were documented in the Zhou Li.

Since Confucius was born during the Spring-Autumn Period of the Zhou Dynasty, he was an ardent advocate of the Zhou Li, and by extension, he taught his disciples to respect, fear and serve Tian (Sky). By serving Tian (Sky), he meant to follow its supreme principles and virtues. Under Confucius's philosophy, Ren is the core virtue and is bestowed and planted into human mind by Tian (Sky). The *Confucius Analects* also mentioned a few times the divine providence and the will of Tian (Sky).

Mencius also believed the existence of a supreme deity, Tian (Sky), which is the Creator of the universe. Mencius also believed that Tian (Sky) has a will (天志), wisdom (天知), perfect and infinite goodness (天道), and principles (天理). All human beings are bestowed with some of these qualities as seeds in our conscience. For example, Ren (仁) corresponds to the qualities of perfect and infinite goodness of Tian (天道), Yi (義) and Li (禮) correspond to the qualities of principles of Tian (天理), and human wisdom (智) corresponds to the quality of wisdom of Tian (天知). Through relentless and ardent observation, learning, practice, self-examination, meditation, and self-improvement, one can be enlightened and follow the will, wisdom, path to goodness, and principles of Tian. Both Confucius and Mencius taught that the goal of following the will, wisdom, path, and principles of Tian is not only personal sanctification, but also the fostering of such greatness to one's family, society, country, and the world. A person who can accomplish such goals completely is called a saint.

It is important to note that although the description of Tian (Sky) under Confucianism has many similarities with the description of God under Judaism and Christianity, there are several important differences. First, Tian (Sky) is not personified under Confucianism, whereas the Christian Bible and Judaist Scriptures described God like the emperor in Heaven, who often communicated with prophets in words. Confucians rarely mention any direct revelation from Tian (Sky) to humans. Second, although Confucians and Taoists believe that Tian (Sky) creates all things in nature and is the fundamental power perpetuating the universe, their description of the Creation is not as vivid and comprehensive as what is described in the Genesis. Third, there is no concept of Divine Trinity under Confucianism. Fourth, there is no concept of the Redemption of human beings by the Son of God. Fifth, there is no concept of Heaven and hell under Confucianism. Sixth, there is no discussion of afterlife under Confucianism. Confucius tried to stay away from such discussions. When Zi Lu ventured to ask Confucius about death and the afterlife, Confucius said, "You don't even know enough about life, why do you bother to know about death?" (Section 11 of Chapter 12, 先進, of *Confucius Analects*). Confucians emphasize pragmatism and discourage the study of supernatural matters. Confucius never talked about myths, violence, revolt, gods, or spirits (Section 21 of Chapter 7, 述而, of *Confucius Analects*).

Because of the differences in the descriptions of Tian (Sky) and God, and the need to prevent confusion, this book avoids the use of the word *God* and adopts the use of *Tian* (*Sky*).

Some translators used the word *Heaven* to translate 'Tian'. This approach has the problem that it could mislead readers to think that Confucians have the same concept of Heaven as described by Christians.

Some translators have used the word *Sky* to translate Tian. This approach also has the problem that sky has the connotation of the physical universe and lacks a supernatural character.

Xin (心, Heart, Mind): This word is often used in the text of *Mencius* written in Chinese. Some translators used the word *heart,* which has biological, as well as emotional and psychological connotations. Under Mencius's philosophy, the word *Xin* has a higher, metaphysical meaning—the moral mind or moral conscience. It is this moral mind that defines human nature and distinguishes human beings from animals. Therefore, the author has aimed to avoid using the word *heart*, instead preferring the term "moral mind" wherever appropriate. The author also avoids the use of the word *soul* since it has a religious connotation. Throughout *Mencius* and *Confucius Analects*, there was never a reference to soul.

Jun Zi, Xiao Ren, Sage, and Saint: The term Jun Zi (君子) is used in Chinese scholarly texts to mean a gentleman, a person of superior and noble character, a prominent and respectable person in society, or a person who upholds high standards of virtuous principles. It was commonly translated as "gentleman" in the past. However, as described throughout *Confucius Analects*, a Jun Zi stands for a much wider range of excellence and a higher standard of morality than what the English word *gentleman* stands for. Therefore, this book retains the transcribed term Jun Zi to preserve its authentic meaning in Chinese. A Xiao Ren (小人) has the opposite character of a Jun Zi. A Xiao Ren is, for example, mean, wicked, cruel, dumb, lacking virtues, dishonest, low class, and so on. Some old translations used "mean man" to describe a Xiao Ren (小人). Since such a character has many inferior and obnoxious qualities, "mean man" is an incomplete description. There is no single English word that conveys all these qualities. To preserve the complete and accurate meaning of this phrase in Chinese culture, this book thus uses the transcription of the Chinese phrase.

A sage is a Jun Zi who is meritorious, wise, learned, competent, visionary, and has outstanding virtues. A sage is one level higher than a Jun Zi in terms of goodness. While there are many Jun Zis, sages are rare.

A saint is a sage who attains an extremely high level of goodness. His or her teachings and actions enlighten people in the world for millennia. The concept of the word *saint* under Confucianism is different from that under Catholicism. Since Confucians do not discuss afterlife matters, they do not consider saints to be spirits in Heaven. For Confucians, saints are just exceptionally virtuous and great men and women who contribute immensely to the world. Therefore, in the following chapters of this book, the word *saint* carries its meaning under Confucianism.

Is Confucianism a Religion? Since this is a controversial topic beyond the scope of this book, the short answer to this question depends on the definition of a religion. If one defines a religion to include not only the belief of the existence of a supreme deity or a number of supernatural gods and spirits, the teaching of moral principles, and the need to be obedient to and in harmony with these deities, but also the belief of the existence of afterlife with the goal of getting eternal happiness in Heaven, Paradise, Nirvana, or some other supernatural worlds, and avoidance of pain and suffering in hell or cycles of reincarnation, then Confucianism should not be regarded as a religion. If religion is defined to be the teachings of the goal of humanity and the approaches and methods to reach that goal, such as what modern Christian theologian Paul Tillich proposed, Confucianism can then be regarded as a religion. During the Song Dynasty and Ming Dynasty, many Confucians, namely Wang Yang Ming (王陽明), have advanced the idea that the goal of a Jun Zi is his unification with Tian (Sky), (天人合一). In the past century, some neo-Confucians attempted to expound on the similarities Confucianism shares with the major religions nowadays, and concluded that Confucianism is a "religion of morality". The key point to note here is that Confucianism focuses on life on Earth and stops short of any discussion about afterlife. According to neo-Confucians, a person can transcend spiritually to the state of sanctification on Earth.

Highlights

Constancy

1. 雖有天下易生之物也 一日暴之 十日寒之 未有能生者也。
Even the most easily growing thing in the world will not grow if it is exposed to cold weather over ten days for every one day under the Sun (Section 9 of Chapter 11).

Dao

2. 天下有道 以道殉身 天下無道 以身殉道。
When the Dao prevails in the country, you follow it. When the country lacks Dao, you sacrifice yourself for it (Section 42 of Chapter 13).

Determination

3. 不為也 非不能也。
It is because you do not want to do it and not because you cannot do it (Section 7 of Chapter 1).

Divine Wisdom

4. 天視自我民視 天聽自我民聽。
Tian (Sky) sees through the eyes of people. Tian hears through the ears of people (Section 5 of Chapter 9).

Fabric of Society

5. 天下之本在國 國之本在家 家之本在身。

The foundation of a country is the state. The foundation of a state is the family. The foundation of a family is the individual member (Section 5 of Chapter 7).

Filial Piety

6. 事孰為大 事親為大 守孰為大 守身為大。
   Who are the most important persons to serve? Serving your parents is most important. What is the most important thing to protect? Protecting the quality of your character is most important (Section 19 of Chapter 7).

Flexibility

7. 可以仕則仕 可以止則止 可以久則久 可以速則速 孔子也。
   Confucius's way was to become an official when it was appropriate to do so, to retire when it was inappropriate to be an official, to offer his service for as long as possible, and to resign quickly when needed (Section 2 of Chapter 3).

Flippant Words

8. 人之易其言也 無責耳矣。
   A glib and flippant talker has no sense of responsibility (Section 22 of Chapter 7).

Forbearance

9. 往者不追 來者不距。
   Do not care about the past of anyone, nor refuse anyone who comes (Section 30 of Chapter 14).

Fortunes vs. Misfortunes

10. 禍福無不自己求之者。
    Fortunes and misfortunes are all caused by one's own actions, and nobody else (Section 4 of Chapter 3).

11. 天作孽 猶可違 自作孽 不可活。
    It is still possible to elude natural catastrophes. There is no way out of a self-inflicted disaster (Section 4 of Chapter 3 and Section 8 of Chapter 7).

12. 永言配命 自求多福。
    Always remember to be in harmony with divine providence so that your good conduct will yield auspicious results (Section 4 of Chapter 3 and Section 4 of Chapter 7).

13. 窮則獨善其身 達則兼善天下。
    When a man is poor and lowly, he should try to perfect his virtues in obscurity. When he is successful and prominent, he should also benefit the world (Section 9 of Chapter 13).

Four Virtuous Beginnings

14. 無惻隱之心 非人也 無羞惡之心 非人也 無辭讓之心 非人也 無是非之心 非人也。惻隱之心 仁之端也 羞惡之心 義之端也 辭讓之心 禮之端也 是非之心 智之端也。
    People without a compassionate mind are inhuman; people without a mind with sense of shame are inhuman; people without humble and modest mind are inhuman; people without the mind to discern right and wrong are inhuman. The compassionate

mind is the beginning of Ren virtue. The mind with a sense of shame is the beginning of Yi virtue. The mind with humility and modesty is the beginning of Li virtue. The mind to discern right from wrong is the beginning of wisdom (Section 6 of Chapter 3).

15. 惻隱之心 人皆有之 羞惡之心 人皆有之 恭敬之心 人皆有之 是非之心 人皆有之。惻隱之心 仁也 羞惡之心 義也 恭敬之心 禮也 是非之心 智也。仁義禮智 非由外鑠我也 我固有之也。

    Everybody has a mind with compassion. Everybody has a mind with a sense of shame. Everybody has a respectful mind. Everybody has a mind with a sense of right and wrong. A compassionate mind is Ren. A mind with a sense of shame is Yi. A respectful mind is Li. A mind with a sense of right and wrong is Wisdom. The virtues of Ren, Yi, Li, and Wisdom are not imposed upon or induced into our minds from outside. We have them inherently and internally. We are not aware of them because we never reflect upon their existence (Section 6 of Chapter 11).

16. 求則得之 舍則失之。

    Pursue and you will get them. Neglect and you will lose them (Section 6 of Chapter 11).

Friendship

17. 不挾長 不挾貴 不挾兄弟而友。友也者 友其德也 不可以有挾也。

    Friendship should not be based on seniority, age, social status, and kinship. You should befriend a person because of his virtues and nothing else (Section 3 of Chapter 10).

Gift vs. Bribe

18. 無處而餽之 是貨之也。
    A gift without a valid reason is a bribe (Section 3 of Chapter 4).

Governance

19. 以若所為求若所欲 猶緣木而求魚也。
    To achieve these goals based on what you are currently doing is like trying to find fish by climbing up a tree (Section 7 of Chapter 1).

20. 樂以天下 憂以天下 然而不王者 未之有也。
    If you take the world's joy as yours and the world's worries as yours, how can you not become a benevolent and magnanimous king? (Section 4 of Chapter 2).

21. 作於其心 害於其事 作於其事 害於其政。
    When one's mind is deluded, his actions will be ruinous, and will lead to ruinous governance policies (Section 9 of Chapter 6).

22. 城郭不完 兵甲不多 非國之災也 田野不辟 貨財不聚 非國之害也 上無禮 下無學 賊民興 喪無日矣。
    Demolished city walls and castles, and inadequate arms are not catastrophic to a country. Undeveloped farmland and depleted treasury coffers are not ruinous to a country. If the ruler is unruly, its people are uneducated, and crimes and revolts abound, the days of the country are numbered (Section 1 of Chapter 7).

23. 順天者存 逆天者亡。
    Those who follow the law of Tian (Sky) will survive and those who are against it will perish (Section 7 of Chapter 7).

24. 國君好仁 天下無敵。
    If a king advocates Ren, he will be invincible (Section 7 of Chapter 7).

25. 夫人必自侮 然後人侮之 家必自毀 而後人毀之 國必自伐 而後人伐之。
    A person must first debase himself and then others will debase him further. A family must first break itself up and then others will break it up further. A country must first ruin itself and then others will destroy it (Section 8 of Chapter 7).

26. 得天下有道 得其民 斯得天下矣 得其民有道 得其心 斯得民矣 得其心有道 所欲與之聚之 所惡勿施爾也。
    There is a way to win the world. If you win the support of people, you win the world. There is a way to win the support of people. If you win their hearts, you win their support. There is a way to win their hearts. You give them what they want and refrain from imposing on them what they hate (Section 9 of Chapter 7).

27. 君之視臣如手足 則臣視君如腹心 君之視臣如犬馬 則臣視君如國人 君之視臣如土芥 則臣視君如寇讎。
    If the king regards his ministers as his limbs, they will regard him as their hearts. If the king regards his ministers as dogs and horses, they will regard him as nobody. If the king regards his ministers as dirt, they will regard him as a robber and an enemy (Section 3 of Chapter 8).

28. 民為貴 社稷次之 君為輕。

People are most important to a state, its sovereignty is next, and its ruler is least (Section 14 of Chapter 14).

Good Timing

29. 雖有智慧 不如乘勢 雖有鎡基 不如待時。

Even if one has wisdom, it is better for him to ride the prevailing trend. Even if one has farming tools, it is better for him to wait for a favorable season (Section 1 of Chapter 3).

Judging Others

30. 人之患在好為人師。

A common flaw of most people is that they like to teach others (Section 23 of Chapter 7).

Learning

31. 學問之道無他 求其放心而已矣。

The role of learning is nothing but to seek the lost mind (Section 11 of Chapter 11).

Li and Yi

32. 非禮之禮 非義之義 大人弗為。

A great man does not practice acts which fake Li and Yi (Section 6 of Chapter 8).

Listening Discerningly

33. 詖辭知其所蔽　淫辭知其所陷　邪辭知其所離　遁辭知其所窮。

    When I hear a biased message, I know that the mind of the speaker is blocked. When I hear a flowery message, I know that the mind of the speaker is decadent. When I hear a wicked message, I know that the mind of the speaker is devious. When I hear an evasive message, I know that the mind of the speaker is illogical (Section 2 of Chapter 3).

34. 生於其心　害於其政　發於其政　害於其事。

    Flaws in the speaker's mind reflect the faults in the speaker's governance policy. A faulty governance policy negatively affects the running of the government (Section 2 of Chapter 3).

Magnanimous Spirit and Character

35. 我知言　我善養吾浩然之氣。

    Mencius said, "I am a discerning listener, and I am good at cultivating my magnanimous spirit and character" (Section 2 of Chapter 3).

36. 持其志　無暴其氣。

    Uphold your will and belief, and do not sap your energy and impetus (Section 2 of Chapter 3).

Mission of Life

37. 窮則獨善其身　達則兼善天下。

When a man is poor and lowly, he should try to perfect his virtues in obscurity. When he is successful and prominent, he should also benefit the world (Section 9 of Chapter 13).

Moral Strength

38. 富貴不能淫 貧賤不能移 威武不能屈 此之謂大丈夫。
    A great man cannot be corrupted by wealth or status, cannot be moved by poverty or lowliness, and cannot be subjugated by threat or force (Section 2 of Chapter 6).

39. 志士不忘在溝壑 勇士不忘喪其元。
    A person with a staunch will is not afraid of being dumped into a drench. A person with great valor is not afraid of being beheaded (Section 7 of Chapter 10).

Morality

40. 養心莫善於寡欲。
    The best way to cultivate one's morality is to reduce his desires (Section 35 of Chapter 14).

Overcoming Adversity

41. 天將降大任於斯人也 必先苦其心志 勞其筋骨 餓其體膚 空乏其身 行拂亂其所為 所以動心忍性 曾益其所不能。
    When Tien (Sky) is about to confer a great role to a person, it first subjects his mind and will with suffering and disappointments, drills his sinews and bones, starves his body, saps his strength, and thwarts his endeavors. By all these methods, it stimulates his mind, hardens his tolerance, and

provides him with the tenacity to accomplish the impossible (Section 15 of Chapter 12).

42. 生於憂患而死於安樂也。
Survival arises from hardship and worries, and death arises from comfort and complacency (Section 15 of Chapter 12).

Patience

43. 助之長者 揠苗者也 非徒無益 而又害之。
Those who artificially promote their moral strength are like those who pull up shoots to promote growth. This action is not only futile but also harmful (Section 2 of Chapter 3).

44. 其進銳者 其退速。
Those who dash forward abruptly will have to retreat rapidly (Section 44 of Chapter 13).

Power of Virtues

45. 以力服人者 非心服也 力不贍也 以德服人者 中心悅而誠也。
If you subdue others by force, their submission is involuntary and necessitated by their weakness to resist you. If you subdue others by your virtues, they will follow you willingly (Section 3 of Chapter 3).

Procrastination

46. 如知其非義 斯速已矣 何待來年。
If you know that your act is wrong, you should correct it

immediately. Why wait until next year? (Section 8 of Chapter 6).

Promoting Wickedness

47. 長君之惡其罪小　逢君之惡其罪大。

Aiding and abetting the wickedness of one's king is a relatively small crime compared with the great crime of anticipating, enticing, and promoting wickedness of the king (Section 7 of Chapter 12).

Purity

48. 大人者　不失其赤子之心者也。

A great person retains a pure heart like that of an infant (Section 12 of Chapter 8).

Ren

49. 見其生　不忍見其死　聞其聲　不忍食其肉。是以君子遠庖廚也。

Having watched them alive, he cannot bear to see them dying, and having heard their pitiful cries, he cannot bear to eat their meat. Therefore, a Jun Zi stays away from the kitchen (Section 7 of chapter 1).

50. 仁者無敵。

A benevolent government is invincible (Section 5 of Chapter 1).

51. 老吾老　以及人之老　幼吾幼　以及人之幼　天下可運於掌。

If you respectfully take good care of elderly people in your family and then extend the same to all elderly people in the world, and if you nurture young people in your family and then extend the same to all young people in the world, the whole world will be in your hands (Section 7 of Chapter 1).

52. 故推恩足以保四海 不推恩無以保妻子。
Therefore, the fostering of kindness can help you protect the whole world. Otherwise, you cannot protect even your wife (Section 7 of Chapter 1).

53. 仁則榮 不仁則辱。
If the ruler implements Ren policies, his country will be peaceful and prosperous. Otherwise, his country will be ruined (Section 4 of Chapter 3).

54. 人人親其親 長其長 而天下平。
If everybody loves and cares for his parents and dear ones and respect elders, the world will be peaceful (Section 11 of Chapter 7).

55. 為富不仁矣 為仁不富矣。
The rich do not care about Ren virtue. Those who care about Ren virtue cannot be rich (Section 3 of Chapter 5).

Ren and Li

56. 愛人者人恆愛之 敬人者人恆敬之。
Those who love others will be constantly loved by them. Those who respect others will be constantly respected by them (Section 28 of Chapter 8).

Ren and Yi

57. 王亦曰仁義而已矣 何必曰利。
    Your Majesty should focus on Ren and Yi rather than benefits (Section 1 of Chapter 1).

58. 行一不義 殺一不辜 而得天下 皆不為也。
    If they needed to commit an act of evil or to kill an innocent person to conquer the whole world, they would refrain from doing so (Section 2 of Chapter 3).

59. 君仁莫不仁 君義莫不義。
    If the king is benevolent, all people below him will be benevolent. If the king is righteous, all people below him will be righteous (Section 5 of Chapter 8).

60. 殺人之父 人亦殺其父 殺人之兄 人亦殺其兄。
    If you kill the father of another person, he will then kill your father. If you kill a brother of another person, he will then kill your brother (Section 7 of Chapter 14).

Reputation

61. 有不虞之譽 有求全之毀。
    There are undeserving and unexpected praises. There are nitpicking criticisms.

    There are undeserving praises of trivial contributions. There are harsh criticisms of near perfect accomplishments.

    There are praises for one's work even though he does not expect them. There are criticisms on one's work even though he aims at perfection.

There are praises for one's work even though he does not expect them. There are curses on a person who renounces honor and strives for existence (Section 21 of Chapter 7).

Sages vs. Fools

62. 賢者以其昭昭 使人昭昭 今以其昏昏 使人昭昭。
    In the old days, virtuous and learned people were enlightened so that they could enlighten others. Nowadays, ignorant and stupid people try to enlighten others (Section 20 of Chapter 14).

Self-cultivation

63. 盡其心者 知其性也 知其性 則知天矣。
    If you make your utmost effort to reflect and explore the goodness of your mind, you can know your own nature. Knowing the nature of your being will enlighten you about the good nature of Tian (Sky) (Section 1 of Chapter 13).

64. 莫非命也 順受其正 是故知命者 不立乎巖牆之下 盡其道而死者 正命也 桎梏死者 非正命也。
    Nothing happens that is not affected by the realities of life. One should accept them with a positive attitude. Therefore, those who understand the realities of life will not stand beneath a wall about to collapse. If one dies because of doing his best in pursuing his moral principles, he has lived positively. If one dies because of criminal offences or decadence, he has ruined his life (Section 2 of Chapter 13).

65. 求則得之 舍則失之 是求有益於得也 求在我者也。

Morality can be obtained by seeking and lost by neglecting. In this case, seeking helps getting because seeking of morality is completely under our control (Section 3 of Chapter 13).

66. 萬物皆備於我矣。反身而誠 樂莫大焉。

The basic nature of everything is in me. There is no greater joy for me to fathom the basic nature of myself by sincere and dedicated effort (Section 4 of Chapter 13).

Self-examination

67. 行有不得者 皆反求諸己 其身正而天下歸之。

If you do not get the desired results from your actions, you need to introspect and rectify yourself. If your actions are proper, everybody in the world will support you (Section 2 of Chapter 7).

Self-rectification

68. 發而不中 不怨勝己者 反求諸己而已矣。

If you do not hit the target, you should not blame your rivals who surpass you. You must examine your own ineptness and rectify it (Section 7 of Chapter 3).

69. 自暴者 不可與有言也 自棄者 不可與有為也。

It is impossible to talk to a person who mutilates himself. It is impossible to work with a person who abandons himself (Section 10 of Chapter 7).

Setting Good Examples

70. 君子之德 風也 小人之德 草也 草尚之風必偃。
    The morality of the king (leader) is like wind, and the morality of the citizenry (subordinates) is like grass. When wind blows over grass, it must bend with the wind (Section 2 of Chapter 5).

Shame

71. 人不可以無恥 無恥之恥 無恥矣。
    A man cannot be without shame. A person who does not recognize this is indeed shameless (Section 6 of Chapter 13).

Sharing

72. 古之人與民偕樂 故能樂也。
    Sharing one's happiness with people is the true happiness (Section 2 of Chapter 1).

73. 獨樂樂 不若與眾樂樂。
    It is more pleasurable to enjoy music with many than alone (Section 1 of Chapter 2).

74. 樂民之樂者 民亦樂其樂 憂民之憂者 民亦憂其憂。
    If a ruler rejoices in the joy of his people, they will also rejoice in his joy. If a ruler agonizes over the worries of his people, they will also agonize over his worries (Section 4 of Chapter 2).

Sincerity

75. 至誠而不動者 未之有也 不誠 未有能動者也。

There has never been a truly sincere person who does not move others. An insincere person can never move anybody (Section 12 of Chapter 7).

76. 恭儉豈可以聲音笑貌為哉。

How can one feign respect and modesty with fawning voices and amiable smiles? (Section 16 of Chapter 7).

Slander

77. 言人之不善 當如後患何。

How would you deal with negative consequences arising from your slander against others? (Section 9 of Chapter 8).

Strong Medicine

78. 若藥不瞑眩 厥疾不瘳。

If the medicine is not strong enough to cause dizziness to the patient, it is ineffective to cure any disease (Section 1 of Chapter 5).

Support of People

79. 得道者多助 失道者寡助。

Whoever follows the Dao gets a lot of support. Whoever departs from the Dao gets little support (Section 1 of Chapter 4).

80. 寡助之至 親戚畔之 多助之至 天下順之。

The lack of support can be so extreme that even close relatives and confidants will become rebels and turncoats. The abundance of support can be so extreme that the whole world will become your followers (Section 1 of Chapter 4).

Unity

81. 天時不如地利 地利不如人和。

Timing advantage is less important than geographic and environmental advantages, which are in turn less important than the support and unity of people (Section 1 of Chapter 4).

Warning

82. 戒之戒之 出乎爾者 反乎爾者也。

Beware, beware! Whatever you have done unto others will be done unto you! (Section 12 of Chapter 2).

Wealth Disparity

83. 庖有肥肉 廄有肥馬 民有飢色 野有餓莩 此率獸而食人也。

Their kitchens have fat meat, and their stables have fat horses, but their people have hungry looks, and their countryside has corpses from starvation. This is equivalent to leading beasts to devour people (Section 9 of Chapter 6).

Wisdom

84. 人有不為也 而後可以有為。

A person should know what he should not do before he can achieve what he ought to do (Section 8 of Chapter 8).

85. 盡信書 則不如無書。

It is better to act without a book than to believe everything written in it (Section 3 of Chapter 14).

Yi

86. 魚 我所欲也 熊掌 亦我所欲也 二者不可得兼 舍魚而取熊掌者也。生 亦我所欲也 義 亦我所欲也 二者不可兼得 舍生而取義者也。

    Fish is my favorite. Bear paws are also my favorite. If I cannot get both, I will forego the fish and take the bear paws. Life is also my desire. Yi is also my desire. If I cannot keep both, I will forego life and chose Yi (Section 10 of Chapter 11).

87. 無為其所不為 無欲其所不欲 如此而已矣。

    Do not do what your conscience tells you not to do. Do not desire what your conscience tells you not to desire. It is that simple (Section 17 of Chapter 13).

Chapter 1: King Hui of Liang (1)

Section 1

孟子見梁惠王。

　王曰　叟　不遠千里而來　亦將有以利吾國乎。

　孟子對曰　王何必曰利　亦有仁義而已矣。王曰　何以利吾國　大夫曰　何以利吾家　士庶人曰　何以利吾身　上下交征利而國危矣。萬乘之國弒其君者　必千乘之家　千乘之國弒其君者　必百乘之家。萬取千焉　千取百焉　不為不多矣。苟為後義而先利　不奪不饜。未有仁而遺其親者也　未有義而後其君者也。王亦曰仁義而已矣　何必曰利。

Mencius went to see King Hui of Liang.

　King Hui asked, "Old man, you have traveled a thousand miles to see me. What benefit will you bring to my country?"

　Mencius replied, "Why must your Majesty talk about 'benefits'? I can talk about Ren (humanity) and Yi (righteousness) with you. If your Majesty asks, 'What can benefit my country?', your senior ministers will ask, 'What can benefit my family?' and your junior officials will ask, 'What can benefit myself?'

　When everyone in the government, from the top to the bottom, struggles to grab more benefit for himself, the country will be in great danger. In a large country of ten thousand chariots, the murderer of its king must be another feudal lord of a state which has a thousand chariots. In a state of a thousand chariots, the murderer of its lord must be another official whose family has a hundred

Chapter 1: King Hui of Liang (1)

chariots. It is not rare in history that countries the size of ten thousand were toppled by countries the size of one thousand, and countries the size of one thousand were toppled by countries the size of one hundred. If everyone emphasizes benefits and ignores Yi (righteousness), nobody will be satisfied without snatching his benefits.

There has never been a humane person who neglects his or her parents and clan. There has never been a righteous person who ignores and disobeys his king or lord. Therefore, your Majesty should focus on Ren (humanity) and Yi (righteousness) rather than benefits."

Commentary:

The word *Ren* has a deep meaning (see Section 4 of the Introduction and the Commentary in Section 2 of Chapter 3). For convenience, it is translated here as humanity. Likewise, the word *Yi* has a deep meaning (see Section 4 of the Introduction and the Commentary of Section 2 of Chapter 3). It is translated here for convenience as righteousness.

King Hui of Liang (梁惠王, 400–319 BC) was the same as King Hui of the state of Wei (魏惠王). His reign lasted from 369 BC to 319 BC. In 362 BC, the kingdom of Wei relocated its capital to the city of Da Liang (大梁, modern-day Kaifeng in Henan Province). Therefore, King Hui was called the King Hui of Liang (梁惠王). The following brief history of the state of Wei is shown below:

The Western Zhou Dynasty (西周) lasted from 1066 BC to 770 (or 771) BC. Since its capital was located at Hao Jing (鎬京) in the west of China, this dynasty was called the Western Zhou Dynasty. When feudalism was introduced, members of the royal family, prominent ministers, and generals were classified into five nobility ranks: duke, marquess, earl, viscount, and baron. Dukes and marquesses were each enfeoffed a territory of one hundred square miles, earls were each enfeoffed a territory of seventy square miles, and viscounts and barons were each enfeoffed a territory of fifty square miles. Feudal lords had autonomy over their enfeoffed territories, which were de facto independent states. Their states had their own armies, which had to be smaller than that of the central government. The states were required to pay taxes and tributes to the central government and respond to summons by the emperor. They also had the responsibility of defending the central government when it was under foreign attack. After 12 successions of emperors of the Western Zhou Dynasty, nomads from the west invaded the country, pillaged the capital, and killed King You (周幽王) of Zhou in 770 BC. His successor King Ping (周平王) moved the capital eastward to Luo Yi (雒邑, modern-day Luo Yang 洛陽 in Henan Province 河南). This began the Eastern Zhou Dynasty (東周). During this regime, the emperor of Zhou lost effective control over many feudal states. They paid homage to the emperor in a ceremonial sense only. Feudal states fought among themselves. Small states were conquered, pillaged, destroyed, and annexed by larger states. Historians call this period (from 771 to 476 BC) the Spring-Autumn period because Confucius wrote the Spring-Autumn Annals, a chronicle of the state of Lu (魯國), between 722 to 479 BC. The political map during the early part of the Spring-Autumn period (from 685 to 591 BC) was dominated by five hegemons: the states of Qi (齊), Song (宋), Jin (晉), Qin (秦), and Chu (楚); or alternatively Qi (齊), Chu (楚), Jin (晉), Wu (吳), and Yue (越). Between 497 to 453 BC, the state of Jin (晉國) broke up into three states: Han (韓), Zhao (趙), and Wei (魏). Therefore, during the second part of the Spring-Autumn period, from about 592 to 474 BC, there were seven hegemons: the states of Qi (齊), Chu (

Chapter 1: King Hui of Liang (1)

楚), Yue (越), Han (韓), Zhao (趙), Wei (魏), and Qin (秦). The Western Zhou Dynasty lasted for 285 years. The Spring-Autumn period lasted for 295 years and was followed by the Warring States Period towards the end of the Eastern Zhou Dynasty. The Warring States Period started in 475 BC and ended in 221 BC. The country was dominated by seven hegemons: Qi (齊), Chu (楚), Yan (燕), Han (韓), Zhao (趙), Wei (魏), and Qin (秦). Many wars broke out during this period.

King Hui of Liang (also known as King Hui of Wei) regarded his kingdom as the old state of Jin (晉國) and wanted to conquer the states of Zhao (趙國) and Han (韓), which were offsprings of the old state of Jin. In 354 BC, the state of Zhao (趙國) invaded the state of Wey (衛國), which was an ally of the state of Wei (魏國). The state of Zhao took away two counties from the state of Wey. Upset with the action of the state of Zhao, King Hui of Wei punished the state of Zhao by sending an army under the command of Pang Juan (龐涓) to besiege the capital, Han Dan (邯鄲), of the state of Zhao. After fighting for one year, the King of Zhao begged King Wei of Qi (齊威王) for rescue. After some debate in the royal court, the king of Qi decided in 353 BC to rescue the state of Zhao by sending an army led by Tian Ji (田忌) as the chief commander and Sun Bin (孫臏) as the strategic advisor. The army of the state of Wei was defeated by Tian Ji and Sun Bin in the Battle of Gui Ling (桂陵).

After the Battle of Gui Ling, in 342 BC, King Hui of Wei was again the aggressor. He attacked the state of Han, a neighbor in the south. The King of Han begged for a rescue from King Wei of Qi, who sent his army to fight against the state of Wei. Tian Ji was again appointed the chief commander of the army and Sun Bin his strategic advisor. Once again, the army of the state of Wei was annihilated in the Battle of Ma Ling (馬陵). King Hui's eldest son, Prince Shen (申), was killed, along with his chief commander, Pang

Juan.

After the Battles of Gui Ling and Ma Ling, the state of Wei declined in power and influence. Mencius visited King Hui after the Battle of Ma Ling.

Section 2

孟子見梁惠王。王立於沼上 顧鴻鴈麋鹿 曰 賢者亦樂此乎。

孟子對曰 賢者而後樂此 不賢者雖有此 不樂也。詩云 經始靈臺 經之營之 庶民攻之 不日成之 經始勿亟 庶民子來 王在靈囿 麀鹿攸伏 麀鹿濯濯 白鳥鶴鶴 王在靈沼 於牣魚躍。文王以民力為臺為沼 而民歡樂之 謂其臺曰靈臺 謂其沼曰靈沼 樂其有麋鹿魚鱉。古之人與民偕樂 故能樂也。湯誓曰 時日害喪 予及女偕亡。民欲與之偕亡 雖有臺池鳥獸 豈能獨樂哉。

On another day, Mencius visited King Hui of Liang, who was standing by a pond in his garden, enjoying a beautiful scene of flying large wild geese and fat deer. King Hui asked Mencius, "Do virtuous people [like you] also enjoy such scenes?"

Mencius replied, "Only virtuous people can peacefully enjoy such serenity. People who are void of virtue cannot enjoy such scenes, even if they own them. The *Book of Poetry* narrated an episode about King Wen of Zhou: 'After he had drawn a plan to build his Miraculous Terrace, his people collaborated to build it in a few days. He did not hurry them, yet his people voluntarily and enthusiastically joined in the project as if they were his children. When King Wen visited the park of the Miraculous Terrace, big and fat female deer rested there in comfort, and cranes were glistering

Chapter 1: King Hui of Liang (1)

with white feathers. When King Wen visited the pond of the Miraculous Terrace, fish in the pond jumped with joy toward him.' Although King Wen spent public money to build his terrace, park, and ponds, his people supported his project, and even called the terrace as the Miraculous Terrace and the pond Miraculous Pond as if they were gifts from Tian (Sky). His people were as happy as the deer and fish in the park. Therefore, our ancestors used to say that sharing one's happiness with people is true happiness. On the contrary, King Tang's *Declaration of Revolt* against Emperor Jie wrote that the people of Emperor Jie yearned for the fall of the Sun so that he would vanish with the Sun [They hated Emperor Jie very much]. Although Emperor Jie owned marvelous terraces, ponds, birds, animals, and pets, he could not enjoy them alone."

Annotation:

Since ancient Chinese did not have the same notion of God as Christians, the word *Tian* (*Sky* 天) was used to represent a supernatural and unknown natural power that governs the world. Therefore, the words *God, Heaven, Sky,* and *Nature* are synonyms in the context of classic Chinese literature. The word *Tian* should not be interpreted astronomically (see the explanation of Tian in the Introduction).

Commentary:

Yu (禹, circa 2237–2139 BC) founded the Xia Dynasty (夏朝, circa 2184–1600 BC) in about 2184 BC. After about 500 years of the dynasty, the 16th successor to the throne was Emperor Jie of Xia (夏桀). His birthname was Lu Gui (履癸). He was an extraordinarily talented person. In addition to being a superb scholar, he was a great fighter and possessed unusual physical strength—he could kill a tiger with his bare hands. However, Emperor Jie was the first tyrant in Chinese history. Years before Jie became Emperor, the Xia Dynasty had already declined substantially. Many feudal states had stopped paying tributes to the central government. Foreign tribes intruded into territories at the border. Class struggles were rampant and wealth disparity was immense.

When Emperor Jie came to power, he hired and trusted many crooked ministers and got rid of many meritorious officials. Evil confidants taught Emperor Jie how to blackmail, rip off, torture, and terrorize people. As a result, the economy tanked, and the treasury coffer was depleted. To make up for the deficit, Emperor Jie started to invade many smaller states and tribes to rob their land and wealth.

Some meritorious ministers advised Emperor Jie to refrain from decadent extravagance. They were all tortured and killed. When Emperor Jie heard that his people hated him, he regarded the report as a rumor, saying, "This is just slander. I owned the whole country, like the sky owns the Sun. When the Sun in the sky vanishes, my country will vanish. Oh, Sun, when will you vanish? I would like to vanish with you!"

King Tang of the state of Shang, a meritorious king, raised an army and formed an alliance with other feudal lords to revolt against Emperor Jie. In his *Declaration of Revolt* (湯誓) against the Xia Dynasty, King Tang mentioned that the people of the Xia Dynasty had yearned for the vanish of the Sun so that Emperor Jie would also vanish. King Tang toppled the Xia Dynasty in about 1600 BC before founding the Shang Dynasty (see Section 3 of Endnote).

Section 3

梁惠王曰 寡人之於國也 盡心焉耳矣。河內凶 則移其民於河

Chapter 1: King Hui of Liang (1)

東 移其粟於河內。河東凶亦然。察鄰國之政 無如寡人之用心者。鄰國之民不加少 寡人之民不加多 何也。

孟子對曰 王好戰 請以戰喻。填然鼓之 兵刃既接 棄甲曳兵而走。或百步而後止 或五十步而後止。以五十步笑百步 則何如。

曰 不可 直不百步耳 是亦走也。

曰 王如知此 則無望民之多於鄰國也。不違農時 穀不可勝食也。數罟不入洿池 魚鱉不可勝食也。斧斤以時入山林 材木不可勝用也。穀與魚鱉不可勝食 材木不可勝用 是使民養生喪死無憾也。養生喪死無憾 王道之始也。五畝之宅 樹之以桑 五十者可以衣帛矣。雞豚狗彘之畜 無失其時 七十者可以食肉矣。百畝之田 勿奪其時 數口之家可以無饑矣。謹庠序之教 申之以孝悌之養 頒白者不負戴於道路矣。七十者衣帛食肉 黎民不饑不寒 然而不王者 未之有也。狗彘食人食而不知檢 塗有餓莩而不知發。人死 則曰 非我也 歲也。 是何異於刺人而殺之 曰 非我也 兵也。王無罪歲 斯天下之民至焉。

King Hui of Liang asked, "Being a humble ruler, I am wholeheartedly devoted to the governance of my country. For example, when the He Nei (the region surrounded by the river) experienced a famine, I relocated its people to He Dong (the region east of the river) and transported food from He Dong to He Nei. When He Dong had a famine, I did the same. I notice that the ruler of my neighboring country is not as devoted as I am. Yet the size of its population has not declined, and my country has not increased in size either. Why?"

Mencius replied, "This is because you like to wage wars. Let me illustrate this point with wars. After fierce and brutal fighting, the defeated soldiers desert with their weapons and armors. Some stopped after running for one hundred steps. Some stopped after fifty steps. The latter group laughed at the former group. Do you think whether the latter is right in laughing?"

The King said, "Of course, they are wrong also. Although they have not run one hundred steps, they are still deserters."

Mencius said, "Since your Majesty understands this, you do not need to worry about the size of your country versus your neighbor. If your people do not miss the planting seasons, they will have an inexhaustible amount of food. If your people do not fish with finely knitted nets, they will have an inexhaustible number of fish to eat. If your people follow a regulated pace of cutting down trees, they will have inexhaustible amount of wood to use. Since your people have abundant food, fish, and wood, they do worry about their livelihood and funerals. This is what a benevolent government should provide for.

If each household has five acres of farming land with mulberry trees, fifty-year-old people can then wear silk clothes. If your people do not neglect the right time to raise poultry and hogs, seventy-year-old people can eat meat regularly. If each household has one hundred acres and does not neglect the right time to farm, all household members will not worry about starvation. If your government then institutes in schools a meritorious education which emphasizes filial and fraternal virtues, we will not see poor elderly people carrying heavy burden and tools on the road. If, in your country, seventy-year-old people can wear silk and eat meat, and nobody need to suffer from cold and hunger, it is impossible for you not to become the emperor of the entire empire.

You lavishly throw away food for humans to dogs and pigs and do not donate and distribute food to starving people on the street.

Chapter 1: King Hui of Liang (1)

When you see poor people dying from starvation, you even say, 'It is not my business. It is their fate.' How is this different from killing a person with a sword and saying, 'I did not kill him; the sword killed him'?

If your Majesty does not blame suffering and misfortunes of your people on famines, everybody in the world will flock to your country."

Annotation:

Mencius mentioned that King Hui of Liang was a warmonger because he tried to invade the state of Zhao and the state of Han but was defeated (see Commentary in Section 1).

Modern Perspective:

Nowadays, many rich people are apathetic to poor people. Rich people feel disgusted at the scene of thousands of homeless people living in tents and cardboards along the street. The mindset and behavior of rich people correspond to the second last paragraph of this section: they lavishly throw away food for humans to dogs and pigs and do not donate and distribute food to starving people on the street. When they see poor people dying from starvation, they even say, 'It is not my business. It is their fate.' How is this different from killing a person with a sword and saying, 'I did not kill him; the sword killed him'?

Section 4

梁惠王曰 寡人願安承教。

孟子對曰 殺人以梃與刃 有以異乎。

曰 無以異也。

(曰) 以刃與政 有以異乎。

曰 無以異也。

曰 庖有肥肉 廄有肥馬 民有饑色 野有餓莩 此率獸而食人也。獸相食 且人惡之。為民父母 行政不免於率獸而食人。惡在其為民父母也。仲尼曰 始作俑者 其無後乎。為其象人而用之也。如之何其使斯民饑而死也。

King Hui of Liang said, "I am glad to listen to your teaching."

Mencius asked, "Is there any difference between killing a person with a cudgel and with a sword?"

King Hui replied, "There is no difference."

Mencius asked further, "Is there any difference between killing people with swords and with political means?"

King Hui replied, "There is no difference also."

Mencius said, "If your kitchen is stocked with fat meat and your stable has fat horses, while your people look hungry and many are dying from starvation in the fields, this situation is like sending out wild beasts to devour people. When wild beasts victimize and devour other beasts, we detest their behaviors. Yet, many rulers who are supposed to be protectors and parents of their people often commit misdeeds that are equivalent to sending out wild beasts to devour people. They betray their role as protectors and parents of their people. Confucius once said, 'Those who invented the use of figurines as burial artefacts deserved to have no descendants.' This is because even the idea of using of human images as burial artefacts is evil. Therefore, why would you let your people die of starvation?"

Chapter 1: King Hui of Liang (1)

Modern Perspective:

The first few sentences in the above paragraph can be rephrased in a modern context: "If your wine cellar is stocked with wines of exotic vintages and fancy cars are parked in your garage, while your neighbors look hungry and many are dying from starvation in the streets, this situation is like sending out wild beasts to devour people."

Section 5

梁惠王曰 晉國 天下莫強焉 叟之所知也。及寡人之身 東敗於齊 長子死焉。西喪地於秦七百里 南辱於楚。寡人恥之 願比死者一灑之 如之何則可。

孟子對曰 地方百里而可以王。王如施仁政於民 省刑罰 薄稅斂 深耕易耨。壯者以暇日修其孝悌忠信 入以事其父兄 出以事其長上 可使制梃以撻秦楚之堅甲利兵矣。彼奪其民時 使不得耕耨以養其父母 父母凍餓 兄弟妻子離散。彼陷溺其民 王往而征之 夫誰與王敵。故曰 仁者無敵。王請勿疑。

King Hui of Liang told Mencius, "The state of Jin used to be the strongest among all states. You know it. During my reign, I was defeated by the state of Qi in the east, and my eldest son was killed in the battle. I was defeated by the state of Qin in the west and lost seven hundred square miles of territory to them. I was also humiliated by the state of Chu in the south. I feel ashamed. I want to revenge on behalf of those who sacrificed their lives for my country. What should I do?"

Mencius replied, "A country does not need to be large. A country with just one hundred square miles of territory is sufficient to implement a benevolent governance so that the whole world will support its leadership. If your Majesty implements humane and benevolent policies, reduces the severity of punishments and the burden of taxation, promotes farming, and encourages young people to spend their free time to learn and practice the virtues of filial piety, fraternity, loyalty, honor, and trust, so that they will seriously take care of their parents and siblings at home and serve their superiors at work, your country will be strong enough to fight even with cudgels against strong armies of the states of Qin and Chu.

These states interfere with and interrupt the timing of planting by their peasants. Their people cannot produce enough food, so their parents suffer from cold and hunger, and their wives, children, and brothers are separated and scattered abroad. These states are in deep trouble. If your Majesty wages a war against them, who will fight against you? Therefore, there is a common saying, 'A benevolent government is invincible.' Your Majesty, please do not doubt this!"

Commentary:

The state of Jin (晉國) was a predecessor of the state of Wei. As mentioned in the Commentary of Section 1 above, between 497 to 453 BC, the state of Jin broke up into three states: Han (韓), Zhao (趙), and Wei (魏). King Hui of the state of Wei (also known as King Hui of Liang) regarded the state of Wei as an offspring of the state of Jin. Therefore, he referred the state of Wei as the state of Jin in the first paragraph of this section. As mentioned in the Commentary of Section 1 above, the state of Wei was defeated twice by the state of Qi in the Battle of Gui Ling and the Battle of Ma Ling. His eldest son, Prince Shen, was killed in the Battle of Ma Ling. According to Shi Ji (史記, *Records of the Grand Historian*), written by Sima Qian

Chapter 1: King Hui of Liang (1)

(司馬遷, 145–86 BC), the state of Wei was defeated by the state of Qin in 342 BC and lost a territory of seven hundred square miles in the west of the Yellow River. In 323 BC, the state of Wei lost eight cities to the state of Chu after a defeat.

Modern Perspective:

Mencius reminded rulers of all eras that the fundamental and underlying strengths of a country are the happiness of its people, their virtues, and the benevolent governance policy, rather than just military strength, as shown in the sentence: "Your country will be strong enough to fight even with cudgels against the strong armies of the states of Qin and Chu."

Section 6

孟子見梁襄王。出 語人曰 望之不似人君 就之而不見所畏焉。

　卒然問曰 天下惡乎定。
　吾對曰 定於一。
　(曰) 孰能一之。
　對曰 不嗜殺人者能一之。
　(曰) 孰能與之。
　對曰 天下莫不與也。王知夫苗乎。七八月之間旱 則苗槁矣。天油然作雲 沛然下雨 則苗浡然興之矣。其如是 孰能禦之。今夫天下之人牧 未有不嗜殺人者也 如有不嗜殺人者 則天下之民皆引領而望之矣。誠如是也 民歸之 由水之就下 沛然誰能禦之。

Mencius saw King Xiang of Liang. After the meeting, Mencius told others, "He does not look majestic from afar. When I got closer to him, I found nothing intimidating about him. He abruptly asked me, 'How can there be peace in the entire country?' I answered, 'There will be peace when the entire country is unified.' He then asked, 'Who can unify the entire country?' I answered, 'A king who hates killing people.' He asked further, 'Who will support such leader?'

I answered, 'Everybody in the world will support and join him. Does your Majesty know how grains germinate? During July and August when the weather is dry, the sprouts will wither. However, after a heavy rain, the sprouts will regenerate again. Who can stop their growth? Nowadays, there is no ruler who hates killing people. If there is one who hates killing people, everybody in the world will yearn for his advent. People will certainly follow and support him like cascading water. Who can stop them?"

Annotation:

King Xiang of Liang (梁襄王, also known as King Xiang of Wei, 魏襄王) was the son of King Hui of Liang.

Modern Perspective:

This section is still relevant today.

Section 7

齊宣王問曰 齊桓 晉文之事可得聞乎。

孟子對曰 仲尼之徒無道桓文之事者 是以後世無傳焉。臣未之聞也。無以 則王乎。

Chapter 1: King Hui of Liang (1)

曰 德何如 則可以王矣。

曰 保民而王 莫之能禦也。

曰 若寡人者 可以保民乎哉。

曰 可。

曰 何由知吾可也。

曰 臣聞之胡齕曰 王坐於堂上 有牽牛而過堂下者 王見之曰 牛何之。對曰 將以釁鐘。王曰 舍之 吾不忍其觳觫 若無罪而就死地。對曰 然則廢釁鐘與。曰 何可廢也 以羊易之。不識有諸。

曰 有之。

曰 是心足以王矣。百姓皆以王為愛也 臣固知王之不忍也。

王曰 然。誠有百姓者。齊國雖褊小 吾何愛一牛。即不忍其觳觫 若無罪而就死地 故以羊易之也。

曰 王無異於百姓之以王為愛也。以小易大 彼惡知之。王若隱其無罪而就死地 則牛羊何擇焉。

王笑曰 是誠何心哉。我非愛其財 而易之以羊也。宜乎百姓之謂我愛也。

曰 無傷也 是乃仁術也 見牛未見羊也。君子之於禽獸也 見其生 不忍見其死。聞其聲 不忍食其肉。是以君子遠庖廚也。

王說曰 詩云 他人有心 予忖度之。夫子之謂也。夫我乃行之 反而求之 不得吾心。夫子言之 於我心有戚戚焉。此心之所以合於王者 何也。

曰 有復於王者曰 吾力足以舉百鈞 而不足以舉一羽。明足

以察秋毫之末 而不見輿薪 則王許之乎。

曰 否。

曰 今恩足以及禽獸 而功不至於百姓者 獨何與。然則一羽之不舉 為不用力焉。輿薪之不見 為不用明焉。百姓之不見保 為不用恩焉。故王之不王 不為也 非不能也。

曰 不為者與不能者之形何以異。

曰 挾太山以超北海 語人曰 我不能 是誠不能也。為長者折枝 語人曰 我不能 是不為也 非不能也。故王之不王 非挾太山以超北海之類也。王之不王 是折枝之類也。老吾老 以及人之老 幼吾幼 以及人之幼。天下可運於掌。詩云 刑於寡妻 至於兄弟 以禦於家邦。言舉斯心加諸彼而已。故推恩足以保四海 不推恩無以保妻子。古之人所以大過人者無他焉 善推其所為而已矣。今恩足以及禽獸 而功不至於百姓者 獨何與。權然後知輕重 度 然後知長短。物皆然 心為甚。王請度之。抑王興甲兵 危士臣 構怨於諸侯 然後快於心與。

王曰 否 吾何快於是 將以求吾所大欲也。

曰 王之所大欲可得聞與。

王笑而不言。

曰 為肥甘不足於口與。輕暖不足於體與。抑為采色不足視於目與。聲音不足聽於耳與。便嬖不足使令於前與。王之諸臣皆足以供之 而王豈為是哉。

曰 否 吾不為是也。

曰 然則王之所大欲可知已。欲辟土地 朝秦楚 蒞中國而撫四夷也。以若所為求若所欲 猶緣木而求魚也。

曰 若是其甚與。

Chapter 1: King Hui of Liang (1)

曰　殆有甚焉。緣木求魚　雖不得魚　無後災。以若所為　求若所欲　盡心力而為之　後必有災。

曰　可得聞與。

曰　鄒人與楚人戰　則王以為孰勝。

曰　楚人勝。

曰　然則小固不可以敵大　寡固不可以敵眾　弱固不可以敵強。海內之地方千里者九　齊集有其一。以一服八　何以異於鄒敵楚哉。蓋亦反其本矣。今王發政施仁　使天下仕者皆欲立於王之朝　耕者皆欲耕於王之野　商賈皆欲藏於王之市　行旅皆欲出於王之塗　天下之欲疾其君者皆欲赴愬於王。其若是　孰能禦之。

王曰　吾惛　不能進於是矣。願夫子輔吾志明以教我。我雖不敏　請嘗試之。

曰　無恒產而有恒心者　惟士為能。若民　則無恒產　因無恒心。苟無恒心　放辟　邪侈　無不為已。及陷於罪　然後從而刑之　是罔民也。焉有仁人在位　罔民而可為也。是故明君制民之產　必使仰足以事父母　俯足以畜妻子　樂歲終身飽　凶年免於死亡。然後驅而之善　故民之從之也輕。今也制民之產　仰不足以事父母　俯不足以畜妻子　樂歲終身苦　凶年不免於死亡。此惟救死而恐不贍　奚暇治禮義哉。王欲行之　則盍反其本矣。五畝之宅　樹之以桑　五十者可以衣帛矣。雞豚狗彘之畜　無失其時　七十者可以食肉矣。百畝之田　勿奪其時　八口之家可以無饑矣。謹庠序之教　申之以孝悌之義　頒白者不負戴於道路矣。老者衣帛食肉　黎民不饑不寒　然而不王者　未之有也。

King Xuan of Qi asked Mencius, "Can you tell me how Qi Huan Gong and Jin Wen Gong became leading hegemons among feudal lords?"

Mencius replied, "Disciples of Confucius never discuss the hegemony of Qi Huan Gong and Jin Wen Gong. Therefore, there is no historical record on their affairs. I have also not heard about them. If you want me to discuss, may I just talk about benevolent governance?"

King Xuan then asked, "What virtues must a ruler have so he can implement a benevolent governance?"

Mencius replied, "If you protect and appease your people, nobody can oppose and deter you."

King Xuan asked, "Can the type of person like myself protect and appease my people?"

Mencius said, "Of course!"

King Xuan asked, "Can you tell me why?"

Mencius said, "I heard from your minister, Hu He, an episode about you. When your Majesty was sitting in your chamber on one day, you saw a servant pulling along an ox. You asked, 'Where is the ox going?' The servant replied, 'I am taking the ox to the slaughter-house to get its blood to consecrate a bell for the altar.' You said, 'Let it go. I cannot bear the sight of its trembling. It is innocent. Why must it be killed?' The servant then asked, 'Shall we not consecrate the bell for the altar?' You replied, 'No, we cannot abolish the tradition. How about substituting it with a lamb?' Did this incident happen?"

King Xuan answered, "Yes, it did."

Then, Mencius said, "Your kind heart is already sufficient for you to be a benevolent and magnanimous ruler! Your people know that your Majesty has a kind heart. Your ministers definitely know that you are a compassionate person."

Chapter 1: King Hui of Liang (1)

King Xuan replied, "Yes, but some people think that I am petty [since a lamb is cheaper than an ox]. Although the state of Qi is small, I do not need to spare an ox. I could not bear to see the ox trembling. Since it is innocent, it should not be killed. I therefore suggested using a lamb as a substitute."

Mencius said, "Your people criticized your pettiness because you substituted a smaller animal for a bigger one. How did they know that you acted out of your kindness? Since your Majesty cannot bear to kill an innocent animal, what is the difference between killing an ox versus a lamb?"

King Xuan laughed and said, "What do you think was in my mind? I substituted an ox with a lamb not because I wanted to save money. No wonder my people misunderstood me."

Mencius said, "It does not matter. It reflected your instinct of humanity since you had only seen the ox and not the lamb. A natural attitude of a Jun Zi toward animals is that, having watched them alive, he cannot bear to see them dying, and having heard their pitiful cries, he cannot bear to eat their meat. Therefore, a Jun Zi stays away from the kitchen."

King Xuan said, "The *Book of Poetry* says, 'I can guess what is in the minds of others.' This applies to you. When I reflect on what I have done in this incident, I cannot figure out my real motivation. After you, my teacher, have spoken these words, I am still perplexed. Why is my kind heart consistent with the establishment of a benevolent and magnanimous government?"

Mencius said, "When someone tells you, 'I can lift a weight of three thousand pounds but cannot lift a feather. I can see the tip of a hair but cannot see a cart of firewood', do you agree with him?"

King Xuan replied, "No, I do not."

Mencius then said, "Your Majesty has a kind heart. Even animals get the benefit of your benevolence; however, your people have not. Why? The truth is that you have the strength to lift a feather, but you do not want to lift your finger, and you can see a cart of firewood, but you deliberately ignore it. Your people are not protected and appeased because you do not want to foster their welfare. Therefore, your Majesty has not implemented a benevolent and magnanimous government and unified the entire empire because you do not want to do it, and not because you are unable to do it."

King Xuan asked, "What is the difference between not wanting to do and unable to do?"

Mencius replied, "If you are asked to grab the Tai Shan mountain under your arms and jump into the North Sea with it, and if you say, 'I am unable to do it,' then you really cannot do it. If you are asked to massage the limbs of an elderly person and you say, 'I am unable to do it,' it is because you do not want to do it, not because you cannot do it. The implementation of a benevolent and magnanimous government and the unification of the empire is not an exercise of the first type but is an exercise of the second type.

If you respectfully take good care of elderly people in your family and then extend the same to all elderly people in the world, and if you nurture young people in your family and then extend the same to all young people in the world, the whole world will be in your hands. The *Book of Poetry* says, 'Be a good model first to your wife, then to your brothers, and finally to the country.' It essentially says that you should apply your kindness to others. Therefore, the fostering of kindness can help you protect the whole world. Otherwise, you cannot protect even your wife. Ancient saintly kings surpassed other rulers only because they were adept in applying their virtues to others. Your Majesty is kind to animals. Why do your people not get the benefit of your kindness?

By weighing, we can differentiate light objects from heavy ones.

Chapter 1: King Hui of Liang (1)

By measuring, we can differentiate long objects from short ones. This applies to objects. The same principle applies to your mind. Your Majesty, please consider it.

Does waging wars, endangering the lives of your people and officials, and becoming enemies of other feudal lords give you pleasure?"

King Xuan said, "No, how can I derive pleasure from these actions? I just want to achieve my grand desires."

Mencius asked, "May I know your grand desires?"

King Xuan laughed and did not answer.

Mencius then said, "Is it because you do not have enough delicious and wholesome food, warm and light clothes to keep you comfortable, enough colorful scenes to fascinate your eyes, good music to entertain your ears, large numbers of concubines and servants to please you? Your officials can provide these to you. Are these what you want?"

King Xuan replied, "No, these are not what I want."

Mencius said, "If so, let me guess what you really want. Your Majesty wants to expand your territory, subdue the states of Qin and Chu, rule the middle part of the empire, and conquer all barbaric tribes in peripheral regions. To achieve these goals based on what you are currently doing is like trying to find fish by climbing up a tree."

King Xuan said, "Is it that serious?"

Mencius said, "It will be worse than that. The worst outcome of climbing up a tree to find fish will only be the failure to find fish. This endeavor will not result in a disaster. If you try to pursue your goals by doing what you are currently doing, you will not only waste your efforts but also bring disaster to your country."

King Xuan asked, "Can you explain why I will bring disaster to my country?"

Mencius asked, "If the state of Cheng and state of Chu go to war, who do you think will win?"

King Xuan said, "The state of Chu will of course win [because the state of Cheng is much smaller]."

Mencius said, "Therefore, a small country cannot withstand a large country, a small army cannot withstand a large army, and a weak country cannot withstand a strong country. There are nine regions in the entire empire, each occupying about one thousand square miles. The state of Qi is only one of them. The attempt to subdue eight regions by one region is equivalent to the fight of the state of Cheng against the state of Chu. Why do you not resort to fundamental means of achieving your goals?

If you implement a benevolent governance, all competent and talented people in the entire empire will work for your government, peasants will flock to the fields of your state, merchants will come to your markets to trade, tourists will visit attractions in your state, and all dissidents from other states with immigrate to your state. If you can accomplish these, who can fight against you?"

King Xuan said, "I was stupid. I have not accomplished these in the past. I hope you, my teacher, can help me achieve my goals. Please teach me. Although I am not quite intelligent, I can try."

Mencius said, "Only educated and virtuous people can persist in upholding their principles, even when they lack any property to maintain a stable livelihood. Common people do not uphold righteous principles because they lack any property and cannot maintain a stable livelihood. Once they do not uphold righteous principles, they will lose their self-esteem and morality, and become licentious. After they have committed crimes, the imposition of punishment on them is equivalent to entrapping them. No benevolent ruler will implement a policy to entrap his people. Therefore, a wise and virtuous ruler will allocate enough property to

Chapter 1: King Hui of Liang (1)

households so that elderly parents in the family can be taken good care of, wives and children will be well fed, and people will not suffer from starvation even during a famine. After this is accomplished, the next step is to educate people with moral principles. In this way, it is easy to get the support from people.

Nowadays, the allocation of property to people is so petty that households cannot have enough food to feed elderly parents, wives, and children. They need to suffer from hunger, even during a good harvest, and from starvation during a famine. Under this condition, it is difficult to ensure the survival of family members. How can people have time and interest to learn moral principles?

If your Majesty wants to unify the entire empire, why not consider the implementation of benevolent governance. If each household has five acres of farming land with mulberry trees, fifty-year-old people can then wear silk clothes. If your people do not neglect the right time to raise poultry and hogs, seventy-year-old people can eat meat regularly. If each household has one hundred acres and does not neglect the right time to farm, all household members will not worry about starvation. If your government then institutes in schools a meritorious education which emphasizes filial and fraternal virtues, we will not see poor elderly people carrying heavy burden and tools on the road. If, in your country, seventy-year-old people can wear silk and eat meat, and nobody need to suffer from cold and hunger, it is impossible for you not to become the emperor of the entire empire."

Annotation:

King Xuan of Qi (齊宣王, 350–301 BC) was the king of the state of Qi (齊).

King Wu (周武王, died 1043 BC) founded the Zhou Dynasty

(周朝) in 1066 BC. His prime minister and chief commander of army, Jiang Zi Ya (姜子牙, circa 1156–1017 BC), helped King Wu of Zhou (周武王) overthrow Emperor Zhou (紂王) of the Shang Dynasty and was enfeoffed the state of Qi by King Wu. After 16 successions to the throne, Jiang Zi Ya's descendant, Qi Huan Gong (also known as Duke Huan of Qi, 齊桓公, died 643 BC) became the top hegemon among all feudal lords during the Spring-Autumn period. His great grandson was Qi Ling Gong (齊靈公, also known as Duke Ling of Qi) who died in 554 BC. Duke Ling of Qi had two sons, Prince Guang (光) and Prince Chu Jiu (杵臼). Prince Guang succeeded Duke Ling of Qi and became Duke Zhuang of Qi in 554 BC. He had an affair with the wife of his powerful minister Cui Zhu (崔杼). In revenge, Cui Zhu plotted and assassinated Duke Zhuang of Qi in 558 BC and supported Prince Chu Jiu to be the Duke Jing of Qi. King Xuan of Qi (齊宣王, also known as Qi Xuan Gong or Duke Xuan of Qi, 齊宣公) was the great grandson of Duke Jing of Qi.

Jin Wen Gong (晉文公, also known as Duke Wen of Jin, 671–628 BC) was one of the five hegemons during the Spring-Autumn Period.

Hu He (胡齕) was a minister for King Xuan of Qi.

Commentary:

Mencius was a great teacher and psychologist. He broke the ice with King Xuan by praising the king for his kind heart before pointing out the errors of King Xuan. Mencius's argument was step-by-step and forceful.

The following quotes in this section are famous:
1. "A natural attitude of a Jun Zi towards animals is that, having watched them alive, he cannot bear to see them

dying, and having heard their pitiful cries, he cannot bear to eat their meat. Therefore, a Jun Zi stays away from the kitchen."
2. "Because you do not want to do it and not because you are unable to do it."
3. "If you respectfully take good care of elderly people in your family and then extend the same to all elderly people in the world, and if you nurture young people in your family and then extend the same to all young people in the world, the whole world will be in your hands."
4. "Therefore, the fostering of kindness can help you protect the whole world. Otherwise, you cannot protect even your wife."
5. "The worst outcome of climbing a tree to find fish will only be the failure to find fish."

Modern Perspective:

The following sentences are still relevant today:
"If you implement a benevolent governance, all competent and talented people in the entire empire will work for your government, peasants will flock to the fields of your country, merchants will come to your markets to trade, tourists will visit attractions in your country, and all dissidents from other countries with immigrate to your country."

One of the key political doctrines of Confucianism is that only after the people of a country are well-fed and well-clothed will they have their sense of pride and honor. This idea is also illustrated in the sentences of this section: "Under this condition, it is difficult to ensure the survival of family members. How can people have time and interest to learn moral principles?" This doctrine is still relevant to modern society.

Many people and rulers fail to do good work not because they cannot do so but because they do not want to. We often hear excuses such as: "It cannot be done because of this or that."

Chapter 2: King Hui of Liang (2)

Section 1

莊暴見孟子曰　暴見於王　王語暴以好樂　暴未有以對也。好樂何如。

　　孟子曰　王之好樂甚　則齊國其庶幾乎。

　　他日見於王曰　王嘗語莊子以好樂　有諸。

　　王變乎色曰　寡人非能好先王之樂也　直好世俗之樂耳。

　　曰　王之好樂甚　則齊其庶幾乎。今之樂猶古之樂也。

　　曰　可得聞與。

　　曰　獨樂樂　與人樂樂　孰樂。

　　曰　不若與人。

　　曰　與少樂樂　與眾樂樂　孰樂。

　　曰　不若與眾。

　　(曰)　臣請為王言樂　今王鼓樂於此　百姓聞王鐘鼓之聲　管籥之音　舉疾首蹙頞而相告曰　吾王之好鼓樂　夫何使我至於此極也。父子不相見　兄弟妻子離散。今王田獵於此　百姓聞王車馬之音　見羽旄之美　舉疾首蹙頞而相告曰　吾王之好田獵　夫何使我至於此極也。父子不相見　兄弟妻子離散。此無他　不與民同樂也。

　　今王鼓樂於此　百姓聞王鐘鼓之聲　管籥之音　舉欣欣然有喜色而相告曰　吾王庶幾無疾病與　何以能鼓樂也。今王田獵於此　百姓聞王車馬之音　見羽旄之美　舉欣欣然有喜色而相告曰　吾王庶幾無疾病與。何以能田獵也。此無他 與民同樂也。今王與百姓同樂 則王矣。

When Zhuang Bao saw Mencius, he said, "I have met King Xuan. He told me that he loves music. I did not respond. Should a king love music?"

Mencius said, "If King Xuan indeed loves music very much, the state of Qi is already in good shape!"

A few days later, Mencius went to see King Xuan of Qi and asked, "Your Majesty once told Zhuang Bao that you love music very much. Was that true?"

King Xuan looked embarrassed and said, "I am not interested in the classical music of our ancestors. I just like pop music."

Mencius said, "Since your Majesty love music, it is a sign that the state of Qi is already well governed. It does not matter whether you like classical or pop music."

King Xuan asked, "Can you explain to me the reason?"

Mencius asked, "Which is more pleasurable—to enjoy music alone or to enjoy it with others?"

King Xuan replied, "It is more pleasurable to enjoy music with others."

Mencius then asked, "Which is more pleasurable—to enjoy music with a few or to enjoy it with many?"

King Xuan replied, "It is more pleasurable to enjoy music with many."

Mencius said, "Let me then discuss the enjoyment of music. Suppose that when your Majesty is playing music, your people, hearing the drum-beats and sound of flutes and pipes, shake their aching heads, knit their eyebrows, and say to one another, 'Our king is enjoying music by himself. Why does he reduce us to such dire distress? Parents are separated from children. Brothers and wives

Chapter 2: King Hui of Liang (2)

are also separated from us.' Suppose that when your Majesty is hunting, your people, hearing the noise of your carriages and horses and watching glamorous flags of your procession, shake their aching heads, knit their eyebrows, and say to one another, 'Our king is enjoying his hunting. Why does he reduce us to such dire distress? Parents are separate from children. Brothers and wives are also separated from us.' Why? It is because you do not share your happiness with people.

Suppose that when your Majesty is playing music, your people, hearing the drum-beats and sound of flutes and pipes, say to one another joyfully, 'It is likely that our king has recovered from sickness. That is why he can play music.' Suppose that when your Majesty is hunting, your people, hearing the noise of your carriages and horses and watching glamorous flags of your procession, say to one another joyfully, 'It is likely that our king has recovered from sickness. That is why he can hunt.' Why? It is because you share your happiness with people. Therefore, if you share your happiness with people, you will become a benevolent and magnanimous ruler of the entire empire."

Annotation:

Zhuang Bao (莊暴) was a minister of the state of Qi.
In this section, Mencius talked with King Xuan of Qi (齊宣王, 350–301 BC).

Commentary:

The sentence, "It is more pleasurable to enjoy music with many than alone" is well-known.

Section 2

齊宣王問曰 文王之囿方七十里 有諸。

　　孟子對曰 於傳有之。

　　曰 若是其大乎。

　　曰 民猶以為小也。

　　曰 寡人之囿方四十里 民猶以為大 何也。

　　曰 文王之囿方七十里 芻蕘者往焉 雉兔者往焉 與民同之。民以為小 不亦宜乎。臣始至於境 問國之大禁 然後敢入。臣聞郊關之內有囿方四十里 殺其麋鹿者如殺人之罪。則是方四十里 為阱於國中。民以為大 不亦宜乎。

King Xuan of Qi asked Mencius, "King Wen of Zhou had a royal garden of seventy square miles. Was that true?"

Mencius replied, "Yes, according to historical record."

King Xuan said, "It was quite large, wasn't it?"

Mencius replied, "Yet his people lamented that it was too small."

King Xuan said, "My royal garden has only forty square miles. Yet my people criticize that it is too large. Why?"

Mencius said, "The garden of King Wen had seventy square miles. His people had the permission to enter it to collect firewood and catch wild chickens and rabbits. He shared the garden with his people. It is natural that his people considered the garden too small. When I, your humble servant, first arrived at your state, I had to check whether a place was prohibited before I entered it. I heard that there was a royal garden of forty square miles. Whoever kills a deer inside that garden is punishable by death sentence. Therefore, this garden is a like a trap of forty square miles in the state. Is it natural that your people consider it too large?"

Chapter 2: King Hui of Liang (2)

Commentary:

This and the above section are about sharing.

Section 3

齊宣王問曰 交鄰國有道乎。

孟子對曰 有。惟仁者為能以大事小 是故湯事葛 文王事昆夷。惟智者為能以小事大 故大王事獯鬻 句踐事吳。以大事小者 樂天者也。以小事大者 畏天者也。樂天者保天下 畏天者保其國。詩云 畏天之威 於時保之。

王曰 大哉言矣 寡人有疾 寡人好勇。

對曰 王請無好小勇。夫撫劍疾視曰 彼惡敢當我哉。此匹夫之勇 敵一人者也。王請大之。詩云 王赫斯怒 爰整其旅 以遏徂莒 以篤周祜 以對於天下。此文王之勇也。文王一怒而安天下之民。書曰 天降下民 作之君 作之師 惟曰其助上帝 寵之四方 有罪無罪 惟我在 天下曷敢有越厥志。一人衡行於天下 武王恥之。此武王之勇也。而武王亦一怒而安天下之民。今王亦一怒而安天下之民 民惟恐王之不好勇也。

King Xuan of Qi asked Mencius, "Is there a method to establish friendly foreign relations with my neighbors?"

Mencius replied, "Yes, there is. Only a ruler of a large state who practices the Ren virtue can treat small states with forbearance and friendliness. This was illustrated by how King Tang of the Shang Dynasty dealt with the state of Ge, and how King Wen of Zhou dealt with the barbaric tribe Kun Yi. Only a wise ruler of a small state can build a harmonious relation with a large state. This was illustrated by how King Tai of the state of Zhou avoided a confrontation with the barbaric tribe Xun Yu, and how King Gou Jian of Yue submitted to the state of Wu. A ruler of a large state, which treats small states with forbearance and friendliness, happily advocates righteous principles of nature. A ruler of a small state, which can build a harmonious relation with a large state, is compliant with righteous principles of nature. Advocates of righteous principles of nature can protect the world. Those who are compliant with righteous principles of nature can protect their states. The *Book of Poetry* says, 'Being fearful of principles of nature will foster peace.' "

King Xuan said, "This is a magnanimous talk. However, I have a weakness. I love valor."

Mencius replied, "Your Majesty should not love trivial valor. By drawing a sword, showing a fierce look, and saying, 'Dare you challenge me?' one displays brute valor, which can subdue only a single person. Your Majesty needs to have great bravery.

The *Book of Poetry* [referring to King Wen of Zhou] states, 'With an outburst of indignation, the king amassed an army to stop invaders and to protect the state of Zhou so that his people can live peacefully.' This showed the great bravery of King Wen. A righteous outburst of indignation can bring peace to the world.

The *Book of Classic History* [referring to King Wu of Zhou] says, 'Tian (Sky) creates people on earth and delegates rulers and teachers to assist Tian to protect people. As a ruler, I have the responsibility to govern both innocent people and criminals. Who dares to violate the will of Tian?' King Wu of Zhou loathed being a bully of the world. This illustrated the great bravery of King Wu. His righteous outburst of indignation brought peace to people in the world. If your Majesty can bring peace to the world with an outburst of indignation, your people will want you to have more bravery."

Chapter 2: King Hui of Liang (2)

Annotation and Commentary:

In the literature of Confucianism, the word *Ren* (仁) embodies all the core virtues of humanity, including love. This word was translated as "kindness" or "humaneness" in the past. Such an interpretation and translation of *Ren* does not convey the full meaning of the word in Chinese. There is no single word in English that encompasses all the meanings of the word in Chinese. Therefore, this translation uses the transcriptions of the Chinese word 仁 to preserve its authentic meanings. In the context of this section, Ren refers to love of humanity. A ruler or a leader of the society who practices Ren tries to bring peace and happiness to all people in the world (see the discussion on Ren in the Commentary of Section 2 of Chapter 3).

The Great Yu (禹, circa 2237–2139 BC) founded the Xia Dynasty (夏朝, circa 2184–1600 BC) in about 2184 BC. After about 500 years of the dynasty, the 16th successor to the throne was Emperor Jie of Xia (夏桀). He was an extraordinarily talented person. In addition to being a superb scholar, he was a great fighter with unusual physical strength. He could kill a tiger with his bare hands. However, he was the first tyrant in Chinese history. When Emperor Jie came to power, he hired and trusted many crooked ministers and got rid of many meritorious officials. Evil confidants taught Emperor Jie how to blackmail, rip off, torture, and terrorize people. As a result, the economy tanked, and the treasury coffer was depleted. To make up for the deficit, Emperor started to invade many smaller states and tribes to rob their land and wealth. King Tang of the state of Shang (商湯, circa 1670–1587 BC) was a feudal lord of the Xia Dynasty. To save the people of the empire from turmoil, he formed an alliance with many other feudal lords to revolt against Emperor Jie. In about 1600 BC, King Tang toppled the Xia Dynasty and founded the Shang Dynasty (商朝).

Before King Tang overthrew Emperor Jie, there was a tribe Ge (葛) next to the state of Shang. Ge Bo (葛伯), the leader of Ge and an ally of Emperor Jie, was another tyrant. He did not organize worship ceremonies. In ancient China, it was extremely important to worship Sky, Earth, and ancestors. King Tang sent his envoy to reprimand Ge Bo, who responded, "My tribe is poor. We cannot afford to sacrifice an animal for the worship." King Tang then provided cows and lambs for Ge Bo's ceremonies. Instead of sacrificing these animals on the altar, Ge Bo ate them. King Tang then sent his envoy to reprimand Ge Bo, who responded, "My tribe does not have enough grain to eat. Why should we waste these animals for the sacrifice to the gods?" King Tang then sent his own peasants to work for tribe Ge and donated food to their elderly and poor people. Ge Bo intercepted the delegates on their way, stole the food, and killed one boy who was carrying the food. In response to Ge Bo's barbaric act, King Tang invaded Ge and killed Ge Bo. The lesson of this story was that a ruler who practices Ren may not necessarily refrain from using arms and waging wars. When there was a need to foster and uphold Ren and to remove evil, it is righteous to wage a war. Another lesson is that the way for a large country to deal with a small country is to apply a "carrot and stick" policy. A policy of "carrot" should first be applied, and if it fails, a "stick" policy can be applied.

The Shang Dynasty lasted for about 600 years. After 30 successions to the throne, a brutal tyrant, Emperor Zhou (紂), also known as Emperor Xin (帝辛), ruled the empire. A smart and strong man and a great warrior, Emperor Zhou considered himself smarter than all his ministers. He had a notoriously decadent and extravagant lifestyle. He spent a fortune on his grand pavilion, called the Deer Terrace (鹿台), on which he indulged in debauchery with beautiful and bewitching concubines, including the malicious Da Ji (妲己). He ruled by brutality and terror. His uncle and private tutor, Bi Gan (比干), once advised Zhou to stop his brutality. Bi Gan wrote that being a counsel of the emperor, he had the responsibility to advise the emperor. He would rather die than keep his mouth shut. The enraged Zhou said to his other ministers, "I heard that a virtuous person's heart has seven holes. Let us verify whether Bi Gan's heart has seven holes." Zhou then ordered Bi Gan's heart be cut out alive and showed to other ministers to prove that Bi Gan's heart did not have seven holes.

Because of his tyranny, Emperor Zhou lost support from his people, including close relatives and good ministers. For example, Ji Zi (箕子) was an uncle of Emperor Zhou and his private tutor. Ji Zi repeatedly advised Zhou to stop his tyranny but failed to change him. Ji Zi then faked madness. Zhou then imprisoned and enslaved Ji Zi. Wei Zi (微子) was Zhou's brother and a viscount. Wei disagreed with Zhou on his brutality, quitted the royal court, and became a turncoat later.

Emperor Zhou was a warmonger also. He expanded his empire by invading many tribes in the east and southeast and captured hundreds of thousands of slaves from his conquests. However, years of invasion depleted his treasury coffers.

In the west part of the country was the state of Zhou (周), which was populated by a tribe in the Wei River valley. Because of the state's fertile land, favorable climate, and prudent government, Zhou gained in prominence in that region. Its meritorious and benevolent ruler, Ji Chang (姬昌), also known as Earl Wen of Zhou, fostered a culture of humaneness, reverence for the elderly, kindness to youth, and respect of knowledge and competency. He implemented policies to protect the underclass and peasants, introduced free trade and emphasized economic development, and lowered the tax rate on peasants to 11.1% so that they could have more disposable incomes and savings. He also ran a clean and lean government, and promoted morality in the society. Through his virtuous behaviors, Earl Wen set a good example.

The state of Zhou prospered as a result of Earl Wen's rule, and its people were happy. Many neighboring tribes joined the state or became its allies. The growing prominence of this state and Earl Wen's heightened reputation alerted officials in the central government of the Shang Dynasty. At the suggestion of his ministers, Emperor Zhou trapped, arrested, and imprisoned Earl Wen. A minister of the state of Zhou spent a large sum of money to acquire precious jewelry, thoroughbreds, silk, and beautiful women as a ransom for Earl Wen. Upon seeing beautiful women, the lascivious Emperor Zhou was gratified and said, "Just these beautiful women are enough. I don't care about other treasures." The satisfied Emperor Zhou then released Earl Wen.

After Earl Wen returned home, he planned to overthrow the Shang Dynasty. He started to build alliance with other feudal lords and states. He also continued to build the economy of his state without raising eyebrows of officials in the central government. He became a model of righteousness and virtue among other feudal lords, and an arbiter of conflicts among them. They later called him King Wen of Zhou and supported him as their spiritual leader.

King Wen of Zhou (周文王, 1152–1056 BC) founded the Kingdom of Zhou which was later called the Zhou Dynasty in 1066 BC. He died at the age of 97. His son Ji Fa (姬發), also called King Wu of Zhou (周武王), was the successor. He continued the same policy of his father. The state grew further while the Empire of Shang continued to decline. Emperor Zhou was troubled by infighting in his government and disturbance at the east border by barbaric tribes in the east and southeast. King Wu of Zhou then

Chapter 2: King Hui of Liang (2)

seized this opportunity to quickly build his army and form an alliance to overthrow Emperor Zhou. In the Spring of 1046 BC, King Wu raised an army of 300 chariots, 3,000 armored warriors and thousands of infantrymen. His small army traveled eastward from his home base to Meng Jin. Other feudal lords in the alliance also brought their own armies to Meng Jin. After the coalition was formed, King Wu declared war against the Shang Dynasty. He defeated Emperor Zhou in the Battle of Mu Ye (牧野), 70 miles south of Chao Ge (朝歌), the capital of the Shang Dynasty. King Wu of Zhou then founded the Zhou Dynasty (周朝) in 1066 BC.

In 1062 BC, four years after King Wen of Zhou founded the Zhou Dynasty, there was a small tribe, Kun Yi, in the west of Zhou. It did not know the power of Zhou's army. It repeatedly made incursions on the territory of Zhou. On one day, they tried to attack the east gate of Zhou three times. King Wen told his people, "Close the gate. No need to fight with them. Ignore them and mind our daily business. They will leave soon."

The state of Zhou was small during the reign of King Tai, the grandfather of King Wen. A barbaric tribe, Xun Yu (獯鬻), in the north of the state of Zhou had a fierce army. It repeatedly made incursions into Zhou and robbed goods and animals. King Tai told his people, "Let them take our goods and animals." A while later, Xun Yu invaded again and demanded the concession from King Kai of territory. The people of Zhou were angry and wanted to fight. King Tai told his people, "People support a king because of his role in providing the welfare to people. I am only a custodian of the land. If the Xun Yu people want it, let them have it. I do not want my people to die for my land." King Tai then left his capital with his family and clan and migrated to the foot of Qi Mountain. People in surrounding tribes and states, having heard about the Ren virtue of King Tai, gradually joined the state of Zhou. It then grew to a large state when his grandson, King Wen, took the reign.

The lesson of this historical example is that the goal of a person with Ren virtue is the protection of humanity. When confronted with the choice between the welfare of his people versus power and property, the ruler of a small country must make a wise decision to uphold Ren principles. The lives of people are more important than power and property.

In 496 BC, during the Spring-Autumn period, King Fu Chai (夫差) of the state of Wu (吳國) succeeded his father who was killed in a war against the state of Yue (越國). In 494 BC, Fu Chai decided to revenge and invaded the state of Yue. King Gou Jian (勾踐) of the state of Yue, unprepared for the invasion, was defeated and besieged. His prime minister Fan Li (范蠡) suggested that King Gou Jian should make a truce with the state of Wu. Under the peace treaty, the state of Yue gave King Fu Chai plenty of gold and jewelry, and many beautiful women, and King Gou Jian agreed to be a subject of the state of Wu. Although the state of Yue was defeated, it was still capable of launching a counterattack on the state of Wu. Instead, King Gou Jian hid his desire to fight back because the timing was not right. After the peace treaty had been signed, King Gou Jian delegated the running of his government to his ministers and left for the state of Wu. He took Fan Li along. Both became servants (prisoners and slaves) of King Fu Chai. Their subservience convinced King Fu Chai that they had no ambition at all. King Gou Jian and Fan Li were set free after three years. After King Gou Jian returned home, he realized his state was much weaker than the state of Wu. His priority was to rebuild his state, which he did stealthily and steadily. To constantly remind himself of the goal of rebuilding the state, he slept on a rough mattress made of sticks of firewood and tasted gall juice every day. This practice reminded him of the need to overcome hardship. There is a famous idiom in

Chinese language related to his practice: "Sleeping on a mattress made of sticks of firewood and tasting gall juice (臥薪嘗膽)."

After leaving his palace, King Gou Jian stayed on a farm, where he grew his own food and his wife weaved cloth for the family. While he lived in austerity, he continued to run his government. He lowered taxes for peasants, introduced land reforms, promoted birth rates, improved infrastructures, and repaired ruined cities. In the meantime, he stealthily trained an elite army. He continued to send valuable gifts and beautiful women to King Fu Chai to show his loyalty. In 478 BC, the state of Wu had a famine and chaos ensued. King Gou Jian took this great opportunity to invade the state of Wu. After years of decadence, corruption, and waste, the state of Wu failed. Its army was annihilated, and King Fu Chai was killed.

This story illustrated Mencius's point that a ruler of a small state must have wisdom to deal with adversity. King Gou Jian endured great humiliation to protect the survival of his state and its people. Again, the goal of this story is the pursuit of Ren principle.

In the second part of this section, Mencius talked about the real meaning of bravery. Brute valor is not true bravery. Great bravery requires the moral courage to uphold Ren principles and the righteous principles of Tian.

This section highlights three inter-related virtues: Ren, wisdom, and bravery. We should have an ideal in life. The ultimate ideal should be guided by the principles of Ren and the mission that Tian (Sky 天命) has bestowed on us. This mission is related to righteous principles of Tian, as well as the era and circumstances in which we live in. One needs wisdom to understand and appreciate what constitute the principles of Ren and our mission in life. One also needs wisdom to make the right choice of actions in our pursuit of such principles. When we are in an advantageous and superior position, we need to treat disadvantaged and inferior people with forbearance and magnanimity. When we are in a disadvantaged and inferior position, we still need to make the right choice to firmly uphold Ren principles and our mission in life. Bad people commit plunders and even crimes when they are poor or desperate. Confucius also said, "Everyone hates poverty and low-class status. If the departure from them is through improper ways, we should not follow them (see *Confucius Analects*, section 5 of Chapter 4). Those who crave bravery, but dread poverty will tend to rebel. Those who lack the Ren virtue will also tend to rebel under a huge stress and crisis (see *Confucius Analects*, section 10 of Chapter 8). A Jun Zi endures poverty firmly. A Xiao Ren commits plunders when he is poor" (Section 2 of Chapter 15).

After deciding upon the right course of action, one must have the moral courage to follow through. The determination and display of moral courage to execute and persist in our chosen goal and to overcome obstacles and opposition to pursue righteousness and Ren principles is great bravery.

The word *Jun Zi* (君子) is used in Chinese scholarly texts to mean a gentleman, a person of superior and noble character, a prominent and respectable person in society, or a person who upholds high standards of virtuous principles. Jun Zi was commonly translated as "gentleman" in the past, but it stands for a much wider range of excellence and a higher standard of morality than what the English word *gentleman* stands for. Therefore, this translation retains the transcribed term *Jun Zi* to preserve its authentic meaning in Chinese. A Xiao Ren (小人) is a person with the opposite character of a Jun Zi. A Xiao Ren is, for example, mean, wicked, cruel, dumb, lacking virtues, dishonest, low class, and so on. Some old translations used "mean man" to describe a Xiao Ren (小人). Since such a character has many inferior and obnoxious qualities, "mean man" is an incomplete description. There is no single English word that conveys all these qualities. To preserve the complete and accurate meaning of this phrase in Chinese culture, this translation therefore uses the transcription of the Chinese phrase.

Section 4

齊宣王見孟子於雪宮。王曰 賢者亦有此樂乎。

　孟子對曰 有。人不得 則非其上矣。不得而非其上者 非也。為民上而不與民同樂者 亦非也。樂民之樂者 民亦樂其樂。憂民之憂者 民亦憂其憂。樂以天下 憂以天下 然而不王者 未之有也。昔者齊景公問於晏子曰 吾欲觀於轉附 朝儛 遵海而南 放於琅邪 吾何修而可以比於先王觀也。晏子對曰 善哉問也 天子適諸侯曰巡狩 巡狩者巡所守也 諸侯朝於天子曰述職 述職者述所職也 無非事者 春省耕而補不足 秋省斂而助不給 夏諺曰 吾王不遊 吾何以休 吾王不豫 吾何以助 一遊一豫 為諸侯度。今也不然 師行而糧食 飢者弗食 勞者弗息。睊睊胥讒 民乃作慝。方命虐民 飲食若流。流連荒亡 為諸侯憂。從流下而忘反謂之流 從流上而忘反謂之連。從獸無厭謂之荒 樂酒無厭謂之亡。先王無流連之樂 荒亡之行。惟君所行也。

　景公說 大戒於國 出舍於郊。於是始興發補不足 召大師曰 為我作君臣相說之樂。蓋徵招角招是也。其詩曰 畜君何尤。畜君者 好君也。

King Xuan of Qi received Mencius in his Winter Palace [with gorgeous buildings, terraces, landscaped gardens, ponds, and rare species of flowers and animals]. The king asked Mencius, "Does a virtuous person like yourself enjoy these?"

Mencius replied, "Yes, I do. When people do not have these, they will blame on their ruler. They are of course wrong in blaming their ruler for not having these. However, if a ruler does not share his enjoyment with people, he is also wrong. If a ruler rejoices in the joy of his people, they will also rejoice in his joy. If a ruler agonizes over the worries of his people, they will also agonize over his worries. If you take the world's joy as yours and the world's worries as yours, how can you not become a benevolent and magnanimous king?

Duke Jing of Qi once asked Yan Ying, 'I plan to travel to the famous mountains, Zhuan Fu and Chao Wu, then south along the seacoast, and finally to the Lang Xie province. What should I prepare so that my tour is comparable to those taken by ancient saintly kings?'

Yan Ying replied, 'Good question! When the imperial emperor visited feudal lords, he took a tour of inspection. When feudal lords visited the imperial emperor, they reported their duties. These visits were all related to governmental matters. In Spring, the emperor assessed the adequacy of cultivation resources and provided aid to peasants if needed. In Autumn, the emperor assessed the harvest and provided aid to peasants if the harvest was poor. A proverb in the Xia Dynasty said, 'If the emperor does not visit us, how can we sleep well? If the emperor does not assess our needs, how can we get aid? This tradition was followed by all feudal lords.' The practice is different nowadays. When an emperor travels, he extorts food from his people to feed an army of guards, attendants, and companions. As a result, hungry people are deprived of food. Laborers cannot get rests. People talk to one another with frustrated and angry eyes about how to revolt. The emperor enslaves his subjects and wastes food like water draining down the river. When the emperor drifts, roams,

Chapter 2: King Hui of Liang (2)

becomes unruly and disoriented, his feudal lords and ministers should worry for him. Traveling downstream and forgetting to return is called 'drifting.' Traveling upstream and forgetting to return is called 'roaming.' If he goes hunting too frequently, he will become unruly. If he drinks excessively, he will be disoriented. Ancient saintly kings avoided these indulgences. You should now know what to do.'

Duke Jing of Qi was impressed with the advice from Yan Ying. After making necessary arrangements, Duke Jing left his capital and stayed in the suburbs. He opened his granary and donated food to people in need. He commissioned a royal musician to compose pieces of music for everyone in court. Therefore, the famous songs 'Zheng Zhao' and 'Jiao Zhao' were written. A line in these songs says, 'What worry does a restrained king have?' A restrained king is a good king!"

Annotation:

Zhuan Fu (轉附), Chao Wu (朝儛), and Lang Xie (琅邪) were names of mountains in modern-day Shandong Province.

Qi Jing Gong (齊景公, also known as Duke Jing of Qi, circa 550–490 BC) was a descendant of Jiang Zi Ya (姜子牙, circa 1156–1017 BC), who helped King Wu of Zhou (周武王) overthrow Emperor Zhou (紂王) of the Shang Dynasty and was enfeoffed the state of Qi by King Wu. The Annotation of Section 7 of Chapter 1 also mentioned Duke Jing of Qi. King Xuan of Qi (齊宣王, also known as Duke Xuan of Qi or Qi Xuan Gong, 齊宣公) was the great grandson of Duke Jing of Qi.

Duke Jing of Qi was assisted by a meritorious prime minister, Yan Ying (晏嬰). During the early part of his reign, Duke Jing of Qi was a responsible and diligent ruler and listened to the advice of Yan

Ying. However, he later indulged in lavishness, pleasure, and lust, and did not care about the welfare of his people. According to Shi Ji (史記, *Records of the Grand Historian*) written by Sima Qian (司馬遷, 145–86 BC), Duke Jing loved grand palaces, dogs, horses, and extravagance. He also levied heavy tax and imposed severe punishments on people.

Yan Ying (晏嬰, also known as Yan Zhong 晏仲, Yan Zi 晏子, circa 578–500 BC) was born in modern-day Gaomi county, Shandong province. He was a meritorious prime minister during the reigns of Duke Ling of Qi, Duke Zhuang of Qi, and Duke Jing of Qi. Confucius met Yan Ying in the state of Qi and gave him high credit. Duke Jing of Qi managed to maintain the integrity of his sovereignty over his state because of Yan Ying's good efforts and advice (see the story of Yan Ying in Section 1 of the Endnotes).

Section 5

齊宣王問曰　人皆謂我毀明堂。毀諸　已乎。

　　孟子對曰　夫明堂者　王者之堂也。王欲行王政　則勿毀之矣。

　　王曰　王政可得聞與。

　　對曰　昔者文王之治岐也　耕者九一　仕者世祿　關市譏而不征　澤梁無禁　罪人不孥。老而無妻曰鰥。老而無夫曰寡。老而無子曰獨。幼而無父曰孤。此四者　天下之窮民而無告者。文王發政施仁　必先斯四者。詩云　哿矣富人　哀此煢獨。

　　王曰　善哉言乎。

　　曰　王如善之　則何為不行。

　　王曰　寡人有疾　寡人好貨。

Chapter 2: King Hui of Liang (2)

對曰 昔者公劉好貨。詩云 乃積乃倉 乃裹餱糧 于橐于囊 思戢用光 弓矢斯張 干戈戚揚 爰方啟行。故居者有積倉 行者有裹糧也 然後可以爰方啟行。王如好貨 與百姓同之 於王何有。

王曰 寡人有疾 寡人好色。

對曰 昔者大王好色 愛厥妃。詩云 古公亶甫 來朝走馬 率西水滸 至於岐下 爰及姜女 聿來胥宇。當是時也 內無怨女 外無曠夫。王如好色 與百姓同之 於王何有。

King Xuan of Qi asked Mencius, "Some people tell me to demolish the Hall of Proclamation. Should I demolish it or not?"

Mencius replied, "The Hall of Proclamation was the place where your ancestors assembled their ministers to proclaim important government decrees. If your Majesty desires to implement benevolent and magnanimous policies, you should not demolish it."

King Xuan then asked, "Can you elaborate what are benevolent and magnanimous policies?"

Mencius replied, "In the past, King Wen of Zhou brought peace and prosperity to his state in the Qi Mountain region by levying a low tax rate of 11.1%, providing salaries and benefits to descendants of senior officials, eliminating custom duty, only performing inspections at borders, removing the prohibition to fish in lakes and ponds, and not punishing wives and children of criminals. An elderly man without a wife is called a widower. An elderly woman without a husband is called a widow. A lonely elderly without children and family members is called a single senior. A young child without parents is called an orphan. The welfare policy of King Wen of Zhou gave priority to these four groups. The *Book of Poetry* said, 'Only the rich can live comfortably. Lonely elderly and orphans are miserable.'"

King Xuan said, "Your words are great!"

Mencius replied, "If your Majesty thinks that these policies are great, why do you not implement them?"

King Xuan said, "I have a weakness. I love wealth."

Mencius replied, "[There is nothing wrong with the love of wealth]. In the past, the earliest founder of the clan of Zhou, Gong Liu, also loved wealth. The *Book of Poetry* narrated his words, "Let us accumulate food and fill up our granaries, pack our bags and sacks with dry food, consider diverse opinions for better knowledge, bring sufficient number of bows, arrows, spears, axes, shields, and swords before we start our expedition.' Therefore, households had abundant food in their warehouses, and travelers had sufficient food in their bags before their journeys. If your Majesty loves wealth and shares it with your people, what is wrong with it?"

King Xuan said, "I have another weakness. I love sexual pleasure."

Mencius said, "[There is nothing wrong with the love of sexual pleasure.] In the past, King Tai loved beautiful women. He loved his beautiful wife. The *Book of Poetry* mentioned about him, 'Gu Gong Tan Fu rode his horse early in the morning, headed west along the river, and arrived at the foot of Mountain Qi. He brought along his wife, who was a native of Jiang and visited families in that area.' At that time, there was no unmarried woman in a household, and no single man outside. If your Majesty loves sexual pleasure and shares it with your people, what is wrong with it?"

Annotation:

Gong Liu (公劉) was an early fore father of the clan of Zhou.

King Tai (also known as Gu Gong Tan Fu, 古公亶父) was the earliest leader of the clan of Zhou, and the grandfather of King Wen of Zhou (周文王).

Chapter 2: King Hui of Liang (2)

Commentary:

The second half of this section shows that Mencius did not endorse asceticism. In Confucianism, food and sex are basic human (and all animal) instincts. Unlike many other religions and philosophy schools, Confucians consider that the satisfaction of these instincts is a basic human need. Greed and the excessive indulgence in these desires are wrong, though, according to the *Doctrine of the Mean* (中庸之道), an important theme under Confucianism. The hoarding of food and wealth is not wrong by itself. Selfishness and the unwillingness to share them with others are wrong. This section points out that the provision of food, wealth, social welfare, sexual satisfaction, self-defense, and peace to people in the country is a goal of a benevolent and magnanimous government.

Section 6

孟子謂齊宣王曰 王之臣有托其妻子於其友 而之楚遊者。比其反也 則凍餒其妻子 則如之何。

　王曰 棄之。

　曰 士師不能治士 則如之何。

　王曰 已之。

　曰 四境之內不治 則如之何。

　王顧左右而言他。

Mencius said to King Xuan of Qi, "Suppose that one of your officials needed to travel to the state of Chu. He entrusted his wife and children to the care of his friend. After your official returned home, he found that his friend had let his wife and children suffer from cold and hunger. How should he deal with his friend?"

King Xuan replied, "Discontinue the friendship."

Mencius asked, "What if a sheriff of a prison does not control his subordinate?"

King Xuan replied, "Fire him."

Mencius asked again, "What if a country is not well governed?"

King Xuan did not reply, and instead looked around and changed the topic.

Commentary:

Mencius's last question embarrassed King Xuan. Mencius subtly implied that King Xuan would lose his throne if his country were not well governed. Since the state of Qi was in decline, Mencius's question was a warning to King Xuan.

Section 7

孟子見齊宣王曰 所謂故國者 非謂有喬木之謂也 有世臣之謂也。王無親臣矣 昔者所進 今日不知其亡也。

王曰 吾何以識其不才而舍之。

曰 國君進賢 如不得已 將使卑踰尊 疏踰戚 可不慎與。左右皆曰賢 未可也。諸大夫皆曰賢 未可也。國人皆曰賢 然後察之 見賢焉 然後用之。左右皆曰不可 勿聽。諸大夫皆曰不可 勿聽。國人皆曰不可 然後察之 見不可焉 然後去之。左右皆曰可殺 勿聽。諸大夫皆曰可殺 勿聽。國人皆曰可殺 然後察之 見可殺焉 然後殺之。故曰 國人殺之也。如此 然後可以為民父母。

Chapter 2: King Hui of Liang (2)

Mencius saw King Xuan and said, "A country is old not because it has old trees and buildings; it is because it has officials who have a long history of loyalty. Your Majesty does not have loyal and intimate officials. Why have they all gone?"

King Xuan asked, "How can I tell who is incompetent and who to dismiss?"

Mencius replied, "When a king tries to hire competent and meritorious officials, he might sometimes have to place low-ranked officials over high-ranked officials, and unrelated people over close relatives. He must be careful in this matter. If all around you consider a candidate to be competent and virtuous, do not listen to them yet. If all ministers consider the candidate to be competent and virtuous, do not listen to them yet. If, however, people in the country consider the candidate to be competent and virtuous, you should then observe further. You can then hire the candidate after witnessing his good qualities. If all around you object to the hiring of a candidate, do not listen to them yet. If all ministers object to the hiring of the candidate, do not listen to them yet. If, however, people in the country object to the hiring of the candidate, you should observe further. You can then dismiss the candidate after witnessing his bad qualities. If all around you consider that a person deserves a death sentence, do not listen to them yet. If all ministers around you consider that the person deserves a death sentence, do not listen to them yet. If, however, people in the country consider that the person deserves a death sentence, you should then investigate further. You can then sentence the person to death if you find valid evidence of his offense. If you take the above approach, you are indeed the parent and guardian of your people."

Commentary:

In this section, Mencius emphasized the importance of objectivity and public opinion. A ruler should not be easily swayed by his ministers and confidants. Public opinion and objective evidence are more important.

Modern Perspective:

Mencius pointed out that, in the choice of government officials, the will of the people is most important.

Section 8

齊宣王問曰 湯放桀 武王伐紂 有諸。

孟子對曰 於傳有之。

曰 臣弒其君 可乎。

曰 賊仁者謂之賊 賊義者謂之殘 殘賊之人謂之一夫。聞誅一夫紂矣 未聞弒君也。

King Xuan of Qi asked Mencius, "King Tang banished Emperor Jie. King Wu of Zhou overthrew Emperor Zhou. Did these events happen?"

Mencius replied, "Yes, according to historical record."

King Xuan said, "Is it alright for an official to kill his king?"

Mencius replied, "Those who damage Ren principles are called bandits. Those who wreck righteousness are called brutes. A brute bandit is called an outcast. We only heard that Emperor Zhou was an outcast. We have not heard that Emperor Zhou was assassinated."

Chapter 2: King Hui of Liang (2)

Annotation:

The story of Emperor Jie of Xia Dynasty and King Tang of Shang Dynasty is narrated in the Commentary of Section 3 of Chapter 1. The story of Emperor Zhou of Shang Dynasty and King Wu of Zhou is also narrated in the same Commentary. King Tang and King Wu were once feudal lords under Emperor Jie and Emperor Zhou, respectively.

Section 9

孟子見齊宣王曰 為巨室 則必使工師求大木。工師得大木 則王喜 以為能勝其任也。匠人斲而小之 則王怒 以為不勝其任矣。夫人幼而學之 壯而欲行之。王曰 姑舍女所學而從我。則何如。今有璞玉於此 雖萬鎰 必使玉人雕琢之。至於治國家 則曰 姑舍女所學而從我 則何以異於教玉人雕琢玉哉。

Mencius saw King Xuan of Qi and said, "If we want to build a big mansion, we must send the best carpenter to look for big pieces of timber. If the carpenter can find them, your Majesty must be pleased and appreciate his competency. If, however, another workman breaks up large pieces of timber, your Majesty must be angry and consider the workman to be incompetent. Having learned since his youth how to run a good government and grown up, a scholar would want to put his knowledge into practice. If your Majesty tells him, 'Put aside what you have learned and follow me', what will be the consequence? Suppose that we have a piece of unwrought jade hidden in a stone. Although it is worth tens of thousands of gold coins, it must be cut, crafted, and sculptured by a skillful artisan.

Likewise, regarding the government of a country, your directive is equivalent to telling an artisan how to sculpture a piece of jade."

Modern Perspective:

In this section, Mencius's point is a good reminder for managers in general. A good manager must respect the professional skills of his or her staff.

Section 10

齊人伐燕 勝之。宣王問曰 或謂寡人勿取 或謂寡人取之 以萬乘之國伐萬乘之國 五旬而舉之 人力不至於此。不取 必有天殃。取之 何如。

孟子對曰 取之而燕民悅 則取之。古之人有行之者 武王是也。取之而燕民不悅 則勿取。古之人有行之者 文王是也。以萬乘之國伐萬乘之國 簞食壺漿 以迎王師。豈有他哉 避水火也。如水益深 如火益熱 亦運而已矣。

The state of Qi attacked and conquered the state of Yan (燕). King Xuan of Qi asked Mencius, "Some people advise me not to take possession of it. Some people advise me to take possession of it. The conquest in fifty days of a country with ten thousand chariots by another country with ten thousand chariots is an achievement beyond human strength. Since this is a divine providence, calamity will come to me if I do not take possession of it. What do you think?"

Mencius replied, "If the people of Yan welcome your possession of Yan, you should then take it. This was what saintly kings like King Wu of Zhou did. If the people of Yan hate your possession of their country, you should not take it. This was what saintly kings like King Wu of Zhou did. After your state with ten thousand chariots has conquered the state of Yan with ten thousand chariots, people of Yan lined up the streets offering baskets of food and vessels of water to your army. There is no other reason but their desire and expectation to escape from fire and water. However, if your conquest of the state of Yan will drown its people in deeper water and burn them with hotter fire, its people will soon revolt against you and seek another conqueror."

Annotation:

The state of Yan (燕) was one of the seven hegemons during the Warring State Period. It was to the northeast of the state of Qi.

Commentary:

This section is a good lesson to leaders of countries nowadays. Conquests and occupations of other countries will be auspicious if the conqueror follows Ren principles and gets the support of people in the conquered country. Otherwise, disasters will befall the conqueror.

Section 11

齊人伐燕 取之 諸侯將謀救燕。宣王曰 諸侯多謀伐寡人者 何以待之。

孟子對曰 臣聞七十里為政於天下者 湯是也。未聞以千里畏人者也。書曰 湯一征 自葛始。天下信之。東面而征 西夷怨 南面而征 北狄怨 曰 奚為後我。民望之 若大旱之望雲霓也。歸市者不止 耕者不變。誅其君而弔其民 若時雨降 民大悅。書曰 徯我後 後來其蘇。

今燕虐其民 王往而征之。民以為將拯己於水火之中也 簞食壺漿 以迎王師。若殺其父兄 系累其子弟 毀其宗廟 遷其重器 如之何其可也。天下固畏齊之強也。今又倍地而不行仁政 是動天下之兵也。王速出令 反其旄倪 止其重器 謀於燕眾 置君而後去之 則猶可及止也。

The state of Qi conquered the state of Yan and took its territory. Other feudal lords plotted to rescue the state of Yan. King Xuan of Qi asked Mencius, "Many feudal lords plot to attack my country. How should I deal with them?"

Mencius replied, "Let me cite an example of King Tang before he founded the Shang Dynasty. He started off with a small territory of seventy square miles. Yet he could unify and lead the whole empire. I have never heard of a state such as yours with thousands of square miles fearful of other states. The *Book of Classic History* said, 'Before King Tang started his revolt against the Xia Dynasty, he invaded the small state of Ge. Everybody in the empire trusted and supported him. When he later attacked eastern states and tribes, people in the Yi tribe in the west yearned for his advent, and when he attacked southern states and tribes, people in the Di tribe also yearned for his advent. They asked, 'Why does he come to us last?' They yearned for their liberation from their own harsh rulers, like waiting for the appearance of a cloud in the sky during a severe drought. In these regions, the markets still boomed, and the fields were still cultivated. After King Tang had removed the tyrants of these states, their people felt like having a rainfall during a drought. They were joyous. The *Book of Classic History* says, 'We have waited so long for the advent of a great king. We are saved!'

Since the ruler of the state of Yan have tyrannized over his people, and your Majesty has gone there and punished him, they think that you can liberate them from their horrendous situation. They therefore line the streets, offering baskets of food and vessels of water to welcome your army. If your Majesty goes in and kill their parents and elder brothers, imprisons their children and younger brothers, destroys their ancestral temples, and loots their valuables, how can such actions be proper? All feudal lords in the empire used to dread the power of the state of Qi. If they now see the doubling of your territory and your actions against Ren principles, they will initiate a coalition to fight against you.

Your Majesty should immediately order the return of all captives and the prohibition of looting. You should also consult with the people of Yan to appoint a new king for them and then leave the state of Yan. In this way, you can avoid a war with all feudal lords."

Annotation:

Ge (葛) was a small state during the Shang Dynasty.
Yi (夷) was a tribe in the west of China.
Di (狄) was a tribe in the north of China.

Section 12

鄒與魯鬨。穆公問曰 吾有司死者三十三人 而民莫之死也。誅之 則不可勝誅。不誅 則疾視其長上之死而不救 如之何則可也。

孟子對曰 凶年饑歲 君之民老弱轉乎溝壑 壯者散而之四方者 幾千人矣。而君之倉廩實 府庫充 有司莫以告 是上慢而殘

Mencius in Modern Perspectives

下也。曾子曰 戒之戒之 出乎爾者 反乎爾者也。夫民今而後得反之也 君無尤焉。君行仁政 斯民親其上 死其長矣。

The state of Zou was at war with the state of Lu. Duke Mu of Zou (also known as Zou Mu Gong) asked Mencius, "Thirty-three officers were killed on my side, but none of my people would die to defend the officers. If I punish these people, there are too many of them. If I do not punish them, they will continue to be antagonistic against the government and apathetic towards the death of their officers. What should I do?"

Mencius replied, "During recent years of depression and famine, many elderly and weak people in your country have died and their corpses were thrown into ditches. Strong people have emigrated abroad by the thousands. Yet the royal granary is overwhelmed with food and your treasury coffer is full. Your officials did not report the dire situation of your people to you. This is indeed a case of a negligent and irresponsible government and cruelty to its people. Zheng Zi once said, 'Beware, beware! Whatever you have done unto others will be done unto you!' Now is the time for your people to revenge on you. If, on the contrary, your Majesty implements a benevolent policy, your people will love you and be willing to die for you and your officers."

Annotation:

The state of Zou (鄒) was a small feudal state in the modern-day Zou county of Shandong province. Mencius was a native of Zou.

Zou Mu Gong (鄒穆公, also known as Duke Mu of Zou, 382–330 BC) was a benevolent king of the state of Zou and a contemporary of Mencius.

Zheng Zi (曾子, also known as Zheng Shen 曾参, born 505 BC)

Chapter 2: King Hui of Liang (2)

was a prominent disciple of Confucius, known for his filial piety. He was the author of *The Book of Great Learning* (大學).

Commentary:

According to Mencius, a benevolent governance policy is the foundation of patriotism and loyalty.

Section 13

滕文公問曰 滕 小國也 間於齊楚。事齊乎 事楚乎。
　孟子對曰 是謀非吾所能及也。無已 則有一焉。鑿斯池也 築斯城也 與民守之 效死而民弗去 則是可為也。

Duke Wen of Teng asked Mencius, "Teng is a small state located between the state of Qi and state of Chu. With whom should I become an ally?"

Mencius replied, "I am incompetent to give you strategic advice. If I must, I have a word for you: Dig a deep and wide moat and build a strong wall around your city. If you unite your people to defend your state and are prepared to die in its defense, your people will not leave you. This may be a viable course of action."

Annotation:

Duke Wen of Teng (滕文公, also known as Teng Wen Gong) was the king of a small state Teng (滕) during the Warring States Period. He was a contemporary of Mencius.

The state of Qi (齊國) was one of the seven hegemons during the Warring States Period.

117

The state of Chu (楚國) was one of the seven hegemons during the Warring States Period.

The state of Teng (滕) is a small state in the southwest of modern-day Teng county in Shandong province.

Section 14

滕文公問曰 齊人將築薛 吾甚恐。如之何則可。

孟子對曰 昔者大王居邠 狄人侵之 去之岐山之下居焉。非擇而取之 不得已也。苟為善 後世子孫必有王者矣。君子創業垂統 為可繼也。若夫成功 則天也。君如彼何哉 強為善而已矣。

Duke Wen of Teng asked Mencius, "The state of Qi is fortifying a city wall for my neighbor, the state of Xue. I am worried. What should I do?"

Mencius replied, "In the past, King Tai of Zhou originally dwelt in the Bin region. He was invaded by the barbaric tribe of Di. He then relocated to the foot of Mountain Qi, not because he chose it but because he had no other choice. If a king implements a benevolent governance, one of his descendants will eventually build a great country because he will follow your legacy. It is, of course, a matter of divine providence as to whether they will be successful. What can you do now? Practicing benevolence is all you can do now."

Annotation:

See the Annotation in Section 13 above for the state of Qi (齊國) and Duke Wen of Teng (滕文公).

Chapter 2: King Hui of Liang (2)

The state of Xue (薛) was a small state in the Warring States Period.

The story of King Tai of Zhou is narrated in both the Commentary of Section 3 of Chapter 2, the Annotation of Section 5 of Chapter 2, and the following section.

Section 15

滕文公問 滕 小國也。竭力以事大國 則不得免焉。如之何則可。

孟子對曰 昔者大王居邠 狄人侵之。事之以皮幣 不得免焉 事之以犬馬 不得免焉。事之以珠玉 不得免焉。乃屬其耆老而告之曰 狄人之所欲者 吾土地也 吾聞之也 君子不以其所以養人者害人 二三子何患乎無君 我將去之。去邠 踰梁山 邑於岐山之下居焉。邠人曰 仁人也 不可失也。從之者如歸市。或曰 世守也 非身之所能為也 效死勿去。君請擇於斯二者。

Duke Wen of Teng asked Mencius, "Teng is a small state. Although I have tried my best to serve large neighboring states, I cannot prevent them from invading me. What can I do?"

Mencius replied, "In the past, King Tai of Zhou originally dwelt in the Bin region. The barbaric tribe, Di, invaded the state of Zhou. Although King Tai gave the Di tribe fur, silk, dogs, horses, and jewels, he could not prevent the invasion. He then assembled elderly representatives in his state and told them, 'The Di people wants our land. I heard from sages that a Jun Zi would not hurt his people with what nourishes him. All of you should not grieve for not having a king. I plan to leave.' He then left Bin, passed the Mountain Liang, and finally settled down at the foot of Mountain Qi. The people of

Bin said to one another, 'He is a man of Ren virtue. We shall not miss him.' They then followed him as if they were hurrying to the market. However, some people also said, 'The land of Bin was a legacy of his ancestors. It is not up to him to relinquish it. He should die for it.' Your Majesty can choose one of these two alternatives."

Annotation:

    King Tai of Zhou (大王) was the grandfather of King Wen of Zhou (周文王). The story of King Tai is narrated in Section 3 of Chapter 2 above.

    Bin (邠) was a place in modern-day Shaanxi Province.

    Di (狄) was a tribe in the north of China during the Spring-Autumn Period.

Section 16

魯平公將出 嬖人臧倉者請曰 他日君出 則必命有司所之。今乘輿已駕矣 有司未知所之 敢請。

    公曰 將見孟子。

    曰 何哉 君所為輕身以先於匹夫者 以為賢乎。禮義由賢者出。而孟子之後喪踰前喪。君無見焉。

    公曰 諾。

    樂正子入見曰 君奚為不見孟軻也。

    曰 或告寡人曰 孟子之後喪踰前喪。是以不往見也。

    曰 何哉君所謂踰者。前以士 後以大夫。前以三鼎 而後以五鼎與。

    曰 否 謂棺槨衣衾之美也。

Chapter 2: King Hui of Liang (2)

曰　非所謂踰也　貧富不同也。

樂正子見孟子曰　克告於君　君為來見也。嬖人有臧倉者沮君　君是以不果來也。

曰　行或使之　止或尼之。行止　非人所能也。吾之不遇魯侯天也。臧氏之子焉能使予不遇哉。

When Duke Ping of Lu was about to leave his palace, his favorite steward, Zang Can, said to him, "When you went out in the past, you used to tell beforehand the butler where you were going. Your carriage and horse are now ready for you, but we do not know where you are going. May I ask?"

Duke Ping replied, "I am going to see Mencius."

Zang Can said, "Why? Are you demeaning yourself by seeing that charlatan? Is he virtuous? A virtuous person should observe the customary Li. However, Mencius arranged a more elaborate funeral for his mother than the earlier funeral for his father [This shows that he violated the customary Li]. You better not see him."

Duke Ping then said, "I am not going then."

Yue Zheng Zi entered the court and asked Duke Ping, "Your Majesty, why did you cancel the meeting with Mencius?"

Duke Ping replied, "Zang Can told me that Mencius arranged a more elaborate funeral for his mother than the earlier funeral for his father. I, therefore, did not go to see Mencius."

Yue Zheng said, "Why? What did he mean by saying that the later funeral was more elaborate than the earlier funeral? Did he mean that the earlier funeral was comparable to those for low-level officials and the later funeral was comparable to those for ministers? Did he mean that the earlier funeral deployed three tripods to hold offerings and the later funeral deployed five tripods to hold offerings?"

Duke Ping said, "No, he meant the quality of the inner coffin, the outer casket, clothes for the dead, and the shroud."

Yue Zheng said, "It was not Mencius's intention to violate customary Li. He was poor when his father died. He was richer when his mother died later [He therefore could afford a more elaborate funeral for his mother]."

Yue Zheng went to see Mencius and said, "I have recommended you to Duke Ping of Lu. He originally planned to see you. However, his favorite steward, Zang Can, dissuaded him. Duke Ping did not come to see you."

Mencius said, "A venture succeeds because it may be aided by some invisible forces. A venture fails because it may be impeded by some invisible forces. Success and failure may be beyond the power of a person. It may be the divine providence that I do not have the opportunity to meet with Duke Ping of Lu. How can that son of Zang preclude my opportunity to meet with Duke Ping?"

Annotation:

Duke Ping of Lu (魯平公, also known as Lu Ping Gong, 314–294 BC) was the son of Lu Jing Gong (魯景公).

Zang Can (臧倉) was a eunuch of Duke Ping of Lu.

Yue Zheng Zi (樂正子) was a disciple of Mencius and a minister of the state of Lu.

The son of Zang was Zang Can.

Chapter 3: Gong Sun Chou (1)

Section 1

公孫丑問曰 夫子當路於齊 管仲 晏子之功 可復許乎。

　孟子曰 子誠齊人也 知管仲 晏子而已矣。或問乎曾西曰 吾子與子路孰賢。曾西蹴然曰 吾先子之所畏也。曰 然則吾子與管仲孰賢。曾西艴然不悅曰 爾何曾比予於管仲 管仲得君如彼其專也 行乎國政 如彼其久也 功烈 如彼其卑也 爾何曾比予於是。

　曰 管仲 曾西之所不為也 而子為我願之乎。

　曰 管仲以其君霸 晏子以其君顯。管仲 晏子猶不足為與。

　曰 以齊王 由反手也。

　曰 若是 則弟子之惑滋甚。且以文王之德 百年而後崩 猶未洽於天下。武王 周公繼之 然後大行。今言王若易然 則文王不足法與。

　曰 文王何可當也 由湯至於武丁 賢聖之君六七作。天下歸殷久矣 久則難變也。武丁朝諸侯有天下 猶運之掌也。紂之去武丁未久也 其故家遺俗 流風善政 猶有存者 又有微子 微仲 王子比干 箕子 膠鬲皆賢人也 相與輔相之 故久而後失之也。尺地莫非其有也 一民莫非其臣也 然而文王猶方百里起 是以難也。齊人有言曰 雖有智慧 不如乘勢 雖有鎡基 不如待時。今時則易然也。夏後 殷周之盛 地未有過千里者也 而齊有其地矣。雞鳴狗吠相聞 而達乎四境 而齊有其民矣。地不改辟矣

民不改聚矣 行仁政而王 莫之能禦也。且王者之不作 未有疏於此時者也。民之憔悴於虐政 未有甚於此時者也。饑者易為食 渴者易為飲 孔子曰 德之流行 速於置郵而傳命。當今之時 萬乘之國行仁政 民之悅之 猶解倒懸也。故事半古之人 功必倍之 惟此時為然。

Gong Sun Chou asked Mencius, "If you, my teacher, had the authority to run the government of Qi, will you repeat Guan Zhong's and Yan Ying's accomplishments?"

Mencius said, "You are indeed a national of the state of Qi. You only know about Guan Zhong and Yan Ying. In the past, somebody asked Zheng Xi, 'Who is more meritorious, you or Zi Lu?' Zheng Xi looked uneasy and said, 'Zi Lu was revered by my grandfather.' That person then asked, 'Who is more meritorious, you or Guan Zhong?' Zheng Xi was angry and said, 'How can you compare me with Guan Zhong?! Guan Zhong got the dedicated trust of his king and had the opportunity to implement his policy for a long time, but his accomplishments were quite insignificant. How can you compare him with me?' Zheng Xi further said, 'I will not imitate Guan Zhong. Do you think that I like to?'"

Gong Sun Chou said, 'Guan Zhong assisted his king to become the top hegemon among all feudal lords. Yan Ying helped his king to stand out. Are these accomplishments insufficient?"

Mencius said, "To turn the state of Qi into a great leader of the empire would be as easy as flipping one's palms."

Gong Sun Chou then said, "I, your student, am quite perplexed by your comment. King Wen of Zhou, who had superior merit, was still unable to implement his benevolent policy to the entire empire before his death at one hundred. It required his successor, King Wu of Zhou, to carry on broadly implementing his father's ideals. You

Chapter 3: Gong Sun Chou (1)

now say that it is easy to become a great leader of the empire. Do you mean that King Wen was not worthy of imitation?"

Mencius said, "How can I measure up to King Wen of Zhou? After the founding of the Shang Dynasty by King Tang, there were six to seven successions of great emperors until Emperor Wu Ding came to power. The Shang Dynasty had earned the loyalty of its people for a long while. Such a long history made it difficult to change a regime. Furthermore, since Emperor Wu Ding had the support of all feudal lords, governing the empire was as easy as manipulating an object in one's hands. Even [the notorious] Emperor Zhou did not depart from Emperor Wu Ding's policy for a long while because good ancestral traditions and practices still prevailed. Emperor Zhou also had the assistance of meritorious mentors, relatives, and ministers such as Wei Zi, Wei Zhong Yan, Bi Gan, Ji Zi, and Jiao Ge. Therefore, it took a long time for Emperor Zhou to lose his throne. During his reign, every foot of land in the entire empire belonged to the Shang Dynasty, and every person was a subject of Shang. Therefore, it was extremely difficult for King Wen of Zhou, who had only a hundred square mile of territory, to revolt against the Shang Dynasty.

People of Qi have a saying, 'Even if one has wisdom, it is better for him to ride the prevailing trend. Even if one has farming tools, it is better for him to wait for a favorable season.' Even the prosperous Xia, Shang, and Zhou dynasties had less than a thousand square miles of territories. The state of Qi has a territory of comparable size. The crows of cocks and barks of dogs inside the state of Qi can be heard in all four corners of the empire. Furthermore, the state of Qi has a big population. It does not need to expand its territory further and increase its population size further. If it implements a benevolent and magnanimous governance, who can conquer it? However, the void of good governance has prevailed unprecedentedly for a long time. People's suffering under tyranny is also unprecedented. Hungry people disregard the poor quality of food. Thirsty people disregard the impurity of water. Confucius once said, 'Implement a benevolent policy speedily, like sending a message by express mail.' In today's era, if a large country with ten thousand chariots were to implement a benevolent and magnanimous governance, its people will be so gratified as if they were relieved from hanging upside down. By just implementing half of what ancient saintly kings did, a modern ruler can reap double benefits. Now is the time to do good."

Annotation:

Gong Sun Chou (公孫丑) was a disciple of Mencius. Some scholars thought that Gong Sun Chou co-authored the book of *Mencius*.

Section 6 of Endnotes narrates the story of Guan Zhong (管仲, 725–645 BC). He was one of the best prime ministers in Chinese history and assisted King Huan of the state of Qi to become the top hegemon during the Spring-Autumn Period.

Section 1 of Endnotes narrates the story of Yan Ying (晏嬰, also known as Yan Zhong 晏仲, Yan Zi 晏子, circa 578–500 BC). He was a meritorious prime minister during the reigns of Duke Ling of Qi, Duke Zhuang of Qi, and Duke Jing of Qi.

Zheng Xi (曾皙, also known as Zheng Dian, 曾點) was a disciple of Confucius and the father of Zheng Zi (曾子), who was a great Confucian. Section 37 of Chapter 14 below also mentions Zheng Xi.

Zi Lu (子路, 542–480 BC also known as Zhong You 仲由) was a disciple of Confucius best known for his ability and success in statesmanship. He was noted for his valor and sense of justice.

Chapter 3: Gong Sun Chou (1)

Section 9 of Endnotes tells the story of Wei Zi (微子), Wei Zhong Yan (微仲衍), Bi Gan (比干), Ji Zi (箕子), and Jiao Ge (膠鬲). The story of Emperor Zhou of the Shang Dynasty and King Wu of Zhou Dynasty is also narrated in the Commentary of Section 8 of Chapter 2.

Section 2

公孫丑問曰 夫子加齊之卿相 得行道焉 雖由此霸王不異矣。如此 則動心否乎。

孟子曰 否。我四十不動心。

曰 若是 則夫子過孟賁遠矣。

曰 是不難 告子先我不動心。

曰 不動心有道乎。

曰 有。北宮黝之養勇也 不膚撓 不目逃 思以一豪挫於人 若撻之於市朝。不受於褐寬博 亦不受於萬乘之君。視刺萬乘之君 若刺褐夫。無嚴諸侯。惡聲至 必反之。孟施舍之所養勇也 曰 視不勝猶勝也。量敵而後進 慮勝而後會 是畏三軍者也 舍豈能為必勝哉 能無懼而已矣。孟施舍似曾子 北宮黝似子夏。夫二子之勇 未知其孰賢 然而孟施舍守約也。昔者曾子謂子襄曰 子好勇乎 吾嘗聞大勇於夫子矣 自反而不縮 雖褐寬博 吾不惴焉 自反而縮 雖千萬人 吾往矣。孟施舍之守氣 又不如曾子之守約也。

曰 敢問夫子之不動心 與告子之不動心 可得聞與。

(曰) 告子曰 不得於言 勿求於心 不得於心 勿求於氣。不得於心 勿求於氣 可。不得於言 勿求於心 不可。夫志 氣之帥也。氣 體之充也。夫志至焉 氣次焉。故曰 持其志 無暴其氣。

(曰) 既曰 志至焉 氣次焉。又曰 持其志無暴其氣者 何也。

曰 志壹則動氣 氣壹則動志也。今夫蹶者趨者 是氣也 而反動其心。

(曰) 敢問夫子惡乎長。

曰 我知言 我善養吾浩然之氣。

(曰) 敢問何謂浩然之氣。

曰 難言也 其為氣也 至大至剛 以直養而無害 則塞於天地之閒。其為氣也 配義與道 無是 餒也。是集義所生者 非義襲而取之也。行有不慊於心 則餒矣。我故曰 告子未嘗知義 以其外之也。必有事焉而勿正 心勿忘 勿助長也。無若宋人然 宋人有閔其苗之不長而揠之者 芒芒然歸。謂其人曰 今日病矣 予助苗長矣。其子趨而往視之 苗則槁矣。天下之不助苗長者 寡矣。以為無益而舍之者 不耘苗者也 助之長者 揠苗者也。非徒無益 而又害之。

(曰) 何謂知言。

曰 詖辭知其所蔽 淫辭知其所陷 邪辭知其所離 遁辭知其所窮。生於其心 害於其政 發於其政 害於其事。聖人復起 必從吾言矣。

(曰) 宰我 子貢善為說辭 冉牛 閔子 顏淵善言德行。孔子兼之曰 我於辭命則不能也。然則夫子既聖矣乎。

曰 惡 是何言也。昔者子貢問於孔子曰 夫子聖矣乎。孔子曰 聖則吾不能 我學不厭而教不倦也。子貢曰 學不厭 智也

Chapter 3: Gong Sun Chou (1)

教不倦 仁也 仁且智 夫子既聖矣。夫聖 孔子不居 是何言也。

（曰）昔者竊聞之 子夏 子遊 子張皆有聖人之一體。冉牛 閔子 顏淵則具體而微。敢問所安。

曰 姑舍是。

曰 伯夷 伊尹何如。

曰 不同道 非其君不事 非其民不使 治則進 亂則退 伯夷也。何事非君 何使非民 治亦進 亂亦進 伊尹也。可以仕則仕 可以止則止 可以久則久 可以速則速 孔子也。皆古聖人也 吾未能有行焉。乃所願 則學孔子也。

（曰）伯夷 伊尹於孔子 若是班乎。

曰 否。自有生民以來 未有孔子也。

曰 然則有同與。

曰 有 得百里之地而君之 皆能以朝諸侯有天下。行一不義 殺一不辜而得天下 皆不為也。是則同。

曰 敢問其所以異。

曰 宰我 子貢 有若智足以知聖人。汙 不至阿其所好。宰我曰 以予觀於夫子 賢於堯舜遠矣。子貢曰 見其禮而知其政 聞其樂而知其德 由百世之後 等百世之王 莫之能違也 自生民以來 未有夫子也。有若曰 豈惟民哉 麒麟之於走獸 鳳凰之於飛鳥 太山之於丘垤 河海之於行潦 類也 聖人之於民 亦類也 出於其類 拔乎其萃 自生民以來 未有盛於孔子也。

Gong Sun Chou asked Mencius, "If you, my teacher, had an opportunity to become a prominent minister of the state of Qi and implement your political ideology, you could undoubtedly assist a hegemon to lead the empire. Does this opportunity appeal to you or

Mencius in Modern Perspectives

are you intimidated by such a responsibility?"

Mencius replied, "No. At 40, I have already developed a resolute, undaunted, and incorruptible heart."

Gong Sun Chou said, "As such, you, my teacher, is superior to Meng Ben!"

Mencius said, "It is not difficult to attain that. Gao Zi has developed a resolute, undaunted, and incorruptible heart before me."

Gong Sun Chou asked, "Is there a method to have a resolute, undaunted, and incorruptible heart?"

Mencius said, "Yes, there is. Bei Gong Yao's method to cultivate his valor is as follows: he does not flinch when his skin is being pinched; he does not dodge when his eyes are being attacked; when a piece of his hair is pulled out by somebody, he considers the attack as if he is beaten publicly in the market place; he does not submit to a commoner nor to a king of a big country; he considers the challenge of assassinating a king to be the same as assassinating a commoner; he is not afraid of any king or lord; he always retaliates against insults on him. On the other hand, Meng Shi She has another method to cultivate his valor. He said, 'I consider a defeat as if it is a victory. If a general assesses the strength and weakness of an enemy before an advance, and to weigh the chance of victory before engaging in a fight, he is indeed afraid of meeting a formidable enemy. How can I guarantee a victory? I am just fearless.' Meng Shi She resembles Zheng Zi, whereas Bei Gong Yao resembles Zi Xia. I do not know whose valor is superior. I think that Meng Shi She has mastered the essence of valor. Zheng Zi once asked his student Zi Xiang, 'Do you love valor? Confucius once said that if on reflection he was wrong, he would not harass a commoner, but if on reflection he was right, he would not be afraid of confronting an army of tens of thousands of men.' Although Meng Shi She resembles Zheng Zi, the essence of Meng's valor is simply fearlessness, which is inferior

Chapter 3: Gong Sun Chou (1)

to the valor based on righteousness."

Gong Sun Chou asked, "May I venture to ask you, my teacher, to tell me the difference between your resolute, undaunted, and incorruptible heart and Gao Zi's resolute, undaunted, and incorruptible heart?"

Mencius replied, "Gao Zi said, 'If you do not discern the words of others, you need not bother with pondering their truth and validity. If you cannot tell what is right or wrong in a matter, you should not be upset and deal with the matter emotionally.' It is correct to avoid dealing with a matter emotionally when one is uncertain of what is right or wrong in the matter. It is incorrect to ignore the words of others and refrain from pondering their truth and validity when one cannot discern such words. The will is the commander of energy and impetus [and emotion], which flow through the body of a person. Wherever the will wants to go and whatever it wants to do, the energy and impetus of the person will follow, hence the saying, 'Uphold your will [and belief], and do not sap your energy and impetus.' "

Gong Sun Chou asked, "You say that the will is the commander of energy and impetus of a person. You also say that one should uphold his will and not sap his energy and impetus. Why? [The two sentences seem to contradict each other]."

Mencius said, "When the mind and will is focused on a matter, they will drive the energy and impetus of a person. On the other hand, when energy and impetus is intensely focused on a matter, they will also affect the will of a person. For example, when one runs fast and stumbles over a pit, he is controlled by his energy and impetus [and emotion] to the extent that his will is affected."

Gong Sun Chou asked, "May I venture to ask about your strengths?"

Mencius said, "I am a discerning listener, and I am good at

cultivating my magnanimous spirit [and character]."

Gong Sun Chou asked, "What does 'magnanimous spirit' mean?"

Mencius replied, "It is hard to describe. If you look at it as a form of energy and impetus, it is extremely great and unsurmountable. If one nurtures it righteously and does not deplete it, his magnanimous spirit will fill and be applicable to every corner of the world. The exercise of this spirit must be in line with Dao and Yi. Otherwise, this spirit will sap. The spirit is accumulated through a long period of righteous practices and cannot be acquired by an incidental act of righteousness. Once one's action deviates from the righteous belief in his heart, this spirit will sap. I, therefore, say that Gao Zi does not know the essence of Yi. He has not internalized it and made it an integral aspect of his character. One should practice righteousness as a matter of course, without the expectation of its explicit benefits to himself. One should also not forget about the constant nurturing of his magnanimous spirit. However, one should not try to artificially groom it. Do not follow the example of a farmer of Song. This farmer was concerned about the slow growth of his plants. He pulled up the shoots of his plants to speed up their growth. He returned home and told his family, 'I am tired from working all day. I have pulled the shoots up so that they are taller.' His son hurried to the fields and found that all plants had withered. Few people in the world abstain from pulling up shoots to promote the growth of plants. Those who do not bother to grow plants are lazy. Those who artificially promote their moral strength are like those who pull up shoots to promote growth. This action is not only futile but also harmful."

Gao Sun Chou asked, "What does a discerning listener mean?"

Mencius said, "When I hear a biased message, I know that the mind of the speaker is blocked. When I hear a flowery message, I

Chapter 3: Gong Sun Chou (1)

know that the mind of the speaker is decadent. When I hear a wicked message, I know that the mind of the speaker is devious. When I hear an evasive message, I know that the mind of the speaker is illogical. These faulty types of messages reflect the flaws in the speaker's mind and heart. Such flaws reflect the faults in the speaker's governance policy. A faulty governance policy negatively affects the running of the government. Even the future saints will agree with me."

Gong Sun Chou said, "Zai Wo, Zi Gong were known for their eloquence. Ran Niu, Min Zi Qian, and Yan Yuan were known for their virtues. Confucius had all their good qualities. Yet, he said, 'I am not good at words.' You, my teacher, now say that you are good at words and you know how to cultivate a magnanimous, undaunted, and incorruptible spirit. Have you then attained sainthood already?"

Mencius exclaimed, "Oh! What words are these? In the past, Zi Gong asked Confucius, 'Are you already a saint?' Confucius replied, 'I am not yet a saint. I just try to learn and teach relentlessly.' Zi Gong said, 'Learning relentlessly shows your wisdom. Teaching relentlessly shows that you have the Ren virtue. Since you have both wisdom and Ren virtue, you, my teacher, are already a saint.' Even Confucius dared not claim to be a saint. What do your words mean?"

Gong Sun Chou asked, "I once heard that Zi Xia, Zi You, and Zi Zhang had each acquired one good quality of Confucius, whereas Ran Niu, Min Zi Qian, and Yan Yuan had acquired all the good qualities of Confucius, albeit to a smaller extent. May I venture to ask you, my teacher, who do you measure up to?"

Mencius said, "Let us stop talking about this now."

Gong Sun Chou asked, "How do you compare Bo Yi and Yi Yin?"

Mencius said, "Their approaches to life were different. Bo Yi's way was not to serve an undeserving king, not to govern an undeserving people, to take up an official post during peace and to retire during chaos. Yi Yin's way was to serve any king, to govern any people, to take up an official post during times of both peace and chaos. Confucius's way was to become an official when it was appropriate to do so, to retire when it was inappropriate to be an official, to offer his service for as long as possible, and to resign quickly when needed. These were ancient saints. I have not yet followed their examples. Given a choice, I would follow Confucius's example."

Gong Sun Chou asked, "Did Bo Yi and Yi Yin belong to the same class as Confucius?"

Mencius said, "No, hardly! Since the beginning of humanity, there never has been another great man like Confucius."

Gong Sun Chou asked, "If so, did they have similarities?"

Mencius said, "Yes. If they had an opportunity to rule a small country of a hundred square miles, they could become the leader of all feudal lords. If they needed to commit an act of evil or kill an innocent person to conquer the whole world, they would refrain from doing so. These are their similarities."

Gong Sun Chou asked, "What were their dissimilarities?"

Mencius said, "Zai Wo, Zi Gong, and You Ruo were intelligent enough to understand Confucius. Although they were imperfect, they would not have flattered their favorite person. Zai Wo said, 'According to my observation, Confucius was superior to Yao and Shun.' Zi Gong said, 'Confucius could tell the character of the government of a country from the knowledge of its Li system. Confucius could tell the character of a person's virtue by listening to his music. Confucius's doctrines can be applied without exceptions to evaluate, after hundreds of generations, the merits, and demerits of rulers during the last hundreds of generations. Since the beginning of humanity, there has never been another Confucius.'

Chapter 3: Gong Sun Chou (1)

You Yo then said, 'Why can only humans be ranked? Unicorns among quadrupeds, phoenix among birds, the Tai Shan Mountain among all the hills, rivers and seas among all the streams and ponds, can be classified to their respective kinds. Likewise, saints among humans are of the same kind. Although unicorns, phoenix, Tai Shan, rivers, seas, and saints belong to their respective categories, they stand out from their respective kinds. Since the beginning of humanity, there has never been another great man like Confucius.' "

Annotation:

Since the ancient Chinese did not have the same notion of God as Christians, the word *Tian* (*Sky* 天) was used to represent a supernatural and unknown natural power that governs the world. Therefore, the words *God, Heaven, Sky,* and *Nature* are synonyms in the context of classic Chinese literature. The word *Heaven* in this translation does not carry the same meaning of Heaven under Christianity. The word *Sky* should not be interpreted astronomically.

Gong Sun Chou (公孫丑) was one of the 18 disciples of Mencius. Some scholars thought that he was a co-author, together with Mencius, of the book *Mencius*. Some other scholars believed that he was a co-author with Wan Zhang (萬章) of the book *Mencius*.

Meng Ben (孟賁) was a famous brave warrior and strong man during the Warring States Period.

Meng Shi She (孟施舍) was another brave warrior during the Warring States Period. Some scholars thought that Meng Shi She and Meng Ben were two names for the same person.

Bei Gong Yao (北宮黝) was a brave warrior of the state of Qi (齊國).

Gao Zi (告子) was a philosopher and contemporary of Mencius.

Zheng Zi (曾子, also known as Zheng Shen 曾参, born 505 BC) was a prominent disciple of Confucius, known for his filial piety. He was the author of *The Book of Great Learning* (大學).

Zai Wo (宰我, also known as Zai Yu, 宰予, 522–458 BC) was among the top disciples of Confucius and a minister for Ai Gong (哀公).

Zi Gong (子貢, also known as Duan Mu Ci 端木賜, born around 520 BC) was one of the top ten disciples of Confucius. He later became the prime minister of the states of Lu (魯國) and Wey (衛國). He also made a fortune in business and was the wealthiest disciple of Confucius. After Confucius's death, Zi Gong observed six years of mourning vigil to show his deep respect for Confucius.

Min Zi Qian (閔子騫, 536–487 BC) was a disciple of Confucius and named as one of the twenty-four models of filial piety in the classic *The Book of Filial Piety* (孝經). He was born of a poor family. His own mother died early. His stepmother abused him and gave him a light coat in a freezing winter, whereas his two younger stepbrothers had warm and heavy coats. His father was upset when he discovered this fact and wanted to punish the stepmother by divorcing her (in the old days, divorcing a wife meant throwing her out of the house). Instead of cheering his father's decision, Min Zi Qian begged his father to stay with the stepmother, arguing that, with the presence of the stepmother, only one boy would suffer in the cold weather, whereas in the absence of the stepmother, all three boys would suffer. His father then changed his mind. His stepmother realized her past misbehavior and repented.

Ran Niu (冉牛, also known as Bo Niu, 伯牛 and Ran Bo Niu, 冉伯牛) was an early disciple, as well as a close friend of Confucius, and accompanied Confucius during Confucius's diplomatic tour of many states. According to Confucius, Yan Yuan, Min Zi Qian, and Ran Niu were outstanding and virtuous students. Little was known

Chapter 3: Gong Sun Chou (1)

about the life of Ran Niu. The *Analects* had a paragraph about him. When he contracted a contagious disease and was terminally ill, Confucius visited him and held Niu's hand from outside the window. Confucius exclaimed, "We will miss a good person. It is fate! Why would a good person get such a disease? Why would a good person get such a disease?"

Yan Yuan (顏淵, also known as Yan Hui 顏回, 521–481 BC) was Confucius's best disciple. Confucius held him in the highest regard among his disciples.

Zi Xia (子夏, born 507 BC) was a disciple of Confucius and later became an official of the state of Wei (魏國).

Zi You (子游, also known as Yan Yan 言偃, 506–443 BC) was a prominent disciple of Confucius.

Zi Zhang (子張, 503–447 BC) was a disciple of Confucius.

Bo Yi (伯夷) and Shu Qi (叔齊) were two princes of the last duke of the feudal state of Gu Zhu (孤竹國) during the Shang Dynasty (商朝, 1766–1066 BC). Bo Yi was the eldest brother, and Shu Qi was the youngest. Before their father died, Shu Qi was nominated to be his successor. Shu Qi abdicated his throne to his eldest brother, Bo Yi, and stressed that the eldest son should be the successor to the throne according to tradition. Bo Yi refused to accept out of the respect for his father's wishes. Both eventually renounced the throne and migrated to the territory of the state of Zhou (周). Later, King Wu of Zhou (周武王) raised an army to invade the Shang Dynasty. Both Bo Yi and Shu Qi knelt in front of King Wu's chariot and begged King Wu not to invade the Shang Dynasty. King Wu eventually conquered the Shang Dynasty and founded the Zhou Dynasty (周朝). Bo Yi and Shu Qi refused to be subjects of the Zhou Dynasty and eat its food. They moved to the mountains and starved to death. Many historians regard these two ancient characters as model Jun Zis, who had the Ren virtue.

Yu (禹, around 2237–2139 BC) founded the Xia Dynasty (夏朝, around 2184–1600 BC) in about 2184 BC. After about 500 years of the dynasty, the 16th successor to the throne was Emperor Jie of Xia (夏桀). He was a notorious tyrant.

Yi Yin (伊尹, around 1649–1549 BC) was born in the era under the terrible reign of Emperor Jie. His real name at birth was unknown. The first word, *Yi* (伊), was derived from the Yi River (伊水), which ran through the village where he was born. The second word, *Yin* (尹), meant a government official. Some historians thought that this meant a prime minister, whereas some others considered it to refer to a low-level official. Therefore, his name referred to the government official who came from Yi River. Yi Yin was one of the greatest prime ministers in the history of China. He assisted King Tang to overthrow the notorious tyrant, Emperor Jie of the Xia Dynasty, and to establish the Shang Dynasty. His story is told in Section 3 of the Endnotes.

You Ruo (有若, about 518–458 BC) was a prominent disciple of Confucius.

Commentary:

This section contains important inter-related concepts of Mencius's philosophy. Many Confucians after him have interpreted and analyzed in depth the dialogue in this section between Mencius and Gong Sun Chou. Different interpretations have led to different schools of thought about Mencius's philosophy. This book tries to stick to the pragmatic, down-to-earth view, which is more in line with pre-Qin Confucianism (先秦) (i.e., Confucianism before the Qin Dynasty, expounded mainly during the Spring-Autumn Period and Warring States Period), and avoids the esoteric and metaphysical interpretations expounded by later generations. The

Chapter 3: Gong Sun Chou (1)

reason is that the primary objective of this book is to teach common readers the principles for self-cultivation rather than to add esoteric sophistication to Confucianism, which is the subject matter for academics only. Therefore, the author has tried to translate the names of some core concepts into modern words which are understandable by most readers, while trying to accurately preserve their meaning in the context of the entire philosophy of pre-Qin Confucianism.

The sequence of presentation of various core concepts in the dialogue between Mencius and Gong Sun Chou seems to be confusing. In fact, there is a framework that connects these core concepts. Figure 1 below illustrates this framework. In this figure, the boxes on the right of the vertical dotted line represent various faculties of the mind (and soul) mentioned by Mencius in this section. The boxes on the left of the dotted line represent information, activities, and the Dao in the external world. The figure is shaded gradually with a darker shade to the right. The darkness of the shade represents the depth in a person's mind. Among the boxes on the right side of the dotted line, the lower the box, the harder and longer it is for the person to cultivate the ability and/or virtue represented by the box. The boxes with thick borders refer to those abilities and/or virtues pointed out by Mencius in this section. The dialogue between Mencius and Gong Sun Chou can then be explained in groups according to the following sequence, starting from the top and left side of Figure 1:

(1) Innate roots of Ren and Yi, External information, Listening discerningly, and Reasoning;
(2) Belief and Will, Energy and Impetus;
(3) Yi;
(4) Magnanimous spirit and character;
(5) Great valor;

Mencius in Modern Perspectives

(6) Resolute, undaunted, and incorruptible heart.

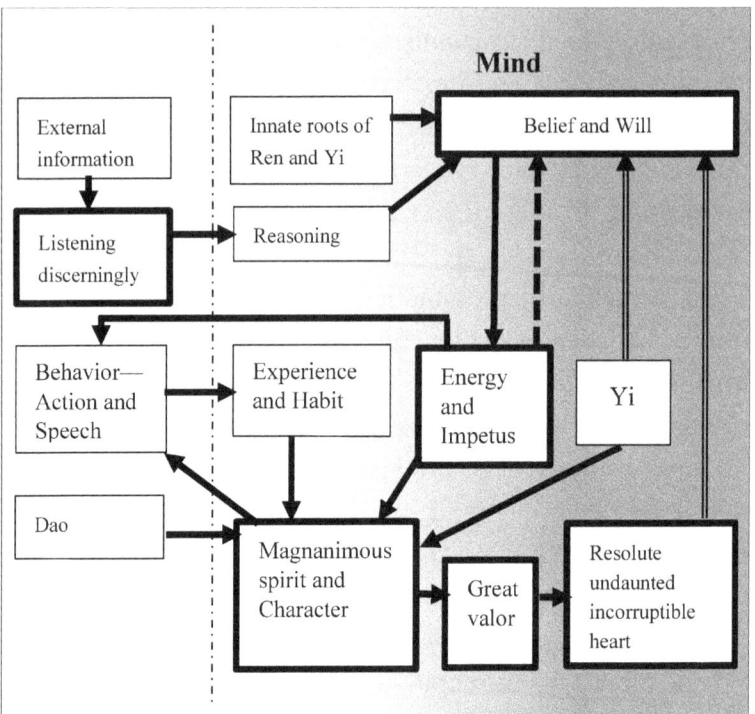

Figure 1. Graphic Illustration of Mencius's Spiritual Framework

Innate roots of Ren (仁) and Yi (義), External information, Listening discerningly (知言), and Reasoning:

Mencius believed that people are born with the innate roots of Ren and Yi. These virtuous roots must be supplemented by a long process of learning for the mind, belief, and will to develop properly.

The second group of boxes describes the process of learning. The term "listening discerningly" can be generalized to include seeing and perception from all senses. The ability to discern right from wrong by careful listening (and learning) and reasoning is wisdom. Mencius hinted his virtue of wisdom when he mentioned his being a discerning listener and said, "When I hear a biased message, I know that the mind of the speaker is blocked. When I hear a flowery message, I know that the mind of the speaker is decadent. When I hear a wicked message, I know that the mind of the speaker is devious. When I hear an evasive message, I know that the mind of the speaker is illogical. These faulty types of messages reflect the flaws in the speaker's mind and heart." These sentences imply that a discerning listener (and learner) needs to have logical thinking and insightful perspective. The word *listening* includes also reading and all means of reception and perception of all external information.

Mencius stressed the importance of reasoning when he said, "Gao Zi said, 'If you do not discern the words of others, you need not bother with pondering their truth and validity. If you cannot tell in your mind what is right or wrong in a matter, you should not be upset and deal with the matter emotionally.' It is correct to avoid dealing with a matter emotionally when one is uncertain of what is right or wrong in the matter. It is incorrect to ignore the words of others and refrain from pondering their truth and validity when one cannot discern such words."

If a person does not use good reasoning when he listens (and sees), he could be misled into believing a fallacy, and he could follow an erroneous belief and path in life.

Belief and Will (志), Energy, and Impetus (氣):

The Chinese word of *Will* (志), as mentioned in the Mencius's original text, also has the meanings of belief, determination, objective, motive, and desire. This book translates it in short as "Belief and will". The Chinese word of *Energy and Impetus* (氣, Qi) mentioned in Mencius's original text has many meanings depending on the context. Practitioners of Qi Kung consider Qi as a mysterious form of energy flow in the body, which can be controlled by the mind through meditation. Since such a skill was unknown in the era of Mencius, the word *Qi* should be interpreted simply as impetus. In modern terms, Mencius's sentence: "The will is the commander of energy and impetus [and emotion] which flow through the body of a person" can be interpreted as: "When the mind wants to do something, the brain sends out neural signals, triggers the flow of adrenaline and other hormones so that the body follows the order of the mind."

Mencius also thought that the level of energy, impetus, and emotion can conversely affect the will. He gave an example, saying, "On the other hand, when energy and impetus is intensely focused on a matter, they will also affect the will of a person. For example, when one runs fast and stumbles over a pit, he is controlled by his energy and impetus [and emotion] to the extent that his will is affected." Therefore, there is a dotted arrow in Figure 1 pointing from the box representing energy and impetus to the box representing belief and will. The converse situation typically occurs when a person is under undue stress, fright or anger, and loses control of himself.

Yi:

The Chinese word *Yi* (義) is usually translated as righteousness. However, according to the explanation in the Introduction chapter, Yi has a deeper meaning. The reader needs to refer to the discussion there.

The philosophy of Mencius focuses mainly on Yi. Mencius believed that everybody is born with an innate root of Yi. However, this virtue needs to be cultivated by learning and practice, so that the desire for righteousness becomes an internal quality of one's mind (and soul) and becomes second nature. Some Confucians after

Confucius and before Mencius advanced the view that the Ren virtue is internal, whereas Yi is external. Gao Zi belonged to this school of thought. Yi was considered to be a set of requirements and expectations of proper conducts imposed by peer influence and the society at large. Mencius believed that this view was dangerous and could lead to the destruction of one's morality, to herd behavior, even herd violence, and eventually, to the collapse of the society. Mencius said, "I therefore say that Gao Zi does not know the essence of Yi. He has not internalized it and made it an integral aspect of his character. One should practice righteousness as a matter of course without the expectation of its explicit benefits to himself." Mencius advocated the need for independent and critical reasoning, so that one can critically and discerningly listen, read, and learn. That was why Mencius criticized Gao Zi for his neglect of the use of reasoning. Mencius stressed the importance of the ability to listen discerningly. Sections 1 to 7 of Chapter 11 below comprise a deep discussion on this point.

Because of Mencius's viewpoint, the box representing Yi in Figure 1 is drawn inside the area representing the mind.

Magnanimous Spirit and Character (浩然之氣):

As shown in Figure 1, energy and impetus motivate the actions and speeches of a person. Such behaviors produce experiences, and over a long time, develop habits in a person. If a person conscientiously directs and controls his or her energy and impetus according to Dao and the inner urge of Yi, his or her experiences and habits will develop a magnanimous spirit. This spirit will further motivate him or her to do good to people and to the world unconditionally. After a long period of accumulation of such spirit, this person will, gradually and naturally, develop a magnanimous character. This character is a second nature of this person. The following bullet points reiterate Mencius's explanation on the substance of magnanimous spirit and character:

(1) <u>As a form of energy and impetus, it is extremely great and unsurmountable</u>. "Extremely great" means magnanimity. "Unsurmountable" here means that the person with a magnanimous spirit and character can stand firm in the face of danger, threats, obstacles, opposition, and so on.

(2) <u>If one nurtures it righteously and does not deplete it, his magnanimous spirit will fill and be applicable to every corner of the world</u>. "Filling every corner of the world" means that the person who has a magnanimous spirit and character will become a model for all people in the world. He will inspire people with his magnanimity so that other people will emulate his virtues. Such magnanimity will be applicable to every place and situation in the world.

(3) <u>The exercise of this spirit must be in line with Dao and Yi</u>. This is a necessary requirement for the accumulation of a magnanimous spirit and development of a magnanimous character. This point is critical. If a person develops a powerful and unsurmountable spirit in lieu of Dao and Yi, he will go astray. For example, gangsters or terrorists may have a powerful and unsurmountable spirit. Some of them are not afraid of death. They consider themselves heroes when, in fact, their actions go against humanity, and therefore, their powerful and unsurmountable spirit cannot be regarded as a magnanimous spirit.

(4) <u>The spirit is accumulated through a long period of righteous practices and cannot be acquired by an incidental act of righteousness</u>. Likewise, this spirit is different from an incidental adrenaline rush, triggered by an external crisis, call to arms, excess fear, or anger. This spirit is a constant

Chapter 3: Gong Sun Chou (1)

and consistent aspect of a person's character.

(5) <u>Once one's action deviates from the righteous belief in his heart, this spirit will sap.</u> The righteous belief in a person's heart is the foundation of magnanimous spirit.

(6) <u>One should also not forget about the constant nurturing of his magnanimous spirit. However, one should not try to artificially groom it.</u> A magnanimous spirit is developed gradually and naturally over a long period of practice, experience, challenges, and tests. It cannot be developed, for example, by a planned schedule of charitable actions, or in a boot camp.

The concept of magnanimous spirit and character is translated from the Chinese term (浩然之氣). There have been many interpretations of the meaning of this term. One common interpretation is based on the literary meanings of the four Chinese characters, which were translated word-by-word into "Free-flowing Qi," "Ubiquitous Energy," "Ubiquitous Qi," and so on. These translations were also supported by a direct word-to-word translation of another sentence mentioned in this section by Mencius: "In the form of Qi, it is extremely magnificent and strong. If one cultivates it properly and does not hurt it, this Qi can fill the Sky and Earth." In this book, however, the author has translated the same sentence into: "If you look at it as a form of energy and impetus, it is extremely great and unsurmountable. If one nurtures it righteously and does not deplete it, his magnanimous spirit will fill and be applicable to every corner of the world." This difference in interpretation and translation is important because it leads to fundamental differences in the understanding of Confucianism.

The former approach extrapolates the meaning of Qi into some mysterious energy flows inside the body, and further, into some mysterious energy or power filling the universe. This view is influenced by Taoist philosophy about the universe and the meaning of Dao (see the discussion on Dao in the Introduction). Once some neo-Confucians saw the phrase "Sky and Earth", they were too ready to bring in Taoist ideas of the universe and Dao into Confucianism. The word *Tian* (*Sky*) has a connotation of something supernatural and mystic. Some were even too ready to convert Confucianism into a religion because of the word *Sky*.

While not trying to refute the theory of some neo-Confucians, this book takes a more mundane and pragmatic interpretation for six reasons:

(1) The pre-Qin Confucianism was different from Taoism. Confucius confessed that he did not understand Dao, although he wished to. Confucius had the humility of admitting that he did not understand the metaphysical version of Dao as expounded by Laozi. He said, "If one is enlightened with True Way (Dao) in the morning, one is willing to die in the evening" (Section 8 of Chapter 4, 里仁, of *Confucius Analects*). He desired to know it but still could not understand it completely.

(2) However, Confucius did not endorse wasting time to ponder on supramundane and supernatural matters before more urgent problems in the world are solved. When his student, Zi Lu, asked about how to serve and worship gods and spirits, Confucius said, "You still have not served men well. Why do you bother serving gods and spirits?" Zi Lu then ventured to ask about death and the afterlife. Confucius said, "You don't even know enough about life, why do you bother to know about death?" (Section 11 of Chapter 12, 先進, of *Confucius*

Chapter 3: Gong Sun Chou (1)

Analects). Confucius emphasized pragmatism and discouraged the study of supernatural and metaphysical matters. Confucius never talked about myths, violence, revolt, gods, or spirits (Section 21 of Chapter 7, 述而, of *Confucius Analects*).

(3) Since even Laozi acknowledged that it was impossible to give a name to Dao, and to understand it, it is impossible for common people to feel the presence of Qi and perceive that Qi flows freely along with Dao in the universe. Therefore, the phrases "Ubiquitous Qi," and "Filling Sky and Earth" become abstract and mysterious concepts without much practical use.

(4) If one were to accumulate Qi like Qi Kung masters or Buddhist monks using transcendental meditation, only a few persons out of millions can acquire such a skill. How can one then foster Mencius's teaching to the public if such skill is needed to acquire this esoteric Qi?

(5) An interpretation and translation of a concept must be coherent with other concepts in the entirety of Confucian philosophy. The interpreter and translator should not distort or extrapolate the entire theory because of a few odd sentences or phrases in the original text.

(6) The introduction of supernatural, metaphysical, and mystic concepts to Confucianism will turn it into a religion or quasi-religion and deviate from the original intention of Confucius.

(7) Throughout the book *Mencius*, there is no reference to supernatural, metaphysical and mystic concepts.

Mencius in Modern Perspectives

Therefore, this book adopts the translation "Magnanimous spirit and character" instead of "Ubiquitous Qi" or "Free-flowing Qi". As shown clearly in the above paragraphs, this book's approach is more practical for self-cultivation.

Great Valor (大勇):

Mencius mentioned three types of valor. The first is Bei Gong Yao's brute valor. He did not flinch when his skin was being pinched; he did not dodge when his eyes were being attacked; when a piece of his hair was pulled out by somebody, he considered the attack as if he was beaten publicly in the market place; he did not submit to a commoner nor to a king of a big country; he considered the challenge of assassinating a king to be the same as assassinating a commoner; he was not afraid of any king or lord; and he always retaliated against insults on him. This valor is faulty because it does no good to anybody. Even some street fighters, gangsters, and terrorists can be trained to possess such valor.

The second type of valor is irrational valor. This was exemplified by Meng Shi She. He said, "I consider a defeat as if it is a victory. If a general assesses the strength and weakness of an enemy before an advance, and to weigh the chance of victory before engaging in a fight, he is indeed afraid of meeting a formidable enemy. How can I guarantee a victory? I am just fearless." A person with this type of valor does not care about whether his actions are right or wrong, or whether his actions will bring disaster to people. If he is ordered to engage in a fight, he just goes for it without fear. What if his mission is evil? This type of valor is, therefore, not only irrational but irresponsible.

The third type of valor is great valor. This was exemplified by what Confucius said, "If on reflection I am wrong, I would not harass a commoner, but if on reflection I am right, I would not be afraid of confronting an army of tens of thousands of men." The great valor is based on righteousness—Yi. Confucius had two points: the courage to admit one's mistake and apologize, and the courage to confront an extremely formidable challenge. Confucius also said, "A hero who is determined to uphold the Ren virtue would not seek to live at the expense of hurting his Ren virtue, but he would sacrifice his life in order to preserve it" (Section 9 of Chapter 15, 衛靈公, of *Confucius Analects*). Therefore, when the course is wrong, a person having great valor will not take any action to pursue the course, even though he might be considered a coward. Therefore, a person having great valor could sometimes be regarded by others as a coward. Therefore, Su Shi (蘇軾), a famous scholar and poet in the Song Dynasty, wrote, "A person with great wisdom may appear idiotic. A person with great valor may appear timid (大智若愚, 大勇若怯)." However, when the course is right, a person having great valor will take all necessary actions to pursue it, even at the expense of sacrificing his own life.

Great valor is a derived and companion virtue of magnanimous character. A person cannot have great valor without a magnanimous character and Yi virtue as foundations. This relationship is depicted by Figure 1 above.

Resolute, Undaunted, and Incorruptible Heart (不動心):

Magnanimous spirit and character, great valor, and resolute, undaunted, and incorruptible heart are three moral strengths discussed in this section. They are shown at the bottom of Figure 1 because these exceptional virtues are deep in the personality of a person. A resolute, undaunted, and incorruptible heart is more demanding than the other two virtues because it requires more than the undaunted strength to pursue Ren and Yi against obstacles and challenges. It also requires the strength to resist all kinds of temptations. This ideal was introduced by Mencius in Section 4 of Chapter 6 below, in which he said, "A great man cannot be corrupted by wealth or status, cannot be moved by poverty or lowliness, and cannot be subjugated by threat or force." A great man sticks resolutely to his principles and original noble mission in life, even under dire poverty. This requires a resolute heart. Confucius also said, "Everyone loves great wealth and high-class status. If these are obtained in improper ways, we should not pursue them. Everyone hates poverty and low-class status. If the departure from them is through improper ways, we should not follow them" (Section 5 of Chapter 4, 里仁, of *Confucius Analects*). Likewise, a great man cannot be corrupted by wealth or status. There are two aspects of this sentence. In the first aspect, the wealthier and more powerful a person, the bigger is the temptation for him or her to degenerate into decadence. In the second aspect, the lure of more wealth and higher status tends to corrupt a person. An incorruptible heart can resist such temptations. A great man cannot be subjugated by threat or force because he possesses a magnanimous spirit and character and has great valor. Therefore, the virtue of having a resolute, undaunted, and incorruptible heart encapsulates all these good qualities. Since this virtue affects the will of a person, an arrow is shown in Figure 1 connecting this virtue with the will.

Some scholars interpret and translate the Chinese term (不動心) differently. They interpret this term as a state of mind which is completely placid, calm, and unruffled to the extent that no ideas can stay in and bother the mind. This state is typically attained by expert masters of transcendental meditation such as holy monks and Taoists. Because of such interpretation, this Chinese term (不動心) is translated into "unperturbed heart," "unperturbable heart," "immovable heart," or "nonchalant heart." This book does not take this view for the following reasons:

Chapter 3: Gong Sun Chou (1)

(1) Throughout the Mencius book and the *Analects*, there is no mention of the practice of meditation and the transcendental state of mind.

(2) Confucianism is not a religion in the narrow sense (see the discussion in the Introduction) and Confucius ignored the study of supernatural, supramundane, and metaphysical matters.

(3) To Confucians, a saint is just a great man, and not some fairy in Heaven nor a Buddha in Nirvana.

(4) It is, therefore, a departure from pre-Qin Confucianism to introduce Taoist and Buddhist concepts to explain and interpret Confucianism.

Modern Perspective:

This section contains many important moral lessons that are still relevant to modern life. The more important ones are: (1) listening discerningly, (2) magnanimous spirit and character and big valor, and (3) a resolute, undaunted, incorruptible heart.

<u>Listening Discerningly</u>:
In today's information era, there is an explosive growth in the generation, availability, and flow of information. One must be extremely cautious to discern truth from falsehood and right from wrong. Otherwise, one's mind, belief, and will can be contaminated or even poisoned. There are an unlimited number of types of immoral players and bad information. The following are a few examples:

(1) Fake news, lies, conspiracy theories, pseudoscience, innuendos, defamation, and propaganda are broadcast and communicated at light speed through the internet.

(2) Lies repeated a thousand times tend to be considered truth by the public, or at least earn a benefit of doubt from some people.

(3) The public is constantly bombarded with subtle brainwashing propaganda and advertising.

(4) Spineless scientists falsify data or mislead the public about scientific facts.

(5) Unethical accountants and auditors produce incomplete or misleading financial reports.

(6) Demagogues spread lies and provoke hatred.

(7) Unprofessional journalists spin and cherry-pick news.

(8) Communication experts artfully manipulate the minds of the public.

Some people may say, "I do not care about the lies that candidate talks about. If his policy benefits me, I will vote for him." However, Mencius thought otherwise, stating that, "These faulty types of messages reflect the flaws in the speaker's mind and heart. Such flaws reflect the faults in the speaker's governance policy. Faulty governance policy negatively affects the running of the government." Therefore, smart voters should not take speeches of politicians lightly.

On the other hand, one should be cautious in his or her speeches. What comes out from the mouth reflects what is in the mind. Smart listeners can get a good idea of the speaker's mind and character from his words.

Chapter 3: Gong Sun Chou (1)

Magnanimous Spirit and Character, and Great Valor:

One does not need to be a hero to cultivate a magnanimous spirit and character. The cultivation is a continuous life-long process, starting from small habits and endeavors. The following are a few examples:

(1) When you see someone fall in the street, you immediately walk up and pull him or her up. You do not worry about the negative consequences of your actions.

(2) When you see a pitiful beggar, you give him or her all the money in your wallet, without thinking about your own needs for the money or what is the right amount to give.

(3) You donate blood without thinking about its consequence to your own health.

(4) You participate in a vaccine trial and take the risk of suffering from the vaccine's side-effects.

(5) You participate in voluntary work and sacrifice your time and energy.

(6) You readily acknowledge your own ignorance and incompetency in public.

(7) You readily apologize in public about your own mistakes.

(8) You stand up against blackmails.

(9) You become a whistle blower against crimes committed by management in your company.

(10) You refuse to be complicit towards malpractice in your organization.

Resolute, Undaunted, and Incorruptible Heart:

The above paragraph has already given some examples regarding the undaunted aspect of this virtue. This paragraph then focuses on the resolute and incorruptible aspects. When one is in a dire situation or a crisis, one must not lose his or her bearings, forget his or her original mission and principles, or trade his or her integrity for the promise of departure from hardship. Some weak people in poverty commit crimes such as larceny, robbery, forgery, drug trafficking, child pornography, or prostitution to make fast money. On the contrary, a person with a resolute heart willingly endures poverty to pursue Ren virtue. For example, some good teachers work in schools in the middle of nowhere not because they cannot find other more lucrative and easier jobs but because they are committed to their mission to teach poor children. Some good physicians practice in the underdeveloped world for a low salary, enduring hardship not because they are unqualified or unable to find a better job in the developed world but because they are committed to helping poor people. Some good doctors stick to their profession as general practitioners, making much less money than what specialists make, not because they have no ability to become specialists but because they believe in their mission of providing basic and affordable medical services to poor people.

There are a few aspects of an incorruptible heart. When a person is wealthy, there is a temptation to lead a lavish lifestyle and to degenerate into decadence. When a person is powerful, there is a temptation to abuse his or her power and to commit corruption. A person with an incorruptible heart is resistant to such temptations, and will stay pure, clean, and uncorrupted in all circumstances. When a person vies for ascension to power or gathering of more wealth, he or she can easily be tempted to commit corruption and betray his or her integrity. This phenomenon is common. For example, suppose that you are being offered a high post but there is a tacit expectation that your appointment will involve some unethical complicity or partisan alignment. Would you accept the offer? If you accept it, you will get high status, great wealth, and fame. Would you trade your integrity for such benefits? If you have an incorruptible heart, you will reject such offers.

Section 3

孟子曰 以力假仁者霸 霸必有大國 以德行仁者王 王不待大。湯以七十里 文王以百里。以力服人者 非心服也 力不贍也。以德服人者 中心悅而誠服也 如七十子之服孔子也。詩云 自西自東 自南自北 無思不服。此之謂也。

Mencius said, "If you use force disguised as Ren and Yi to become a hegemon, your hegemony must be based on the large size of your state. If you apply virtuous actions to implement Ren principles and become a magnanimous leader of all states, your leadership is independent of the size of your state. King Tang of the Shang Dynasty became an emperor from a base of only seventy square miles. King Wu of the Zhou Dynasty became an emperor from a base of only one hundred square miles. If you subdue others by force, their submission is involuntary and necessitated by their weakness to resist you. If you subdue others by your virtues, they will follow you willingly. This was why seventy disciples followed Confucius. This is the meaning of the verse in the *Book of Poetry*: 'From west to east, from south to north, nobody will defy you.'"

Mencius in Modern Perspectives

Annotation:

King Tang (湯, 1670–1587 BC) overthrew the last Emperor Jie of the Xia dynasty (夏朝, circa 2184–1600 BC) and founded the Shang Dynasty (商朝, circa 1600–1066 BC), which was also called the Yin Dynasty (殷朝). He was the king of a small state before he led a revolution against the Xia Dynasty.

The Shang Dynasty lasted for about 600 years. After 30 successions to the throne, the empire was ruled by a brutal tyrant, Emperor Zhou (紂), who was also known as Emperor Xin (帝辛). King Wu of Zhou (周武王, died 1043 BC), whose father was King Wen of Zhou (周文王, circa 1152–1056 BC), overthrew Emperor Zhou and founded the Zhou Dynasty (周朝, circa 1066–256 BC). King Wu of Zhou was the king of a small state in the west of the Yangtze River before he led a revolution against the Shang Dynasty.

Confucians regarded King Tang, King Wen, and King Wu as saintly kings. During their regimes, ancient China had a near utopian society.

The Book of Poetry (詩經) was compiled during the Zhou Dynasty (周朝, circa 1043 to 256 BC) as a collection of national folk songs (國風), royal paeans (大雅), royal poems (小雅), and hymns (頌). National folk songs were a collection of folk songs of various states. On formal occasions, the emperor and princes would chant royal paeans. Royal poems were recited in feasts. Hymns were sung during ceremonies of sacrifice in temples. The quotation in this section was from the royal paeans in praise of King Wen of Zhou.

Modern Perspective:

This section is still relevant today.

Chapter 3: Gong Sun Chou (1)

Section 4

孟子曰 仁則榮 不仁則辱。今惡辱而居不仁 是猶惡溼而居下也。如惡之 莫如貴德而尊士 賢者在位 能者在職。國家閒暇 及是時明其政刑。雖大國 必畏之矣。詩云 迨天之未陰雨 徹彼桑土 綢繆牖戶。今此下民 或敢侮予。孔子曰 為此詩者 其知道乎。能治其國家 誰敢侮之。

今國家閒暇 及是時般樂怠敖 是自求禍也。禍福無不自己求之者。詩云 永言配命 自求多福。太甲曰 天作孽 猶可違 自作孽 不可活。此之謂也。

Mencius said, "If the ruler implements Ren policies, his country will be peaceful and prosperous. Otherwise, his country will be ruined. Nowadays, rulers hate to ruin their countries but do not implement Ren policies. Their approach is analogous to dreading swamps but continuing to stay in low-lying land. If they seriously hate ruining their countries, they should start hiring meritorious and competent ministers to run their governments. When the country is free from external threat and internal troubles, the ruler should take this window of opportunity to reform and improve governance and legislation. If so, even large enemies will be awed by the achievement of his country. The *Book of Poetry* says, 'Before the storm comes, let us peel off the bark from mulberry trees to cover our windows and doors, so that people below will not blame us.' Confucius said, 'The author of this poem knew the Dao. If a country is well governed, who can humiliate it?' When the country is free from external threat and internal troubles, the ruler is asking for trouble and ruin if he indulges in pleasure, extravagance, and complacency. Fortunes and misfortunes are all caused by one's own actions, [and nobody else]. The *Book of Poetry* said, 'Always remember to be in harmony with divine providence so that your good conduct will yield auspicious results.' Therefore, *Tai Jia* also said, 'It is still possible to elude natural catastrophes. There is no way out of a self-inflicted disaster.' "

Annotation:

The Annotation in Section 2 above narrated the story of Yi Yin, who was the prime minister of King Tang (湯, died in 1587 BC). Yi Yin then became the prime minister and the guardian teacher to the subsequent three successors to the throne. The third emperor was the young Emperor Tai Jia (太甲), who was a spoiled kid. He ignored the rules and laws laid down by his ancestor, Emperor Tang. To teach Tai Jia a lesson, Yi Yin confined Tai Jia to a cottage erected next to the tomb of Emperor Tang. Tai Jia was asked to study books on governance and politics written by Yi Yin. The book *Tai Jia* was the teaching material written by Yi Yin. Tai Jia was not allowed to leave the cottage until he repented. After three years, Tai Jia repented and wrote a confession of his past misbehaviors. Convinced that Tai Jia had sincerely repented, Yi Yin then welcomed Tai Jia back to the throne. Tai Jia later became one of the best rulers of the Shang Dynasty.

The last sentence in the section is the same as the sentence in Section 8 of Chapter 7.

Commentary and Modern Perspective:

This section has four lessons:
(1) **Ren policies are conducive to the peace and prosperity to a country**: This is the main theme in the political philosophy of Confucianism.

Chapter 3: Gong Sun Chou (1)

(2) **A ruler should not miss the opportunity to reform and improve his government during peace and prosperity**: However, many rulers become complacent during good times. When the treasury coffers are full, there is a tendency to waste money on projects that fatten the pockets of vested interests and political allies. Over-optimistic budgets are made. When the society is peaceful, there is a tendency to ignore underlying but emerging inequality and social grievances. A rising tide floats all boats. When the tide recedes, dirt and ugliness will then emerge.

(3) **Fortunes and misfortunes are all caused by one's own actions, and nobody else**: A few examples can illustrate this point:

(a) Many self-starters were born in impoverished families and had little formal education. Yet, they become successful in life through good vision, hard work, perseverance, strict discipline, and other good qualities in their personalities. Therefore, a loser in life should not blame his or her parents for not providing them a good springboard.

(b) Losers tend to blame other people, the society, government, environment, and the world rather than themselves for their demise.

(c) There is a tendency nowadays for parents to blame teachers for the misbehavior and poor scholastic performance of their children. These parents do not introspect on their own mistakes—being a bad role model for their children, neglect of their children, lack of moral teaching and training of children, extravagant and decadent lifestyle of the parents, and so on.

(4) **Self-made disasters are more ruinous than natural disasters**: A few examples can illustrate this point:

(a) Earthquakes, tsunamis, and hurricanes are known natural calamities. Modern science can provide some early warnings of such occurrences so that preventive and mitigative measures can be taken. If a government ignores warnings from scientists and technologists, the damage arising from a natural calamity will be multiplied. The damage to the lives and health of its people and to the world environment will be immeasurable and irreversible.

(b) Before an epidemic becomes a full-blown pandemic, there are means to control the growth of the epidemic in its early stage. If a government is tardy and does not take appropriate controls, the resulting damage to public health and the economy is more ruinous because of such inertia.

(c) On a personal level, it is well-known that alcoholism and addiction to drugs are damaging to the physical and mental health of a person. If a person ignores such warning and continues to indulge in alcoholism and drug use, the damage to his or her health is self-inflicted and often irreparable.

(d) The same applies to gluttony. Over-consumption of fat, refined sugars, and other high-calorie foods is known to be a major cause of type-2 diabetes, obesity, and heart disease. If one does not control his or her gluttony, the damage to his or her health is self-inflicted.

Section 5

孟子曰　尊賢使能　俊傑在位　則天下之士皆悅而願立於其朝矣。市廛而不征　法而不廛　則天下之商皆悅而願藏於其市矣。關譏而不征　則天下之旅皆悅而願出於其路矣。耕者助而不稅　則天下之農皆悅而願耕於其野矣。廛無夫里之布　則天下之民皆悅而願為之氓矣。信能行此五者　則鄰國之民仰之若父母矣。率其子弟　攻其父母　自生民以來　未有能濟者也。如此　則無敵於天下。無敵於天下者　天吏也。然而不王者　未之有也。

Mencius said, "If a ruler values meritocracy and fills government positions with individuals of distinction, all learned and competent people will be glad to serve in his government. If his government provides rent-free warehouses to merchants and buys their unsold inventories at market prices, merchants from all countries will love to come to his country to trade. If, at the border of his country, only travelers are inspected, and goods are not subject to duties, travelers and tourists will love to visit his country. If, instead of paying land taxes, farmers are only required to cultivate one public plot of field for every eight private plots of field belonging to them and to surrender the yield from the public plot to the government, farmers from all countries will love to cultivate in his country. If there is no per capita tax on residents of his country, all people will love to reside in his country. If the ruler can implement these five benevolent policies, all people in neighboring countries will look up to him as their parents. From the beginning of mankind, there has never been a successful case where a ruler of a neighboring country can lead its people to attack their own parents. Therefore, a benevolent ruler will be invincible. An invincible ruler is like an angel from *Tian* (*Sky*). It is impossible for such a benevolent ruler not to become a magnanimous emperor."

Annotation:

Since ancient Chinese did not have the same notion of God as Christians, the word *Tian* (*Sky* 天) was used to represent a supernatural and unknown natural power that governs the world. Therefore, the words *God, Heaven, Sky,* and *Nature* are synonyms in the context of classic Chinese literature. The word *Heaven* in this translation does not carry the same meaning of Heaven under Christianity. The word *Tian* (*Sky*) should also not be interpreted astronomically.

Modern Perspective:

This section is still relevant today.

Section 6

孟子曰 人皆有不忍人之心。先王有不忍人之心 斯有不忍人之政矣。以不忍人之心 行不忍人之政 治天下可運之掌上。所以謂人皆有不忍人之心者 今人乍見孺子將入於井 皆有怵惕惻隱之心。非所以內交於孺子之父母也 非所以要譽於鄉黨朋友也 非惡其聲而然也。由是觀之 無惻隱之心 非人也 無羞惡之心 非人也 無辭讓之心 非人也 無是非之心 非人也。惻隱之心

Chapter 3: Gong Sun Chou (1)

仁之端也　羞惡之心　義之端也　辭讓之心　禮之端也　是非之心　智之端也。人之有是四端也　猶其有四體也。有是四端而自謂不能者　自賊者也　謂其君不能者　賊其君者也。凡有四端於我者　知皆擴而充之矣　若火之始然　泉之始達。苟能充之　足以保四海　苟不充之　不足以事父母。

Mencius said, "Everybody has compassion. The compassionate mind of ancient saintly kings prompted them to implement compassionate policies. If a ruler implements compassionate policies based on his compassionate mind, he can govern the world in one hand. To illustrate the point that everybody has a compassionate mind, let us suppose that we see a toddler falling into a well. All of us will be shocked with grief and sympathy. We grieve not because we are friends of the toddler's parents, want to earn credit from friends, or cannot bear to hear the toddler's cries. From this observation, and upon introspection, we can conclude that people without a compassionate mind are inhuman; people without a mind with sense of shame are inhuman; people without humble and modest mind are inhuman; and that people without the mind to discern right and wrong are inhuman. The compassionate mind is the beginning of Ren virtue. The mind with a sense of shame is the beginning of Yi virtue. The mind with humility and modesty is the beginning of Li virtue. The mind to discern right from wrong is the beginning of wisdom. These four beginning seeds of virtue in the mind of a person are like his or her four limps. Anyone processing these four virtuous seeds while claiming his or her inability to develop and practice these four virtues is self-deceptive and abandoning. If one claims that his or her king (boss) is incapable of practicing these virtues, he or she is undermining the king (boss). People who are aware of the presence of these four virtuous seeds

Mencius in Modern Perspectives

know the need to nurture and grow them like the start of a fire or a gush of spring water. After sufficient nourishment, these virtues can be applied to protect the world. Without any nourishment, these virtues are insufficient to serve one's parents."

Annotation:

The Chinese terms (不忍人之心) and (惻隱之心) can be translated as "compassion" or "commiseration". This book adopts the first translation because compassion not only means the awareness and feeling of grief of suffering of others but also the desire to help others. The word "commiseration" only means the awareness and feeling of grief of suffering of others. In addition, in the context of this section, a "compassionate government policy" makes more sense than "commiserating government policy."

Commentary:

Mencius used the example of the fall of a toddler into a well to illustrate his theory that there are innate seeds of Ren, Yi, Li, and Wisdom in the mind of everybody. They are the Four Virtuous Beginnings of Mencius's philosophy. The Introduction has elaborated the nature and content of these four virtues. This section sketches Mencius's theory: (1) human beings are born with innate seeds of virtues, (2) these virtues must be further developed by learning and practice, (3) when they are fully developed, they can be applied everywhere.

Section 7

孟子曰　矢人豈不仁於函人哉。矢人唯恐不傷人　函人唯恐傷

Chapter 3: Gong Sun Chou (1)

人。巫匠亦然 故術不可不慎也。孔子曰 里仁為美 擇不處仁 焉得智。夫仁 天之尊爵也 人之安宅也 莫之禦而不仁 是不智也。不仁 不智 無禮 無義 人役也。人役而恥為役 由弓人而恥為弓 矢人而恥為矢也。如恥之 莫如為仁。仁者如射 射者正己而後發。發而不中 不怨勝己者 反求諸己而已矣。

Mencius said, "Is the arrow-maker less humane than the armor-maker? The arrow-maker is concerned that his arrows cannot hurt people, whereas the armor-maker is concerned that his armors cannot protect people. This role conflict also exists between the coffin-maker and the priest whose job is to pray for the well-being of people. Therefore, one must choose his profession with caution. Confucius said, 'People prefer to live in a village where the Ren virtue flourishes. If one chose to reside in a place void of Ren virtue, how can he be wise?' The Ren virtue takes the highest place among all blessings bestowed upon people by Tian (Sky), and Ren is the safest home for people. It is unwise for a person, free of duress, not to practice Ren. People void of the Ren, Yi, Li, and wisdom deserve to be enslaved by others. Those slaves who feel ashamed of being slaves are like bow-makers who feel ashamed of being bow-makers, or like arrow-makers who feel ashamed of being arrow-makers. If these slaves feel ashamed, why not practice Ren? A person with the Ren virtue is like an archer who always sets up a proper posture before shooting. If he does not hit the target, he does not blame his rivals who surpass him. He must examine his own ineptness and rectify it."

Commentary:

The questions of the choice of profession and role conflict are complex. Mencius did not offer any definitive answers to these questions and only said that one should be cautious in his choice of profession. For example, since the job of an arrow-maker is to manufacture sharp arrows to hurt people, one can infer superficially that such a job violates the Ren virtue. However, if the arrows are made for national defense, does this job violate the Ren virtue? Suppose that a modern scientist is involved in the development of a weapon of mass destruction. Should this scientist, free from duress, quit his or her job for the sake of Ren virtue and forsake patriotism? Mencius did not give a clear answer to resolve such role conflict but only suggested the exercise of wisdom, which is an open-ended mechanism to weigh one good against another or to discern right from wrong. A wise decision depends on many circumstantial factors and cannot be generalized. Mencius just hinted a guide to resolve such ambiguous dilemma by saying that "the Ren virtue takes the highest place amount all blessings bestowed upon people." This means that the Ren virtue should be given the highest priority.

Section 8

孟子曰 子路 人告之以有過則喜。禹聞善言則拜。大舜有大焉 善與人同。舍己從人 樂取於人以為善。自耕 稼 陶 漁以至為帝 無非取於人者。取諸人以為善 是與人為善者也。故君子莫大乎與人為善。

Mencius said, "Zi Lu was glad to hear criticisms of him. Yu respectfully thanked speakers of good words. The great Shun was even greater. He loved to do good work with others. He humbled himself to follow others and learn their good qualities. During his careers as a farmer, pottery maker, fisherman, and finally, the

Chapter 3: Gong Sun Chou (1)

emperor, he continuously learned from others. Learning the good qualities of others is equivalent to the encouragement, support, help, and leadership given to others, and the cooperation with others to do good work. Therefore, this is no greater deed for a Jun Zi than such deeds."

Annotation:

Zi Lu (子路, 542–480 BC), also called Zhong You (仲由), was a disciple of Confucius and was best known for his ability and success in statesmanship. He was also noted for his valor and sense of justice.

Historians regarded Emperor Yan (炎), Huang Di (黃帝, Yellow Emperor), Yao (堯), Shun (舜), and Yu (禹) as the five saintly emperors in the Period of the Five Emperors. This period started between 5000 and 6000 years ago. Shun (舜, circa 2294–2184 BC) started as a lowly person in the grassroots. He ascended in society because of his great virtues and eventually succeeded Emperor Yao (堯, circa 2356–2255 BC). Before Emperor Shun died in circa 2184 BC, he chose the Great Yu (禹, circa 2237–2139 BC) to be his successor. The Great Yu and his father were engineering ministers in charge of flood control, irrigation, and water management. The Great Yu earned immense credit from people for completing a large-scale water conservancy and flood control project.

Commentary and Modern Perspective:

The main themes of this section are (1) humility, and (2) encouragement, support, help, and leadership given to others, and cooperation with others to do good work. The promotion of good work by the society is more important and greater than individual endeavors and achievements.

Section 9

孟子曰 伯夷 非其君不事 非其友不友。不立於惡人之朝 不與惡人言。立於惡人之朝 與惡人言 如以朝衣朝冠坐於塗炭。推惡惡之心 思與鄉人立 其冠不正 望望然去之 若將浼焉。是故諸侯雖有善其辭命而至者 不受也 不受也者 是亦不屑就已。柳下惠 不羞汙君 不卑小官 進不隱賢 必以其道 遺佚而不怨 阨窮而不憫。故曰 爾為爾 我為我 雖袒裼裸裎於我側 爾焉能浼我哉。故由由然與之 偕而不自失焉 援而止之而止。援而止之而止者 是亦不屑去已。

　　孟子曰 伯夷隘 柳下惠不恭。隘與不恭 君子不由也。

Mencius said, "The character of Bo Yi was that he would not serve any undeserving king, befriend undeserving people, stand in the court of a corrupt government, and talk to wicked people. He considered that the act of standing in the court of a corrupt government and of talking to wicked people would spoil his attire with dirt. He extended his aversion to wickedness to his interaction with his clansmen. Whenever he met a villager, whose hat was improperly worn, he would leave abruptly as if he could be contaminated. Therefore, he turned down many articulate invitations for appointment offered by feudal lords. He turned them down because he was obsessed with his lofty purity.

On the contrary, Liu Xia Hui did not feel ashamed to work for evil kings and embarrassed to take lowly positions. In his jobs, he never concealed his caliber and virtue and he always adhered to his principles. He did not complain when he was neglected or fired. He did not grieve when he was poor and destitute. Therefore, he said, 'You are you. I am I. Even if you stand naked by my side, how can

Chapter 3: Gong Sun Chou (1)

you seduce or upset me?' Therefore, being suave and self-confident, he was able to handle people smoothly without violating his own principles. He stayed in his job when his boss asked him to stay. He did not resign at the urge of his boss because he considered an abrupt departure a violation of his lofty principles."

Mencius then said, "Bo Yi was narrow-minded. Liu Xia Hui was suave. A Jun Zi loathes being narrow-minded or suave."

Annotation:

The story of Bo Yi (伯夷) and Shu Qi (叔齊) is narrated in Section 5 of Endnotes.

Liu Xia Hui (柳下惠, 720–621 BC) was once an official of the state of Lu (魯國). He later resigned and became a hermit. He was repeatedly fired as the chief justice. When asked, "Why can't you go elsewhere?" he replied, "Since I deal with people based on righteousness, which country would not fire me repeatedly? If I am required to bend my righteousness to serve my boss, why should I leave my motherland?" (Section 2 of Chapter 18, 微子, of *Confucius Analects*).

There was also a famous episode about him. It was a freezing, snowy evening when he was traveling. He went into a ruined temple for shelter. Soon afterward, a beautiful woman came in. She shivered and begged to sit on his lap and embrace each other to keep warm. He refused at first, claiming that it was inappropriate. However, she insisted, and said that if she died, nobody would take care of her elderly mother. He finally agreed, held the woman on his lap, and shared his coat with her. During the entire evening, while she was being warmed, he did not harass her sexually. He was later praised by historians for being able to resist sexual temptation, even with a beauty sitting on his lap.

Commentary:

Mencius discussed the flaws of two extreme types of character. Bo Yi was obsessed with his lofty purity, rigidity, and narrow-mindedness. This type of person contributes little to society because they reject and despise almost everybody, and therefore do not want to work for and with others. The second type, such as Liu Xia Hui, is suave externally but internally overconfident of their ability to uphold their virtues. They think that they can handle wicked bosses, accommodate harsh environment, and resist temptations while trying to please everybody. They think that they can adapt to all situations smoothly and flexibly without violating their own principles. This type of person could also be dangerous to society because they are too ready to plunge into situations of role conflict (see Commentary in Section 7 above). When their wicked bosses force them to do evil, it will be impossible for them to please their bosses and adhere to righteous principles at the same time. They will be complicit by then.

The question is how to strike the right balance between these extremes. Mencius did not give a definitive answer here because it depends on the circumstance. In Section 1 of Chapter 10, Mencius gave an answer by referring to Confucius's behavior: "When it was proper to leave quickly, he did so. When it was proper to stay longer, he did so. When it was proper to retire, he did so. When it was proper to take up an official post, he did so. This was the way of Confucius." The *Book of the Mean* (中庸, also known as the *Doctrine of the Mean*) also offers some guidance to this question.

Modern Perspective:

Extremism should be avoided even with good intention.

Chapter 3: Gong Sun Chou (1)

Confucius's pragmatic and flexible behavior can be a good reference: "When it was proper to leave quickly, he did so. When it was proper to stay longer, he did so. When it was proper to retire, he did so. When it was proper to take up an official post, he did so." Propriety should be determined by Ren, Yi, and Li.

Chapter 4: Gong Sun Chou (2)

Section 1

孟子曰 天時不如地利 地利不如人和。三里之城 七里之郭 環而攻之而不勝。夫環而攻之 必有得天時者矣 然而不勝者 是天時不如地利也。城非不高也 池非不深也 兵革非不堅利也 米粟非不多也 委而去之 是地利不如人和也。

故曰 域民不以封疆之界 固國不以山谿之險 威天下不以兵革之利。得道者多助 失道者寡助。寡助之至 親戚畔之 多助之至 天下順之。以天下之所順 攻親戚之所畔 故君子有不戰 戰必勝矣。

Mencius said, "Timing advantage is less important than geographic and environmental advantages, which are, in turn, less important than the support and unity of people. Take, for example, a city with an area of three square miles enclosed by a city wall of seven miles in diameter. The enemy tries to besiege it but fails to conquer it. The enemy must have chosen the right time to attack. Its failure to conquer is not due to the timing advantage but to the strong defense provided by the geographic and environmental advantages of the city. Suppose again that the city wall is tall, the moat surrounding the city is deep, and the city has strong arms and ample food inventory. If its defending soldiers desert the city, it can be easily conquered. This illustrates that geographic and environment advantages are less important than the support and unity of people. Therefore, we can infer that, 'The control of population movement does not depend on the erection of fences and walls at the border. National security does not depend on the existence of hazardous mountain ranges surrounding the country. Domination over the world by a country does not depend on the strength of its army. Whoever follows the Dao gets a lot of support. Whoever departs from the Dao gets little support. The lack of support can be so extreme that even close relatives and confidants will become rebels and turncoats. The abundance of support can be so extreme that the whole world will become your followers. The result is predictable if a country with the support of the whole world attacks another country whose relatives and confidants have become rebels and turncoats. Unless a Jun Zi with the support of the whole world does not initiate an attack, he will certainly be the victor in a war if he needs to fight.' "

Annotation:

The meaning of the Dao in Confucianism has been explained in detail in the Introduction. In the context of this section, it means the principles of Ren and Yi.

The word *Jun Zi* (君子) means a gentleman, a person of superior and noble character, a prominent and respectable person in society, or a person who upholds high standards of virtuous principles. Jun Zi was commonly translated as "gentleman" in the past, but it stands for a much wider range of excellence and a higher standard of morality than what the English word *gentleman* stands for (see Section 4 of the Introduction).

Commentary:

This section contains a key point of Mencius's geopolitical

philosophy. The first eight sentences of this section establish the logic of the assertion: "Timing advantage is less important than geographic and environmental advantages, which are, in turn, less important than the support and unity of people." The subsequent sentences emphasize the importance of support of people. The support of people is derived from the implementation of Ren and Yi principles (i.e., the Dao approach).

To Mencius, strong fortifications at the border, geographic advantages, and a strong army are not the determinant factors for the establishment of power and influence of a country. Instead, the Dao approach is invincible. It is interesting to note the relevance to modern-day geopolitics of the sentences: "The control of population movement does not depend on the erection of fences and walls at the border. National security does not depend on the existence of hazardous mountain ranges surrounding the country. Domination over the world by a country does not depend on the strength of its army."

Modern Perspective:

Modern rulers tend to do the opposite of what Mencius said.

Section 2

孟子將朝王 王使人來曰 寡人如就見者也 有寒疾 不可以風。朝將視朝 不識可使寡人得見乎。

對曰 不幸而有疾 不能造朝。

明日 出吊於東郭氏 公孫丑曰 昔者辭以病 今日吊 或者不可乎。

Chapter 4: Gong Sun Chou (2)

曰 昔者疾 今日愈 如之何不吊。

王使人問疾 醫來。孟仲子對曰 昔者有王命 有采薪之憂 不能造朝。今病小愈 趨造於朝 我不識能至否乎。使數人要於路 曰 請必無歸 而造於朝。

不得已而之景丑氏宿焉。景子曰 內則父子 外則君臣 人之大倫也。父子主恩 君臣主敬。丑見王之敬子也 未見所以敬王也。

曰 惡 是何言也 齊人無以仁義與王言者 豈以仁義為不美也。其心曰 是何足與言仁義也。云爾 則不敬莫大乎是。我非堯舜之道 不敢以陳於王前 故齊人莫如我敬王也。

景子曰 否 非此之謂也。禮曰 父召無諾 君命召不俟駕。固將朝也 聞王命而遂不果 宜與夫禮若不相似然。

曰 豈謂是與。曾子曰 晉楚之富 不可及也 彼以其富 我以吾仁 彼以其爵 我以吾義 吾何慊乎哉。夫豈不義而曾子言之 是或一道也。天下有達尊三 爵一 齒一 德一。朝廷莫如爵 鄉黨莫如齒 輔世長民莫如德。惡得有其一 以慢其二哉。故將大有為之君 必有所不召之臣。欲有謀焉 則就之。其尊德樂道 不如是不足與有為也。故湯之於伊尹 學焉而後臣之 故不勞而王 桓公之於管仲 學焉而後臣之 故不勞而霸。今天下地醜德齊 莫能相尚。無他 好臣其所教 而不好臣其所受教。湯之於伊尹 桓公之於管仲 則不敢召。管仲且猶不可召 而況不為管仲者乎。

When Mencius was about to go to the royal court to see the King of Qi, a messenger came in with a note from the king, "I originally planned to come to see you. However, I have a cold and cannot expose myself to wind. I will hold a ministerial meeting in the royal court tomorrow. I wonder if I can see you there?"

Mencius replied, "Unfortunately, I also have a cold. I cannot come tomorrow."

On the next day, Mencius wanted to attend the funeral vigil of a member of the Dong Guo family. Gong Sun Chou, the student of Mencius, asked, "You just recovered from yesterday's cold. You are going to attend the funeral today. Can you not go?" Mencius replied, "I was sick yesterday, but am feeling well now. Why can't I go?"

The King of Qi sent a messenger accompanied with a physician to inquire about Mencius's sickness. Meng Zhong Zi, another student of Mencius, told the messenger, "Mencius has already received the invitation from the king. However, he was sick yesterday and could not see the king. He is getting better today. I think he is already on his way to the royal court. I don't know whether he has already arrived at the court." Meng Zhong Zi immediately sent a messenger to intercept Mencius on the road to tell him, "Please do not return home. Go to the court right away!"

Mencius reluctantly changed his plan, visited his good friend, Jing Chou, a minister of the state of Qi, and stayed overnight at his home. After hearing what happened with Mencius during the day, Jing Chou said, "The relations between parents and children in a family, and between the king [boss] and ministers [subordinates] are the basic social fabrics. There should be love between parents and children, and respect between the king and ministers. I can see the king's respect of you, but I have not seen your showing any respect of the king."

Mencius replied, "Oh! What do you mean? No minister in the state of Qi speaks to the king about Ren and Yi. Do all ministers consider Ren and Yi unwanted? They perhaps think that the king does not deserve to be told about Ren and Yi. If so, their attitude is most disrespectful. I dare not present to and discuss with the king anything which is not as good as the principle of Yao and Shun, the two ancient saintly kings. Therefore, no one in the state of Qi can surpass me regarding my respect of the king."

Jing Chou said, "I disagree with you on this. The *Book of Rites* says, 'One should not ignore the call from the parent; upon a summon from the king, one should immediately go to see him without waiting for the carriage to be ready.' You originally planned to meet the king in court. After you have received the king's invitation to a meeting in the royal court, you changed your mind and turned him down. Your behavior does not seem to be in line with Li [being disrespectful and lack of courtesy]."

Mencius said, "Is this what concerns you? Zheng Zi once said, 'The wealth of the states of Jin and Chu are unsurpassable. They rely on their wealth, but I rely on my Ren virtue. They rely on their noble status, but I rely on my Yi virtue. Why should I feel inferior to them?' If such words are wrong, why did Zheng Zi say so? These words make sense. In today's world, people regard three things to be respectable: noble status, age, and virtue. In the royal court, the noble status of a person is the most important. In the clan, the age of a person is the most important. In the governance of people, a person's virtue is the most important. It is wrong to rely on one's noble status to debase people who have the other two qualities.

Therefore, a king with the potential for great accomplishments must have some ministers whom he would not summon. If the king needs to seek advice from them, he will visit them in person. In this way, the king shows deep respect for virtuous and meritorious ministers. If not, he does not deserve to be their king. Therefore, this was how King Tang of the Shang Dynasty treated Yi Yin. King Tang humbled himself as the student of Yi Yin before appointing him as the prime minister. As a result, King Tang easily became the emperor of the Shang Dynasty. This was also how Duke Huan of the state of Qi treated Guan Zhong. Duke Huan humbled himself as the student of Guan Zhong before appointing him as the prime minister. As a result, Duke Huan easily became the top hegemon among all feudal lords. Nowadays, no state stands out among others in terms of virtue and merit. There is no other reason but one. A typical king prefers to appoint ministers who can be taught by him. The king does not like to appoint ministers who can teach him. Even Guan Zhong cannot be summoned by Duke Huan of Qi; what about more superior people who have disdain for Guan Zhong? [I am one of them.]"

Annotation:

Dong Guo (東郭) was a minister of the state of Qi (齊).
Gong Sun Chou (公孫丑) was a disciple of Mencius. Some scholars thought that Gong Sun Chou co-authored with Mencius the book *Mencius*.
Meng Zhong Zi (孟仲子) was a cousin and a disciple of Mencius.
Jing Chou (景丑) was a minister of the state of Qi and a good friend of Mencius.
The Book of Rites (禮記) was written by Zheng Zi (曾子). *The Book of Great Learning* (大學) was one of the *Four Books* in Confucianism and a chapter of *The Book of Rites* (禮記). In the South Song Dynasty of China (1127–1279 AD), a prominent Confucian, Zhu Xi (朱熹), designated the Four Books—*The Book of Great Learning* (大學), *The Book of the Mean* (中庸, also known as The Doctrine of the Mean), *The Analects* (論語), and *Mencius*

Chapter 4: Gong Sun Chou (2)

(孟子)—to be the required syllabus for the imperial examination for recruitment to the civil service.

Zheng Zi (曾子, also known as Zheng Shen 曾参, born 505 BC) was a prominent disciple of Confucius, known for his filial piety. He was the author of *The Book of Great Learning* (大學).

The story of Yi Yin (伊尹) and King Tang (湯) of the Shang Dynasty (商朝, circa 1600–1066 BC) is narrated in the Annotation of Section 2 of Chapter 3 above.

The story of Qi Huan Gong (齊桓公, also known as Duke Huan of Qi,), Guan Zhong (管仲), and Bao Shu Ya (鮑叔牙) is narrated in Section 6 of Endnotes.

Commentary:

This section has four key points. The first point was embodied in the words of Mencius: "No minister in the state of Qi speaks to the king about Ren and Yi. Do all ministers consider Ren and Yi unwanted? They perhaps think that the king does not deserve to be told about Ren and Yi. If so, their attitude is most disrespectful." Mencius believed that it was the responsibility of a minister to advise the king about the principles of Ren and Yi.

The second key point was presented by Zheng Zi's words: "The wealth of the states of Jin (晉) and Chu (楚) are unsurpassable. They rely on their wealth, but I rely on my Ren virtue. They rely on their noble status, but I rely on my Yi virtue. Why should I feel inferior to them?" To Zheng Zi, Ren and Yi virtues were more important than wealth.

The third key point was presented by Mencius's words: "In today's world, people regard three things to be respectable: noble status, age, and virtue. In the royal court, the noble status of a person is the most important. In the clan, the age of a person is the most important. In the governance of people, a person's virtue is the most important. It is wrong to rely on one's noble status to debase people who have the other two qualities." Mencius criticized several noblemen and high-ranking officials of his time for debasing meritorious and elderly people with wisdom.

The fourth key point was about people management. King Tang of the Shang Dynasty and Duke Huan of Qi were cited as good examples of great leaders who respected talented staff. Mencius cited these examples to convey his frustration that the king of Qi did not treat him with due respect as King Tang and Duke Huan of Qi did.

Modern Perspective:

Respect your staff. Be an honest advisor to your boss.

Section 3

陳臻問曰 前日於齊 王饋兼金一百而不受。於宋 饋七十鎰而受。於薛 饋五十鎰而受。前日之不受是 則今日之受非也。今日之受是 則前日之不受非也。夫子必居一於此矣。

孟子曰 皆是也。當在宋也 予將有遠行 行者必以贐。辭曰 饋贐。予何為不受。當在薛也 予有戒心。辭曰 聞戒。故為兵饋之 予何為不受。若於齊 則未有處也。無處而饋之 是貨之也。焉有君子而可以貨取乎。

Chen Zhen asked Mencius, "When you were in the state of Qi the other day, you declined the gift of 2,000 oz. of refined gold from the king of Qi. When you were in the state of Song, you accepted the

Chapter 4: Gong Sun Chou (2)

gift of 1,400 oz. of refined gold from the king of Song. When you were in the state of Xue, you also accepted the gift of 1,000 oz. of refined gold from the king of Xue. If you were right in declining the gift from the king of Qi, your acceptance of the gifts from Song and Xue must be wrong. If you were right in accepting the gifts from Song and Xue, your decline of the gift from Qi must be wrong. You, my teacher, must choose one of these alternatives."

Mencius replied, "I was right in all these cases. When I was in the state of Song, I needed to take a long journey to the next destination. A traveler needs travel expenses. The gift from the king of Song was intended to pay for my travel expenses. How could I decline his gift? When I was in the state of Xue, I was concerned of my safety. When the king of Xue heard about my concern, he gave me money to buy arms for self-defense. How could I decline his gift? When I was in the state of Qi, there was no reason for the gift. A gift without a valid reason is a bribe. How is it possible for a Jun Zi to accept a bribe?"

Annotation:

Chen Zhen (陳臻) was a disciple of Mencius.

The unit of gold mentioned in the original text in Chinese was "yi," which was equivalent to about 20 oz. The text mentioned the gift by the king of Qi was 100 yi, which was equivalent to 2000 oz. Furthermore, gold at that time might not be pure gold but rather an amalgamate of bronze and gold, or just bronze. Therefore, the refined gold mentioned in the Chinese text was most likely pure gold.

The state of Song (宋) was a hegemon during the Spring-Autumn Period but became a small state during the Warring States Period.

Mencius in Modern Perspectives

The small state of Xue (薛) was enfeoffed to Tian Ying (田嬰), the younger brother of King Xuan of Qi.

Modern Perspective:

The key sentence in this section is: "A gift without a valid reason is bribery." Although there is no obvious string attached to the gift, you owe the doner a favor and you may be obliged to return the favor in future. A wise person should decline such gifts.

Section 4

孟子之平陸。謂其大夫曰 子之持戟之士 一日而三失伍 則去之否乎。

曰 不待三。

(曰) 然則子之失伍也亦多矣。凶年饑歲 子之民 老羸轉於溝壑 壯者散而之四方者 幾千人矣。

曰 此非距心之所得為也。

曰 今有受人之牛羊而為之牧之者 則必為之求牧與芻矣。求牧與芻而不得 則反諸其人乎。抑亦立而視其死與。

曰 此則距心之罪也。

他日 見於王曰 王之為都者 臣知五人焉。知其罪者 惟孔距心。為王誦之。

王曰 此則寡人之罪也。

Mencius arrived at Ping Lu city and asked its mayor, Kong Ju Xi, "If a guard defending the city misses the call of duty three times a day, will you dismiss him?"

Chapter 4: Gong Sun Chou (2)

Kong Ju Xin replied, "I would not wait three times to dismiss him."

Mencius said, "You are also derelict of your duty in many ways. During calamitous years and famines, your old and feeble citizens perish in ditches, and thousands of strong citizens are scattered over all places."

Kong Ju Xin said, "This is beyond my reach."

Mencius said, "Suppose there is a shepherd who is hired to take care and feed herds of cows and lambs. He must find pasture and grass to feed the animals. If he cannot find feeding ground and grass, should he return the animals to the owner, or should he stand by and watch them die?"

Kong Ju Xin replied, "I, Ju Xin, am sorry. It is my fault."

On another day, Mencius met and told the king of Qi, "Among your mayors of cities, I know five of them. There is only one called Kong Ju Xin who admits his fault." Mencius then narrated his dialogue with Kong Ju Xin.

King Xuan of Qi said, "It is in fact my fault."

Annotation:

Ping Lu (平陸) was a city at the border of the state of Qi.
Kong Ju Xin (孔距心) was a mayor of Ping Lu.

Modern Perspective:

This section is relevant today. It points out common misconduct of rulers of countries, leaders of organizations, and senior executives of companies. First, harsh rules and laws are imposed on common citizens and low-level employees who are punished disproportionately for trivial violations, but rulers and managers at the top can find numerous excuses to avoid blame, impeachment, and punishment for major plunders. Second, misconduct and violations of common people are incomparable in scale and severity to those committed by people at the top. A mistake made by a ruler could cause major suffering and even death to millions. A mistake made by the chief executive could cause the failure of the company. However, people at the top are seldom held accountable for their mistakes and dereliction of duty. Third, when a disaster occurs, the typical responses from rulers and top managers are: "I am not responsible for it," "It is an unavoidable natural disaster," "Nobody expects it," "It is the fault of somebody else or of a foreign country," and so on. Fourth, some rulers and top executives even double-down on their mistakes and wrong decisions. Fifth, a meritorious leader should have the wisdom, honesty, and courage to acknowledge his or her mistakes, and the commitment to correct them.

Section 5

孟子謂蚳鼃曰 子之辭靈丘而請士師 似也 為其可以言也。今既數月矣 未可以言與。

蚳鼃諫於王而不用 致為臣而去。齊人曰 所以為蚳鼃 則善矣 所以自為 則吾不知也。

公都子以告。

曰 吾聞之也 有官守者 不得其職則去。有言責者 不得其言則去。我無官守 我無言責也 則吾進退 豈不綽綽然有餘裕哉。

Mencius said to Qi Wa, "You resigned from the post of the mayor of Ling Qiu and asked to be appointed as the royal counsel. Your move seemed to make sense because your new job gives you an opportunity to advise the king. Why have you not given any advice to the king for months?"

Qi Wa tried to advise the king but was ignored. The frustrated Qi Wa resigned and left.

People of Qi commented, "Mencius has advised Qi Wa to do the right thing. What about Mencius himself? We don't know."

Gong Du Zi, disciple of Mencius, reported this hearsay to Mencius.

Mencius said, "I have also heard such criticism. A government official who cannot perform his duties properly should resign. An advisor who is ignored should also resign. I do not have any official post and I am not an advisor. Therefore, I am free to do anything without any constraint."

Annotation:

Qi Wa (蚳蛙) was an official of the state of Qi.
Ling Qiu (靈丘) was a city at the border of the state of Qi.
Gong Du Zi (公都子) was a disciple of Mencius.

Commentary:

Confucius also said, "If the government of a country is good and clean, and you collect a salary as an official, and if the government is corrupt and decadent, and you still collect a salary as an official, shame on you" (See Section 1 of Chapter 14, 憲問, of *Confucius Analects)*. Confucius's way was to become an official when it was appropriate to do so, to retire when it was inappropriate to be an official, to offer his service for as long as possible, and to resign quickly when needed (Section 2 of Chapter 3).

Modern Perspective:

There are many situations where a Jun Zi should consider seriously resigning from his or her job. The following are a few examples:

(1) Suppose that you are a public health official, an environmental protection official, a nuclear scientist, or a seismologist, and your job is to issue warning to the authority and the public about looming catastrophes. If your boss prohibits you from issuing an early warning for inappropriate reasons, you should seriously consider resigning from your job; else you are complicit.

(2) Suppose that you are a financial risk manager, and your job is to advise the company of financial risks and proper balance-sheet management. If the senior management ignores your good advice and the level of risks in the financial position of the company, you should seriously consider resigning from your job; else you are complicit. When the company fails, you will lose your job or be sued.

(3) Suppose that you are an architect or construction engineer, and it is your job to provide safety margin in the construction of buildings or public works. If your boss pressures you to lower the safety margin to reduce the construction cost, you should seriously consider resigning from your job; else you will be legally liable.

(4) Suppose that you are an accountant and if your boss pressures you to cook the books of the company, you should consider resigning from your job.

Chapter 4: Gong Sun Chou (2)

Section 6

孟子為卿於齊 出吊於滕 王使蓋大夫王驩為輔行。王驩朝暮見 反齊滕之路 未嘗與之言行事也。

　公孫丑曰 齊卿之位 不為小矣 齊滕之路 不為近矣。反之 而未嘗與言行事 何也。

　曰 夫既或治之 予何言哉。

Mencius was a minister of the state of Qi. He was sent on a mission of condolence of Teng Wen Gong. The king of Qi also sent Wang Huan, the governor of the county of Gai, to accompany Mencius. Although Wang Huan saw Mencius day and night during the entire journey, the two did not talk about official matters.

Gong Sun Chou asked Mencius, "A minister of the state of Qi is an important position. The road between the state of Qi and the state of Teng is quite long. Why did you and Wang Huan not talk about official matters on the way?"

Mencius replied, "Wang Huan is complacent of the governance of his county. What else can I talk about with him?"

Annotation:

　Teng Wen Gong (滕文公, also known as Duke Wen of Teng) was the king of a small state of Teng during the Warring States Period. He was a contemporary of Mencius.

　Wang Zi Ao (王子敖, also known as Wang Huan 王驩) was a prime minister of the state of Qi. Wang Zi Ao was mentioned also in Section 6 of Chapter 4. On that occasion, he was only a governor of the county of Gai. He was also mentioned in Sections 24 and 25 of Chapter 7. Mencius did not like him.

187

Modern Perspective:

Since a complacent person does not listen to good advice from others, he cannot make any progress.

Section 7

孟子自齊葬於魯　反於齊　止於嬴。充虞請曰　前日不知虞之不肖　使虞敦匠事　嚴　虞不敢請。今願竊有請也　木若以美然。

曰　古者棺槨無度　中古棺七寸　槨稱之。自天子達於庶人。非直為觀美也　然後盡於人心。不得　不可以為悅　無財　不可以為悅。得之為有財　古之人皆用之　吾何為獨不然。且比化者　無使土親膚　於人心獨無恔乎。吾聞之君子　不以天下儉其親。

Mencius took a leave of absence from his job in the state of Qi to bury his mother in the state of Lu. On his return to the state of Qi, he stopped by the city of Ying.

Chong Yu, a disciple of Mencius, asked respectfully, "You did not know my incompetency the other day and asked me to supervise the making of a coffin. Since you were in a hurry, I dared not ask you any questions. I want to ask you a question now. The wood of the coffin seems to be too good."

Mencius replied, "In the old days, there was no rule regarding the thickness of the inner coffin and the outer casket. The Zhou Li specified seven inches for the inner coffin and the outer casket. This standard was applicable to everyone, from the emperor to common people. It was not about the beauty of the wood but about people's sentiment. If the thickness was prohibited by regulation, descendants were upset. If the descendants could not afford such a

Chapter 4: Gong Sun Chou (2)

thickness, they were upset also. If such a thickness was allowed and affordable, the descendants in the past used this standard. Why should I deviate from this tradition? Descendants do not feel comfortable if the bodies of their deceased parents are too close to the earth. I heard that a Jun Zi should not be mean to their deceased parents for the sake of extreme frugality."

Annotation:

The state of Lu (魯國) was a small state next to the state of Qi. It was the birthplace of Confucius.

Ying (嬴) was a city in the state of Lu.

Chong Yu (充虞) was a disciple of Mencius.

Zhou Li (周禮) was a system of Li instituted during early Zhou Dynasty by Zhou Gong (周公, also known as Duke of Zhou), the younger brother of King Wu of Zhou (周武王, died 1043 BC) and the first prime minister of the Zhou Dynasty. Zhou Gong formalized and further developed the prevailing social norms at that time into a set of official mandates. These mandates were decreed in the Zhou Li (周禮) system. This system was very elaborate and detailed. It covered many aspects of how a person should behave from birth to death; for example, the paternal lineage of family names, the prohibition of marriages between siblings and close cousins, the prohibition of marriages between two persons with the same family name, inheritance of estate, the definition of relatives within the extended family, how relatives in the extended family should interact with one another, the rituals of celebrations, worship of ancestors, and funerals. More importantly, the Zhou Li system literally defined the political and social system of the Zhou Dynasty. It defined the roles, power, and entitlement of the Imperial Emperor versus feudal lords. It also defined the protocols in courts, as well as in local and central governments. It also specified the rituals and ceremonies for worships of Tian (Sky), Earth, ancestors, and other gods. The purpose of this Li system was to maintain an orderly and peaceful society at that time.

Commentary:

According to Zhou Li, funerals and burials were serious matter. Confucius and Mencius were ardent advocates of Zhou Li. On the contrary, Mo Zi, another prominent philosopher during the Warring States Period, advocated frugality in organizing funerals.

The key point of this section is not about coffin making but about filial piety. The main sentence is: "A Jun Zi should not be mean to their deceased parents for the sake of extreme frugality."

Section 8

沈同以其私問曰 燕可伐與。

孟子曰 可。子噲不得與人燕 子之不得受燕於子噲。有仕於此 而子悅之 不告於王而私與之吾子之祿爵。夫士也 亦無王命而私受之於子 則可乎。何以異於是。

齊人伐燕。或問曰 勸齊伐燕 有諸。

曰 未也。沈同問 燕可伐與。吾應之曰 可。彼然而伐之也。彼如曰 孰可以伐之。則將應之曰 為天吏 則可以伐之。今有殺人者 或問之曰 人可殺與。則將應之曰 可。彼如曰 孰可以殺之。則將應之曰 為士師 則可以殺之。今以燕伐燕 何為勸之哉。

Chapter 4: Gong Sun Chou (2)

Historical Background:

The state of Yan (燕國) was one of the seven hegemons during the Warring State Period. Its territory was in modern-day Liaoning and Harbin provinces in China, north and north-west of North Korea. King Wu of the Zhou Dynasty (周武王, died 1043 BC) enfeoffed the state of Yan to his cousin Shao Gong Shi (召公奭), who was the ancestorial founder of the state. This state lasted until 222 BC, when it was conquered by the state of Qin (秦). The 35th successor to the throne after Shao Gong Shi was King Kuai of Yan (燕王噲, also known as Zi Kuai, 子噲, died 316 BC). When Zi Kuai was old, he delegated many of his duties to his prime minister, Zi Zhi (子之, died 314 BC), who had the ambition to overthrow his king. Zi Zhi had a relative Su Dai (蘇代) who was a famous lobbyist.

Su Dai visited the state of Yan after his lobbying journey to the state of Qi. King Zi Kuai asked Su Dai, "Can the state of Qi become a dominant hegemon?" Su Dai replied, "No." King Zi Kuai asked, "Why?" Su Dai answered, "The king of Qi does not trust his ministers." After this conversation, King Zi Kuai delegated even more power to Zi Zhi. Lu Mao Shou (鹿毛壽), a minister and a comrade of Zi Zhi, later advised King Zi Kuai, saying: "If you want to be remembered as a saintly king in history, you should take the ancient saintly king, Shun, as a model. When Shun was old, he tried to abdicate his throne to his prime minister, Xu You (許由). However, Xu You turned down the offer. Both Shun and Xu You earned great credit for doing so. If you abdicate your throne to Zi Zhi, he will also turn down the offer, and suggest your son, Prince Ping (太子平), to be your successor. In this way, you will be remembered in history as a saintly king." King Zi Kuai took the advice and abdicated his throne to Zi Zhi, who accepted the offer. Before King Zi Kuai died, Zi Zhi was able to grab all ruling power from Prince Ping.

Prince Ping subsequently waged a civil war against Zi Zhi. Prince Ping and tens of thousands of Yan nationals were killed in the civil war.

The king of the state of Qi waged a war to punish Zi Zhi for his atrocity. Zi Zhi was brutally killed by soldiers of the state of Qi. His body was chopped into small pieces.

The second son of King Zi Kuai returned to the state of Yan after the war with the state of Qi. He was then crowned King Zhao of Yan (燕昭王).

Text of *Mencius*:

Shen Tong asked Mencius privately, "Should the state of Yan be invaded?"

Mencius replied, "Yes. Zi Kuai should not relinquish the state of Yan to someone else. Zi Zhi should not accept the state of Yan from Zi Kuai. Suppose that there is an official who is your good friend. He privately gives you his position and salary without informing the king. Suppose also that you give to the same official your position and salary without informing the king. Are these transactions appropriately? Are these transactions different from the transaction between Zi Kuai and Zi Zhi?"

The state of Qi later invaded the state of Yan. Somebody asked Mencius, "Did you advise the state of Qi to invade the state of Yan?" Mencius replied, "No, I did not. When Shen Tong asked, 'Should the state of Yan be invaded?' my answer was that it should be invaded. If he had asked me differently, 'Who may invade the state of Yan?' my answer would be, 'Only an official from Tian (Sky) may invade it.' Suppose there is a murderer. If somebody asked, 'Should he be executed?' The correct answer is 'Yes.' If the

Chapter 4: Gong Sun Chou (2)

question is, 'Who should execute him?' the answer should be, 'Only the official executioner may kill him.' Since the state of Qi and state of Yan are both atrocious, the invasion was effectively a war between two states. Why should I have advised such atrocity?"

Annotation:

Shen Tong (沈同) was a minister of the state of Qi.

Since ancient Chinese did not have the same notion of God as Christians, the word *Tian* (*Sky* 天) was used to represent a supernatural and unknown natural power that governs the world. Therefore, the words *God, Heaven, Sky,* and *Nature* are synonyms in the context of classic Chinese literature. The word *Heaven* in this translation does not carry the same meaning of Heaven under Christianity. The word *Sky* should not be interpreted astronomically.

Commentary:

This section has three lessons. The first is about the mistake made by King Zi Kuai. The head of a state should not take his country as his personal asset. Instead, he has the responsibility to bring peace and prosperity to his people. He betrayed his people by relinquishing his responsibility. This action was against the Yi virtue. In addition, he fantasized about becoming a saintly king like Shun by an artificial maneuver. This was vanity. He also lacked wisdom and did not realize Zi Zhi's hypocrisy. His action resulted in a horrible civil war in his country.

The second lesson was about the wickedness of Zi Zhi, who was a tiger in a sheep's skin. He pretended to be a meritorious official in the beginning to earn the trust of King Zi Kuai. After he had grabbed power, he ruined the country for his personal interest.

The third lesson was about the mistake committed by the state of Qi. The king of Qi was greedy. He took advantage of the chaos and vulnerability of the state of Yan. He invaded the state of Yan under the guise of being a benevolent conqueror and a savior from Tian (Sky). Instead of saving the state of Yan from turmoil, he plundered and pillaged it. This was hypocrisy.

Mencius loathed these mistakes.

Section 9

燕人畔。王曰 吾甚慚於孟子。

陳賈曰 王無患焉。王自以為與周公 孰仁且智。

王曰 惡 是何言也。

曰 周公使管叔監殷 管叔以殷畔。知而使之 是不仁也 不知而使之 是不智也。仁智 周公未之盡也 而況於王乎。賈請見而解之。

見孟子問曰 周公何人也。

曰 古聖人也。

曰 使管叔監殷 管叔以殷畔也 有諸。

曰 然。

曰 周公知其將畔而使之與。

曰 不知也。

(曰) 然則聖人且有過與。

曰 周公 弟也 管叔 兄也。周公之過 不亦宜乎。且古之君子 過則改之 今之君子 過則順之。古之君子 其過也 如日月之食 民皆見之 及其更也 民皆仰之。今之君子 豈徒順之 又從為之辭。

Chapter 4: Gong Sun Chou (2)

Historical Background:

King Wu of Zhou (周武王, died 1043 BC) overthrew the Shang Dynasty (商朝, circa 1600–1066 BC), which was also called the Yin Dynasty (殷朝), and founded the Zhou Dynasty (周朝, 1066–256 BC) in 1066 BC. He had four younger brothers in the order of Guan Shu (管叔), Zhou Gong (周公, also known as Duke of Zhou), Cai Shu (蔡叔), and Huo Shu (霍叔). King Wu appointed the Duke of Zhou as the prime minister and the son, Wu Geng (武庚), of the defeated Emperor of the Shang Dynasty (also known as Yin Dynasty), Emperor Zhou (紂), as the governor of the territory of the old Shang Dynasty. King Wu died in 256 BC and was succeeded by his son King Cheng of Zhou (周成王). Since King Cheng of Zhou was young, the Duke of Zhou became the regent to govern the country temporarily. Duke of Zhou appointed Guan Shu, Cai Shu, and Huo Shu to monitor Wu Geng. Guan Shu and Wu Geng ganged up to rebel against King Cheng and Duke of Zhou. The Duke of Zhou crushed Guan Shu's rebellion and killed Guan Shu.

Text of *Mencius*:

The people of the state of Yan revolted against the state of Qi two years after Qi's conquest and established a new king of Yan (see Section 8 above). The king of Qi said, "I feel ashamed for not listening to Mencius."

Chen Jia consoled him and said, "Your Majesty needs not regret. Comparing yourself with the Duke of Zhou, who has more wisdom and Ren virtue?"

The king of Qi exclaimed, "Oh, what do you mean?"

Chen Jia said, "The Duke of Zhou sent Guan Shu to govern the old territory of the Yin Dynasty. Guan Shu later ganged up with Wu

Geng to revolt against the Zhou Dynasty. If the Duke of Zhou expected that Guan Shu would one day rebel, and purposely sent Guan Shu to monitor Wu Geng, the Duke of Zhou acted against Ren. If the Duke of Zhou did not expect that Guan Shu would one day rebel, and still sent Guan Shu to monitor Wu Geng, the Duke of Zhou was not wise. Therefore, even the Duke of Zhou was deficient in Ren and wisdom. How can your Majesty be better than the Duke of Zhou? Let me go to see Mencius and explain this."

Chen Jia went to see Mencius and asked, "What kind of man was the Duke of Zhou?"

Mencius replied, "He was an ancient saint."

Chen Jia then asked, "Was it true that the Duke of Zhou sent Guan Shu to supervise Wu Geng, and then Guan Zhu rebelled?"

"Yes," Mencius replied.

Chen Jia asked, "Did the Duke of Zhou know that Guan Shu would one day rebel, and did he purposely send Guan Shu to Yan?"

Mencius replied, "He did not know."

Chen Jia said, "If so, even the ancient saint made mistakes?"

Mencius said, "The Duke of Zhou was the younger brother. Guan Shu was the elder brother. The mistake made by the Duke of Zhou [for not doubting his brother] was understandable. In the old days, when a ruler made a mistake, he corrected it. Today, when a ruler makes a mistake, he persists in it. In the old days, the mistakes made by a ruler were like the eclipses of the sun and moon. They were so transparent that everybody could see them. After the mistakes were corrected, everybody respectfully looked up to the ruler. Today, a ruler not only persists in his mistakes but is appeased by his sycophantic ministers, who readily find excuses for his mistakes."

Chapter 4: Gong Sun Chou (2)

Annotation:

Chen Jia (陳賈) was a crooked minister of the state of Qi.

In the original Chinese text, the last paragraph of this section included the term *Jun Zi* (君子). This book interprets a Jun Zi in this context as a person of high social status, and therefore, a ruler. With this interpretation, the last paragraph sounds logical. If the word *ruler* in this paragraph is replaced by "a virtuous person of noble character," then the paragraph is illogical.

Zhou Gong (周公, also known as Duke of Zhou) was the brother of King Wu of Zhou (周武王, died 1043 BC) and the first prime minister of the Zhou Dynasty.

Commentary:

Confucians regarded the ancient Duke of Zhou as a saintly ruler. Mencius thought that the Duke of Zhou was innocent in this historical episode. As the younger brother of Guan Shu, the Duke of Zhou had no reason to doubt Guan Shu, did not know Guan Shu's intention to rebel in future, and, therefore, did not set a trap for Guan Shu. Chen Jia presented a crooked argument to justify the mistake made by the king of Qi. In the last paragraph, Mencius reprimanded Chen Jia for misleading the king of Qi. A good minister should advise the king to be righteous and to correct past mistakes.

Modern Perspective:

This section has the following lessons:

- (1) A leader should have the wisdom to recognize his mistakes, the courage to admit them, and the commitment to correct them.

197

(2) A subordinate should not be sycophantic and appease the boss when the boss makes a mistake. It is the duty of a subordinate to advise and guide the boss along the path of righteousness.

Section 10

孟子致為臣而歸。王就見孟子 曰 前日願見而不可得 得侍 同朝甚喜。今又棄寡人而歸 不識可以繼此而得見乎。

對曰 不敢請耳 固所願也。

他日 王謂時子曰 我欲中國而授孟子室 養弟子以萬鐘 使諸大夫國人皆有所矜式。子盍為我言之。

時子因陳子而以告孟子 陳子以時子之言告孟子。

孟子曰 然。夫時子惡知其不可也 如使予欲富 辭十萬而受萬 是為欲富乎。季孫曰 異哉子叔疑 使己為政 不用 則亦已矣 又使其子弟為卿 人亦孰不欲富貴 而獨於富貴之中 有私龍斷焉。古之為市也 以其所有易其所無者 有司者治之耳。有賤丈夫焉 必求龍斷而登之 以左右望而罔市利。人皆以為賤 故從而征之。征商 自此賤丈夫始矣。

The frustrated Mencius resigned from his position as the advisor to the king of Qi and was about to return to his home state. The king of Qi went to see Mencius and said, "In the past, I wished to see you but in vain. I am glad that I can now listen to your advice and work with you in the government. You want to leave me and go home today. I wonder when we can meet again?" Mencius replied, "I dare not ask for my return in future because I have made up my mind."

On the next day, the king of Qi spoke to his minister Shi Zi, "I

Chapter 4: Gong Sun Chou (2)

want to give Mencius a building in the center of the country and support his disciples with an emolument of ten thousand zhongs, so that the officials and people of our state can pay homage to Mencius. Can you tell Mencius about my plan?"

Shi Zi related this message to the Chen Zi, who, in turn, told Mencius.

Mencius said, "Yes. Does Shi Zi not know that I am determined to leave? They want to entice me with money. If I wanted more wealth, would I resign from a job paying a salary of hundred thousand zhongs and take up another job paying ten thousand zhongs? Ji Sun once said, 'Zi Shu Yi is a sinister person indeed! He tried to get an official appointment but was rejected by the king. He should give up his ambition. Instead, he schemed to get his disciples appointed as ministers. Who does not want to be rich and powerful? In the circle of the rich and powerful, there are many unworthy people who manipulate to gain monopolistic wealth and power.' In the old days, markets were established to allow people to exchange what they want with what they had, and an official was appointed to ensure fair and orderly transactions. There was then a despicable merchant who manipulated and monopolized the market. He made profit by ripping off people on the right and left. Since people deplored his behavior, the government began to tax his profit. This was the origin of the profit tax nowadays."

Annotation:

Shi Zi (時子) was a minister of the state of Qi. Shi was his family name. Zi meant "Mister."

Chen Zi (陳子, also known as Chen Qin 陳臻) was a disciple of Mencius.

In ancient times, the salary of officials was paid in bushels of grains. A zhong was equal to 64 bushels. Therefore, ten thousand zhongs was equal to 640,000 bushels. When Mencius was appointed as the top advisor to the king, his salary was 100 thousand zhongs, which equated to 6.4 million bushels.

Ji Sun (季孫) was an unknown person in ancient history.

Zi Shu Yi (子叔疑) was another unknown person in ancient history.

Commentary:

This section showed that Mencius's objective, as a high-ranking minister of the state of Qi, was to implement his political ideology. He was frustrated that the king of Qi did not take his advice seriously and invaded the state of Yan for greed under the guise of righteousness. Seeing no future for his mission, he resigned. Money was irrelevant and he could not change his mind. The salary of 6.4 million bushels of grain was huge for the time, but he did not hang on his job for the sake of the salary. The king of Qi underestimated Mencius's nobility and thought that Mencius can be lured by money. Therefore, Mencius mentioned that, if money mattered, he would have stayed as a high-ranking minister.

Mencius detested spineless officials interested in their power and wealth only.

Modern Perspective:

Suppose that you are a government official or a senior executive of a company. You need to resign from a powerful and/or lucrative job when your ideals and righteous principles are ignored and rejected. Suppose you are a lawyer and an evil gangster wants to hire you as his defense attorney. You should turn down his appointment.

Chapter 4: Gong Sun Chou (2)

No amount of money should lure you away from righteous principles.

Section 11

孟子去齊　宿於晝。有欲為王留行者　坐而言。不應　隱几而臥。客不悅曰　弟子齊宿而後敢言　夫子臥而不聽　請勿復敢見矣。

　曰　坐　我明語子。昔者魯繆公無人乎子思之側　則不能安子思　泄柳　申詳　無人乎繆公之側　則不能安其身。子為長者慮而不及子思。子絕長者乎　長者絕子乎。

Mencius left the capital of the state of Qi and stayed overnight in the city of Zhou. A national of the state of Qi wanted to retain Mencius on behalf of the king of Qi. That person sat down and tried to speak to Mencius. However, Mencius ignored him and slept on his stool. The visitor was upset, and said, "I have observed a fasting vigil for a day before I venture to speak to you. Yet, you sleep and ignore me. I will not dare to come to see you again."

Mencius said, "Sit down. Let me make it clear to you, my friend. In the past, Duke Mu of Lu assigned aides to stand by all the time to assist Zi Si. Otherwise, Zi Si would not feel comfortable working for Duke Mu. If Xie Liu and Shen Xiang did not have their supporters by the side of Duke Mu, they would not feel secure in their positions and stay in their jobs. You do not consider my situation that I was not given as much respect by the king of Qi as that given to Zi Si by Duke Mu. Are you disrespectful to me, an old man? Or am I, an old man, disrespectful to you, sir?"

Annotation:

The city of Zhou (畫) of a city in the southwest corner of the state of Qi.

Duke Mu of Lu (魯缪公, also known as 魯穆公, Lu Mu Gong, died 377 BC) was a good king of the state of Lu (魯國) during the Spring-Autumn Period.

Zi Si (子思, 483–402 BC) was the grandson of Confucius and a student of Zheng Zi. He was once a minister for Duke Mu of Lu. He authored the *Book of the Mean* (also known as the *Doctrine of the Mean*, 中庸).

Xie Liu (泄柳) was a meritorious scholar in the state of Lu. He later became a minister for Duke Mu of Lu.

Shen Xiang (申詳) was the son of Zi Zhang (子張) and the son-in-law of Zi You (子游). Both Zi Zhang and Zi You were disciples of Confucius. Shen Xiang was a meritorious scholar in the state of Lu and became a minister for Duke Mu of Lu.

Commentary:

Mencius mentioned two historical cases to justify his resignation and departure from the state of Qi. He used the case of Zi Si to point out that the king of Qi did not respect Mencius's advice. The king of Qi did not implement a magnanimous policy and ignored Mencius's advice. He invaded the state of Yan. In comparison, Duke Mu of Lu's respect for Zi Si was greater. Mencius also did not want to leave his disciples in the state of Qi because they did not have supporters in the government of the state of Qi. In the old days, Xie Liu and Shen Xiang needed to have supporters by the side of the king; otherwise, they did not feel safe.

Chapter 4: Gong Sun Chou (2)

Section 12

孟子去齊。尹士語人曰　不識王之不可以為湯武　則是不明也　識其不可　然且至　則是干澤也。千里而見王　不遇故去。三宿而後出畫　是何濡滯也。士則茲不悅。

高子以告。

曰　夫尹士惡知予哉。千里而見王　是予所欲也　不遇故去　豈予所欲哉　予不得已也。予三宿而出畫　於予心猶以為速。王庶幾改之。王如改諸　則必反予。夫出畫而王不予追也　予然後浩然有歸志。予雖然　豈舍王哉。王由足用為善。王如用予　則豈徒齊民安　天下之民舉安。王庶幾改之　予日望之。予豈若是小丈夫然哉。諫於其君而不受　則怒　悻悻然見於其面。去則窮日之力而後宿哉。

尹士聞之曰　士誠小人也。

When Mencius left the state of Qi, Yin Shi criticized him to others: "If Mencius did not know that the king of Qi could not become King Tang of the Shang Dynasty and King Wu of the Zhou Dynasty, the two saintly kings, this showed that Mencius lacked intelligence. If Mencius knew that the king of Qi could not become a saintly king, but still worked for the king notwithstanding, this showed that Mencius coveted the salary. He traveled a thousand miles to see the king and left after his ideas were ignored. Why did he linger in the city Zhou for three nights before he left the state of Qi? I am perplexed."

Gao Zi heard Yin Shi's comment and related it to Mencius, who then said, "Yin Shi does not know my motive, does he? It was my desire to travel a thousand miles to see and advise the king of Qi.

How could my failure in mission and departure be my desire? I had no choice. I originally thought that staying in the city of Zhou for three nights was too short. I was hoping that the king of Qi might change and repent. If he repented, he would recall me. However, the king of Qi did not pursue me after my departure from the city of Zhou. I, therefore, decided to leave like water flowing downstream. Should my good intentions be misunderstood to be my giving up on the king? The king has the potential to do good. If he follows my teachings, not only will the people of the state of Qi enjoy peace and happiness, but so too will the people of the entire empire have the same benefit. I hope that the king will repent one day. Am I like a Xiao Ren, who will get upset and show his angry face when his advice is rejected by the king? If so, I would have departed in one day and not bothered to stay overnight."

When Yin Shi heard Mencius's comment, he said, "I am indeed a Xiao Ren!"

Annotation:

Yin Shi (尹士) was a national of the state of Qi.

Gao Zi (高子) was a disciple of Mencius.

The city of Zhou (晝) was a small city at the southwest corner of the state of Qi.

In Chinese scholarly texts, a Jun Zi (君子) was a gentleman, a person of superior and noble character, a prominent and respectable person in society, or a person who upholds high standards of virtuous principles. A Xiao Ren is the opposite of a Jun Zi (君子). A Xiao Ren is, for example, mean, wicked, cruel, dumb, lacking virtues, dishonest, low class, and so on (see Section 4 of the Introduction).

Chapter 4: Gong Sun Chou (2)

Commentary:

This section shows that Mencius was disappointed because the king of Qi did not follow Ren and Yi principles. Mencius originally thought that he could guide the king of Qi on the path towards magnanimity. Having failed in his mission, Mencius had no choice but to leave.

Section 13

孟子去齊。充虞路問曰 夫子若有不豫色然。前日虞聞諸夫子曰 君子不怨天 不尤人。

曰 彼一時 此一時也。五百年必有王者興 其間必有名世者。由周而來 七百有餘歲矣。以其數則過矣 以其時考之則可矣。夫天 未欲平治天下也 如欲平治天下 當今之世 舍我其誰也。吾何為不豫哉。

After Mencius had left the state of Qi, Chong Yu asked Mencius, "Master, you looked sad. In the past, I have heard you say, 'A Jun Zi does not blame Tian (Sky) and has no grudge against others.'"

Mencius replied, "Now is different from the past. History has shown that a magnanimous sovereign must emerge every 500 years, and during this period, a famous [and great] leader must emerge. It has been 700 years since the founding of the Zhou Dynasty. The length of this period has exceeded the average of 500 years. Alas, Tian (Sky) has not yet provided peace on earth! Who else in today's world, other than myself, wishes to foster peace on earth? How can I not feel sad?"

Annotation:

Chong Yu (充虞) was a disciple of Mencius.

Since ancient Chinese did not have the same notion of God as Christians, the word *Tian* (*Sky* 天) was used to represent a supernatural and unknown natural power that governs the world. The word *Sky* should not be interpreted astronomically.

Section 14

孟子去齊　居休。

公孫丑問曰　仕而不受祿　古之道乎。

曰　非也。於崇　吾得見王。退而有去志　不欲變　故不受也。繼而有師命　不可以請。久於齊　非我志也。

After Mencius had left the state of Qi, he stayed in the city of Xiu. Gong Sun Chou asked him, "Was it common practice in ancient times for an official to relinquish his salary?"

Mencius said, "No, it was not. When I was in Chong, I had the chance to meet the king of Qi [and then serve him as a guest advisor]. Disappointed with his behavior, I was determined to leave. I therefore relinquished my salary. Subsequently, a war broke out. It was inappropriate for me to resign at that time. It was not my original intention to stay in the state of Qi for a long time."

Annotation:

Xiu (休) was a city near the home of Mencius.
Chong (崇) was a city in the state of Qi.
Gong Sun Chou (公孫丑) was a disciple of Mencius.

Chapter 4: Gong Sun Chou (2)

Commentary:

Mencius stayed in the state of Qi for about five years as a guest advisor to the king. However, the king of Qi did not adopt Mencius's ideology of magnanimous governance. The disappointed Mencius wanted to resign from his job soon after his appointment. However, since a war broke out between the states of Qi and Yan, Mencius was obliged to stay for a few more years. However, owing to his failure in this mission, Mencius relinquished his salary, which amounted to hundreds of thousands of zhongs.

Modern Perspective:

It is extremely rare nowadays that a company executive or a government official would return his or her earned salary for being derelict of his or her duties.

Chapter 5: Teng Wen Gong (1)

Section 1

滕文公為世子　將之楚　過宋而見孟子。孟子道性善　言必稱堯舜。

　世子自楚反　復見孟子。

　孟子曰　世子疑吾言乎　夫道一而已矣。成覸謂齊景公曰　彼丈夫也　我丈夫也　吾何畏彼哉。顏淵曰　舜何人也　予何人也　有為者亦若是。公明儀曰　文王我師也　周公豈欺我哉。今滕絕長補短　將五十里也　猶可以為善國。書曰　若藥不瞑眩　厥疾不瘳。

When Teng Wen Gong was a prince of the state of Teng, he was on a diplomatic mission to the state of Chu. On his way, he passed by the state of Song and met Mencius, who preached to the prince the doctrine of innate good nature of humans. In his speech, Mencius always lauded the virtues of Yao and Shun.

After the prince had returned from the state of Chu, he met Mencius again. Mencius said, "Honorable Prince, do you still doubt my doctrine? There is only one Dao. In the past, Cheng Gan told Qi Jing Gong, 'He is a strong man. I am also a strong man. Why should I be afraid of him?' Yan Yuan once said, 'What kind of man was Shun? What kind of man am I? A worthwhile person should be like him.' Gong Ming Yi said, 'King Wen of Zhou is my model. Why should the Duke of Zhou deceive us by saying these words?' Today, the state of Teng has a territory of 50 square miles. Although it is small, it can still become a well-run state. The *Book of Classic History* said, 'If the medicine is not strong enough to cause dizziness to the patient, it is ineffective to cure any disease.' "

Annotation:

Teng Wen Gong (滕文公, also known as Duke Wen of state of Teng, successor to the throne in 326 BC) was a believer of Mencius's ideology.

The state of Teng (滕) was a small country during the Spring-Autumn and Warring States Periods.

The state of Chu (楚國) was a hegemon in the Warring States Period.

The state of Song (宋國) was a small state in the Warring States Period.

Yao (堯) and Shun (舜) were two saintly kings in ancient China.

Dao (道) under Confucianism is the collection of principles in line with the Confucian doctrines (see a further explanation of Dao in Section 4 of the Introduction).

Cheng Gan (成覵) was a minister of the state of Qi during the reign of Duke Jing of Qi.

Qi Jing Gong (齊景公, also known as Duke Jing of Qi, died 490 BC) was the duke of Qi.

Yan Yuan (顏淵, also known as Yan Hui, 顏回, 521–481 BC) was the best disciple of Confucius. Confucius held him in the highest regard among his disciples.

Gong Ming Yi (公明義) was a student of Zheng Zi (曾子, 505–432 BC), a disciple of Confucius. The reputation of Gong Ming Yi was higher than Mencius at that time.

King Wen of Zhou (周文王, 1152–1056 BC) was the father of King Wu of Zhou (周武王, died 1043 BC), who founded the Zhou

Dynasty. Both King Wen and King Wu were regarded saintly kings by Confucians.

Zhou Gong (周公, also known as Duke of Zhou) was the brother of King Wu of Zhou (周武王, died 1043 BC) and the first prime minister of the Zhou Dynasty.

The *Book of Classic History* (書, also known as The *Book of Documents, Classic of History, Shangshu* 尚書, and *Shu Jing* 書經) is one of the five classics of ancient Chinese literature.

Commentary:

This section hints at some key points of Mencius's philosophy: (1) everybody is born with a good nature; (2) therefore, everybody can become as good as Yao and Shun (3) by trying hard enough.

Modern Perspective:

This last sentence of this section is enlightening: "If the medicine is not strong enough to cause dizziness to the patient, it is ineffective to cure any disease." One cannot hope to achieve anything in life without hard experience.

Section 2

滕定公薨。世子謂然友曰 昔者孟子嘗與我言於宋 於心終不忘。今也不幸至於大故 吾欲使子問於孟子 然後行事。

然友之鄒問於孟子。

孟子曰 不亦善乎 親喪固所自盡也。曾子曰 生 事之以禮 死 葬之以禮 祭之以禮 可謂孝矣。諸侯之禮 吾未之學也 雖

Chapter 5: Teng Wen Gong (1)

然 吾嘗聞之矣。三年之喪 齊疏之服 饘粥之食 自天子達於庶人 三代共之。

然友反命 定為三年之喪。

父兄百官皆不欲 曰 吾宗國魯先君莫之行 吾先君亦莫之行也 至於子之身而反之 不可。且志曰 喪祭從先祖。曰 吾有所受之也。

謂然友曰 吾他日未嘗學問 好馳馬試劍。今也父兄百官不我足也 恐其不能盡於大事 子為我問孟子。

然友復之鄒問孟子。

孟子曰 然。不可以他求者也。孔子曰 君薨 聽於冢宰 歠粥 面深墨 即位而哭 百官有司 莫敢不哀 先之也。上有好者 下必有甚焉者矣。君子之德 風也 小人之德 草也。草尚之風必偃。是在世子。

然友反命。

世子曰 然 是誠在我。五月居廬 未有命戒。百官族人可謂曰知。及至葬 四方來觀之 顏色之戚 哭泣之哀 弔者大悅。

Teng Ding Gong died. When Prince Teng Wen Gong asked his teacher, Ran You, to consult Mencius, the prince said, "In the past, Mencius told me in the state of Song about his doctrine. I have not forgotten his words. I am now confronted with the unfortunate death of my father. I want to send you to consult Mencius before I organize the funeral."

Ran You went to ask Mencius in the state of Zou.

Mencius said, "The prince asked a good question! In organizing the funeral of a parent, the children should try their utmost to show their filial piety. Zheng Zi once said, 'When parents are alive, you serve them according to Li. On their death, you bury them according to Li and pay homage to them according to Li. If you do so, you are indeed filial pious.' I have not learned the rituals practiced by feudal lords. Notwithstanding this, I have heard the following: a child should observe a mourning vigil for three years, during which he should wear coarse clothes with the lower edges cut even and eat light congee. This was practiced by kings and citizenry during the Xia, Shang, and Zhou dynasties."

Ran You reported back to prince Teng Wen Gong, who then decreed a three-year mourning vigil. His senior relatives and ministers objected to this decree, and said, "The state of Lu, which has the same ancestors as our state, does not implement a three-year mourning vigil. Our own ancestors did not observe this either. It is inappropriate for you to violate this tradition. Furthermore, our *Book of Records* says, 'Follow ancestorial practices in the handling of funerals.' This means that we must follow our ancestorial practice."

Prince Teng Wen Gong spoke to Ran You, "I have ignored academic learning in the past since I like horse riding and fencing only. I am now being challenged by my senior relatives and ministers. I am afraid I may not be able to handle this important matter according to my wish. Please consult Mencius on my behalf."

Ran You again went to the state of Zou and asked Mencius, who said, "Well, you cannot rely on their opinion in this matter. Confucius once said, 'When the last king is dead and the prince is observing a mourning vigil, the prime minister then takes over the administration of the government. The prince eats light congee, shows his darkened face, and weeps at the memorial altar. All officials dare not refrain from mourning because the prince took the lead.' Subordinates tend to do more of what the boss likes to do. 'The morality of the king (leader) is like wind, and the morality of the citizenry (subordinates) is like grass. When wind blows over

Chapter 5: Teng Wen Gong (1)

grass, it must bend with the wind.' Therefore, it is up to the prince to decide what to do."

Ran You then reported back to the prince, who said, "Yes, it is up to me." For the next five months, Prince Teng Wen Gong stayed in a shed and did not issue any administrative orders. All his relatives and officials lauded him as the one who knew Li. On the day of the funeral, mourners arrived from all places. They saw the prince with a sad face and in tears. They were impressed with his filial piety.

Annotation:

Teng Ding Gong (滕定公, died 327 BC) was the 28th successor to the throne of the small state of Teng, and the father of Teng Wen Gong.

Teng Wen Gong (滕文公, also known as Duke Wen of state of Teng, successor to the throne in 326 BC) was a believer of Mencius's ideology.

Ran You (然友) was the teacher of Teng Wen Gong.

The state of Zou (鄒國) was a small state, forty miles from the state of Teng.

Commentary:

In ancient China, a funeral was an important matter.

The key sentence in this section is: "The morality of the king (leader) is like wind, and the morality of the citizenry (subordinates) is like grass. When wind blows over grass, it must bend with the wind." This passage was taken from Section 19 of Chapter 12, Yan Yuan 顏淵, of *Confucius Analects*, which concerns leadership and setting a good example for subordinates.

Mencius in Modern Perspectives

Modern Perspective:

Leaders, teachers, and parents are role models for followers, students, and children, respectively.

Section 3

滕文公問為國。

　　孟子日　民事不可緩也。詩云　晝爾於茅　宵爾索綯　亟其乘屋　其始播百谷穀。民之為道也　有恒產者有恒心　無恒產者無恒心。苟無恒心　放辟邪侈　無不為已。及陷乎罪　然後從而刑之　是罔民也。焉有仁人在位　罔民而可為也。是故賢君必恭儉禮下　取於民有制。陽虎日　為富不仁矣　為仁不富矣。夏后氏五十而貢　殷人七十而助　周人百畝而徹　其實皆什一也。徹者徹也　助者　藉也。龍子日　治地莫善於助　莫不善於貢。貢者校數歲之中以為常。樂歲　粒米狼戾　多取之而不為虐　則寡取之。凶年　糞其田而不足　則必取盈焉。為民父母　使民盻盻然將終歲勤動　不得以養其父母　又稱貸而益之。使老稚轉乎溝壑　惡在其為民父母也。夫世祿　滕固行之矣。詩云　雨我公田　遂及我私。惟助為有公田。由此觀之　雖周亦助也。設為庠序學校以教之　庠者　養也。校者　教也。序者　射也。夏曰校　殷曰序　周曰庠　學則三代共之　皆所以明人倫也。人倫明於上　小民親於下。有王者起　必來取法　是為王者師也。詩云　周雖舊邦　其命惟新。文王之謂也。子力行之　亦以新子之國。

　　使畢戰問井地。

　　孟子日　子之君將行仁政　選擇而使子　子必勉之。夫仁政

Chapter 5: Teng Wen Gong (1)

必自經界始。經界不正 井地不鈞 穀祿不平。是故暴君汙吏必慢其經界。經界既正 分田制祿可坐而定也。夫滕壤地褊小 將為君子焉 將為野人焉。無君子莫治野人 無野人莫養君子。請野九一而助 國中什一使自賦。卿以下必有圭田 圭田五十畝。餘夫二十五畝。死徙無出鄉 鄉田同井。出入相友 守望相助 疾病相扶持 則百姓親睦。方里而井 井九百畝 其中為公田。八家皆私百畝 同養公田。公事畢 然後敢治私事 所以別野人也。此其大略也。若夫潤澤之 則在君與子矣。

Teng Wen Gong asked Mencius about the governance of a country.

Mencius said, "People's productive activities cannot endure delays. The *Book of Poetry* says, "Collect the thatch in the day. Twist it into ropes at night. Cover your roof with twisted thatch. Then begin to sow seeds." The normal behavior of people is as follows: If they can make a stable living, they will feel secure. If they cannot make a stable living, they will feel insecure. If they feel insecure, they will be unruly and devious and do anything to get their needs. Upon their commitment of crimes, any punishment imposed on them is equivalent to entrapping them. Is there a benevolent king who wants to entrap his people? Therefore, a virtuous ruler should be modest, austere, and respectful to meritorious and talented officials. He should levy limited tax on people. Yang Huo once said, 'The rich do not care about Ren virtue. Those who care about Ren virtue cannot be rich.' Under the contributory system of taxation of the Xia Dynasty, every man was allotted 50 acres of land. Under the cooperative system of taxation of the Shang Dynasty, every man was allotted 70 acres of land. Under the sharing system of taxation of the Zhou Dynasty, every man was allotted 100 acres of land. Their tax rates were effectively

10 percent. Under the sharing system, a commune of eight families was formed. They cultivated the eight plots of land together and shared the yield of the harvest. They also cultivated another plot of land owned by the government, and the yield from this plot was submitted as a tax. Under the cooperative system, a commune of eight families was formed. Each family cultivated its own plot of land and got the yield from it. The eight families also cooperated to cultivate the ninth plot of land owned by the government and the yield from it was submitted as a tax. Long Zi once said, 'The cooperative system was the best land policy. The contributory system was the worst.' Under the contributory system, the average yield of an allotted plot of land over the past few years was first calculated. A 10 percent tax was levied on the average number and payable to the government for the following few years. Therefore, in a year of good harvest, the peasants had large after-tax surpluses, which often remained unconsumed and wasted. However, in a year of bad harvest, the total amount of produce was insufficient to pay the required tax, no matter how much fertilizer was applied to the land. As a result, the government, which was supposed to be the parental protector of its people, caused unbearable distress to its people. Although they had toiled during the whole year, they could not make enough to feed their parents and they had to live on debts. Babies and elderly people starved and were thrown into ditches. How can the government claim to be the parental protector of its people?

The state of Teng has implemented a system of hereditary salaries for noblemen for a long time. [However, it has not yet implemented a cooperative system of taxation]. The *Book of Poetry* says, 'May the rain fall on our public field, and then on our private fields.' Only the cooperative system of taxation can justify the existence of public fields. On close analysis, the sharing system of

Chapter 5: Teng Wen Gong (1)

taxation of the Zhou Dynasty was effectively a cooperative system.

On the topic of education, you should set up four types of schools: Xiang, Xu, Xue, and Xiao. Teachers in the Xiang-type of schools are retirees so that they can make a living. The Xiao-type of schools are regular teaching institutions. The Xu-type of schools teaches archery. The Xia Dynasty had Xiao-type of schools. The Yin Dynasty has Xu-type of schools. The Zhou Dynasty has Xiang- type of schools. The Xue-type of schools were common in all three dynasties. Their rulers all understood the importance of the principles governing human and social relations. If the top echelon of your country understands the principles of government and social relations, your people will follow. If a magnanimous king emerges in future, he will visit your country and learn from you. You will then become the teacher of a magnanimous king. The *Book of Poetry* said, 'Although the Zhou is an old country, it is rejuvenated.' This verse referred to King Wen of Zhou. If your Majesty seriously implements my suggestions, your country will also be rejuvenated."

Teng Wen Gong further sent Bi Zhan to consult Mencius about the nine-squares system of land allotment and taxation.

Mencius said, "Your king wants to implement a benevolent governance policy. Since he has assigned you a great responsibility, you must take it seriously. The starting point of a benevolent land policy is the accurate delineation of boundaries of plots of land to be allotted. If the delineation is inaccurate, the allotment will be unfair, and the resulting yield from the land will be uneven. Therefore, corrupted rulers and government officials are tardy in the delineation of boundaries of land. Once the boundaries are accurately defined, the system of tax collection on the plots of land follows.

The territory of the state of Teng is small. Should its land policy take care of the interest of the ruler and officials, or should it take

Mencius in Modern Perspectives

care of the interest of its people? Without government officials, it is impossible to govern its people. Without its people, it is impossible to pay government officials. I suggest that the allotment to common people in rural areas follows the nine-squares cooperative system, whereby the ninth square plot is owned by the government. In the cities, a tax rate of 10 percent should be levied on the produce of a family. The allotment to government officials below the rank of top ministers should be 50 acres for each head of a family. This land can be inherited by the successor heir of the family. The other sons of the family are allotted 25 acres each. People are not allowed to leave their village, even on occasions of death or relocation of residence. Families in the commune of nine-squares of land work together on the public plot, help each other out, and take care of the sick and disabled. In this way, they will live harmoniously. A square mile of land can be divided into nine plots of land of 100 acres each. The center plot belongs to the government. The eight families in the commune each own 100 acres of private plot. They cooperate to cultivate the public plot. They cultivate their individual private plots afterwards. This is the skeleton. It is your call to fill in other details."

Annotation:

Yang Huo (陽貨, also known as Yang Hu 陽虎) was the top official working for the Ji Si family.

The Xia Dynasty (夏朝, circa 2184–1600 BC) preceded the Shang Dynasty (商朝, circa 1600–1066 BC), which was also called the Yin Dynasty (殷朝). King Wu of Zhou (周武王, died 1043 BC), whose father was King Wen of Zhou (周文王, 1152–1056 BC), founded the Zhou Dynasty (周朝, 1066–256 BC).

Xiang (庠), Xu (序), Xue (學), and Xiao (校) were four types of schools during three ancient dynasties.

Chapter 5: Teng Wen Gong (1)

Long Zi (龍子) was a sage during the Spring-Autumn Period.

Bi Zhan (畢戰) was a minister of the state of Teng.

The Shang and Zhou Dynasties practiced the nine-squares system of land allotment and taxation. A large plot of land was divided into nine squares of equal size. The subdivided plots were arranged in a 3 x 3 pattern. The central plot belonged to the government. The surrounding plots were allotted to eight families in a commune. They were responsible for cultivating together the central plot, and the yield from that plot was submitted to the government as a tax. In a cooperative system, each of the eight families owned and cultivate their allotted plot individually. In a sharing system, the eight families worked on the eight plots together and shared the yield produced by the eight plots.

Commentary:

This section mainly discussed land and taxation policy. Mencius cited the example of the flaw of the contributory system of taxation in the Xia Dynasty to illustrate how a faulty government policy could bring turmoil to its people. Although the tax rate imposed by the Xia Dynasty was about the same as those during the latter two dynasties, the flaw in the details of the contributory system caused unbearable hardship to its people.

Modern Perspective:

A notable quote in this section is: "The rich do not care about Ren virtue. Those who care about Ren virtue cannot be rich." This is true throughout human history. Nowadays, the economic and political systems enable some smart and/or lucky people to become rich and/or powerful. Although many of them are good people in heart on a personal level, they are unaware of or apathetic to the fact that their accumulation of wealth and power may have hurt poor and/or unlucky people struggling to survive. The rich and powerful think that the villain is the system, not themselves. According to Mencius, this view is analogous to saying, "I did not kill them. The knife killed them." On the contrary, many people in the grassroots contribute greatly to the society by their lowly but essential work. They are exploited by the system, are not rewarded fairly, and remain poor and destitute.

Section 4

有為神農之言者許行 自楚之滕 踵門而告文公曰 遠方之人聞君行仁政 願受一廛而為氓。文公與之處 其徒數十人 皆衣褐 捆屨 織席以為食。

陳良之徒陳相與其弟辛 負耒耜而自宋之滕 曰 聞君行聖人之政 是亦聖人也 願為聖人氓。

陳相見許行而大悅 盡棄其學而學焉。

陳相見孟子 道許行之言曰 滕君 則誠賢君也 雖然 未聞道也。賢者與民並耕而食 饔飧而治。今也滕有倉廩府庫 則是厲民而以自養也 惡得賢。

孟子曰 許子必種粟而後食乎。

曰 然。

(曰) 許子必織布而後衣乎。

曰 否 許子衣褐。

(曰) 許子冠乎。

曰 冠。

Chapter 5: Teng Wen Gong (1)

曰 奚冠。

曰 冠素。

曰 自織之與。

曰 否 以粟易之。

曰 許子奚為不自織。

曰 害於耕。

曰 許子以釜甑爨 以鐵耕乎。

曰 然。

(曰) 自為之與。

曰 否 以粟易之。

(曰) 以粟易械器者 不為厲陶冶 陶冶亦以其械器易粟者 豈為厲農夫哉。且許子何不為陶冶。舍皆取諸其宮中而用之 何為紛紛然與百工交易。何許子之不憚煩。

曰 百工之事 固不可耕且為也。

(曰) 然則治天下獨可耕且為與。有大人之事 有小人之事。且一人之身 而百工之所為備。如必自為而後用之 是率天下而路也。故曰 或勞心 或勞力 勞心者治人 勞力者治於人 治於人者食人 治人者食於人 天下之通義也。

當堯之時 天下猶未平 洪水橫流 泛濫於天下。草木暢茂 禽獸繁殖 五穀不登 禽獸偪人。獸蹄鳥跡之道 交於中國。堯獨憂之 舉舜而敷治焉。舜使益掌火 益烈山澤而焚之 禽獸逃匿。禹疏九河 瀹濟漯 而註諸海 決汝漢 排淮泗 而註之江 然後中國可得而食也。當是時也 禹八年於外 三過其門而不入 雖欲耕 得乎。

后稷教民稼穡。樹藝五穀 五穀熟而民人育。人之有道也

飽食　暖衣　逸居而無教　則近於禽獸。聖人有憂之　使契為司徒　教以人倫　父子有親　君臣有義　夫婦有別　長幼有序　朋友有信。放勳曰　勞之來之　匡之直之　輔之翼之　使自得之　又從而振德之。聖人之憂民如此　而暇耕乎。

堯以不得舜為己憂　舜以不得禹　皋陶為己憂。夫以百畝之不易為己憂者　農夫也。分人以財謂之惠　教人以善謂之忠　為天下得人者謂之仁。是故以天下與人易　為天下得人難。孔子曰　大哉堯之為君　惟天為大　惟堯則之　蕩蕩乎民無能名焉　君哉舜也　巍巍乎有天下而不與焉。堯舜之治天下　豈無所用其心哉　亦不用於耕耳。

吾聞用夏變夷者　未聞變於夷者也。陳良　楚產也。悅周公仲尼之道　北學於中國。北方之學者　未能或之先也。彼所謂豪傑之士也。子之兄弟事之數十年　師死而遂倍之。昔者孔子沒三年之外　門人治任將歸　入揖於子貢　相向而哭　皆失聲　然後歸。子貢反　築室於場　獨居三年　然後歸。他日　子夏　子張　子遊以有若似聖人　欲以所事孔子事之　強曾子。曾子曰　不可　江漢以濯之　秋陽以暴之　皓皓乎不可尚已。今也南蠻鴃舌之人　非先王之道　子倍子之師而學之　亦異於曾子矣。吾聞出於幽谷遷於喬木者　未聞下喬木而入於幽谷者。魯頌曰　戎狄是膺　荊舒是懲。周公方且膺之　子是之學　亦為不善變矣。

(曰)　從許子之道　則市賈不貳　國中無偽。雖使五尺之童適市　莫之或欺。布帛長短同　則賈相若　麻縷絲絮輕重同　則賈相若。五穀多寡同　則賈相若　屨大小同　則賈相若。

曰　夫物之不齊　物之情也　或相倍蓰　或相什伯　或相千萬。子比而同之　是亂天下也。巨屨小屨同賈　人豈為之哉。從許子

Chapter 5: Teng Wen Gong (1)

之道 相率而為偽者也 惡能治國家。

An advocate of the Shen Nong [agriculturalist] school of thought, Xu Xing, came to the state of Teng from the state of Chu. When he arrived at Teng Wen Gong's palace, he said, "I am a man from afar. I have heard that your Majesty is practicing a magnanimous governance policy. I wish to be granted a site and to become your citizen." Teng Wen Gong then gave him a residence. Tens of his disciples came and lived with him. They wore coarse clothes. They made shoes with hemp and wove mats to make a living.

Chen Xiang, a disciple of Chen Liang, and his brother Chen Xin, carrying ploughing tools, came from the state of Song to the state of Teng. Chen Xiang told Teng Wen Gong, "I heard that you are practicing a magnanimous policy. You must be a saint also. We wish to be your citizens." Chen Xiang then met Xu Xing and was impressed with Xu Xing's philosophy. Chen Xiang abandoned his old learning and became a disciple of Xu Xing.

Chen Xiang met Mencius and related Xu Xing's criticism on Teng Wen Gong, saying, "Teng Wen Gong tries to be a meritorious ruler. However, he does not know its real doctrine. A meritorious ruler should make his living by cultivating in the fields like his people. He should prepare his own meals while simultaneously running the government. Today, he owns his granaries and treasures. These show that he is robbing his people to nourish himself. How can he be meritorious?"

Mencius asked, "Does Xu Xing grow food himself?"
Chen Xiang replied, "Yes."
Mencius asked, "He weaves cloth himself, doesn't he?"
Chen Xiang replied, "No, he wears coarse clothes."
Mencius asked, "Does Xu Xing wear a hat?"
Chen Xiang replied, "Yes, he wears a hat."

Mencius asked, "What kind of hat?"

Chen Xiang replied, "He wears a white hat made of raw silk."

Mencius asked, "Was the silk woven by him?"

Chen Xiang replied, "No, he bought the hat by bartering grains."

Mencius asked, "Why does he not weave the silk himself?"

Chen Xiang replied, "That will interfere with his farming work."

Mencius asked, "What kind of cooking pots does he use? Are they made of metal?"

Chen Xiang replied, "Yes."

Mencius asked, "Are these utensils made by him?"

Chen Xiang replied, "No, he bought them by bartering grains."

Mencius said, "When a farmer exchanges cooking pots and pans with grains, he has not hurt the potter and the founder. When the potter and the founder exchange food with pots and pans, have they hurt the farmer? Moreover, why does Xu Xing not make pots and smelt iron himself, and manufacture all utensils for his household? Why should he waste time busily bartering? Why should he take all these troubles?"

Chen Xiang replied, "If he undertakes those activities, he will not have time to do farming."

Mencius said, "If so, do you think that it is uniquely possible for a person to run a government along with farming at the same time? Rulers have their jobs as rulers, and common people have their jobs as common people. Hundreds of skills are required to provide all necessities for a person. If all these necessities are to be self-made before they can be used, everybody in the world will need to run around in all directions. Therefore, some work with their brains and some with their brawn. Those who work with their brains become rulers. Those who work with their brawn are ruled. People who are ruled mutually support themselves. The livelihood of the ruling class depends on those they rule. This is common sense.

Chapter 5: Teng Wen Gong (1)

In the era of Yao, the world was still primordial. The country was inundated with floods. Jungles were everywhere. Birds and wild animals propagated fast. It was difficult to grow grains because wild birds and animals often attacked people, and the paths of these animals crisscrossed the heartland of the country. Only Yao was concerned of the situation. He appointed Shun to manage the hostile environment. Shun, in turn, appointed his subordinate Yi to manage forest fire. Yi set fire to mountain ranges to drive away wild animals. Shun also sent Yu to dredge nine rivers, and re-direct the waters of the Ji and Luo Rivers to the sea. He also opened a vent for the Ru and Han Rivers to re-direct the waters of the Huai and Si Rivers into the Yangtze River. After these accomplishments, people in the country could then cultivate food. During that time, Yu was away from home for eight years. Even when he passed by the door of his house three times, he did not enter it. Even if he wished to cultivate food for himself, could he do so?

Hou Ji taught people husbandry to grow five types of grains, and, as a result, people then had enough food to eat. It is human nature that when people are well fed, warmly clad, and comfortably housed, they will behave like animals if they lack moral education. Aware of this issue, Shun then appointed Xie as the education minister to teach people about social norms: love between parents and children, honor and righteousness between sovereigns and officials, separate roles between husbands and wives, order between old and young, honesty and trust between friends. Emperor Yao said, 'Give them work, lead them, rectify them, straighten them, help them, and give them wings so that they are free to do what they want. Promote their moral standard afterward.' Since the saintly king cared about his people so much, how could he have time to grow food for himself?

Emperor Yao was anxious that he could not find Shun as his

successor. Emperor Shun was anxious that he could not find Yu as his successor. Gao Yao was anxious about his own position. If a person is concerned about the harvest from his land of one hundred acres, he is a mere peasant. Donating money to others is called charity. Teaching others about propriety is called loyalty. Finding a meritorious person to rule the country is called Ren. It is easy to give away the throne to another person. It is difficult to find a meritorious person to rule the country.

Confucius said, 'Yao was a great emperor. The Tian (Sky) is the highest. Only Yao was next to it. His virtue was so boundless that his people could not find a name for it. Shun indeed deserved to be an emperor. His virtue was towering since he did not own the country after he became the emperor. How could Yao and Shun not devote their whole minds to attain great achievements in their governance?

I have heard of the possibility of changing barbarians with Chinese culture, but I have not heard of changing us with the barbaric culture. Your old teacher, Chen Liang, was a native of the state of Chu. Since he admired the doctrines of Duke of Zhou and Confucius, he moved north to China. Among scholars in the north, no one could excel him. He was indeed an outstanding scholar. You and your brother have been his students for decades; yet after his death, you immediately renege on his teaching. In the past, the disciples of Confucius observed three years of mourning vigil upon the death of Confucius. When they were about to pack up their luggage to return home, they bade farewell to Zi Gong. Before they departed, they wailed together until they lost their voices. When Zi Gong returned to the burial site of Confucius, he built a shed there, where he stayed to observe three more years of mourning vigil in memory of Confucius. After a while, Zi Xia, Zi Zhang, and Zi You thought that You Ruo looked like Confucius and wanted to honor

Chapter 5: Teng Wen Gong (1)

You Ruo as their teacher. They asked Zheng Zi to join them. Zheng Zi refused, saying, 'It is wrong to do so. We have been cleansed with the water of Jiang and Han River, and tanned by the Sun in the summer. Nobody can attain the altitude and brightness of virtues of our teacher, Confucius.' Now that barbaric guy with a southern tongue wants to repudiate the doctrines of our ancient saintly kings. You renege on the teachings of your old teacher to follow this guy. You differ from Zheng Zi. I have heard of birds leaving dark valleys to find refuge on tall trees, but I have not heard of birds leaving tall trees to find refuge in dark valleys. The *Hymn of Lu* said, 'Fight against barbarians from the west and north, stop barbarians from Jing and Shu [in the south].' Even Duke of Zhou was determined to fight against barbarians; yet you want to be their followers. Your change is inappropriate."

Chen Xiang said, "According to Xu Xiang's doctrines, prices of goods will be standardized and uniform. There will be no deceit in the country. Even juveniles will not be cheated in the market. All pieces of cloth of the same length, regardless of their qualities, will have the same price. Raw silk and linen with the same weight will have the same price. All kinds of grains will be priced the same. Shoes will be priced the same regardless of their sizes."

Mencius said, "Goods of the same kind may have different qualities and characteristics. This is their objective nature. Some goods of the same kind may need be priced twice, ten times, a hundred times, or even tens of thousands of times higher than others of the same kind. If you set the same price for all of them, the market will be chaotic. For example, if a pair of large shoes has the same price as that of a pair of small shoes, who would make large shoes? Xu Xiang's doctrine will then incentivize people to cheat. How can his doctrine be applied to run a country?"

Annotation:

Shen Nong (神農) was a legendary leader in the pre-historic era of China. The Shen Nong Clan (神農氏), headed by Emperor Yan (炎帝), was a legendary clan in the pre-historic era of China. They developed agriculture further and grew five types of grains for food staples. Emperor Yan was also the forerunner of herbal medicine.

Xu Xing (許行, circa 372–289 BC) was a native of the state of Chu and a prominent leader of the Agriculturist School of thought. During the Warring States Period, there were nine competing schools of thought: Confucians, Taoists, Yin-Yang, Legalists, Logicians, Mohists, Diplomatic Strategists, Eclectics, and Agriculturists. Xu Xing advocated the lifestyle and social structure of pre-historical times in China.

The state of Chu (楚國) was one of the seven hegemons during the Spring-Autumn Period and the Warring States Period. Since it was in the south of China, people in northern states considered people in Chu as southern barbarians.

Chen Liang (陳良) was a native of the state of Chu who went north, attended Confucian schools, and returned home as a prominent Confucian.

Chen Xiang (陳相) and Chen Xin (陳信) were students of Chen Liang.

Yao (堯, circa 2356–2255 BC), Shun (舜, circa 2294–2184 BC), and Yu (禹, circa 2237–2139 BC) were three emperors in the Period of Five Emperors (circa 3000–2200 BC). The other two emperors were Emperor Yan (炎帝) and Huang Di (黃帝, Yellow Emperor). These emperors were considered saintly kings.

Yi (益) was an official under Yao in charge of forest management.

Ji (濟水), Luo (濼水), Ru (汝水), Han (漢水), Huai (淮水), and

Chapter 5: Teng Wen Gong (1)

Si (泗水) are main rivers in the central part of China. Yangtze River (長江) is the longest river of China.

Hou Ji (后稷) was a legendary Chinese agriculturist regarded as the God of Agriculture. During the time of the Xia Dynasty, Hou Ji introduced millet to humanity as a major food staple before wheat. He also perfected the technology of growing five types of staple grains and many vegetables.

Xie (契) was the earliest minister of education in China during the era of Shun.

Gao Yao (皋陶) was the earliest Chief Justice in China during the era of Shun. His name stood for the best judge.

Zi Xia (子夏, born 507 BC) was a disciple of Confucius and later became an official of the state of Wei (魏國).

Zi Zhang (子張, 503–447 BC) was a disciple of Confucius.

Zi You (子有, also known as Ran You, 冉有, Ran Qiu, 冉求, born in 522 BC) was a disciple of Confucius.

You Ruo (有若, also known as You Zi 有子, born around 518 BC) was a disciple of Confucius.

Zheng Zi (曾子, also known as Zheng Shen 曾參, born 505 BC) was a prominent disciple of Confucius, known for his filial piety. He was the author of *The Book of Great Learning* (大學).

Hymn of Lu (魯頌) was a chapter of the *Book of Poetry*, praising the accomplishment of Lu Xi Gong (魯僖公, on the throne 659–627 BC) who was the duke of the state of Lu (魯國).

Commentary:

It is amazing that, about two and a half millennia ago, Mencius already explained two topics of modern economics theory: (1) division of labor, (2) market prices.

Today, there are still some hermitical groups who advocate the lifestyle and socio-economic structures of pre-historic times, like those expounded by Xu Xing. They think that departure from modern life is the best way to cultivate purity of mind and to attain sainthood. Confucians do not endorse such attitude. They instead insist that the goals of a Jun Zi, meritorious sage, and saint are not only self-cultivation but also the fostering of welfare and peace to people in the world. Confucianism stresses the importance of active participation in the society. This is illustrated by repeated references to Yao, Shun and Yu, who were great leaders of their times, as saintly kings throughout Confucian literature.

The two main goals for Confucians—self-cultivation and the fostering of welfare and peace to the world correspond to the doctrines of Theravada (also known as Hinayana 小乘) and Mahayana (大乘) of Buddhism, respectively.

Section 5

墨者夷之 因徐辟而求見孟子。孟子曰 吾固願見 今吾尚病 病愈 我且往見 夷子不來。

他日又求見孟子。

孟子曰 吾今則可以見矣。不直 則道不見 我且直之。吾聞夷子墨者。墨之治喪也 以薄為其道也。夷子思以易天下 豈以為非是而不貴也。然而夷子葬其親厚 則是以所賤事親也。

徐子以告夷子。

夷子曰 儒者之道 古之人 若保赤子 此言何謂也。之則以為愛無差等 施由親始。

徐子以告孟子。

孟子曰 夫夷子 信以為人之親其兄之子為若親其鄰之赤子

Chapter 5: Teng Wen Gong (1)

乎。彼有取爾也。赤子匍匐將入井 非赤子之罪也。且天之生物也 使之一本 而夷子二本故也。蓋上世嘗有不葬其親者。其親死 則舉而委之於壑。他日過之 狐狸食之 蠅蚋姑嘬之。其顙有泚 睨而不視。夫泚也 非為人泚 中心達於面目。蓋歸反虆梩而掩之。掩之誠是也 則孝子仁人之掩其親 亦必有道矣。

徐子以告夷子。夷子憮然為閒曰 命之矣。

A Mohist, Yi Zi, asked Xu Bi to introduce him to Mencius, who said, "I would like to see him. However, I am sick today. I will visit him after I recover. He needs not come to see me."

A few days later, Yi Zi requested to see Mencius again. Mencius said, "I can see him now. If I am not candid with him, he will not see the truth in Confucianism. Let me correct his mistakes now. I heard that Yi Zi was a disciple of Mo Zi. Mohists adhere to the principle of frugality in organizing funerals. Yi Zi wants to apply this principle to change the customs of the country. Does he not consider that the deviation from his advocacy would reflect a lack of noble virtues? However, he buried his parents extravagantly. Therefore, [according to his logic], he served his dead parent in an ignoble way."

Xu Bi told Yi Zi about Mencius's comments.

Yi Zi said, "Confucians teaches the doctrine that ancient rulers should take care of their people as if they are babies. Are they serious about it? I love everyone indiscriminately, starting from my parents."

Xu Bi related Yi Zi's words to Mencius.

Mencius said, "Does Yi Zi really think that a person's love of the child of his brother is merely like his love of a baby of his neighbor? In fact, the phrase "taking care of people as if they are babies" in the *Book of Records* has a different meaning. It means that, when an innocent baby crawls on the ground and is about to fall into a well, it is not its fault. Likewise, when innocent people commit offences and crimes, they are like innocent babies crawling on the ground. It is the duty of the ruler to prevent them from committing crimes by education.

By the way, every creature in Nature has one single origin and root. [For example, the parent is the root of a child]. Yi Zi's doctrine implies that a child can have two [and more] roots [because he advocates that a child should serve everyone as his parent].

In ancient times, there was a man who did not bury his dead parent. He threw the dead body of his parent into a drench. After a while, he passed by the dead body and saw it eaten by foxes and swarmed by flies, gnats, and worms. Sweat exuded on his forehead instinctively at such a horrible sight. He turned his head away and closed his eyes, unable to bear the sight. The sweat on his forehead was an emotional reaction from his heart and not a gesture to impress others. He immediately went home, brought back baskets and shovels, and buried the dead body. It was appropriate for him to do so. Therefore, filial and virtuous children have good reasons to bury their dead parents in sophisticated manners."

Xu Bi related Mencius's discussion to Yi Zi. After pondering for a while on what Xu Bi told him, Yi Zi said, "Mencius has taught me a lesson."

Annotation:

Mo Zi (墨子, circa 470–391 BC, also known as Mo Di, 墨翟) was a prominent philosopher and a native of the state of Lu (魯國人) during the Warring States Period. He was the founder of the Mohist school of philosophy, which advocated universal and

Chapter 5: Teng Wen Gong (1)

indiscriminative love (兼愛), and defensive wars (非攻), among other teachings (see Section 2 of Endnotes for details).

Yi Zi (夷子) was a follower of the Mohist school.

Xu Bi (徐辟) was a disciple of Mencius.

Commentary:

The Mohist school advocated the universal and indiscriminative love of everybody in the world. In theory, this ideal is noble and there is nothing wrong with it. In practice, this is inconsistent with human nature. Confucianism also preaches universal love, but not indiscriminative love. Therefore, Mencius said, "Does Yi Zi really think that a person's love of the child of his brother is merely like his love of a baby of his neighbor?" Mencius also repudiated Mo Zi's philosophy in Section 9 of Chapter 6, Sections 26 and 27 of Chapter 13. The practice of Ren virtue needs to be pragmatic and in different steps and degrees, starting from our roots, which are our parents, brothers and sisters, spouses, and children. This love is then extended to the society, country, and world in steps and in order of priority. Therefore, unlike the Mohist school of thought, Confucianism is not just a rhetoric but a realistic set of principles.

Confucians treat funeral and memorable vigils seriously. In this section, Mencius criticized the doctrine of frugality when applied to the administration of a funeral.

Chapter 6: Teng Wen Gong (2)

Section 1

陳代曰 不見諸侯 宜若小然 今一見之 大則以王 小則以霸。且誌曰 枉尺而直尋。宜若可為也。

　孟子曰 昔齊景公田 招虞人以旌 不至 將殺之。志士不忘在溝壑 勇士不忘喪其元。孔子奚取焉。取非其招不往也 如不待其招而往 何哉。且夫枉尺而直尋者 以利言也。如以利 則枉尋直尺而利 亦可為與。昔者趙簡子使王良與嬖奚乘 終日而不獲一禽。嬖奚反命曰 天下之賤工也。或以告王良。良曰 請復之。強而後可 一朝而獲十禽。嬖奚反命曰 天下之良工也。簡子曰 我使掌與女乘。謂王良。良不可 曰 吾為之範我馳驅 終日不獲一 為之詭遇 一朝而獲十。詩云 不失其馳 舍矢如破。我不貫與小人乘 請辭。御者且羞與射者比。比而得禽獸 雖若丘陵 弗為也。如枉道而從彼 何也。且子過矣 枉己者 未有能直人者也。

Chen Dai said to Mencius, "Since you are reluctant to request meetings with feudal lords, are you a bit squeamish? If you take initiatives to see them, you could, at best, meet a magnanimous king who might endorse your doctrine. At least, you could meet a hegemon. The *Book of Records* says, 'By bending one foot, one can straighten eight feet.' You should try your luck."

Mencius said, "Once upon a time, when Duke Jing of Qi was hunting, he summoned the guardian of the hunting ground with a

Chapter 6: Teng Wen Gong (2)

flag. The guardian felt demeaned and would not comply. The upset duke was about to execute him. Confucius heard about this event and said to the duke, 'A person with a staunch will is not afraid of being dumped into a drench. A person with great valor is not afraid of being beheaded.' Why did Confucius praise the guardian? That was because the guardian adhered to the spirit of Li. If the summon was not issued with proper protocol and respect, he should not go. If I voluntarily go to see feudal lords without being invited respectfully, what is my objective? Those who try to straighten eight feet by bending one foot are motivated by the prospect of material gains. What if one is required to bend eight feet to straighten one foot? Should he do so?

In the past, Zhao Jian Zi's favorite minister, Xi, went on a hunting expedition, and Zhao Jian asked Wang Liang to drive Xi around on a chariot. The two spent the whole day without getting a single trophy. The frustrated Xi told Zhao Jian Zi afterwards, saying, 'Wang Liang was the most inept driver in the country.' Somebody told Wang Liang about Xi's comment. Wang Liang then spoke to Xi, saying, 'Let us try again.' Xi agreed reluctantly. During the next trip, they got 10 trophies in one day. Xi then praised Wang Liang to Zhao Jian Zi, saying, 'Wang Liang is the best driver in the country.' Zhao Jian Zi then appointed Wang Liang to be Xi's permanent driver. Wang Liang rejected the offer and said, 'When I followed proper and safety rules in driving the chariot, he could not get any trophy. I had to violate proper rules to facilitate his success in getting 10 preys in one day. The *Book of Poetry* says that the archer should be able to kill the target upon every shooting when the driver follows proper driving rules. I am not used to be a driver of an incompetent archer. I beg to decline the appointment.' Even a driver felt ashamed to drive an incompetent archer. Despite the potential of getting a mountain of trophies, he did not take the offer.

If I were to bend my principles and follow unworthy feudal lords, what kind of man am I? Moreover, you are wrong because it is impossible for a subservient and spineless person to rectify others."

Annotation:

Chen Dai (陳代) was a student of Mencius.
Qi Jing Gong (齊景公, also known as Duke Jing of Qi, on the throne from 547 to 490 BC, died 490 BC) was the ruler of the state of Qi during the Spring-Autumn Period.
Zhao Jian Zi (趙簡, also known as Zhao Yang, 趙軮) was one of the top six ministers of the state of Jin (晉國) during the Spring-Autumn Period.
Wang Liang (王良) was a skillful chariot driver.
Xi (奚) was a favorite subordinate of Zhao Jian Zi.

Commentary:

During the Warring States Period, rulers of states tried to recruit brilliant strategists and advisors to help them conquer other states or to defend against hegemons. Therefore, many lobbyists and scholars tried to make a fortune and rise to prominence by selling their crooked or defective ideologies to rulers. Many of them were shameless since their objectives were personal wealth and fame rather than magnanimity and the desire to foster peace to the empire. Mencius detested such behavior. The examples in this section highlight two pre-conditions under which Mencius would consider an appointment: (1) the king must be respectful, (2) the king deserved Mencius's service. Mencius did not want to bend his principles for personal gains.

Chapter 6: Teng Wen Gong (2)

Modern perspective:

When you apply for a senior job and are invited to an interview, you need to carefully note the words, attitude, air, and body language of the hiring manager and other interviewers. If you sense any hints of disparaging and debasing attitude, bias, or immoral tendency of the hiring manager and other employees of the company, you need to be cautious. If you were hired, you could be required to bend your principles to toe the party line and to be complicit in unethical or even illegal activities.

Section 2

景春曰 公孫衍 張儀豈不誠大丈夫哉。一怒而諸侯懼 安居而天下熄。

孟子曰 是焉得為大丈夫乎。子未學禮乎。丈夫之冠也 父命之 女子之嫁也 母命之 往送之門 戒之曰 往之女家 必敬必戒 無違夫子。以順為正者 妾婦之道也。居天下之廣居 立天下之正位 行天下之大道。得志與民由之 不得志獨行其道。富貴不能淫 貧賤不能移 威武不能屈。此之謂大丈夫。

Jing Chun asked Mencius, "Are not Gong Sun Yan and Zhang Yi great men? Feudal lords were terrified by their anger, and the flames of conflict were extinguished by their calls to peace."

Mencius replied, "How can they be regarded as great men? Have you not learned Li? During the capping ceremony to symbolize the coming-of-age of a young man, the father heads the ceremony and reminds his son of righteous principles. During the wedding of a young girl, the mother heads the ceremony, bids farewell to her daughter, and reminds her, 'In your new home, you must be respectful and control yourself. Do not offend your husband.' Obedience is the expected norm for a wife. When a person lives in the biggest mansion, occupies the highest office, traverses the broadest path in the country, and has accomplished his lofty goals, he should practice his principles for the good of people. Otherwise, he should adhere to his principles himself. A great man cannot be corrupted by wealth or status, cannot be moved by poverty or lowliness, and cannot be subjugated by threat or force. This is what a great man should be."

Annotation:

Jing Chun (景春) was a disciple of the School of Diplomacy (縱橫家) founded by Guiguzi (鬼谷子).

Gong Sun Yan (公孫衍) was a prominent figure in the School of Diplomacy.

Zhang Yi (張儀) and Su Qin (蘇秦) were two famous disciples of Guiguzi. Zhang Yi was a key statesman and diplomat for the state of Qin (秦) and was able to build a hegemon for the state of Qin by sheer diplomacy.

In the era of Zhou Dynasty, a capping ceremony was organized to celebrate the coming-of-age of a young man when he reached the age of 20.

Commentary and Modern Perspective:

The last sentence: "A great man cannot be corrupted by wealth or status, cannot be moved by poverty or lowliness, and cannot be subjugated by threat or force" has become a famous quote in Chinese literature. This sentence is still relevant today and is a good reminder for people.

Chapter 6: Teng Wen Gong (2)

Section 3

周霄問曰 古之君子仕乎。

孟子曰 仕。傳曰 孔子三月無君 則皇皇如也 出疆必載質。公明儀曰 古之人三月無君則弔。

(曰) 三月無君則弔 不以急乎。

曰 士之失位也 猶諸侯之失國家也。禮曰 諸侯耕助 以供粢盛 夫人蠶繅 以為衣服。犧牲不成 粢盛不潔 衣服不備 不敢以祭。惟士無田 則亦不祭。牲殺器皿衣服不備 不敢以祭 則不敢以宴 亦不足弔乎。

(曰) 出疆必載質 何也。

曰 士之仕也 猶農夫之耕也 農夫豈為出疆舍其耒耜哉。

曰 晉國亦仕國也 未嘗聞仕如此其急。仕如此其急也 君子之難仕 何也。

曰 丈夫生而願為之有室 女子生而願為之有家。父母之心 人皆有之。不待父母之命 媒妁之言 鑽穴隙相窺 踰牆相從 則父母國人皆賤之。古之人未嘗不欲仕也 又惡不由其道。不由其道而往者 與鑽穴隙之類也。

Zhou Xiao asked Mencius, "In the past, did Jun Zis take government jobs?"

Mencius said, "Yes they did. A history book says, "If Confucius was unemployed by any ruler for three months, he became anxious and uneasy. After he left a state, and looked for a position in another state, he must bring an introductory gift to the ruler of the latter state. Gong Ming Yi also said, 'If a person were without an official job for three months, he would need to be condoled with.' "

Zhou Xiao said, "Would it be too hasty to condole with a person who is out of an official job for three months?"

Mencius said, "The loss of a job to an official is like the loss of a state to a feudal lord. *Li Ji* says, 'Feudal lords ploughed land and grew millet to be used as sacrifice. The wives of feudal lords raised silkworms and unwound their cocoons to make garments for sacrificial ceremonies. If the sacrificial animals were too slim, the millet was unclean, and the garments were incomplete, they were not used as sacrifice. If an official did not own a piece of land to grow sacrificial grains, he could not participate in the ceremony.' If the sacrificial animals, utensils, and garments are lacking, one dares not perform a sacrificial ceremony and arrange a banquet afterwards. Is this a good reason for condolence?"

Zhou Xiao asked, "Why must an unemployed official looking for a position in another state bring an introductory gift?"

Mencius said, "This was how an official looked for a job. It is analogous to the need for a farmer to bring along his ploughing tools when he migrates to another state."

Zhou Xiao said, "The state of Jin is one of the states that recruit officials in their governments, but I have not heard of any meritorious scholar who is so eager in finding an official job. If so, why are many Jun Zis reluctant to become officials?"

Mencius said, "After a son is born, his parents hope that they can find a good wife for him. After a daughter is born, his parents hope that they can find a good husband for her. This is the common desire of all parents. If a couple of youngsters ignore the wish of their parents and the recommendation of the match maker, bore holes through the walls of their family houses to get a peep of each other, or jump over walls to secretly meet each other, their parents will

Chapter 6: Teng Wen Gong (2)

despise them. Ancient scholars indeed desired to find official jobs. However, they also detested the seeking of jobs through improper ways. If a person gets an appointment through improper ways, he is like the youngsters who bore holes through the family walls."

Annotation:

Zhou Xiao (周霄) was a native of the state of Wei (魏國).

Gong Ming Yi (公明義) was a student of Zheng Zi (曾子, 505–432 BC), a disciple of Confucius. During Mencius's time, the reputation of Gong Ming Yi was remarkably high.

Li Ji (禮記) was a collection of 49 chapters/books which documented the historical background, contents, and the philosophy of *Li* (rites, rituals and so on) from the ancient times to the Zhou Dynasty. It also documented many teachings of Confucius and his disciples. *Li Ji* also contained two important books: The *Doctrine of Zhong Yong* (中庸) and the *Book of Great Learning* (大學).

The state of Jin (晉國) was broken up into three states in 403 BC—the states of Han (韓), Zhao (趙), and Wei (魏). Therefore, when Zhou Xiao, who was a native of the state of Wei, mentioned the state of Jin, he referred to his own state of Wei also.

During the Spring-Autumn and Warring States Periods, ordinary government officials were not enfeoffed with plots of land. Their salaries just enabled them to survive without conducting farming themselves. If they lost their jobs, they could not support their families and sacrifice food during sacrificial ceremonies.

In ancient China, parents dictated the marriages of young men and women through a process of match making. Secret marriages without the consent of parents were considered violations of *Li*.

Mencius in Modern Perspectives

Commentary and Modern Perspective:

This key point in this section is: "If a person gets an appointment through improper ways, he is like the youngsters who bore holes through the family walls." Nowadays, many people get appointments to good jobs through improper ways, and they are not ashamed.

Section 4

彭更問曰 後車數十乘 從者數百人 以傳食於諸侯 不以泰乎。

孟子曰 非其道 則一簞食不可受於人 如其道 則舜受堯之天下 不以為泰 子以為泰乎。

曰 否。士無事而食 不可也。

曰 子不通功易事 以羨補不足 則農有餘粟 女有餘布。子如通之 則梓匠輪輿皆得食於子。於此有人焉 入則孝 出則悌 守先王之道 以待後之學者 而不得食於子。子何尊梓匠輪輿而輕為仁義者哉。

曰 梓匠輪輿 其志將以求食也。君子之為道也 其志亦將以求食與。

曰 子何以其志為哉。其有功於子 可食而食之矣。且子食志乎 食功乎。

曰 食志。

曰 有人於此 毀瓦畫墁 其志將以求食也 則子食之乎

曰 否。

曰 然則子非食志也 食功也。

Chapter 6: Teng Wen Gong (2)

Peng Geng asked Mencius, "You, my master, have traveled from state to state with an entourage of tens of carriages and hundreds of disciples, and stayed in hotels paid for by feudal lords. Is it a bit excessive?"

Mencius replied, "If there is no righteous ground for a gift, we should not take even one bowl of rice from people. If there a righteous ground, even a gift of the empire of Yao and Shun is not excessive. Why do you consider it excessive?"

Peng Geng said, "No. However, it is improper for a scholar performing no service to receive any reward."

Mencius said, "You do not understand that the essence of trade is to exchange some goods in surplus for other goods in shortage. Therefore, farmers have surpluses of grains, and female weavers have surpluses of cloth. If you provide a market for trading them, potters, carpenters, wheel makers, and carriage makers can trade their surpluses of their goods for food from you. Suppose that there is a scholar who is filial at home and fraternal outside, compliant with the principles of ancient saintly kings, and who teaches his disciples. He then cannot get food from the market [because he has no physical goods to trade for food]. Why should you honor the potter, carpenter, wheel maker, and carriage maker, but turn away a person with Ren and Yi virtues?"

Peng Geng replied, "The motive of the potter, carpenter, wheel maker, and carriage maker is to make a living. Is the motive of a virtuous scholar about making a living?"

Mencius asked, "Why should you bother about their motives? If someone's service or product is valuable, you will give him food in exchange for the service or product for what it is worth. Do you provide food for people because of their motives, or because of the value of services or products they provide?"

Peng Geng replied, "I provide food for people based on their motives."

Mencius said, "Suppose there is a handyman who breaks the tiles on the roof of your house and mess up the paint on its wall. His motive is to make a living. Would you pay him because of his motive?"

Peng Geng replied, "No."

Mencius said, "You then pay people for the values of their services or products rather than their motives."

Annotation:

Peng Geng (彭更) was a disciple of Mencius.

Commentary and Modern Perspective:

This section is on basic economic theory. Commodities, physical goods, products, and services all provide values to people. A market facilitates trades among them based on their values. One cannot disregard the value of services, especially those in teaching and promoting virtuous principles. Another point of this section is about payment for performance.

Section 5

萬章問曰 宋 小國也。今將行王政 齊楚惡而伐之 則如之何。

孟子曰 湯居亳 與葛為鄰 葛伯放而不祀。湯使人問之曰 何為不祀。曰 無以供犧牲也。湯使遺之牛羊。葛伯食之 又不以祀。湯又使人問之曰 何為不祀。曰 無以供粢盛也。湯使亳

Chapter 6: Teng Wen Gong (2)

眾往為之耕　老弱饋食。葛伯率其民　要其有酒食黍稻者奪之　不授者殺之　有童子以黍肉餉　殺而奪之。書曰　葛伯仇餉。此之謂也。為其殺是童子而征之　四海之內皆曰　非富天下也　為匹夫匹婦復讎也。湯始征　自葛載。十一征而無敵於天下。東面而征　西夷怨　南面而征　北狄怨　曰　奚為後我。民之望之　若大旱之望雨也。歸市者弗止　芸者不變。誅其君　弔其民　如時雨降　民大悅。書曰　徯我后　后來其無罰　有攸不惟臣　東征　綏厥士女　匪厥玄黃　紹我周王見休　惟臣附於大邑周。其君子實玄黃於匪以迎其君子　其小人簞食壺漿以迎其小人　救民於水火之中　取其殘而已矣。太誓曰　我武惟揚　侵於之疆　則取於殘　殺伐用張　於湯有光。不行王政云爾　苟行王政　四海之內皆舉首而望之　欲以為君。齊楚雖大　何畏焉。

Wan Zhang asked, "The state of Song is small. It plans to implement magnanimous governance policy. The states of Qi and Chu hate such policy and attacked Song. What should they do?"

    Mencius said, "King Tang lived in the area Bo and was a neighbor of the tribe of Ge. The head of the tribe, Ge Bo, was a dissolute person and did not organize worship ceremonies. Tang sent his envoy to ask Ge Bo, 'Why don't you organize worship ceremonies?' Ge Bo answered, 'We cannot afford to sacrifice an animal for the worship.' King Tang then provided cows and lambs for Ge Bo's ceremonies. Instead of sacrificing these animals, Ge Bo ate them. King Tang sent his envoy to ask Ge Bo again, 'Why don't you organize worship ceremonies?' Ge Bo responded, 'My tribe does not have enough grain to eat. [Why should we waste these animals for the sacrifice to gods?]' King Tang then sent his own peasants in Bo to work for tribe Ge and donated food to their elderly and poor people. Ge Bo led his people to rob the grains, food and wine from carriers sent by King Tang, and kill those carriers who resisted the robbery. Ge Bo's gang even robbed and killed a boy carrying millet and meat. This was why the *Book of Classic History* said, "Ge Bo killed the carrier of food." King Tang waged a war against Ge Bo because of the killing of a boy. Everybody in the world commented, "King Tang was not interested in enriching himself. He just wanted to avenge the murderer of common people." After the conquest of the Ge tribe, King Tang then waged eleven wars against other barbaric tribes and was invincible. When his army went to the east, barbarians in the west yearned for its advent. When his army went to the south, barbarians in the north yearned for its advent. They said, 'When will his army come and liberate us?' People longed for his advent like their longing for the rain during a long drought. Wherever his army went to, trading did not stop in bazaar markets, and peasants continued to cultivate their land. King Tang removed tyrants in these territories and brought peace to their people like timely rain. People were joyous. The *History Book of Shang* says, 'When will the good king come? When he comes, we will no longer suffer under tyranny. During the revolutionary campaign by King Wu of Zhou against the tyrannical Emperor Zhou of Shang, some heads of states did not want to surrender to King Wu, who then needed to attack and subdue the eastern states, and liberate their people. They brought baskets of black and yellow silk as tributes to the big state of Zhou and begged to become its subjects.' The upper class in the Shang Dynasty offered black and yellow silk to the upper class in the state of Zhou. Common people in the Shang Dynasty offered bowls of rice and bottles of wine to common people in the state of Zhou. King Wu saved people from their turmoil and eliminated their oppressors. The *Great Manifesto* of King Wu announced, 'Let us raise an army,

Chapter 6: Teng Wen Gong (2)

invade his territory, remove the tyrant, and bring peace by war. Our great accomplishment will be more glorious than that of King Tang.'

Regarding the state of Song, its king does not want to implement a magnanimous government policy. If he does, all people in the entire country will look up to him as their leader. If so, how can the state of Song be threatened by great powers like the states of Qi and Chu?"

Annotation:

Wan Zhang (萬章) was a disciple of Mencius.

The state of Song (宋國) was a small state in modern-day Henan Province in China. King Yan (宋王偃) of Song was an ambitious warmonger. According to the *Book of Records* (*Shi Ji* 史記), he attempted to destroy the state of Teng (滕) and invade the state of Xue (薛). He defeated the state of Qi (齊) in the east and took five cities from Qi. He defeated the state of Chu (楚) in the south and took a territory of three hundred square miles from Chu. He defeated the state of Wei (魏) in the west. He was, therefore, an enemy of Qi, Chu, and Wei. He was also a brutal person. He trained his soldiers by hanging bags of human blood and asking them to shoot the bags until blood splashed out from the bags. He also indulged in women and wine. He killed meritorious advisors in his court. In 286 BC, the coalition of the states of Qi, Chi, and Wei conquered Song and killed him. The state of Song was annexed by its three enemies. The dialogue between Wan Zhang and Mencius occurred before 286 BC when the states of Qi, Chi, and Wei were about to invade Song.

Yu (禹, circa 2237–2139 BC) founded the Xia Dynasty (夏朝, circa 2184–1600 BC) in about 2184 BC. After about 500 years of the dynasty, the 16th successor to the throne was Emperor Jie of Xia (夏桀). He was an extraordinarily talented person. In addition to being a superb scholar, he was a great fighter with unusual physical strength. However, he was the first tyrant in Chinese history. Years before Jie became Emperor, the Xia Dynasty had already declined substantially. Foreign tribes intruded into territories at the border. Class struggles were rampant, and wealth disparity was immense. Common people suffered immensely. King Tang of the state of Shang formed an alliance, revolted against the Xia Dynasty, and defeated the army of Emperor Jie. The Shang Dynasty (商朝) was then founded in about 1600 BC by King Tang.

The Shang Dynasty lasted for about 600 years. After 30 successions to the throne, the empire was ruled by a brutal tyrant, Emperor Zhou (紂), who was also called Emperor Xin (帝辛). He was a smart and strong man, and a great warrior. He lived a notoriously decadent and extravagant lifestyle. He indulged in debauchery with beautiful and bewitching concubines, including the malicious Da Ji (妲己). He ruled by brutality and terror. The state of Zhou (周) in western China was populated by a tribe in the Wei River valley. Because of fertile land, favorable climate, and a prudent government, this state emerged in prominence in that region. They had a meritorious and benevolent ruler, Ji Chang (姬昌), who was called Earl Wen of Zhou. He fostered a culture of humaneness, reverence for the elderly, kindness to youth, and respect of knowledge and competency. He implemented policies to protect the underclass and peasants. He ran a clean and lean government. He also promoted morality in society. He set a good example by his virtuous behaviors. The state of Zhou prospered as a result, and its people were happy. Many neighboring tribes joined the state or became its allies. They later called him King Wen of Zhou and supported him as their spiritual leader.

King Wen of Zhou (周文王, 1152–1056 BC) died at the age of 97. His son, Ji Fa (姬發), also called King Wu of Zhou (周武王),

Chapter 6: Teng Wen Gong (2)

was the successor. He continued the same policy of his father. The state grew further while the Empire of Shang continued to decline. In 1048 BC, King Wu formed an alliance of 800 feudal lords. In the spring of 1046 BC, King Wu raised an army of 300 chariots, 3,000 armored warriors and thousands of infantrymen. His small army traveled eastward from his home base to Meng Jin. Other feudal lords in the alliance also brought their own armies to Meng Jin, where King Wu announced his *Great Manifesto* (太誓) and declared war against the Shang Dynasty. The coalition army defeated the army of Shang Dynasty in Mu Ye (牧野), which was only 70 miles south of the capital of the Shang Dynasty. King Wu founded the Zhou Dynasty in 1048 BC.

Commentary:

This section has two teachings of Mencius. The first is that a corrupt, brutal, and warmongering country like the state of Song will eventually be destroyed by its enemies. If the state of Song had implemented a magnanimous policy and stopped its warmongering behavior, it would have avoided its fall.

The second is that, according to Mencius, invading another country is justified if the goal is to remove its evil ruler and to bring peace, prosperity, and happiness to its people, and the act of invasion is welcomed by its people. Mencius cited the military campaigns of King Tang of Shang and King Wu of Zhou, both regarded as saintly kings, to justify his point of view. During the Warring States Period, China was extremely tumultuous and common people lived under the terror of tyranny and wars. Many philosophic schools, including Confucians, Mohists, and Strategists, advanced their respective approaches of bringing peace to the country. Mencius's point of view was contended by Mohists, who expounded their doctrine of non-aggression. The Strategist School emphasized the importance of diplomacy over the use of force. There is no clear answer to this debate as this is an extremely complex question throughout human history.

Modern Perspective:

History does not repeat itself, but it rhymes.

Section 6

孟子謂戴不勝曰 子欲子之王之善與 我明告子。有楚大夫於此 欲其子之齊語也 則使齊人傅諸 使楚人傅諸。

曰 使齊人傅之。

曰 一齊人傅之 眾楚人咻之 雖日撻而求其齊也 不可得矣。引而置之莊嶽之間數年 雖日撻而求其楚 亦不可得矣。子謂薛居州 善士也。使之居於王所。在於王所者 長幼卑尊 皆薛居州也 王誰與為不善。在王所者 長幼卑尊 皆非薛居州也 王誰與為善。一薛居州 獨如宋王何。

Mencius spoke to Dai Bu Sheng, "Do you want your king to be virtuous? Let me tell you how. In the past, there was a minister of the state of Chu who wanted his son to be able to speak the language of Qi. Should he hire a native of Qi or a native of Chu to teach his son?"

Dai Bu Sheng replied, "He should hire a native of Qi."

Mencius said, "The son was taught by only one speaker of the Qi language but was surrounded by a multitude of speakers of the Chu language. Even if he was beaten daily to speak the Qi language,

Chapter 6: Teng Wen Gong (2)

it did not work. After the son was taken to reside in the streets of Qi, Zhuang and Yue, for a few years, the son could no longer speak the language of Chu even if the father beat him. You regard Xue Ju Zhou to be a virtuous person. You should place him near your king. If all officials surrounding your king, irrespective of their ages and ranks, are as virtuous as Xue Ju Zhou, how can your king not be virtuous? If all officials surrounding your king, irrespective of their ages and ranks, are unlike Xue Ju Zhou, from whom can your king learn virtues? Just one Xue Ju Zhou cannot make a big difference to the state of Song."

Annotation:

Dai Bu Sheng (戴不勝) was a minister of the state of Song (宋國).

The states of Qi (齊) and Chu (楚) were two hegemons in the Warring States Period.

Zhuang (莊) and Yue (嶽) were names of two streets in the capital of Qi.

Xue Ju Zhou (薛居州) was a known meritorious scholar in the state of Song.

Commentary and Modern Perspective:

In this section, Mencius pointed out the importance of environmental and peer influence.

Section 7

公孫丑問曰 不見諸侯 何義。

孟子曰 古者不為臣不見。段幹木踰垣而辟之 泄柳閉門而

不內 是皆已甚。迫 斯可以見矣。陽貨欲見孔子而惡無禮 大夫有賜於士 不得受於其家 則往拜其門。陽貨瞷孔子之亡也 而饋孔子蒸豚。孔子亦瞷其亡也 而往拜之。當是時 陽貨先 豈得不見。曾子曰 脅肩諂笑 病於夏畦。子路曰 未同而言 觀其色赧赧然 非由之所知也。由是觀之 則君子之所養可知已矣。

Gong Sun Chou asked Mencius, "Why you don't want to see feudal lords?"

Mencius replied, "In the old days, if a scholar is not an official of a state, he did not go to see the head of that state. Duan Gan Mu leaped over the wall of his house to avoid seeing Duke Wen of the state of Wei. Xie Liu shut his door to Duke Mu of the state of Lu. The two scholars were too extreme. Since the two feudal lords were so urgent and earnest, it was proper to see them. For example, Yang Huo wanted to summon Confucius but did not want to be impolite. It was a rule that when a minister sent a gift to a scholar who was away and unable to receive the gift, the scholar was obliged to return a visit to the minister and thank him in person. Yang Huo then watched when Confucius was out and sent Confucius a roast pig. Confucius then visited Yang Huo while he was out [to avoid seeing Yang Huo in person]. At that time, if Yang Huo had taken the initiative to visit Confucius, how could Confucius decline to see Yang Huo? Zheng Zi said, 'The act of shrugging one's shoulders and putting on fawning smiles is as torturous as toiling in a large field during the summer.' Zi Lu also said, 'When I see someone flattering others despite a difference in interest and goals, and showing a red face in shame, I do not understand his psychology.' From these remarks, we know the meaning of the virtuous character of a Jun Zi."

Chapter 6: Teng Wen Gong (2)

Annotation:

Gong Sun Chou (公孫丑) was a disciple of Mencius.

Duan Gan Mu (段干木) was a native of the state of Jin (晉國) during the Warring States Period. He lived in the state of Wei. He did not want to work for the government of the state of Wei. When Duke Wen of Wei tried to recruit him and visited his home, Duan leaped over the wall of his house to avoid seeing the duke.

Xie Liu (泄柳) was a meritorious scholar of the state of Lu during the Warring States Period. Duke Mu of the state of Lu wanted to recruit him into his government. When the duke paid a visit to Xie Liu, he closed his door to the duke.

Yang Huo (陽貨, also known as Yang Hu 陽虎) was the top official working for the Ji Sun Si (季孫氏) family which controlled the government of the state of Lu (魯). Confucius despised him and regarded him as a malicious official. Yang Huo wanted to recruit Confucius to work for him, but Confucius had turned down his offer before. Since Yang Huo sent him a roast pig, Confucius needed to pay him a visit to thank him according to normal etiquette. Since Confucius did not want to see Yang Huo in person, Confucius visited Yang Huo while he was out. They later met on the road. Yang Huo said to Confucius, "Come, I need to talk to you." He then said, "If one possesses an outstanding caliber like a precious jewel but stands aloof from chaos in the country, can he be regarded to have Ren virtue?" Confucius said, "No, he cannot." Yang Huo then said, "If one is interested in public services but misses great opportunities, is he wise?" Confucius said, "No, he is not." Yang Huo then said, "Time flies. It does not wait for us." Confucius replied, "Yes. I will look for an official job then" (see Section 1 of Chapter 17, 陽貨, of *Confucius Analects*).

Zheng Zi (曾子, also known as Zheng Shen 曾參, born 505 BC)

was a prominent disciple of Confucius, known for his filial piety. He was the author of *The Book of Great Learning* (大學).

Zi Lu (子路, 542–480 BC, also known as Zhong You 仲由) was a disciple of Confucius and was best known for his ability and success in statesmanship. He was noted for his valor and sense of justice.

Commentary:

In this section, Mencius spoke about the balance between courtesy and dogma. He criticized Duan Gan Mu and Xie Liu to be too extreme in shunning sincere invitations by the dukes, and cited the example of how Confucius behaved courteously while, at the same time, avoided meeting Yang Huo. Mencius did not want to take the initiative to meet many feudal lords because they did not take his doctrines seriously.

Modern Perspective:

One should be courteous and give people the benefit of doubt and not reject people by judging their motives and sincerity too quickly. Even Confucius changed his mind after his meeting with Yang Huo on the road.

The following words of Zheng Zi are worth noting: 'The act of shrugging one's shoulders and putting on fawning smiles is as torturous as toiling in a large field during the summer.' Zi Lu's comment, 'When I see someone flattering others despite a difference in interest and goals, and showing a red face in shame, I do not understand his psychology,' also applies to many shameless people nowadays.

Chapter 6: Teng Wen Gong (2)

Section 8

戴盈之曰 什一 去關市之征 今茲未能。請輕之 以待來年 然後已 何如。

孟子曰 今有人日攘其鄰之雞者 或告之曰 是非君子之道。曰 請損之 月攘一雞 以待來年 然後已。如知其非義 斯速已矣 何待來年。

Dai Ying Zhi said to Mencius, "You suggest that we levy a 10 percent tax rate on land and eliminate duties at our ports and markets. We cannot implement it this year. We plan to reduce our taxation a little now and wait until next year to implement your suggestion. What do you think?"

Mencius replied, "There is a man who daily steals chickens belonging to his neighbor. He was told by others, 'This is not the way of a Jun Zi.' He replied, 'Alright, I will reduce my theft. I will steal once a month from now and will stop stealing by next year.' If you know that your act is wrong, you should correct it immediately. Why wait until next year?"

Annotation:

Dai Ying Zhi (戴盈之) was a minister of the state of Song.

Commentary:

Mencius advocated low taxation and duty-free imports. His philosophy on economics was more than two millennia ahead of his time.

Mencius in Modern Perspectives

Modern Perspective:

The key sentence in this section is: "If you know that your act is wrong, you should correct it immediately." Do not procrastinate. The tendency of procrastination is often mistaken by many policy makers to be pragmatism.

Section 9

公都子曰 外人皆稱夫子好辯 敢問何也。

孟子曰 予豈好辯哉。予不得已也。天下之生久矣 一治一亂。當堯之時 水逆行泛濫於中國 蛇龍居之 民無所定 下者為巢 上者為營窟。書曰 洚水警余。洚水者 洪水也。使禹治之。禹掘地而注之海 驅蛇龍而放之菹 水由地中行 江 淮 河 漢是也。險阻既遠 鳥獸之害人者消 然後人得平土而居之。

堯舜既沒 聖人之道衰 暴君代作 壞宮室以為汙池 民無所安息 棄田以為園囿 使民不得衣食 邪說暴行又作 園囿 汙池 沛澤多而禽獸至。及紂之身 天下又大亂。周公相武王 誅紂伐奄 三年討其君 驅飛廉於海隅而戮之 滅國者五十 驅虎豹犀象而遠之 天下大悅。書曰 丕顯哉 文王謨 丕承哉 武王烈 佑啟我後人 咸以正無缺。

世衰道微 邪說暴行有作 臣弒其君者有之 子弒其父者有之。孔子懼 作春秋。春秋 天子之事也 是故孔子曰 知我者 其惟春秋乎 罪我者 其惟春秋乎。

聖王不作 諸侯放恣 處士橫議 楊朱 墨翟之言盈天下 天下之言 不歸楊則歸墨。楊氏為我 是無君也。墨氏兼愛 是無父

Chapter 6: Teng Wen Gong (2)

也。無父無君 是禽獸也。公明儀曰 庖有肥肉 廄有肥馬 民有飢色 野有餓莩 此率獸而食人也。楊墨之道不息 孔子之道不著 是邪說誣民 充塞仁義也。仁義充塞 則率獸食人 人將相食。吾為此懼。閑先聖之道 距楊墨 放淫辭 邪說者不得作。作於其心 害於其事 作於其事 害於其政。聖人復起 不易吾言矣。

昔者禹抑洪水而天下平。周公兼夷狄驅猛獸而百姓寧。孔子成春秋而亂臣賊子懼。詩云 戎狄是膺 荊舒是懲 則莫我敢承。無父無君 是周公所膺也。我亦欲正人心 息邪說 距詖行 放淫辭 以承三聖者。豈好辯哉 予不得已也。能言距楊墨者 聖人之徒也。

Gong Du Zi asked Mencius, "Many people outside say that you, Master, like to argue. May I ask why?"

Mencius said, "Why do I like to argue? I am compelled to. Since the beginning of mankind in the world, periods of peace have been followed by periods of chaos.

In the era of Yao, water overflew the rivers and inundated the country. Snakes and dragons lived there. People had nowhere to live but in nests built on trees or camps inside caves. The *Book of Classic History* says, 'Be warned of overflowing water.' By overflowing water, it refers to a big flood. Yao assigned Yu to controlling floods. Yu dug channels and tributaries to redirect water to the sea. He drove away snakes and dragons to the marshes. He redirected water from the land to the Yangtze, Yellow, Wei, and Han rivers. After the water obstruction was removed, birds and wild animals no longer threatened people. They could then live on land in comfort.

After the death of Yao and Shun, the meritorious principles of these saintly leaders gradually decayed. The country was ruled by tyrants who pulled down homes to build their private ponds. Displaced people became homeless. Farmland were converted to royal gardens so that farmers could not make a living. Heresy and violence abounded. The abundance of gardens, ponds, and marshes provided breeding grounds for wild animals once again. During the reign of Emperor Zhou of the Shang Dynasty, the country was in tremendous chaos and turmoil. The Duke of Zhou assisted King Wu of Zhou to revolt against Emperor Zhou. It took them three years to conquer the Shang Dynasty. King Wu drove Fei Lian to the seaside and killed him. King Wu then conquered fifty more enemies, and repelled tigers, leopards, rhinoceroses, and elephants to the wilderness. As a result, people in the country were gratified. The *Book of Classic History* said, 'The grand plan of King Wen was indeed luminous. The accomplishment of King Wu was indeed unprecedented. Their examples have helped to enlighten our descendants so that they can follow their flawless principles.'

As time passed, the country became rotten and heresies were everywhere. There were instances of assassinations of kings by ministers and the slaying of fathers by sons. The worried Confucius then wrote the *Annals of Spring-Autumn*. This book recorded the affairs of monarchs. Therefore, Confucius said, 'The Annals of Spring-Autumn shows people my concerns. People will also criticize me because of this book.'

Nowadays, there is no saintly king anymore. Feudal lords are unruly. Rogue scholars spread their heresies. The words of Yang Zhu and Mo Di filled the country. Ideologies in the country are either Yang Zhu's or Mo Di's. Yang's individualism implies the irrelevance of the sovereign. Mo's theory of indiscriminative love implies the irrelevance of parents. People who disregard the relevance of the sovereign and parents are animals. Gong Ming Yi

Chapter 6: Teng Wen Gong (2)

said, 'Their kitchens have fat meat, and their stables have fat horses, but their people have hungry looks, and their countryside has corpses from starvation. This is equivalent to leading beasts to devour people.' If the ideologies of Yang and Mo are not extinguished, Confucius's philosophy will not flourish. The theories of Yang and Mo are heresies and deceptive, void of Ren and Yi. The obstruction of the principles of Ren and Yi is equivalent to the leading of beasts to devour people and will result in people devouring one another. Since I am concerned, I need to uphold the principles of ancient saints and oppose Yang and Mo so that their unruly words and heretical theories will not spread. When one's mind is deluded, his actions will be ruinous, and will lead to ruinous governance policies. Even if saints are reborn today, they will not disagree with me.

In the past, Yu's control of floods established a new order in the country, the conquest of barbarians and repulsion of wild animals by Duke of Zhou enabled people to live in comfort, and the completion of the *Annals of Spring-Autumn* by Confucius terrified rebellious ministers and villainous sons. In the *Book of Poetry,* it is said, 'We defeated barbarians in the west and north, and repelled the Jing and Shu tribes. Who dared to resist us?' Duke of Zhou has defeated those who disregard their kings and parents. I just want to rectify the minds of people, extinguish heresies, oppose devious behaviors, and banish their licentious words, and uphold the principles of the three saints. Do I like to argue? No, I am obliged to. A disciple of the saints should be able to oppose Yang and Mo."

Annotation:

Gong Du Zi (公都子) was a disciple of Mencius.
Fei Lian (飛廉) was a strong warrior and a general for Emperor

Zhou of the Shang Dynasty. He was defeated and killed by King Wu of Zhou. He had two sons. One son was the ancestor of the royal family of the state of Qin and the other son was the ancestor of the royal family of the state of Zhao.

Yang Zhu (楊朱, circa 440–360 BC) was a famous philosopher during the Warring States Period. His school, the Mohist school, and Confucianism were the three dominant and competing schools during that period. Mencius was critical against both Yang Zhu and Mohists. In his early days, Yang Zhu learned Taoism, but he later deviated from it and founded his own philosophy, which had four key themes:

> (1) He advocated individualism. He claimed that the world revolved around oneself. He thought that our lives were constrained by the environment and social norms, and we must break away from such bondages to enjoy true happiness and freedom endowed by Nature on us.

> (2) On politics, he objected to hegemony and de-emphasized the concept of sovereignty. He thought that the world belonged to everybody, and that all its resources should be shared equally among everybody. He thought that laws, social norms, regulations, and Li all have the negative effects of restricting one's freedom.

> (3) On a personal level, he endorsed selfishness. He once said that one should not sacrifice even one piece of hair to benefit the world. He thought that if everyone takes care of his or her self-interest, the society and its economy will flourish naturally.

> (4) On the topic of morality, he endorsed the close attention to one's health and physical existence, and the maximization of one's physical and emotional

Chapter 6: Teng Wen Gong (2)

enjoyment. He also endorsed the concept of insatiability of desire.

Yang Zhu's philosophy sounds familiar today.

Mo Zi (墨子, circa 470–391 BC, also known as Mo Di, 墨翟) was a prominent philosopher and a native of the state of Lu (魯國人) during the Warring States Period. He was the founder of the Mohist school of philosophy, which advocated universal and indiscriminative love (兼愛), non-offensive warfare (非攻), and other teachings (see Endnote 2 for more details on Mo Zi's philosophy).

Zhou Gong (周公, also known as Duke of Zhou) was the brother of King Wu of Zhou (周武王, died 1043 BC) and the first prime minister of the Zhou Dynasty.

Commentary:

During the time of Mencius, the schools of thought of Yang Zhu and Mo Di were competitors of Confucianism. Therefore, this section showed the harsh criticism of Mencius on his competitors. It is obvious from the description of the philosophy of Yang Zhu in the above Annotation that Confucians were strong opponents of Yang Zhu. Section 2 in the Endnotes chapter provides an explanation of the difference between Confucianism and Mohism.

Section 10

匡章曰 陳仲子豈不誠廉士哉。居於陵 三日不食 耳無聞 目無見也。井上有李 螬食實者過半矣 匍匐往將食之 三咽 然後耳有聞 目有見。

孟子曰　於齊國之士　吾必以仲子為巨擘焉。雖然　仲子惡能廉。充仲子之操　則蚓而後可者也。夫蚓　上食槁壤　下飲黃泉。仲子所居之室　伯夷之所築與。抑亦盜跖之所築與。所食之粟　伯夷之所樹與。抑亦盜跖之所樹與。是未可知也。

曰　是何傷哉。彼身織屨　妻辟纑　以易之也。

曰　仲子　齊之世家也。兄戴　蓋祿萬鐘。以兄之祿為不義之祿而不食也　以兄之室為不義之室而不居也　辟兄離母　處於於陵。他日歸　則有饋其兄生鵝者　己頻顣曰　惡用是鶃鶃者為哉。他日　其母殺是鵝也　與之食之。其兄自外至曰　是鶃鶃之肉也。出而哇之。以母則不食　以妻則食之　以兄之室則弗居　以於陵則居之。是尚為能充其類也乎。若仲子者　蚓而後充其操者也。

Kuang Zhang asked Mencius, "Was Chen Zhong Zi austere and pure indeed? While he was in Wu Ling, he fasted for three days until he could not hear and see. The plums fallen from the plum-tree next to a well were half-eaten by worms. He crawled to pick up the plums and ate them. After three mouthfuls, his sight and hearing recovered."

Mencius said, "Among all the scholars in the state of Qi, I would raise my thumb to Zhong Zi. Notwithstanding this, how can he be regarded an austere and pure person? To follow his behavior, one must become an earthworm. Earthworms eat dirt and drink muddy water. Was Zhong Zi's house built by Bo Yi or by a thief? Was his food grown by Bo Yi or by a thief? We don't know."

Kuang Zhang said, "Why does it matter? He weaved sandals with hemp himself. His wife twisted threads of hemp to be exchanged for other necessities."

Chapter 6: Teng Wen Gong (2)

Mencius said, "Zhong Zi was born to a noble family of Qi. His elder brother was a prominent official of Qi and paid a salary of ten thousand zhongs [i.e., 640,000 bushels] of grains. Zhong Zi considered that his brother's salary was earned improperly and refused to depend on it. Likewise, Zhong Zi considered that his brother's house was earned improperly and refused to live in it. He stayed away from his brother, left his mother, and lived in Wu Ling alone. One day, he returned home. Somebody gave a live goose to his brother. Upon seeing the goose, Zhong Zi was upset, knitted his eyebrows, and exclaimed, 'What are you going to use that quacking goose for?' On the next day, his mother cooked that goose and treated Zhong Zi with its meat. His elder brother came in and told him, 'That is the meat of that quacking goose.' Zhong Zi immediately ran out of the house and vomited. Zhong Zi did not like eating the meals his mother prepared, but he did not mind eating the meals prepared by his wife. He did not like to live in the house of his brother, but instead lived alone in Wu Ling. Can his behavior be considered austere and pure? To follow Zhong Zi's austere and pure ways, one must be an earthworm."

Annotation:

Kuang Zhang (匡章) was a general of the state of Qi.

Chen Zhong Zi (陳仲子) was a native of the state of Qi and a philosopher. Since he lived in the city of Ling, he was also called Ling Zi (陵子). His brother was a top minister of the state of Qi. He belonged to the philosophy school of Yang Zhu (楊朱) and advocated purity and asceticism.

Wu Ling (於陵) was a city of the state of Qi in modern-day Shandong Province.

Bo Yi (伯夷) was an ancient saint. He and his brother Shu Qi

(叔齊) were two princes of the last duke of the feudal state of Gu Zhu (孤竹國), during the Shang Dynasty (商朝, circa 1766–1066 BC). Bo Yi was the eldest brother, and Shu Qi was the youngest. Before their father died, Shu Qi was nominated to be his successor. Shu Qi abdicated his throne to his eldest brother, Bo Yi, and stressed that the eldest son should be the successor to the throne according to tradition. Bo Yi refused to accept out of the respect of his father's wish. Both eventually renounced the throne and migrated to the territory of the state of Zhou (周). Later, King Wu of Zhou (周武王) raised an army to invade the Shang Dynasty. Both Bo Yi and Shu Qi knelt in front of King Wu's chariot and begged King Wu not to invade the Shang Dynasty. King Wu eventually conquered the Shang Dynasty and founded the Zhou Dynasty (周朝). Bo Yi and Shu Qi refused to be subjects of the Zhou Dynasty and eat its food. They moved to the mountains and starved to death. Historians regarded these two ancient characters to be model Jun Zis who possessed the Ren virtue.

Commentary:

Kuang Zhang admired Chen Zhong Zi and considered the austere and ascetic behavior of Chen Zhong Zi to be noble. On the contrary, Mencius considered that since humans needed to live in a society, the practice of loving others and living harmoniously with others is more important than the practice of austerity and abstinence. Mencius therefore objected to the unnatural and extreme behavior of stoics.

Chapter 7: Li Lou (1)

Section 1

孟子曰 離婁之明 公輸子之巧 不以規矩 不能成方員。師曠之聰 不以六律 不能正五音。堯舜之道 不以仁政 不能平治天下。今有仁心仁聞而民不被其澤 不可法於後世者 不行先王之道也。故曰 徒善不足以為政 徒法不能以自行。詩云 不愆不忘 率由舊章。遵先王之法而過者 未之有也。聖人既竭目力焉 繼之以規矩準繩 以為方員平直 不可勝用也。既竭耳力焉 繼之以六律 正五音 不可勝用也。既竭心思焉 繼之以不忍人之政 而仁覆天下矣。故曰 為高必因丘陵 為下必因川澤。為政不因先王之道 可謂智乎。是以惟仁者宜在高位。不仁而在高位 是播其惡於眾也。

上無道揆也 下無法守也 朝不信道 工不信度 君子犯義 小人犯刑 國之所存者幸也。故曰 城郭不完 兵甲不多 非國之災也 田野不辟 貨財不聚 非國之害也。上無禮 下無學 賊民興 喪無日矣。

詩曰 天之方蹶 無然泄泄。泄泄 猶沓沓也。事君無義 進退無禮 言則非先王之道者 猶沓沓也。故曰 責難於君謂之恭 陳善閉邪謂之敬 吾君不能謂之賊。

Mencius said, "Even if one has sharp eyes as Li Lou, and skills of Gong Shu Zi, he cannot draw circles and squares without a compass and a set square ruler. Even if one has acute ears like the music

265

master Shi Kuang, he cannot tune the five notes accurately without the six pitch-tubes. Even if one has the talents of Yao and Shun, he cannot foster peace to the country without the implementation of Ren policies. Some rulers today have the intention and reputation of implementing Ren policies, but their people do not receive any benefit, and these rulers cannot set a good example for future generations because they do not follow the way of ancient saintly kings. Therefore, a benevolent heart alone is insufficient to rule a country. Likewise, laws alone are insufficient to ensure their compliance. The *Book of Poetry* states, 'Do not deviate, do not forget. Follow ancient rules.' Those who follow rules of ancient kings will never make mistakes. Since ancient saints have already exhausted their eyesight and invented the compass and set square, we can draw an unlimited number of shapes. Since the ancient saints have already exhausted their hearing ability and invented the six pitch-tubes and five notes, we can compose an unlimited number of music pieces. They have thought hard to develop compassionate governance policies so that benevolence flourished in the country. Therefore, we say that, to reach high mountains, we must begin with mounds and, to reach deep places, we must begin with rivers and marshes. Is it wise to rule a country without following the principles of ancient saintly kings?

It is desirable to have people with the Ren virtue to lead the country. If people void of the Ren virtue occupy high posts in the government, they will spread their wickedness to people. If the ruling class does not have governance principles, their subjects will have no rules to follow. If government officials do not believe in principles, laborers do not believe in standards, the elite class is not righteous, and common people commit crimes, it is a matter of luck that the country can survive. Therefore, demolished city walls and castles and inadequate arms are not catastrophic to a country.

Chapter 7: Li Lou (1)

Undeveloped farmland and depleted treasury coffers are not ruinous to a country. If the ruler is unruly, its people are uneducated, and crimes and revolts abound, the days of the country are numbered.

The *Book of Poetry* said, 'Tian (Sky) is about to punish us. Do not just talk and talk.' Just talking endlessly is effectively abetting. When an official does not serve his king with righteousness, does not advance nor retreat according to Li, does not talk about the principles of ancient saintly kings, he is just abetting. Therefore, we say that admonishing the mistakes of one's king is, in fact, honoring him, and giving good advice and preventing evil are, in fact, respecting him. To think that one's king cannot do any good is harmful to the king."

Annotation:

Ancient Chinese music had five notes, which are equivalent to Do, Re, Mi, Sol, and La. In addition, there were also 12 pitches. An octave was divided into 12 semi-pitches, equivalent to C, C#, D, D#, E, E#, F, G, G#, A, A#, and B in Western music. The odd numbered semi-pitches were called Lu (律) and the even numbered semi-pitches were called Ryo (呂). Six pitch-tubes (六律) of different lengths were used to tune these semi-pitches and the five major notes.

Li Lou (離婁) was a legendary person with sharp eyes, who lived during the period of Yellow Emperor. Li Lou could see the tips of leaves on a tree one hundred steps away.

Gong Shu Zi (公輸子, also known as Lu Ban 魯班) was a famous carpenter, craftsman, and builder, who lived during the Spring-Autumn Period.

Shi Kuang (師曠) was a famous musician, who lived during the Spring-Autumn Period.

Mencius in Modern Perspectives

Since ancient Chinese did not have the same notion of God as Christians, the word *Tian* (*Sky* 天) was used to represent a supernatural and unknown natural power that governs the world (see Section 4 of the Introduction).

Commentary and Modern Perspective:

The following two quotes in this section are still relevant to the modern world:

"Therefore, demolished city walls and castles, and inadequate arms are not catastrophic to a country. Undeveloped farmland and depleted treasury coffers are not ruinous to a country. If the ruler is unruly, its people are uneducated, and crimes and revolts abound, the days of the country are numbered."

"Just talking endlessly is effectively abetting."

Section 2

孟子曰 規矩 方員之至也。聖人 人倫之至也。欲為君盡君道 欲為臣盡臣道 二者皆法堯舜而已矣。不以舜之所以事堯事君 不敬其君者也。不以堯之所以治民治民 賊其民者也。孔子曰 道二 仁與不仁而已矣。暴其民甚 則身弒國亡。不甚 則身危國削。名之曰 幽厲 雖孝子慈孫 百世不能改也。詩云 殷鑒不遠 在夏后之世。此之謂也。

Mencius said, "The compass and set squares are tools to make perfect circles and squares. Saints are perfect models for human relations. To be a good king, one must try his best to follow proper principles for a king. To be a good minister, one must try his best to follow proper principles for a minister. If one does not follow the approach of Shun in serving Yao, he does not respect his king. If one does not follow the approach of Yao in ruling his people, he is ruining them.

Confucius said, 'There are only two courses to run a country: a magnanimous course or otherwise.' If a ruler is oppressive, he will be slain, and his country will fall in the worst case. At least, his life will be endangered, and his country will weaken. He will be designated with an infamous posthumous title of a 'loser' or a 'tyrant.' Even his filial and forgiving descendants over hundreds of generations cannot change his bad name. The *Book of Poetry* states, 'The mirror for the Yan (Shang) Dynasty was not far away. It was the history of the Xia Dynasty.' This is the meaning of this verse."

Annotation:

Shun (舜, circa 2294–2184 BC) was a minister of Yao (堯, circa 2356–2255 BC). Both were regarded ancient saintly kings.

The Yan (Shang) Dynasty (商朝, circa 1766–1046 BC) followed the Xia Dynasty (夏朝, circa 2184–1600 BC).

Commentary:

There was a historical tradition in China to designate posthumous titles to kings that summarized the pros and cons of their reign. These titles were entered into historical records for millennia. Therefore, most kings were concerned about such titles. Mencius used this as a reminder to kings.

Likewise, we should be concerned that our contribution or damage to the society will be remembered for a long time.

Section 3

孟子曰 三代之得天下也以仁 其失天下也以不仁。國之所以廢興存亡者亦然。天子不仁 不保四海 諸侯不仁 不保社稷 卿大夫不仁 不保宗廟 士庶人不仁 不保四體。惡死亡而樂不仁 是猶惡醉而強酒。

Mencius said, "The Xia, Shang, and Zhou dynasties rose because of Ren policies, and fell because of the lack of Ren policies. The rise and fall of all countries are due to the same reason. If the imperial emperor does not implement a Ren policy, he cannot protect his country. If a feudal lord does not implement a Ren policy, he cannot protect his state. If a minister does not implement a Ren policy, he cannot protect his clan. If a common person does not have Ren virtue, he cannot protect his body. If a person dreads death but is delighted to oppose Ren, he is like an alcoholic who dreads getting drunk."

Section 4

孟子曰 愛人不親反其仁 治人不治反其智 禮人不答反其敬。行有不得者 皆反求諸己 其身正而天下歸之。詩云 永言配命 自求多福。

If you try to be kind to others but do not receive a reciprocal affection, you must reflect on your Ren approach. If you try to rule your people but they are still not submissive, you must question your wisdom. If you try to be polite to others but they do not return with politeness, you must reflect whether you are respectful enough. If

Chapter 7: Li Lou (1)

you do not get the desired results from your actions, you need to introspect and rectify yourself. If your actions are proper, everybody in the world will support you. The *Book of Poetry* said, 'Be observant to fate. Those who help and demand on themselves are blessed with fortunes.'

Commentary and Modern Perspective:

This section points out some common mistakes made by people. They tend to blame their failures on others, the society, country, environment, and circumstance. They do not reflect on their own inadequacy and flaws. They criticize and demand on others, not themselves.

The last sentence is a good reminder. We must relentlessly improve ourselves and demand on ourselves rather than others. This sentence is often misinterpreted to be: "Those who take care of their self-interest will be blessed with fortunes." This interpretation is erroneous because it encourages selfishness and differs from the context of this section.

Section 5

孟子曰　人有恒言皆曰　天下國家。天下之本在國　國之本在家　家之本在身。

Mencius said, "There is a popular saying, 'The empire, the state, and the family.' The foundation of an empire is the state. The foundation of a state is the family. The foundation of a family is the individual member."

Commentary:

Although this is a simple sentence, this is an important point on social and political structures. First, we have seen historically that countries descended into civil wars when their states, segments, or regions fought among themselves. We have also seen how broken families affected the social fabric of the society and ruined their communities and countries. We have also seen many cases of how families are broken by irresponsible and selfish members.

Section 6

孟子曰　為政不難　不得罪於巨室。巨室之所慕　一國慕之。一國之所慕　天下慕之。故沛然德教溢乎四海。

Mencius said, "It is not difficult to run a government. The key is not to offend popular political parties. If they support and revere you, the entire state will follow. If all states support and revere you, the entire country will follow. Your magnanimity will be unstoppable and flourish in the whole world."

Annotation:

The second sentence in the original text was also interpreted and translated word-by-word to be: "The key is not to offend great families (巨室)." Even Zhu Xi (朱熹, 1130–1200 AD), a prominent Confucian in the Song Dynasty, annotated the phrase "great families" to be "Powerful nobilities, ministers, and families entrenched for generations."

This sentence is interpreted and translated differently as shown above for two good reasons. The first is to make Mencius's teaching

Chapter 7: Li Lou (1)

more relevant to the modern world. The second is explained below.

Commentary:

During the Spring-Autumn Period and the Warring States Period, states and the entire country were either run or dominated by feudal lords, nobilities, and great families who inherited their power and wealth from generations of ancestors. Many of these "great families" were rotten, oppressive, abusive, and corrupt. They often ganged together to overthrow or decapitate the sovereign rulers. For example, the motherland of Confucius, the state of Lu (魯國), was dominated by three abusive and corrupt families, Ji Sun Si (季孫氏), Meng Sun Si (孟孫氏), and Su Sun Si (叔孫氏). Confucius detested them.

If the phrase "great families" in the second sentence of Mencius's teaching is interpreted to mean these families, one can then infer that Mencius recommended complicity and cowardice, submission to, and abetment of evil for the purpose of expedience in running a government or the temporary maintenance of political power. This interpretation has indeed poisoned many dynasties of rulers and bureaucrats in China. The fear of offending powerful dignitaries and families has made the country ungovernable. Therefore, this interpretation negates the main theme of the teachings of Mencius.

During the Warring States Period, there was another type of "great family" which arose from the grassroots and was led by scholars, opinion leaders, and lords interested in fostering peace in the country along righteous principles. They were supported by many followers, talented strategists, and strong warriors. A typical example is that of the Mohists (see Section 2 of Endnotes). There were also four other dominant political gangs, led by Meng Chang

273

Jun (孟嘗君), Ping Yuan Jun (平原君), Xin Ling Jun (信陵君), and Chun Shen Jun (春申君). The modern-day analogies of these gangs are political parties. In addition to popular support from the grassroots, these gangs had armies strong enough to defeat the army of a state.

If the phrase "great families" is interpreted to represent the political parties formed from the grassroots during that period, then Mencius's sentence can be interpreted as shown above. Mencius endorsed the power of people rather than the power of corrupt nobilities and families.

Section 7

孟子曰 天下有道 小德役大德 小賢役大賢。天下無道 小役大 弱役強。斯二者天也。順天者存 逆天者亡。齊景公曰 既不能令 又不受命 是絕物也。涕出而女於吳。今也小國師大國而恥受命焉 是猶弟子而恥受命於先師也。如恥之 莫若師文王。師文王 大國五年 小國七年 必為政於天下矣。詩云 商之孫子 其麗不億 上帝既命 侯於周服 侯服於周 天命靡常 殷士膚敏 祼將於京。孔子曰 仁不可為眾也 夫國君好仁 天下無敵。今也欲無敵於天下而不以仁 是猶執熱而不以濯也。詩云 誰能執熱 逝不以濯。

Mencius said, "When a country is properly governed, officials with inferior virtues take orders from senior officials with superior virtues, and the less competent officials take orders from more competent officials. When a country is chaotic, the lower echelon is enslaved by the upper echelon, and the weak is enslaved by the strong. These two phenomena are laws of Tian (Sky). Those who follow the law of Tian (Sky) will survive and those who are against it will perish.

Duke Jing of Qi once said, 'I cannot command them, and I do not want to submit to them. I have no choice.' In tears, he sent off his daughter to be married to the king of Wu.

Nowadays, small states follow the decadent and corrupt ways of large states but are ashamed to be subservient. They are like disciples who want to learn from the teacher but are ashamed to be taught. If they feel ashamed, why not implement the magnanimous policies of King Wen of Zhou? It will only take large states five years and small states seven years to reap the benefits of such policy in their states. The *Book of Poetry* said, 'There were tens of thousands of descendants of the Shang Dynasty. It was divine providence that they had to submit to the Zhou Dynasty. Their submission to Zhou showed that divine providence is never constant. All the elegant and smart elites of the Shang Dynasty needed to pour wine at the altar of Zhou to assist the emperor of Zhou in his ancestorial worship.' Confucius lamented, 'In the eyes of a person with Ren virtue, tens of thousands of enemies are insignificant. If a king advocates Ren, he will be invincible.' If a king wishes to be invincible but does not endorse Ren, he is like a man who touches a hot object without dipping his hand into cold water beforehand. The *Book of Poetry* said, 'Who can touch a hot object without dipping his hand into cold water beforehand?' "

Annotation:

Duke Jing of Qi (齊景公) was the ruler of the state of Qi from 547 to 490 BC. King He Lu (闔閭, 537–496 BC) of the state of Wu (吳國) planned to invade the state of Qi. Duke Jing of Qi considered the state of Wu as barbaric but too formidable to fight against. To

Mencius in Modern Perspectives

fend off the war, Duke Jing reluctantly agreed to the marriage of his daughter to a prince of the state of Wu.

King Wen of Zhou (周文王, circa 1152–1056 BC) founded the Kingdom of Zhou, which was a state of the Shang Dynasty. As a result of King Wen's magnanimous governance policy, his state grew in prominence. He died at the age of 97. His son Ji Fa (姬發), also called King Wu of Zhou (周武王), followed the same policy of his father, overthrew the Shang Dynasty (商朝, circa 1766–1066 BC), and founded the Zhou Dynasty (周朝) in 1066 BC.

Commentary and Modern Perspective:

The key sentence in this section is: "Those who follow the law of Tian (Sky) will survive and those who are against it will perish." This doctrine is still true today.

This section reiterated a Confucian theme: "If a king advocates Ren, he will be invincible."

Section 8

孟子曰 不仁者可與言哉。安其危而利其菑 樂其所以亡者。不仁而可與言 則何亡國敗家之有。有孺子歌曰 滄浪之水清兮 可以濯我纓 滄浪之水濁兮 可以濯我足。孔子曰 小子聽之 清斯濯纓 濁斯濯足矣 自取之也。夫人必自侮 然後人侮之。家必自毀 而後人毀之。國必自伐 而後人伐之。太甲曰 天作孽 猶可違 自作孽 不可活。此之謂也。

Mencius said, "How can we talk to those who are against the Ren principle? They are complacent even in danger and covetous during

Chapter 7: Li Lou (1)

a looming calamity. They enjoy things that will cause their downfall. If it were possible to talk to those who are against the Ren principle, why are there so many failed states and broken families?

A children song said, 'Oh, the water of the river Cang Lang is so pure. I can wash the strings of my cap with it. Oh, the water of the river Cang Lang is so muddy. I can only wash my feet with it.' Upon hearing this, Confucius exclaimed, 'Listen, you guys! Pure water is used to wash the strings of caps. Dirty water is used to wash the feet. It is the quality of water that matters.' Therefore, a person must first debase himself and then others will debase him further. A family must first break itself up, and then other people will break it up further. A country must first ruin itself, and then other countries will destroy it. The *Book of Tai Jia* said, 'It is still possible to elude natural catastrophes. There is no way out of a self-inflicted disaster.' This is what this sentence means."

Annotation:

River Cang Lang (滄浪) is a tributary of the river Han (漢水) in the Hebei Province in China.

King Tang (湯) founded the Shang Dynasty in 1600 BC. He died in 1587 BC. Yi Yin became the prime minister and the guardian-teacher to the subsequent three successors to the throne. The third emperor was the young Emperor Tai Jia (太甲), who was a spoiled kid. He ignored the rules and laws laid down by his ancestor Emperor Tang. To teach Tai Jia a lesson, Yi Yin confined Tai Jia to a cottage erected next to the tomb of Emperor Tang. Tai Jia was asked to study books on governance and politics written by Yi Yin. Tai Jia was not allowed to leave the cottage until he repented. After three years, Tai Jia repented and wrote a confession of his past misbehaviors. This confession constituted the *Book of Tai Jia*.

Commentary:

The key sentences in this section are: 'It is still possible to elude natural catastrophes. There is no way out of a self-inflicted disaster (天作孽猶可違, 自作孽不可活).' These are popular quotes in Chinese literature.

The teaching of the section is relevant to the modern world. We should learn from the following sentences: "Therefore, a person must first debase himself and then other people will debase him further. A family must first break itself up, and then other people will break it up further. A country must first destroy itself, and then other countries will destroy it further."

Section 9

孟子曰 桀紂之失天下也 失其民也。失其民者 失其心也。得天下有道 得其民 斯得天下矣。得其民有道 得其心 斯得民矣。得其心有道 所欲與之聚之 所惡勿施爾也。

民之歸仁也 猶水之就下 獸之走壙也。故為淵驅魚者 獺也。為叢驅爵者 鸇也。為湯武驅民者 桀與紂也。今天下之君 有好仁者 則諸侯皆為之驅矣。雖欲無王 不可得已。

今之欲王者 猶七年之病求三年之艾也。苟為不畜 終身不得。苟不志於仁 終身憂辱 以陷於死亡。詩云 其何能淑 載胥及溺。此之謂也。

Mencius said, "Emperor Jie of the Xia Dynasty and Emperor Zhou of the Shang (Yan) Dynasty lost their empires because they lost the support of their people. They lost the support of their people because they lost the hearts of people. There is a way to win the world. If

Chapter 7: Li Lou (1)

you win the support of people, you win the world. There is a way to win the support of people. If you win their hearts, you win their support. There is a way to win their hearts. You give them what they want and refrain from imposing on them what they hate. It is as simple as this. People turn to benevolent policies like water flowing downstream and wild animals running in the wilderness. Therefore, otters drive fish into deep waters and vultures drive birds into thick forest. Jie and Zhou drove their people towards King Tang of Shang and King Wu of Zhou. Nowadays, if an emperor endorses Ren policies, feudal lords will drive their people towards him. Even if he is reluctant to be an emperor, he cannot avoid the honor. However, an unworthy feudal lord who craves to be an emperor is like curing a seven-year sickness with mugwort straws, which must be weathered for three years. If the feudal lord does not start weathering and storing the mugwort straws now, he will not get the straws for life. Likewise, if one is not determined to practice Ren, he will regret, be in disgrace for life, and die as a loser. The *Book of Poetry* said, 'How can they be good? They will drown everyone.' This is what it means."

Annotation:

Yu (禹, circa 2237–2139 BC) founded the Xia Dynasty (夏朝, circa 2184–1600 BC) in approximately 2184 BC. After approximately 500 years of the dynasty, the 16th successor to the throne was Emperor Jie of Xia (夏桀). He was a brutal tyrant. King Tang (湯) overthrew him and founded the Shang (Yan) Dynasty (商朝) in 1600 BC.

The Shang Dynasty lasted until 1066 BC. The last emperor was another brutal tyrant, Emperor Zhou (紂). He was overthrown by King Wu (周武王) of the Zhou Dynasty (周朝) in 1066 BC.

Both King Tang and King Wu were regarded as saintly kings by Confucians.

Chinese physicians used dried mugwort straws to cure some diseases. It must be dried for years before it can be used.

Commentary:

This section delineates the logical sequence of good governance: benevolent policy, meeting the needs of people, wining their hearts, getting their support, and finally ruling the country. Mencius's philosophy pointed out the essence of good governance.

Section 10

孟子曰 自暴者 不可與有言也。自棄者 不可與有為也。言非禮義 謂之自暴也。吾身不能居仁由義 謂之自棄也。仁 人之安宅也。義 人之正路也。曠安宅而弗居 舍正路而不由 哀哉。

Mencius said, "It is impossible to talk to a person who mutilates himself. It is impossible to work with a person who abandons himself. Talking against the principles of Li and Yi is self-mutilation. Behaving against the principles of Ren and Yi is self-abandonment. Ren is the home of humanity. Yi is the path to that home. It is tragic indeed to vacate a comfortable home and to deviate from a straight path."

Annotation:

The meanings of Ren (仁), Yi (義) and Li (禮) are explained in the Introduction.

Chapter 7: Li Lou (1)

Section 11

孟子曰　道在爾而求諸遠　事在易而求之難。人人親其親　長其長而天下平。

Mencius said, "The way to accomplishment is nearby, but people seek remote paths. There are easy ways to get things done, but people take difficult ways. If everybody loves and cares for his parents and dear ones and respects his elders, the world will be peaceful."

Commentary:

　　This section is relevant today. The modern society lacks the virtue of the love of parents and the respect for elders.

Section 12

孟子曰　居下位而不獲於上　民不可得而治也。獲於上有道　不信於友　弗獲於上矣。信於友有道　事親弗悅　弗信於友矣。悅親有道　反身不誠　不悅於親矣。誠身有道　不明乎善　不誠其身矣。是故誠者　天之道也。思誠者　人之道也。至誠而不動者未之有也。不誠　未有能動者也。

Mencius said, "If a subordinate fails to win the trust of his superiors, he cannot rule his people effectively. There is a way to win the trust of superiors: If one is not trusted by his friends, he will not win the trust of his superiors. There is a way to win the trust of his friends: If he displeases his parents and dear ones, he cannot win the trust of

281

his friends. There is a way to please his parents and dear ones: If he does not behave sincerely, he cannot please his parents and dear ones. There is a way to behave sincerely: If he cannot discern right from wrong, there is no sincerity in his behavior. Therefore, sincerity is a heavenly standard. The pursuance of sincerity is a human standard. There has never been a truly sincere person who does not move others. An insincere person can never move anybody."

Commentary and Modern Perspective:

This section emphasizes the importance of sincerity, which is the basis of the success in establishing good human relations. The sequence of positive inferences is sincerity, filial piety and fraternity, trust by friends, and finally, trust by the boss.

Section 13

孟子曰 伯夷辟紂 居北海之濱 聞文王作 興曰 盍歸乎來 吾聞西伯善養老者。太公辟紂 居東海之濱 聞文王作 興曰 盍歸乎來 吾聞西伯善養老者。二老者 天下之大老也 而歸之 是天下之父歸之也。天下之父歸之 其子焉往。諸侯有行文王之政者 七年之內 必為政於天下矣。

Mencius said, "To escape from the tyranny of Emperor Zhou, Bo Yi migrated to the shore of the North Sea. When he heard about the achievements of Earl Wen of Zhou, he exclaimed, 'I want to move to his state. I heard that he treats elderly people well.' To escape from the tyranny of Emperor Zhou, Jiang Zi Ya migrated to the shore of the East Sea. When he heard about the achievements of Earl

Chapter 7: Li Lou (1)

Wen, he exclaimed, 'I want to move to his state. I heard that he treats elderly people well.' These two elderly persons were reputable sages in the country. Since they wanted to join King Wu, all elderly people also wanted to follow suit. Would their children not follow? If a feudal lord implements the policy of King Wen, his policy can be applied to the entire country in seven years."

Annotation:

The Shang Dynasty last from 1600 BC to 1066 BC. The last emperor was another brutal tyrant, Emperor Zhou (紂). During his reign, a tribe emerged in prominence in the western part of the country. Emperor Zhou gave the title of Earl Wen to the head of this tribe and appointed him to govern other neighboring feudal lords. Therefore, Earl Wen was also called the West Earl (西伯). Earl Wen implemented a magnanimous policy to his subjects. He later started a revolution against the Shang Dynasty. His son, King Wu (周武王), conquered the Shang Dynasty and founded the Zhou Dynasty (周朝) in 1066 BC.

Bo Yi (伯夷) was an ancient saint. He and his brother Shu Qi (叔齊) were two princes of the last duke of the feudal state of Gu Zhu (孤竹國), during the Shang Dynasty (商朝, circa 1766–1066 BC). Bo Yi was the eldest brother, and Shu Qi was the youngest. Before their father died, Shu Qi was nominated to be his successor. Shu Qi abdicated his throne to his eldest brother, Bo Yi, and stressed that the eldest son should be the successor to the throne according to tradition. Bo Yi refused to accept out of respect for his father's wish. Both eventually renounced the throne and migrated to the territory of the state of Zhou (周) (Section 5 of Endnotes narrates the story of Bo Yi).

Jiang Zi Ya (姜子牙, circa 1156–1017 BC) was born in a poor

family. The Great Yu of the Xia Dynasty once enfeoffed the territory Lu (呂) to an ancestor of Jiang Zi Ya. The descendants of the ancestor grew to the tribe of Lu. Another ancestor was later enfeoffed the territory of Shen (申), whose inhabitants had the surname of Jiang (姜). Therefore, Jiang Zi Ya acquired his family name—Jiang. He was also called Lu Shang (呂尚) because he was born to the tribe of Lu. After many centuries, only a few descendants retained their status as noblemen, whereas most had become common peasants. Therefore, Jiang Zi Ya's parents were common peasants.

When he was young, Jiang Zi Ya had been a butcher, a bartender, owner of a restaurant and bar, and a small businessman. He could barely make a living from all his trades. He had also been a junior official in the government of the Shang Dynasty (商朝). Disgusted with the corruption of the Shang government, he resigned shortly after. His wife divorced him because of his poverty and lack of future. Although he lived a hermit-like life until he was 70, he did not give up his aspiration to serve the country in a leadership role. He diligently and relentlessly studied all subjects related to military affairs, politics, governance, philosophy, economics, classics, and so on. He kept waiting for an opportunity to be hired by a good leader until he was 72.

Jiang Zi Ya then became the top strategic advisor to Earl Wen. With the assistance of Jiang Zi Ya, the state of Zhou grew in prominence and reach. Earl Wen then declared himself the King of Zhou and started a revolution against the Shang Dynasty. When King Wen died, Jiang Zi Ya assisted King Wu of Zhou, son of King Wen of Zhou, to fight against the Shang Dynasty under Emperor Zhou (紂王). Jiang Zi Ya was the chief commander of an army and assisted King Wu in defeating Emperor Zhou (Section 7 of Endnotes narrates the story of Jiang Zi Ya).

Chapter 7: Li Lou (1)

Section 14

孟子曰 求也為季氏宰 無能改於其德 而賦粟倍他日。孔子曰 求非我徒也 小子鳴鼓而攻之可也。由此觀之 君不行仁政而富之 皆棄於孔子者也。況於為之強戰。爭地以戰 殺人盈野 爭城以戰 殺人盈城。此所謂率土地而食人肉 罪不容於死。故善戰者服上刑 連諸侯者次之 辟草萊 任土地者次之。

Mencius said, "Ran Qiu was the chief of staff of the Ji Zi family. He could not change the bad behavior of Ji Kang Zi and even recommended to double the taxation on the people of the state of Lu. Confucius said, 'He does not deserve to be my disciple anymore. You guys can openly criticize him with a trumpet.' We see from this episode that, if a ruler violates Ren and his minister assists him to garnish wealth, the minister is condemned by Confucius. How much worse will it be if the minister recommends the waging of a war? In a war for a territorial contention, the battlefield will be filled with dead bodies. In a war to struggle for a city, it will also be filled with dead bodies. Waging a war to capture more land is equivalent to devouring human flesh. Even a death sentence is insufficient to punish such crime to humanity. Therefore, warmongers should be on the top of the list of punishment. Lobbyists who canvass strategic alliance among feudal lords should be next on the list. Those who force peasants to cultivate in undeveloped land and levy heavy taxes on them are next on the list."

Annotation:

Ji Kang Zi (季康子, died 468 BC) was the prime minister of the state of Lu (魯國) during the reign of Ai Gong (哀公) and was the

285

most powerful official. His family, the Ji Si family, was a prominent and wealthy family in the state.

Zi You (子有, also known as Ran You, 冉有, Ran Qiu, 冉求 born in 522 BC) was the chief of staff of the Ji Si family and a disciple of Confucius.

The wealth of the Ji Si family was more than the Duke of Zhou in ancient times. However, Ran Qiu still assisted them to garnish assets from people to further enrich the family. Confucius said, "He does not deserve to be my disciple anymore. You guys can openly criticize him with a trumpet" (see Section 17 of Chapter 11, 先進, of *Confucius Analects*).

Zhou Gong (周公, also known as Duke of Zhou) was the brother of King Wu of Zhou (周武王, died 1043 BC) and the first prime minister of the Zhou Dynasty.

Commentary and Modern Perspective:

During the Warring States Period, numerous wars were waged for the same purpose mentioned in this section and resulted in huge human tragedies. This background prompted Mencius to condemn the waging of wars. This section is still relevant today.

Section 15

孟子曰 存乎人者 莫良於眸子。眸子不能掩其惡。胸中正 則眸子瞭焉。胸中不正 則眸子眊焉。聽其言也 觀其眸子 人焉廋哉。

Mencius said, "The best way to observe the character of a person is to watch the pupils of his eyes. If a person is upright in his heart, his

Chapter 7: Li Lou (1)

pupils appear bright. If his heart is not upright, his pupils appear dull. You listen to his words and watch his pupils. What can he hide?"

Commentary and Modern Perspective:

This is an excellent way to observe whether a person is telling a lie or not. This technique is especially useful in a business setting.

Section 16

孟子曰 恭者不侮人 儉者不奪人。侮奪人之君 惟恐不順焉 惡得為恭儉。恭儉豈可以聲音笑貌為哉。

Mencius said, "A truly respectful person never humiliates others. A truly modest person never plunders others. A king who is fond of humiliating and plundering others demands subservience. How can he be a respectful and modest person? How can one feign respect and modesty with fawning voices and amiable smiles?"

Modern Perspective:

This point is important for all staff working for a boss. If the boss demands absolute subservience and obedience, he cannot be respectful to you. He may also be abusive and arrogant. When you first see him initially during a job interview, he may show amiable smiles and appear friendly. His appearance is pretentious.

Section 17

淳於髡曰 男女授受不親 禮與。

孟子曰 禮也。

曰 嫂溺則援之以手乎。

曰 嫂溺不援 是豺狼也。男女授受不親 禮也。嫂溺援之以手者 權也。

曰 今天下溺矣 夫子之不援 何也。

曰 天下溺 援之以道。嫂溺 援之以手。子欲手援天下乎。

Chun Yu Kun asked, "Is there a rule under Li that a male and female should not touch each other's hands when they give and receive things?"

Mencius replied, "Yes, there is."

Chun Yu Kun asked, "If the sister-in-law of a man is drowning, should he rescue her then?"

Mencius said, "If the sister-in-law is drowning and you do not rescue her, you are a wolf. The rule under Li, that a male and female should not touch each other's hands when they give and receive things, is applicable in general only. When the sister-in-law is drowning, the rescue of her is an exception in an emergency."

Chun Yu Kun asked, "The world is drowning today. Why don't you rescue it then?"

Mencius said, "You rescue the drowning world with magnanimous principles. You rescue the sister-in-law with your hands. Do you want to save the world with your bare hands only?"

Annotation:

Chun Yu Kun (淳于髡) was a minister of the state of Qi under King Wei (齊威王, 378–320 BC) and King Xuan (齊宣王, 350–301 BC) of Qi. Chun Yu Kun was known for his eloquence and humor. King Wei inherited the state of Qi from his father Qi Huan Gong (齊

Chapter 7: Li Lou (1)

桓公, also known as Duke Huan of Qi), who was the leading hegemon among all feudal lords. The state of Qi gradually declined in strength during the early years of the reign of King Wei because he was young and spoiled. He also had an erratic and hot temper. His ministers did not dare to give him good advice and rectify him for fear of severe punishment. Knowing that King Wei liked to listen to jokes and play with puzzles, Chun Yu Kun devised a subtle method to reprimand King Wei. One day, Chun Yu Kun went to see King Wei and said, "There is a big eagle in our country. It has taken a shelter in your palace for a few years already. It does not fly or screech. Do you know why?" King Wei immediately realized that Chun Yu Kun was referring to him, and said emphatically, "This bird does not fly now but when it flies, it will reach the top of the sky. This bird does not screech now, but when it screeches, it will shock everybody." Chun Yu Kun immediately followed through and said, "Your Majesty is very smart. All ministers are waiting to see this bird fly and to hear its screech." King Wei subsequently recognized his past mistakes and repented.

Commentary:

Chun Yu Kun deployed the same subtle tactic to persuade Mencius to work for King Huan of Qi. Mencius repudiated Chun Yu Kun's argument by saying that a drowning world can only be saved by magnanimous principles, not by just one person. Mencius subtly hinted that King Huan of Qi, the boss of Chun Yu Kun, neglected to implement a magnanimous policy in his state.

Another lesson of this section is that one should not be dogmatic. One should exercise his wisdom to determine the right course of action in all circumstances. Saving the life of the sister-in-law is more important than the ancient social norm.

Section 18

公孫丑曰 君子之不教子 何也。

孟子曰 勢不行也。教者必以正。以正不行 繼之以怒 繼之以怒 則反夷矣。夫子教我以正 夫子未出於正也。則是父子相夷也。父子相夷 則惡矣。古者易子而教之。父子之間不責善。責善則離 離則不祥莫大焉。

Gong Sun Chou asked, "People used to say that a Jun Zi does not teach his own son. Why?"

Mencius said, "This is to avoid an embarrassing situation. The teacher must demand his student to adhere strictly to righteous principles. If such demand does not work, the teacher will get angry. The teacher's anger will antagonize the student. He would then think, 'You, old guy, demand my adherence to strict principles, and yet you do not follow them yourself.' Therefore, if a father teaches his son, they will soon be unfriendly. Such unfriendly relationship is undesirable. Therefore, ancient people exchanged their sons, and one parent taught the son of another parent. There should be no admonition between the father and the son. Admonition between them will break their relationship. It will be extremely inauspicious that their relationship is broken."

Annotation:

Gong Sun Chou (公孫丑) was a disciple of Mencius. Some scholars thought that Gong Sun Chou co-authored the book *Mencius* with Mencius himself.

Chapter 7: Li Lou (1)

Commentary and Modern Perspective:

Mencius pointed out a salient reason why home-schooling was inappropriate. If education is only about the teaching of academic and technical knowledge, home-schooling may perhaps work. However, regarding disciplinary training, home-schooling may be deficient in general. (Of course, there are special circumstances where home-schooling is justified and necessary).

Although many well-off, noble, and royal families in ancient China did not send their children to schools, they hired private tutors who were learned and meritorious scholars. To the student, the status of the teacher was as important and high as the parent. In the ceremony of the appointment of the teacher, the student was required to kowtow to the teacher and take a vow of strict obedience to the teacher. The high respect of the teacher has been ingrained in the Chinese culture for millennia, before and after the era of Mencius.

Section 19

孟子曰 事孰為大 事親為大。守孰為大 守身為大。不失其身而能事其親者 吾聞之矣。失其身而能事其親者 吾未之聞也。孰不為事 事親 事之本也。孰不為守 守身 守之本也。曾子養曾皙 必有酒肉。將徹 必請所與。問有餘 必曰 有。曾皙死 曾元養曾子 必有酒肉。將徹 不請所與。問有餘 曰 亡矣。將以復進也。此所謂養口體者也。若曾子 則可謂養志也 事親若曾子者 可也。

Mencius said, "Who are the most important persons to serve? Serving your parents is most important. What is the most important thing to protect? Protecting the quality of your character is most important. I have heard of people who can protect the quality of their character and serve their parents well. I have not heard of people who ruin their character but can serve their parents well. Who does not serve other people? Serving your own parents is fundamental. Who does not protect things? Protecting the quality of your character is fundamental.

When Zheng Zi provided a meal for his father, Zheng Xi, wine and meat were always available in the meal. At the end of it, Zheng Zi then asked to whom the left-over food should be given. When the father asked whether he could take a bit more food, Zheng Zi always said yes. After the death of Zheng Xi, it was Zheng Yuan's turn to provide food for his father, Zheng Zi. Wine and meat were also available in the meal. At the end of it, Zheng Yuan did not ask to whom the left-over food should be given. When Zheng Zi asked whether he could take a bit more food, Zheng Yuan replied that no more food was left. In fact, he wanted to keep the left-over food for the next meal. Zheng Yuan just tried to nourish the body and mouth of his parent. Zheng Zi tried to satisfy the wish of his parent. Zheng Zi's approach in serving his parent is recommendable."

Annotation:

Zheng Zi (曾子, also known as Zheng Shen 曾參, born 505 BC) was a prominent disciple of Confucius, known for his filial piety. He was the author of *The Book of Great Learning* (大學).

Zheng Xi (曾皙) was the father of Zheng Zi and another disciple of Confucius.

Zheng Yuan (曾元) was the son of Zheng Zi.

Chapter 7: Li Lou (1)

Commentary:

Mencius pointed out the spirit of filial piety here. Confucius said, "Most people nowadays think that filial piety is just about feeding your old parents. Even dogs and horses are fed by people. If you do not respect your parents, how do you differentiate feeding your parents from feeding dogs and horses?" (see Section 7 of Chapter 2, 為政, of *Confucius Analects*). Confucius also said, "The most difficult behavior is to show respectful, obedient, and amiable manners. If the young person handles chores on behalf of seniors when there is a need, or if seniors are treated with food and wine when available, are such acts enough to show filial piety according to Zheng Zi? [Of course not!]" (see Section 8 of Chapter 2, 為政, of *Confucius Analects*).

Section 20

孟子曰 人不足與適也 政不足間也。惟大人為能格君心之非。君仁莫不仁 君義莫不義 君正莫不正。一正君而國定矣。

Mencius said, "It is not enough to criticize your king for his mismanagement of staff. It is not enough to reprimand your king for his errors in governance. Only a great man can rectify the mind (and ideology) of his king. Once the king's mind is benevolent, everybody in the country will be benevolent. Once his mind is righteous, everybody in the country will be righteous. Once his mind is proper, everybody in the country will be proper. Once the mind of the king is rectified, the country will be in order."

Commentary:

In this section, Mencius thought that the cause of mismanagement of people and errors in governance policy is a wrong political mindset (and ideology). It is futile to correct every mistake made by the ruler if his mindset is fundamentally wrong. It is more effective to rectify the mindset of the ruler. If his political ideology is based on the principles of benevolence, righteousness, and propriety, everything else in the country will naturally fall into place.

Section 21

孟子曰 有不虞之譽 有求全之毀。

Mencius said, "There are undeserving and unexpected praises. There are nitpicking criticisms."

Or,

Mencius said, "There are undeserving praises of trivial contributions. There are harsh criticisms of near perfect accomplishments."

Or,

Mencius said, "There are praises for one's work, even though he does not expect them. There are criticisms on one's work, even though he aims at perfection."

Or,

Mencius said, "There are praises for one's work, even though he does not expect them. There are curses on a person who renounces honor and strives for existence."

Commentary and Modern Perspective:

This famous quote by Mencius can be interpreted in many ways. The above shows four possible interpretations, and the top three are more popular. All of them make sense.

The lesson from the first two quotes is that we should not expect the world to be fair. There are people awarded with recognition, fame, appointment to high positions, promotion, and prizes from trivial and undeserving contribution to society. They earned such awards through disgraceful means. On the other hand, there are great people who have contributed immensely to the society or people who have done a near-perfect job. Yet, they often receive harsh and nitpicking criticisms. Another lesson from the first two quotes is that we should not be moved by praises or criticisms because these are often unfair and superficial. If we carry on with our righteous mission and continue to do good work, praises or criticisms are irrelevant.

The lesson from the third quote is that we should try our best to do good work and stay low-key. We should not expect any praise. Our good work will one day be recognized beyond our expectations. We should also accept the fact that, despite our perfect work, fault-finding criticisms will always be made. Not receiving praise should not discourage our effort. Harsh criticisms should not deter us from trying our best.

The first sentence in the fourth quote teaches the same lesson as above. The second sentence is a reminder that our infamy will be in the historical records if we renounce honor and bend against righteousness to strive for existence. Such behavior is common in the modern world. Mencius told us that our virtuous character should not be compromised.

Section 22

孟子曰 人之易其言也 無責耳矣。

Mencius said, "A glib and flippant talker has no sense of responsibility."

Modern Perspective:

We need to beware of glib and flippant talkers—salesmen, our dates, business partners, politicians, and so on. Their sense of responsibility is doubtful.

Section 23

孟子曰 人之患在好為人師。

Mencius said, "A common flaw of most people is that they like to teach others."

Modern Perspective:

This is quite true. This flaw impedes our relationship with others. In a work environment, this flaw alienates our colleagues. In a family setting, this flaw hurts the relationship between spouses and siblings.

Chapter 7: Li Lou (1)

Section 24

樂正子從於子敖之齊。樂正子見孟子。
　孟子曰　子亦來見我乎。
　曰　先生何為出此言也。
　曰　子來幾日矣。
　曰　昔昔。
　曰　昔昔　則我出此言也　不亦宜乎。
　曰　舍館未定。
　曰　子聞之也　舍館定　然後求見長者乎。
　曰　克有罪。

Yue Zheng Zi followed Wang Zi Ao and arrived at the state of Qi.
　Yue Zheng Zi came to see Mencius, who asked, "Do you care to come to see me?"
　Yue Zheng Zi said, "Master, why do you say these words?"
　Mencius asked, 'How many days have you been here?"
　Yue Zheng Zi replied, "A few days ago."
　Mencius said, "A few days ago! Am I right to say such words?"
　Yue Zheng Zi replied, "I have to settle down in the hotel."
　Mencius said, "Have you ever heard that a student should first settle down in his hotel before coming to see his teacher?"
　Yue Zheng Zi said, "It is my fault."

Annotation:

　Yue Zheng Zi (樂正子) was a disciple of Mencius.
　Wang Zi Ao (王子敖, also known as Wang Huan 王驩) was a powerful minister of the state of Qi.

Commentary:

This section illustrates that ancient Chinese expected a high level of respect of the teacher from the student.

Section 25

孟子謂樂正子曰 子之從於子敖來 徒餔啜也。我不意子學古之道 而以餔啜也。

Mencius said to Yue Zheng Zi, "You followed Wang Zi Ao to come to the state of Qi only because of food and drinks. I cannot accept that, having learned ancient doctrines, you acted to just get food and drinks."

Commentary:

Mencius expected his disciples to have a noble mission, which is more than just making a living.

Section 26

孟子曰 不孝有三 無後為大。舜不告而娶 為無後也 君子以為猶告也。

Mencius said, "There are three unfilial behaviors. Having no children is the worst of them. Shun did not consult his parents before his marriage because he worried of having no children. A Jun Zi should keep this point in mind."

Chapter 7: Li Lou (1)

Annotation:

Ancient Chinese considered the following three behaviors to be unfilial: (1) causing one's parents to act improperly, (2) idling, (3) staying single and having no children. The third behavior was regarded most unfilial because, in ancient times, heritage and the propagation of the gene pool, ancestorial family, the clan, and the state were important.

Section 27

孟子曰 仁之實 事親是也。義之實 從兄是也。智之實 知斯二者弗去是也。禮之實 節文斯二者是也。樂之實 樂斯二者 樂則生矣。生則惡可已也 惡可已 則不知足之蹈之 手之舞之。

Mencius said, "A concrete manifestation of the Ren virtue is filial piety. A concrete manifestation of the Yi virtue is obedience to your elder brothers. The concrete manifestation of wisdom is to understand Ren and Yi and hold onto them. The concrete manifestation of Li is the practice of Ren and Yi in a disciplined and civilized way. The concrete manifestation of music is the joy derived from the practice of Ren and Yi virtues. Once this joy is cultivated, it is unstoppable. This unstoppable joy will unconsciously motivate the feet to dance and the hands to wave."

Annotation:

The Introduction has explained the meaning of Ren, Yi, Li, and wisdom and their relationship. The Introduction has also explained the relationship among these virtues.

Commentary:

This section says that Ren, Yi, Li, and wisdom are not just rhetoric. There are concrete starting steps to cultivate these virtues, and these steps are filial piety and fraternity. Since parents and siblings are closest to a person, it is natural and easiest to practice Ren, Yi, and Li with them in mind. If a person treats his or her parents badly and is unfriendly with other members of his or her family, then his or her character is questionable.

Section 28

孟子曰 天下大悅而將歸己。視天下悅而歸己 猶草芥也。惟舜為然。不得乎親 不可以為人 不順乎親 不可以為子。舜盡事親之道而瞽瞍底豫 瞽瞍底豫而天下化 瞽瞍底豫而天下之為父子者定。此之謂大孝。

Mencius said, "Suppose that people in the world are pleased to support you and want to become your subjects. Only Shun can regard such a great achievement as a bundle of grass. Shun thought that if one could not win the heart of his parents, he did not deserve to be a man, and that if one did not obey his parents, he did not deserve to be a son. Shun tried his best to be filial, and eventually pleased his father Gu Sou. The conversion of the attitude of his father set a model for everyone in the world. Such an example solidified the bondage between parents and children. This is called great filial piety."

Chapter 7: Li Lou (1)

Annotation:

Shun (舜, circa 2294–2184 BC) was a minister of Yao (堯, circa 2356–2255 BC). Before he died, Yao appointed Shun as his successor. Both were regarded ancient saintly kings.

There was a legend about Shun. His father, Gu Sou (瞽瞍), was stubborn, his stepmother, Yin (嚚), was wicked, and his stepbrother, Xiang (象), was arrogant. They plotted to kill Shun a few times but failed. On one occasion, they asked Shun to repair the roof of a granary tower. After Shun had climbed up the roof, they set fire to the granary tower. Shun escaped the fire by using his big hat as a parachute and jumped down unscathed. On another occasion, Gu Sou and Xiang asked Shun to descend a well to clear the water channel. After Shun had descended the well, Gu and Xiang poured mud and threw stone into the well to bury Shun alive. Fortunately, Shun was able to dig a tunnel from the well and emerged from another spot. Shun forgave their atrocity, continued to be filial to his father and to love his stepbrother. The legend even said that Tian (Sky) was impressed and sent elephants to help Shun plough his farmland and birds to help him sow the seeds. Emperor Yao heard about Shun's virtue and appointed him to be a minister. Emperor Yao even set up the marriages of his two daughters with Shun. Before Yao died, he appointed Shun to be his successor. After Shun became the emperor, he returned home and paid homage to his father. Shun also granted Xiang a feudal lordship.

Chapter 8: Li Liao (2)

Section 1

孟子曰 舜生於諸馮 遷於負夏 卒於鳴條 東夷之人也。文王生於岐周 卒於畢郢 西夷之人也。地之相去也 千有餘里 世之相後也 千有餘歲。得志行乎中國 若合符節 先聖後聖 其揆一也。

Mencius said, "Shun was born in Zhu Feng, moved to Fu Xia, and died in Ming Tiao. He was a native of an eastern barbaric tribe. King Wen was born in mount Qi Zhou and died Bi Ying. He was a native of a western barbaric tribe. The two places were thousands of miles apart, and they lived about a thousand years apart. After they got the power to implement their visions in their countries, their policies danced to the same tune and beat. The policies of the earlier and later saints followed the same principle."

Annotation:

    Zhu Feng (諸馮) and Fu Xia (負夏) were counties in modern-day Shandong Province.
    Ming Tiao (鳴條) was a county in the modern-day Shanxi Province.
    Qi Zhou (岐周) was a county in the modern-day Mount Qi in Shaanxi Province.
    Bi Ying (畢郢) was a county in modern-day Shaanxi Province.

Chapter 8: Li Liao (2)

Section 2

子產聽鄭國之政 以其乘輿濟人於溱洧。

　　孟子曰 惠而不知為政。歲十一月徒杠成 十二月輿梁成 民未病涉也。君子平其政 行辟人可也。焉得人人而濟之。故為政者 每人而悅之 日亦不足矣。

Zi Chan was the prime minister of the state of Cheng. He carried common people across the Zhen and Wei rivers in his own carriage. Mencius said, "Zi Chan's charitable act was trivial, and he did not know the essence of running a government. If foot-bridges were built in the eleventh month of the year and carriage bridges were built in twelfth month of the year, his people needed not take the trouble of wading the water. If a ruler's policies are fair and beneficial to his people at large, it is acceptable to clear the road to give way for the carriage of the ruler. How can he carry each person across the river? If a ruler wants to please everybody, he will not have enough days to do so."

Annotation:

　　Zi Chan (子產, died 552 BC, also known as Gong Sun Qiao, 公孫僑) was a prominent statesman and reputed prime minister of the state of Zheng (鄭國).

　　The Zhen and Wei rivers are in the north-east and east, respectively, of the modern-day Henan Province.

Commentary:

　　This section has an implication that a government policy should focus on the big picture rather than minor benevolence to individual interest groups. The same applies to a company and an individual.

Section 3

孟子告齊宣王曰 君之視臣如手足 則臣視君如腹心。君之視臣如犬馬 則臣視君如國人。君之視臣如土芥 則臣視君如寇讎。

　王曰 禮 為舊君有服 何如斯可為服矣。

　曰 諫行言聽 膏澤下於民。有故而去 則君使人導之出疆 又先於其所往 去三年不反 然後收其田里。此之謂三有禮焉。如此 則為之服矣。今也為臣。諫則不行 言則不聽 膏澤不下於民。有故而去 則君搏執之 又極之於其所往 去之日 遂收其田里。此之謂寇讎。寇讎何服之有。

Mencius told King Xuan of Qi, "If the king regards his ministers as his limbs, they will regard him as their hearts. If the king regards his ministers as dogs and horses, they will regard him as nobody. If the king regards his ministers as dirt, they will regard him as a robber and an enemy.

King Xuan asked, "According to Li, ministers must wear mourning attire at the death of their deceased king. How can a king motivate his minister to wear mourning attire at his death?"

Mencius said, "Suppose that a minister's good advice is taken by the king so that his people are benefited. Suppose that when the minister needs to resign for some reason, the king arranges an escort to accompany the minister beyond the border of the country, provides accommodation for the minister at his destination, and refrains from confiscating the enfeoffed land and residence of the minister, unless the minister does not return after three years. These are the three proper actions of the king according to Li. If so, his ministers will voluntarily wear mourning attire at his death. Nowadays, admonishments by ministers are not followed, their advice is ignored, and their good suggestions cannot benefit the people of the country. When a frustrated minister resigns, he and his family members are immediately arrested, his foreign residence is pillaged, and his land is confiscated on the day of his departure. Such treatments are akin to robbery and antagonism. Why would a minister wear mourning attire in memory of a robber and enemy?"

Modern Perspective:

Many companies treat departing employees with similarly unfriendly and humiliating practices. Employees who are laid off are given a short time to pack up their belongings and are escorted by security guards to the exit of the building, as if the employees are criminals. The departing employees are not allowed to bid farewell to colleagues. The management of these companies do not realize that they are burning the bridge of friendship with departing employees. What goes around comes around. The departing employees may one day become important customers or endorsers of the old company.

Section 4

孟子曰　無罪而殺士　則大夫可以去。無罪而戮民　則士可以徙。

Mencius said, "If a king kills innocent officials, top ministers should resign immediately. If a king kills innocent people, officials should quit the country."

Modern Perspective:

It is lamentable that, nowadays, many officials and executives in high places are complicit with their wicked bosses.

Section 5

孟子曰 君仁莫不仁 君義莫不義。

Mencius said, "If the king is benevolent, all people below him will be benevolent. If the king is righteous, all people below him will be righteous."

Modern Perspective:

A leader should set a good example for his people.

Section 6

孟子曰 非禮之禮 非義之義 大人弗為。

Mencius said, "A great man does not practice acts which fake Li and Yi."

Section 7

孟子曰 中也養不中 才也養不才 故人樂有賢父兄也。如中也棄不中 才也棄不才 則賢不肖之相去 其間不能以寸。

Mencius said, "Meritorious and achieved people should enlighten

Chapter 8: Li Liao (2)

those who are not. Capable people should educate those who are not. Therefore, people are glad to have meritorious parents and elder brothers (and seniors in the family and clan). If meritorious people abandon those who are not, and capable people abandon those who are not, the gap between the meritorious and unworthy groups is less than a few inches."

Annotation:

The original text in Chinese of the first phrase here can also be translated as: "People who have attained the virtuous standard according to Zhong Yong." For brevity, this sentence is translated as: "Meritorious and achieved people." Zhong Yong (中庸) is a doctrine described in the *Book of the Mean*, *The Doctrine of the Mean*, or *Book of Zhong Yong*. Zhong means the right path, not devious, unbiased, not in excess in one way or the other. Yong means ordinary, firm, unwavering, and perpetual truth.

Commentary:

Mencius emphasized the importance of education and the enlightening of the mass. If meritorious and capable people mind their own business only, what good are they? They are then not different from mediocre people.

Section 8

孟子曰 人有不為也 而後可以有為。

Mencius said, "A person should know what he should not do before he can achieve what he ought to do."

Commentary:

Mencius's advice seems negative, but it is salient, prudent, and moral. When one is confronted with a myriad of choices, he must draw a boundary to rule out immoral, high-risk, detrimental activities. He must exercise his wisdom to decide what is right versus wrong and appropriate versus inappropriate. Without such wisdom, he cannot make the right choice and have the conviction to follow through his right choice.

Section 9

孟子曰 言人之不善 當如後患何。

Mencius said, "How would you deal with the negative consequences arising from your slander against others?"

Commentary and Modern Perspective:

Mencius gave a good advice. This should be a motto placed on our desktops.

Section 10

孟子曰 仲尼不為已甚者。

Mencius said, "Confucius refrained from extreme behaviors."

Section 11

孟子曰 大人者 言不必信 行不必果 惟義所在。

Mencius said, "A great person may not (stubbornly) keep his words and act resolutely, provided that he acts according to Yi principles."

Commentary:

The original text in Chinese has many interpretations, and therefore, can be translated in many ways. The above translation highlights that the focus should be on Yi principle. The objective of maintaining trust by keeping one's words and following through one's action should be determined by and secondary to Yi (righteous) principles. Although Confucians consider trustworthiness a virtue, they do not endorse stubborn, blind trust, and dogmatism. Since nobody is perfect and has perfect foresight, and since the environment is dynamic, one may discover that his original promise has led or will lead him to act against Ren and Yi, or that he has been misled by wicked counterparts. By that time, he should not continue to err for the sake of keeping his promise and honor. If trust is not guided by the principle of Yi, even gangsters who keep their evil promises to their comrades could be regarded as having the virtue of trustworthiness. Mencius, in fact, repeated Confucius's point illustrated by a dialogue between Zi Gong and Confucius:

Zi Gong asked, "What qualities must one have to entitle him to be called an intellectual and honorable official?" Confucius said, "He must conduct himself with a sense of shame. When he is sent as an envoy to other countries, he must not disgrace his mission. If he can do so, he deserves to be called an intellectual and honorable official." Zi Gong then asked, "May I ask what qualities are secondary?" Confucius said, "He must be praised for being filial to his clan and for being brotherly with his fellow men." Zi Gong asked further, "What is next?" Confucius said, "He talks honestly, keeps his promises, and follows through with his actions. However, even some stubborn Xiao Ren's do so! Even so, these are still good secondary qualities."

It is important to note the word *may*, the condition "provided that he acts according to Yi principles," and the word *stubbornly* in parenthesis in Mencius's sentence. Mencius did not say that a person can make frivolous, deceptive, and cunning promises a priori when he utters his words, or act with an ulterior motive. One should always speak his mind, which should always be guided by Yi principles. One should always act with genuine and righteous motives.

Therefore, the following interpretation and translation of the original text is problematic:

Mencius said, "A great person does not think beforehand of his words that they may be sincere, nor of his actions that they may be resolute. It is alright if he acts according to righteous principles."

Another interpretation and translation of the original text is also problematic:

Mencius said, "A great person does not need to keep his words in every promise he makes, and follow through in every action he takes, provided that he acts according to Yi principles."

This interpretation implies that a person can determine a priori that some promises he makes do not need to be kept, and some actions need not be followed through. Since other people do not know his mind and what percentage of promises he will keep, nobody will ever trust him.

Unfortunately, Mencius's sentence has been misinterpreted by several scholars to mean that it is acceptable to be cunning and deceptive sometimes, and that the end goal of Yi thus justifies wicked means. Many Chinese have been misguided in the past by this misinterpretation.

Chapter 8: Li Liao (2)

Another interpretation and translation of the original text in Chinese is as follows:

Mencius said, "For a great person, his words do not need to be trusted by others and his actions may not produce desirable results. It is alright if he sticks to Yi principles."

This translation makes sense because it re-iterates the same theme in previous chapters: If one acts according to Yi principles, other people's lack of faith in his endeavors and the uncertain future should not deter him from his goals. Confucius once said that if on reflection he was wrong, he would not harass a commoner, but if on reflection he was right, he would not be afraid of confronting an army of tens of thousands of men (see Section 2 of Chapter 3 above).

Section 12

孟子曰 大人者 不失其赤子之心者也。

Mencius said, "A great person retains a pure heart like that of an infant."

Commentary:

Many religions and philosophers teach the same point above.

Section 13

孟子曰 養生者不足以當大事 惟送死可以當大事。

Mencius said, "Supporting and nourishing the livelihood of your parents is a commonplace norm. Arranging a proper funeral for your deceased parents is a big deal."

311

Mencius in Modern Perspectives

Section 14

孟子曰　君子深造之以道　欲其自得之也。自得之　則居之安。居之安　則資之深。資之深　則取之左右逢其原　故君子欲其自得之也。

Mencius said, "A Jun Zi should follow a proper course to learn deep and broad knowledge with the goal of self-improvement, enlightenment, and internalizing it into his inner nature. After the knowledge is internalized, it will be firm and unwavering. After it is firmly secured, it will continue to accumulate and grow. Having such vast and deep knowledge, you can then be so resourceful in handling all matters, like the ability to collect underground water from all sources on the left and on the right. Therefore, a Jun Zi wishes to internalize his knowledge."

Commentary:

The word *knowledge* here includes not only technical know-how and skills but also the enlightenment of truth and accumulation of virtues. The key point of this section is the internalization of knowledge so that it becomes second nature of oneself and it is embedded deep in one's mind (and soul). The main goal of knowledge is not to impress others, earn credit from others, get accreditation for a professional qualification, compete, or make more money. It should be for self-improvement, self-fulfillment, and contribution to the world

The analogy of a tree can help to further explain the spirit of this section. Mencius said that we need to strive to acquire deep and broad knowledge. A tree needs to grow its branches to a wide span and its roots deep into the ground. The proper way to learn is

Chapter 8: Li Liao (2)

relentless effort, persistence, and endurance of hardship. A tree grows relentlessly to where there is sunlight and endures storms and snowfall. The accumulated knowledge is for self-improvement. A tree acquires its nourishments for its survival and growth. After the knowledge is internalized, it can then be firm and unwavering. A grown-up tree can withstand storms and cold winter. After the knowledge is firmly secured, it can continue to accumulate and grow deeper. A firm tree can then grow its root deeper. Such vast and deep knowledge can then be applied. A mature tree can then produce flowers and fruit. You can be versatile in handling all matters, like the ability to collect irrigated water from all sources on the left and on the right. The tree can then receive nourishments from sunlight and underground water from all sources. This analogy explains that the entire process is natural. Therefore, the acquisition of knowledge by a Jun Zi should be steadfast and natural. If the knowledge has not been internalized, it is not part of him and will soon be forgotten or abandoned.

Section 15

孟子曰 博學而詳說之 將以反說約也。

Mencius said, "The ultimate goal of extensive learning and thorough analyses is to discover basic and simple truth."

Commentary:

Only the very learned can appreciate this sentence. If one understands this sentence from experience, one is already enlightened and achieved.

Section 16

孟子曰 以善服人者 未有能服人者也。以善養人 然後能服天下。天下不心服而王者 未之有也。

Mencius said, "If one tries to subdue others with his excellence and advantage, he will fail. If one tries to nourish others with his excellence and advantage, others will submit to him willingly. It is impossible for anyone to become a ruler without earning the heart of his people."

Section 17

孟子曰 言無實 不祥。不祥之實 蔽賢者當之。

Mencius said, "Words not in line with reality (or untrue) are inauspicious. Those who hinder virtuous people should be responsible for the resulting inauspicious consequences."

Section 18

徐子曰 仲尼亟稱於水 曰 水哉 水哉。何取於水也。

孟子曰 原泉混混 不舍晝夜。盈科而後進 放乎四海 有本者如是 是之取爾。苟為無本 七八月之間雨集 溝澮皆盈。其涸也 可立而待也。故聲聞過情 君子恥之。

Xu Zi said, "Confucius repeatedly praised the nature of water and exclaimed, 'Oh, water. Oh, water.' What did he find in water to praise?"

Chapter 8: Li Liao (2)

Mencius said, "Water gushes out from the springs day and night, fills up depressed ground, advances, and flows to the ocean. Everything with an origin is like water. Therefore, Confucius took water as an example. If the water has no original source, like showers during July and August, the ditches and water channels are flooded but the water will dry up in a short time. Therefore, a Jun Zi is ashamed of an undeserving reputation that will soon fade away."

Annotation:

Xu Zi (徐子, also known as Xu Pi 徐辟) was a disciple of Mencius.

Confucius said, "A wise person loves to behave like water [being versatile and flexible], whereas a person with Ren virtue loves to behave like a mountain [being steadfast, firm, and unwavering]" (see Section 23 of Chapter 6, 雍也, of *Confucius Analects*).

Commentary:

In this section, Mencius hinted that many other schools of thought did not have proper origins. He maintained that Confucianism originated from the saintly kings like Yao, Shun, Yu, and King Wen of Zhou, and many ancient sages. Because of this, the philosophy of Confucianism will not be dried up soon.

Section 19

孟子曰 人之所以異於禽於獸者幾希 庶民去之 君子存之。舜明於庶物 察於人倫 由仁義行 非行仁義也。

Mencius said, "There are only a few differences between humans and animals. The common people throw away such differences, whereas Jun Zi's keep them. Shun understood many things and clearly noted their relations with humanity. His practice of Ren and Yi was motivated by his innate nature. He did not practice Ren and Yi because he was expected to do so."

Commentary:

This section points out two core themes of Confucianism. The first is the difference between humans and animals, and the second is that Ren and Yi are two innate virtues of humans.

Regarding the first point, Mencius acknowledged that animals and humans are similar in most aspects. They are creatures with physical bodies, various sensory cognitions, and various mental functions. They have common needs and desires for food, sex, health, comfort, shelter, and survival. Mencius did not reject such needs and desires. However, Mencius maintained that there are important differences that make humans superior to animals. However, he did not elaborate on what such differences were. Referring to other chapters of his book, we know that the differences are the innate nature of Ren, Yi, Li, and human wisdom. Without such innate nature, there is no difference between humans and animals. In Section 4 of Chapter 5 above, Mencius said, "It is human nature that when people are well fed, warmly clad, and comfortably housed, they will behave like animals if they lack moral education." If we are like common people who care about food, clothes, shelter, comfort, and basic survival, we are just animals.

Every person is born with the seeds of Ren and Yi virtues. Jun Zis and saints keep and grow them to fruition so that it is part of their good nature to practice Ren and Yi voluntarily. They practice

Chapter 8: Li Liao (2)

Ren and Yi without the objective of conformance to social norms. This is the fundamental theme of Mencius's philosophy.

Section 20

孟子曰 禹惡旨酒而好善言。湯執中 立賢無方。文王視民如傷 望道而未之見。武王不泄邇 不忘遠。周公思兼三王 以施四事 其有不合者 仰而思之 夜以繼日 幸而得之 坐以待旦。

Mencius said, "Yu of the Xia hated gourmet wine and loved reasonable words. Tang of the Shang upheld balanced policies and hired talented ministers without regard to their origins. King Wen of Zhou treated his people like caring for the wounded and looked far beyond current horizon. King Wu of Zhou did not spoil nor abuse people close to him and did not ignore people far away. Duke of Zhou tried to emulate the kings of these three eras and follow their virtuous deeds. If he had any doubt regarding the appropriateness of these behaviors, he thought them over day and night. If he was fortunate enough to find a solution, he stayed awake during the night and executed it immediately after daybreak."

Annotation:

Yu (禹, circa 2237–2139 BC) founded the Xia Dynasty (夏朝, circa 2184–1600 BC) in about 2184 BC. King Tang (湯) founded the Shang (Yan) Dynasty (商朝) in 1600 BC. King Wen of Zhou (周文王, 1152–1056 BC) founded the Kingdom of Zhou, which was a state of the Shang Dynasty. As a result of King Wen's magnanimous governance policy, his state grew in prominence. He died at the age of 97. His son, Ji Fa (姬發), also called King Wu of

Zhou (周武王, died 1043 BC), followed the same policy of his father, overthrew the Shang Dynasty (商朝, 1766–1066 BC), and founded the Zhou Dynasty (周朝) in 1066 BC. Zhou Gong (周公, also known as Duke of Zhou) was the younger brother of King Wu of Zhou (周武王) and the first prime minister of the Zhou Dynasty. These historical figures were regarded as saintly kings and rulers.

The *History Book of the Warring State Period* (戰國策) recorded an episode that a good friend of Yu produced a gourmet wine. After drinking it, Yu exclaimed, "This is indeed a great wine!" He later told people, "There will surely be rulers in future generations who will ruin their kingdoms because of their indulgence in wine." Yu then stayed away from the wine maker and abstained from drinking good wine.

Commentary and Modern Perspective:

In this section, Mencius gave examples of meritorious rulers and their behaviors.

Such exemplary behaviors are still relevant for rulers today: abstinence from extravagance, humility to listen to good advice, balanced policies, no discrimination, caring of people, long-term vision, no favoritism and nepotism, broad horizon, and earnestness.

Section 21

孟子曰 王者之跡熄而詩亡 詩亡然後春秋作。晉之乘 楚之檮杌 魯之春秋 一也。其事則齊桓 晉文 其文則史。孔子曰 其義則丘竊取之矣。

Mencius said, "Since King Ping of Zhou moved eastward, he could

Chapter 8: Li Liao (2)

not govern feudal lords. Poetry in praise of good government or condemning bad government no longer prevailed. Therefore, the Spring-Autumn Annals took its place. The history books *Sheng of the state of Jin*, *Tao Wu of the state of Chu*, and *Spring-Autumn Annals of the state of Lu* were similar in purpose. They recorded the history of hegemons, such as Duke Huan of Qi and Duke Wen of Jin. The facts were taken from records of various ministries of history. Confucius said, 'I have copied the records from various ministries of history onto the *Spring-Autumn Annals*.'"

Annotation:

King Wu of Zhou (周武王, died 1043 BC), whose father was King Wen of Zhou (周文王, 1152–1056 BC), overthrew Emperor Zhou and founded the Zhou Dynasty in 1066 BC. From 1066 BC to 770 (or 771) BC, the new dynasty was called the Western Zhou Dynasty (西周) because its capital was located at Hao Jing (鎬京) in the west of China. When feudalism was introduced, members of the royal family, prominent ministers, and generals were classified into five nobility ranks: duke, marquess, earl, viscount, and baron. Dukes and marquesses were each enfeoffed a territory of one hundred square miles; earls were each enfeoffed a territory of seventy square miles; and viscounts and barons were each enfeoffed a territory of fifty square miles. The feudal lords had autonomy over their enfeoffed territories, which were de facto independent states. The states had their own armies, which had to be smaller than that of the central government. The states had to pay taxes and tributes to the central government and respond to summons by the emperor. They also had the responsibility of defending the central government when it was under foreign attack. After 12 successions of emperors of the Western Zhou Dynasty, nomads from the West invaded the country, pillaged the capital, and killed King You (周幽王) of Zhou in 770 BC. His successor, King Ping (周平王), moved the capital eastward to Luo Yi (雒邑, modern-day Luo Yang 洛陽 in Henan Province 河南). This began the Eastern Zhou Dynasty (東周). During this regime, the emperor of Zhou lost effective control over many feudal states. They paid homage to the emperor only ceremonially. Feudal states fought among themselves, and small states were conquered, pillaged, and annexed by larger states. Historians call this period, which stretched from 771 to 476 BC, the Spring-Autumn period because Confucius wrote the Spring-Autumn Annals, a chronicle of the state of Lu (魯國), between 722 to 479 BC.

After King Wu founded the Zhou Dynasty, his brother, Zhou Gong (周公, also known as Duke of Zhou) became the prime minister. He introduced the Li and music frameworks as governance tools. The Introduction has explained the essence of the Li system. Duke of Zhou also thought that the sounds of Sky and Earth (such as the sounds of wind, storm, thunder, rain, waves, birds, rivers and so on) were the communication between Tian (Sky) and humans. The combination of these sounds was a musical symphony that inspired and enlightened the hearts of people. At times, it bestowed joy to people, and at other times, it reprimanded and punished people for their sins. In addition, music was a common language for communication among people. Good music resonated in the hearts of people, nurtured them towards purity and virtue, and unified them. Filthy music, on the other hand, rotted, agitated, and provoked people. The ruler, therefore, could tell from the content and quality of folk songs, dances, and instrumental music the culture of the governed people, their joy or pain, satisfaction or grievances, and loyalty or anger. Therefore, the ruler must ensure that good music was propagated in the country. He must also survey folk songs and note their content and subtle meanings. Because of such belief, Duke of Zhou instituted an elaborate system of music and set up the ministry of music. This consisted of expert musicians, regulators, and educators. The ministry was responsible for composing good music that promoted harmony and submission to Tian (Sky) and Earth, respect for ancestors, and loyalty to the regime. In addition, they were also responsible for propagating good culture through music. Lastly, they were also responsible for the survey and compilation of folk songs in all feudal states for reference by the central government (this was analogous to modern-day opinion surveys).

Most musical performances were accompanied by songs. The lyrics of songs conveyed subtle messages that reflected the opinions of people. These lyrics were then called poetry. They contained subtle messages in praise of good governance or criticisms against bad governance. *The Book of Poetry* (詩經) was compiled during the Zhou Dynasty (周朝, circa 1043 to 256 BC) as a collection of national folk songs (國風), royal paeans (大雅), royal poems (小雅), and hymns (頌). The official national folk songs were a collection of songs praising the great virtues, magnanimity, and achievements of King Wen and King Wu, the founders of the Zhou Dynasty. These poems reminded later generations of rulers and the populace to follow the same footsteps of their ancestors. Royal paeans and royal poems were chanted and recited in formal meetings of the emperor and princes and reminded them of the good historical records of their ancestors. Hymns were sung in temples during ceremonies of sacrifice in the worship of Sky, Earth, and ancestors.

After King Ping of Zhou moved eastward and founded the Eastern Zhou Dynasty, he lost the support and respect from feudal lords. They gradually abandoned both the Li and music system instituted during the Western Zhou Dynasty. The ministry of music was degraded, and their role of monitoring public opinions was reassigned to the minister of history. Many music masters lost their jobs. This phenomenon was mentioned in the *Confucius Analects*: "The grand music master, Zhi (摯), went to the state of Qi. Gan (干), the bandmaster of the second course of the meal went to the state of Chu. Liao (繚), the bandmaster at the third course of the meal, went to the state of Cai. Que (缺), the bandmaster of the fourth course of the meal, went to the state of Qin. Fang Shu (方叔), the drum master, moved to the banks of the Yellow River. Wu (武), the master of the castanets, went to the banks of the Han River. Yang (陽), the assistant music master, and Xiang (襄), the master of the stone percussion, went to the seaside" (see Section 9 of Chapter 18, 微子, of *Confucius Analects*). Over time, music gradually lost its role of nurturing the public and monitoring the performance of their rulers.

The decline in the role of music led to the diminished role of poetry, which no longer became a tool for educating Ren and Yi to people, and monitoring rulers. The political contents of poetry had faded away during the era of Confucius.

Recognizing the lack of tools for praising meritorious deeds and reprimanding evil, Confucius wrote the Spring-Autumn Annals, a collection of historical records of the Spring-Autumn Period. This history book first focused on the history of the state of Lu (魯國), and then extended to the history of other states. In a subtle manner, it praised meritorious actions according to the principles of Ren and Yi of states and their feudal lords, and condemned deeds against Ren and Yi. Since the central government was powerless in regulating feudal lords, Confucius thought that a fair history book would be an effective tool to rein in misbehaving feudal lords and teach future generations of rulers about good governance and universal law of morality.

Confucius was humble in stating that he stole the historical records from ministers of history of various states and confessed that he had not added or deleted any facts. Therefore, **Confucius** said, "I just narrate the classics and do not create new ideas. I believe in and appreciate ancient culture" (see Section 1 of Chapter 7, 述而, of *Confucius Analects*).

Sheng (乘) of the state of Jin (晉國), Tao Wu (檮杌) of the state of Chu, and Spring-Autumn (春秋) were names of history books.

Section 22

孟子曰 君子之澤五世而斬 小人之澤五世而斬。予未得為孔子徒也 予私淑諸人也。

Mencius said, "The influence of a Jun Zi does not last more than five generations. Likewise, the influence of a Xia Ren does not last more than five generations. Although I do not have the opportunity to be a disciple of Confucius, I have learned his teachings from his followers."

Annotation:

A *Jun Zi* (君子) is used in Chinese scholarly texts to mean a gentleman, a person of noble character, a prominent and respectable person in society, or a person who upholds virtuous principles. A *Xiao Ren* (小人) is a person with the opposite characteristics of a Jun Zi. A Xiao Ren is, for example, mean, wicked, cruel, dumb, and/or lacking in virtues.

Commentary and Modern Perspective:

If Jun Zi is interpreted as a successful entrepreneur or a founder of a kingdom, then the following sentence is noteworthy: "The influence of a Jun Zi does not last more than five generations." The five generations can be interpreted as five stages: founding of a new establishment, preservation of accomplishments of previous generations, becoming spoiled and decadent, corruption, collapse of the establishment. This phenomenon is common throughout history.

Section 23

孟子曰 可以取 可以無取 取 傷廉。可以與 可以無與 與傷惠。可以死 可以無死 死傷勇。

Mencius said, "If you are confronted with an ambivalent choice of taking versus not taking, be mindful that taking could hurt your probity. If you are confronted with an ambivalent choice of giving versus not giving, be mindful that giving could abuse your generosity. If you are confronted with an ambivalent choice of dying versus not dying, be mindful that dying may hurt your valor."

Or,

Mencius said, "If you are confronted with an ambiguous choice of taking versus not taking, then you should protect your probity by not taking. If you are confronted with an ambiguous choice of giving versus not giving, then you should not abuse your generosity by giving. If you are confronted with an ambiguous choice of dying for a course versus not dying, you should be aware that dying may not be an act of great valor."

Or,

Mencius said, "If you can take something but, upon a deeper

analysis, you should not take it, taking will hurt your probity. If you can give to someone but, upon a deeper analysis, you should not give, giving will abuse your generosity. If you want to die for a course but, upon deeper analysis, you should not die, dying will hurt your valor."

Commentary and Modern Perspective:

The above three interpretations are similar but slightly different in practical applications. The first two are almost identical, except that in the first case, the two choices have about equal moral values, whereas in the second case, you are uncertain whether the two choices have about equal moral values. The third interpretation emphasizes that you should think twice before making your choice.

In all three interpretations, the subject matter is about probity, generosity, and valor. To cultivate the virtue of probity, you must learn to forego opportunities to take possession of something or make a claim on something, although your taking does not hurt anybody, and is legally and morally acceptable. If you have developed a habit of taking possession on moral ambivalence or circumstantial ambivalence, your greed will gradually grow. You are walking on a slippery slope. You will then develop a habit of taking things for granted and finding justifications for your greed. Very soon, you will become corruptible.

When you want to give, you must be mindful of situations where you should not do so. For example, you should not give to somebody who does need or value your gift. Giving to the rich and powerful is sycophancy. The *Confucius Analects* narrated a related episode. Zi Hua, a disciple of Confucius, was sent as an envoy to the state of Qi.

Zi You, another disciple of Confucius, asked Confucius to give Zi Hua's mother some grains. Confucius said, "Give her 6.4 bushels." Zi You then asked for more. Confucius said, "Give her another 2.4 bushels then." Zi You secretly gave her eighty bushels instead. Confucius said, "I heard that Zi Hua traveled to the state of Qi on a chariot carried by fat horses, wearing a light warm fur coat. A Jun Zi should help the poor and needy rather than enrich the wealthy" (see Section 4 of Chapter 6, 雍也, of *Confucius Analects*).

If your gift hurts the recipient more than helping him, you should not give. One should give poor people fishing rods rather than fish so that they can learn how to make their living on their own. The same situation occurs in spoiling your young children with too many toys and candies.

The third reminder about giving is that you need to think deeper about the consequence of your generosity before you give. Your act of generosity and charity may benefit Peter but hurt Paul. In some other situations, your generosity will benefit a small group with a vested interest but hurt the entire nation or organization, or trigger jealousy and infighting.

Section 2 of Chapter 3 extensively discussed the essence of great valor. Confucius said, "A hero who is determined to uphold the Ren virtue would not seek to live at the expense of hurting his Ren virtue, but he would sacrifice his life in order to preserve it" (Section 9 of Chapter 15, 衛靈公, of *Confucius Analects*). However, just dying may not be a simple answer to uphold and pursue Ren and Yi. Sometimes, staying alive and continuing to struggle for Ren and Yi for a great course may be warranted and more honorable. In such situations, staying alive and enduring hardship until the end of the struggle may even be harder than just dying. The desire to die to avoid the responsibility of righteous struggles or the pain and suffering of life in general is suicidal and cowardice.

Section 24

逢蒙學射於羿 盡羿之道 思天下惟羿為愈己 於是殺羿。

　孟子曰 是亦羿有罪焉。

　公明儀曰 宜若無罪焉。

　曰 薄乎云爾 惡得無罪。鄭人使子濯孺子侵衛 衛使庾公之斯追之。子濯孺子曰 今日我疾作 不可以執弓 吾死矣夫。問其僕曰 追我者誰也。其僕曰 庾公之斯也。曰 吾生矣。其僕曰 庾公之斯 衛之善射者也 夫子曰 吾生 何謂也。曰 庾公之斯學射於尹公之他 尹公之他學射於我。夫尹公之他 端人也 其取友必端矣。庾公之斯至 曰 夫子何為不執弓。曰 今日我疾作 不可以執弓。曰 小人學射於尹公之他 尹公之他學射於夫子 我不忍以夫子之道反害夫子 雖然 今日之事 君事也 我不敢廢。抽矢扣輪 去其金 發乘矢而後反。

Pang Meng learned archery from Yi, the best archer in the country during the Xia Dynasty. After Pang Meng had learned all the skill of his teacher, Pang Meng could not bear the existence of Yi, his only competitor in the country, and murdered Yi.

　Mencius said, "In this case, Yi was to blame."

　Gong Ming Yi said, "Yi should not bear any blame."

　Mencius said, "Yi indeed made a small mistake. How can Yi not be blamed? In the past, the state of Cheng sent Zi Zhuo Ru to attack the state of Wey, which subsequently sent Yu Gong Zhi to pursue Zi Zhuo Ru. In desperation, Zi Zhuo Ru said, 'I am suddenly sick today. I cannot draw my bow. I am afraid I will soon be killed.' He then asked his servant, 'Who is pursuing me?' His servant replied, 'Yu Gong Zhi.' Zi Zhuo Ru then exclaimed, 'I will be alive, then.' His servant asked, 'Yu Gong Zhi is the best archer in the state of Wey. Why do you say that you will be alive?' Zi Zhuo Ru said, 'Yu Gong Zhi learned archery from Yin Gong Tuo, who, in turn, learned archery from me. Yin Gong Tuo is an upright person. Therefore, he must have chosen an upright friend and student.' Yu Gong Zhi arrived and asked Zi Zhuo Ru, 'Why don't you draw your bow?' Zi Zhuo Ru replied, 'I am sick today and cannot draw my bow.' Yu Gong Zhi said, 'I learned archery from Yin Gong Tuo, who, in turned, learned it from you, my master teacher. I cannot bear to kill you, my master teacher, with your own skill. However, I cannot betray my responsibility to my country.' Yu Gong Zhi then took out four arrows, knocked off their arrowheads against the carriage wheel, and shot those arrows without heads towards Zi Zhuo Ru."

Annotation:

Pang Meng (逄蒙) was originally a hunter in the mountains. Yi (羿) was a legendary archer in the Xia Dynasty. Yi met Pang Meng and took Pang Meng as his student. After many years, Pang Meng learned almost all the skills of Yi. The two were later regarded by their countrymen as equals in archery. Pang Meng was unhappy that his teacher could be a potential rival and planned to murder Yi. One day, Yi went out hunting, and Pang Meng followed him stealthily. Pang Meng shot an arrow towards Yi behind his back. Sensing the sound of the incoming arrow in flight, Yi turned around, drew his bow, and shot his arrow against the incoming arrow. The Yi's arrow intercepted and cut Pang Meng's arrow in half. Pang Meng repeated his attack ten times, and each time, Yi's arrow intercepted and cut

Pang Meng's arrow in half. After the tenth attempt, Yi ran out of arrows, but Pang Meng had one arrow left. Pang Meng hit Yi with his last arrow. Believing Yi was dead, Pang Meng came close to Yi's body. Yi suddenly jumped up and scared Pang Meng. The last arrow hit Yi's mouth, but Yi was able to stop and bite it with his teeth. Yi told Pang Meng, "You have not yet learned all my skills!" The humiliated Pang Meng did not give up his plan to murder Yi. On another occasion, Pang Meng followed Yi stealthily from behind and killed Yi with a cudgel.

Gong Ming Yi (公明儀) was a disciple of Mencius.

Zi Zhuo Ru (子濯孺子) was a general of the state of Cheng (鄭) and an accomplished archer.

Yu Gong Zhi (庾公之斯) was a general of the state of Wey (衛) and another good archer.

Yin Gong Tuo (尹公之他) was another good archer and the teacher of Yu Gong Zhi.

Commentary and Modern Perspective:

Mencius told these stories to teach a few lessons. First, one should try to select upright people to be friends and students. Second, a righteous person should honor and respect his teacher. Killing and hurting one's teacher are condemned. Third, Yu Gong Zhi was a good example who knew how to resolve his role conflict. To Yu, the practice of Ren and Yi virtue towards his teacher's teacher had a higher priority to his loyalty to his country. In ancient China, a teacher was regarded as important as a parent.

Section 25

孟子曰　西子蒙不潔　則人皆掩鼻而過之。雖有惡人　齊戒沐浴則可以祀上帝。

Mencius said, "If lady Xi Shi, the famous beauty in history, were covered with filthy dirt, people would cover their noses when they passed by her. If, on the contrary, a wicked person fasts and bathes [i.e., repents], he may take part in a worship ceremony of Tian (Sky)."

Annotation:

Xi Shi (西施) was one of the four most beautiful women in Chinese history. A popular folklore in Chinese literature exaggerated that, once upon a time, she dipped her face into water in a stream. At the sight of her beautiful face, fishes below were so charmed that they forgot to swim and sank. There is a phrase in Chinese literature, "Even fishes sink at the sight of her (沉魚)." Xi Shi was a young girl in a small village in the state of Yue (越國). On a beautiful day in spring, when Xi Shi was washing clothes in a stream, Fan Li (范蠡), a minister for the King of Yue, ran into her. Fan Li was on a mission to search all over the country for beautiful women to be offered as concubines to King Fu Chai (夫差) of the state of Wu (吳國). He was stunned by her beauty. Fan Li told her that he and King Gou Jian (勾踐) of the state of Yue had a plot against King Fu Chai. She was supposed to become a concubine of King Fu Chai so that she could eventually ruin him. Since she was patriotic, she agreed to take part in a long-term plot against King Fu Chai. Fan Li brought her to see King Gou Jian, who then sent her to a training school for three years to learn music, singing, dancing, poetry, literature, painting, etiquette, and other seductive skills. When King Fu Chai met Xi Shi, he was enchanted and fell in love with her. He built palaces, theaters, dancing halls, pavilions,

Chapter 8: Li Liao (2)

gardens, swimming pools, and chapels for her. He spent so much time with her that he forgot about his official duties. He often skipped official meetings in the royal court. His decadence and lasciviousness ruined him. He was later conquered by the state of Yue and was killed by King Gou Jian. Xi Shi disappeared.

Commentary:

In this section, the words *fasts* and *bathes* mean "repents" or "purifies." This section talks about the importance of repentance.

Section 26

孟子曰 天下之言性也 則故而已矣。故者以利為本。所惡於智者 為其鑿也。如智者若禹之行水也 則無惡於智矣。禹之行水也 行其所無事也。如智者亦行其所無事 則智亦大矣。天之高也 星辰之遠也 苟求其故 千歲之日至 可坐而致也。

Mencius said, "Many people in the world wrongly say that human nature is firmly ingrained and unchangeable, like other creatures in Nature. Therefore, they argue that it is fundamentally beneficial to just follow our firmly ingrained and unchangeable nature. I also dislike those supposedly wise men who recommend the artificial forging of virtues, like boring a wall with a chisel. If those supposedly wise men can learn how Yu managed flood, I cannot find any fault with those wise men. The way Yu managed water flow was not to go against its nature. If those wise men do not artificially go against their nature, their wisdom is indeed great. The sky is high, and the stars are far away. If one can figure out the nature of their perpetual characteristics, one can deduce the dates of all Summer and Winter solstices a thousand years from now."

Or,

Mencius said, "Many people in the world say that human nature is firmly ingrained and unchangeable, like other creatures in Nature. Therefore, it is fundamentally beneficial to just follow our firmly ingrained and unchangeable nature. I also dislike those supposedly wise men who recommend the artificial forging of virtues, like boring a wall with a chisel. If those supposedly wise men can learn how Yu managed floods, I cannot find any fault with those wise men. The way Yu managed water flow was not to go against its nature. If those wise men do not artificially go against their nature, their wisdom is indeed great. The sky is high, and the stars are far away. If one can figure out the nature of their perpetual characteristics, one can deduce the dates of all Summer and Winter solstices a thousand years from now."

Or,

Mencius said, "People in the world want to understand human nature. We can deduce human nature from human behavior and track records in the past. Many supposedly wise men are objectionable because they ignore fundamental human nature and recommend the artificial forging of virtues, like boring a wall with a chisel. If those supposedly wise men can learn how Yu managed floods, I cannot find any fault with those wise men. The way Yu managed water flow was not to go against its nature. If those wise men do not artificially go against their nature, their wisdom is indeed great. The sky is high, and the stars are far away. If one can figure out the nature of their perpetual characteristics, one can deduce the dates of all Summer and Winter solstices a thousand years from now."

Chapter 8: Li Liao (2)

Or,

Mencius said, "People in the world want to understand human nature. All characteristics of human beings [including their minds and bodies] are already built at birth as his nature. Since these characteristics are unchangeable, we just need to follow with the flow of our nature and do not need to do anything else. Many supposedly wise men are objectionable because they ignore fundamental human nature and recommend the artificial forging of virtues, like boring a wall with a chisel. If those supposedly wise men can learn how Yu managed floods, I cannot find any fault with those wise men. The way Yu managed water flow was not to go against its nature. If those wise men do not artificially go against their nature, their wisdom is indeed great. The sky is high, and the stars are far away. If one can figure out the nature of their perpetual characteristics, one can deduce the dates of all Summer and Winter solstices a thousand years from now."

Or,

Mencius said, "People in the world want to understand human nature. We can find the answer by analyzing history and past behavior of people. Such historical analyses should be based on the criteria of benefits to people. Many supposedly wise men are objectionable because they ignore fundamental human nature and recommend the artificial forging of virtues, like boring a wall with a chisel. If those supposedly wise men can learn how Yu managed floods, I cannot find any fault with those wise men. The way Yu managed water flow was not to go against its nature. If those wise men do not artificially go against their nature, their wisdom is indeed great. The sky is high, and the stars are far away. If one can figure out the nature of their perpetual characteristics, one can deduce the

333

dates of all Summer and Winter solstices a thousand years from now."

Annotation:

The second interpretation and translation of the original text is in line with the annotation of Zhao Qi (趙岐, 108–201 AD) of the Eastern Han Dynasty. The third version is in line with the annotation by Zhu Xi (朱熹, 1130–1200 AD) of the Song Dynasty. The fourth version is in line with the annotation by Sun Shi (孫奭, 962–1033 AD) of the Song Dynasty. The fifth version is in line with the annotation by Jiao Xun (焦循, 1763–1820 AD) of the Qing Dynasty. The differences in their annotations are mainly in the first three to four sentences of Mencius's speech. Such differences led to fundamental disagreements about Mencius's philosophy of human nature.

Commentary:

The first version seems to be more consistent with Mencius's philosophy of human nature for the following reasons.

According to Mencius, human beings are different from physical matters and animals because human beings have moral conscience (will, mind, or heart 心 in Chinese). Human beings can act according to their instinct like animals, and can also act against it according to their moral conscience, which is independent of their instinct. Human beings are superior to animals because they have the autonomy and freedom to act beyond their animal instincts and according to their moral conscience. Human beings are endowed with innate seeds (or roots) of Ren, Yi, Li, and wisdom in their conscience. As mentioned in Section 2 of Chapter 3, such seeds (or roots) need to be nurtured to fully grow to into the virtues of Ren, Yi, Li, and wisdom. Without careful nurturing, education, and learning, these seeds will wither, and the person will be void of virtue and become wicked and decadent. As pointed out in that same section, the process of nurturing is dynamic. If the seeds are neglected, they will not grow. On the other hand, one should not try to pull up the shoots of his plants to speed up their growth. In this section, Mencius used the analogy of trying to bore a wall with a chisel. After blossom and fruits are grown from the virtuous seeds, the person will be a meritorious Jun Zi and eventually a saint. This is the summary of Mencius's theory of "Good Human Nature (性善論)."

Some scholars misunderstand his theory to mean that human nature is virtuous at birth, and therefore, if a person follows the flow of nature, he will naturally be a good person, a Jun Zi, and eventually a saint, and be incapable of being wicked. Such misunderstanding is in line with the Taoist philosophy that one just needs to follow with the flow of nature and act in harmony with it, and that one does not need to make extra effort to nurture and cultivate one's virtues. Such attitude deviates from the long-standing teaching of Confucius and other Confucians that education and persistent self-improvement are important. Some Confucians, such as Xun Zi (荀子), then criticized Mencius by pointing out that his theory was not in line with historical facts. If human nature is good, why were there so many atrocities in history? They misunderstood Mencius. When Mencius said that human nature was good, he only meant that human beings were born only with the seeds (roots) of virtue, not a fully grown plant of virtue. Without proper nurturing and education, a person can do evil.

Therefore, Mencius objected to the view that human nature is firmly ingrained and unchangeable like other creatures in Nature and that it is fundamentally beneficial to just follow our firmly ingrained and unchangeable nature. The first two sentences of the first version above show this point.

The first two sentences of the second version above state: "Many people in the world say that human nature is firmly ingrained and unchangeable, like other creatures in Nature. Therefore, it is fundamentally beneficial to just follow our firmly ingrained and unchangeable nature." The first sentence here does not indicate clearly whether Mencius objected or not. The second sentence negates Mencius's point.

The first two sentences of the third version above state: "People in the world want to understand human nature. We can deduce human nature from human behavior and track records in the past." Although the second sentence looks scientific and objective, it does not indicate Mencius's point that human beings are born with a moral conscious and seeds of virtues. This is the a-priori basis of his theory and has nothing to do with a-posteriori observations of historical records. Worse still, historical records have shown more evil activities than good activities of mankind. Therefore, objective observations of historical records will refute Mencius's theory of "good human nature."

The first three sentences of the fourth version state: "People in the world want to understand human nature. All characteristics of human beings, [including their minds and bodies], are already built at birth as his nature. Since these characteristics are unchangeable, we just need to follow with the flow of our nature and do not need to do anything else." As pointed out above, these sentences have a Taoist flavor, which is fundamentally different from pre-Qin Confucianism.

The first three sentences of the fifth version state: "People in the world want to understand human nature. We can find the answer by analyzing the history and past behavior of people. Such historical analyses should be based on the criteria of benefits to people." The last sentence here mentioned "benefits" as the criteria to define human nature. Mencius rejected the idea of using benefits as a criterion throughout his book. For example, in the first section of Chapter 1, Mencius said to King Hui of Liang, "Therefore, your Majesty should focus on Ren (humanity) and Yi (righteousness) rather than benefits." Mencius objected to the Mohists, who insisted that "benefits" to people should be the basis to evaluate Ren and Yi. Therefore, the fifth version negates Mencius's theory.

All versions show the following sentence: "I also dislike those supposedly wise men who recommend the artificial forging of virtues like boring a wall with a chisel." This re-iterates Mencius's point in Section 2 of Chapter 3 that one should not try to pull up the shoots of his plants to speed up their growth. The process of nurturing one's virtue must be gradual and natural. One cannot be impatient.

All versions show the next few sentences: "If those supposedly wise men can learn how Yu managed floods, I cannot find any fault with those wise men. The way Yu managed water flow was not to go against its nature. If those wise men do not artificially go against their nature, their wisdom is indeed great." Some scholars misinterpret these sentences to mean that Mencius recommended inertia and complacency, and that one can be laid-back and let Nature play out its course. By citing the example of Yu and his management of floods, Mencius hinted that one must take the initiative to deal with Nature. When there is a flood, one cannot ignore it and let the country be swamped. Rather, one must proactively manage the situation in the same way as Yu did. However, one must handle the situation according to natural principles and avoid counterproductive plunders.

Mencius in Modern Perspectives

All versions show the last two sentences: "The sky is high, and the stars are far away. If one can figure out the nature of their perpetual characteristics, one can deduce the dates of all Summer and Winter solstices a thousand years from now." Some scholars misinterpret Mencius's point here and think that human nature is like the stars in the sky, whose motion is perpetual and predictable. Therefore, it is futile to modify human nature. The last four versions show this view. However, this view is dangerous and defeats the core theme of Confucianism. Mencius taught that human nature is different from the nature of other physical objects and animals. Human beings have a moral conscience, which has an independent will and can change. Human nature is also dynamic. Since human beings have free will, they can act differently from their instincts, and their behavior is difficult to control and predict. It is much easier to predict the dates of the solstices from the motion of the stars. It is difficult to predict human behavior, and even harder to improve human nature. Therefore, a relentless process of education and self-improvement is needed.

Section 27

公行子有子之喪 右師往弔 入門 有進而與右師言者 有就右師之位而與右師言者。孟子不與右師言 右師不悅曰 諸君子皆與驩言 孟子獨不與驩言 是簡驩也。

孟子聞之曰 禮 朝廷不歷位而相與言 不踰階而相揖也。我欲行禮 子敖以我為簡 不亦異乎。

Gong Hang Zi held a funeral for his son. The Right Prime Minister, Wang Huan of the state of Qi, went to show his condolence. After he had entered the funeral hall, many guests greeted him and spoke

Chapter 8: Li Liao (2)

with him. Some went near his seat and spoke with him. Mencius did not speak with him.

Wang Huan was displeased and said, "All prominent people here, except Mencius, spoke with me. He slighted me."

Mencius heard about Wang Huan's comment and said, "According to Li, officials are not supposed to move around in the royal court and talk to each other. They are not supposed to cross their assigned aisles to bow to each other. I followed these rules. How strange that he thought I slighted him?"

Annotation:

Gong Hang Zi (公行子) was a minister of the state of Qi.

Wang Zi Ao (王子敖, also known as Wang Huan 王驩) was the Right Prime Minister of the state of Qi. At that time, the six top-ranked ministers in the state of Qi were the Right Prime Minister (右師), Left Prime Minister (左師), Minister of Defense (司馬), Minister of Home Affairs (司徒), Minister of Justice (司寇), and Minister of Environment (司城). Wang Zi Ao was mentioned also in Section 6 of Chapter 4. On that occasion, he was only a governor of the county of Gai. He was also mentioned in Sections 24 and 25 of Chapter 7. Mencius did not like him.

Commentary and Modern Perspective:

It was the norm in ancient China that the deceased person in a funeral should receive the highest respect and status. Even when a king attended a funeral, he would still bow to the deceased person. Likewise, a funeral hall was a solemn place, and as important as the royal court. It was a lack of etiquette to chat and socialize with other mourners during a funeral.

However, it is common nowadays that many mourners of funerals take such opportunities to socialize rather than to mourn and give condolence to the family of the deceased. Such behavior is disrespectful to the deceased.

This section shows that Mencius detested sycophancy.

Section 28

孟子曰 君子所以異於人者 以其存心也。君子以仁存心 以禮存心。仁者愛人 有禮者敬人。愛人者人恒愛之 敬人者人恒敬之。有人於此 其待我以橫逆 則君子必自反也。我必不仁也 必無禮也 此物奚宜至哉。其自反而仁矣 自反而有禮矣 其橫逆由是也 君子必自反也 我必不忠。自反而忠矣 其橫逆由是也 君子曰 此亦妄人也已矣 如此則與禽獸奚擇哉 於禽獸又何難焉。是故 君子有終身之憂 無一朝之患也。乃若所憂則有之 舜人也 我亦人也。舜為法於天下 可傳於後世 我由未免為鄉人也 是則可憂也。憂之如何。如舜而已矣。若夫君子所患則亡矣。非仁無為也 非禮無行也。如有一朝之患 則君子不患矣。

Mencius said, "Jun Zis are different from common people because of what is kept in their hearts. Jung Zis keep Ren and Li in their hearts. Ren means love of people and Li means respect of people. Those who love others will be constantly loved by them. Those who respect others will be constantly respected by them. Suppose there is an abusive person who treats the Jun Zi in an unreasonable and objectionable manner. A Jun Zi should reflect on his behavior: 'I must have been unkind or impolite to him. What should I do to improve my relationship with him?' After the Jun Zi has become kinder and more polite, the abusive person continues his unreasonable and objectionable behavior. A Jun Zi should again reflect on his behavior: 'I must have been disloyal to him.' Even after the Jun Zi has subsequently become more loyal, the abusive person continues his unreasonable and objectionable behavior. The Jun Zi should say, 'He is just an ignorant and uncivilized person, not different from an animal. Why should I get upset with an animal?' Therefore, a Jun Zi should be concerned with his life-long objective rather than temporary adversity. What a Jun Zi should worry about is the following: 'Shun was a human being. I am also a human being. However, he was a model for the world and his virtue enlightened many generations after him. I am just a common villager.' This is indeed worrisome. What can a Jun Zi do to overcome such worry? The answer is to follow the good model of Shun. If a Jun Zi can do so, all his troubles will be gone. If a Jun Zi does not act against Ren and Li, he will not be troubled by a temporary adversity."

Commentary and Modern Perspective:

This section has four lessons. Mencius first explained in simple terms the essence of Ren and Li. He then pointed out: "Those who love others will be constantly loved by them. Those who respect others will be constantly respected by them." He next taught forbearance with the sentence: "He is just an ignorant and uncivilized person, not different from an animal. Why should I get upset with an animal?" He taught us to control our anger and to avoid fighting with minions.

The last point is to have a long-term perspective of life. We should not lose our bearings and be troubled, discouraged, or swayed by temporary adversity.

Section 29

禹 稷當平世 三過其門而不入 孔子賢之。顏子當亂世 居於陋巷 一簞食 一瓢飲。人不堪其憂 顏子不改其樂 孔子賢之。

孟子曰 禹 稷 顏回同道。禹思天下有溺者 由己溺之也。稷思天下有饑者 由己饑之也 是以如是其急也。禹 稷 顏子易地則皆然。今有同室之人鬭者 救之 雖被髮纓冠而救之 可也。鄉鄰有鬭者 被髮纓冠而往救之 則惑也 雖閉戶可也。

Yu and Ji lived in a peaceful era. They were so devoted to their work that, during their official missions, they passed by the doors of their homes three times without entering. Confucius praised them. Yan Hui lived during a warring period. He lived in a ghetto, ate with a bowl made of bamboo, and drank with a cup made of the skin of a melon. Other people could not withstand such austerity. He, on the contrary, enjoyed it. Confucius praised him also. Mencius said, "Yu, Ji and Yan Hui followed the same principle of life. Yu agonized over the drowning of anybody in the world as if it was his own drowning. Ji agonized over the hunger of anybody in the world as if it was his own hunger. Therefore, they were earnest to save people. If Yu, Ji, and Yan Hui had exchanged their respective circumstances and places, they would do the same thing. Suppose that some members in your family fight. You must stop the fight as soon as possible, even when your hat is not properly attached to your unbound hair. It is appropriate for you to do so. If neighboring villages fight, and you try to stop the fight when your hat is not properly attached to your unbound hair, you are imprudent. In such a case, it is appropriate for you to shut your door and ignore the fight."

Chapter 8: Li Liao (2)

Annotation:

Yu (禹, circa 2237–2139 BC) founded the Xia Dynasty (夏朝, circa 2184–1600 BC) in about 2184 BC. His father was a civil engineer and a minister in charge of water management under Yao. The father died before his construction projects were completed. Yao assigned Yu to control floods. Yu dug channels and tributaries to redirect water to the sea and succeeded in controlling floods. He stayed away from home for many years, and on three occasions, he had the opportunity to return to his village. He was so engaged in his project that he did not have time to visit his family.

Hou Ji (后稷) was a legendary Chinese agriculturist regarded as the God of Agriculture. He introduced millet to humanity during the time of the Xia dynasty as a major food staple before wheat. He also perfected the technology of growing five types of staple grains and many vegetables.

Yan Hui (顏回, also known as Yan Yuan 顏淵, 521–481 BC) was the best disciple of Confucius, who held him in the highest regard among his disciples.

Commentary and Modern Perspective:

There are two points in this section. The first point is that the principle and spirit of Ren is universal and independent of the era, place, and circumstance. Although Hou Ji, Yu, and Yan Hui were hundreds of years apart, they followed the principle of Ren. The second point is that the actual implementation of Ren must be governed by prudence. In the cases of Hou Ji and Yu, their countries were peaceful but had different challenges. They devoted their lives to overcome the challenges for the good of people. In the case of Yan Hui, the country was chaotic, and he had no opportunity to contribute his talents to the country. He then devoted his energy in self-improvement and spiritual development. Mencius further gave another example. Since one knows the background and cause of a fight within a family, one can and should stop the fight as soon as possible. On the other hand, one may not know the background and cause of a fight between two villages well enough; therefore, it is futile to be an arbitrator and imprudent to side with either village.

Section 30

公都子曰　匡章　通國皆稱不孝焉。夫子與之遊　又從而禮貌之　敢問何也。

　　孟子曰　世俗所謂不孝者五　惰其四支　不顧父母之養　一不孝也。博弈好飲酒　不顧父母之養　二不孝也。好貨財　私妻子　不顧父母之養　三不孝也。從耳目之欲　以為父母戮　四不孝也。好勇鬥很　以危父母　五不孝也。章子有一於是乎。夫章子　子父責善而不相遇也。責善　朋友之道也。父子責善　賊恩之大者。夫章子　豈不欲有夫妻子母之屬哉。為得罪於父　不得近。出妻屏子　終身不養焉。其設心以為不若是　是則罪之大者　是則章子已矣。

Gong Du Zi said, "Everyone in the country regarded Kuang Zhang as unfilial. Yet you, Master, befriended him and treated him politely. May I ask why?"

　　Mencius said, "People consider five behaviors to be unfilial. First, being lazy, and hence unable to support the livelihood of one's elderly parents. Second, being an alcoholic and addicted to gambling, and hence unable to support the livelihood of one's elderly parents. Third, being greedy and selfish, catering to the needs of one's wife and children, but unwilling to support the livelihood of one's elderly parents. Fourth, being indulgent in sensual pleasure to the extent of disgracing one's parents. Fifth, being fond of confrontation and fighting with people, thus endangering one's parents. Does Kuang Zhang have any of these vices? After Kuang Zhang admonished his father, their relationship broke and Kuang Zhang left home. Reproofs between friends are appropriate in friendship. However, admonishment between a parent and a child can seriously damage their relationship. Did Kuang Zhang not wish to have an affectionate relationship between him and his wife, and between his wife and his son? Since he had offended his father and was not permitted to approach his wife and son, he had no choice but to divorce his wife and be separated from his son. For all his life, he refused to receive any cherishing support from them. He thought that if he did not do so, he could not show his repentance for his grave sin. This was his motive."

Annotation:

Gong Du Zi (公都子) was a disciple of Mencius.
Kuang Zhang (匡章) was a disciple of Mencius and an official of the state of Qi. Kuang Zhang's mother was killed by his father. Kuang Zhang reproved his father and left home.

Commentary and Modern Perspective:

The lesson of this section is about forbearance. Before we form an opinion about a person, we should give him or her a benefit of doubt. We should try to understand the person's motivation and rationale first.

Mencius in Modern Perspectives

Section 31

曾子居武城 有越寇。或曰 寇至 盍去諸。

　曰 無寓人於我室 毀傷其薪木。寇退 則曰 修我墻屋 我將反。寇退 曾子反。

　左右曰 待先生 如此其忠且敬也。寇至則先去以為民望 寇退則反 殆於不可。

　沈猶行曰 是非汝所知也 昔沈猶有負芻之禍 從先生者七十人 未有與焉。

　子思居於衛 有齊寇。或曰 寇至 盍去諸。子思曰 如伋去 君誰與守。

　孟子曰 曾子 子思同道。曾子 師也 父兄也。子思 臣也 微也。曾子 子思易地則皆然。

When Zheng Zi lived in the city Wu Cheng in the state of Lu, soldiers from the state of Yue raided the city. Someone asked him, "The enemy is coming. Why are you not leaving?" Before Zheng Zi left, he told the keeper of the house, "Don't let soldiers stay in my house, lest they destroy the stuff in the house and plants and trees in the yard." After the war was over and the enemy was gone, Zheng Zi told the keeper, "Please repair the walls of my house. I will return." After the enemy had left, Zheng Zi returned. Some people around Zheng Zi criticized him, saying, "The king of the state of Lu had treated you with sincerity and respect. You left the country right away when it was under attack. Your action has disappointed the people of the state of Lu. You returned immediately after the enemy had left. Your action is not honorable." Shen You Xing, a disciple of Zheng Zi, told them, "You do not understand the real situation.

In the past, Zheng Zi and his disciples stayed in the estate of my parents. Some bandits came and raided the estate. Zheng Zi also escaped with all his 70 disciples. None of the disciples were hurt."

When Zi Si lived in the state of Wey, the army of the state of Qi invaded Wey. Someone asked him, "The enemy is coming. Why are you not leaving?" Zi Si replied, "If I leave, who can assist the king to defend this country?"

Mencius said, "Zheng Zi and Zi Si followed the same moral principle. In the case of Zheng Zi, he was a teacher, with a status of a father and elder brother, of the king of Lu. Zi Si was an official working for the king of Wey. If Zheng Zi and Zi Si had exchanged their roles, either of them would have done what the other did."

Annotation:

Zheng Zi (曾子, also known as Zheng Shen 曾參, born 505 BC) was a prominent disciple of Confucius, known for his filial piety. He was the author of *The Book of Great Learning* (大學).

Yuan Si (原思, also known as Yuan Xian 原憲 and Zi Si 子思, born 515 BC) was a disciple of Confucius, and later became an official of the state of Wey.

The states of Lu (魯國) and Wey (衛國) were two small states during the Spring-Autumn Period. The state of Qi (齊國) was a hegemon. Wu Cheng (武城) was a city in the state of Lu.

Shen You Xing (沈猶行) was a disciple of Zheng Zi and a son of a rich parent who owned a large estate. Zheng Zi set up his school in the estate.

Commentary:

In this section, Mencius reminded his disciples against being dogmatic. The same principle, when applied to different situations and roles, may warrant different actions.

Section 32

儲子曰 王使人瞯夫子 果有以異於人乎。

孟子曰 何以異於人哉 堯舜與人同耳。

Chu Zi told Mencius, "The king sent a person to spy on you, Master, to see whether you are indeed extra-ordinary."

Mencius said, "How am I different from other people? Even Yao and Shun were just the same as other people."

Annotation:

Chu Zi (儲子) was a native of the state of Qi (齊國).
Yao and Yun were the two ancient saintly kings.

Section 33

齊人有一妻一妾而處室者 其良人出 則必饜酒肉而後反。其妻問所與飲食者 則盡富貴也。其妻告其妾曰 良人出 則必饜酒肉而後反 問其與飲食者 盡富貴也 而未嘗有顯者來 吾將瞯良人之所之也。蚤起 施從良人之所之 遍國中無與立談者。卒之東郭墦閒 之祭者 乞其餘 不足 又顧而之他 此其為饜足之道也。其妻歸 告其妾曰 良人者 所仰望而終身也 今若此。與其妾訕其良人 而相泣於中庭。而良人未之知也 施施從外來 驕其妻妾。

Chapter 8: Li Liao (2)

由君子觀之 則人之所以求富貴利達者 其妻妾不羞也 而不相泣者 幾希矣。

A man of the state of Qi had a wife and a concubine living together with him in the same house. Whenever the husband went out, he had gotten himself very full of food and drinks before he returned home. When his wife asked him with whom he ate and drank, his reply was that he had wined and dined with wealthy friends and dignitaries. His wife said to his concubine, "Whenever our husband goes out, he must have taken a lot of food and drinks before he returns. When I ask him with whom he has wined and dined, his reply is that they are all wealthy friends and dignitaries. However, nobody of any distinction ever visits us. I will spy on him to see where he goes." The wife then got up early in the morning and stealthily followed the husband. No one throughout the whole city stood and talked with him. After eventually arriving at the graveyard on the east end of the city, he waited at the side of a tomb until a mourning party had finished their sacrificial ritual. He then begged for the remains of the sacrifice. If he were not yet full, he would look for another mourning party and begged for more food. This was the way he got himself full of food and drinks. His wife returned home and told his concubine, saying, "Our livelihood and future depend on our husband. Yet he is so unworthy and shameless." They reviled their husband, hugged each other, and cried. The husband returned, not knowing what had happened. He walked into the house with a jaunty gait and boasted to his wife and concubine again.

Mencius said, "In the eyes of a Jun Zi, if a person shamelessly gets wealth, power, gain, and status, it is rare that his wife and concubine would not feel ashamed and weep together."

Commentary and Modern Perspective:

This is a famous story, often quoted in Chinese literature. Mencius told this interesting parable to illustrate how shameless a hypocrite is. We often see many people who, despite appearing gracious and virtuous, having an impeccable reputation and credentials, occupying high places in society, and so on, do unsightly and wicked things behind the scenes.

If we reflect on ourselves, we should ask whether we have also committed similarly shameless behaviors.

Chapter 9: Wan Zhang (1)

Section 1

萬章問曰 舜往於田 號泣於旻天 何為其號泣也。

孟子曰 怨慕也。

萬章曰 父母愛之 喜而不忘。父母惡之 勞而不怨。然則舜怨乎。

曰 長息問於公明高曰 舜往於田 則吾既得聞命矣 號泣於旻天 於父母 則吾不知也。公明高曰 是非爾所知也。夫公明高以孝子之心 為不若是恝 我竭力耕田 共為子職而已矣 父母之不我愛 於我何哉。帝使其子九男二女 百官牛羊倉廩備 以事舜於畎畝之中。天下之士多就之者 帝將胥天下而遷之焉。為不順於父母 如窮人無所歸。天下之士悅之 人之所欲也 而不足以解憂。好色 人之所欲 妻帝之二女 而不足以解憂。富 人之所欲 富有天下 而不足以解憂。貴 人之所欲 貴為天子 而不足以解憂。人悅之 好色 富貴 無足以解憂者 惟順於父母 可以解憂。人少 則慕父母。知好色 則慕少艾 有妻子 則慕妻子 仕則慕君 不得於君則熱中。大孝終身慕父母。五十而慕者 予於大舜見之矣。

Wan Zhang asked Mencius, "When Shun worked in the field, he cried and prayed for the forgiveness of Tian (Sky). What made him cry?"

Mencius said, "He was remorseful."

Mencius in Modern Perspectives

Wan Zhang said, "When his parents loved him, he did not forget their love. When his parents hated him, he continued to do his job and did not grumble. Why should he be remorseful?"

Mencius said, "Chang Xi asked Gong Ming Gao, 'I can understand why Shun went to work in the fields. I do not understand why he should cry out for the forgiveness of Tian and of his parents.' Gong Ming Gao replied, 'This is beyond your comprehension.' According to Gong Ming Gao, a filial person cannot be apathetic to whether his parents love or hate him. He cannot think that if he cultivates diligently in the field and fulfils the responsibility of a son, his parents' lack of love of him is irrelevant. In the past, Emperor Yao ordered nine sons to be the students of Shun and two daughters to be the wives of Shun. Yao also assigned hundreds of officials to assist Shun. They brought with them cattle and cargoes of grain as gifts to Shun, who was still working in the field. When Shun got the support of people in the country, Yao then transferred his power to Shun. However, if a person cannot please his parents, he is like a poor homeless person. Anyone would be overjoyed if he gets the support of all people in the country, yet Shun was still remorseful. Anyone would be overjoyed with the possession of beautiful women and the marriages with two princesses, yet Shun was still remorseful. Anyone would be overjoyed with great fortunes and the possession of a country, yet Shun was still remorseful. Anyone would be overjoyed with the rise to prominence and becoming an emperor, yet Shun was still remorseful. The support of people, the possession of beautiful women, riches and power were insufficient to alleviate the sorrow of Shun, yet the reconciliation with his parents would remove his sorrow. A young child craves for the love of his parents, while an adolescent craves for sex and beautiful girls. After marriage, a man desires a good wife and children. A government official desires the trust of his king and bosses, and if he is not trusted, he will be uneasy. A man of great filial piety yearns for the love of his parents. It is rare for a person over 50 years old to still remember his parents and yearn for their love. I see Shun as such an example."

Annotation:

Wan Zhang (萬章) was a disciple of Mencius.
Gong Ming Gao (公明高) was a disciple of Zheng Zi (曾子), who was the disciple of Confucius (see Annotation of Section 31 of Chapter 8).
Chang Xi (長息) was a disciple of Gong Ming Gao.
For the story of Shun, see the Annotation of Section 28 of Chapter 7 above.

Commentary:

Here, Mencius emphasized the greatness of filial piety.

Section 2

萬章問曰 詩云 娶妻如之何 必告父母。信斯言也 宜莫如舜。舜之不告而娶 何也。

孟子曰 告則不得娶。男女居室 人之大倫也。如告 則廢人之大倫 以懟父母 是以不告也。

萬章曰 舜之不告而娶 則吾既得聞命矣。帝之妻舜而不告 何也。

曰 帝亦知告焉則不得妻也。

萬章曰 父母使舜完廩 捐階 瞽瞍焚廩。使浚井 出 從而揜之。象曰　謨蓋都君咸我績　牛羊父母　倉廩父母　干戈朕　琴朕　弤朕　二嫂使治朕棲。象往入舜宮　舜在床琴。象曰　鬱陶思君爾。忸怩。舜曰　惟茲臣庶　汝其於予治。不識舜不知象之將殺己與。

　　曰　奚而不知也。象憂亦憂　象喜亦喜。

　　曰　然則舜偽喜者與。

　　曰　否。昔者有饋生魚於鄭子產　子產使校人畜之池。校人烹之　反命曰　始舍之圉圉焉　少則洋洋焉　攸然而逝。子產曰　得其所哉　得其所哉。校人出曰　孰謂子產智。予既烹而食之曰　得其所哉　得其所哉。故君子可欺以其方　難罔以非其道。彼以愛兄之道來　故誠信而喜之　奚偽焉。

Wan Zhang asked, "The *Book of Poetry* said, 'What should a man do to marry a wife? He must consult his parents.' Shun was not one of those who followed this ancient rule. He got married without seeking the approval of his parents. Why?"

Mencius replied, "If he had consulted his parents, he would not get married. The marriage of a man and woman is the most important human bond. If he had consulted his parents, he would certainly not get their approval, and therefore, could not consummate his marriage and have any children. This was against the interest of his parents. He therefore did not consult his parents."

Wan Zhang asked, "I now take your explanation about why Shun did not consult his parents about his marriage. Emperor Yao set up his daughters' marriages with Shu without consulting Shun's parents. Why?"

Mencius replied, "Emperor Yao also knew that Shun's parent would not approve Shun's marriage and therefore did not consult them."

Chapter 9: Wan Zhang (1)

Wan Zhang said, "Shun's parents sent Shun to repair the roof of the family's granary tower. After Shun had reached the roof, they removed the ladder. His father, Gu Sou, set fire to the granary tower to kill Shun. Later, his parents sent Shun to drain a well. His father and brother Xiang threw mud and stones into the well to bury Shun alive. Thinking the Shun had died, his brother Xiang proclaimed, 'I have the merit of burying Shun, the governor of Du. His cattle of oxen and sheep now goes to my parents. His granaries go to my parents also. His shield and spear shall be mine. His lute and bow shall also be mine. His two wives should sleep with me from now on.' When Xiang arrived at the palace of Shun, he was surprised to find Shun alive, playing his lute on his couch (Shun had escaped through a tunnel connected to the well). Feeling embarrassed and blushed, Xiang said to Shun, 'I come here because I have been thinking of you.' Shun told Xiang calmly, 'I have too many officials and people to govern. Can you help me govern them?' Did Shun know that Xiang had tried to kill him?"

Mencius said, "How could he be ignorant of that? However, Shun felt sorrowful when Xiang was sorrowful. Shun was joyful when Xiang was joyful."

Wan Zhang said, "If so, Shun was a hypocrite!"

Mencius said, "No. In the past, someone gave a live fish to Zi Chan of the state of Zheng. Zi Chan ordered the pond keeper to keep the fish in the pond. The pond keeper cooked the fish and ate it. He then reported to Zi Chan, 'At first, the fish swam sluggishly. After a few rounds, it swam energetically. It has now swum away and disappeared from our sight.' Zi Chan replied, 'It has found its new home. It has found its new home.' The pond keeper went out and said, 'Is Zi Chan smart? I have cooked the fish and eaten it. Yet he said repeatedly that it had found its new home.' Therefore, a Jun Zi can be cheated by a rational approach but cannot be cheated by an irrational approach. Xiang faked his love of Shun. Therefore, Shun believed in him and was pleased. How can we say that Shun was a hypocrite?"

Annotation:

Gu Sou (瞽瞍) was the father of Shun.

Xiang (象) was the younger brother of Shun. At that time, the father, Gu Sou, was a lord of a small state, and Shun was the governor of a small county, Du (都), within the state, and called the governor of Du.

Zi Chan (子產, died 552 BC, also known as Gong Sun Qiao, 公孫僑) was a prominent statesman and reputed prime minister of the state of Zheng (鄭 國). He was praised by Confucius (see Section 16 of Chapter 5, 公冶長, of *Confucius Analects*).

Commentary:

The dialogue between Mencius and his disciple, Wan Zhang, was a record of discussions during a history class. Wan Zhang was an inquisitive and critical student. In this section, Mencius used the example of Shun to teach Wan Zhang the essence of filial piety and fraternal love. Shun did not hold a grudge against his father and brother, who plotted to kill Shun. His father listened to his second wife, who wanted to kill Shun so that her own son, Xiang, could succeed Gu Sou.

Section 3

萬章問曰 象日以殺舜為事 立為天子 則放之 何也。

　　孟子曰 封之也 或曰放焉。

Chapter 9: Wan Zhang (1)

萬章曰 舜流共工於幽州 放驩兜於崇山 殺三苗於三危 殛鯀於羽山 四罪而天下咸服 誅不仁也。象至不仁 封之有庳。有庳之人奚罪焉。仁人固如是乎。在他人則誅之 在弟則封之。

曰 仁人之於弟也 不藏怒焉 不宿怨焉 親愛之而已矣。親之欲其貴也 愛之欲其富也。封之有庳 富貴之也。身為天子 弟為匹夫 可謂親愛之乎。

(曰) 敢問或曰放者 何謂也。

曰 象不得有為於其國 天子使吏治其國 而納其貢稅焉 故謂之放 豈得暴彼民哉。雖然 欲常常而見之 故源源而來。不及貢 以政接於有庳。此之謂也。

Wan Zhang asked, "Xiang plotted every day to kill Shun. Yet, after Shun became the emperor, he only sent Xiang to exile. Why?"

Mencius said, "In fact, Xiang was enfeoffed a land by Shun. Some people say that Xiang was sent in exile."

Wan Zhang said, "Shun sent the chief water engineer in exile to You Zhou, Huan Dou into exile to mountain Gong, the king of San Mei in exile to San Wei, and killed Gun on mountain Yu. People in the country agreed to the punishment of these four notorious criminals. They were punished for their lack of Ren virtue. However, Xiang was most in lack of Ren. He was even enfeoffed the province of You Bei. What wrong had the people of You Bei done for them to be ruled by Xiang? Should a benevolent ruler punish others but enfeoff his own brother?"

Mencius said, "A man with Ren virtue does not hold anger and grudges against his brother because of fraternal love. Shun's affection prompted him to wish his brother to be dignified, and

Shun's love prompted him to wish his brother to be rich. With the enfeoffment of You Bei, Xiang would become dignified and rich. Since Shun was the emperor, allowing his brother to be a commoner was not a sign of affection and love."

Wan Zhang asked, "May I ask why some people said that Xiang was sent into exile?"

Mencius said, "In fact, Xiang did not have the power to run the government of You Bei. Emperor Shun appointed other officials to rule that place. Only its tax revenue was paid to Xiang. Therefore, some people said that Xiang was banished. Therefore, how can we say that Xiang oppressed his people? Shun wished to see his brother frequently. Therefore, Xiang visited the court regularly. A quote from a history book said, 'Do not wait for the times of tributes to the emperor or official meetings of the court to receive the feudal lord of You Bei.' This referred to the relationship between Shun and Xiang."

Annotation:

Wan Zhang (萬章) was a disciple of Mencius.

You Zhou (幽州) was one of the twelve big provinces at that time, located in the northeast of China.

Huan Dou (驩兜) was a minister under Emperor Yao. He colluded with the chief water engineer to form a gang of corrupted officials.

Mountain Chong (崇山) was in modern-day Hunan Province.

San Mei (三苗) was the name of a small county in modern-day Hunan Province.

San Wei (三危) was in modern-day Dunhuang (敦煌) city in Gansu Province (甘肅).

Chapter 9: Wan Zhang (1)

Gun (鯀) was the father of Great Yu (禹). Gun oversaw flood control and water management. He failed in his project and was punished to death by Shun. Yu later took his father's role and succeeded in saving the country from flooding.

Mountain Yu (羽山) was in modern-day Shandong Province.

You Bei (有庳) was the ancient name of a small county in modern-day Hunan Province.

Commentary:

This section should not be misunderstood to mean that Mencius endorsed nepotism—"blood is thicker than water." To Wan Zhang, Xiang was as evil as the other notorious criminals. Therefore, Xiang should be punished for his crime of trying to kill Shun. Instead, Xiang was enfeoffed a land. This was a flagrant sign of nepotism. However, Mencius rationalized the actions of Shun differently. Mencius considered that Xiang's intention to kill Shun arose from the rivalry between siblings, which was a family matter. On the contrary, the violations of the other four criminals hurt the entire country. Mencius thought that Shun did not care about Xiang's original antagonism and had forgiven Xiang. The saintly Shun considered Xiang innocent. Furthermore, Xiang later repented and tried to rebuild the brotherly relationship with Shun. Therefore, Shun continued to show his affection and love of his brother. On the contrary, the other four criminals were punished because of their evil acts against the country or incompetency. Shun did not empower Xiang to run You Bei. Instead, Shun appointed other officials to run the government for Xiang. This showed that Shun did not endorse nepotism in his government. This section showed how Shun tried to achieve a balance between private versus public matters.

Section 4

咸丘蒙問曰　語云　盛德之士　君不得而臣　父不得而子。舜南面而立　堯帥諸侯北面而朝之　瞽瞍亦北面而朝之。舜見瞽瞍　其容有蹙。孔子曰　於斯時也　天下殆哉　岌岌乎。不識此語誠然乎哉。

　孟子曰　否。此非君子之言　齊東野人之語也。堯老而舜攝也。堯典曰　二十有八載　放勳乃徂落　百姓如喪考妣　三年　四海遏密八音。孔子曰　天無二日　民無二王。舜既為天子矣　又帥天下諸侯以為堯三年喪　是二天子矣。

　咸丘蒙曰　舜之不臣堯　則吾既得聞命矣。詩云　普天之下　莫非王土　率土之濱　莫非王臣。而舜既為天子矣　敢問瞽瞍之非臣　如何。

　曰　是詩也　非是之謂也。勞於王事　而不得養父母也。曰　此莫非王事　我獨賢勞也。故說詩者　不以文害辭　不以辭害志。以意逆志　是為得之。如以辭而已矣。雲漢之詩曰　周餘黎民　靡有孑遺。信斯言也　是周無遺民也。孝子之至　莫大乎尊親　尊親之至　莫大乎以天下養。為天子父　尊之至也　以天下養　養之至也。詩曰　永言孝思　孝思維則。此之謂也。書曰　祗載見瞽瞍　夔夔齊栗　瞽瞍亦允若。是為父不得而子也。

Xian Qiu Meng said, "There is an ancient saying, 'A person of sublime virtue should not be treated like a subordinate by a king, and like a son by a father.' When Shun became the emperor and stood in his court facing the south, his predecessor, Yao, led other feudal lords to hail him by facing the north. Shun's father Gu Sou did the same. When Shun saw his father standing among feudal lords and officials, Shun appeared embarrassed. Confucius once commented, 'At that time, the country's stability was impaired.' I do not know whether Confucius actually said so."

Mencius said, "No. These were not the words of a Jun Zi. This was just a rumor among uneducated people in the east of the state of Qi. At that time, the old Yao deputized Shun to rule the country. The historical records of Yao's era said, 'Shun ruled the country on behalf of Yao for 28 years. When Yao died, all ministers and official felt as if they had lost their parents. They observed a mourning vigil for three years, and people in the country ceased to play music.' Confucius said, 'The sky does not have two Suns. Likewise, a country cannot have two kings.' If Shun was an emperor when Yao was still alive and led all officials to observe the mourning vigil, there were then two kings in the country."

Xian Qiu Meng said, "I now accept your explanation that Shun did not treat Yao as a subordinate. The *Book of Poetry* said, 'Every piece of land in the whole country belongs to the emperor. Everyone within the border of the whole country is a subject of the emperor.' When Shun became the emperor, why should his father Gu Sou not be treated as a subject also?"

Mencius replied, "This poem does not mean so. The author of this poem lamented that he had worked for the king wholeheartedly and had no time to take care of his parents. He therefore said later, 'Everything here concerns the king, and there are so many brilliant people working for the king. Why should I be singled out to handle all these matters alone because of my competency and virtue?' Therefore, when you interpret a poem, you should not misinterpret a sentence because of a single word, and misinterpret the meaning of a verse because of a sentence. You should stretch your insight to read the mind of the author. You can then get the subtle meaning of the poem. If you interpret a poem word by word, you will also misinterpret the verse in the chapter Yun Han of the *Book of Poetry*, which said, 'People of Zhou Dynasty; nobody is left behind.' You will then misinterpret it to mean that every citizen of the Zhou Dynasty has vanished (whereas it should be interpreted to mean that everybody in the country has become a subject of the Zhou Dynasty).

Among all the merits of a filial son, nothing is greater than honoring his parents. Among all the activities of honoring his parents, nothing is greater than nourishing his parents with the whole country. Gu Sou became the father of an emperor. This was the ultimate honor. Shun nourished his parents with the whole country. This was the ultimate nourishment. The *Book of Poetry* said, 'Cherish filial thoughts constantly and set an example for future generations.' This was what Shun did. The *Book of Classic History* said, 'Shun served his father dutifully and with awe. Gu Sou, henceforth, trusted Shun for his filial piety and acquiesced Shun.' This illustrates the meaning of the earlier sentence: 'A person of sublime virtue should not be treated like a son by a father.'"

Annotation:

Xian Qiu Meng (咸丘蒙) was a disciple of Mencius.

Yun Han of the Book of Poetry (詩經:大雅, 雲漢篇) is a chapter of the *Book of Poetry*.

When Emperor Yao was old, he deputized Shun to be his regent for 28 years. When Emperor Yao died at the age of over 100 years, Shun became the emperor.

Commentary:

This section contains two good points. The first point is related

Chapter 9: Wan Zhang (1)

to role conflict. The relationship between Shun and his father Gu Sou was bifurcated. On one hand, Shun was the emperor and had a status above Gu Sou. On the other hand, Shun was the son of Gu Sou and had a status below Gu Sou. Shun handled this conflict well. Although Gu Sou had to pay homage to Shun in official occasions, Shun still maintained his filial piety in private. The same role conflict occurred between Yao and Shun. Yao was the retired ruler and the old boss of Shun, whereas Shun was the person in power. Both Yao and Shun behaved appropriately.

The second point is related to management of talented people, as spelled out in the sentence: "A person of sublime virtue should not be treated like a subordinate by a king, and like a son by a father."

Section 5

萬章曰 堯以天下與舜 有諸。

孟子曰 否。天子不能以天下與人。

(曰) 然則舜有天下也 孰與之。

曰 天與之。

(曰) 天與之者 諄諄然命之乎。

曰 否。天不言 以行與事示之而已矣。

曰 以行與事示之者如之何。

曰 天子能薦人於天 不能使天與之。天下諸侯能薦人於天子 不能使天子與之諸侯。大夫能薦人於諸侯 不能使諸侯與之大夫。昔者堯薦舜於天而天受之 暴之於民而民受之。故曰 天不言 以行與事示之而已矣。

曰 敢問薦之於天而天受之 暴之於民而民受之 如何。

曰 使之主祭而百神享之 是天受之。使之主事而事治 百姓安之 是民受之也。天與之 人與之。故曰 天子不能以天下與人。舜相堯二十有八載 非人之所能為也 天也。堯崩 三年之喪畢 舜避堯之子於南河之南。天下諸侯朝覲者 不之堯之子而之舜。訟獄者 不之堯之子而之舜。謳歌者 不謳歌堯之子而謳歌舜 故曰天也。夫然後之中國 踐天子位焉。而居堯之宮 逼堯之子 是篡也 非天與也。太誓曰 天視自我民視 天聽自我民聽。此之謂也。

Wan Zhang asked, "Yao gave the country to Shun. Was that true?"

Mencius replied, "No. An emperor cannot give his country to another person."

Wan Zhang asked, "However, Shun owned the country. Who gave it to him?"

Mencius said, "Tian (Sky) gave it to him."

Wan Zhang asked, "Did Tian give it to him? Did Tian speak to him?"

Mencius said, "No. Tian does not talk. It shows its will by actions and facts."

Wan Zhang asked, "What does 'showing its will by actions and facts' mean?"

Mencius said, "The emperor can recommend a candidate to Tian but cannot force Tian to give the country to the candidate. Feudal lords can recommend a candidate to the emperor but cannot force the emperor to appoint him as a feudal lord. Ministers of a feudal state can recommend a candidate to the feudal lord but cannot force the feudal lord to appoint him as a minister. In the past, Yao recommended Shun to Tian and it accepted his recommendation. Yao presented Shun to people of the country and they accepted

Chapter 9: Wan Zhang (1)

Shun. Therefore, I say that Tian does not talk but it shows its will by actions and facts."

Wan Zhang asked, "May I ask the meaning of the sentences: 'Yao recommended Shun to Tian and it accepted his recommendation. Yao presented Shun to people of the country and they accepted Shun.'"

Mencius said, "When Yao ordered Shun to head a sacrificial rite, all gods were pleased. This showed that Tian accepted Shun. When Yao ordered Shun to administer the government, Shun did his job well and the people of the country could live in comfort and peace. This showed that people accepted Shun. Both Tian and people accepted Shun. Therefore, we say that an emperor cannot give a country to another person.

Shun was a regent for Yao for 28 years. It was beyond the ability of a man. It was due to the will of Tian. When Yao died, Shun observed a mourning vigil for three years. Shun moved afterwards to the south of the South River to concede his power to the son of Yao. However, all feudal lords continued to pay homage to Shun instead of the son of Yao. All litigants wanted their cases to be arbitrated by Shun instead of the son of Yao. Songs were sung in praise of Shun instead of the son of Yao. This showed the will of Tian. Because of these phenomena, Shun returned to the capital and accepted the throne. If Shun had forced the son of Yao to surrender the throne, Shun would have committed an act of treason and his throne was not given by Tian. The *Grand Oath* said, 'Tian sees through the eyes of people. Tian hears through the ears of people.' This is indeed true."

Annotation:

Wan Zhang (萬章) was a disciple of Mencius.

Commentary:

Although Mencius seemed to emphasize the importance of divine providence in this section, he essentially equated the power bestowed on a ruler by Tian to be the power derived from the support of the people. The will of people reflects the will of Tian. This point is hinted by the last two sentences: "Tian sees through the eyes of people. Tian hears through the ears of people." This section underpins Mencius's governance ideals.

Section 6

萬章問曰 人有言 至於禹而德衰 不傳於賢而傳於子。有諸。

孟子曰 否 不然也。天與賢 則與賢。天與子 則與子。昔者舜薦禹於天 十有七年 舜崩。三年之喪畢 禹避舜之子於陽城。天下之民從之 若堯崩之後 不從堯之子而從舜也。禹薦益於天 七年 禹崩。三年之喪畢 益避禹之子於箕山之陰。朝覲訟獄者不之益而之啟 曰 吾君之子也。謳歌者不謳歌益而謳歌啟 曰 吾君之子也。丹朱之不肖 舜之子亦不肖。舜之相堯 禹之相舜也 歷年多 施澤於民久。啟賢 能敬承繼禹之道。益之相禹也 歷年少 施澤於民未久。舜 禹 益相去久遠 其子之賢不肖 皆天也 非人之所能為也。莫之為而為者 天也。莫之致而至者 命也。匹夫而有天下者 德必若舜禹 而又有天子薦之者 故仲尼不有天下。繼世以有天下 天之所廢 必若桀紂者也 故益 伊尹 周公不有天下。伊尹相湯以王於天下。湯崩 太丁未立 外丙二年 仲壬四年。太甲顛覆湯之典刑 伊尹放之於桐。三年 太甲悔過 自怨自艾 於桐處仁遷義。三年 以聽伊尹

Chapter 9: Wan Zhang (1)

之訓己也　復歸於亳。周公之不有天下　猶益之於夏　伊尹之於殷也。孔子曰　唐虞禪　夏后　殷　周繼　其義一也。

Wan Zhang asked, "Some people say, 'Morality declined during the reign of Yu. He picked his son, rather than a meritorious and competent person as his successor.' Was this correct?"

Mencius replied, "No. This is incorrect. If Tian wants to give the throne to a meritorious and competent person, it will be given to him. If Tian wants to give the throne to a son, it will be given to the son. In the past, Shun recommended Yu to Tian. Shun died after 17 years. After Yu observed a mourning vigil on the death of Shun for three years, Yu retreated to Yang Cheng to make room for the son of Shun. However, people in the country followed Yu, just as the people who followed Shun instead of the son of Yao after Yao's death. Yu recommended Yi to Tian and died seven years afterwards. Yi observed a mourning vigil on the death of Yu and retreated to the south of mountain Qi. Feudal lords paid homage to Qi, the son of Yu, instead of Yi. All litigants in the country went to Qi instead of Yi to arbitrate on their cases. They said, 'Qi is the son of our king.' Songs were sung in praise of Qi instead of Yi, such as 'Qi is the son of our king.' Dan Zhu, the son of Yao, lacked merit. The son of Shun also lacked merit. Shun assisted Yao and Yu assisted Shun in running the government for many years and had fostered welfare to people. Qi, the son of Yu was meritorious and competent enough to carry on the policy of Yu. Yi had only assisted Yu for a short time and fostered little welfare to people. The difference in the lengths of services, Qi versus Yi, and the lack of merits of their sons were determined by the will of Tian rather than man. All matters that happen beyond human ability are due to the will of Tian. All accomplishments without being caused by man are due to fate. For a commoner to rise to the top of a country, he must process

Mencius in Modern Perspectives

exceptional virtue like Shun and Yu, and be fortunate enough to be recommended by his king. Therefore, Confucius could not become an emperor. If a son inherits the throne from his father but Tian wants to dispose of him, he will be overthrown like Jie of the Xia Dynasty and Zhou of the Shang Dynasty. Therefore, Yi, Yi Yin, and the Duke of Zhou could not become the emperor. Yi Yin assisted King Tang to conquer and unify the country. After King Tang's death, his son Tai Ding also died before he was crowned. Wai Bing then ruled the country for two years, and Zhong Ren for four years. The next successor, Tai Jia, threw out the statues and policies of King Tang. Yi Yin then sent Tai Jia to exile in the province Tong. After three years, Tai Jia repented. When he was in Tong, Tai Jia practiced Ren and Yi, and learned the teachings of Yi Yin. Then, Yi Yin sent Tai Jia back to Bo and crowned him. The Duke of Zhou could not be the emperor of his country. Likewise, Yi could not be the emperor of Xia Dynasty and Yi Yin could not be the emperor of Yin Dynasty. Confucius said, 'Yao of Tang tribe and Shun of Yu tribe conceded their thrones to competent ministers. The throne was inherited during the Xia, Yin, and Zhou dynasties. The principle was the same in all cases.' "

Annotation:

Wan Zhang (萬章) was a disciple of Mencius.

The meaning of Tian (天) is explained in the Introduction.

Yang Cheng (陽城) was the name of a mountain in modern-day Henan Province.

Shun (舜) was the emperor of the Yu (虞) tribe, and Yu (禹) was a minister under Shun, who later conceded his throne to Yu.

Yi (益) was a minister under Yu.

Dan Zhu (丹朱) was the son of emperor Yao.

Chapter 9: Wan Zhang (1)

Mountain Qi (箕山) was the name of a mountain in modern-day Henan Province.

Qi (啟) was the son of Yu.

Yi Yin (伊尹, circa 1649–1549 BC) was born in the era under the terrible reign of Emperor Jie (桀), the last emperor of the Xia Dynasty (夏朝). Yi Yin later assisted King Tang (湯) to overthrow Emperor Jie and founded the Shang Dynasty (商朝, also known as Yin Dynasty 殷朝). The story of Yi Yin and Tai Jia (太甲) is narrated in the Annotation of Section 2 of Chapter 3 above and Section 3 of Endnotes.

Emperor Zhou (紂王) of the Shang Dynasty was a tyrant and the last emperor of the Shang Dynasty.

Tai Ding (太丁) was the eldest son of King Tang.

Wai Bing (外丙) was the second son of King Tang and the successor of King Tang.

Zhong Ren (仲壬) was the third son of King Tang and the successor of Tai Ding.

Tai Jia (太甲) was the son of Tai Ding and the fourth emperor of the Shang Dynasty. He was young when he was enthroned.

Yi Yin was the regent of the second to the fourth emperors, and therefore, the mentor of Tai Jia.

Zhou Gong (周公) of the Zhou Dynasty was the brother of King Wu (周武王, died 1043 BC), the founder of the Zhou Dynasty. Duke Zhou was also the prime minister under King Wu.

Commentary:

This and the last few sections recorded discussions between Wan Zhang and Mencius during a history class. In this section, Mencius discussed three topics: popular support, succession to the throne, and divine providence. Contrary to criticisms by some modern scholars on Confucianism, Confucius and Mencius did not endorse the inheritance of monarchy per se. They thought that succession to the throne depended on popular support, the circumstantial needs, and historical development of the country, which are collectively called divine providence. If an emperor who inherited the throne failed in his role, he would be removed by Tian. Confucius cited the examples of Emperors Jie and Zhou, who were tyrants.

Section 7

萬章問曰 人有言 伊尹以割烹要湯 有諸。

　　孟子曰 否 不然。伊尹耕於有莘之野 而樂堯舜之道焉。非其義也 非其道也 祿之以天下 弗顧也。繫馬千駟 弗視也。非其義也 非其道也 一介不以與人 一介不以取諸人 湯使人以幣聘之 囂囂然曰 我何以湯之聘幣為哉 我豈若處畎畝之中 由是以樂堯舜之道哉。湯三使往聘之 既而幡然改曰 與我處畎畝之中 由是以樂堯舜之道 吾豈若使是君為堯舜之君哉 吾豈若使是民為堯舜之民哉 吾豈若於吾身親見之哉 天之生此民也 使先知覺後知 使先覺覺後覺也 予 天民之先覺者也 予將以斯道覺斯民也 非予覺之 而誰也。思天下之民匹夫匹婦有不被堯舜之澤者 若己推而內之溝中。其自任以天下之重如此 故就湯而說之以伐夏救民。吾未聞枉己而正人者也 況辱己以正天下者乎。聖人之行不同也 或遠或近 或去或不去 歸潔其身而已矣。吾聞其以堯舜之道要湯 末聞以割烹也。伊訓曰 天誅造攻自牧宮 朕載自亳。

Chapter 9: Wan Zhang (1)

Wan Zhang asked, "Some people say, 'Yi Yin managed to get the trust of King Tang with culinary art.' Was it true?"

Mencius replied, "No, it is not. When Yi Yin was a farmer in the field of You Xin, he was already an advocate of the magnanimous principles of Yao and Shun. If an opportunity was against his principles of Yi and Dao, even a reward of the whole country will not entice him to take the opportunity. He would disregard even a reward of a thousand chariots driven by four horses. In any matter contrary to his principles of Yi and Dao, he would not give even a penny to anyone or take a penny from anyone. King Tang once sent his messenger carrying rolls of silk as an initial employment offer to Yi Yin, who calmly said, 'What can I do with such big present of silk from King Tang? I love to work in the fields and practice the way of Yao and Shun.' Three times, King Tang sent his messenger to present Yi Yin with job offers. Yi Yin finally changed his mind and said, 'I enjoy being a farmer and practice the way of Yao and Shun here. Why should I not convert this king to be like Yao and Shun? Why should I not rule people of this country under the governance of Yao and Shun? Why should I not hope to see this happen during my lifetime? Among all people created by Tian, there must be someone with the foresight to lead others without, and someone with enlightenment to lead others without. I am an enlightened person. I should enlighten others. If not, who will do so?' He thought that if there were a single man and single woman in the country who could not enjoy the benevolence of Yao and Shun, he would feel as if he himself pushed them into the ditch and drown them. He took such a great responsibility on his shoulder. Therefore, he joined King Tang and persuaded Tang to overthrow Emperor Jie. I have never heard of a debased person to be able to rectify others, much less a disgraced person to be able to rectify the entire country. Saints have their own ways: some keep a distance from the king, some approach him, some quit their jobs, and some stay. Preservation of purity is their common objective. I have heard that Yi Yin convinced King Tang with the doctrines of Yao and Shun. I have not heard that Yi Yin did so with his culinary art. The *Teachings of Yi Yin* states, 'Tian's punishment on Emperor Jie started from his palace Mu. Our conquest of him started from city Bo.' "

Annotation:

The story of Yi Yin is narrated in Section 3 of Endnotes provides the background of this section.

Commentary:

There are two lessons in the section. The first is that one's responsibility and mission in life are more important than wealth. This is especially relevant to leaders of a country. The second is hinted by the last sentence: "Tian's punishment on Emperor Jie started from his palace Mu. Our conquest of him started from the city of Bo." Emperor Jie was a notorious tyrant and had a decadent lifestyle. His demise was caused by his own making. City Bo was a small and insignificant place. Despite its insignificance, a revolution started there and snowballed into a formidable force that overthrew an evil empire.

Section 8

萬章問曰 或謂孔子於衛主癰疽 於齊主侍人瘠環 有諸乎。

　孟子曰　否　不然也。好事者為之也。於衛主顏讎由。彌子

Chapter 9: Wan Zhang (1)

之妻與子路之妻 兄弟也。彌子謂子路曰 孔子主我 衛卿可得也。子路以告。孔子曰 有命。孔子進以禮 退以義 得之不得曰 有命。而主癰疽與侍人瘠環 是無義無命也。孔子悅於魯衛 遭宋桓司馬將要而殺之 微服而過宋。是時孔子當阨 主司城貞子 為陳侯周臣。吾聞觀近臣 以其所為主。觀遠臣 以其所主。若孔子主癰疽與侍人瘠環 何以為孔子。

Wan Zhang asked, "Some people say that when Confucius was in the state of Wey, he stayed in the home of the eunuch Yong Ju (who was also an ulcer doctor), and when Confucius was in the state of Qi, he stayed in the home of eunuch Qi Huan. Was it true?"

Mencius said, "No, it was not true. It was a rumor spread by gossipers. When Confucius was in the state of Wey, he stayed in the home of Yan Chou You. The wives of Mi Zi, a minister of Wey, and Zi Lu, were sisters. Mi Zi told Zi Lu, 'If Confucius had stayed in my home, he would become a minister of the state of Wey.' Zi Lu related this message to Confucius, who then said, 'It is a matter of fate.' Confucius stepped forward according to Li and retreated according to Yi. It was a matter of fate whether he got an official appointment or not. Confucius would have reneged on his principles of Yi and deviated from fate by being a guest of Yong Ju and Qi Huan. Confucius was disappointed with his experience in the states of Lu and Wey. He was later pursued by the chief commander of the state of Song, Huan Tui, who plotted to kill him. Confucius managed to escape from the state of Song disguised as a commoner. Confucius was in a dire situation at that time. Fortunately, he was received by Si Cheng Zhen Zi, who was a minister under maquis Chen Zhou. I have heard that the character of a minister in court can be discerned from his guests, and the character of an unfamiliar minister can be discerned from his hosts. If Confucius had stayed with eunuchs Yong Ju and Qi Huan, how could he be regarded as the honorable Confucius?"

Annotation:

Yong Ju (癰疽) was a eunuch and a confidant of Duke Ling of Wey (衛靈公). Some scholars thought that Yong Ju was a doctor who treated the ulcer of the Duke of Wey. Confucius once worked for Duke Ling of Wey and left after nine months, frustrated with the bad character of Duke of Wey. Yong Ju was complicit with the Duke.

Qi Huan (瘠環) was a eunuch of Qi Jing Gong (齊景公, also known as Duke Jing of Qi). The state of Qi (齊國) was a large hegemon during the Spring-Autumn Period. Qi Huan also had a bad reputation.

Yan Chou You (顏讎由) was a meritorious minister of the state of Wey and a friend of Confucius.

Mi Zi (彌子) was a prominent minister of the state of Wey and a confidant of Duke Ling of Wey. Confucius did not like him.

Zi Lu (子路, also known as Zhong You 仲由, 542–480 BC) was a disciple of Confucius and was best known for his ability and success in statesmanship. He was also noted for his valor and sense of justice.

The meanings of Li (禮) and Yi (義) are explained in the Introduction.

The states of Lu (魯國) and Wey (衛國) were small states during the Spring-Autumn Period.

Huan Tui (桓魋) was a powerful and notorious chief commander of the state of Song (宋國). Some scholars believed that he was the brother of Si Ma Niu (司馬牛), a disciple of Confucius. In 492 BC,

Chapter 9: Wan Zhang (1)

Confucius passed by the state of Song. Huan Tui heard about Confucius's visit to his country and planned to assassinate Confucius. While Confucius was teaching his disciples under a tree on the principles of Li, Huan Tui's men tried to kill Confucius by cutting down the tree. Fortunately, his disciples protected him so that he could escape (see Section 23 of Chapter 7, 述而, of *Confucius Analects*).

Si Cheng Zhen Zi (司城貞子) was a minister of the state of Chen (陳), a small state during the Spring-Autumn Period. The head of the state was marquis Chen Zhou (陳周).

Commentary:

The lesson of this section is that we should be cautious of who we befriend. People judge our character by our friends and peers.

During the Spring-Autumn and Warring Periods, a guest in a minister's home and estate was almost equivalent to be an aide, advisor, or comrade of the minister.

Section 9

萬章問曰 或曰 百里奚自鬻於秦養牲者 五羊之皮 食牛 以要秦穆公。信乎。

孟子曰 否 不然。好事者為之也。百里奚 虞人也。晉人以垂棘之璧與屈產之乘 假道於虞以伐虢。宮之奇諫 百里奚不諫。知虞公之不可諫而去 之秦 年已七十矣 曾不知以食牛干秦穆公之為汙也 可謂智乎。不可諫而不諫 可謂不智乎。知虞公之將亡而先去之 不可謂不智也。時舉於秦 知穆公之可與有行也而相之 可謂不智乎。相秦而顯其君於天下 可傳於後世不賢而能之乎。自鬻以成其君 鄉黨自好者不為 而謂賢者為之乎。

Wan Zhang asked, "Some people say, 'Bai Li Xi sold himself to a cattle owner for five pieces of ram skin. He then used his cattle raising skill to get an official job under Qin Mu Gong.' Was that true?"

Mencius said, "No, that was not true. This story was made up by rumor-mongers. Bai Li Xi was a native of the state of Yu. The state of Jin presented pieces of top-quality jade produced in Chui Ji and thoroughbreds to the king of the state of Yu and asked for permission to pass through Yu to attack the state of Guo, [a neighbor and ally of the state of Yu]. A minister of Yu, Gong Zhi Qi, advised the king of the state of Yu to grant the permission, whereas Bai Li Xi did not. Knowing that the king of Yu would not take his advice, Bai Li Xi left the state of Yu and went to the state of Qin. When he arrived at the state of Qin, he was already 70 years old. If he did not know that it would be a shameful act to seek an introduction to Qin Mu Gong by feeding oxen, could he be considered wise? Knowing that it was futile to give advice to his boss, Bai Li Xi refrained from giving advice. Was he not wise in doing so? Knowing that the king of the state of Yu would soon be ruined, Bai Li Xi left before the event. Was he not wise in doing so? When he had an opportunity in the state of Qin, he knew that he could partner with Qin Mu Gong for major achievements and accepted the offer of being the prime minister. Was he not wise in doing so? He assisted Qin Mu Gong to shine in the country and left behind a great legacy for future generations. Can a person without virtue and competency accomplish his achievements? The act of selling oneself as a slave to seek an introduction to a king is loathed by even a villager with self-esteem. Would a meritorious and competent person do so?"

Chapter 9: Wan Zhang (1)

Annotation:

Bai Li Xi (百里奚, circa 725–621 BC) was a scholar and a meritorious and competent prime minister of the state of Qin (秦) during the Spring-Autumn Period. He assisted the Duke of Qin, Qin Mu Gong (秦穆公), to become a prominent hegemon and to foster great peace and prosperity to the state of Qin. Before working for the state of Qin, he was a minister in the state of Yu (虞國) (Section 4 of Endnotes narrates the inspiring story of Bai Li Xi).

The state of Jin (晉國), located in the central north of China, was another hegemon during the Spring-Autumn Period.

The state of Yu (虞國) was a small state which used to be the enfeoffed territory of Shun (舜) before his rise to prominence.

Chui Ji (垂棘) was a place in the state of Jin famous for its production of top-quality jade.

The state of Guo (虢國) was small and a neighbor and ally of the state of Yu.

Gong Zhi Qi (宮之奇) was a bad minister and a confidant of the king of the state of Yu.

Commentary and Modern Perspective:

In this section, the discussion between Wan Zhang and Mencius showed that Wan Zhang was frustrated with Mencius for his reluctance to take official jobs. Wan Zhang cited the example of Bai Li Xi, who was rumored in folklores to be willing to debase himself for an opportunity to get a good job. Mencius corrected the myth and reminded Wan Zhang that a meritorious and virtuous person should not cheapen himself for the opportunity to obtain wealth and power. The last two sentences were the conclusion: "The act of selling oneself as a slave to seek an introduction to a king is loathed by even a villager with self-esteem. Will a meritorious and competent person do so?"

In modern times, there are numerous situations where people are too ready to betray their integrity, dignity, and nobility for money and power.

Chapter 10: Wan Zhang (2)

Section 1

孟子曰 伯夷 目不視惡色 耳不聽惡聲。非其君不事 非其民不使 治則進 亂則退。橫政之所出 橫民之所止 不忍居也。思與鄉人處 如以朝衣朝冠坐於塗炭也。當紂之時 居北海之濱 以待天下之清也。故聞伯夷之風者 頑夫廉 懦夫有立志。

伊尹曰 何事非君 何使非民。治亦進 亂亦進。曰 天之生斯民也 使先知覺後知 使先覺覺後覺 予 天民之先覺者也 予將以此道覺此民也。思天下之民匹夫匹婦有不與被堯舜之澤者 若己推而內之溝中 其自任以天下之重也。

柳下惠 不羞汙君 不辭小官。進不隱賢 必以其道。遺佚而不怨 阨窮而不憫。與鄉人處 由由然不忍去也。爾為爾 我為我 雖袒裼裸裎於我側 爾焉能浼我哉。故聞柳下惠之風者 鄙夫寬 薄夫敦。

孔子之去齊 接淅而行。去魯 曰 遲遲吾行也。去父母國之道也。可以速而速 可以久而久 可以處而處 可以仕而仕 孔子也。

孟子曰 伯夷 聖之清者也。伊尹 聖之任者也。柳下惠 聖之和者也。孔子 聖之時者也。孔子之謂集大成。集大成也者 金聲而玉振之也。金聲也者 始條理也。玉振之也者 終條理也。始條理者 智之事也。終條理者 聖之事也。智 譬則巧也。聖 譬則力也。由射於百步之外也 其至 爾力也。其中 非爾力也。

Mencius said, "Bo Yi would not look at ugly sights or listen to disgusting sounds. He would not serve an undeserving king and govern an undeserving people. He took an official post during peace and retired during chaos. He would not dwell in a country ruled by a tyrannical government or populated with lawless people. He considered that sitting next to a villager would dirty his official garment and hats. During the reign of Emperor Zhou, he resided on the north shore and waited for the coming of a cleansed society. Therefore, among those who follow the example of Bo Yi, the corrupt will become pure, and cowards will be emboldened.

Yi Yin said, 'No king is undeserving to be served. No people are undeserving to be governed.' He would take up an official post during peace and chaos. He said, 'Among all people created by Tian, there must be someone with foresight to lead others without, and someone with enlightenment to lead others without. I am an enlightened person. I should enlighten others.' He believed that if there were a single man and single woman in the country who could not enjoy the benevolence of Yao and Shun, he would feel as if he himself pushed them into the ditch and drown them. He took such a great responsibility on his shoulder.

Liu Xia Hui was not ashamed to serve a filthy king. He did not mind taking up a lowly official post. When he advanced to a high position, he did not conceal his virtue but adhered to his principles. He had no grudge on his dismissal, or grief during poverty. He got along with villagers and was reluctant to leave them. He said, 'You are you. I am I. Even if you stand naked by my side, how can you seduce or upset me?' Among those who follow the example of Liu

Xia Hui, the mean would become generous and the hypercritical would become forbearing.

When Confucius left the state of Qi, he had no time to cook his meal and simply packed up the grains already soaked in water. When he left the state of Lu, he said, 'Let us walk slowly. This should be way to leave my motherland.' When it was proper to leave quickly, he did so. When it was proper to stay longer, he did so. When it was proper to retire, he did so. When it was proper to take up an official post, he did so. This was the way of Confucius."

Mencius said, "Bo Yi was the pure type among sages. Yi Yin was the responsible type. Liu Xia Hui was the accommodative type. Confucius was the pragmatic type. Confucius's virtue encompassed all their virtues. What does an encompassing virtue mean? It is like an orchestral concert. It begins with the ringing of bells and ends with the percussion of jade vessels. The initial ringing of bells is orderly and meticulously performed, and the percussion of jade vessels in the finale is also orderly and meticulously done. The execution of an orderly beginning requires wisdom. The accomplishment of an orderly end requires sageness. Wisdom is like skill in a game, and sageness is like the strength and endurance in a game. For example, in an archery game, the ability to shoot a target one-hundred steps away requires an immense amount of strength. To be able to shoot the bull's eye requires a sophisticated skill."

Annotation:

Section 2 of Chapter 3 has similarly compared Bo Yi and Yi Yin with Confucius. Section 9 of Chapter 3 also contains a discussion on Bo Yi (伯夷) and Liu Xia Hui (柳下惠, 720–621 BC). Section 7 of Chapter 9 also mentions Yi Yin. Section 3 of Endnotes contains the story of Yi Yin (伊尹). Section 4 of Endnotes contains the story of

Bo Yi. These stories provide a solid background for the discussion in this section. It is important to read these sections again before reading the following commentary.

Commentary:

There are two main lessons in this section. The first lesson is that one should be pragmatic and avoid being stubborn and dogmatic. Mencius mentioned Confucius as a good example of pragmatism. Although all three ancient sages, Bo Yi, Yi Yin, and Liu Xia Hui, were praised by Confucians to be virtuous, they were still imperfect. For example, Bo Yi was stubborn and narrow-minded. Bo Yi upheld purity to the extreme. He looked at the world through a narrow lens. Everything was classified to be either right or wrong and black or white according to his narrow concept of Ren and Yi. He rejected King Wu of Zhou by asserting that King Wu should not wage a war during a mourning vigil of his diseased father, King Wen, and that King Wu should not revolt against his boss, the imperial Emperor Zhou. Bo Yi considered that King Wu's action was against the narrow concept of Ren, Yi, and filial piety. In fact, Emperor Zhou was a notorious tyrant. If Emperor Zhou had continued to stay in power a bit longer, more people would have been victimized, and the country would have been hellish. King Wu could not waste any more time trying to remove evil from the country. The elimination of evil from the country and saving its people from hell were more urgent than the observance of the mourning vigil of the diseased father, and more upright than the loyalty to a boss. Bo Yi failed to see this because he looked at the world in a binary and unidimensional view. History showed that King Wu did the right thing by waging a revolution against Emperor Zhou and founding a new dynasty, the Zhou Dynasty, which had hundreds of years of

Chapter 10: Wan Zhang (2)

peace and prosperity thereafter. King Wu was regarded a saintly king by Confucians, including Confucius himself.

Yi Yin was one of the best prime ministers in Chinese history. He took upon himself a responsibility to foster peace and prosperity for the country. He was lucky to have met the great King Tang, and that was Yi Yin's fate. What if Yi Yin had no opportunity to meet King Tang? He would then stay in the field as a peasant, and perhaps become a hermit for the rest of his life.

Liu Xia Hui was very adaptable and easy-going. His ability to mingle with ugly, lowly, and filthy people without compromising his upright principles was highly respectable. However, the circumstance and environment may not allow one to do so all the time. If it is proper and time to go, one should go and not linger any longer. Confucius's approach was: "When it was proper to leave quickly, he did so. When it was proper to stay longer, he did so. When it was proper to retire, he did so. When it was proper to take up an official post, he did so. This was the way of Confucius."

The key question here is how to know when it is proper to come or go? The second lesson of this section brings out the relevance of wisdom. The observance and upholding of Ren, Yi, and Li require the moral strength, whereas wisdom tells one to make the right call at the right circumstance.

This section also highlights the need to look at things from different angles and in a multidimensional view. If one looks at a matter under a single dimension, one can easily and naively tell what is right from wrong, right from left, north from south. But when one looks at worldly matters from a higher dimension, the identification of right from wrong, right from left, or north from south will be ambiguous and even irrelevant.

It is interesting to also note that the discussion of this section coincides with the philosophies of various branches of Buddhism.

Bo Yi's approach was close to Hinayana (or Theravada) Buddhism, whereas the approaches of Yi Yin and Liu Xia Hui were close to Mahayana Buddhism, and Confucius's approach was close to Zen Buddhism.

Section 2

北宮錡問曰 周室班爵祿也 如之何。

孟子曰 其詳不可得聞也。諸侯惡其害己也 而皆去其籍。然而軻也 嘗聞其略也。天子一位 公一位 侯一位 伯一位 子男同一位 凡五等也。君一位 卿一位 大夫一位 上士一位 中士一位 下士一位 凡六等。天子之制 地方千里 公侯皆方百里 伯七十里 子 男五十里 凡四等。不能五十里 不達於天子 附於諸侯 曰附庸。天子之卿受地視侯 大夫受地視伯 元士受地視子 男。大國地方百里 君十卿祿 卿祿四大夫 大夫倍上士 上士倍中士 中士倍下士 下士與庶人在官者同祿 祿足以代其耕也。次國地方七十里 君十卿祿 卿祿三大夫 大夫倍上士 上士倍中士 中士倍下士 下士與庶人在官者同祿 祿足以代其耕也。小國地方五十里 君十卿祿 卿祿二大夫 大夫倍上士 上士倍中士 中士倍下士 下士與庶人在官者同祿 祿足以代其耕也。耕者之所獲 一夫百畝。百畝之糞 上農夫食九人 上次食八人 中食七人 中次食六人 下食五人。庶人在官者 其祿以是為差。

Bei Gong Qi asked, "How was the hierarchy and enfeoffment system of the Zhou Dynasty?"

Mencius said, "The details of it are not clear now. Feudal lords

Chapter 10: Wan Zhang (2)

worried that the disclosure of such details would hurt them, and so they have kept them off records. However, I know its general outline.

The nobilities were ranked as follows: the imperial emperor was ranked on top; dukes second; marquises third; counts fourth; viscounts and barons fifth. Government officials were ranked as follows: the king was ranked on top; prime ministers second; ministers third; senior officials fourth; middle officials fifth; junior officials sixth. In terms of enfeoffments to nobilities, the imperial emperor was allotted a territory of one thousand square miles, each duke and marquis got one hundred square miles, each count got seventy square miles, and each viscount and baron got fifty square miles. Rulers of a territory smaller than fifty miles were not governed by the imperial court. Such a region was governed by a feudal lord as his colony. In terms of enfeoffments to government officials, the allotments to prime ministers were the same as those to marquises, the allotments to ministers were the same as those to counts, and the allotments to senior officials were the same as those to viscounts and barons.

In a state of the size of one hundred square miles ruled by a duke or marquis, the head of the state earned a salary, ten times that of his chief minister. The chief minister earned a salary, four times that of a minister. A minister earned a salary, double that of a senior official. A senior official earned a salary, double that of a middle official. A middle official earned a salary, double that of a junior official. A junior official earned the same salary as any other low-level government employee. Such a salary was enough to spare them from cultivating in the field.

In a state the size of seventy square miles, the head of the state got a salary that was ten times that of his chief minister. The chief minister earned a salary that was three times that of a minister. A minister earned a salary that was double that of a senior official. A senior official earned a salary that was double that of a middle official. A middle official earned a salary that was double that of a junior official. The salary of a junior official was the same as that earned by a low-level government employee. Such a salary was enough to spare them from working in the fields.

In a state of the size of fifty square miles, the head of the state earned a salary that was ten times that of his chief minister. The chief minister earned a salary that was double that of a minister. A minister earned a salary that was double that of a senior official. A senior official earned a salary that was double that of a middle official. A middle official earned a salary that was double that of a junior official. A junior official earned the same salary as any other low-level government employee. Such a salary was enough to spare them from working in the fields.

Regarding the incomes of peasants, each family of a farmer had one hundred acres of land. These plots of land were classified into levels of fertility. A top level of fertility supported a family of nine persons. A second-tier plot supported a family of eight persons. A third-tier plot supported a family of seven persons. A fourth-tier plot supported a family of six persons. A fifth-tier plot supported a family of five persons. Common people who were low-level staff in the government were paid according to a similar scale."

Commentary and Modern Perspective:

It is interesting to note that, for a large state of the size of one hundred square miles, the head of the state earned a salary 320 times that of a junior official or common staff in the government. This was a disparity of income. This disparity is comparable to the prevailing disparity in modern-day corporations.

Chapter 10: Wan Zhang (2)

Section 3

萬章問曰 敢問友。

　孟子曰 不挾長 不挾貴 不挾兄弟而友。友也者 友其德也 不可以有挾也。孟獻子 百乘之家也 有友五人焉 樂正裘 牧仲 其三人 則予忘之矣。獻子之與此五人者友也 無獻子之家者也。此五人者 亦有獻子之家 則不與之友矣。非惟百乘之家為然也。雖小國之君亦有之。費惠公曰 吾於子思 則師之矣 吾於顏般 則友之矣。王順 長息則事我者也。非惟小國之君為然也 雖大國之君亦有之。晉平公之於亥唐也 入云則入 坐云則坐 食云則食。雖疏食菜羹 未嘗不飽 蓋不敢不飽也。然終於此而已矣。弗與共天位也 弗與治天職也 弗與食天祿也 士之尊賢者也 非王公之尊賢也。舜尚見帝 帝館甥於貳室 亦饗舜 迭為賓主 是天子而友匹夫也。用下敬上 謂之貴貴。用上敬下 謂之尊賢。貴貴 尊賢 其義一也。

Wan Zhang asked, "May I ask about friendship?"

　Mencius said, "Friendship should not be based on seniority, age, social status, and kinship. You should befriend a person because of his virtues and nothing else. Meng Xian Zi was the head of a family with a hundred chariots. He had five friends: Yue Zheng Qiu and Mu Zhong. I forget the names of the other three. He befriended them because they did not care about the wealth and status of Meng's family. If anyone among them cared about the wealth of status of Meng's family, Meng would cease to befriend him. This applied not only to a family of a hundred chariots, since a king of a small state would do the same. Duke Hui of Bi said, 'I treat Zi Si as my teacher and Yan Ban as my friend. Wang Shun and Chang Xi are my staff only.' Not only did the kings of small states display such behavior, but the kings of large states also did the same. Duke Ping of Jin did the same to his friend, Hai Tang. When Hai invited Duke Ping to his house, Duke Ping went. When Hai told Duke Ping to be seated, Duke Ping sat down. When Hai told Duke Ping to eat, Duke Ping ate. Although there were only coarse rice and vegetable soup for dinner, Duke Ping ate fully and dared not do otherwise. Duke Ping treated Hai Tang as a friend only. Duke Ping did not share his sovereignty with Hai Tang, appoint Hai Tang to an official post, and pay Hai Tang an emolument. Duke Ping honored a virtuous person in his capacity as a scholar and friend. Duke Ping did not honor a virtuous person in his capacity as a king. When Shun visited Emperor Yao, who lodged Shun, his son-in-law, in the annex to the palace, they enjoyed meals together, ignoring their respective roles as the host and the guest. This exemplified how an emperor maintained a friendship with a private individual. The respect shown by inferiors to superiors is called the honoring of dignities. The respect shown by superiors to inferiors is called the honoring of the virtuous. The same principle applies to both the honoring of dignities and the honoring of the virtuous."

Annotation:

Meng Xian Zi (孟獻子) was a prime minister of the state of Lu (魯國).

Yue Zheng Qiu (樂正裘) and Mu Zhong (牧仲) were friends of Meng Xian Zi.

Duke Hui of Bi (費惠公, also known as Bi Hui Gong) was the head of a small state, Bi (費).

Jin Ping Gong (晉平公, also known as Duke Ping of Jin, reigned

from 557–532 BC) was the head of the hegemon, the state of Jin (晉).

Hai Tang (亥唐) was a friend of Jin Ping Gong.

Commentary and Modern Perspective:

In this section, Mencius talked about the essence of true friendship. He also gave the example of Duke Ping of Jin, who did not practice nepotism. Mencius also mentioned the humility of Emperor Yao. This is a valuable lesson for us.

Section 4

萬章問曰 敢問交際何心也。

孟子曰 恭也。

曰 卻之卻之為不恭 何哉。

曰 尊者賜之 曰 其所取之者 義乎 不義乎。而後受之 以是為不恭 故弗卻也。

曰 請無以辭卻之 以心卻之 曰 其取諸民之不義也。而以他辭無受 不可乎。

曰 其交也以道 其接也以禮 斯孔子受之矣。

萬章曰 今有禦人於國門之外者 其交也以道 其餽也以禮 斯可受禦與。

曰 不可。康誥曰 殺越人於貨 閔不畏死 凡民罔不譈。是不待教而誅者也。殷受夏 周受殷 所不辭也。於今為烈 如之何其受之。

曰 今之諸侯取之於民也 猶禦也。苟善其禮際矣 斯君子受

之 敢問何說也。

曰 子以為有王者作 將比今之諸侯而誅之乎。其教之不改而後誅之乎。夫謂非其有而取之者盜也 充類至義之盡也。孔子之仕於魯也 魯人獵較 孔子亦獵較。獵較猶可 而況受其賜乎。

曰 然則孔子之仕也 非事道與。

曰 事道也。

(曰) 事道奚獵較也。

曰 孔子先簿正祭器 不以四方之食供簿正。

曰 奚不去也。

曰 為之兆也。兆足以行矣 而不行 而後去 是以未嘗有所終三年淹也。孔子有見行可之仕 有際可之仕 有公養之仕也。於季桓子 見行可之仕也。於衛靈公 際可之仕也。於衛孝公 公養之仕也。

Wan Zhang asked, "What should be our right attitude in the giving and acceptance of presents in a social setting?"

Mencius replied, "Respect."

Wan Zhang asked, "Some people say that repeatedly declining a present is disrespectful. Why?"

Mencius said, "Suppose that your superior gives you a present. You then say in your mind, 'Did he get this present righteously or not?' and then accept the present. This is disrespectful. Therefore, you should not decline the present."

Wan Zhang asked, "Suppose I do not decline the present verbally but decline it in my heart and think that he took it from people improperly. I then find another excuse to decline the present. What is wrong with my approach?"

Chapter 10: Wan Zhang (2)

Mencius said, "Interpersonal interactions should be in accordance with propriety, and the giving and acceptance of presents should be in accordance with Li. This is Confucius's principle of accepting a present."

Wan Zhang said, "Suppose there is a bandit who robs and kills victims in a foreign land. He befriends me in accordance with propriety and gives me the robbed goods in accordance with Li. Should I accept his present?"

Mencius said, "No, you should not. The *Declaration of Kang* said, 'Bandits who kill victims to rob their goods, act fearlessly, and defy death are hated by everyone in the country.' These criminals should immediately be executed without probation. The Yin Dynasty inherited this law from the Xia Dynasty, and the Zhou Dynasty inherited this law from the Yin Dynasty. They did not want to change this law. The law against this crime is even tougher nowadays. How can you accept such presents from these criminals?"

Wan Zhang said, "Nowadays, feudal lords take from their people, just like bandits who kill and rob their victims. If their way of giving a present is perfectly in line with propriety and Li so that a Jun Zi would accept the present accordingly, may I ask the justification?"

Mencius said, "Do you think that, if there arises a truly magnanimous emperor, he will need to kill all feudal lords or he will put them on probation and admonish them, and if they do not repent, they need to be killed? Calling a person who takes what does not belong to him a robber is pushing an idealistic point to the extreme. When Confucius was an official in the state of Lu, the people of Lu liked a hunting competition. Confucius also participated in the hunting game. Even the competition for hunted trophies was acceptable. Why is the acceptance of gifts from feudal lords not acceptable?"

Wan Zhang asked, "If so, when Confucius was a government official, did he not put his doctrines into practice?"

Mencius said, "He put his doctrines into practice."

Wan Zhang asked, "If he put his doctrines into practice, why did he participate in the hunting game?"

Mencius said, "Confucius kept a strict register of all sacrificial materials. He did not indiscriminately enter food items from all over the place into the register."

Wan Zhang asked, "Why did he not leave the state of Lu?"

Mencius said, "It was about the prospect of putting his doctrines into practice. If the initial prospect of putting his doctrines into practice failed to crystalize, he would then leave his job. Therefore, he did not stay in any job for longer than three years. There were three conditions under which Confucius took an official job. If there was a favorable prospect of putting his doctrines into practice, he would take the official job. If the sovereign treated him with respect and politeness, he would take the official job. If the sovereign provided for his retirement, he would take the official job. Confucius worked for Ji Huan Zi because there was a prospect of putting Confucius's doctrines into practice. Confucius worked for Wey Ling Gong because Confucius was treated with respect and politeness. Confucius worked for Wey Xiao Gong because he provided for Confucius's retirement."

Annotation:

The meaning of Li (禮) was explained in the Introduction.

The "Declaration of Kang" is a chapter about the history of the Zhou Dynasty in the *Book of Documents* or *Book of Classic History*, also known as the *Shangshu* (尚書) and *Shu Jing* (書經). It is one of

Chapter 10: Wan Zhang (2)

the Five Classics of ancient Chinese literature and served as the foundation of Chinese political philosophy during the Yao, Shun, Xia Dynasty, Yin Dynasty, and Zhou Dynasty.

Ji Huan Zi (季桓子, died 492 BC) was the prime minister of the state of Lu (魯國). During the time of Confucius, the state of Lu was ruled by three prominent and wealthy families. The Ji Si family was the dominant family, and the other two families were Meng Sun Si (孟孫氏) and then Su Sun Si (叔孫氏). Ji Huan Zi inherited the position from his father Ji Ping Zi (季平子) in 505 BC. However, the Ji family was controlled by a wicked chief of staff (or governor), Yang Huo (陽貨, also known as Yang Hu 陽虎). Yang Huo imprisoned Ji Huan Zi and ruled the Ji family for three years. Later, Yang Huo plotted to kill Ji Huan Zi, who was fortunate to escape the assassination. Ji Huan Zi then obtained the support of the Meng Sun Si to topple and kill Yang Huo. Confucius was hired by Ji Huan Zi as the chief of justice (大司寇). In the beginning, Ji Huan Zi trusted Confucius, who helped Ji Huan Zi eliminate many wicked officials in the state. However, Confucius proposed to demolish three major cities occupied by wicked elements of the three prominent families. Two cities belonging to the Ji family and Su family, respectively, were conquered and destroyed. With the support of the state of Qi, the city belonging to the Meng family resisted, so Confucius's plan failed. Ji Huan Zi later realized that Confucius's motive for the plan was to reduce the power of the three families and raise the power of the duke of the state of Lu. Ji Huan Zi then started to keep a distance from Confucius. The state of Qi wanted to conquer the state of Lu for a while. It was mentioned in the *Confucius Analects* that the state of Qi sent a troupe of beautiful and sexy female dancers and singers as a gift to the duke of Lu, Lu Ding Gong, and Ji Huan Zi. Both gratefully accepted the gift. Ji Huan Zi indulged in their entertainment so much that he did not attend the royal court meeting for three days. The disappointed Confucius then quit his official job and left the state of Lu.

Wey Ling Gong (衛靈公, 540–493 BC) was the duke of Wey (衛國). Confucius once worked for him but later became frustrated. According to *Confucius Analects*, Confucius once commented on Wey Ling Gong's incompetent and unprincipled governance style. Wey Ling Gong was succeeded by his grandson, Wey Xiao Gong (衛孝公, died 456 BC). After Confucius left the state of Wey, his disciples, who were still officials of Wey, begged Confucius to return to the state of Wey. Since Wey Xiao Gong treated Confucius respectfully and paid him a good salary, and since Wey Xiao Gong was a good leader trying to foster prosperity to his state, Confucius agreed to return to the state of Wey.

Commentary:

This and the following few sections recorded the discussion between Wan Zhang and Mencius. The central theme of this discussion was related to why Mencius was reluctant to take an official job. Wan Zhang was a sharp and cunning debater. He wanted to persuade Mencius to readily accept official appointments from feudal lords. Wan Zhang tried to trap Mencius and put the words into Mencius's mouth in that it was acceptable to work for undeserving feudal lords. However, Wan Zhang could not trap Mencius.

Wan Zhang asked, "Suppose I do not decline the present verbally but decline it in my heart and think that he took it from people improperly. I then find another excuse to decline the present. What is wrong with my approach?" Wan Zhang hinted that Mencius had repeatedly given excuses to decline presents and job offers from feudal lords. If Mencius replied that it was wrong to do so, Mencius

Chapter 10: Wan Zhang (2)

would fall into Wan Zhang's trap. Mencius would then agree that he had made mistakes in the past. Mencius was smart enough to dodge Wan Zhang's question and just said, "Interpersonal interactions should be in accordance with propriety, and the giving and acceptance of presents should be in accordance with Li. This is Confucius's principle of accepting a present."

Wan Zhang then initiated another line of attack. He raised the topic of the parallelism between bandits and feudal lords. He had already anticipated that Mencius would answer that there was a difference between bandits and feudal lords, and that it was acceptable to accept presents and offers from feudal lords. Mencius was almost trapped by Wan Zhang when Mencius mentioned that even Confucius would find no problem in accepting gifts from feudal lords. When Wan Zhang asked, "If Confucius put his doctrines into practice, why did he participate in the hunting game?" he expected Mencius to surrender and agree to taking offers from feudal lords.

Realizing he was almost trapped, Mencius dodged the question and said instead, "Confucius kept a strict register of all sacrificial materials. He did not indiscriminately enter food items from all over the place into the register." These sentences seem out of place and unrelated to the ongoing discussion. This was also pointed out by Zhu Xi (朱熹), a prominent Confucian in the Song Dynasty. If these sentences are interpreted metaphorically, they might not be out of place and might reflect Mencius's wisdom. Sacrificial materials represented the noble qualities of a person's conscience to be presented to Tian. One must keep track of such qualities and uphold them. This is a serious matter, like keeping a registry of sacrificial stuff. One cannot let inferior and undeserving things, such as food and job opportunities from all directions, to enter to our sacred registry, which is our moral conscience. These two sentences reminded Wan Zhang that one must have a noble red line before considering the acceptance of gifts and offers from feudal lords. This is the same message for people nowadays. No amount of money should lure us to betray our morality.

Knowing that he was defeated by Mencius's argument, Wan Zhang then changed the subject and asked the reason why Confucius took and leave his jobs. Wan Zhang tried to convince Mencius that he was not as pragmatic as Confucius. Mencius, however, pointed out that the priority was the prospect of putting his doctrines into practice. If such hope turns out to be in vain, like Confucius, one must leave his job. Therefore, Mencius was a good follower of Confucius.

Section 5

孟子曰 仕非為貧也 而有時乎為貧。娶妻非為養也 而有時乎為養。為貧者 辭尊居卑 辭富居貧。辭尊居卑 辭富居貧 惡乎宜乎。抱關擊柝。孔子嘗為委吏矣 曰 會計當而已矣。嘗為乘田矣 曰 牛羊茁壯 長而已矣。位卑而言高 罪也。立乎人之本朝 而道不行 恥也。

Mencius said, "In general, a scholar should not take an official job because he is poor. However, it is sometimes necessary to do so. In general, one should not marry a wife simply to have children. However, it is sometimes necessary to do so. A scholar who needs to take an official job because of poverty must be ready to humble himself for a junior role and to forsake wealth for a mean salary. What jobs would match one's readiness to humble himself for a junior role and to forsake wealth for a mean salary? Gate-keepers and night-watchmen are good examples. Confucius was once a keeper of a warehouse. He said, 'I try to keep good accounts.' He was once a farm manager also. He said, 'I try to raise fat and strong oxen and sheep.' It is a misconduct to talk about high-level matters when one is in a low position in the government. It is a shame to fail to implement one's policy when one is in a high position in the government."

Commentary and Modern Perspective:

This section has five points. The first point is that we should have a sense of mission when we take a government job. We should not become a government official just for money, fame, or power. The second point is that we need to be pragmatic, and in exceptional situations, we should be ready to humble ourselves and take on a low-level job. The third point is that, when we are in a low-level position that is incomparable to one's caliber, we should try our best to do a good job. The fourth point is that we should be modest and avoid being a loose cannon talking about matters above our roles and boasting around. The fifth point is a reminder for all government officials and politicians—it is a shame to fail to implement one's policy when one is in a high position in the government. This point also hinted at the reason why Mencius had serious reservations in taking job offers from feudal lords.

Section 6

萬章曰 士之不托諸侯 何也。

孟子曰 不敢也。諸侯失國 而後托於諸侯 禮也。士之托於諸侯 非禮也。

萬章曰 君饋之粟 則受之乎。

曰　受之。

(曰)　受之何義也。

曰　君之於氓也　固周之。

曰　周之則受　賜之則不受　何也。

曰　不敢也。

曰　敢問其不敢何也。

曰　抱關擊柝者　皆有常職以食於上。無常職而賜於上者　以為不恭也。

曰　君餽之　則受之　不識可常繼乎。

曰　繆公之於子思也　亟問　亟餽鼎肉。子思不悅。於卒也　摽使者出諸大門之外　北面稽首再拜而不受。曰　今而後知君之犬馬畜伋。蓋自是臺無餽也。悅賢不能舉　又不能養也　可謂悅賢乎。

曰　敢問國君欲養君子　如何斯可謂養矣。

曰　以君命將之　再拜稽首而受。其後廩人繼粟　庖人繼肉　不以君命將之。子思以為鼎肉　使己僕僕爾亟拜也　非養君子之道也。堯之於舜也　使其子九男事之　二女女焉　百官牛羊倉廩備　以養舜於畎畝之中　後舉而加諸上位。故曰　王公之尊賢者也。

Wan Zhang asked, "Why should scholars not become aides and get financial support from a foreign feudal lord?"

Mencius said, "They dare not. When a feudal lord loses his state and finds refuge and support from another allied feudal lord, this is in accordance with the social norm under Li. However, it is against the social norm under Li for a scholar to become an aide and get

Chapter 10: Wan Zhang (2)

financial support from a foreign feudal lord."

Wan Zhang asked, "If the feudal lord donates food to the scholar, should he accept it?"

Mencius said, "Yes, he can."

Wan Zhang asked, "Why can he accept?"

Mencius said, "It is a common practice for feudal lords to donate food to refugees from foreign states as an act of charity."

Wan Zhang asked, "Why it is proper to accept donations but improper to accept official support?"

Mencius said, "The scholars dare not accept official support."

Wan Zhang asked, "Why do they not accept such support?"

Mencius said, "Gate-keepers and night-watchmen are entitled to earn their living from their job responsibilities. If a scholar does not have a specific responsibility, it is disrespectful to receive financial support."

Wan Zhang asked, "If the feudal lord donates food to the scholar continually for a long time, is it proper to accept it?"

Mencius said, "Duke Mu of the state of Lu treated Zi Si in the following way: he frequently sent a messenger to visit Zi Si, asked about his well-being, and give him caldrons of meat. Zi Si was upset about this. After a long while, Zi Si pushed the messenger out the main door and bowed his head to the ground twice with his face to the north. He turned down the present and said, 'I now know that the duke wants to treat me like a dog and horse.' Since then, the messenger stopped sending food to Zi Si. When a feudal lord pretends to value the virtue and talents of a scholar but does not give him a defined job nor support him properly, does the feudal lord really value him?"

Wan Zhang asked, "May I ask what a feudal lord should do if he wants to properly support a virtuous and competent scholar?"

Mencius said, "If the feudal lord sends the present in his name, the scholar should receive the present by bowing his head down to the ground twice. Subsequently, the pantry keeper of the lord continued to send grains and the chef continued to send caldrons of meat to Zi Si, albeit not in the name of the feudal lord. Zi Si was annoyed about having to repeatedly bow to these messengers for the meat in the caldrons. This should not be the proper way to support a virtuous and competent scholar. Yao treated Shun in the following way: Yao sent nine sons to serve Shun and two daughters to marry Shun. Yao arranged various officers, oxen and sheep, and storehouses of grains to support Shun, who was still working in the fields. Yao later promoted Shun to a high position in the government. From this example, we can say, 'This is the way how a king honors a virtuous and competent person.' "

Annotation:

During the Spring-Autumn Period and Warring States Period, there was a practice for feudal lords, prominent officials of government, and wealthy families to keep and support a group of courtiers who had no specific jobs and responsibilities. These courtiers stayed in the host's estate and offered occasional assistance and advice to the host, who did not regard and honor the courtiers highly. In his opening question, Wan Zhang referred to these courtiers.

Lu Mu Gong (魯穆公, also known as Duke Mu of Lu, 410–377 BC) was the twenty ninth sovereign of the state of Lu (魯國).

Zi Si (子思, 483–402 BC) was the grandson of Confucius and the teacher of Mencius and the author of Zhong Yong (中庸), *The Book of Zhong Yong* (*The Doctrine of the Mean*), *The Doctrine of the Mean*, or *Book of Zhong Yong*, a central doctrine of Confucianism.

Chapter 10: Wan Zhang (2)

Commentary:

This section has two points. The first point is that we should earn our living by doing an honorable and responsible job. This is highlighted by the sentences: "Gate-keepers and night-watchmen are entitled to earn their living from their job responsibilities. If a scholar does not have a specific responsibility, it is disrespectful to receive financial support."

The second point is about the proper way of valuing and respecting a virtuous and competent subordinate.

Section 7

萬章曰 敢問不見諸侯 何義也。

孟子曰 在國曰市井之臣 在野曰草莽之臣 皆謂庶人。庶人不傳質為臣 不敢見於諸侯 禮也。

萬章曰 庶人 召之役 則往役。君欲見之 召之 則不往見之 何也。

曰 往役 義也。往見 不義也。且君之欲見之也 何為也哉。

曰 為其多聞也 為其賢也。

曰 為其多聞也 則天子不召師 而況諸侯乎。為其賢也 則吾未聞欲見賢而召之也。繆公亟見於子思 曰 古千乘之國以友士 何如。子思不悅 曰 古之人有 曰事之云乎 豈曰友之云乎。子思之不悅也 豈不曰 以位 則子君也 我 臣也 何敢與君友也 以德 則子事我者也 奚可以與我友。千乘之君求與之友 而不可得也 而況可召與。齊景公田 招虞人以旌 不至 將殺之。志

士不忘在溝壑　勇士不忘喪其元。孔子奚取焉。取非其招不往也。

曰　敢問招虞人何以。

曰　以皮冠。庶人以旃　士以旂　大夫以旌。以大夫之招招虞人　虞人死不敢往。以士之招招庶人　庶人豈敢往哉。況乎以不賢人之招招賢人乎。欲見賢人而不以其道　猶欲其入而閉之門也。夫義　路也。禮　門也。惟君子能由是路　出入是門也。詩云　周道如砥　其直如矢　君子所履　小人所視。

萬章曰　孔子　君命召　不俟駕而行。然則孔子非與。

曰　孔子當仕有官職　而以其官召之也。

Wan Zhang asked, "Some say that a scholar should not take an initiative to see a feudal lord. What does this mean?"

Mencius said, "People living in cities are urbanites. People living elsewhere are called people in the grassroots. Both types are called commoners. Commoners who do not have official roles dare not go and see their feudal lords. This is the rule according to Li."

Wan Zhang asked, "When a commoner is drafted into to the army, he must obey. On the contrary, when a feudal lord summons a commoner for a meeting, the commoner does not need to go. Why?"

Mencius said, "It is a responsibility to comply with a draft order. There is, however, no established responsibility for a commoner to see a feudal lord. Moreover, one needs to ask the reason why the feudal lord wants to see him."

Wan Zhang said, "The feudal lord may want to see the scholar because of his great knowledge and virtue."

Mencius said, "Even the emperor does not summon his teacher to see him. Why can a feudal lord summon his teacher? If the reason

Chapter 10: Wan Zhang (2)

for the summon is the great virtue of the scholar, I have never heard of the practice of summoning a virtuous person for a meeting. Eager to see Zi Si, Duke Mu of the state of Lu said to Zi Si, 'I am the sovereign of a state with a long history and with a thousand chariots. I want to be your friend. May I?' Zi Si was upset and said, 'There is an ancient saying that the relationship between a boss and employee should not be confused with friendship.' Zi Si was upset because he also said to Duke Mu, 'In respect of status, you are my boss, and I am your staff. How dare I be your friend? In respect of virtue, you are my student. How can you be my friend?' Even the lord of a state with a thousand chariots cannot request to befriend a virtuous scholar. How much less can he summon a scholar? Once upon a time, when Duke Jing of Qi was hunting, he summoned the guardian of the hunting ground with a flag. The guardian would not comply. The upset duke was about to execute him. There is a saying: 'A person with a staunch will is not afraid of being dumped into a drench. A person with great valor is not afraid of being beheaded.' What did Confucius recommend in this situation? He endorsed the guardian's refusal to respond to the summon because of its improper protocol."

Wan Zhang asked, "What should be the proper protocol to summon the guardian?"

Mencius replied, "He should be summoned with a skin cap. A commoner should be summoned with a plain banner. A low-level official should be summoned with a banner with dragons embroidered on it. A minister should be summoned with a flag having feathers attached to the top of the staff. The guardian was summoned with a flag designated for a minister. Therefore, the guardian refused to go to see the duke. When a commoner is summoned with the protocol designated for a low-level official, the commoner dares not go. It is even more inappropriate to summon a

403

virtuous and competent person with a protocol that applies to people without virtue and competency. Trying to see a virtuous and competent scholar while ignoring the scholar's principles is like trying to walk through a closed door. Yi is the path and Li is the door. A Jun Zi follows the path and goes in and out through the door. The *Book of Poetry* said, 'The path laid down by the Zhou Dynasty is the foundation and is as straight as an arrow. Jun Zis follow it but Xiao Rens see it.' "

Wan Zhang asked, "When Confucius was summoned by his king, Confucius did not wait for his carriage to be ready and instead walked in a hurry to see the king. Was Confucius wrong in doing so?"

Mencius replied, "At that time, Confucius was a minister. When he was summoned, he was obliged to respond to the summon."

Annotation:

The annotations regarding Duke Mu of the state of Lu and Zi Si were included in Section 6 above. The episode regarding Duke Jing of Qi and the guardian was also mentioned in Section 1 of Chapter 6.

Commentary and Modern Perspective:

Although this section discussed the rules under Li during the time of Mencius, the modern lesson of this section is that a boss should pay due respect to virtuous and competent staff.

Section 8

孟子謂萬章曰　一鄉之善士　斯友一鄉之善士。一國之善士　斯友一國之善士。天下之善士 斯友天下之善士。以友天下之善士為未足 又尚論古之人。頌其詩 讀其書 不知其人 可乎。是以論其世也。是尚友也。

Mencius told Wan Zhang, "A distinguished and virtuous scholar in a village wants to befriend all distinguished and virtuous scholars in the village. A distinguished and virtuous scholar in a country wants to befriend all distinguished and virtuous scholars in the country. A distinguished and virtuous scholar in the world wants to befriend all distinguished and virtuous scholars in the world. If it is insufficient to befriend all distinguished and virtuous scholars in the world, one must learn from ancient sages. Is it appropriate to just recite their poems and read their books without knowing their characters? Therefore, we must study their eras and backgrounds. This is equivalent to befriending them."

Section 9

齊宣王問卿。孟子曰 王何卿之問也。
　王曰 卿不同乎。
　曰 不同。有貴戚之卿 有異姓之卿。
　王曰 請問貴戚之卿。
　曰 君有大過則諫 反覆之而不聽 則易位。
　王勃然變乎色。
　曰 王勿異也。王問臣 臣不敢不以正對。
　王色定 然後請問異姓之卿。
　曰 君有過則諫 反覆之而不聽 則去。

Mencius in Modern Perspectives

King Xuan of Qi asked Mencius about matters related to prime ministers.

Mencius asked, "Do you want to hear about types of prime ministers?"

King Xuan replied, "Are there different types of prime ministers?"

Mencius replied, "Yes, there are different types. Some are noblemen and relatives of the king. Some have different family names."

King Xuan asked, "How do you characterize those who are noblemen and relatives of the king?"

Mencius replied, "When the king commits mistakes, this type of prime ministers will try to remonstrate him. If he repeatedly ignores them, they will overthrow him."

King Xuan immediately reacted with unease. Mencius said, "Your Majesty, please do not feel offended. Since you ask this question, I dare not hide the truth." After King Xuan had calmed down, he then asked about the other type of prime ministers.

Mencius said, "When the king commits mistakes, the second type will try to remonstrate him. If he repeatedly ignores them, they will simply quit."

Annotation:

King Xuan of Qi (齊宣王, 350–301 BC) was mentioned repeatedly in Chapter 2, Sections 3 and 4 of Chapter 4, and Section 17 of Chapter 7.

Commentary:

Mencius subtly spoke about himself. He hinted to King Xuan

that he was disappointed with the king and would be ready to quit. Mencius also warned the king that the other type of prime ministers who were noblemen and relatives of the king could overthrow him.

Chapter 11: Gao Zi (1)

Section 1

告子曰 性 猶杞柳也。義 猶桮棬也。以人性為仁義 猶以杞柳為桮棬。

　孟子曰 子能順杞柳之性而以為桮棬乎。將戕賊杞柳而後以為桮棬也。如將戕賊杞柳而以為桮棬 則亦將戕賊人以為仁義與。率天下之人而禍仁義者 必子之言夫。

Gao Zi said, "Human nature is like the qi-willow tree, and Ren and Yi are like wooden cups and bowls. Your deduction of Ren and Yi from human nature is like the making of wooden cups and bowls from qi-willow trees."

　Mencius said, "Can you keep the nature of the willow tree untouched to make wooden cups and bowls? You must cut the wood of the tree and cast it into cups and bowls. Since you must cut up the tree and destroy its nature to make cups and bowls, must you not, according to your analogy, destroy human nature to produce Ren and Yi? Your words will definitely lead all men in the world to destroy Ren and Yi."

Annotation:

　Gao Zi (告子) was a philosopher and contemporary of Mencius and was mentioned in the Introduction and Section 2 of Chapter 3. Gao Zi adopted the ancient theory that human nature consisted only of the inborn physical (biological, physiological, psychological, and

Chapter 11: Gao Zi (1)

instinctive) characteristics of human beings. Gao Zi also advocated the view that Yi was externally determined and not an internal virtue. Mencius refuted Gao Zi's views.

Commentary:

This section and the following sections in this chapter constitute the crux of Mencius's philosophy on humanity. His philosophy was hotly contended during his time. His philosophy was a path-breaking development for Confucianism. Confucius regarded Ren as the core and ultimate virtue of humans. Mencius took a step further. He considered that Ren, Yi, Li, and wisdom are innate properties of human nature. Humanity is not just about physical characteristics of human beings but also about the moral characteristics covering Ren, Yi, Li, and wisdom. Mencius raised human nature to humanity, which is a higher level in terms of the value of the existence of human life. Under this idealism, human beings are different from animals because humans are rational beings and, have free will, and therefore, morals. The set of moral principles defines humanity from morality standpoint.

The ancient concept of human nature before Confucius's and Mencius's time was encapsulated in the statement: "The collection of natural properties of human existence (and life) is human nature (生之謂性)." This statement sounds circular. Natural properties include the set of biological, physiological, psychological, and instinctive characteristics and functions. This was a basic understanding of humanity and excluded the dimension of morality. Mencius objected to this rudimentary concept of human nature, which does not differentiate human beings from animals. Animals do not have free will and morals.

Gao Zi looked at human natures materialistically like the wood

409

of a willow tree, which must first be cut and crafted to become wooden cups and bowls. In Gao Zi's analogy, wooden cups and bowls are like Ren and Yi. In his view, human nature was extremely rudimentary and must be trained and nurtured before the Ren and Yi virtues are acquired. This implies that Ren and Yi are not innate, not inside human nature, only obtained through external means later in life, and therefore, are artificial and unnatural. In modern philosophic terms, Gao Zi's view looked at the relationship between human nature and Ren and Yi virtues both empirically and synthetically. On the other hand, Mencius looked at the relationship analytically—the distinction between human nature and animal nature must imply the presence of morals inside human nature and Ren and Yi are two moral principles.

When Mencius asked, "Must you not, according to your analogy, destroy human nature to produce Ren and Yi?" Mencius refuted Gao Zi's view that human nature must be crafted and modified to obtain Ren and Yi. According to Gao Zi's argument, Ren and Yi are unnatural, dependent on external processes, and therefore, do not have absolute certainty of prevalence among human beings. Worse still, one must destroy basic human nature to achieve the higher goals of Ren and Yi. By doing so, one would also destroy Ren and Yi. Therefore, Mencius said to Gao Zi, "Your words will definitely lead all men in the world to destroy Ren and Yi."

Section 2

告子曰 性猶湍水也 決諸東方則東流 決諸西方則西流。人性之無分於善不善也 猶水之無分於東西也。

　　孟子曰 水信無分於東西。無分於上下乎。人性之善也 猶

Chapter 11: Gao Zi (1)

水之就下也。人無有不善　水無有不下。今夫水　搏而躍之　可使過顙。激而行之　可使在山。是豈水之性哉。其勢則然也。人之可使為不善　其性亦猶是也。

Gao Zi said, "Human nature is like flowing water. If you open a passage for it to the east, it will flow to the east. If you open a passage for it to the west, it will flow to the west. Human nature is not intrinsically good or evil, just as water can be directed towards the east or west."

Mencius said, "Water definitely does not tend towards east or west, but does it tend to flow downward, though? Human nature tends towards goodness as if water tends to flow downwards. There is nobody whose nature does not tend towards goodness. No water does not flow downwards. In the case of water, it will leap over your forehead if you strike it. It can cross the mountain if you pump it up. Is this the intrinsic nature of water? It is the applied force that causes its behavior. Likewise, human beings can be made to do evil, like how water reacts to external force."

Commentary:

Both Gao Zi and Mencius used analogies to present their theses. Their arguments should not be analyzed with formal logic.

Gao Zi continued with his view that human nature is neutral. Human nature is not intrinsically good or evil. Therefore, morality is irrelevant to human nature. This view was popular during the time of Mencius. There were at least four contending views: (1) according to Gao Zi, human nature was neither good nor evil and that external environment, influences, and other factors that caused human nature to exhibit goodness or evil; (2) some human natures were good and some evil; (3) according to Sun Zi, human nature was innately evil but could be corrected by upbringing, education, and law; (4) according to Mencius, human nature was innate goodness. On deeper analysis, one can see that the first three schools claimed that goodness, Ren, and Yi are all externally determined or even non-existent in some cases. They were not intrinsic properties of human nature. Proponents of these views argued from the ancient principle: "The collection of natural properties of human existence (and life) is human nature (生之謂性)" and their conclusions were derived empirically. Mencius objected to this principle and defined human nature on a morality level.

Gao Zi said the first three sentences to present his argument with the analogy of water. There are two implicit points in these sentences. First, human nature is neither intrinsically good nor evil. Second, the goodness or evil of human nature depends on external forces. If you direct human beings towards goodness, like directing water towards east, they will tend towards goodness. If you direct human beings towards evil, like directing water to the west, they will tend towards evil. This thesis has dangerous implications for the society. This thesis implies that the citizenry of a country is a herd of sheep, which can be manipulated through brainwashing and propaganda spread by hypocrites, wicked opinion leaders, demagogues, and dictators. Citizenry of the country do not have a universal and inherent moral standard to judge good from evil and right from wrong. The consequence will bring chaos and destructive wars to the country. That was why, in the last section, Mencius said to Gao Zi, "Your words will definitely lead all men in the world to destroy Ren and Yi." Because of this moral vision, Mencius objected to Gao Zi's thesis. It should be noted that Mencius did not deduce his views from empirical arguments. All arguments presented by his opponents relied on empirical observations and

Chapter 11: Gao Zi (1)

existential analyses of the physical, biological, psychological, and instinctive characteristics of human life. Based on this view, human beings are not much different from animals, and the value of humanity and the value of human civilization are therefore debased. Eventually, such debasement will morally ruin human civilization.

Mencius then used the same analogy of water to explain his point that human nature was intrinsically good. Mencius then explained the difference between intrinsic property versus empirically observed behavior caused by external force in the next two sentences: "In the case of water, it will leap over your forehead if you strike it. It can cross the mountain if you pump it up. Is this the intrinsic nature of water? It is the applied force that causes its behavior." In the last two sentences, Mencius thus explained that human nature was intrinsically good, but evil behaviors were the result of external influences.

Section 3

告子曰 生之謂性。

　孟子曰 生之謂性也 猶白之謂白與。

　曰 然。

　(曰) 白羽之白也 猶白雪之白。白雪之白 猶白玉之白與。

　曰 然。

　(曰) 然則犬之性 猶牛之性。牛之性 猶人之性與。

Gao Zi said, "The collection of natural properties of human existence (and life) is human nature."

Mencius said, "By saying that the collection of natural properties of human existence is human nature, do you mean that this statement is the same as saying white is white?"

Gao Zi said, "Yes."

Mencius said, "Is the white color of a white feather the same as the white color of white snow, and the white color of the white snow the same as the white color of white jade?"

Gao Zi again said, "Yes."

Mencius said, "Therefore, is the nature of a dog the same as the nature of an ox, and is the nature of an ox the same as human nature?"

Commentary:

It should be noted that there was a trick in Mencius's argument. The statement: "white is white" is a tautology. Mencius tricked Gao Zi into stating that the collection of natural properties of human existence is tautologically the same as human nature. Mencius further tricked Gao Zi into agreeing that the white colors of white feather, white snow and white jade were the same. Gao Zi did not realize that he was trapped by replying "yes" to Mencius's first two questions. If he had answered that the white colors of white feather, white snow, and white jade were slightly different, Mencius would have forced Gao Zi to agree that the collection of natural properties of human existence was not the same as human nature, and that the nature of a dog was different from the nature of an ox, and the nature of an ox was different from human nature. This was the answer that Mencius wanted to put into the mouth of Gao Zi. If Gao Zi had replied "yes" to the last two questions, he would be trapped into negating the empirical reality that the natures of dogs and oxen were different from human beings.

Mencius's goal in this discussion was the objection to the assertion (A) that the collection of natural properties of human existence is human nature. Although not strictly logical, Mencius tried to use contrapositive inference here. Since this statement (A) implies statement (B)—that the natures of dogs and oxen are the same as human nature—and since statement (B) is negated by Gao Zi's belief in empiricism, statement (A) must then be false.

Mencius stressed that human nature was not just the collection of natural properties of human existence but also included morality, which is innate goodness. This innate goodness covers the four basic virtues: Ren, Yi, Li, and wisdom. From a purely moral (and human) standpoint, human nature consists of just these virtues. Sections 4 to 10, and 15 below will elaborate this point further.

Section 4

告子曰 食色 性也。仁 內也 非外也。義 外也 非內也。

孟子曰 何以謂仁內義外也。

曰 彼長而我長之 非有長於我也。猶彼白而我白之 從其白於外也 故謂之外也。

曰 異於白馬之白也 無以異於白人之白也。不識長馬之長也 無以異於長人之長與。且謂長者義乎。長之者義乎。

曰 吾弟則愛之 秦人之弟則不愛也 是以我為悅者也 故謂之內。長楚人之長 亦長吾之長 是以長為悅者也 故謂之外也。

曰 耆秦人之炙 無以異於耆吾炙。夫物則亦有然者也 然則耆炙亦有外與。

Gao Zi said, "Food and sex are basic human nature. Ren is internal and not external whereas Yi is external and not internal."

Mencius in Modern Perspectives

Mencius asked, "What do you mean by saying that Ren is internal, and Yi is external?"

Gao Zi said, "When I meet an elderly person, I respect him. My respect of this person arises from his being elderly, not from my predetermined mind. It is like the case when I see a white man and I perceive him as white. His being white is an external phenomenon and my perception is induced by this phenomenon."

Mencius said, "It is correct to say that the white color of a white horse is the same as the white color of a white man. However, do you know that our regard to the old age of an old horse is different from our respect to an elderly person? Does our respect arise from the objective fact of his old age? Or does it arise from our internal respect of elderly persons?"

Gao Zi said, "I love my younger brother. I do not love the brother of a native of Qin. My feeling of love is determined by myself. I therefore say that Ren is internal. I respect elderly persons of Chu and elderly persons of my own state. My respect is determined by age. I, therefore, say that Yi external."

Mencius said, "The enjoyment of the taste of roasted meat of Qin is not different from the enjoyment of the taste of roasted meat of our state. Many things can be analyzed similarly. How can you assert that the enjoyment of roasted meat is external?"

Commentary and Modern Perspective:

When Gao Zi said that food and sex are basic human nature, he repeated the theme that the collection of natural properties of human existence (and life) is human nature (生之謂性). These are the common needs of animals.

Gao Zi then jumped to another thesis that Ren was internal, and Yi was external. By saying that Ren was internal, he meant that Ren

Chapter 11: Gao Zi (1)

came from the heart (mind) and was not induced, influenced, or forced by external objects, events, environments, and phenomena. By saying that Yi was external, he meant that Yi (the virtue of righteousness) was induced by external objects, events, environment, and phenomena. The implication of this view is that righteous acts must be externally imposed on people. This further leads to the legislation of laws and imposition of harsh punishments, which were endorsed and implemented by the School of Legalists. In Section 2 of Chapter 3, Mencius objected to this view and criticized Gao Zi.

Gao Zi said, "When I meet an elderly person, I respect him. My respect of this person arises from his being elderly, not from my predetermined mind. It is like the case when I see a white man and I perceive him as white." Gao Zi made a false analogy here. The respect given to an elderly person is not the same as the perception of white color of a white man. Respect is a moral issue, whereas perception of color is a cognitive issue. The two are totally different. While it is correct to say that the perception of color was induced externally, it is incorrect to link this mental activity to respect, which is an internal morality of the observer. Therefore, Mencius asked Gao Zi the question: "Does our respect arise from the objective fact of his old age? Or does it arise from our internal respect of elderly persons?" Mencius could further explain that, without the virtue of respect, which was an aspect of Yi, we would not pay respect to anybody, irrespective of whether there was an old man or not. The virtue of respect is a subjective and internal matter.

Mencius said, "However, do you know that our regard to the old age of an old horse is different from our respect to an elderly person?" Our regard to the old age of an old horse is different from our respect to an elderly person. We pity the horse for its old age, whereas we respect an elderly for his or her age. The former related

417

to Ren, and the latter is related to Yi.

Mencius said, "The enjoyment of the taste of roasted meat of Qin is not different from the enjoyment of the taste of roasted meat of our state. Many things can be analyzed similarly. How can you assert that the enjoyment of roasted meat is external?" Mencius used the analogy of taste to refute Gao Zi's assertion that respect is determined by external factors. Regarding the concept of "respect of old age", the subject matter should be "respect" rather than the objective target of "old age". Gao Zi confused the subject matter with the object matter. If respect exists internally, it does not matter who is old or not, or where the elderly comes from. If we do not have the attitude of respect, it also does not matter where the elderly comes from. Therefore, the origin of the elderly person has no bearing to whether 'respect' is internal or external.

Modern people often make Gao Zi's mistake. There is an over-emphasis on objective observations, and hence, scientific knowledge and disregard for moral imperatives. In many situations, the subject matter is a moral question: "what ought to be", much like the "respect" for people. Instead, common people focus their attention on the objective question: "what is it", like whether the person is an elderly or not or where he comes from. This is a cause of decadence in modern society.

Section 5

孟季子問公都子曰 何以謂義內也。

　　曰 行吾敬 故謂之內也。

　　(曰) 鄉人長於伯兄一歲 則誰敬。

　　曰 敬兄。

　　(曰) 酌則誰先。

Chapter 11: Gao Zi (1)

曰 先酌鄉人。

(曰) 所敬在此 所長在彼 果在外 非由內也。

公都子不能答 以告孟子。

孟子曰 敬叔父乎 敬弟乎。彼將曰 敬叔父。曰 弟為尸則誰敬。彼將曰 敬弟。子曰 惡在其敬叔父也。彼將曰 在位故也。子亦曰 在位故也。庸敬在兄 斯須之敬在鄉人。

季子聞之曰 敬叔父則敬 敬弟則敬 果在外 非由內也。

公都子曰 冬日則飲湯 夏日則飲水 然則飲食亦在外也。

Meng Ji Zi asked Gong Du Zi, "What do you mean by saying that Yi is internal?"

Gong Du Zi said, "We act according to our inner feeling of respect. Therefore, Yi is internal."

Meng Ji Zi asked, "Suppose there is a villager who is older than your elder brother by one year. Whom do you respect?"

Gong Du Zi replied, "I respect my brother."

Meng Ji Zi asked further, "To whom you pour out wine first during a banquet?"

Gong Du Zi replied, "The villager first."

Meng Ji Zi said, "You respect your elder brother during one occasion, but you honor the villager during another. This shows that you action is determined externally, not internally."

Gong Du Zi could not answer. He related the conversation to Mencius, who then said, "You can ask him, 'Do you respect your uncle? Do you respect your younger brother?' He would then reply that he respects his uncle. You then ask further, 'If your younger brother is ordained a holy role which personates ancestors during a worship ceremony, whom do you respect?' He would then reply, 'I respect my younger brother.' You then ask him, 'Why not the uncle?' He would then reply, 'Because my younger brother is in an honorable position.' You then say to him, 'That is exactly because of different positions. I ordinarily respect my elder brother, but in a special situation, I first need to pour wine to the villager.' "

Meng Ji Zi heard the above conversation and said to Gong Du Zi, "When respect is due to my uncle, I respect him. When respect is due to my younger brother, I respect him. Therefore, your respect is externally determined, not internally."

Gong Du Zi said to Meng Ji Zi, "You drink hot soup during winter and cool water during summer. Is the desire for food and water also determined externally?"

Annotation:

Meng Ji Zi (孟季子) was the younger brother of Meng Zhong Zi (孟仲子) who was a cousin and disciple of Mencius.

Gong Du Zi (公都子) was a disciple of Mencius.

Commentary:

The discussion between Meng Ji Zi and Gong Du Zi was about whether Yi was intrinsic to human nature or externally determined. Meng Ji Zi's viewpoint was the same as Gao Zi's. They both argued that since the observed behavior of Yi changes with external environment and circumstance, it must be determined by external factors. Therefore, Meng Ji Zi said, "You respect your elder brother during one occasion, but you honor the villager during another. This shows that you action is determined externally, not internally." Meng Ji Zi made the same mistake as Gao Zi mentioned in Section 4 above. Regarding the concept of "respect of a person", the subject matter is "respect" rather than the objective target of "a person".

Meng Ji Zi confused the subject matter with the object matter. If respect exists internally, it does not matter who that person is and under what situation that person is present. If we do not have the attitude of respect, it also does not matter who that person is, and under what situation that person is present. There is no inferential relationship between the subject matter "respect" and the object matter "a person". Therefore, it is wrong to deduce from the observation of different behaviors under different circumstances that respect is internal or external.

Gao Zi and Meng Ji Zi adopted the narrow meaning of Yi: "Yi is appropriateness (義者宜也)." Under this interpretation, Yi is dependent on the environment and circumstance. This concept was also adopted by Mo Zi (see Endnotes). Mencius's concept of Yi is on a morality level.

At the end of this section, Gong Du Zi said, "You drink hot soup during winter and cool water during summer. Is the desire for food and water also determined externally?" The first two sentences in fact supported Meng Ji Zi's view that Yi is appropriateness, and thus weakened Gong Du Zi's argument.

Section 6

公都子曰 告子曰 性無善無不善也。或曰 性可以為善 可以為不善 是故文武興 則民好善 幽厲興 則民好暴。或曰 有性善 有性不善 是故以堯為君而有象 以瞽瞍為父而有舜 以紂為兄之子且以為君 而有微子啟 王子比干。今曰 性善 然則彼皆非與。

孟子曰 乃若其情 則可以為善矣 乃所謂善也。若夫為不善 非才之罪也。惻隱之心 人皆有之。羞惡之心 人皆有之。恭敬

之心 人皆有之。是非之心 人皆有之。惻隱之心 仁也。羞惡之心 義也。恭敬之心 禮也。是非之心 智也。仁義禮智 非由外鑠我也 我固有之也 弗思耳矣。故曰 求則得之 舍則失之。或相倍蓰而無算者 不能盡其才者也。詩曰 天生蒸民 有物有則。民之秉夷 好是懿德。孔子曰 為此詩者 其知道乎 故有物必有則 民之秉夷也 故好是懿德。

Gong Du Zi spoke to Mencius, "Gao Zi said, 'Human nature is neither good nor evil.' Some also said, 'Human nature can be made to do good, or to do evil. Under the reigns of King Wen and King Wu of Zhou, people loved to do good. Under the reigns of Emperor You and Emperor Li of the Zhou Dynasty, people loved cruelty.' Or they said, 'The nature of some people is good, and the nature of some others is bad. Therefore, during the reign of the saintly emperor Yao, there was the wicked Xiang. The wicked Gu Sou fathered the saintly Emperor Shun. The cruel tyrant Emperor Zhou had a virtuous brother, Wei Zi Qi, and a virtuous uncle, Bi Gan.' You now say that human nature is good. Are they all wrong?"

Mencius said, "It is a reality that human nature has the potential to do good. This is what I mean by saying that human nature is good. If a person does evil, we cannot say that his nature is originally bad. Everybody has a mind with compassion. Everybody has a mind with sense of shame. Everybody has a respectful mind. Everybody has a mind with sense of right and wrong. A compassionate mind is Ren. A mind with a sense of shame is Yi. A respectful mind is Li. A mind with sense of right and wrong is Wisdom. The virtues of Ren, Yi, Li, and Wisdom are not imposed upon or induced into our minds from outside. We have them inherently and internally. We are not aware of them because we never reflect upon their existence. Therefore, I say, 'Pursue and you will get them. Neglect and you

Chapter 11: Gao Zi (1)

will lose them.' Men differ from one another regarding these virtues. Some have equal, double, or five times as much as others. Some even have incalculable amounts. Many are unable to carry out their full potential. The *Book of Poetry* said, 'The Tian (Sky) creates man with physical body and moral principles. If people uphold invariable moral principles, they will have great virtues.' Confucius said, 'The author of this poem has moral insight! Therefore, all matters have their respective principles. The upholding of invariable moral principles is the love of great virtues.' "

Annotation:

Gong Du Zi (公都子) was a disciple of Mencius.

Emperor You of Zhou (周幽王, died 771 BC) was mentioned in the Annotation of Section 21 of Chapter 8 above. He was the twelfth emperor of the Western Zhou Dynasty and was on the throne for eleven years only (782–771 BC). He was decadent and corrupt. His ministers were incompetent and wicked. In the second year of his reign, a beautiful girl, Bao Si (褒姒), became his favorite concubine. She gave birth to a son, Bo Fu (伯服). To please her, Emperor You relinquished the title of successor to the throne from his eldest son, Yi You (宜臼), and gave it to Bo Fu. Emperor You also divorced Queen Shen (申后), the mother of Bo Fu. Bao Si seldom smiled. To induce her to smile, Emperor You devised a dramatic show. He ordered border guards to start fires on watch-towers along the Great Wall surrounding the country. The fires sent out signals to feudal lords that barbarians from the north were invading the country. Therefore, many feudal lords came to rescue the emperor. After the feudal lords had arrived at the gate of the palace, they found no barbarian enemy. Emperor You and his concubine, Bao Si, watched the frustrated feudal lords and the hassle of their armies from the tower of the palace and laughed heartily at feudal lords. This episode was repeated a few times to entertain Bao Si. Thereafter, deceived and angered feudal lords no longer responded to the call by Emperor You. The father of the disposed Queen Shen later colluded with western barbarians to invade the Zhou Dynasty. Emperor You then started the fires on watch-towers along the border wall to send out calls to feudal lords for rescue. Having been deceived a few times, no feudal lord responded to the call. Emperor You was defeated and killed. His beautiful concubine committed suicide and his empire, the Western Zhou Dynasty, ended. After the death of his father, Yi You ascended to the throne, became Emperor Ping of Zhou (周平王), moved his capital east, and founded the Easter Zhou Dynasty. The story of Emperor You of Zhou and Emperor Ping of Zhou is also described in Section 21 of Chapter 8, Section 6 of Chapter 11 above, and Section 3 of this chapter below.

Emperor Li of Zhou (周厉王, 890–828 BC) was the tenth emperor of the Zhou Dynasty. Confucians considered him to be an incompetent tyrant. In 842 BC, a popular riot occurred, and he had to escape from the capital. The government was run by his good ministers until the son of Emperor Li was enthroned.

Gu Sou (瞽瞍) was the father of Shun. Xiang (象) was the younger brother of Shun. The story of Shun, Gu Sou, and Xiang is mentioned in the Annotation of Section 28 of Chapter 7, and Sections 2 and 4 of Chapter 9.

The story of King Wen of Zhou (周文王, 1152–1056 BC), King Wu of Zhou (周武王, died 1043 BC), Emperor Zhou (紂), Wei Zi Qi (微子啟), and Bi Gan (比干) is narrated in the Commentary of Section 3 of Chapter 2 and the Annotation of Section 3 of Chapter 3 above.

The Ren, Yi, Li, and Wisdom virtues are discussed in greater detail in the Introduction.

Chapter 11: Gao Zi (1)

Commentary:

Confucians consider that human beings are rational beings and have free will and that there is an inner morality in human nature. This inner morality has a set of moral principles that are real and subjective. These moral principles motivate human behaviors, which can be observed externally. However, these moral principles are not externally imposed or induced. The above sections mentioned that Mencius rejected the narrow view that human nature is only the collection of natural properties of human existence and life (生之謂性). The collection of natural properties includes biological, physiological, psychological, instinctive properties of all animals, but excludes moral principles. Gao Zi and other contemporary philosophers of Mencius thus considered that: "Human nature is neither good nor evil. Or human nature can be made to do good, or to do evil. Or the nature of some people is good, and the nature of some others is bad." They used historical observations to refute Mencius's argument that human nature was inherently good.

Mencius countered by saying, "It is a reality that human nature has the potential to do good. This is what I mean by saying that human nature is good." Mencius's view that human nature is inherently good was misunderstood by many scholars. He only meant that there are *seeds* of virtues in the mind of people. These seeds have the *potential* to grow into great virtues, but if they are neglected, they will wither. Therefore, he said, "Pursue and you will get them. Neglect and you will lose them. Men differ from one another regarding these virtues. Some have equal, double, or five times as much as others. Some even have incalculable amounts. Many are unable to carry out their full potential."

To make the concept "human nature is inherently good" more

concrete, Mencius related this concept to the mind (or heart in another translation of the Chinese text) of people. By "mind", Mencius did not refer to the cognitive mind, which has the function of understanding, nor the emotional and sensational mind, but more importantly, the moral mind. This mind is dynamic and subjective, has free will, and is independent of external forces. Mencius also described the four important characteristics of this moral mind, which were called the Four Virtuous Beginnings (四端). These four characteristics are: Ren, Yi, Li, and Wisdom. He also asserted that these characteristics are *universal* to all human beings. Therefore, he said, "Everybody has a mind with compassion. Everybody has a mind with sense of shame. Everybody has a respectful mind. Everybody has a mind with sense of right and wrong. A compassionate mind is Ren. A mind with a sense of shame is Yi. A respectful mind is Li. A mind with a sense of right and wrong is Wisdom."

Another important point is that these seeds of virtues are innate. Mencius therefore said, "The virtues of Ren, Yi, Li, and Wisdom are not imposed upon or induced into our minds from outside. We have them inherently and internally. We are not aware of them because we never reflect upon their existence." Mencius then explained why people have different levels of virtues and why some people are evil. His answer laid in the two sentences: "Pursue and you will get them. Neglect and you will lose them."

The last few sentences of this section defined what constitutes "goodness": "The Tian (Sky) creates man with physical body and moral principles. If people uphold invariable moral principles, they will have great virtues." The upholding of moral principles means the response to our inner moral mind, which is bestowed on us by Tian (Sky). Since this moral mind is subjective, internal, and independent of external forces, our response should be unconditional. For example, if we do good deeds for the sake of earning credit from people, or if we refrain from doing evil to avoid punishment, our response is conditional and, therefore, not good.

Section 7

孟子曰 富歲 子弟多賴。凶歲 子弟多暴。非天之降才爾殊也 其所以陷溺其心者然也。

今夫麰麥 播種而耰之 其地同 樹之時又同 浡然而生 至於日至之時 皆熟矣。雖有不同 則地有肥磽 雨露之養 人事之不齊也。故凡同類者 舉相似也 何獨至於人而疑之。聖人與我同類者。故龍子曰 不知足而為屨 我知其不為蕢也。屨之相似 天下之足同也。

口之於味 有同耆也。易牙先得我口之所耆者也。如使口之於味也 其性與人殊 若犬馬之與我不同類也 則天下何耆皆從易牙之於味也。至於味 天下期於易牙 是天下之口相似也惟耳亦然。至於聲 天下期於師曠 是天下之耳相似也。惟目亦然 至於子都 天下莫不知其姣也。不知子都之姣者 無目者也。故曰 口之於味也 有同耆焉。耳之於聲也 有同聽焉。目之於色也 有同美焉。至於心 獨無所同然乎。心之所同然者何也。謂理也 義也。聖人先得我心之所同然耳。故理義之悅我心 猶芻豢之悅我口。

Mencius said, "In prosperous years, young people tend to be lazy. During a famine, young people tend to be violent. They are not born to be so. Their minds are drowned in decadence. Take, for example, the growing of barley. We plough the soil and sow the seeds. If the field and the time of planting are the same, the plant will grow up rapidly and be ripe uniformly by Winter solstice. There may be differences in the output of produce despite good fertility of the soil and abundant rainfall. This is due to the difference in the efforts of the farmers. Therefore, there must be commonalities among things in the same category. Why should we doubt that human beings are different? Therefore, Long Zi said, 'Although I do not know the measurements of the feet of a person, I know that I will not make for him shoes that look like baskets.' Shoes should have similar shapes because feet of all people in the world are alike.

Regarding mouth and taste, we all have similar relishes. The famous culinary artist, Yi Ya, had mastered our common relishes before he cooked dishes. If our tastes vary among us as much as the differences between dogs, horses, and human beings, why would the world crave the taste of Yi Ya's dishes? Regarding taste, the world craves the taste of Yi Ya because our mouth and tastes are similar. Regarding the ear and music, the world craves to hear the music of virtuoso Shi Kuang because our ears are similar. Regarding beauty, the world recognizes the handsomeness of Zi Du. Those who do not recognize the beauty of Zi Du have no eyes. Therefore, I can say that, regarding the mouth and taste, we all have the same relishes, and regarding the ears and music, we all have the same hearing, and regarding the eyes and vision, we all recognize the same beauty. Regarding our minds, why should they be different? What are the commonalities of our minds? They are our moral principles and Yi. Saints knew before us such commonalities. Therefore, moral principles and Yi are endearing to our minds just as grass-eating and grain-fed animals are pleasurable to our mouths."

Chapter 11: Gao Zi (1)

Annotation:

Long Zi (龍子) was a famous shoes maker during the Spring-Autumn Period.

Yi Ya (易牙) was a famous culinary artist during the Spring-Autumn Period. He was also a favorite minister of Qi Huan Gong (齊桓公, also known as Duke Huan of Qi), the leading hegemon.

Shi Kuang (師曠) was a famous musician during the Spring-Autumn Period.

Zi Du (子都) was a legendary handsome man, and his name has since become a generic description of a handsome man.

Commentary:

This section reinforces the same theme in the last few sections. There are four main points here: (1) there are seeds of virtue inherent and internal in our mind, (2) these seeds need to be nurtured to grow, and the difference in nurturing explains the difference in characters and observed behaviors of people, (3) these seeds are universal to all men, (4) our inner moral principles are endearing to our minds.

When Mencius said that human nature was inherently good, he must justify why observed behaviors of people vary from person to person and from time to time. His opening sentences here were: "In prosperous years, young people tend to be lazy. During a famine, young people tend to be violent." In the last section, he needed to explain why there were saints like Shun and wicked people like Xiang and Gu Sou, who lived in the same environment and were closely related. Mencius ascribed the variation to be due to the differences in human effort and nurturing after birth. He, therefore, said, "We plough the soil and sow the seeds. If the field and the time of planting are the same, the plant will grow up rapidly and be ripe uniformly by Winter solstice. There may be differences in the output of produce despite of good fertility of the soil and abundant rainfall. This is due to the difference in the efforts of the farmers."

The external manifestation of our internal virtues may vary but the seed of virtue is common and universal to all men. He used the analogies of the shape of feet of people, taste, hearing, perception of beauty. He then extended the commonalities of physical characteristics, perceptions, and cognitive functions of people to morals of people. Although these analogies are not strictly logical, this was the usual style of teaching by saints. Mencius was not an analytic philosopher but an inspirational teacher and a saint.

At the end of this section, Mencius said, "Therefore, moral principles and Yi are endearing to our minds." The word 'endearing' is important. This word has the connotation of positive and active motivation rather than passive compliance of moral principles. He did not say that we need to comply with moral principles in our minds because passive compliance implies the lack of free will and contradicts his characterization of human nature. This point will be elaborated in Section 10 below.

Section 8

孟子曰 牛山之木嘗美矣 以其郊於大國也 斧斤伐之 可以為美乎。是其日夜之所息 雨露之所潤 非無萌櫱之生焉 牛羊又從而牧之 是以若彼濯濯也。人見其濯濯也 以為未嘗有材焉 此豈山之性也哉。

雖存乎人者 豈無仁義之心哉。其所以放其良心者 亦猶斧斤之於木也 旦旦而伐之 可以為美乎。其日夜之所息 平旦之氣 其好惡與人相近也者幾希 則其旦晝之所為 有梏亡之矣。梏之反覆 則其夜氣不足以存 夜氣不足以存 則其違禽獸不遠

Chapter 11: Gao Zi (1)

矣。人見其禽獸也 而以為未嘗有才焉者 是豈人之情也哉。

故苟得其養 無物不長 苟失其養 無物不消。孔子曰 操則存 舍則亡 出入無時 莫知其鄉。惟心之謂與。

Mencius said, "The trees on Niu mountain were once beautiful. Unfortunately, the mountain is situated near a large state, whose citizens cut down the trees for firewood. How can the trees retain their beauty? The trees are still growing day and night and are nourished by rain and dew so that they are not without new buds and sprouts. However, cattle and sheep graze on them. Therefore, the mountain looks bare. When people see its bare appearance, they think that it never has any vegetation. Is this the original nature of the mountain? Applying this analogy to men, can we assert that Ren and Yi are not inherently in our minds? People who neglect the goodness of their minds are like axes to trees on the mountain whose trees are cut down daily. How can the beautiful mind manifest? Those people who neglect their inner goodness of their minds can still get some refreshing and good spirit in the morning after a good night sleep. However, this spirit is too weak for them to choose goodness and refrain from evil like normal people. Their actions during daytime suffocate such spirit. When the spirit is suffocated repeatedly, it cannot recover at night. Since their good spirit cannot recover at night, they are not far from being animals. When people observe such animal behaviors, people consider that the inner goodness of their minds is absent originally. Is this the reality of humanity? Therefore, if nourishment is applied, nothing will stop growing. If nourishment is not applied, nothing will survive. Confucius said, 'You can keep it by upholding and practicing it. You will lose it by letting it go. It comes in and goes out unpredictably, and you do not know where it is and where it goes.' "

Annotation:

Niu mountain was in modern-day Shandong Province.

Commentary:

This section repeats the first two points of last section. Mencius said that our moral mind is inherently with us, but it needs to be nourished relentlessly by upholding and practicing it. The word *it* in the last three sentences referred to the moral mind.

Section 9

孟子曰 無或乎王之不智也 雖有天下易生之物也 一日暴之 十日寒之 未有能生者也。吾見亦罕矣 吾退而寒之者至矣。吾如有萌焉何哉。今夫弈之為數 小數也。不專心致志 則不得也。弈秋 通國之善弈者也。使弈秋誨二人弈 其一人專心致志 惟弈秋之為聽。一人雖聽之 一心以為有鴻鵠將至 思援弓繳而射之 雖與之俱學 弗若之矣。為是其智弗若與。曰 非然也。

Mencius said, "I do not wonder why the king is not wise. Even the most easily growing thing in the world will not grow if it is exposed to cold weather over ten days for every one day under the Sun. I seldom saw the king, but after I departed, naysayers arrived and poured cold water on good ideas. I have tried to sow good seeds in his mind, without avail. Take, for example, the chess game, which is a trivial game. If one does not devote his mind to it, he cannot master it. Yi Qiu is the best chess player in the country. Suppose that he has two students. One of them is devoted and listens attentively to Yi Qiu's teaching; the other seems to be listening but fantasizes that he has already mastered the art as if he had a great fortune to shoot down a swan flying by. Although the two students are learning together, the second student cannot accomplish much. Why? Are their levels of intelligence different? Not so."

Annotation:

The word *king* in this section referred to King Xuan of Qi (齊宣王, 350–301 BC). He was also mentioned in Chapter 2, Sections 3 and 4 of Chapter 4, Section 17 of Chapter 7, and Section 9 of Chapter 10.

Yi Qi (弈秋) was a famous chess master.

For ancient Chinese hunters, the unexpected arrival of a swan in the sky symbolized a great fortune.

Commentary:

This section has two main points. Mencius first explained his disappointment with King Xuan of Qi. Mencius then used the example of the two students of Yi Qiu to highlight the importance of human effort. Although innate seeds of virtues are inherently the same across all men, the variation in human efforts makes the difference in the manifestation of virtues.

Section 10

孟子曰 魚 我所欲也。熊掌 亦我所欲也。二者不可得兼 舍魚而取熊掌者也。生 亦我所欲也。義 亦我所欲也 二者不可得兼 舍生而取義者也。生亦我所欲 所欲有甚於生者 故不為苟得也。死亦我所惡 所惡有甚於死者 故患有所不辟也。如使人之所欲莫甚於生 則凡可以得生者 何不用也。使人之所惡莫甚於死者 則凡可以辟患者 何不為也。由是則生而有不用也 由是則可以辟患而有不為也。是故所欲有甚於生者 所惡有甚於死者 非獨賢者有是心也 人皆有之 賢者能勿喪耳。

　一簞食 一豆羹 得之則生 弗得則死。嘑爾而與之 行道之人弗受。蹴爾而與之 乞人不屑也。萬鐘則不辨禮義而受之。萬鐘於我何加焉。為宮室之美 妻妾之奉 所識窮乏者得我與。鄉為身死而不受 今為宮室之美為之。鄉為身死而不受 今為妻妾之奉為之。鄉為身死而不受 今為所識窮乏者得我而為之 是亦不可以已乎。此之謂失其本心。

Mencius said, "Fish is my favorite. Bear paws are also my favorite. If I cannot get both, I will forego the fish and take the bear paws. Life is also my desire. Yi is also my desire. If I cannot keep both, I will forego life and chose Yi. Life is also my desire, but there are things more desirable than life. I, therefore, will not hang on to life just to survive. Death is what I dread, but there are things more dreadful than death. Therefore, there are dangers that I will not avoid. If survival is all that matters to people, will they not use all means to survive? If death is the most dreadful thing, will they not adopt all means to avoid dangers? Some people do not adopt all means just for survival, and others do not adopt all means just to avoid danger. Therefore, there are things that matter more than life. There are things more dreadful than death. Not only virtuous people have such an idea; all men have it. The difference is that virtuous people stick to it. Take, for instance, a basket of rice and a bowl of soup, and a situation that the availability of them will keep people

Chapter 11: Gao Zi (1)

alive and the want of them will mean death. If the food is offered in an insulting voice, even pedestrians will not accept it, and if it is kicked around and stepped on, even beggars will refuse to take it. If you accept a salary of ten thousand zhongs of grains and ignore Li and Yi, what benefit will you get really? The glamor of your palace, the service of your wife and concubines, or the gifts to your poor friends? In the past, you rejected such a big salary at the risk of losing your life, and now accept it for the sake of a glamorous palace. In the past, you rejected such a big salary at the risk of losing your life, and now accept it for the sake of supporting your wife and concubines. In the past, you rejected such a big salary at the risk of losing your life, and now accept it for the sake of gifts to your poor friends. Can you forego all these now? Not foregoing is called the loss of your original moral mind."

Annotation:

Ten thousand zhongs is equal to 640,000 bushels. Ancient government officials are paid with bushels of grains. Only top-level ministers received such a salary.

Commentary:

In this section, Mencius eloquently presented a very emphatic and key point of his teachings. This section is famous in Chinese literature. The first few sentences, "Fish is my favorite. Bear paws are also my favorite. If I cannot get both, I will forego the fish and take the bear paws. Life is also my desire. Yi is also my desire. If I cannot keep both, I will forego life and chose Yi." have been widely quoted.

The first theme of the section is: "There are things more desirable than life. There are things more dreadful than death."

Although Mencius did not spell out explicitly what those things were, he meant that morality was more important than life and the loss of morality is more dreadful than death. Mencius presented neatly a contra-positive inference in his argument. 'If survival is all that matters to people, they will use all means to survive.' However, some people do not adopt all means just for survival. This negates the second clause "they will use all means to survive." By contrapositive inference, the statement "survival is all that matter" is negated. Therefore, survival is not all that matters and there must be something else more important than life. The same argument applies to death. Mencius further cited an example of beggars rejecting food for survival to demonstrate that some people in some situations will not take all means to survive.

In this section, Mencius repeated the same theme discussed in previous sections that human nature has morality, in addition to physical and biological needs.

In the later part of this section, Mencius warned against the temptation of wealth and power. Many people take these as more important than life and death.

The last key words are "original moral mind." Mencius warned against the loss of this original moral mind, which is more valuable than life and death.

Mencius's teaching here underpinned the spirit of numerous heroes and saints in Chinese history. His teachings are still relevant today.

Section 11

孟子曰 仁 人心也。義 人路也。舍其路而弗由 放其心而不知求 哀哉。人有雞犬放 則知求之。有放心 而不知求。學問之

Chapter 11: Gao Zi (1)

道無他 求其放心而已矣。

Mencius said, "Ren is man's moral mind. Yi is man's path. It is indeed lamentable to neglect the path and go astray, and to lose this mind and not know to seek it again. When people lose their fowls and dogs, they are eager to seek them back. When they lose their mind, they do not bother to seek it back. The role of learning is nothing but to seek the lost mind."

Section 12

孟子曰 今有無名之指 屈而不信 非疾痛害事也 如有能信之者 則不遠秦楚之路 為指之不若人也。指不若人 則知惡之。心不若人 則不知惡 此之謂不知類也。

Mencius said, "There is a man whose fourth finger is bent and cannot stretch straight. It is not painful but causes some inconvenience to him. If there were a doctor who could straighten it, the man would travel a long distance to the states of Qin and Chu to see the doctor because the finger is abnormal. The man hates the abnormality of his finger. Yet he does not hate the abnormality of his mind. This is called the ignorance of relative importance."

Modern Perspective:

Mencius's comment is still relevant today. Most people pay more attention to and spend more money on cosmetics, manicure, pedicure, nutritional supplements, gym subscription, social club subscriptions, fashion, dancing lessons, fitness equipment, sports, minor ailments, games on the internet, entertainments, alcohol, drugs, and so on than on good books, charitable donations, children education, and so on.

Section 13

孟子曰 拱把之桐梓 人苟欲生之 皆知所以養之者。至於身 而不知所以養之者 豈愛身不若桐梓哉。弗思甚也。

Mencius said, "Take, for example, young tong and zi trees, which can be grasped with one or both hands. When people want to cultivate these trees, they know how to nourish them. In the case of their own bodies and minds, they do not know or care how to nourish them. Is their love of themselves inferior to their love of tong and zi trees? It is indeed ridiculous."

Commentary and Modern Perspective:

Sections 11 to 13 have the same theme. Mencius's words are still relevant today. People spend too much time on trivial matters and ignore the need to correct their rotten minds and decadent characters. For example, many people have more affection for their pets than their parents, siblings, and spouses.

Section 14

孟子曰 人之於身也 兼所愛。兼所愛 則兼所養也。無尺寸之膚不愛焉 則無尺寸之膚不養也。所以考其善不善者 豈有他哉。於己取之而已矣。體有貴賤 有小大。無以小害大 無以賤害貴。養其小者為小人 養其大者為大人。今有場師 舍其梧檟

Chapter 11: Gao Zi (1)

養其樲棘　則為賤場師焉。養其一指而失其肩背　而不知也　則為狼疾人也。飲食之人　則人賤之矣　為其養小以失大也。飲食之人無有失也　則口腹豈適為尺寸之膚哉。

Mencius said, "Man loves every part of his body. Because of such love, they try to nourish every part. Since they love every inch of their skin, they try to nourish every inch. To evaluate what approach is good or not, their rely on their own judgement. Some parts of the body are critical, and some other parts are trivial. Some parts are large while others are small. It is inappropriate to damage the large parts for the sake of small ones, and to damage the critical parts for the sake of trivial ones. Those who try to nourish small parts are little people, while those who try to nourish the large parts are great people. A forester who abandons big trees in favor of weed trees is an inferior forester. If a person nourishes his fingers while he loses his shoulder and back, and is not aware of his mistake, he is like a hurried wolf. A person who cares about food and drinks only is despised by other people because he loses big things for the sake of small things. If a person who only cares about food and drinks wants to lose nothing, should he fill his stomach just for the sake of nourishing an inch of his skin?"

Annotation:

"A person who cares about food and drinks only" is translated from a common Chinese idiom (飲食男女).

Commentary and Modern Perspective:

In this section, although Mencius did not explicitly mention that the moral mind is the most important part of a person, this point is apparent from the context of other sections. This section follows through the same theme of previous sections. He reminded people not to ignore the most important aspect of life and humanity while focusing all their energy on unimportant or even trivial matters.

Section 15

公都子問曰 鈞是人也 或為大人 或為小人 何也。

孟子曰 從其大體為大人 從其小體為小人。

曰 鈞是人也 或從其大體 或從其小體 何也。

曰 耳目之官不思 而蔽於物 物交物 則引之而已矣。心之官則思 思則得之 不思則不得也。此天之所與我者 先立乎其大者 則其小者弗能奪也。此為大人而已矣。

Gong Du Zi said, "We are all human. Some are great men, but some are little men. Why?"

Mencius said, "Those who pay attention to their important parts are great men. Those who pay attention to their trivial parts are little men."

Gong Du Zi said, "We are all human. Some pay attention to their important parts, and some pay attention to their trivial parts. What do you mean?"

Mencius said, "Our eyes and ears do not think. They can be obscured and misled by external matters. When a material comes into contact with another material, they set forth a chain of interaction, reaction, and perception. That is all. The mind has a thinking ability. Thinking can reveal truth. The lack of thought cannot reveal truth. This is what Tian (Sky) bestows on us. It gives

Chapter 11: Gao Zi (1)

us this great ability. Other inferior organs cannot overtake it. This is what makes man great."

Commentary:

This section follows through the same theme as the last few sections. Mencius emphasized the importance and superiority of the mind. Great men care about their moral mind, whereas little men care about inferior sensory satisfaction.

Another point in this section is also insightful: "Our eyes and ears do not think. They can be obscured and misled by external matters." Many philosophers, religious leaders, and psychologists have also raised this point.

Section 16

孟子曰 有天爵者 有人爵者。仁義忠信 樂善不倦 此天爵也。公卿大夫 此人爵也。古之人修其天爵 而人爵從之。今之人修其天爵 以要人爵。既得人爵 而棄其天爵 則惑之甚者也 終亦必亡而已矣。

Mencius said, "There is supramundane nobility. There is also mundane nobility. Ren, Yi, loyalty, fidelity and trust, and relentless affinity to goodness constitute supramundane nobility. Dukes, prime ministers, and senior government officials are examples of mundane nobility. Ancient sages cultivated their supramundane nobility, and then mundane nobility came along without asking. Nowadays, people cultivate supramundane nobility to seek mundane nobility. Once they have obtained mundane nobility, they abandon supramundane nobility. They are indeed deluded and will eventually lose all their nobility.

441

Commentary:

The first two sentences of the Chinese text of this section were sometimes translated as: "There is nobility of Tian (Sky) (天爵) and there is nobility of man (人爵)," or "There is nobility bestowed by Tian (Sky) and there is nobility of man." Both translations do not accurately convey the philosophy of Mencius. The term "mundane nobility" is more in line with the context of this chapter and Mencius's philosophy. Such nobility is the high social status, honor, and credit given by worldly people. Since such nobility is externally derived, it is given and obtained with conditions. For example, a king can give an honorable title and high position to a person because of many reasons and conditions. The king can also take the nobility position away from a person when these conditions vanish. The same applies to all other aspects of mundane nobility.

On the other hand, supramundane nobility is internal to a person. It is about virtues, self-respect, and self-esteem. It is about whether a person is responsive to his own moral mind and can answer to it without any regret. A person with supramundane nobility is noble with respect to Dao Te and not to worldly criteria. It is independent of external factors and therefore cannot be removed by worldly people. Under Confucianism, such nobility is unconditional and is completely under the control of a person.

The sentence: "Ancient sages cultivated their supramundane nobility, and then mundane nobility came along without asking" should not be interpreted logically as cause and effect. A misinterpretation of this is: "If you cultivate supramundane nobility, you will get mundane nobility as a result." In common language, this means that good virtue will yield good results, happiness, and honor in the world. This is obviously not the case in the real world. Mencius said this sentence as an encouragement and general observation. The key words here are "without asking." We should not expect or ask for good results by being virtuous advertently. In the next few sentences, Mencius criticized some people who tried to cultivate fake supramundane nobility with the purpose of getting high positions and status in society. Such a nobility is fake supramundane nobility because it is conditional. Lastly, Mencius warned that such hypocrites will eventually lose their self-respect and self-esteem and be abandoned by other people.

Modern Perspective:

Many people nowadays confuse supramundane nobility with mundane nobility or are even ignorant of the concept of supramundane nobility. For example, common people regard earning prestigious honors, prizes, medals, hall of fame recognition, great reputation, designations of high status and rank in the society, and so on, as attainments of nobility. If such prestigious recognition and status are obtained through worldly conditions and means, or if they are sought after as means to gain other worldly advantages, they are just mundane nobility. Such nobility is inferior to supramundane nobility. Mundane nobility is conferred by other people and can be repealed and forgotten. Supramundane nobility lasts long.

Section 17

孟子曰 欲貴者 人之同心也。人人有貴於己者 弗思耳。人之所貴者 非良貴也。趙孟之所貴 趙孟能賤之。詩云 既醉以酒 既飽以德。言飽乎仁義也 所以不願人之膏粱之味也。令聞廣譽施於身 所以不願人之文繡也。

Mencius said, "All men desire to be honored. In fact, all men have nobility within themselves, but they are not aware of it. The honor conferred by others is not good honor. Zhao Meng can honor you one day, but he can also debase you on another. The *Book of Poetry* says, 'Wine can make you drunk. Virtue can satisfy you though.' It says that if you are satiated with Ren and Yi, you will not crave fat meat and fine millet from men. If you earn your reputation from your inner nobility, you do not need elegant embroidery on your garment given by others."

Annotation:

Zhao Meng (趙孟) was a powerful minister of the state of Jin (晉國).

Commentary and Modern Perspective:

When people give you money, power, honor, food, wine, and so on, these treatments usually come with conditions. The phrase "elegant embroidery on your garment" symbolizes flowery praise, prizes, titles, medals, and other worldly means of honoring a person. These are superficial. Only your inner nobility is real.

Section 18

孟子曰 仁之勝不仁也 猶水勝火。今之為仁者 猶以一杯水 救一車薪之火也。不熄 則謂之水不勝火 此又與於不仁之甚者也。亦終必亡而已矣。

Mencius said, "The Ren virtue can overcome its opposite just as water can extinguish fire. Nowadays, people with little Ren virtue behave like a cup of water used to extinguish the fire on a cart of firewood. When the fire cannot be extinguished by that small amount of water, they say that water cannot extinguish fire. Their behavior greatly encourages those without Ren virtue. Their character will eventually be ruined."

Section 19

孟子曰　五穀者　種之美者也。苟為不熟　不如荑稗。夫仁亦在乎熟之而已矣。

Mencius said, "The five kinds of grains are the best among all seeds. However, if they are not ripe, they are worse than weed. Therefore, the value of Ren virtue depends on its being brought to maturity."

Annotation:

The five kinds of grains that Mencius referred to were: rice, soybean, barley, millet, and wheat. Another possible list was wheat, broomcorn, foxtail millet, hemp, and soybean. These were staple cereals in ancient China.

Commentary:

This section repeats the same theme that although the seeds of virtues are innate, they must be cultivated to fruition.

Section 20

孟子曰　羿之教人射　必志於彀。學者亦必志於彀。大匠誨人

必以規矩 學者亦必以規矩。

Mencius said, "When the archery master Yi taught students how to shoot, he insisted on drawing the bow to the full. His students then followed his rule rigorously. When a master craftsman teaches students, he must teach them how to use the compass and the set square correctly. His students also follow his rules."

Annotation:

Yi (羿, also known as Hou Yi, 后羿) was a legendary archer during the time of Emperor Yao. An ancient legend said that he shot down nine Suns.

Commentary:

In this section, Mencius reminded his disciples that they must learn basic rules rigorously and build a solid foundation to learning. Mencius's concept of learning was not just the acquisition of knowledge but also the cultivation of virtues.

Chapter 12: Gao Zi (2)

Section 1

任人有問屋廬子曰 禮與食孰重。
　曰 禮重。
　(曰) 色與禮孰重。
　曰 禮重。
　曰 以禮食 則饑而死。不以禮食 則得食 必以禮乎。親迎則不得妻 不親迎 則得妻 必親迎乎。
　屋廬子不能對 明日之鄒以告孟子。
　孟子曰 於答是也何有 不揣其本而齊其末 方寸之木可使高於岑樓。金重於羽者 豈謂一鉤金與一輿羽之謂哉。取食之重者 與禮之輕者而比之 奚翅食重。取色之重者 與禮之輕者而比之 奚翅色重。往應之曰 紾兄之臂而奪之食 則得食。不紾則不得食 則將紾之乎。踰東家墻而摟其處子 則得妻。不摟則不得妻 則將摟之乎。

A man of the state of Ren asked Wu Lu Zi, "Which is more important, food versus Li?"
　Wu Lu Zi replied, "Li is more important."
　The man then asked, "Which is more important, sex versus Li?"
　Wu Lu Zi replied, "Li is more important."
　The man pursued, "If the observance of Li will result in starvation and death, and if one can get food by disregarding Li, should he abide by Li? If the customary practice of receiving a bride

from her home according to Li will result in not marrying her, and if the disregard of Li will result in marrying her, should one abide by Li?"

Wu Lu Zi could not answer those questions and told Mencius the next morning. Mencius said, "Why are those questions difficult to answer? That man did not understand the fundamental nature of things and make judgements on their superficial manifestations. A block of wood, one inch in height, placed on top of a tall building, is higher than the building below. Gold is heavier than feather, but can we say that a small piece of gold is heavier than a large cargo of feather? If we compare the case where eating is utmost important with the case where the observance of trivial rules under Li is of little importance, is it wrong to generalize that food is categorically and far more important than Li? If we compare the case where sex is utmost important with the case where the observance of trivial rules under Li is of little importance, is it wrong to generalize that sex is categorically and far more important than Li? You should go and ask that man the question, 'If you can snatch his food from your elder brother by twisting his arms, and if you have no food otherwise, will you twist your brother's arms? If, by climbing over the wall of your neighbor's house and kidnapping his virgin daughter, you can get a wife, and if not doing so will result in not getting a wife, will you kidnap her?"

Annotation:

The state of Ren (任) was a small state in modern-day Shandong Province.

Wu Lu Zi (屋廬子) was a disciple of Mencius.

In ancient China, receiving a bride from her maiden home was an official recognition of the legitimacy of the marriage.

Chapter 12: Gao Zi (2)

Commentary and Modern Perspective:

In the last chapter, Mencius asserted that morality was more important than physical and psychological needs and satisfaction. This view was challenged by some of his contemporaries and the man of the state of Ren was an example. Although brief, the discussion in this section is critically important. It covers a few core ideas of Mencius.

The man of the state of Ren used an artificial and forced dichotomy between physical needs and morality to refute Mencius's thesis that morality was what made human being noble. The man of the state of Ren contrived an extreme, hypothetical, and life versus death situation to declare that food is categorically more important than morality. He also used the practice of receiving the bride, a minor and customary rule under Li, to declare that sex is categorically more important than Li. In fact, in his two situations, Li was relatively trivial and could be ignored, but it does not mean that Li can be ignored in *all* situations and for *all* aspects of Li and physical needs are more important than morality in *all* situations and *all* aspects of morality.

Mencius countered that, in the choice between physical needs and morality, there were other considerations in the realm of wisdom. These considerations are typically: (1) the fundamental nature of things versus their superficial manifestation, (2) relative weights and values, (3) the yardstick to evaluate weights (objective in character) and values (subjective in character), (4) the red line drawn on morality.

Before one makes a choice, one must see the true and fundamental nature of things and events. One must distinguish between fundamentals and superficial appearances. Most people often commit the mistake of failing to see fundamentals behind

449

superficial appearances and phenomena. This mistake is common in all walks of life. Mencius illustrated this with the example of a block of wood which was one inch tall. Fundamentally, it is short and when it is placed on the ground, it appears low. However, when placed on top of a tall building, the block of wood appears high. There are some inferior, mean, lowly, and wicked people in the world, whose true stature in terms of morality are as tall as a block of wood. Yet, when they occupy high places in society by luck, nepotism, money, or manipulative tactics, they are acclaimed and adored. These people are like wood blocks of one-inch height placed in high positions. They appear adorable but have lowly fundamentals. In the choice between physical needs versus morality, if we construct a situation where physical needs would occupy an extremely high place and morality would occupy a trivial role, we will conclude that physical needs are more important than morality. Mencius further explained this point by saying, "If we compare the case where food is utmost important with the case where the observance of trivial rules under Li is of little importance, is it wrong to generalize that food is categorically and far more important than Li? If we compare the case where sex is utmost important with the case where the observance of trivial rules under Li is of little importance, is it wrong to generalize that sex is categorically and far more important than Li?"

When we assess relative weights and values, we need to consider the circumstance and factor into all relevant variables. The concept of weight and value is vacuous without the specification of the parameters defining weight and value. Mencius cited a good example of gold versus feather. The statement that gold is heavier than feather is meaningless without the specification of the quantities of gold and feather. The same point applies to weighing choices in life. In Mencius's example, gold represented morality and

Chapter 12: Gao Zi (2)

feather represented food. Another example can illustrate the point of relative weight and value. Suppose that you and your family are trapped in a supermarket which has collapsed due to an earthquake and suppose that all other people in the supermarket have died and you and your family are the only survivors. Suppose that rescue has not arrived for days. Will you steal water and food in the supermarket to keep alive? Stealing is immoral and against the law, whereas not stealing will lead to death of the family. In this situation, the stealing of water and food is a trivial violation of law and morality. How much harm you will do to others versus how much harm you will do to your family? At worst, the supermarket will lose a few hundred dollars, which are trivial in comparison to the loss of life. A third example can illustrate further the point of relative weight and value. Suppose you are a biological scientist. Suppose that someone puts a gun to your head to force you to create bioweapons. Will you surrender to this threat? In this situation, the relative weights will be your own life versus millions of lives, and the relative values will be the value of your life versus the value of millions of lives. Confucius said, "A hero who is determined to uphold the Ren virtue would not seek to live at the expense of hurting his Ren virtue, but he would sacrifice his life in order to preserve it" (Section 9 of Chapter 15, 衛靈公, of *Confucius Analects*). Will you follow his advice?

The next question is what yardstick or common denominator should be used to assess relative weights and values. According to Mencius, the yardstick should be Ren and Yi. He touched upon this point in the section with the examples of twisting the arms of one's brother to snatch food from him and of the kidnapping a virgin daughter of one's neighbor. Both were in violation of the Ren and Yi virtues.

The last question is where to draw the red line of morality. It is lamentable that the modern, permissive society draws a low red line of morality, and that the red line keeps falling over time due to the feedback loop of social influence. With a low red line, everything is permissible, and physical, sensory, psychological, and material needs and desires are given top priority and importance. It is not easy to provide definitive answers to the four considerations discussed here. One needs wisdom to figure them out.

Section 2

曹交問曰 人皆可以為堯舜 有諸。

孟子曰 然。

(曰) 交聞文王十尺 湯九尺 今交九尺四寸以長 食粟而已 如何則可。

曰 奚有於是。亦為之而已矣。有人於此 力不能勝一匹雛 則為無力人矣。今日舉百鈞 則為有力人矣。然則舉烏獲之任 是亦為烏獲而已矣。夫人豈以不勝為患哉。弗為耳。徐行後長者謂之弟 疾行先長者謂之不弟。夫徐行者 豈人所不能哉。所不為也。堯舜之道 孝弟而已矣。子服堯之服 誦堯之言 行堯之行 是堯而已矣。子服桀之服 誦桀之言 行桀之行 是桀而已矣。

曰 交得見於鄒君 可以假館 願留而受業於門。

曰 夫道 若大路然 豈難知哉。人病不求耳。子歸而求之 有餘師。

Cao Jiao asked, "It is said that everyone can be a Yao and a Shun. Is it true?"

Mencius replied, "Yes."

Cao Jiao then asked, "I heard that King Wen of Zhou was ten feet tall, and King Tang Shang was nine feet tall. I am nine feet and four inches tall. Yet, I am just ordinary man feeding on grains. What can I do to be like them?"

Mencius said, "What has the question of size to do with the matter? It is all about your actions. There is a man who cannot lift even a baby chicken. He is then a man with little physical strength. Suppose there is a man who can lift 3000 pounds. He is then a man with great strength. A person who can lift the same weight as Wu Huo is just another Wu Huo. Why should a person grieve (and find excuses) for his lack of strength? He just does not want to make an effort. To walk slowly behind elders is the expected modesty of juniors. To walk fast ahead of elders is a disregard of such modesty. Can any junior person not walk slowly behind elders? The junior person does not do so because he does not want to. The virtues of Yao and Shun were simply filial piety and fraternal love. If you wear the clothes of Yao, study the words of Yao, and follow the actions of Yao, you will become a Yao. If you wear the clothes of Jie, study the words of Jie, and follow the actions of Jie, you will become a Jie."

Cao Jie said, "I have an appointment to see the king of Zou and can ask him to grant me a residence in the state of Zou. I now want to stay here and be your student."

Mencius said, "The way to Dao is very wide. It is not difficult to find. The only problem is that people do not seek it. You should go home and search for it. You can find many teachers like me."

Annotation:

Cao Jiao (曹交) was a brother of the princeling of Cao, a small state in decline. He was a spoiled kid.

Mencius in Modern Perspectives

Historians regarded Emperor Yan (炎), Huang Di (黃帝, Yellow Emperor), Yao (堯, circa 2356–2255 BC), Shun (舜, circa 2294–2184 BC), and Yu (禹) as the five saintly emperors in the Period of the Five Emperors.

Wu Huo (烏獲) was a legendary weight-lifter.

Emperor Jie of the Xia Dynasty (夏桀) was a notorious tyrant.

Commentary and Modern Perspective:

This section has four lessons. The first is that physical (and mental) strength should not be confused with moral strength. Cao Jiao confused the two and wondered why he could not become a saint like Yao and Shun. Mencius cited the examples of lifting a baby chicken and Wu Huo to explain that physical strength had nothing to do with morality. Although the distinction seems obvious, people often find excuses for not doing good work, such as "I do not have the energy or ability to do so," "I am not intelligent enough to understand deep ideas," or "I do not have time."

The second lesson is that, regarding the cultivation of virtue and doing good work, people do not do so not because they cannot, but rather because they do not want to. Mencius also mentioned this point in Section 7 of Chapter 1 above. Mencius cited the example of walking slowly behind elders. This is an act to show respect, courtesy, and modesty. Everybody can do so if they care to. They do not do so because they do not want to.

The third lesson is that everybody has the potential to become a saint if they want to and work towards such a goal.

The fourth lesson is that the way to Dao is available everywhere. It is around the corner, and, in fact, inside everyone's mind. One can easily find it if one cares to. Mencius told Cao Jiao to go home for two reasons. The first was this reason. The second was that Cao Jiao was a spoiled kid and not sincere in following Mencius.

Chapter 12: Gao Zi (2)

Section 3

公孫丑問曰 高子曰 小弁 小人之詩也。

　孟子曰 何以言之。

　曰 怨。

　曰 固哉 高叟之為詩也。有人於此 越人關弓而射之 則己談笑而道之。無他 疏之也。其兄關弓而射之 則己垂涕泣而道之。無他 戚之也。小弁之怨 親親也。親親 仁也。固矣夫 高叟之為詩也。

　曰 凱風何以不怨。

　曰 凱風 親之過小者也。小弁 親之過大者也。親之過大而不怨 是愈疏也。親之過小而怨 是不可磯也。愈疏 不孝也。不可磯 亦不孝也。孔子曰 舜其至孝矣 五十而慕。

Gong Sun Chou said, "Gao Zi said, 'The Xiao Pan is an ode of a Xiao Ren.'"

　Mencius asked, "Why did he say so?"

　Gong Sun Chou replied, "It is full of grudges."

　Mencius said, "The criticism of that ode by the old Gao is indeed rigid and outdated! Suppose that a barbaric native is pulling a bow and trying to shoot at another person. I will smilingly and unemotionally advise the native not to shoot. There is no other reason but my being unrelated to them. Suppose that my elder brother is pulling a bow and trying to shoot at another person. I will weep and cry and beg him not to shoot. There is no other reason but my being related to him. The grudge in the ode "Xiao Pan" is an expression of affection to a dear relative. That affection shows Ren. The old Gao's criticism of it is indeed rigid and outdated!"

Gong Sun Chou asked, "Why is there no expression of grudge in the ode of Kai Feng?"

Mencius said, "The parent's fault referred to in Kai Feng was small. The parent's fault referred to in Xiao Pan was great. When the parent's fault is great, not expressing a grudge is equivalent to distancing the parent. When the parent's fault is small, expressing a grudge is equivalent to stirring up ill feeling. Distancing your parents is against filial piety. Stirring up ill feeling is also against filial piety. Confucius said, 'Shun was indeed filial. When he was 50 years old, he still yearned for his parents.' "

Annotation:

Gong Sun Chou (公孫丑) was a disciple of Mencius. Some scholars thought that Gong Sun Chou co-authored with Mencius the book of *Mencius*.

A Jun Zi (君子) is a gentleman, a person of noble character, a prominent and respectable person in society, or a person who upholds virtuous principles. A Xiao Ren (小人) is the opposite of a Jun Zi.

Xiao Pan (小弁) is a poem in the *Book of Poetry*. The background of this poem was about the story of Emperor You of Zhou (周幽王) and his prince, Yi You (宜臼), which was narrated in the Annotation of Section 6 of Chapter 11 above. Emperor You led a decadent life, lost his empire, and was killed by rebels. His fault was great. The teacher of Yi You wrote the ode Xiao Pan to express his sadness and grudge against Emperor You for losing the Western Zhou empire. Yi You's title of the successor to the throne was originally relinquished by his father. After the death of his father, Yi You ascended to the throne, became Emperor Ping of

Zhou (周平王), moved his capital east, and founded the Easter Zhou Dynasty.

Kai Feng (凱風) is another poem in the *Book of Poetry*. The background of this poem was about the story of a widow who raised seven sons. After her sons had grown up, she wanted to remarry. In the ancient time, the remarrying of a widow was denounced by society as her disloyalty to her diseased husband and the loss of her celibacy. Although her seven sons were displeased with her desire, they did not object to her decision and voice any grudge against her. They instead blamed themselves for not taking good care of their mother and not making her happy. They wrote this poem to express their deep regret. After the mother had read the poem, she dropped the idea of remarriage. This poem has often been quoted in Chinese literature and was beautifully written. A translated version is shown below:

Gentle breeze from the South,
Touches the heart of young spine trees.
That heart swings tenderly back and forth.
Our mother has endured great toil and pain.

Gentle breeze from the South,
Blows on the branches of spine trees.
Our mother is saintly and good.
None of us is worthy of her.

There is a cool spring,
Below the village of Jun.
Although she has seven sons,
Our mother still needs to toil.

Beautiful yellow birds,
Chirp their pleasant songs.
She has seven sons,
But none can make her happy.

Commentary:

This section is about filial piety and continues the discussion on weight and value. Before Mencius's time, Confucians considered that holding grudges against parents was unfilial. Confucius said, "When your parents are wrong, you should advise them tactfully. If they do not take your advice, you should not irritate them. You cater to their needs without complaint" (Section 18 of Chapter 4, 里仁, of *Confucius Analects*). Confucius advised against holding grudges against parents as a matter of principle in general and did not differentiate between major versus minor faults of parents. Mencius took one step further based on his argument of relative weight and value.

The fault of Emperor You of Zhou was huge. He messed up the entire empire. Therefore, Mencius thought that his son, Yi You, should not stand aloof and distance himself from his father. It was righteous for Yi You to complain with the hope of correcting his father's mistake.

The fault of the mother of seven sons was small, if any. Her remarriage only affected her life, and nobody else, since her seven sons were grown up. She may have been criticized by her neighbors for her loss of celibacy, but her remarriage should not be regarded as evil. Therefore, it was appropriate for her sons not to complain.

The yardstick to assess weight and value is still Ren. Therefore, Mencius said, "The grudge in the ode Xiao Pan is an expression of affection to a dear relative. That affection shows Ren."

Chapter 12: Gao Zi (2)

Section 4

宋牼將之楚　孟子遇於石丘。曰　先生將何之。

曰　吾聞秦楚構兵　我將見楚王說而罷之。楚王不悅　我將見秦王說而罷之　二王我將有所遇焉。

曰　軻也請無問其詳　願聞其指。說之將何如。

曰　我將言其不利也。

曰　先生之志則大矣　先生之號則不可。先生以利說秦楚之王　秦楚之王悅於利　以罷三軍之師　是三軍之士樂罷而悅於利也。為人臣者懷利以事其君　為人子者懷利以事其父　為人弟者懷利以事其兄。是君臣　父子　兄弟終去仁義　懷利以相接　然而不亡者　未之有也。先生以仁義說秦楚之王　秦楚之王悅於仁義而罷三軍之師　是三軍之士樂罷而悅於仁義也。為人臣者懷仁義以事其君　為人子者懷仁義以事其父　為人弟者懷仁義以事其兄　是君臣　父子　兄弟去利　懷仁義以相接也。然而不王者　未之有也。何必曰利。

When Song Keng was going to the state of Chu, Mencius met him in Shi Qiu. Mencius asked, "Master, where are you going?"

Song Keng replied, "I have heard that the states of Qin and Chu are about to fight. I am going to persuade the king of Chu to cease hostilities. If the king of Chu ignores my advice, I will go to see the king of Qin and persuade him to cease hostilities. I hope one of them will listen to me."

Mencius asked, "May I ask about the details of your plan? Please enlighten me. How will you persuade them?"

Song Keng said, "I will tell them that fighting is not beneficial to them."

Mencius said, "Your aim is great, but your argument is not. If you lobby the kings of Qin and Chu with the argument of benefits, and if they are convinced after the consideration of benefits and stop the movements of their armies, the soldiers of their armies will rejoice in the cessation of war because of resulting benefits. Ministers then serve their kings for the sake of personal benefits, sons then serve their fathers for the sake of personal benefits, and younger brothers then serve their elder brothers for the sake of personal benefits. This means that kings, ministers, fathers, sons, and brothers will abandon Ren and Yi and deal with each other based on personal benefits. There never has been such a state that did not collapse. If you persuade the kings of Qin and Chu with arguments based on Ren and Yi, and if they are convinced after the consideration of Ren and Yi and stop the movements of their armies, soldiers of their armies will rejoice in the cessation of war because of Ren and Yi. Ministers then serve their kings for the sake of Ren and Yi, sons then serve their fathers for the sake of Ren and Yi, and younger brothers serve their elder brothers for the sake of Ren and Yi. This means that kings, ministers, fathers, sons, and brothers will abandon personal benefits and deal with each other based on Ren and Yi. There never has been such a state which did not rise to rule the empire. Therefore, why should you talk about benefits?"

Annotation:

Song Keng (宋牼) was an elderly scholar and lobbyist.
Shi Qiu (石丘) was the name of a place.
The states of Qin (秦) and Chu (楚) were two hegemons during the Warring States Period.

Chapter 12: Gao Zi (2)

Commentary:

The theme of this section is the same as Section 1 of Chapter 1.

Section 5

孟子居鄒 季任為任處守 以幣交 受之而不報。處於平陸 儲子為相 以幣交 受之而不報。他日由鄒之任 見季子。由平陸之齊 不見儲子。

屋廬子喜曰 連得閒矣。問曰 夫子之任見季子 之齊不見儲子 為其為相與。

曰 非也。書曰 享多儀 儀不及物曰不享 惟不役志於享。為其不成享也。

屋廬子悅。或問之。屋廬子曰 季子不得之鄒 儲子得之平陸。

When Mencius was residing in the state of Zou, Ji Ren, the younger brother of the king of the state of Ren, became the regent of the state. Ji Ren sent valuable gifts to Mencius to initiate friendship. Mencius received the gifts but did not thank Ji Ren in person, nor reciprocated with gifts. When Mencius was passing by Ping Lu, Chu Zi, the prime minister of the state of Qi, sent valuable gifts to Mencius to initiate friendship. Mencius received the gifts but did not thank Chu Zi in person nor did he reciprocate with gifts. On another occasion, Mencius traveled from the state of Zou to the state of Ren. He visited Ji Zi. However, when Mencius traveled to Ping Lu in the state of Qi, he did not visit the prime minister, Chu Zi.

Later, Wu Lu Zi gladly said, "I can now have the opportunity to see my teacher when he is free." He then asked Mencius, "Master,

461

when you went to the state of Ren, you visited Ji Zi, but when you went to the state of Qi, you did not see Chu Zi. Was it because Chu Zi was only a minister?"

Mencius replied, "No. The *Book of Classic History* said, 'In the presentation of gifts, it is most important to demonstrate respect. If the demonstration of respect is less than the value of the material gift, we can say that there is no presentation. This is because there is no sincerity in the presentation.'

Wu Lu Zi was satisfied with the answer. When somebody asked him about the episode, Wu Lu Zi said, "Since Ji Zi could not leave the state of Ren and go to the state of Zou, he could not present the gift to Mencius in person. However, Chu Zi could go to Ping Lu, but he did not go."

Annotation:

The state of Zou (鄒) and the state of Ren (任) were two small states next to the state of Qi (齊).

Ji Ren (季任) was the brother of the king of the state of Ren. He was also referred to as Ji Zi here because the word Zi is a respectful title of a person. When the king of the state of Ren was away, Ji Ren ruled the state temporarily as a regent. As such, he had a higher status in society than a prime minister.

Chu Zi (儲子) was the prime minister of the state of Qi.

Ping Lu (平陸) was a city in the state of Qi.

Wu Lu Zi (屋廬子) was a disciple of Mencius.

At that time, Mencius was famous. He had the status of a teacher and top advisor of the king of state of Qi, King Xuan of Qi (齊宣王). Therefore, Ji Zi and Chu Zi wanted to befriend Mencius.

According to Zhou Li, when a gift was presented to a senior and superior, the presenter should present it in person. Not doing so was a sign of disrespect and the recipient need not accept the gift. If the recipient accepted it, he need not reciprocate with another gift nor give thanks to the presenter in person.

In this episode, both Ji Zi and Chu Zi did not present the gift to Mencius in person. Therefore, Mencius needed not return a gift nor give thanks in person.

Mencius excused Ji Zi for not appearing in person because Ji Zi could not leave his office as a regent. However, Chu Zi could see Mencius in person when Mencius was in Ping Lu, which was in the state of Qi. Not presenting a gift to Mencius in person was a sign of disrespect. Therefore, Mencius did not bother to visit Chu Zi when Mencius was in Ping Lu.

Commentary and Modern Perspective:

The lesson of this section is that sincerity and goodwill are more important than the material value of a gift.

The word *gift* can be extended to any other acts of kindness and charity.

Section 6

淳於髡曰 先名實者 為人也。後名實者 自為也。夫子在三卿之中 名實未加於上下而去之 仁者固如此乎。

孟子曰 居下位 不以賢事不肖者 伯夷也。五就湯 五就桀者 伊尹也。不惡汙君 不辭小官者 柳下惠也。三子者不同道 其趨一也。一者何也。曰 仁也。君子亦仁而已矣 何必同。

曰 魯繆公之時 公儀子為政 子柳 子思為臣 魯之削也滋甚。若是乎賢者之無益於國也。

曰 虞不用百里奚而亡 秦穆公用之而霸。不用賢則亡 削何可得與。

曰 昔者王豹處於淇 而河西善謳。綿駒處於高唐 而齊右善歌。華周 杞梁之妻善哭其夫 而變國俗。有諸內必形諸外。為其事而無其功者 髡未嘗睹之也。是故無賢者也 有則髡必識之。

曰 孔子為魯司寇 不用 從而祭 燔肉不至 不稅冕而行。不知者以為為肉也。其知者以為為無禮也。乃孔子則欲以微罪行 不欲為苟去。君子之所為 眾人固不識也。

Chun Yu Kun said, "Some people take fame and real achievements as their primary objectives in life because they want to do something good for people. Some people take fame and real achievements as secondary objectives in life because they are selfish. You, Master, are ranked among the top three ministers. However, before your fame and achievement have reached either to the king or his people, you want to resign and leave the state. Should a man with Ren virtue do this?"

Mencius said, "Although Bo Yi was in an inferior situation, he would not serve an unworthy boss. Yi Yin served Emperor Jie for five times and King Tang for five times. Liu Xia Hui did not feel disdain to serve a rotten king, nor decline a lowly position. The three honorable men took different courses, but their aims were the same. What was their common aim? We can say that it is Ren. Provided that Jun Zis strive for Ren, they do not need to pursue the same course."

Chun Yu Kun said, "During the reign of Lu Mu Gong of the state of Lu, he appointed Gong Yi Zi as prime minister and Zi Liu and Zi

Chapter 12: Gao Zi (2)

Si as ministers. Yet, the state of Lu declined substantially. This shows that virtuous and competent persons cannot bring benefit to a country."

Mencius said, "The king of Yu did not use Bai Li Xi and thereby lost his state. Qin Mu Gong used Bai Li Xi and became a dominant hegemon. Ruin is the result of not employing virtuous and competent people. How can such people bring decline?"

Chun Yu Kun pressed on, "In the past, when the famous singer Wang Bao resided on the bank of the Qi river, people living on the west side of the river learned his aggressive style of singing. When Mian Ju lived in Gao Tang, people living in the east side of the state of Qi became skillful in singing and reciting poems. The wives of Hua Zhou and Qi Liang bewailed at the deaths of their husbands so painfully that crying loud at the deaths of husbands became a norm in the state of Qi. When there is a virtue or vice inside a person, it must manifest outside. I have never seen a person who tries to do work but fails to produce results. Therefore, there is no competent and virtuous person. If there are, I must notice them."

Mencius said, "When Confucius was the Chief of Justice in the state of Lu, the king of Lu did not follow his counsel. When Confucius took part in a sacrificial ceremony of the state, the king did not distribute to Confucius a piece of sacrificial meat after the ceremony. The upset Confucius immediately left the state without even taking off his hat. Those who did not know him thought that he left because of the meat. Those who knew him thought that he left because of the neglect of Li by the king. The truth was that Confucius wanted to shoulder a small blame on himself rather than leaving without an obvious reason. Most people do not usually understand the rationale of the conduct of Jun Zis."

Mencius in Modern Perspectives

Annotation and Commentary:

Chun Yu Kun (淳于髡) was a prominent scholar and advisor to the King Xuan of Qi (齊宣王). Both he and Mencius were members of an academy set up by the king to accommodate a think-tank of talented scholars and strategists. This academy was equivalent to a modern-day advanced institute of politics. Mencius was the lead member there. Chun Yu Kun and Song Keng (宋牼) mentioned in Section 4 above were competitors of Mencius, whose position at that time was equivalent to modern-day top national security advisor. Therefore, Mencius was ranked among the top three ministers of the state. However, since Mencius never said flowery words to please the king, and instead admonished the king for misdeeds, the king often ignored Mencius's advice. The frustrated Mencius wanted to resign and leave the state of Qi. This was the background of the conservation between Chun Yu Kun and Mencius in the section.

The motive of Chun Yu Kun was not clear. He might want to criticize and shame Mencius, or at the urge of King Xuan, he might try to persuade Mencius to stay behind. Chun Yu Kun sounded antagonistic. In the first paragraph, he hinted that Mencius had done nothing good for the state, did not deserve to be in a high position, and was not a virtuous person. This was indeed a big insult to Mencius.

Mencius was smart not to defend his achievements, strengths, and weaknesses to his colleague. Instead, he used three historical figures to convey the concept that great people may have different ways and courses of actions, but they are all motivated by Ren virtue. Mencius subtly hinted: 'I have my own way and you should not criticize me because you do not understand me."

Bo Yi (伯夷), Yi Yin (伊尹), and Liu Xia Hui (柳下惠) are mentioned in Section 2 of Chapter 3, Section 9 of Chapter 3, Section

7 of Chapter 9, and Section 1 of Chapter 10. The story of Bo Yi is narrated in Section 5 of Endnotes. The story of Yi Yin, Emperor Jie of Xia (夏桀), and King Tang of Shang (湯) is narrated in Section 3 of Endnotes. The story of Liu Xia Hui is narrated in the Annotation of Section 9 of Chapter 3. The three Jun Zis took different approaches in life, but they all pursued the same goal of Ren. The last sentence in the paragraph was key: 'Provided that Jun Zis strive for Ren, they do not need to pursue the same course."

Lu Mu Gong (魯穆公, also known as Duke Mu of Lu, 410–377 BC) was the twenty-ninth sovereign of the state of Lu (魯國).

Gong Yi Zi (公儀子) was a prime minister for Lu Mu Gong. Zi Liu (子柳) was a minister for Lu Mu Gong.

Zi Si (子思, 483–402 BC) was the grandson of Confucius and the teacher of Mencius and the author of Zhong Yong (中庸), *The Book of Zhong Yong* (*The Doctrine of the Mean*), a central doctrine of Confucianism. Zi Si also worked for Lu Mu Gong as a minister. Chun Yu Kun insulted Mencius by debasing Zi Si, the teacher of Mencius. In the past, criticizing one's teacher was a big insult.

Mencius restrained his anger but instead cited the example of Bai Li Xi (百里奚) to illustrate his point that ruin is the result of not employing virtuous and competent people. The story of Bai Li Xi is narrated in Section 4 of Endnotes. Mencius subtly hinted that the state of Qi will soon be ruined because King Xuan of Qi did not listen to his advice.

In the next paragraph, Chun Yu Kun pressed on and hinted that Mencius was useless since Chun Yu Kun had not seen any good achievement by Mencius. He cited the examples of Wang Bao, Mian Ju, and wives of Hua Zhou (華周) and Qi Liang (杞梁) to prove his point. Wang Bao (王豹) was a famous singer at that time. Mian Ju (緜駒) was another famous singer. Hua Zhou and Qi Liang were minister of the state of Qi who were war heroes. There was a legend

Mencius in Modern Perspectives

that the wife, Meng Jiang Nu (孟姜女), of Qi Liang cried so loud at the death of Qi Liang that part of the Great Wall collapsed. Chun Yu Kun's argument was illogical. He used a false premise that a competent and virtuous person must produce notable results. By contrapositive argument, since Mencius had not produced visible results, he must not be a competent nor virtuous person. Chun Yu Kun's premise was wrong in the first place. Competency and virtue are not sufficient conditions for notable results. There are many other contributory factors for notable results. Competency and virtue are necessary conditions though. Mencius pointed this out with the example of Bai Li Xi.

Lastly, Mencius countered with an episode in Confucius's life. Confucius was once the Chief of Justice of the state of Lu, his motherland. He worked for Lu Ding Gong (魯定公, 556–495 BC, also known as Duke Ding of Lu). The king of the state of Qi, Qi Jing Gong (齊景公, died 490 BC), was concerned that, because of the competency and virtue of Confucius, the state of Lu could one day become a threat to the state of Qi. The prime minister, Yan Ying (晏嬰, 578–500 BC), of the state of Qi suggested to Qi Jing Gong a plot to cause the resignation of Confucius from his post. Qi Jing Gong sent a troupe of beautiful and sexy female singers and dancers as a gift to Lu Ding Gong. Ignoring Confucius's objection, Lu Ding Gong gladly accepted the gift. Lu Ding Gong was enchanted by the singers and dancers, indulged in entertainment by beautiful women, and neglected his official duties. The frustrated and disappointed Confucius planned to quit his job, but he could not find a good excuse to resign. He did not want the rest of the country to know about the misbehavior of the Lu Ding Gong. In the meantime, an important ceremony to worship ancestors of the king was organized by the state. Being a senior minister, Confucius needed to attend the ceremony. It was a tradition under Li that, after the ceremony was over, the king would send a piece of sacrificial meat to the homes of all participating ministers to show a sign of affection and unity. Lu Ding Gong forgot to give a piece to Confucius, who took this opportunity to take this as an excuse to quit. He told his students to pack up right away because he was upset. Quitting without an official resignation violated Li at that time. Confucius chose to bear the criticism on himself instead of defaming Lu Ding Gong for his lascivious behavior. Confucius's colleagues and disciples thought the Confucius quitted because of the piece of meat, and that he should not quit for such a trivial matter. Therefore, Mencius said that Confucius was misunderstood.

Section 7

孟子曰 五霸者 三王之罪人也。今之諸侯 五霸之罪人也。今之大夫 今之諸侯之罪人也。天子適諸侯曰巡狩 諸侯朝於天子曰述職。春省耕而補不足 秋省斂而助不給。入其疆 土地辟 田野治 養老尊賢 俊傑在位 則有慶 慶以地。入其疆 土地荒蕪 遺老失賢 掊克在位 則有讓。一不朝 則貶其爵。再不朝 則削其地。三不朝 則六師移之。是故天子討而不伐 諸侯伐而不討。五霸者 摟諸侯以伐諸侯者也 故曰 五霸者 三王之罪人也。五霸 桓公為盛。葵丘之會諸侯 束牲 載書而不歃血。初命曰 誅不孝 無易樹子 無以妾為妻。再命曰 尊賢育才 以彰有德。三命曰 敬老慈幼 無忘賓旅。四命曰 士無世官 官事無攝 取士必得 無專殺大夫。五命曰 無曲防 無遏糴 無有封而不告。曰 凡我同盟之人 既盟之後 言歸於好。今之諸侯 皆犯此五禁 故曰 今之諸侯 五霸之罪人也。長君之惡其罪小 逢君之惡其罪大。今之大夫 皆逢君之惡 故曰 今之大夫 今之諸侯之罪人也。

Mencius said, "The Five Hegemons were sinners against the Three Kings. Feudal lords nowadays are sinners against the Five Hegemons. Ministers nowadays are sinners against feudal lords.

During the periods of the Three Kings, the Imperial Emperor used the excuse of unofficial hunting tours to travel to the states of feudal lords to inspect the conditions of the states, whereas feudal lords were required to officially visit the Imperial Emperor in the royal court and to report the conditions of their states to the central government. The central government then examined the process of ploughing in the states in Spring and provided for any deficiency of seeds. The central government also examined the amount of harvest in the states in the Fall and provided aid in case of deficiency. If the Emperor noticed on entering the territory of a state that new land was reclaimed and developed, existing fields were well cultivated, elderly people were taken care of, virtuous people were respected, and government officials were competent, the feudal lord would be awarded for his good performance and he would be enfeoffed with more land. If the Emperor noticed on entering the territory of a state that its land was deserted and barren, elderly people were neglected, virtuous people were ignored, and government offices were filled with wicked crooks, the feudal lord of the state would be reprimanded. If the feudal lord missed his attendance in the royal court to report his improved performance, his rank would be degraded. If he missed his attendance in the royal court twice, a portion of his territory would be taken away from him. If he missed his attendance in the royal court thrice, the Emperor would order to remove the feudal lord. Therefore, the Emperor would only order the punishment on a bad feudal lord but would not execute the

Chapter 12: Gao Zi (2)

punishment himself. Other good feudal lords then executed the punishment upon the order of the Emperor, but they would not initiate the punishment themselves. The Five Hegemons instead formed coalitions with their allied feudal lords and initiated the conquest of other feudal lords. Therefore, the Five Hegemons were sinners against the Three Kings.

Of the Five Hegemons, Qi Huan Gong was the most powerful. He established a league of allied feudal lords and organized an assembly at Kui Qui. Before the declaration of manifestos, he bound an animal, pasted a writing on it, but did not slay it to smear its blood on the mouths of participants. The first manifesto stated, 'We will not kill people except for the unfilial. We will not change our originally designated heirs. We will not replace the positions of our wives with concubines.' The second manifesto stated, 'We will honor sages and nurture the talented. We will praise virtuous people.' The third manifesto stated, 'We will respect the elderly and be kind to the young. We will not ignore visitors and travelers.' The fourth manifesto stated, 'Our official posts will not be hereditary. We will avoid nepotism and interference of public matters by relatives of key leaders of the government. Our official appointments will be based on merit and competency. We will not kill a minister without the approval by the Emperor.' The fifth manifesto stated, 'We will not erect embankments and dams to block and redirect water flow from rivers to hurt our neighboring states. When our neighboring states suffer famines, we will not hoard food but rather give them aid. When we enfeoff a territory to a person, we will report this act to the Emperor.' Nowadays, all feudal lords have violated these manifestos. Therefore, I say that feud lords of today are sinners against the Five Hegemons.

Aiding and abetting the wickedness of one's king is a relatively small crime compared with the great crime of anticipating, enticing, and promoting wickedness of the king. Today's ministers all anticipate, entice, and promote wickedness of their kings. Therefore, I say that ministers of today are sinners against feudal lords."

Annotation:

In this section, Mencius lamented at the deterioration of political decency throughout Chinese history before and during his time. The Introduction has summarized the Chinese history up to the era of Mencius.

For many scholars, the term "Three Kings" referred to Yao (堯, circa 2356–2255 BC), Shun (舜, circa 2294–2184 BC), and Yu (禹, circa 2237–2139 BC). However, some other scholars, such as Zhu Xi (朱熹, 113–1200 AD), considered the "Three Kings" as the three regimes of the Great Yu of the Xia Dynasty, King Tang of the Shang Dynasty, and King Wen and Wu of the Zhou Dynasty, respectively. All these emperors and kings were regarded by Confucians as saintly kings.

The Five Hegemons were: Qi Huan Gong (齊桓公, died 643 BC, also known as Duke Huan of Qi), Jin Wen Gong (晉文公, 671–628 BC, also known as Duke Wen of Jin), Qin Mu Gong (秦穆公, 683–621 BC, also known as Duke Mu of Qin), Song Xiang Gong (宋襄公, died 637 BC, also known as Duke Xiang of Song), and King Zhuang of Chu (楚莊王, died 591 BC). Among them, Qi Huan Gong was the most powerful. Section 6 of Endnotes narrates the story of Qi Huan Gong and his prime minister, Guan Zhong (管仲).

Kui Qui (葵丘) was a city in modern-day Henan Province.

Modern Perspective:

The last few sentences of this section are relevant today: "Aiding and abetting the wickedness of one's king is a relatively small crime compared with the great crime of anticipating, enticing, and provoking wickedness of the king. Today's ministers all anticipate, entice, and provoke wickedness of their kings.' In modern context, the word "king" can stand for "boss" and the word "minister" can stand for "staff" or "subordinate."

Section 8

魯欲使慎子為將軍。孟子曰 不教民而用之 謂之殃民。殃民者不容於堯舜之世。一戰勝齊 遂有南陽 然且不可。

慎子勃然不悅曰 此則滑釐所不識也。

曰 吾明告子。天子之地方千里 不千里 不足以待諸侯。諸侯之地方百里 不百里 不足以守宗廟之典籍。周公之封於魯為方百里也 地非不足 而儉於百里。太公之封於齊也 亦為方百里也 地非不足也 而儉於百里。今魯方百里者五 子以為有王者作 則魯在所損乎。在所益乎。徒取諸彼以與此 然且仁者不為 況於殺人以求之乎。君子之事君也 務引其君以當道 志於仁而已。

The king of the state of Lu wanted to appoint Shen Zi as the chief commander of army. Mencius said, "Sending untrained personnel to war is equivalent to ruining them. A leader who ruins his people was not tolerated in the times of Yao and Shun. Although you might be able to defeat the state of Qi and take Nan Yang from them, you should not do so."

Shen Zi was furious and said, "This is what I, Gu Li, do not understand."

Mencius said, "Let me explain to you clearly. The imperial emperor is appropriated 1000 square miles of territory. With less than 1000 square miles, he cannot govern the feudal lords. The territory appropriated to a feudal lord is 100 square miles. With less than 100 square miles, he cannot maintain the culture and ancestorial traditions of his land. The Duke Zhou was enfeoffed the state of Lu, which originally had a territory of 100 square miles. It was not because of the lack of land at that time, but rather that the size of 100 square miles was subject to established rule. Tai Gong (Jiang Zi Ya) was enfeoffed the state of Qi, which originally had a territory of 100 square miles. It was not because of the lack of land at that time, but rather that the size of 100 square miles was subject to established rule. The territory of the state of Lu has now expanded to 500 square miles. If a prudent person becomes the next emperor, will he increase the territory of the state of Lu, or will he reduce to it? A person with Ren virtue will not enrich his own state by capturing land from another feudal lord, and much less by killing people. A Jun Zi should serve his king by leading the king on the right path towards Ren."

Annotation:

Shen Zi (慎子, also known as Shen Gu Li, 慎滑釐) was a minister of the state of Lu (魯國).

Zhou Gong (周公, also known as Duke of Zhou) was the brother of King Wu of Zhou (周武王, died 1043 BC) and the first prime minister of the Zhou Dynasty. He was enfeoffed with the state of Lu and was therefore the ancestor of the king of the state of Lu during Mencius's time.

The story of Jiang Zi Ya (姜子牙, circa 1156–1017 BC) is narrated in Section 7 of Endnotes.

Chapter 12: Gao Zi (2)

Commentary:

The section can be viewed as a parable for modern people. The sentence: "A person with Ren virtue will not enrich his own state by capturing land from another feudal lord, and much less by killing people" can analogously be reworded as: "A person with Ren virtue will not enrich himself by grabbing money from others, and much less by immoral or illegal acts." Mencius reminded people against their greed. Some people are not yet satisfied even when their incomes and wealth are many times more than the average person in their countries. They still want more.

Section 9

孟子曰 今之事君者曰 我能為君辟土地 充府庫。今之所謂良臣 古之所謂民賊也。君不鄉道 不志於仁 而求富之 是富桀也。我能為君約與國 戰必克。今之所謂良臣 古之所謂民賊也。君不鄉道 不志於仁 而求為之強戰 是輔桀也。由今之道 無變今之俗 雖與之天下 不能一朝居也。

Mencius said, "Nowadays, government officials say, 'We can assist our kings to expand his territory and enrich his treasury coffers' They are now regarded as good ministers, whereas ancient people called them robbers of the people. If a king does not follow the right path and abide by the principles of Ren, but instead focuses on enriching himself, these officials are just enriching a Jie. Or these officials will say, 'We can help our king to form alliances with other states and we can win any war.' They are now regarded as good ministers, whereas ancient people called them robbers of the people. If a king does not follow the right path and abide by the principles of Ren, but instead focuses on conquests, these officials are just abetting a Jie. Although a king in pursuit of rotten ways of the present day were to have a throne given to him, he cannot keep it for one day."

Annotation:

"Jie" here referred to Emperor Jie of Xia Dynasty (夏桀) who was a notorious tyrant. He is also mentioned in Section 3 of Endnotes.

Modern Perspective:

Mencius reminded people not to be complicit with their wicked bosses.

Section 10

白圭曰 吾欲二十而取一 何如。

孟子曰 子之道 貉道也。萬室之國 一人陶 則可乎。

曰 不可 器不足用也。

曰 夫貉 五穀不生 惟黍生之。無城郭 宮室 宗廟 祭祀之禮 無諸侯幣帛饔飧 無百官有司 故二十取一而足也。今居中國 去人倫 無君子 如之何其可也。陶以寡 且不可以為國 況無君子乎。欲輕之於堯舜之道者 大貉小貉也 欲重之於堯舜之道者 大桀小桀也。

Bai Gui said, "I suggest the government to levy a tax rate of five percent. What do you think?"

Chapter 12: Gao Zi (2)

Mencius replied, "Your suggested approach would be that of the barbaric tribe, Mo. Will just one potter be enough for a country of ten thousand households?"

Bai Gui said, "No, there will not be enough supply of pots."

Mencius said, "The five grains cannot be grown in Mo and its people need to eat millet. They do not have fortified cities, palaces, temples, ceremonial rituals, currencies, banquets, and governmental organizations. Therefore, a tax rate of five percent is enough for them. In the middle kingdom where we live in, can we abolish established social order and banish all capable Jun Zis? Even the lack of potters will be problematic for a country; how big a problem will a country face with the lack of Jun Zis? If the tax rate is below what Yao and Shun levied, the country will be like a big or small Mo. If the tax rate is above what Yao and Shun levied, the country will be like a big or small country under Jie."

Annotation:

According to *Shi Ji* (史記, *Records of the Grand Historian*) written by Sima Qian (司馬遷, 145–86 BC), Bai Gui (白圭) was a tycoon from dire poverty. He was also extremely frugal. He advocated austerity, low tax, and small government to the country. Therefore, he proposed a tax rate of 5 percent.

Mo (貉) was a barbaric tribe in the north of China at that time. It had little civilization and infrastructure.

The word *Jie* referred to Emperor Jie of Xia Dynasty who was a notorious tyrant.

Commentary and Modern Perspective:

It is interesting to note that the discussion in this section was like the modern-day debate on taxation and the size of the government. Mencius argument was that too low a tax rate would be insufficient to build infrastructure, provide necessary social services, and attract talented people to work for the government. On the other hand, too high a tax rate was punitive. Mencius advocated the tax rate during the regimes of Yao and Shun, which was about 10 percent.

Section 11

白圭曰 丹之治水也愈於禹。

孟子曰 子過矣。禹之治水 水之道也。是故禹以四海為壑 今吾子以鄰國為壑。水逆行 謂之洚水。洚水者 洪水也 仁人之所惡也。吾子過矣。

Bai Gui said, "My management of the waters is better than Yu's."

Mencius said, "You are wrong, Sir! Yu managed the waters according to the nature of water. Therefore, he made the four seas as receptacles of water. You instead made the neighboring states as receptacles of water. You caused water to flow backwards, causing inundation. The huge inundation resulted in flood. This is what a man with Ren virtue detests. You are indeed wrong."

Annotation:

The details of Bai Gui were shown in Section 10 above.

Yu (禹, around 2237–2139 BC) founded the Xia Dynasty (夏朝, around 2184–1600 BC) in about 2184 BC. He once worked for Emperor Shun as the minister of water management. His father was also the minister of water management, but he tried to control the water by building levees over riverbanks. After 9 years of hard work, he failed and died. There were two versions about his death. One version said that he committed suicide. Another version said that he was punished to death by Emperor Shun. Yu succeeded his father. Over the course of the next 13 years, he succeeded in controlling flood from rivers by dredging riverbeds, re-directing the flow of water, and leading the water to the sea instead of building levees and embankments to block water. More details of Yu were mentioned in Section 8 of Chapter 3, Section 4 of Chapter 5, Section 26 of Chapter 8, and Section 29 of Chapter 8.

Section 12

孟子曰 君子不亮 惡乎執。

Mencius said, "A Jun Zi does not show off his talents and is not stubborn."

Annotation:

Zhu Xi (朱熹, 113–1200 AD) interpreted this short sentence differently as: "If a Jun Zi does not stick to his faith, he cannot uphold any virtue."

Section 13

魯欲使樂正子為政。孟子曰 吾聞之 喜而不寐。
　　公孫丑曰 樂正子強乎。
　　曰 否。
　　(曰) 有知慮乎。

曰　否。
(曰)　多聞識乎。
曰　否。
(曰)　然則奚為喜而不寐。
曰　其為人也好善。
(曰)　好善足乎。
曰　好善優於天下　而況魯國乎。夫苟好善　則四海之內　皆將輕千里而來告之以善。夫苟不好善　則人將曰　訑訑　予既已知之矣。訑訑之聲音顏色　距人於千里之外。士止於千里之外　則讒諂面諛之人至矣。與讒諂面諛之人居　國欲治　可得乎。

The king of the state of Lu wanted to appoint disciple Yue Zheng Zi to administer the government. Mencius said, "After I heard of the news, I am so glad that I could not sleep."

Gong Sun Chou asked, "Is Yue Zheng Zi competent?"

Mencius replied, "No."

Gong Sun Chou asked, "Is he intelligent?"

Mencius replied, "No."

Gong Sun Chou asked, "Is he knowledgeable?"

Mencius replied, "No."

Gong Sun Chou then asked, "Why are you so glad to lose your sleep?"

Mencius replied, "He is a man who loves goodness."

Gong Sun Chou asked, "Is just the love of goodness sufficient?"

Mencius said, "The love of what is good is sufficient for governing the whole world, not just the state of Lu. If a leader loves goodness, all good people in the entire country will travel a thousand miles to present good ideas to him. If a leader does not love goodness, those people will say, 'He is so conceited to think that he knows everything.' His conceited voice and manners will keep people off one thousand miles away. When good scholars are deterred a thousand miles away, flatterers and sycophants will approach him. When he is surrounded by flatterers and sycophants, will it be possible for him to govern the country well?"

Annotation:

Yue Zheng Zi (樂正子) was a disciple of Mencius.

Commentary and Modern Perspective:

This section is relevant not only to governments but also corporations and any other organizations.

Section 14

陳子曰 古之君子何如則仕。

孟子曰 所就三 所去三。迎之致敬以有禮 言將行其言也 則就之。禮貌未衰 言弗行也 則去之。其次 雖未行其言也 迎之致敬以有禮 則就之。禮貌衰 則去之。其下 朝不食 夕不食 饑餓不能出門戶。君聞之曰 吾大者不能行其道 又不能從其言也 使饑餓於我土地 吾恥之。周之 亦可受也 免死而已矣。

Chen Zi asked, "What were the criteria on which Jun Zi's in the past accepted official appointments?"

Mencius said, "There were three cases in which they accept the offers, and three cases in which they resign from their posts. If the king received them respectfully and politely and told them that he will keep his words, they would accept the offers. If they were treated politely but the king did not keep his words, they would quit. In the second case, if the king had not kept his words but maintained his courtesy, they would stay. If the courtesy also deteriorated, they would quit. In the last case, the Jun Zi had nothing to eat day and night so that he could not walk outside his house. The king heard about the dire situation of the Jun Zi and said, 'I cannot follow the major points of his doctrine and put his teachings into practice. If I let him starve to death on my soil, shame on me!' The king then hired him based on charitable intention. In this case, it is alright for the Jun Zi to accept the offer to just avert death."

Annotation:

Chen Zi (陳子) was a disciple of Mencius.

Section 15

孟子曰　舜發於畎畝之中　傅說舉於版築之間　膠鬲舉於魚鹽之中　管夷吾舉於士　孫叔敖舉於海　百里奚舉於市。故天將降大任於斯人也　必先苦其心志　勞其筋骨　餓其體膚　空乏其身　行拂亂其所為　所以動心忍性　曾益其所不能。人恆過　然後能改。困於心　衡於慮　而後作。徵於色　發於聲　而後喻。入則無法家拂士　出則無敵國外患者　國恆亡。然後知生於憂患而死於安樂也。

Mencius said, "Shun rose from the farming fields. Fu Yue was appointed to a high position from being an unemployed construction laborer. Jiao Ge was appointed to a high position from being a salt

Chapter 12: Gao Zi (2)

and fish merchant. Guan Yi Wu was appointed to a high position from being a prisoner. Sun Shu Ao was appointed to a high position when he was hiding on the lakeside. Bai Li Xi was appointed to a high position from the marketplace. Therefore, when Tien (Sky) is about to confer a great role to a person, it first subjects his mind and will with suffering and disappointments, drills his sinews and bones, starves his body, saps his strength, and thwarts his endeavors. By all these methods, it stimulates his mind, hardens his tolerance, and provides him with the tenacity to accomplish the impossible. A man can then learn from his repeated mistakes. When he is perplexed in his mind, he should think deeply and thoroughly before he takes actions. He should watch the looks of others and listen to their words before he understands others. If a country does not have sages and honest counsellors inside the country, and is not threatened by enemies, this country will sooner or later fail. From these points, we know that survival arises from hardship and worries, and death arises from comfort and complacency."

Annotation:

Fu Yue (傅說, circa 1335–1246 BC) was a great politician, militarist, and structural engineer in the Shang Dynasty (商朝). The story of Fu Yue is narrated in Section 8 of the Endnotes.

Jiao Ge (膠鬲) was a national of the Shang Dynasty during the reign of Emperor Zhou (紂王). He started off as hawker selling fish and sea salt and lived in poverty when he was young. He later assisted King Wu of the state of Zhou to overthrow Emperor Zhou. The story of Jiao Ge is narrated in Section 9 of Endnotes.

Guan Yi Wu (管夷吾, also known as Guan Zhong 管仲, 725–645 BC) was the prime minister for Qi Huan Gong (齊桓公) of the state of Qi during the Spring-Autumn period. The story of Guan

Mencius in Modern Perspectives

Zhong is narrated in Section 6 of Endnotes.

Sun Shu Ao (孫叔敖, circa 630–593 BC) was the prime minister of the state of Chu (楚) during the regime of King Zhuang of Chu (楚莊王) in the Spring-Autumn Period. The story of Sun Shu Ao is narrated in Section 10 of Endnotes.

Bai Li Xi (百里奚, circa 725–621 BC) was the prime minister for **Qin Mu Gong** (秦穆公, also known as Duke Mu of the state of Qin) of the state of Qin during the Spring-Autumn period. The story of Bai Li Xi is narrated in Section 4 of Endnotes.

Commentary and Modern Perspective:

This section is famous in Chinese literature. Mencius cited five examples to substantiate his point: "When Tien (Sky) is about to confer a great role to a person, it first subjects his mind and will with suffering and disappointments, drills his sinews and bones, starves his body, saps his strength, and messes up his endeavors. By all these methods, it stimulates his mind, hardens his tolerance, and provides him with the tenacity to accomplish the impossible." These sentences offer powerful encouragement to people who face adversity, failures, defeat, misfortunes, desperation, and depression. Mencius also reminded people not to be complacent by saying, "Survival arises from hardship and worries, death arises from comfort and complacency." This sentence is also frequently quoted in Chinese culture. These two sentences give people the moral strength to overcome hardship and achieve success.

This section is relevant today.

Section 16

孟子曰 教亦多術矣 予不屑之教誨也者 是亦教誨之而已矣。

Chapter 12: Gao Zi (2)

Mencius said, "There are many ways to teach a person. I sometimes refuse to teach a person because my refusal is already a good lesson to him."

Commentary and Modern Perspective:

Section 20 of Chapter 17, Yang Huo, 陽貨, of *Confucius Analects* narrated an episode as follows: "Ru Bei wanted to see Confucius, but Confucius declined with an excuse of being sick. After the messenger left the house, Confucius played the lute deliberately so that the messenger could hear the music." Confucius did not consider Ru Bei (孺悲) sincere in learning, and Confucius's refusal was a good lesson to Ru Bei.

Many conceited people consider themselves knowledgeable and intelligent. They resist to open their minds to another spiritual teaching. They often refute a new teaching with crooked counter arguments before they understand the depth of such teaching. It is futile to teach them. The refusal to teach them not only saves the teacher's time but also sends a message to them about their intellectual arrogance. In some other cases, the listener is not yet up to standard in wisdom to appreciate sophisticated ideas. Trying to educate him will also hurt their egos. Zhuang Zi (莊子), a Taoist saint, told a parable in chapter 6 of his book, *Zhuang Zi*, that the God of River met the God of Sea and was amazed and humbled by the amount of water in the sea. Zhuang Zi then wrote the following dialogue between them:

"You cannot talk about the sea to a frog under a well because the frog is confined to a limited space all its life. You cannot talk about ice to a summer worm because it is confined to a limited time frame all its life. You cannot talk about a straight highway to a person living by a winding road all his life because of his lack of education."

This section is also relevant today.

Chapter 13: Utmost Dedication (1)

Section 1

孟子曰 盡其心者 知其性也。知其性 則知天矣。存其心 養其性 所以事天也。殀壽不貳 修身以俟之 所以立命也。

Mencius said, "If you make your utmost effort to reflect and explore the goodness of your mind, you can know your own nature. Knowing the nature of your being will enlighten you about the good nature of Tian (Sky). Accumulate and maintain the goodness of your mind and cultivate your character by putting the goodness into practice—this is the way to emulate the good nature of Tian. Whether you will die young or live a long life, your need to irrespectively cultivate and perfect your character and await the moment of death at which you will have fulfilled your life."

Commentary:

This chapter encapsulates the acme of the teachings of Mencius on self-cultivation. He taught the path to sanctification. In addition, in the following sections, he also explained the right mindset and the approach to reconcile morality with the reality of life.

The above sentences are interpreted and translated into a simple language without vague jargons to facilitate comprehension by common readers. The first two sentences, although written in a plain language, are the crux of the method of sanctification. (In the Buddhist belief, if one can see the true nature of his being and understand the true good nature of Tian of which he is part, he is already a Buddha. The Chinese translation of this concept is called 明心見性). In Confucianism, he is already a saint.

In the first sentence, the term *goodness of mind* referred to the inner morality, which has four good characteristics: compassion, sense of shame, sense of respect, sense of propriety. These are the Four Virtuous Beginnings (四端) mentioned in Section 6 of Chapter 11. The same good characteristics of the mind are also mentioned in Section 6, 7, and 8 of Chapter 11 above. These correspond to the virtues of Ren, Yi, Li, and Wisdom. Some translators used the word *heart* instead of *goodness of mind*. As mentioned in the Introduction, and throughout Chapter 11, the word *heart* conveys the connotation of feelings, sentiments, emotions, and other biological and psychological functions of a person. It does not convey the deeper morality aspect (or the soul) of a person.

The phrase *utmost effort* in the first sentence is important. Without an effort, one cannot realize the existence of these seeds of virtue. Without serious effort, one cannot grow these seeds to fruition. Thus, one must make relentless and utmost effort to make these virtues flourish. Mencius cited many analogies to explain this point in Sections 7 to 13 of Chapter 11 above.

The other two words *reflect* and *explore* in the first sentence need to be noted. The realization and growth of the goodness of mind is an internal matter, and hence, they cannot be forced, imposed, or even perceived by external revelation. Therefore, one must take his own initiatives to reflect on his own mind and explore the inherent goodness, beauty, and purity of it, and then develop it internally.

The Confucian concept of Tian (Sky) is that it is a name given to ultimate, infinite, and perfect goodness. Since human beings are microcosms of Tian, human nature inherently reflects the nature of Tian, although the goodness of human nature is limited and

Chapter 13: Utmost Dedication (1)

imperfect. Therefore, the second sentence said, "Knowing the nature of your being will enlighten you about the good nature of Tian."

The first two sentences of this section talked about enlightenment of truth—knowing about oneself and about Tian. These sentences focus on the spiritual and morality aspects of the mind. This enlightenment is easy to say but difficult to have. Therefore, the phrase *utmost effort* is essential here. This cannot be obtained by straightforward logical deduction, meditation, or casual practice.

The next two sentences refer to necessary actions. The words *accumulate* and *maintain* refer to the continuous, lifelong, conscientious, and active process of accumulating good thoughts, learning, practicing, and experiencing the application of virtues, and the retention of such acquired virtues. The word *cultivate* refers not only to the purification of one's mind, the rectification of one's errors, and the cultivation of one's virtues, but also the application of them to the world. Such applications include all actions, words, ideas, teachings, writings, reasoning, cognition, and desires of a person.

Therefore, this section delineates two important aspects for sanctification: spiritual enlightenment together with putting into practice one's virtues to benefit others (this corresponds to the philosophy of Hinayana (or Theravada 小乘) and Mahayana (大乘) of Buddhism).

In the last sentence, the phrase "emulates the good nature of Tian" is used instead of "serves Tian," "serves God," and "serves Heaven" which have been adopted by other translators. The word *Tian* here does not refer to some divine spirit above us, but rather refers to the ultimate standard of infinite and perfect goodness. The word *emulate* means "to follow," "to act in accordance with," or "to match by imitation." It has an active and voluntary connotation. The voluntary aspect is important. As mentioned in the Commentary of Section 1 of Chapter 11, human beings are different from animals because humans are rational beings, have free will, and therefore morals. The word *serve* has a passive, subservient, and obligatory connotation, and is inappropriate in the context of teachings of Mencius (and Buddhism), although this word can be translated literally from the Chinese word (事). Furthermore, "serves God" and "serves Heaven" have connotations of Christian religion.

The last sentence is extremely important for mortals born into reality and subject to all sorts of constraints. There is no escape from the four critical events of life: birth, aging, sickness, and death. Many actual realizations of these events are out of our control. It is not up to us to determine when, where, and to which parents we were born. Aging is inevitable and irreversible. Nobody can live without sickness for life. We cannot avoid death, and with few exceptions, determine when we will die. Our lives are filled with ups, downs, fortunes, misfortunes, successes, failures, wealth, and poverty, health, sickness, and so on, and we cannot completely control them according to our wishes. To a large extent, external factors affect the outcomes of such realizations. On the other hand, the morality aspect of our lives is completely under our control. If we make our best efforts to relentlessly cultivate our mind and spirit, we can perceive the true nature of Tian, emulate its goodness, and attain sainthood in Confucian sense. There is no limit to how high and how quickly we can achieve such goals. If we want them, we can get them. The timing of our death and other physical aspects of our lives are irrelevant. Confucius said, "If one is enlightened with True Way in the morning, one is willing to die in the evening" (Section 8 of Chapter 4, 里仁, of *Confucius Analects*). Therefore, the word *wait* in the last sentence has a positive connotation. If we constantly pursue the goal of sanctification, we will have fulfilled our mission

Chapter 13: Utmost Dedication (1)

in life and have no fears or regrets at death.

In the last paragraph of this section, the word *life* refers to the morality aspect of life, not the physical aspect of life. Fulfillment does not mean great success in society, great wealth, good health, long life, love and respect from family members and friends, and so on. Although nice and mundane attributes, they are irrelevant to the morality aspect of life. Confucius said, "Yan Hui is indeed virtuous. He eats with a bowl made of bamboo, drinks with a cup made of the skin of a melon, and lives in a ghetto. Other people cannot withstand such austerity. He, on the contrary, enjoys it. Yan Hui is indeed virtuous" (Section 11 of Chapter 6, 雍也, of *Confucius Analects*). Confucius held Yan Hui, his disciple, to a high regard as a saintly person. Sadly though, he died young.

It is important to note that this section does not teach fatalism. Although we must accept our fate since it is the reality of life and is out of our control, we should cultivate our virtue with utmost effort irrespective of our fate. Later sections will discuss how we reconcile our fate with our goal of sanctification.

We also note that the book *Mencius* does not mention afterlife but sanctification can be achieved during the current life. Confucius said, "Is Ren virtue far away? If you desire to have Ren virtue, it is here right now" (Section 30 of Chapter 7, 述而, of *Confucius Analects*).

Section 2

孟子曰　莫非命也　順受其正。是故知命者　不立乎巖墙之下。盡其道而死者　正命也。桎梏死者　非正命也。

Mencius said, "Nothing happens that is not affected by the realities of life. One should accept them with a positive attitude. Therefore, those who understand the realities of life will not stand beneath a wall about to collapse. If one dies because of doing his best in pursuing his moral principles, he has lived positively. If one dies because of criminal offences or decadence, he has ruined his life."

Commentary:

The Commentary of the last section has explained the concept of realities of life or fate. It is an important concept for Confucians. However, they do not ascribe to fatalism, which is negative, and instead teach people to deal with fate positively. One should try his best to improve his situation through proper and prudent means, and leave the rest to fate. One should not give up his moral principles and other real means. The sentence "one should accept them with a positive attitude" implies many virtues, such as patience, endurance, forbearance, gratitude, modesty, calmness, and not blaming others, the society, and Tian for misfortunes. It also implies activities to overcome hardship and remediate losses. Living a life positively requires much discipline and practice. For example, the Introduction has mentioned the Buddhist Eight Righteous Ways to behave properly. In simple terms, these eight righteous ways are: right view, right resolve, right speech, right conduct, right livelihood, right effort, right mindfulness, and right concentration.

Section 3

孟子曰 求則得之 舍則失之 是求有益於得也 求在我者也。求之有道 得之有命 是求無益於得也 求在外者也。

Mencius said, "Morality can be obtained by seeking and lost by

Chapter 13: Utmost Dedication (1)

neglecting. In this case, seeking helps getting because seeking of morality is completely under our control. Fortune and happiness from worldly matters can be obtained by seeking with proper means. Whether one can get them depends on the realities of life (and fate). In this case, seeking may not help getting because seeking is subject to external factors."

Commentary and Modern Perspective:

The Commentary of Section 1 above explained that our lives have two aspects: morality and physical existence. Our moral mind is under our complete control. On the other hand, fortune and happiness arising from worldly matters, such as wealth, fame, power, success, food, health, family, friendship, comfortable shelter, luxury, entertainment, sensual satisfaction, love, and respect from others, safety, longevity, and so on depend on many external factors which are often outside of our control. In this section, the term *good fortune* (福) refers to the fact of possession and attainment of good aspects of life in the real world. The word *happiness* (樂) is the mental satisfaction arising from such fact. The unexplainable, unexpected, unpredictable, often random, and uncontrollable factors are lumped together and called "fate" by most people. More accurately, these should be called "realities of life."

Therefore, according to the discussion in Section 1 above, we can and should actively pursue our virtues. Mencius said that we can try our best in seeking fortune and happiness only through proper means, but we must accept the fact that we may not get them. Whether we can get good fortune depends on fate. Many people stubbornly refuse to accept realities of life. In the process of acquiring happiness beyond their limits and rights, they hurt not only themselves but also others and the society.

Section 4

孟子曰 萬物皆備於我矣。反身而誠 樂莫大焉。強恕而行 求仁莫近焉。

Mencius said, "The basic nature of everything is in me. There is no greater joy for me to fathom the basic nature of myself by sincere and dedicated effort. Force yourself to forgive others in all your actions, and you will get close to Ren."

Commentary and Modern Perspective:

The sentence: "the basic nature of everything is in me" is extremely important. The word *me* here does not refer to Mencius but anybody. This sentence underpinned Mencius's philosophy. As mentioned in the Commentary of Section 1 above, the Confucian concept of Tian (Sky) is that it is a name given to ultimate, infinite, and perfect goodness. Since human beings are microcosms of Tian, human nature inherently reflects and has the same nature of Tian, although the goodness of human nature is limited and imperfect. Therefore, everybody has the potential to emulate the nature of Tian and become a saint (this is close to the teaching of Buddhism. According to the Tathagata-garbha Sutra, the basic true nature called the "tathagata-garbha" is the universal basis of existence of everything. One becomes a Buddha when he has uncovered, exhibited, and returned to this basic nature. Furthermore, Zhuang Zi (莊子), a prominent Taoist, also wrote, "We have the same root as Tian and Earth. Everything in the universe is part of one body").

Mencius taught that one did not need to seek enlightenment by external means. All principles in the pursuit of goodness are already deep in our mind (conscience). We just need to find them internally

Chapter 13: Utmost Dedication (1)

by sincere and dedicated self-cultivation and self-examination. Here, the word *fathom* must to be noted. Our basic nature resides very deeply in our mind (and deeper than what Carl Jung called "collective unconscious"). One must try hard to fathom it and listen to its "voice."

The first part of this section talks about the enlightenment of truth. The second part of this section talks about the applications of such enlightenment to the world. Just enlightenment alone is not enough. We must put it to action. Mencius only cited the most important virtue, Ren, as an example. The sentence: "Force yourself to forgive others in all your actions" has two key points. The word *force* highlights the first point. The second point is to forgive others. Very often, we are reluctant to forgive others when we are victimized. We must force ourselves to overcome our emotion and forgive others. This sentence leads to the motto: "Control yourself harshly and treat others nicely."

Section 5

孟子曰 行之而不著焉 習矣而不察焉 終身由之而不知其道者眾也。

Mencius said, "Most people do not understand what they practice and examine why they do so habitually. They follow a path all their lives without knowing its principles."

Commentary and Modern Perspective:

There are two interpretations of this section. The first interpretation is that we are all living under the Dao without

495

knowing its presence. We take it for granted because our habits prevent us from perceiving it. For example, we wake up every morning and never think about why we can wake up, why we can walk around, why the world does not end, and so on. We are not aware and do not bother to think about the quadrillions of factors, forces, motions, activities, and principles in nature which are supporting our existence for even a moment. We never seriously ask about why we are in this world, and where we will go, what we should do, why we are practicing this or that, and so on, and we just pursue our daily lives as usual. We do not think about why we have our thoughts, emotions, sensation, and dreams, and whether they are real, unreal, permanent, or transient. There are two Chinese phrases describing some people who only cater to their physical lives. They are called "men and women of food and drinks (飲食男女)" or "walking corpses (行屍走肉)." Unless they change their lifestyle, they cannot see the Dao and the basic nature of themselves and of Tian.

The second interpretation is that some people follow a wrong path of life. They do so because they have acquired a habit from learning, environment, peer influence, tradition, and past experiences, mistakes, thoughts, and attitudes. It will be difficult for them to be enlightened because their habits, biases, and prejudice form an opaque shell that covers their moral mind, and new light cannot penetrate through the shell.

Section 6

孟子曰 人不可以無恥。無恥之恥 無恥矣。

Mencius said, "A man cannot be without shame. A person who does not recognize this is indeed shameless."

Chapter 13: Utmost Dedication (1)

Commentary and Modern Perspective:

In Section 6 of Chapter 3, Mencius said, "The mind with sense of shame is the beginning of Yi virtue." Shame is the driving force to motivate people to do righteous things and avoid mistakes. A person with a sense of shame will reflect on his mistakes and rectify them. Without shame, he cannot make any progress in his moral life. However, there are many powerful and successful people who are shameless but never admit their being shameless. When they have made mistakes, they blame on others, find crooked arguments to justify their mistakes, deny their mistakes, or even spin the mistakes as heroic deeds. These people are indeed shameless.

Section 7

孟子曰 恥之於人大矣。為機變之巧者 無所用恥焉。不恥不若人 何若人有。

Mencius said, "The sense of shame is extremely important to a man. The sense of shame is no use to a person who uses witty and slimy arguments to defend his mistakes. Do not feel inferior to others but just ask yourself why you are inferior."

Or,

Mencius said, "The sense of shame is extremely important to a man. The sense of shame is no use to a person who uses witty and slimy arguments to defend his mistakes. If you are not ashamed to be inferior to others, how can you be equal to them?"

Or,

Mencius said, "The sense of shame is extremely important to a man. The sense of shame is no use to a person who uses witty and slimy arguments to defend his mistakes. If your sense of shame is inferior to others, you are inferior to others in most aspects."

Commentary:

The last sentence of this section can be interpreted in a few meaningful ways. The last two versions were advocated by Zhu Xi (朱熹, 1130–1200 AD), a prominent Confucian during the Song Dynasty. These versions emphasized the importance of the sense of shame in slightly different angles.

The first version reminded people not to have an inferiority complex and be affected by the sense of shame negatively. The sense of shame should be a driving force to improve rather than regress. If we feel ashamed that we are inferior to others, we should ask ourselves why we are inferior. We should then try to improve ourselves. We should amass courage to overcome our weaknesses. Therefore, Zhong Yong (中庸, *The Doctrine of the Mean,* or *Book of the Mean*) said, "The feeling of shame is close to bravery (知恥近乎勇)." In Section 6 of Chapter 11, Mencius said that a mind with a sense of shame is Yi.

Section 8

孟子曰 古之賢王好善而忘勢 古之賢士何獨不然。樂其道而忘人之勢。故王公不致敬盡禮 則不得亟見之。見且由不得亟 而況得而臣之乎。

Chapter 13: Utmost Dedication (1)

Mencius said, "Ancient virtuous kings devoted themselves to goodness and forgot about their power and exalted position. How could ancient sages be any different? They relished their own principles and disregarded the power and exalted position of others. Therefore, when kings and dukes did not show utmost respect and courtesy, they could not see the sages frequently. If seeing frequently the sages was difficult, how much more so to employ them?"

Commentary and Modern Perspective:

This section has a few lessons. By referring to ancient virtuous kings as models, Mencius taught rulers of his time that they should be benevolent to their people and put the well-being of their countries and people as the top priority. They should put aside the question of how to increase his power and influence, how to eliminate opposition, and how to defeat or dominate another state. Leadership was about people being led and not about the leader himself. It is lamentable that, in the modern world, some rulers are more concerned of their own power than the overall well-being of their countries. Likewise, if we have great power and influence on the society or great wealth, we should humble ourselves and work for the benefit of others, rather than for more power and wealth to ourselves. We should not look down upon poor and disadvantaged people but treat them as equals.

The second lesson is about the nobility of character and self-esteem of an individual. Mencius referred to ancient sages as models. The power, status, and wealth of others should not influence our decision on whether and how we will befriend and deal with others. In Rudyard Kipling's words, a true man should: "Talk with crowds and keep your virtue; or walk with kings nor lose the common touch." Confucius said, "Who does not feel ashamed when he, dressed in a shabby and worn-out gown, stands next to another guy dressed in an expensive fur coat? Perhaps Zhong You is the person" (Section 27 of Chapter 9, 子罕, of *Confucius Analects*). We should not be sycophants and attempt to approach, appease, or flatter another person because of his power, influence, or wealth. We should also not attempt to avoid poor friends and relatives. The yardstick for friendship and personal relationship should be virtue and mutual respect rather than power or wealth.

Section 9

孟子謂宋句踐曰 子好遊乎。吾語子遊。人知之 亦囂囂。人不知 亦囂囂。

曰 何如斯可以囂囂矣。

曰 尊德樂義 則可以囂囂矣。故士窮不失義 達不離道。窮不失義 故士得己焉 達不離道 故民不失望焉。古之人 得志 澤加於民。不得志 修身見於世。窮則獨善其身 達則兼善天下。

Mencius said to Song Guo Jian, "Are you fond of traveling from state to state and offering advice to rulers? Let me give you some advice. You should be at ease and content whether you are recognized or not."

Song Gou Jian asked, "How to be at ease and content?"

Mencius said, "By honoring virtue and loving Yi, you can be at ease and content. Therefore, a scholar in destitution should never abandon Yi, nor depart from the Dao when he is successful and wealthy. By not abandoning Yi, he can preserve his good character.

Chapter 13: Utmost Dedication (1)

By not departing from the Dao, he will not disappoint his people. When ancient people were successful, they conferred benefits to people, and when ancient people were unsuccessful, they cultivated their exemplary characters to show to the world. When a man is poor and lowly, he should try to perfect his virtues in obscurity. When he is successful and prominent, he should also benefit the world."

Annotation:

Song Guo Jian (宋勾践) was an unknown person whose family name was Song and personal name was Guo Jian.

Commentary and Modern Perspective:

This section is summarized by the last two sentences: "When a man is poor and lowly, he should try to perfect his virtues in obscurity. When he is successful and prominent, he should also benefit the world." These sentences have been quoted extensively in Chinese literature.

This motto reminds us not to give up, become depressed, become addicted to drugs, or commit crimes when we are poor and destitute. When we are successful and prominent, we should do good to the world.

Section 10

孟子曰 待文王而後興者 凡民也。若夫豪傑之士 雖無文王猶興。

Mencius said, "Dignitaries who ride the coattails of a King Wen were just ordinary people. Outstanding men can rise to prominence even without a King Wen."

Commentary and Modern Perspective:

In this section, "King Wen" refers to a powerful and influential supporter, endorser, or benefactor. The first sentence relates to nepotism, favoritism, and collusion, which are common in all societies. Some people rise to prominence not because of their capabilities or virtue but rather family relationship, social network, collusion, and subservience to powerful leaders. An outstanding man does not need all these to rise to prominence.

Section 11

孟子曰 附之以韓魏之家 如其自視欿然 則過人遠矣。

Mencius said, "If you are related to the Han and Wei family but still feel deficient and inferior, you are indeed superior to most people by far."

Annotation:

The Han (韓) and Wei (魏) families were feudal lords of the states of Han and Wei, respectively. They were two of the seven hegemons during the Warring States Period and were known to be powerful and wealthy.

Commentary and Modern Perspective:

This section talks about modesty.

Chapter 13: Utmost Dedication (1)

Section 12

孟子曰 以佚道使民 雖勞不怨。以生道殺民 雖死不怨殺者。

Mencius said, "If your policy is intended to let your people live comfortably, they will not complain, even when they are hard driven. If your policy is intended to preserve their lives, they will not complain, even when you need to kill some people."

Commentary:

The second point in this section relates to the punishment for serious criminal offences. It is the intention of the ruler to keep everybody safe from attacks by enemies and violent criminals. Although he does not like to kill people, he has no choice but to eliminate enemies and violent criminals from the society.

Section 13

孟子曰 霸者之民 驩虞如也。王者之民 皞皞如也。殺之而不怨 利之而不庸 民日遷善而不知為之者。夫君子所過者化 所存者神 上下與天地同流 豈曰小補之哉。

Mencius said, "Citizens of a hegemonic state can be exhilarated. On the other hand, citizens of a magnanimous kingdom are broadly content. They have no grudge even when put to death. They do not give credit to the ruler for the benefits they receive. They do not know who contributes to the daily progress in the quality of their lives. Wherever a Jun Zi passes, the place goes through a meritorious transformation. He works wonders where he resides. His influence

503

flows up and down and from the earth to the sky. How can anyone say that he mends the society in a small way?"

Commentary and Modern Perspective:

This section describes an ideal of Mencius's philosophy of governance. This should not be interpreted to be laissez faire. A good ruler does good work for the country constantly, consistently, and tacitly. He does not need to apply fanfare and rhetoric to invoke nationalism and populism to earn loyalty. He does not need to dole out huge amounts of benefit to get support. He has already built a prosperous, peaceful, and stable society that his people have great trust in him and are content. Since the good quality of life in the country is a norm and is taken for granted, people never bother to give extraordinary credit to the government.

The first two sentences spell out the difference between the governance of a hegemon versus that of a magnanimous king. The former can provide a burst of ecstasy to his people through a victory in a war, an extraordinary reduction in taxation, or a benevolent decree. However, such ecstasy does not last long. A magnanimous king follows the Dao and builds his country steadfastly through meritorious transformation of the society. Little by little, good things happen to the society like air and water being circulated between the earth and the sky, nourishing all living things in between. As an analogy, we receive so much benefit from the circulation of air and water between the earth and the sky that we cannot survive without it. Yet, we never give much credit to it. This shows the greatness of Nature. A magnanimous king should take this as a model.

In this section, the phrase Jun Zi is meant to be a saint, who can transform the society and leave behind an exemplary legacy.

Chapter 13: Utmost Dedication (1)

Section 14

孟子曰　仁言　不如仁聲之入人深也。善政　不如善教之得民也。善政民畏之　善教民愛之。善政得民財　善教得民心。

Mencius said, "Benevolent words are not as profound as the substance of those words of Ren. A good governance does not win the support of the people as much as good education. A good government is feared by people, whereas a government which gives good education to people is loved by them. A good government can get adequate tax revenues from people, whereas a good education can win the hearts of people."

Commentary and Modern Perspective:

This section has two points. The first point refers to empty and flowery promises of rulers who usually cannot deliver those promises. The substance of those words is more important and profound.

The second point is Mencius's emphasis on education. Confucius also emphasized this point. The foundation of good governance is education, which includes not only literary and technical knowledge but also moral education.

There was the Legalist School of philosophers and practitioners during the Spring-Autumn and Warring States periods. This school advocated and implemented tough laws to rule the country. Confucius strongly objected to this philosophy and said, "If you govern a country by upholding moral and ethical principles, your position will be as secure as the North Star, which is surrounded and adored by other stars" (Section 1 of Chapter 2, 為政, of *Confucius*

Analects). Confucius also said, "If you use laws and regulations to guide and rule your people, and punishment to enforce their compliance, they will be decadent and shameless because they are motivated just by their desire for avoidance of punishment. If you foster moral and ethical principles, and regulate your people with Li (禮), they will not only have their sense of shame but will also be compliant" (Section 3 of Chapter 2, 為政, of *Confucius Analects)*.

This was the central theme of Confucian's political philosophy. Modern societies also have a common flaw: overreliance on the legal system and a deficiency of moral and ethical education.

Section 15

孟子曰 人之所不學而能者 其良能也。所不慮而知者 其良知也。孩提之童 無不知愛其親者。及其長也 無不知敬其兄也。親親 仁也。敬長 義也。無他 達之天下也。

Mencius said, "Men possess some abilities without prior learning because these are intuitive abilities. Men possess some knowledge without prior thought process because such knowledge is intuitive knowledge. All toddlers naturally know to love their parents. After they have grown up a little, they know to respect their elder brothers. Loving one's parents is Ren; respecting one's elder brothers is Yi. There is no other reason but the fact that these virtues are universally innate."

Commentary:

This section reiterates Mencius's philosophy that both Ren and Yi are innate.

Chapter 13: Utmost Dedication (1)

Section 16

孟子曰 舜之居深山之中 與木石居 與鹿豕遊 其所以異於深山之野人者幾希。及其聞一善言 見一善行 若決江河 沛然莫之能禦也。

Mencius said, "When Shun was living in remote mountains, surrounded by woods and rocks, wandering among deer and swine, the difference between him and barbarians was quite small. When he heard a single good word and witnessed a single good deed, he considered them like irresistible water from the rivers breaching the dikes."

Annotation:

Shun (舜, circa 2294–2184 BC) was a saintly king and a model revered by Confucians.

Section 17

孟子曰 無為其所不為 無欲其所不欲 如此而已矣。

Mencius said, "Do not do what your conscience tells you not to do. Do not desire what your conscience tells you not to desire. It is that simple."

Commentary and Modern Perspective:

In another words, "Listen to the voice of your conscience." The second sentence is fundamental because desires motivate actions.

Section 18

孟子曰 人之有德慧術知者 恒存乎疢疾。獨孤臣孽子 其操心也危 其慮患也深 故達。

Mencius said, "Men with great virtues, wisdom, skills, and knowledge always rise from adversity and hardship. They consider themselves as estranged ministers or sons of concubines. They focus on perils and their worries are deep. This is how they succeed."

Commentary and Modern perspective:

In this section, estranged ministers have lost their power and influence in the government. In the old days, the sons of a concubine were ranked below the sons of the wife in their quest of inheritance or succession to the throne. This section reminds people of high caliber and great virtues that their future may not be easy. They must prepare for the worst but try their best. This section is related to Section 15 of Chapter 12 above.

Section 19

孟子曰 有事君人者 事是君則為容悅者也。有安社稷臣者 以安社稷為悅者也。有天民者 達可行於天下而後行之者也。有大人者 正己而物正者也。

Mencius said, "There are men whose purpose is to serve their kings. Pleasing their kings is what they do. There are men whose aim is to bring peace and prosperity to their countries. They are gratified by bringing this about. There are men who are servants of Tian. After

Chapter 13: Utmost Dedication (1)

their missions in the world, they retreat behind others. There are great men who rectify and purify themselves so that others are rectified and purified alike."

Commentary and Modern Perspective:

Most people belong to the first category. They try to please their bosses, do a good job, or climb the social ladder. Mencius gave a low rank to this type of people. The other types of people are great. Servants of Tian (Sky) are people who follow good principles of Tian and bring great benefit to the world. After their success, they do not claim credit for their achievements. The last type are sages and saints who enlighten the world and leave behind an exemplary legacy to future generations. Yao, Shun, Confucius, and Mencius were examples. Mencius omitted the worst type who do not even try to do a good job and climb the social ladder.

Section 20

孟子曰 君子有三樂 而王天下不與存焉。父母俱存 兄弟無故 一樂也。仰不愧於天 俯不怍於人 二樂也。得天下英才而教育之 三樂也。君子有三樂 而王天下不與存焉。

Mencius said, "A Jun Zi has three kinds of happiness. Even an emperor may not have them. His parents are alive, and his brothers are well. This is the first kind of happiness. He is not ashamed to face Tian on top and face people below. This is the second kind of happiness. He has the fortune to educate the most talented students in the world. This is the third kind of happiness. Even an emperor may not have them."

Commentary and Modern Perspective:

Mencius mentioned three kinds of happiness in real life. He did not mention great wealth, power, reputation, and sensory satisfaction as sources of happiness. In modern context, the three kinds of happiness can be summed up as: a happy family, no regret in life, and a chance to educate talented students. Since our lives are subject to constraints and fate, many people do not have these kinds of happiness even if they desire and try hard to get them.

For example, emperors have great power and wealth, but history has shown that many emperors suffered immensely from broken families, infighting, persecution, and killings of parents and siblings. Fighting over estate among children of rich families is common. Even saints such as Shun of the Xia Dynasty did not have a happy family. Confucius and Mencius did not have the fortune to have the first gratification. Confucius was raised by his stepmother. Mencius was an orphan and was raised by his poor mother and uncles.

Having no regret in life is difficult. Few people can say that they can sleep well at night and will owe nobody at death. This peace of mind is invaluable. The higher one rises in the society, the more successful one's career is, and the more complex one's environment is, the more difficult it is to get a peace of mind.

Confucius and Mencius had the good fortune to educate talented disciples who propagated Confucianism. It is a matter of fate though. Even if one is the best teacher, one may not have good students.

Section 21

孟子曰 廣土眾民 君子欲之 所樂不存焉。中天下而立 定四海

Chapter 13: Utmost Dedication (1)

之民 君子樂之 所性不存焉。君子所性 雖大行不加焉 雖窮居不損焉 分定故也。君子所性 仁義禮智根於心。其生色也 睟然見於面 盎於背 施於四體 四體不言而喻。

Mencius said, "A wide territory with large population is what a Jun Zi desires to have, but this does not bring happiness to him. To be at the center of the world and bring peace to its people is a happiness to a Jun Zi, but his moral nature is something else. The moral nature of a Jun Zi cannot be increased by great successes and accomplishments, nor diminished by destitution, because he knows his role in life. The moral nature of a Jun Zi consists of the roots of Ren, Yi, Li, and wisdom in his mind. These virtues are manifested in his gleaming appearance on his face, upright back, and energetic limbs, and, of course, in the whole body."

Commentary and Modern Perspective:

This and Section 20 discuss three concepts: desire, happiness in life, and morality. The first two are related to our physical nature. The last relates to our morality. As explained in previous sections and emphasized again here, our physical nature and morality are different and should be independent.

The possession of great wealth and power, which is desired by many, may not bring happiness to life. The owner needs to worry about the loss of them and to spend time and effort to keep them.

The higher level of happiness is to bring peace to the world. The feeling of happiness from such success is still irrelevant to the morality of a person. A person, such as Yan Hui, the poor disciple of Confucius, upheld his high level of morality, even when he was a beggar. A person, such as Emperor Jie, the tyrant of the Shang

Dynasty, lost his morality even when his was a powerful emperor.

The last point of this section concerns the benefits of virtues to our physical body. Because of peace of mind and inner joy acquired from self-cultivation of virtues, our body will also show healthy signs. A virtuous person often smiles, shows happiness in his appearance, and is upbeat and energetic.

Section 22

孟子曰 伯夷辟紂 居北海之濱 聞文王作興 曰 盍歸乎來 吾聞西伯善養老者。太公辟紂 居東海之濱 聞文王作興 曰 盍歸乎來 吾聞西伯善養老者。天下有善養老 則仁人以為己歸矣。五畝之宅 樹牆下以桑 匹婦蠶之 則老者足以衣帛矣。五母雞 二母彘 無失其時 老者足以無失肉矣。百畝之田 匹夫耕之 八口之家足以無饑矣。所謂西伯善養老者 制其田里 教之樹畜 導其妻子 使養其老。五十非帛不暖 七十非肉不飽。不暖不飽謂之凍餒。文王之民 無凍餒之老者 此之謂也。

Mencius said, "Bo Yi fled from Emperor Zhou and settled at the coast of the North Sea. When he heard of the rise of King Wen, he said, 'Why not go home? I heard that Earl Wen in the West takes good care of the elderly.' Jiang Tai Gong also fled from Emperor Zhou and settled at the coast of the East Sea. When he heard of the rise of King Wen, he said, 'Why not go home? I heard that Earl Wen in the West takes good care of the elderly.' If there were a ruler who takes good care of the elderly, all virtuous people would find refuge under him. King Wen allocated five acres of land to each elderly couple. The spaces between walls were planted with mulberry trees and the woman of the house bred silkworms so that the elderly

Chapter 13: Utmost Dedication (1)

couple could wear silk. Each family had five hens and two female pigs. If the family did not miss the feeding and breeding season, the elderly couple could eat meat. Given a field of one hundred acres, a single farmer could support a family of eight and keep them from hunger. People said that Earl Wen in the West took good care of the elderly because he instituted a good land policy, taught elderly people how to plant trees and breed animals, and educated their wives and children how to take care of the elderly. At the age of 50, a person needs to wear silk to keep warm. At the age of 70, a person needs to eat meat to have a full stomach. Deprived of warm clothes and full meals, a person is said to be cold and hungry. Among the people of King Wen, no elderly person was cold and hungry. This was what people said about King Wen."

Annotation:

The story of Bo Yi (伯夷) is narrated in Section 5 of Endnotes.
King Wen of Zhou (周文王, 1152–1056 BC) was also called the Earl of Wen in the West. He was the father of King Wu of Zhou (周武王, died 1043 BC) who overthrew Emperor Zhou (紂) of the Shang Dynasty with the help of Jiang Tai Gong (姜太公), also known as Jiang Zi Ya (姜子牙, circa 1156–1017 BC).

Section 23

孟子曰 易其田疇 薄其稅斂 民可使富也。食之以時 用之以禮 財不可勝用也。民非水火不生活 昏暮叩人之門戶 求水火 無弗與者 至足矣。聖人治天下 使有菽粟如水火。菽粟如水火 而民焉有不仁者乎。

Mencius said, "If you make sure that the fields of your people are well cultivated and levy a low tax, your people will then be affluent. If your people cultivate and harvest their crops on time and you do not draft them inconsiderately, they will have more than enough wealth for consumption. People cannot survive without water and fire. If you knock at the door of a neighbor and ask for some water and fire, nobody will turn you down because water and fire are so abundant. In the governance of a country, a sage will try to make beans and grains as plentiful as water and fire. If so, how can your people not be benevolent?"

Commentary:

In this section, "beans and grains" stand for food and consumption goods.

During the Spring-Autumn and Warring States periods, wars between states occurred frequently. When a war broke out, peasants were drafted into the army and could not cultivate and harvest their crops on time. If they missed the growing season, they would have no food during the winter.

Section 24

孟子曰 孔子登東山而小魯 登太山而小天下。故觀於海者難為水 遊於聖人之門者難為言。觀水有術 必觀其瀾。日月有明 容光必照焉。流水之為物也 不盈科不行。君子之志於道也 不成章不達。

Mencius said, "After Confucius had ascended the East Mountain, the capital of the state of Lu appeared small to him. After he had

Chapter 13: Utmost Dedication (1)

ascended Tai Shan, everything beneath the sky appeared small to him. Therefore, after one has seen the sea, all ponds of water are negligible to him. No words can describe the awe of disciples of saints whose virtues are unattainably great. To study the nature of water, one must watch its waves. The light from the Sun and Moon reaches every corner on earth. The nature of flowing water is that it fills up all hollows before it moves forward. A Jun Zi in pursuit of Dao must shine at every milestone before reaching his destination."

Annotation:

Confucius was a native of the small state Lu (魯國). East Mountain was at the suburb of the capital of Lu. Tai Shan (太山) was the highest mountain in China at that time.

Commentary and Modern Perspective:

In this section, Mencius talked about learning and self-cultivation. The first three sentences present the analogy that after one has reached a higher level of knowledge and enlightenment, things at the lower level appear trivial, negligible, and irrelevant. The perception of things depends on the level, position, prior knowledge, experience, prejudice, bias, and condition of the observer. When one's view is fixated at the lower level because of the lack of exposure and experience, one cannot perceive and understand the greatness of things at a higher level. Zhuang Zi, a prominent Taoist, also wrote, "You cannot talk about the sea to a frog under a well because the frog is confined to a limited space all its life. You cannot talk about ice to a summer worm because it is confined to a limited time frame all its life. You cannot talk about a straight highway to a person living by a winding road all his life

515

because of his lack of education" (Section 16 of Chapter 12 above). Likewise, an elementary school student who only knows arithmetic cannot understand the sophistication of calculus. A college student who knows calculus considers arithmetic to be elementary. These analogies also teach us to be humble. The world of knowledge and virtues is more immense than we can imagine. Therefore, Mencius mentioned the next sentence, "No words can describe the awe of disciples of saints whose virtues are unattainably great."

In the next two sentences, Mencius used the analogies of the nature of water and sunlight and moonlight to illustrate the complexity, depth, and width of principles of Nature and the Dao. Waves of water can exhibit an infinite number of patterns. Sometimes calm and sometimes violent, these waves are dynamic and changing continuously. Even waves of water are complex and dynamic. How much so for the principles of Nature and the Dao? Sunlight and moonlight reach every corner and pass through every crack on earth. The same applies to ultimate enlightenment.

In the last two sentences, Mencius used the analogy of flowing water to teach his disciples that, on the path of learning and self-cultivation, one must not rush. One must steadfastly achieve firm success at each stage before moving on to the next. There is no short-cut.

Section 25

孟子曰 雞鳴而起 孳孳為善者 舜之徒也。雞鳴而起 孳孳為利者 蹠之徒也。欲知舜與蹠之分 無他 利與善之閒也。

Mencius said, "People who get up early at cock-crowing time to do good earnestly are disciples of Shun. People who get up early at

Chapter 13: Utmost Dedication (1)

cock-crowing time to pursue gains earnestly are disciples of robbers. What is the difference between Shun and a robber? It is nothing but the difference between gains and goodness."

Commentary and Modern Perspective:

Nowadays, most people get up early to beat the traffic so that they are not late to work. Everybody takes this for granted that it is their necessary way of living. Few people bother to get up early to do voluntary work.

Section 26

孟子曰 楊子取為我 拔一毛而利天下 不為也。墨子兼愛 摩頂放踵利天下 為之。子莫執中 執中為近之 執中無權 猶執一也。所惡執一者 為其賊道也 舉一而廢百也。

Mencius said, "Yang Zi preaches individualism. He would not pull out a piece of his hair to benefit the world. Mo Zi preaches universal and indiscriminative love. He does not mind shaving bald his head and walking bare-foot to do good to the world. Zi Mo advocates the middle of the two. Holding onto the middle is closer to the correct approach, but without the right weights and balance, this approach is no different from sticking to one extreme. The fault of holding onto one extreme is that it deviates from the Dao. One approach is chosen at the expense of hundreds of other approaches."

Annotation:

The philosophy of Yang Zhu (楊朱, circa 440–360 BC, also

known as Yang Zi) is explained in the Commentary of Section 9 of Chapter 6 above.

The philosophy of Mo Zi (墨子, circa 470–391 BC, also known as Mo Di, 墨翟) is explained in Section 2 of Endnotes.

Both Yang Zhu and Mo Zi were two prominent philosophers during the Warring States Period.

Zi Mo (子莫) was an unknown person.

In the ancient China, shaving one's head bald was considered unfilial and as a proxy to beheading.

Commentary and Modern Perspective:

This section has two key points. The first point is that Confucians reject extremist philosophies. Yang Zhu and Mo Zi were two extremes on the spectrum of selfishness versus selflessness. The "middle of the road" approach advocated by Zi Mo was closest to Confucian philosophy. The second point is that Mencius cautioned that even holding onto the middle ground is still faulty and is another form of extremism. The position of the middle ground needs to be determined by a balancing act with relative weights of importance of all relevant factors. One must not be stubborn, but instead pragmatic and objective. Such weights change over time and depend on the circumstance under consideration. There is no approach which is correct and applicable all the time (his view is same as the teaching of Buddhism).

Section 27

孟子曰 饑者甘食 渴者甘飲 是未得飲食之正也 饑渴害之也。豈惟口腹有饑渴之害。人心亦皆有害。人能無以饑渴之害為心

Chapter 13: Utmost Dedication (1)

害 則不及人不為憂矣。

Mencius said, "The hungry find any food tasty, and the thirsty find the same of any drink, because their appetite and thirst are not satisfied. Their hunger and thirst distort their sensations. Are the distortions from hunger and thirst the only problem? The minds of men are also subject to a similar problem. If a man can prevent the similar problem from interfering his mind, he needs not worry about his being inferior to others."

Commentary and Modern Perspective:

In this section, Mencius repeated the same point mentioned in the Commentary of Section 24 above: "The perception of things depends on the level, position, prior knowledge, experience, prejudice, bias, and condition of the observer." Mencius also pointed out here that the subjective perception and cognition of things may be different from their objective realities. This is where wisdom comes in. A wise person can see the true reality better than others by being objective and unbiased.

This section is also related to Section 26 above. During the Warring States Period, governments were oppressive and common people yearned for personal freedom. The philosophy of individualism of Yang Zhu was therefore superficially considered to be the correct cure of evils at that time. Some other people who were victims of tyranny and wars yearned for more love and peace in the country. Therefore, the philosophy of indiscriminative love of Mo Zi appealed to people at that time.

To distinguish right from wrong, one must be objective, be aware of his own bias rising from impurities of mind and remove such impurities.

Section 28

孟子曰　柳下惠不以三公易其介。

Mencius said, "Liu Xia Hui did not compromise his integrity for the sake of becoming one of the top three ministers."

Annotation:

Details about Liu Xia Hui (柳下惠, 720–621 BC) are shown in the Annotation of Section 9 of Chapter 3.

Commentary:

This section is the continuation of the last section. Mencius cited the example of Liu Xia Hui to teach his disciples that they should not compromise their integrity and be swayed by power, wealth, fame, or circumstance.

Section 29

孟子曰　有為者辟若掘井　掘井九軔而不及泉　猶為棄井也。

Mencius said, "Trying to achieve a goal is like digging a well. If you if give up after digging a depth of 72 feet and finding no water, you are just abandoning the well."

Commentary and Modern Perspective:

You should not give up before you have achieved your goal.

Chapter 13: Utmost Dedication (1)

Section 30

孟子曰 堯舜 性之也。湯武 身之也。五霸 假之也。久假而不歸 惡知其非有也。

Mencius said, "Yao and Shun were virtuous by their nature. King Tang and King Wu acquired their virtue through practice. The five hegemons pretended that they are virtuous. Since they had pretended to be virtuous for a long time, they did not even realize that they were void of virtues."

Annotation:

Emperor Yao (堯, circa 2356–2255 BC) and Shun (舜, circa 2294–2184 BC) were two ancient saintly kings. King Tang (湯) founded the Shang Dynasty (商朝, circa 1600–1066 BC) and King Wu of Zhou (周武王, died 1043 BC) founded the Zhou Dynasty. Both were also regarded as saintly kings.

The Five Hegemons were: Qi Huan Gong (齊桓公, died 643 BC, also known as Duke Huan of Qi), Jin Wen Gong (晉文公, 671–628 BC, also known as Duke Wen of Jin), Qin Mu Gong (秦穆公, 683–621 BC, also known as Duke Mu of Qin), Song Xiang Gong (宋襄公, died 637 BC, also known as Duke Xiang of Song), and King Zhuang of Chu (楚莊王, died 591 BC).

Commentary and Modern Perspective:

Like Yao and Shun, some people are born virtuous, whereas others developed their virtues by learning and practice. Some hypocrites, like the five hegemons, pretend that they are virtuous

521

and use deception, lies, rhetoric, and manipulation to get the support of their followers, and they even deceive themselves. Over a long time, their characters go bankrupt.

Section 31

公孫丑曰 伊尹曰 予不狎於不順。放太甲於桐 民大悅。太甲賢。又反之 民大悅。賢者之為人臣也 其君不賢 則固可放與。

孟子曰 有伊尹之志 則可。無伊尹之志 則篡也。

Gong Sun Chou said, "Yi Yin said to Tai Jia, 'I cannot stand your being devious.' Yi Yin then banished Tai Jia to Tong and the people of the country were greatly pleased. After Tai Jia had repented and become virtuous, Yi Yin restored him to the throne. The people of the country were greatly please again. If a king is bad, it is permissible for a meritorious minister to banish the king?"

Mencius said, "It is permissible only if the minister has the motive of Yi Yin. Otherwise, the minister is committing an act of usurpation."

Annotation:

The story of Yi Yin (伊尹, circa 1649–1549 BC) and Tai Jia (太甲) is narrated in Section 3 of Endnotes. Yi Yin was a meritorious minister and a patriarch of the Shang Dynasty. He assisted King Tang in the founding of the dynasty. Tai Jia, the young grandson of Tang, became the third emperor. He was a spoiled and devious kid. Yi Yin, in his role as the patriarch and guardian of the dynasty, banished Tai Jia to Tong (桐). Tai Jia repented after three years and

Chapter 13: Utmost Dedication (1)

was then restored to the throne by Yi Yin.

Gong Sun Chou (公孫丑) was a disciple of Mencius.

Section 32

公孫丑曰 詩曰 不素餐兮。君子之不耕而食 何也。

孟子曰 君子居是國也 其君用之 則安富尊榮。其子弟從之 則孝弟忠信。不素餐兮 孰大於是。

Gong Sun Chou asked, "The *Book of Poetry* said, 'Don't eat unearned food.' Why should a Ju Zi then eat food without laboring in the fields?"

Mencius said, "When a Jun Zi lives in a country and works for the king, he can bring security, prosperity, and honor to the country. When his disciples spread his teachings, the virtues of filial piety, fraternity, loyalty, and trustworthiness will be fostered in the country. Comparing this with the principle of not eating unearned food, which is greater?"

Annotation:

In ancient China, people presented food on the altar during worship ceremonies of deities and ancestors. Dolls, figurines, idols, statutes, or later inscribed plagues were placed on the altar to symbolize the worshipped spirits. People imagined that such spirits would eat the food on the altar. Later, there was an idiom that described a person who earned food without doing work as a figurine on the altar. It just sat there doing nothing but was offered food by people. This idiom is defamatory against a person, typically a government official. The *Book of Poetry* used this analogy to remind people against idleness.

In this section, a Jun Zi stands for a scholar and a government official.

Commentary:

Mencius's reply in this section repeated his point during his discussion with Chen Xiang (see Section 4 of Chapter 5).

Section 33

王子墊問曰 士何事。

孟子曰 尚志。

曰 何謂尚志。

曰 仁義而已矣。殺一無罪 非仁也。非其有而取之 非義也。居惡在 仁是也。路惡在 義是也。居仁由義 大人之事備矣。

Prince Dian asked, "What is the business of a scholar?"
    Mencius answered, "Pursue his noble principles."
    Prince Dian asked, "What do noble principles mean?"
    Mencius answered, "They are just Ren and Yi. Punishing one innocent person to death is against Ren. Taking what one is not entitled is against Yi. The home is Ren, and the path is Yi. If you start from Ren and follow the path of Yi, all businesses of great men can be accomplished."

Annotation:

Prince Dian (王子墊) was a son of King Xuan of Qi (齊宣王).

Chapter 13: Utmost Dedication (1)

In this section, "great men" referred to top government officials and nobilities. The phrase "all business of great men" specifically referred to all matters related to the governance of a country. Mencius mentioned this because he tried to educate a future ruler of the state of Qi.

Commentary:

Mencius singled out punishments and confiscation of property as two examples against Ren and Yi because these immoral actions were common. Mencius taught prince Dian not to be a tyrant and not to confiscate property from people.

Section 34

孟子曰 仲子 不義與之齊國而弗受 人皆信之 是舍簞食豆羹之義也。人莫大焉亡親戚 君臣 上下。以其小者信其大者 奚可哉。

Mencius said, "Zhong Zi refused to go to the state of Qi and take an official appointment because he considered it against the principle of Yi. People believed that he was righteous. However, his righteousness was based on just his refusal to accept a basket of rice and a bowl of soup. There is nothing more immoral than the neglect of one's parent, disloyalty to one's king, and disobedience to superiors. Is it correct to infer one's merit on a major morality issue based his minor acts of righteousness?"

Annotation:

Zhong Zi (also known as Chen Zhong Zi, 陳仲子) was a native

of the state of Qi. Since he lived in the city of Ling, he was also called Ling Zi (陵子). His brother was a top minister of the state of Qi. He belonged to the philosophy school of Yang Zhu (楊朱) and advocated purity and asceticism. His story is narrated in Section 10 of Chapter 6 above, in which Mencius criticized his behavior as inhuman.

Commentary:

Mencius considered filial piety, fraternity, and loyalty more important than abstinence and austerity.

Section 35

桃應問曰 舜為天子 皋陶為士 瞽瞍殺人 則如之何。
 孟子曰 執之而已矣。
 (曰) 然則舜不禁與。
 曰 夫舜惡得而禁之。夫有所受之也。
 (曰) 然則舜如之何。
 曰 舜視棄天下 猶棄敝蹝也。竊負而逃 遵海濱而處 終身訢然 樂而忘天下。

Tao Ying asked Mencius, "Suppose that during the reign of Shun as the emperor, Gao Yao were the chief justice, and Gu Sou had killed a person. What would have been done in this situation?"
 Mencius said, "Gao Yao should prosecute Gu Sou."
 Tao Ying asked, "In this case, would Shun not stop it?"
 Mencius replied, "How could Shun have stopped it? Gao Yao had the delegated authority according to law."

Chapter 13: Utmost Dedication (1)

Tao Ying asked, "If then, what else would Shun have done?"

Mencius replied, "Shun would have abandoned his kingdom as if throwing away a pair of worn-out sandals. He would then secretly carry his father on his back and escape to the seashore where they could retire and live happily for the rest of their lives."

Annotation:

Tao Ying (桃應) was a disciple of Mencius.

Gao Yao (皋陶) was the earliest chief justice in China during the era of Shun. His name represents the best judge in history (see Section 4 of Chapter 5).

Gu Sou (瞽瞍) was the father of Shun (see also Section 28 of Chapter 7).

Commentary:

Tao Ying raised a hypothetical dilemma, a choice between two evils, to Mencius. As a righteous emperor, Shun needed to obey the laws of the country. He could not ignore the authority of the chief justice of the country. On the other hand, Shun was known for his filial piety. He would not want to see his father receive the death penalty.

This section shows that Mencius considered filial piety to be most important. The ownership and power over a country can be thrown away like a pair of worn-out sandals. By escaping, Shun would have avoided a dilemma.

Section 36

孟子自范之齊 望見齊王之子。喟然嘆曰 居移氣 養移體 大哉

527

Mencius in Modern Perspectives

居乎。夫非盡人之子與。

　　孟子曰　王子宮室　車馬　衣服多與人同　而王子若彼者　其居使之然也。況居天下之廣居者乎。魯君之宋　呼於垤澤之門。守者曰　此非吾君也　何其聲之似我君也。此無他　居相似也。

Mencius went to the state of Qi from Fan and saw the prince of Qi from a distance. He sighed and exclaimed, "The environment transforms the air of a person. The food also changes his body. The effect of environment on a person is indeed great! Aren't we all sons of somebody?" He then added, "The house, carriage, and clothes of the prince are not so different from common people. What causes the distinctive appearance of the prince is his environment. What about the immense environment under the sky that we are living in? The king of the state of Lu once went to the state of Song. He called out aloud at the gate of Die Ze. The gate-keeper said, 'He is not our king. Yet, his voice sounds like our king's.' There is no reason but the similarity of environments of the two kings."

Annotation:

　　The prince of Qi was the same prince Dian mentioned in Section 33 above.
　　Fan (范) was the name of a city.
　　Die Ze (垤澤) was the name of a gate in the state of Song.

Commentary and Modern Perspective:

　　In this section, Mencius used the distinctive air of the prince and the similarity in the voices of the two kings to teach his disciples that the environment can have significant impact on a person. By the

Chapter 13: Utmost Dedication (1)

question, "What about the immense environment under the sky that we are living in?" Mencius hinted that the environment that all human beings live in was immense and complex. Therefore, we must be aware of its influence on us.

Section 37

孟子曰 食而弗愛 豕交之也。愛而不敬 獸畜之也。恭敬者 幣之未將者也。恭敬而無實 君子不可虛拘。

Mencius said, "To feed a man but not love him is to treat him like a pig. To love him but not respect him is to treat him like a pet. Respect should precede monetary gifts. If the respect is insincere, one cannot employ a Jun Zi by an empty show."

Commentary and Modern Perspective:

Mencius said this in reaction to the behavior of King Xuan of Qi who sent him gifts but did not visit Mencius in person to show respect.

Confucius also said, "Most people nowadays think that filial piety is just about feeding your old parents. Even dogs and horses are fed by people. If you do not respect your parents, how do you differentiate feeding your parents from feeding dogs and horses?" (Section 7 of Chapter 2, 為政, of *Confucius Analects*).

Section 38

孟子曰 形色 天性也。惟聖人 然後可以踐形。

Mencius said, "The functions and appearance of our bodies and

529

emotions are our innate nature. However, a saint knows how to regulate them."

Commentary and Modern Perspective:

This short section has a practical point. Our bodies and mind are interrelated. A healthy mind promotes physical health, and vice versa. A saint knows how to regulate his mind, and therefore, can also improve the health of his body.

Section 39

齊宣王欲短喪。公孫丑曰 為朞之喪 猶愈於已乎。

孟子曰 是猶或紾其兄之臂 子謂之姑徐徐云爾 亦教之孝弟而已矣。

王子有其母死者 其傅為之請數月之喪。公孫丑曰 若此者何如也。

曰 是欲終之而不可得也。雖加一日愈於已 謂夫莫之禁而弗為者也。

King Xuan of Qi wanted to shorten by decree the period of mourning vigil. Gong Sun Chou spoke to Mencius, "To have a mourning period of one year is better than to throw away it altogether."

Mencius said, "This is just as if one is twisting the arm of his elder brother and you tell him that you are doing so gently. You should instead remind the king about filial piety and fraternity."

The mother of a son of King Xuan died, and the tutor of the prince asked the court on behalf of the prince for the permission to observe a few months of mourning vigil. Gong Sun Chou asked

Chapter 13: Utmost Dedication (1)

Mencius, "What do you think of this?"

Mencius said, "This is the case where the son wants to observe the traditional mourning period, but he is not permitted to do so. In this case, even mourning for one more day is better than no mourning at all. I previously referred to those who do not observe any mourning vigil, even when there is no restriction."

Annotation:

Mencius was once a top advisor to King Xuan of Qi but later left the state of Qi, frustrated with the lack of sincerity of King Xuan in reforming his governance. King Xuan later hired Gong Sun Chou, the top disciple of Mencius, as a minister. King Xuan wanted to shorten the three-year period of mourning vigil at the death of parents. Gong Sun Chou consulted Mencius about this decree.

In ancient China, filial piety was utmost important. For millennia, from the Shang Dynasty to the Ming Dynasty, observance of mourning vigil at the death of parents was a norm. Even emperors and ministers were required to observe this norm. Violators were dejected by society and even punished by the government. The Zhou Li stipulated a three-year mourning period.

The *Confucius Analects* recorded a dialogue between Zai Wo and Confucius. Zai Wo asked, "After our parents have died, we are supposed to observe mourning vigil for three years. It is too long. If a Jun Zi does not practice Li rituals for three years, the rituals will become slackened. If he does not play music for three years, his musical skills will be gone. Old grains will be exhausted and replaced by new grains. Firewood will need to be replenished. Therefore, one year of vigil should be enough." Confucius said, "Are you comfortable with that?" "If you feel comfortable, do it then! During a mourning period, a Jun Zi does not find food tasty, music enjoyable, and daily life comfortable. Since you feel comfortable, you can do so for one year." Zai Wo left. Confucius then said, "He does not have Ren virtue. After a child is born, parents need to nurse the child for three years. Therefore, it is a common norm that children need to observe three years of mourning after the death of parents. Will Zai Wo give his parents three years of love?"

The ancient tradition in royal families of China regarded the concubines of a king to be inferior to the queen. A concubine was not regarded as the "official" mother but a "surrogate" mother of her sons. The queen was instead regarded as their official mother. Therefore, when a concubine died, her sons were not permitted to observe a mourning vigil because, in theory, their official mother, the queen, was still alive. Observing a mourning vigil means a curse to the "official" mother.

Section 40

孟子曰 君子之所以教者五 有如時雨化之者 有成德者 有達財者 有答問者 有私淑艾者。此五者 君子之所以教也。

Mencius said, "A Jun Zi teaches in five ways. The first is to foster his influence like timely rain. The second is to help students perfect their virtues. The third is to help students develop their talents. The fourth is to answer their questions. The fifth is to induce people who cannot attend his school to emulate him privately. These five are the ways in which a Jun Zi teaches."

Commentary and Modern Perspective:

In this section, a Jun Zi is already a sage. Very few teachers nowadays follow these five ways.

There are few teachers nowadays following such practices.

Section 41

公孫丑曰 道則高矣 美矣 宜若登天然 似不可及也。何不使彼為可幾及而日孳孳也。

孟子曰 大匠不為拙工改廢繩墨 羿不為拙射變其彀率。君子引而不發 躍如也。中道而立 能者從之。

Gong Sun Chou said, "The Dao is so lofty and beautiful. It is so unattainable, like climbing up the sky. Why not make it into a set of concrete rules so that we can follow them every day?"

Mencius said, "A master of crafts does not put aside plumb lines for the sake of his clumsy apprentices. Yi did not change the arc of the bow for the sake of clumsy archers. A Jun Zi inspires but does not push further, so that his teaching style is dynamic and lively. He is balanced and unbiased, so that students with the potential of learning can follow him."

Annotation:

Gong Sun Chou (公孫丑) was a disciple of Mencius.

Yi (羿, also known as Hou Yi, 后羿) was a legendary archer during the time of Emperor Yao.

The meaning of Dao has been explained in the Introduction.

Commentary and Modern Perspective:

The Dao is immensely broad and deep. Teaching of moral

principles cannot be formula based. The teacher can only inspire his students and let them develop their own awakening and enlightenment. Once inspired, talented students will actively develop their own enlightenment like arrows shot from a bow. The teacher should stay balanced and unbiased and avoid extremes so that his students will not be misled.

The best teacher inspires his or her students but does not spoon-feed them.

Section 42

孟子曰　天下有道　以道殉身。天下無道　以身殉道。未聞以道殉乎人者也。

Mencius said, "When the Dao prevails in the country, you carry it. When the country lacks Dao, you sacrifice yourself for it. I have not heard of the abandonment of Dao to accommodate others."

Annotation:

The meaning of Dao is explained in the Introduction.

Commentary and Modern Perspective:

This short section should be taken seriously.

When the country is peaceful, orderly, civilized, and has a clean government and high moral standards, and so on, it is your mission to bring these to higher levels. In this way, you carry the Dao with you. Confucius also said, "If the world is governed properly, you offer your service. If not, you quit" (Section 13 of Chapter 8, 泰伯,

Chapter 13: Utmost Dedication (1)

of *Confucius Analects*). He also said, "When the government was good, he joined as a minister. When the government was bad, he quit" (Section 7 of Chapter 15, 衛靈公, of *Confucius Analects*). In Section 9 of this Chapter, Mencius also said, "When a man is successful and prominent, he should also benefit the world."

When the country is uncivilized, decadent, war-torn, and has a corrupt government and low moral standards and so on, there are two ways to follow. You can either quit or fight to defend the Dao. If you quit, you are like Bo Yi, who retired in seclusion. You are still sacrificing yourself for Dao because you may have to give up a good life ahead. If you fight, you should be ready to die for it. Confucius said, "A hero who is determined to uphold the Ren virtue would not seek to live at the expense of hurting his Ren virtue, but he would sacrifice his life in order to preserve it" (Section 9 of Chapter 15, 衛靈公, of *Confucius Analects*).

Many people abandon their moral principles to go along a morally bankrupt peer group, to fit into a decadent culture of the society, or to seek wealth, power, and fame. These behaviors are abandonment of Dao to accommodate others.

Section 43

公都子曰 滕更之在門也 若在所禮。而不答 何也。

孟子曰 挾貴而問 挾賢而問 挾長而問 挾有勳勞而問 挾故而問 皆所不答也。滕更有二焉。

Gong Du Zi asked Mencius, "Tang Geng wanted to be your student. He appeared to deserve your courtesy. Yet you refused. Why?"

Mencius replied, "I do not answer questions from a person who has an attitude of being a nobleman, a sage, an elderly, or an elite, or from a person who has an antagonistic agenda. Teng Geng fits in two of these criteria."

Annotation:

Teng Geng (滕更) was the brother of Teng Wen Gong (滕文公), the king of the small state of Teng (滕).

Modern Perspective:

It is annoying to have to answer questions from a person who has the attitude that he is superior, more knowledgeable, more experienced, or older than us. Some already have the answer but try to test us. Some other may try to embarrass us with leading and crooked questions. The best way to deal with them is to refrain from answering their questions.

Section 44

孟子曰　於不可已而已者　無所不已。於所厚者薄　無所不薄也。其進銳者　其退速。

Mencius said, "Some people obstinately do things knowing that they cannot do so. There is nothing which they will not do (and mess up). Some people slight things which are, in fact, more important. There is nothing which they will not slight. Those who dash forward abruptly will have to retreat rapidly."

Or,

Mencius said, "Some people stop short of the finish line knowing

Chapter 13: Utmost Dedication (1)

that they should not stop. There is nothing which they will not stop short of. Some people slight others who are in fact more prominent. There is nobody whom they will not slight. Those who advance sharply will have to retreat rapidly."

Commentary and Modern Perspective:

The first interpretation seems better because it talked about the same personality trait throughout the section and therefore its sentences were more coherent. The second interpretation was however proposed by Zhu Xi (朱熹), a prominent Confucian during the Song Dynasty. This interpretation talked about three different personality traits. Both interpretations are meaningful though. The following focuses on the first interpretation.

Some people are like bulls in a China shop. They are over-confident and think that they can accomplish everything, whereas in fact they lack capability, or they do not have the objectivity and mindset to assess risks. They tend to mess up most of their endeavors. They tend to slight everything since they cannot distinguish heavy from light, right from wrong, and top from bottom. They are impatient and like to rush. They will soon be stopped when they hit a brick wall. The faster they try to achieve unrealistic goals beyond their limits, the harder and faster they will fall.

In this section, Mencius taught his disciples about humility, objectivity, and patience. There is no short cut in the process of self-cultivation.

Section 45

孟子曰　君子之於物也　愛之而弗仁。於民也　仁之而弗親。親

Mencius in Modern Perspectives

親而仁民 仁民而愛物。

Mencius said, "Regarding all creatures other than human beings, a Jun Zi should love them but needs not be benevolent to them. Regarding people in general, he should be benevolent to them but needs not be affectionate to them. He should first be affectionate to his parents and then be benevolent to other people. After being benevolent to people, he should then love all other creatures."

Commentary and Modern Perspective:

This important section is about Ren. The Introduction has explained the concept of Ren in more details. Although Ren is about love in general, there are different levels of Ren. Confucians consider that the affection to parents is at the top level, followed in sequential order by fraternity, loyalty, love of one's country, love of all people in the world, and lastly, love of everything else on earth. This section abbreviates these priorities into three main sequential levels: affection to parents, benevolence to people in general, and love of all other creatures. This is a key tenet of Confucianism. In this section, the phrase "all creatures other than human beings" includes animals, plants, minerals, and natural resources, and not just animals. This love leads to the concept of respect and protection of the environment, and to harmony with Nature.

Unlike Mo Zi, who advocated universal and indiscriminative love of all people, the Confucians insisted that there should be different levels of Ren. Confucians think that indiscriminative love of all people is too idealistic, against human nature, and therefore impractical. Without graded and differential levels of Ren, the society will be in chaos. An example can explain Confucian reasoning versus Mo Zi's. Suppose that both Mo Zi and Mencius

Chapter 13: Utmost Dedication (1)

stood together at a riverbank. Their mothers fell into the river. Mencius would jump into the river and save his mother first before saving Mo Zi's mother. However, Mo Zi could not decide whose mother to save first because Mo Zi was indifferent between the mothers. This example shows the fundamental flaw in Mo Zi idealistic philosophy.

This discussion is not just theoretical. Nowadays, there are people who do not support their elderly parents financially or let their lonely parents wither in nursing homes. Yet they actively donate to charities and participate in voluntary work to earn praise from friends. There are also people who are kind to their pets but cold to their parents and siblings. The pets are their babies, and their parents are just discarded bones in the garbage. Some dog owners walk their dogs every day but do not bother to take their elderly and infirmed parents for a walk for years. If we were parents of these children, how would we feel?

Section 46

孟子曰　知者無不知也　當務之為急。仁者無不愛也　急親賢之為務。堯舜之知而不遍物　急先務也。堯舜之仁不遍愛人　急親賢也。不能三年之喪　而緦小功之察。放飯流歠　而問無齒決　是之謂不知務。

Mencius said, "There is nothing which is unknown to a wise man, but he takes the most urgent task as the top priority. There is nobody whom a man with Ren virtue does not love, but he would take the building of friendship with meritorious persons as the top priority. Yao and Shun could not know everything. They just handled the most urgent tasks at hand. Yao and Shun could not show their affection to everybody. They urgently befriended meritorious persons. Some people do not observe the three-year mourning vigil at the deaths of their parents. Yet, they debate over what to dress during the shortened mourning vigils for three and five months, respectively. Some people eat impolitely by gobbling up food and drinks. Yet, they insist on the minor etiquette of not biting apart small pieces of meat. This is what I call their ignorance of priorities and relative importance."

Commentary and Modern Perspective:

This section is the elaboration of the same point in the last section.

Chapter 14: Utmost Dedication (2)

Section 1

孟子曰 不仁哉 梁惠王也。仁者以其所愛及其所不愛 不仁者以其所不愛及其所愛。

公孫丑問曰 何謂也。

(曰) 梁惠王以土地之故 糜爛其民而戰之 大敗。將復之 恐不能勝 故驅其所愛子弟以殉之。是之謂以其所不愛及其所愛也。

Mencius said, "King Hui of Liang was indeed inhuman. A person with Ren virtue extends his love from those he loves to those he does not care much. An inhuman person extends his ruthlessness from those he does not care much to those he loves."

Gong Sun Chou asked, "What do you mean?"

Mencius said, "For the sake of conquering more territory, King Hui of Liang pulverized his people by sending them to war. He suffered a great defeat. In the next round, worried about another defeat, he sent his own son and other loved ones to war and sacrificed them. This is what I call 'extending his ruthlessness from those he does not care much to those he loves.' "

Annotation:

The detailed story of King Hui of Wei (also known as King Hui of Liang because the capital of Wei was located at the city Da Liang) is shown in the Annotation of Section 1 of Chapter 1 above. He was a warmonger. In the first war in 354 BC mentioned by Mencius, King Hui of Liang invaded the state of Zhao (趙), which begged King Wei of Qi (齊威王) for rescue. The army of Qi, led by Tian Ji (田忌) as the chief commander and Sun Bin (孫臏) as the strategic advisor, defeated the army of King Hui of Liang in the Battle of Gui Ling (桂陵).

After the Battle of Gui Ling, King Hui of Liang was the aggressor again in 342 BC. He attacked a neighbor in the south, the state of Han (韓). The King of Han begged for a rescue from King Wei of Qi who sent his army to fight against the state of Wei. Tian Ji was again appointed the chief commander of the army and Sun Bin was his strategic advisor. To ensure victory, King Hui of Liang ordered his eldest son, Prince Shen (申), and his chief commander, Pang Juan (龐涓), to lead the army, which was again annihilated in the Battle of Ma Ling (馬陵). Prince Shen and Pang Juan were both killed in that battle.

Commentary:

In Section 45 of Chapter 13 above, Mencius mentioned the three levels of Ren: affection to parents, benevolence to people in general, and love of all other creatures. A Jun Zi should start with loving his dearest parents and brothers, then extend his love to other people, and lastly to all other creatures. This explains the sentence: "A person with Ren virtue extends his love from those his loves to those he does not care much."

An inhuman person applies what he dislikes to other creatures, then to other people, and even to his most beloved ones. Mencius cited the example of King Hui of Liang to illustrate his point: "An inhuman person extends his ruthlessness from those he does not care much to those he loves." King Hui not only brought disaster to his

Chapter 14: Utmost Dedication (2)

people but also caused the deaths of his eldest son and his best general.

Section 2

孟子曰 春秋無義戰。彼善於此 則有之矣。征者 上伐下也 敵國不相征也。

Mencius said, "There was no just war during the Spring-Autumn Period. There might be instances of one war relatively more justified than another. Punitive expeditions were waged against inferior feudal lords by feudal lords of higher authority. Peers did not wage wars against each other."

Commentary:

During the Spring-Autumn Period (771 to 476 BC), the imperial emperor of the Zhou Dynasty lost effective control over feudal states. Feudal lords had autonomy over their enfeoffed territories, which were de facto independent states. The states had their own armies. They paid homage to the emperor ceremonially only. There was a rule that feudal lords had the responsibility of defending the central government when it was under attack by foreign invaders. There was another rule that when a feudal state did not obey the central government, attacked another feudal state, or committed other atrocities, the imperial emperor could summon senior feudal states to punish the devious state. A punitive war would be waged against it. This was why Mencius said, "Punitive expeditions were waged against inferior feudal lords by feudal lords of higher authority."

There was also a tradition that feudal lords of the same ancestorial lineage did not fight against each other, because they were distant cousins. This was why Mencius said, "Peers did not wage wars against each other."

However, the above rules were violated repeatedly. Feudal lords fought against each other for greed, ambition, hatred, and revenge. About 52 states were destroyed or annexed by more powerful states during the Spring-Autumn Periods. Therefore, Mencius said that there was no just war during the period.

Section 3

孟子曰 盡信書 則不如無書。吾於武成 取二三策而已矣。仁人無敵於天下 以至仁伐至不仁 而何其血之流杵也。

Mencius said, "It is better to act without a book than to believe everything written in it. Regarding the book *Wu Cheng*, I only believe two or three passages in it. A man with Ren virtue is invincible in the world. If an utmost benevolent state wages a war against an utmost inhuman adversary, why so much blood was shed that staves floated in streams of blood?"

Annotation:

Wu Cheng (武成) was a chapter of the *History Book of Zhou Dynasty*. This chapter described the battle at Mu Ye (牧野) where the coalition army led by King Wu of Zhou annihilated the army of Emperor Zhou of the Shang Dynasty. So much blood was shed that staves floated in streams of blood.

Some scholars consider that the word *book* in the first sentence

Chapter 14: Utmost Dedication (2)

refers specifically to *Wu Cheng*, not just any book. This interpretation confines Mencius's point to a specific book.

Commentary:

Mencius cited the flaw in the history book *Wu Cheng* to support his point that one should not believe everything in a book. He argued that since King Wu was the most benevolent leader and Emperor Zhou was the cruelest tyrant, it was easy for King Wu to defeat Emperor Zhou without a hard fight. Therefore, the description in Wu Cheng was incredible.

The sentence, "It is better to do without a book than to believe everything written in it," is a famous quote in *Mencius*.

Section 4

孟子曰 有人曰 我善爲陳 我善爲戰。大罪也。國君好仁 天下無敵焉。南面而征 北夷怨。東面而征 西夷怨 曰 奚爲後我。武王之伐殷也 革車三百兩 虎賁三千人。王曰 無畏 寧爾也 非敵百姓也。若崩厥角稽首。征之爲言正也 各欲正己也 焉用戰。

Mencius said, "If someone says, 'I am expert at military formations. I am expert at waging wars,' he is a great criminal. A benevolent ruler of a country is invincible. When the army of King Tang marched to the south, barbarians in the north complained, and when his army marched to the east, barbarians in the west complained. They all said, 'When will be our turn to be liberated?' When King Wu revolted against the Shang Dynasty, he had only three hundred chariots and three-thousand elite warriors. He told people of Shang,

545

'Don't be afraid. I am bringing peace to you. I am not your enemy.' The people of Shang knelt and knocked their heads on the ground so hard that the knocking sounded like horns of animals falling off. To wage a punitive war is to rectify. If everyone desires rectification, why is a war necessary?"

Annotation:

Section 5 of chapter 6 also mentioned how King Tang, the founder of the Shang Dynasty, won the support of all tribes in the country.

Commentary:

Sections 1 to 4 of this Chapter all showed Mencius's attitude against war.

Section 5

孟子曰 梓匠輪輿能與人規矩 不能使人巧。

Mencius said, "A carpenter or a carriage-maker can teach his apprentices the basic rules of his craft, but he cannot make them skillful."

Commentary:

This section repeated the same point mentioned in Section 41 of Chapter 13 above. A teacher can only inspire his students, but it is up to them to develop their skills and learning.

Chapter 14: Utmost Dedication (2)

Section 6

孟子曰 舜之飯糗茹草也 若將終身焉。及其爲天子也 被袗衣 鼓琴 二女果 若固有之。

Mencius said, "When Shun lived on coarse rice and wild vegetables, he thought that he would eat such food for the rest of his life. After he became the emperor, he had embroidered clothes, a lute to play, and two daughters of Yao in attendance. He considered that he had such blessings long before."

Commentary and Modern Perspective:

This section said that we should view poverty the same as prosperity. Neither poverty nor prosperity can affect us.

Section 7

孟子曰 吾今而後知殺人親之重也。殺人之父 人亦殺其父 殺人之兄 人亦殺其兄。然則非自殺之也 一閒耳。

Mencius said, "From now on, we know the seriousness of killing the parents and brothers of another person. If you kill the father of another person, he will then kill your father. If you kill a brother of another person, he will then kill your brother. Although you do not kill your father directly, killing your father is just one step away."

Commentary:

What goes around comes around.

Section 8

孟子曰 古之為關也 將以禦暴。今之為關也 將以為暴。

Mencius said, "In ancient times, fortresses were built at the border to defend against invaders. Nowadays, they are built for offensive purposes."

Section 9

孟子曰 身不行道 不行於妻子。使人不以道 不能行於妻子。

Mencius said, "If you do not practice Dao yourself, you cannot have your way, even among your wife and children. If you do not order people properly according to Dao, you cannot order even your wife and children."

Commentary and Modern Perspective:

Dao here refers to the principles related to the virtues of Ren, Yi, Li, and wisdom. This section is valid even today. Many people complain that their families are broken and blame their problems on other members of their families, teachers, schools, or the society at large. They need to reflect and examine their own behaviors first. If they act improperly, they will set bad examples for their children, and their wives will not trust and respect them.

Section 10

孟子曰 周於利者 凶年不能殺。周於德者 邪世不能亂。

Chapter 14: Utmost Dedication (2)

Mencius said, "Those who manage properly their wealth will not be ruined in a bad year. Those who cultivate their virtues will not be corrupted in an evil world."

Commentary and Modern Perspective:

The phrase "manage properly" includes many aspects of wealth: making profits righteously, prudent risk management, saving for the rainy days, prudent lifestyle, donation to charity and so on. The focus of this section is the second sentence. The first sentence just leads to the second sentence.

Section 11

孟子曰 好名之人 能讓千乘之國。苟非其人 簞食豆羹見於色。

Mencius said, "A person craving fame is willing to give away a state of ten thousand chariots, but if he is not really the man to do such a thing, he will haggle and quarrel over a basket of rice and a bowl of soup."

Annotation:

When Mencius made this statement, he was referring to King Kuai of Yan (燕王噲, also known as Zi Kuai, 子噲, died 316 BC), who, like Shun, abdicated his throne to his prime minister to earn a reputation of being a saintly king. His story is narrated in Section 8 of Chapter 4. King Kuai was not genuinely interested in being meritorious. He just wanted to earn a good name in history.

549

Mencius in Modern Perspectives

Commentary:

There are many hypocrites who pretend to be charitable, gracious, and virtuous in the outside world, whereas they are mean inside. Nowadays, we see many cases of famous gentlemen and philanthropists who commit domestic violence at home or have the attitude of "not in my backyard."

Section 12

孟子曰 不信仁賢 則國空虛。無禮義 則上下亂。無政事 則財用不足。

Mencius said, "If competent and meritorious officials are not trusted, the country will be void of talents. If Li and Yi are not observed, the chain of command in the government will be chaotic. If the government is not well regulated, it will have fiscal deficits."

Annotation:

The words *Li* (禮) and *Yi* (義) here not only include moral standards but also secular and worldly laws and rules. These two aspects are complementary. Having solely laws and rules is not sufficient. Confucius said, "If you use laws and regulations to guide and rule your people, and punishment to enforce their compliance, they will be decadent and shameless because they are motivated just by their desire for avoidance of punishment. If you foster moral and ethical principles, and regulate your people with Li, they will not only have their sense of shame but will also be compliant" (Section 3 of Chapter 2, 為政, of *Confucius Analects*).

Chapter 14: Utmost Dedication (2)

Section 13

孟子曰 不仁而得國者 有之矣。不仁而得天下 未之有也。

Mencius said, "There are cases of inhuman persons gaining possession of states, but it has never happened that an inhuman person gained possession of the entire empire."

Commentary:

If the phrase "gaining possession" is interpreted narrowly as possession by political or military means, Mencius's point has been contradicted repeatedly in history. If "gaining possession" includes the winning of hearts and support of people, Mencius had a valid point. Losing the support of people may enable a king to rule a country for a short time, but his people will eventually turn against him.

Section 14

孟子曰 民為貴 社稷次之 君為輕。是故得乎丘民而為天子 得乎天子為諸侯 得乎諸侯為大夫。諸侯危社稷 則變置 犧牲既成 粢盛既絜 祭祀以時 然而旱乾水溢 則變置社稷。

Mencius said, "People are most important to a state; its sovereignty is next; and its ruler is least. Therefore, getting the support of people is the way to be an emperor. Getting the support and favor of the emperor is the way to be a feudal lord. Getting the support and favor of a feudal lord is the way to be a minister. When a feudal lord endangers a state, he will be removed from his position. If, after people have flawlessly offered sacrificial animals and pure millets in worship ceremonies conducted duly, flood and drought still occur, the altar will be dedicated to different gods of land and of grains."

Or,

Mencius said, "People are most important to a state; the god of land and god of grains are next; and its ruler is least. Therefore, getting the support of people is the way to be an emperor. Getting the support and favor of the emperor is the way to be a feudal lord. Getting the support and favor of a feudal lord is the way to be a minister. When a feudal lord endangers a state, he will be removed from his position. If, after people have flawlessly offered sacrificial animals and pure millets in worship ceremonies conducted duly, flood and drought still occur, the altar will be dedicated to different gods of land and of grains."

Annotation:

This section contains a crucial point of the political philosophy of Mencius and Confucians. The following paragraphs will explain the ancient tradition and culture of China to help readers better understand Mencius's words here and to explain the relation between the two interpretations above.

The worship of the god of land probably originated before or during the era of Yao and Shun. The name of this god was called "She (社)." There is a legend that, during the pre-historical reign of Emperor Zhuan Xu (顓頊), about 5,000 to 6,000 years ago, there were huge floods in the country. A nobleman, Ju Long (句龍), was assigned to manage the problem. He resettled the population on hills

Chapter 14: Utmost Dedication (2)

to avoid the floods and set up communities of 20 to 30 households on each hill. Each community became a small society and was called She (社) in Chinese. This social structure lasted until the floods were over. Zhuan Xu and later kings honored Ju Long and considered him to be a hero who saved the population. People in later generations and centuries worshipped him as the god of land, She (社), and prayed to him for the protection of the land from floods and natural disasters.

According to legend, the worship of the god of grains originated during or after the era of emperor Yu of the Xia Dynasty. This god was called Ji (稷), named after Hou Ji (后稷). The story of Hou Ji was narrated in *Shi Ji* (史記, *Records of the Grand Historian*) written by Sima Qian (司馬遷, 14–86 BC). Emperor Ku (嚳) reigned after Emperor Zhuan Xu. On one day, his concubine, Jiang Yuan (姜原), saw a huge footprint on the ground while she was hanging out in the countryside. Driven by curiosity, she stepped on the footprint to compare it with the size of her feet. Suddenly, a strange energy flew through her body and she felt a conception in her womb. She went home scared. A few months later, she gave birth to a baby with a strange look. She thought that it was a demon. She threw the newborn on the street. It was strange that all horses and carriages passing by avoided the baby. Failing to kill the baby, she tried to secretly place the baby in the forest. However, the baby was later discovered by foresters. She then tried to drop the baby into freezing water in a ditch. However, big birds flew by, picked up the baby, and carried it to her home. She was then convinced that the baby was a god. She then changed her mind and brought up the baby. Emperor Yu later called this baby Hou Ji, who became the minister of agriculture. A genius, Hou Ji made many agricultural discoveries. He taught people how to grow the five grains, which solved the country's food problem. He was the pioneer of farming and agriculture in ancient China. Later generations worshipped him as the god of grains. His name, Ji, became the name of this god.

For many centuries, and even until the Qing Dynasty, many Chinese peasants worshipped the god of land, Shi, and the god of grains, Ji, for their blessing of good harvests. During the Zhou Dynasty, the name of the two gods were put together as She Ji (社稷) and this subsequently meant a country, its sovereignty, territory, or well-being. Therefore, the first interpretation above refers to the sovereignty of the state whereas the second interpretation refers to the god of land and god of grains.

The concept of "god" in ancient Chinese culture was unlike the western notion of God, who created and controls everything on earth. The ancient Chinese created their own notion of gods, who can protect people and bring benefits to them. Like She and Ji, these gods could be named after great men in history. If these gods do not respond to the prayers of people, such gods will no longer be worshipped. This was why Mencius mentioned the last sentence: "If, after people have flawlessly offered sacrificial animals and pure millets in worship ceremonies conducted duly, flood and drought still occur, the altar will be dedicated to different gods of land and of grains."

Commentary:

This commentary is based on the first interpretation because it is more relevant to the modern world.

The first sentence is the key: "People are most important to a state, its sovereignty is next, and its ruler is least." This sentence is the core of political philosophy under many meritorious and great rulers in China for millennia. According to Mencius, the people of a country is its foundation. Because of the existence of its people,

Chapter 14: Utmost Dedication (2)

there is a need to build a country. Because of the existence of the country, there is a need for a ruler. People build their country, and the ruler is just an incidental position to run the country. Therefore, the relative importance between people, the country, and its ruler is clear. The ruler works for the people and not the other way around. All governance policies should be based on the interest of its people. Ancient Confucians before Mencius had already advanced this political philosophy. From the ancient time to the Qing Dynasty, emperors and kings used to consider and declare that their power came from Tian (Sky), and that they were, therefore, officers and messengers of Tian. Because of this posture, they considered that they had absolute power over their people. Confucians took the opposite view. They preached that since Tian is wise, it sees the needs and hears the voices of people. Since it is benevolent, it provides for their needs. Therefore, people's wishes are identical to the wishes of Tian. If the ruler ignores the wishes of people and does not do a good job, Tian will remove the ruler through the power of people. It is worth noting the following analogy: "The ruler is like a boat, and common people are like water. Water can float a boat, but water can sink it too." People has the power to choose and support a ruler, but also has the power to overthrow him. Regarding the relation between people and the country, people have the power to change the identity, territory, constitution, laws, and governance structure, and the government of a country. All these are established on behalf of people rather than to subjugate people. Therefore, the sovereignty of a country and the country itself are behind in importance its people.

In the next few sentences of this section, Mencius explained how the authority of the emperor, feudal lords, and ministers of states were derived. Most importantly, he said that the emperor's authority did not come from Tian, but rather from people. The authority of feudal lords and other ministers came from their bosses, whose authorities came indirectly from people also. Furthermore, lords and government officials can obtain their authority by pleasing their bosses, but this authority can easily be rescinded. Without genuine support of people, the authority of such government officials can be removed by the whim of their bosses.

Therefore, Mencius cited the analogy of the worship of the gods of land and grains. If these gods did not do a good job, people would replace them. Since people can do so, even to gods, why can't they do so to under-performing rulers and government officials?

Modern Perspective:

The word *ruler* in this section also refers to monarchs, presidents, party chiefs, and other top government officials nowadays. Irrespective of the type of political system and government structure, the concept of "people are the most important to a country" is universally relevant.

Section 15

孟子曰 聖人 百世之師也 伯夷 柳下惠是也。故聞伯夷之風者 頑夫廉 懦夫有立志。聞柳下惠之風者 薄夫敦 鄙夫寬。奮乎百世之上 百世之下 聞者莫不興起也。非聖人而能若是乎。而況於親炙之者乎。

Mencius said, "Saints are teachers of hundreds of generations. Bo Yi and Liu Xia Hui are good examples. Therefore, after learning about the character of Bo Yi, a corrupt person will be pure, and a coward will become determined. After learning about the character

Chapter 14: Utmost Dedication (2)

of Liu Xia Hui, a mean person will become kind, and a base person will become forbearing. Their distinguished examples were unprecedented for hundreds of generations before them, and would be unsurpassed for hundreds of generations after them. All people who heard of them were motivated. If they were not saints, how could they inspire so many people? How much more did they inspire their students and close affiliates?"

Annotation:

The story of Bo Yi (伯夷) is shown in Section 5 of Endnotes. The story of Liu Xia Hui is shown in Section 9 of Chapter 3, and the discussions on him are shown in Section 1 of Chapter 10, Section 6 of Chapter 12, and Section 28 of Chapter 13.

Bo Yi was known to be upright, pure, uncorruptible, determined, and unyielding. He would rather die than give up his righteous principles. Liu Xia Hui was known to be accommodating, flexible, and forbearing. He did not mind bearing criticisms and debasement but still maintained his purity while doing good work.

Commentary:

A saint contributes to humanity by his teachings and venerable examples, which can illuminate hundreds of generations. His greatness need not bring personal gain, success, power, influence, or recognition during his life but will be acknowledged and emulated by people for millennia afterwards. Confucius and Mencius were such examples. They were unsuccessful as government officials and statesmen because their philosophies went against the interest of rulers during their eras. Yet, their teachings have illuminated the Chinese society for millennia. On the contrary,

557

Mencius in Modern Perspectives

many prominent statesmen during the Warring States Period were forgotten soon after their deaths.

Modern Perspective:

Personal wealth, success, fame, power, influence, and bodily satisfaction are more valuable to most people than their legacy of good teachings and examples for future generations. For example, good teachers are paid much less than speculative traders in Wall Street, and authors of humanity books earn much less than authors of comic and fantasy books. How can the moral standard of the world not decay?

Section 16

孟子曰 仁也者 人也。合而言之 道也。

Mencius said, "The principle of Ren is the same as the principle governing humanity. Put together in short, it is the Dao."

Commentary:

These two short sentences repeat the same concepts and philosophy explained in the paragraph about Ren and the paragraph about Dao in the Introduction and in Section 1 of Chapter 13 above.

Section 17

孟子曰 孔子之去魯 曰 遲遲吾行也。去父母國之道也。去齊 接淅而行 去他國之道也。

Chapter 14: Utmost Dedication (2)

Mencius said, "When Confucius was about to leave the state of Lu, he said, 'I like to procrastinate my journey.' This was his attitude about leaving his motherland. When he decided to leave the state of Qi, he said, 'Let us leave this place as soon as possible.' This was his attitude about leaving a foreign land."

Commentary:

Everybody has the same feeling. Mencius used this example to illustrate that the different levels of Ren and affinity are human nature. Mencius disagreed with the philosophy of indiscriminative love proposed by Mo Zi but advocated differential degrees of Ren and affinity, starting from filial piety.

Section 18

孟子曰 孔子之戹於陳 蔡之間 無上下之交也。

Mencius said, "Confucius was stuck in a dire situation at a place between the states of Chen and Cai because he had no friends in their governments."

Annotation:

After Confucius had left the state of Wey (衛), he took his disciples along and arrived at the place between the states of Chen (陳) and Cai (蔡). They were besieged by a gang of strangers. Confucius and his school of disciples were in great danger and starved for a few days. Yet, Confucius stayed calm and relaxed. This episode was also narrated in Section 2 of Chapter 15, 衛靈公, of *Confucius Analects*:

Mencius in Modern Perspectives

Confucius was stuck in the state of Chen, and his food and provisions were exhausted. His followers were so hungry and sick that they could not get up. The worried and frustrated Zi Lu (子路, 542–480 BC, a disciple of Confucius) complained to Confucius, "Why does a Jun Zi also need to suffer poverty?" Confucius said, "A Jun Zi endures poverty firmly. A Xiao Ren commits plunders when he is poor."

Confucius later lamented: "All my disciples who followed me to the states of Chen (陳) and Cai (蔡) have left my school already" (Section 2 of Chapter 11, 先進, of *Confucius Analects*).

Modern Perspective:

There are two lessons in this section. The first is that we need friends in the society. The second is that personal, public, and political relationships are important.

Section 19

貉稽曰 稽大不理於口。

孟子曰 無傷也。士憎茲多口。詩云 憂心悄悄 慍於群小。孔子也。肆不殄厥慍 亦不隕厥問 文王也。

Mo Qi told Mencius, "I am bothered by people badmouthing me behind my back."

Mencius replied, "It does not matter. All scholars hate gossips. The *Book of Poetry* says, 'I am worried covertly. I am hated by a crowd of mean people.' This was the feeling of Confucius. It also says, 'I cannot crush antagonism against me, but it cannot hurt my reputation and principles.' This was the feeling of King Wen."

Chapter 14: Utmost Dedication (2)

Annotation:

Mo Qi (貉稽) was a scholar. Little was known about him.
King Wen of Zhou (周文王) was regarded a saintly king by Confucians.

Commentary:

This section relates to gossip and badmouthing. Mencius cited the examples of Confucius and King Wen, both saints, to comfort Mo Qi.

Modern Perspective:

The greater a man, the more antagonism he draws. Bad-mouthing and backstabbing are unavoidable in any organization. We need to ignore them, keep our antipathy private, avoid fighting with and confronting antagonists, continue to keep our principles, and move on.

Section 20

孟子曰 賢者以其昭昭 使人昭昭。今以其昏昏 使人昭昭。

Mencius said, "In the old days, virtuous and learned people were enlightened so that they could enlighten others. Nowadays, ignorant and stupid people try to enlighten others."

Modern Perspective:

This phenomenon is common. Many self-proclaimed experts,

sages, healers, forecasters, visionaries, advisors, counselors, and so on, mislead others for profit. The blind leads the blind.

Section 21

孟子謂高子曰 山徑之蹊閒 介然用之而成路。為閒不用 則茅塞之矣。今茅塞子之心矣。

Mencius told Gao Zi, "A trail in the mountain will become a wide road over time after people start walking on it. If it is deserted, it will be covered and blocked by tall grass again. You mind is now filled up with tall grass."

Annotation:

Gao Zi (高子) was a disciple of Mencius.

Commentary:

The first two sentences in this section raise two points. The first sentence is related to the development of new solutions and discoveries, the overcoming of challenges, learning and self-cultivation. The second sentence related to the need of constant practice after a path has been developed.

Modern Perspective:

This section is relevant to many aspects of our lives.

Section 22

高子曰 禹之聲 尚文王之聲。

Chapter 14: Utmost Dedication (2)

孟子曰 何以言之。

曰 以追蠡。

曰 是奚足哉。城門之軌 兩馬之力與。

Gao Zi said, "Music during the era of Yu was more popular and developed than the music during the era of King of Wen."

Mencius asked, "Why do you say so?"

Gao Zi replied, "Because the pivot knobs of the bells used during the era of Yu was worn out."

Mencius said, "This is not yet sufficient proof. Look at the ruts at the city gate. Can the wheels of a carriage driven by just two horses make such deep ruts?"

Annotation:

Gao Zi (高子) was a disciple of Mencius.

There were five major notes in ancient Chinese music, which are equivalent to Do, Re, Mi, Sol, La. In addition, there were also 12 pitches. An octave was divided into 12 semi-pitches, equivalent to C, C#, D, D#, E, E#, F, G, G#, A, A#, and B in Western music. The odd numbered semi-pitches were called Lu (律) and the even numbered semi-pitches were called Ryo (呂). Pipes and tubes of different lengths, and bells of different sizes were used to produce these pitches. Bells were hung on strings attached to metal pivots arranged on a hanging frame. Percussion sounds of different notes were produced by hitting the bells with hammers. When a bell was hit, it swung around the pivot. The knob of the pivot was then rubbed against the hanging frame when the bell swung. After the bell was hit many times, the knob was worn out. Gao Zi noted that the knobs of bells used during the Yu era were more worn out than those used during the era of King Wen. Therefore, he deduced that the bells of Yu era must be used more often, and music must be more popular then.

In the old days, trunk roads in a city used to have nine tracks for horse carriages. However, since gates of a city were narrower, they allowed only two tracks. Therefore, a track at a city gate was used more frequently. After heavy traffic over a long period, deep ruts were developed at the track of a city gate.

Commentary:

This section is the continuation of the last section. The dialogue between Mencius and Gao Zi illustrated the same point: "Repeated exercises lead to perfection."

Gao Zi noted that the pivot knobs of bells used during the era of Yu were more worn out than the bells used during the era of King Wen. Gao Zi then concluded that music was more developed and popular during the Yu era. Mencius pointed out that Gao Zi drew the wrong conclusion. Mencius told Gao Zi that the knobs of the Yu era were more worn out because they had been used for a long time. Mencius further supported his point with the observation of deep ruts at gates of cities. The depth of ruts was caused by frequent and heavy carriages traffic, not just by a single carriage.

With repeated usage over a long time, a narrow path can become a wide road, a bell knob can be worn out, and the rut of a track can be deepened. These are analogies that relentless and frequent drills can perfect one's skills and learning. In contrast to physical materials, mental skills are sharpened by repetitive usage.

Chapter 14: Utmost Dedication (2)

Section 23

齊饑。陳臻曰 國人皆以夫子將復為發棠 殆不可復。

孟子曰 是為馮婦也。晉人有馮婦者 善搏虎 卒為善士。則之野 有眾逐虎。虎負嵎 莫之敢攖。望見馮婦 趨而迎之。馮婦攘臂下車 眾皆悅之 其為士者笑之。

The state of Qi suffered a famine. Chen Zhen said to Mencius, "The people of Qi are thinking that you will ask the king of Qi to open the granary of Tang for them. I am afraid you would not do so the second time."

Mencius said, "If I do so, I would act like Feng Fu. There was a native of the state of Jin called Feng Fu. He has great skill and strength to kill tigers with bare hands. He later changed his career and became a scholar. On one day, he traveled to the countryside on carriages with his friends and saw a group of hunters chasing a tiger. The tiger took refuge in a corner of a hill. No one dared to confront the tiger. When the hunters saw Feng Fu, they approached him and asked for help. He immediately rolled up his sleeves, raised his arms and descended the carriage. All people around were impressed and pleased. However, the scholars who accompanied him laughed at him."

Annotation:

Chen Qin (陳臻, also known as Chen Zi, 陳子) was a disciple of Mencius.

Mencius was once a senior advisor to King Xuan of Qi (齊宣王). Section 7 of Chapter 1 and Sections 1 to 11 of Chapter 2 have shown what happened to Mencius during his tenor in the state of Qi.

565

It had a famine when Mencius was there. Section 4 of Chapter 2 recorded a conversation between Mencius and King Xuan. In the dialogue, Mencius persuaded King Xuan to open the royal granary in the city of Tang (棠) to save starving people. King Xuan took Mencius's advice. As a result, the people of Qi praised Mencius for his good advice to the king.

Later, King Xuan ignored Mencius and continued to misbehave. The frustrated Mencius left Qi in a hurry and vowed never to return even after repeated attempts by King Xuan to persuade Mencius to stay.

Feng Fu (馮婦) was an unknown person.

The state of Jin (晉) was a hegemon during the Spring-Autumn Period.

Commentary and Modern Perspective:

Mencius's reluctance to advise King Xuan of Qi the second time should not be interpreted as his desire for avoidance of criticism. Unlike Feng Fu, Mencius did not want to repeat his past deed after he had moved on to the next stage in life. Since he had already left the state of Qi and given up his hope of a decent King Xuan, he knew that his advice to King Xuan would be futile.

Mencius's refusal to repeat his past had a deep lesson: "Do not hold onto your past. Let bygones be bygones. Do not look back but rather look forward." Whether your past was successful or not, you need to move on. After you have left an old position, place, or environment, you do not have any role in it. This attitude is close to the same Buddhist teaching that one should not hold onto anything.

After you have retired, you should start a new leaf of your life. Your past glory, successes, happiness, shame, failures, and sadness are irrelevant to your future. You should erase from your mind such

Chapter 14: Utmost Dedication (2)

the memory of your past and move on with a fresh breath.

You should have the same attitude after you have stepped down or resigned from a position. You should not interfere with the activities of your successor and should keep your mouth shut about the affairs of your old job.

Section 24

孟子曰 口之於味也 目之於色也 耳之於聲也 鼻之於臭也 四肢之於安佚也 性也。有命焉 君子不謂性也。仁之於父子也 義之於君臣也 禮之於賓主也 智之於賢者也 聖人之於天道也 命也。有性焉 君子不謂命也。

Mencius said, "It is human nature for the mouth to sense and desire good tastes, for the eyes to sense and desire beautiful colors, for the ears to sense and desire pleasant sound, for the nose to sense and desire flagrant odor, and for the limb to feel and desire comfort and rest. These senses are controlled by the constraints of life (and fate) though. A Jun Zi does not yield to these desires by saying, 'It is my nature.' The existence of Ren between father and son, Yi between king and minister, Li between host and guest, wisdom of sages, and the adherence to the Dao by saints are affected by constraints of life (and fate), but the underlying moral nature of a person also matters. A Jun Zi should try to overcome the constraints of life here.

Commentary:

This section is a continuation of Section 1 and 2 of Chapter 13 on Mencius's philosophy of human nature and fate.

This section has two parts. The first part is related to the physical

567

aspects of human nature. Our senses, physical abilities, and functions are subject to constraints of life and fate. We cannot go beyond such constraints and seek unlimited satisfaction of our mundane desires. To do so is to spoil and abandon our life. Therefore, a Jun Zi does not yield to these desires by saying, "It is my nature." Such an excuse will prompt one to disregard his health, indulge in lust, become addicted to alcohol and drugs, or commit crimes.

The second part is related to the morality aspect of human nature. Although one desires a loving relation with parents, it may not exist in real life due to uncontrollable circumstances and backgrounds. For example, Emperor Shun wanted to have a kind father who wanted to kill him instead. Likewise, relations with brothers, bosses, and friends may not be friendly and trusting all the time. The existence of favorable relations with people is affected by many external factors. Mencius called these factors as realities of life. However, there is a morality aspect in all such situations. A morally strong person can still practice Ren, Yi, Li, and wisdom and overcome hardship in adverse situations. It is up to a Jun Zi to take the initiative. For example, Emperor Shun took the initiative to show filial piety to his father who eventually repented.

Section 25

浩生不害問曰 樂正子何人也。

　孟子曰 善人也 信人也。

　(曰) 何謂善 何謂信。

　曰 可欲之謂善 有諸己之謂信 充實之謂美 充實而有光輝之謂大 大而化之之謂聖 聖而不可知之之謂神。樂正子 二之中 四之下也。

Chapter 14: Utmost Dedication (2)

Hao Sheng Bu Hai asked, "What sort of man is Yue Zheng Zi?"

Mencius said, "He is a good man and a true man."

Hao Sheng Bu Hai asked, "What do you mean by a 'good man' and a 'true man'?"

Mencius said, "A good man has emanating warmth in his heart. A true man has intrinsic goodness in his character. A perfect man fills the world with his goodness. A great man fills the world with goodness and shines. A great man who enlightens the world is a saint. A saint with unthinkable virtue is supermundane. Yue Zheng Zi's character is between the first and the second types. He has not yet reached the last four."

Annotation:

Hao Sheng Bu Hai (浩生不害) was a disciple of Mencius.

Yue Zheng Zi (樂正子) was another disciple of Mencius and was mentioned in Section 16 of Chapter 2, Section 24 of Chapter 7, Section 7 of Chapter 7, and Section 13 of Chapter 12. When Yue Zheng Zi got a job offer from the king of the state of Lu, Mencius was so happy that he could not sleep. Mencius said the Yue Zheng Zi was a good man.

Commentary:

Mencius pointed out five ascending characters: good man, true man, perfect man, great man, and saint. A supermundane character is above sainthood. The two first characters can be grouped under the category of Jun Zi. The next two characters can be grouped under the category of sage. As mentioned in Section 2 of Chapter 3, a perfect man and a great man possess magnanimous character and spirit. Their greatness fills every corner of the world.

Having emanating warmth in one's heart is equivalent to having the Ren virtue.

The phrase *perfect man* is also translated as "beautiful man" by some translators. This book uses instead the word *perfect* to avoid the connotation of physical beauty.

Section 26

孟子曰 逃墨必歸於楊 逃楊必歸於儒。歸 斯受之而已矣。今之與楊墨辯者 如追放豚 既入其苙 又從而招之。

Mencius said, "The deserters from the Mohist school must turn to the school of Yang Zhu. After they are disappointed, they will turn to Confucianism. If they do so, we simply welcome them. Nowadays, debaters with followers of the Mohist school and the Yang school are chasing strayed pigs and then tying their feet after they have returned to the pen."

Annotation:

Mo Zi and the Mohist philosophy are discussed in Section 2 of Endnotes. Yang Zhu and his philosophy are discussed in Section 9 of Chapter 6 above. Mencius regarded both schools of thought as being too extreme. Yang Zhu advocated extreme individualism while Mo Zi advocated universal and indiscriminative love. These schools were opposite extremes. Confucianism was in the middle.

Modern Perspective:

This section shows Mencius's attitude toward education. When a person goes astray and is brainwashed with a fallacy, it is futile to

Chapter 14: Utmost Dedication (2)

debate with, criticize, and reprimand them. They will not wake up until they hit a brick wall and realize that they have erred. Therefore, a teacher should let them learn from failures. After the student has returned to the right path, it is wrong to force feed them with another dogma. This comment is also relevant to parents raising children.

Section 27

孟子曰 有布縷之徵 粟米之徵 力役之徵。君子用其一 緩其二。用其二而民有殍 用其三而父子離。

Mencius said, "There are taxes on clothes, grains, and labor. A Jun Zi should only impose tax on one of them and exempt the other two. If taxes are levied on two of them, people will die of hunger. If taxes are levied on three of them, fathers will be separated from sons."

Commentary:

The sentence: "Fathers will be separated from sons" means that young people must emigrate from the country to look for jobs and food elsewhere.

Mencius objected to oppressive taxation on people.

Section 28

孟子曰 諸侯之寶三 土地 人民 政事。寶珠玉者 殃必及身。

Mencius said, "The three treasures of a feudal lord are: land of the state, its people, and its governance. The possession of precious jewelry and jade will certainly ruin him."

Mencius in Modern Perspectives

Modern Perspective:

On a personal level, the three analogous treasures are: the means of making a living, the personal quality and capability, and discipline and self-control. A lavish lifestyle will result in ruin.

Section 29

盆成括仕於齊。

　孟子曰　死矣　盆成括。

　盆成括見殺　門人問曰　夫子何以知其將見殺。

　曰　其為人也小有才　未聞君子之大道也　則足以殺其軀而已矣。

Peng Cheng Kuo became a minister of the state of Qi. Mencius commented, "He is going to die." Later, Peng Cheng Kuo was indeed killed.

　Disciples of Mencius asked him, "Master, how did you know that he was going to be killed?"

　Mencius replied, "He was a man with limited talents. He did not know the great way of a Jun Zi. This was enough to cost his life."

Annotation:

Peng Cheng Kuo (盆成括) was an unknown person.

Modern Perspective:

This section is a reminder for corporate executives as well.

Chapter 14: Utmost Dedication (2)

Section 30

孟子之滕 館於上宮。有業屨於牖上 館人求之弗得。

或問之曰 若是乎從者之廋也。

曰 子以是為竊屨來與。

曰 殆非也。夫子之設科也 往者不追 來者不拒。苟以是心至 斯受之而已矣。

Mencius went to the state of Teng and stayed at the upper palace as a guest of the king. A housekeeper left an unfinished pair of sandals on the sill of a window. When he returned, the sandals disappeared. He asked, "Were the sandals stolen by one of your followers?"

A disciple of Mencius retorted, "Do you think that we come here to steal sandals?"

The housekeeper said, "Is that not so?"

The disciple replied, "The policy of the school founded by my master is that he does not care about the past of anyone, nor refuse anyone who comes. If the student comes with the right attitude, he will teach him."

Commentary:

What happened in this trivial episode was unimportant. The key point is: "He does not care about the past of anyone, nor refuse anyone who comes." It is about magnanimity and forbearance.

Modern Perspective:

This attitude of magnanimity and forbearance is important not only to teachers but in personal relations in general.

Section 31

孟子曰 人皆有所不忍 達之於其所忍 仁也。人皆有所不為 達之於其所為 義也。人能充無慾害人之心 而仁不可勝用也。人能充無穿踰之心 而義不可勝用也。人能充無受爾汝之實 無所往而不為義也。士未可以言而言 是以言餂之也。可以言而不言 是以不言餂之也 是皆穿踰之類也。

Mencius said, "All men have something or some situations that arouse their feeling of compassion. To extend such feeling to things and situations that they are apathetic about is Ren. All men have somethings that they refrain from doing. To extend this feeling to all actions that they are compelled to take is Yi. If a man can fully develop his mind of not hurting others, his Ren virtue will be inexhaustible. If a man can fully develop his dislike for pilferage, his Yi virtue will be inexhaustible. If a man can fully develop his dislike for being disregarded as nobody, he will act righteousness in all places and situations. If a scholar speaks before his rightful turn to speak, his speech must be beguiling. If a scholar keeps quiet when it is his turn to speak, he is also beguiling. In either case, his action is still pilferage."

Commentary:

The first few sentences remind us to exercise deliberate efforts to overcome our apathy and disregard of righteousness. If a person can fully develop his dislike for being disregarded, he will reciprocate this feeling to others. He will then treat others as equals.

When a person speaks before his rightful turn to speak, he tries to steal the limelight, trap, provoke, bait, and rob the other person of

Chapter 14: Utmost Dedication (2)

the chance to speak. This is a subtle act of pilferage.

Likewise, if a person keeps quiet when it is his turn to speak, he tries to use his silence as a bait too. This is also a beguiling act.

Section 32

孟子曰 言近而指遠者 善言也。守約而施博者 善道也。君子之言也 不下帶而道存焉。君子之守 修其身而天下平。人病舍其田而芸人之田 所求於人者重 而所以自任者輕。

Mencius said, "People who cite recent and nearby examples to infer far-reaching implications are good at words. People who adhere strictly to principles themselves before they apply such principles broadly are good at the Dao. When a Jun Zi talks, his words never go below his belt, but great principles are contained in them. A Jun Zi holds onto the principle that his personal cultivation precedes his fostering of peace and order to the country. The trouble with many people is that they abandon their own fields to eradicate weeds in fields of others. They are too stringent to others but too lenient to themselves."

Annotation:

The phrase "talking below one's belt" was an idiom during the era of Mencius. It meant to talk unrealistically and rhetorically.

Commentary:

There are three lessons in this section. A good speaker uses simple words, concrete and recent examples, and comprehensible concepts. He talks subtly and avoids babbling. His speeches are short and to-the-point, but their messages are deep and far-reaching.

The second lesson is related to the Confucian teaching that a Jun Zi's mission in life should be self-cultivation followed by doing good work for the society. This order should not be reversed.

The third lesson is to be stringent to oneself while being lenient to others.

Modern Perspectives:

Most people nowadays ignore the above principles.

Section 33

孟子曰 堯 舜 性者也。湯 武 反之也。動容周旋中禮者 盛德之至也。哭死而哀 非為生者也。經德不回 非以干祿也。言語必信 非以正行也。君子行法 以俟命而已矣。

Mencius said, "Yao and Shun were virtuous by their nature. King Tang and King Wu made their efforts to return to their innate virtue. When the attitude, countenance, and actions of a man are in line with Li, his Dao Te is extremely immense. Mourning over the dead should arise from genuine sorrow and not to impress the living. Following unswervingly the path of Dao Te should not be for the purpose of earning a salary. Always keeping one's words should not be for the purpose of earning approval and trust. If a Jun Zi follows these rules, he will fulfill his mission in life."

Annotation:

Yao and Shun were two saintly kings. King Tang, the founder of the Shang Dynasty, and King Wu, the founder of the Zhou

Chapter 14: Utmost Dedication (2)

Dynasty, were also regarded by Confucians as saintly kings.

The Introduction has explained the terms Dao and Te. Together, Dao Te means virtue.

The Introduction has also explained the meaning of Li and Jun Zi.

Commentary:

During the era of Yao and Shun, the society was simple and pure. It was therefore easier for Yao and Shun to exhibit their natural virtues. The society during the Shang and Zhou dynasties was more materialistic and mundane. Therefore, King Tang and King Wu needed to make additional effort to overcome social bondage and influence to exhibit their virtues.

In the next few sentences, Mencius explained a few examples of how to overcome social bondages. Genuine goodness is the key. Compassion, goodness, and sincerity should be intrinsic rather than extrinsic.

Modern Perspective:

Many eulogies nowadays are speeches that mourn for the dead to impress the living. Some people explore loopholes or cut corners to get good jobs or a promotion. People pay their credit cards on time to maintain good credit rating scores. These behaviors have no place in self-cultivation of virtues since they are done to fulfill their worldly obligations or to earn credit from others.

Section 34

孟子曰 說大人則藐之 勿視其巍巍然。堂高數仞 榱題數尺 我

得志 弗為也。食前方丈 侍妾數百人 我得志 弗為也。般樂飲酒 驅騁田獵 後車千乘 我得志 弗為也。在彼者 皆我所不為也。在我者 皆古之制也。吾何畏彼哉。

Mencius said, "When I meet and counsel prominent and high-ranking persons, I look at them with contempt. I am not awed by their towering pomp and display. Halls many yards high built with beams several feet thick are not coveted by me, even if I were successful. Food spread across a dinner table ten feet long, and hundreds of attendants and concubines are not coveted by me, even if I were successful. Pleasure, wine, and hunting expeditions on thoroughbreds escorted by a thousand chariots are not coveted by me, even if I were successful. I would not do what they are doing. My way is to follow ancient norms. Why should I feel inferior and cower before them?"

Commentary:

In the section, the word *I* could also mean *You* since Mencius was talking to his disciples. The lesson of this section is that self-confidence is derived from the conviction that the value of a person has nothing to do with external glamor, power, pleasure, and display of prominence. The phrase "ancient norms" means simplicity and purity.

Modern Perspective:

When we see or meet a person who owns private jets, fancy cars, grand mansions, villas, and accompanied by a beautiful wife or girlfriend, or a troupe of bodyguards, a few thoughts may cross our minds: admiration, adoration, awe, jealousy, self-degradation, self-pity, anger, hatred, animosity, and so on. All these sentiments are unhealthy according to Mencius. All these external displays of success, fortunes, or happiness should mean nothing. Our minds should not be swayed an iota in both positive and negative directions. This is in line with the concept of resolute, undaunted, and incorruptible heart discussed in Section 2 of Chapter 3.

Section 35

孟子曰 養心莫善於寡慾。其為人也寡慾 雖有不存焉者 寡矣 其為人也多慾 雖有存焉者 寡矣。

Mencius said, "The best way to cultivate one's morality is to reduce his desires. A man with few desires may fail to resist temptations sometimes, but his failures to resist are rare. A man with many desires may try to resist temptations sometimes, but his successes to resist temptation are also rare."

Commentary:

This is a crucial point in the process of self-cultivation. The root cause of sins, decadence, corruption, and crimes is the lack of control of one's desires. To strengthen one's morality, the starting point is the reduction of desires. Buddhism teaches people to get rid of all desires. Confucians are more pragmatic and recognize that it is impossible for common mortals to eliminate all desires. They then teach the exercise of self-control.

This section is related to the last section. Mencius taught his disciples that the way to reduce one's desires is to have the right concept of the value of life. It was mentioned in the above section that external glamor, power, pleasure, and prominence are irrelevant. Since they are irrelevant, one does not covet the possession of them.

Section 36

曾皙嗜羊棗　而曾子不忍食羊棗。公孫丑問曰　膾炙與羊棗孰美。

　　孟子曰　膾炙哉。

　　公孫丑曰　然則曾子何為食膾炙而不食羊棗。

　　曰　膾炙所同也　羊棗所獨也。諱名不諱姓　姓所同也　名所獨也。

Zheng Xi was fond of sheep-dates. Zheng Zi, his son, could not bear to eat sheep-dates. Gong Sun Chou asked, "Which tastes better, minced and roasted meat, or sheep-dates?"

Mencius said, "Minced and roasted meat, of course!"

Gong Sun Chou asked, "Why did Zheng Zi eat minced and roasted meat and refrain from eating sheep-dates?"

Mencius answered, "Minced and roasted meat was a common preference while sheep-dates was uniquely preferred by Zheng Xi. As an analogy, people avoid addressing superiors by their personal names, but do not avoid addressing superiors by their family names. This is because the family name is common to many persons while the personal name is special."

Annotation:

Zheng Xi (曾皙, also known as Zheng Dian, 曾點) was a

Chapter 14: Utmost Dedication (2)

disciple of Confucius.

Zheng Zi (曾子, also known as Zheng Shen, 曾參, born 505 BC) was a prominent disciple of Confucius, known for his filial piety. He was the author of *The Book of Great Learning* (大學). He was the son of Zheng Xi.

"Sheep-dates" is an approximate translation of (羊棗). Some past scholars thought that it was a type of plum while some thought that it was an organ of the intestine of a sheep. The identity of this food does not, however, affect the message of this section.

Commentary:

Zheng Zi was a filial son of Zheng Xi. A sheep-date brought back the memory of his diseased father since his father liked to eat sheep-dates. Therefore, Zheng Zi did not eat sheep-dates.

Gong Sun Chou, a disciple of Mencius, asked his teacher a tough question. Since minced and roasted meat was more tasteful according to Mencius, Zheng Xi must have eaten and liked minced and roast meat. If so, why did Zheng Zi not stay away from minced and roast meat?

Mencius answered that sheep-dates was uniquely preferred by Zheng Xi and therefore, only sheep-dates brought back the memory of Zheng Xi.

The essence of this section is in the last sentence. It explains the rationale for the Chinese tradition that people addressed their parents with family names and not personal names.

Modern Perspective:

Chinese tradition is different from western tradition. Western children address their fathers as "John," "Joe," or "Harry," for

581

example, and their mothers as "Mary," "Liz," "Sue," and so on. In ancient China, and even today, it was and is considered rude to address parents with their personal names.

Section 37

萬章問曰 孔子在陳曰 盍歸乎來。吾黨之士狂簡 進取不忘其初。孔子在陳 何思魯之狂士。

孟子曰 孔子 不得中道而與之 必也狂獧乎 狂者進取 獧者有所不為也。孔子豈不欲中道哉。不可必得 故思其次也。

(曰) 敢問何如斯可謂狂矣。

曰 如琴張 曾晳 牧皮者 孔子之所謂狂矣。

(曰) 何以謂之狂也。

曰 其志嘐嘐然 曰 古之人 古之人。夷考其行 而不掩焉者也。狂者又不可得 欲得不屑不絜之士而與之 是獧也 是又其次也。孔子曰 過我門而不入我室 我不憾焉者 其惟鄉原乎。鄉原 德之賊也。

曰 何如斯可謂之鄉原矣。

曰 何以是嘐嘐也 言不顧行 行不顧言 則曰 古之人 古之人 行何為踽踽涼涼 生斯世也 為斯世也 善斯可矣。閹然媚於世也者 是鄉原也。

萬章曰 一鄉皆稱原人焉 無所往而不為原人 孔子以為德之賊 何哉。

曰 非之無舉也 刺之無刺也 同乎流俗 合乎污世 居之似忠信 行之似廉潔 眾皆悅之 自以為是 而不可與入堯舜之道 故曰 德之賊 也。孔子曰 惡似而非者 惡莠 恐其亂苗也 惡佞

Chapter 14: Utmost Dedication (2)

恐其亂義也。惡利口 恐其亂信也。惡鄭聲 恐其亂樂也。惡紫 恐其亂朱也。惡鄉原 恐其亂德也。君子反經而已矣。經正 則庶民興。庶民興 斯無邪慝矣。

Wan Zhang asked, "When Confucius was in the state of Chen, he exclaimed, 'Alas, let us go home! Scholars of my school are vehement and unfettered, moving forward while not forgetting their original vow.' When Confucius was in the state of Chen, why did he think of the vehement and unfettered scholars in the state of Lu?"

Mencius replied, "Failing to find students who follow the doctrine of the mean, his only other choices are vehement and unfettered students at one extreme and restrained and principled students at the other extreme. The former is aggressive and enterprising while the latter scrupulously draw red lines. Of course, Confucius wanted to have students who follow the doctrine of the mean. Since this is infeasible, he took the second-best choice."

Wan Zhang asked, "May I ask what sort of men can be called vehement and unfettered?"

Mencius replied, "For example, Qin Zhang, Zheng Xi, and Mu Pi were considered by Confucius to be vehement and unfettered."

Wan Zhang asked, "Why are they called vehement and unfettered?"

Mencius said, "They have lofty aims and always say, 'Ancient people did this, ancient people did that.' They never cover up their actions even when they are scrutinized. If Confucius could not find vehement and unfettered characters, he would turn next to the restrained and principled characters. Such characters are scrupulous and would not involve in any impure and undeserving matters. Confucius said, "Among all my students who have entered my school but not yet reached the top class, I do not regret dropping those students who are spineless. Spinelessness is the enemy of virtue."

Wan Zhang asked, "How do you characterize spineless people?"

Mencius said, "They always criticize others, saying, 'Why are you so high sounding? Your words and actions are incoherent. You always say that ancient people did this, and ancient people did that. Why are your actions so peculiar and unpopular? Being in this world, one must behave in a manner pleasing to the world. So long as one is happy, it is all right.' Spineless people are like eunuchs trying to appease the world."

Wan Zhang asked, "The whole village regards such characters to be urbane and down-to-earth. People everywhere like urbane and down-to-earth men. Why did Confucius say that spinelessness is the enemy of virtue?"

Mencius said, "If you want to find fault with them, you cannot find anything. If you want to criticize them, you cannot find anything to criticize. They drift along current trends and consent with filth in the world. Their principles appear to be faithful and honest. Their actions appear to be uncorrupted and clean. All men are pleased with them, and they are self-righteous. It is impossible to lead them to the way of Yao and Shun. Therefore, they are enemies of virtue. Confucius said, 'We should detest hypocrisy. We should detest the foxtail for fear that it will overwhelm seedlings. We should detest flattery for fear that it will mess up righteousness. We should detest glibness for fear that it will distort truth. We should detest the music of Cheng for fear that it will confound with good music. We should detest the violet color for fear that the red color will be tarnished. We should detest spineless people for fear that they will be confounded with virtuous people.' A Jun Zi goes back to the norm. That is all. Once the social norm is on the right path, common people will be awakened, and wickedness will disappear."

Chapter 14: Utmost Dedication (2)

Annotation:

Wan Zhang (萬章) was a disciple of Mencius. Some scholars think that he was a co-author of the book *Mencius*.

Mu Pi (牧皮) was a native of the state of Lu and a disciple of Confucius.

Qin Zhang (琴張, also known as Zi Zhang 子张) was a disciple of Confucius. The best friend, Zi Sang Hu (子桑户), of Qin Zhang died. All guests of the funeral mourned and wept. However, Qin Zhang joined the funeral showing no sign of sorrow. He said to the corps, "You are leaving us. That is all right. Let me sing a song for you." He sang a song aloud and left. He already understood that death was but a step in a long journey, and there is no point in mourning for it.

Zheng Xi (曾晳, also known as Zheng Dian, 曾點) was a disciple of Confucius and the father of Zheng Zi (曾子). His best friend Ji Wu Zi (季武子) died. He also did the same as what Qin Zhang did.

Confucius regarded the music of the state of Cheng (鄭) as rotten.

In ancient Chinese culture, the red color represented nobility, righteousness, and good fortune. A violet color was considered a tarnished red color.

Commentary:

Mencius mentioned three types of characters in this section. The first type is vehement and unfettered. Such characters have lofty ideals and goals, and are unyielding, enterprising, and aggressive. They do not care about what others think of them. The word *impossible* is not in their dictionaries. Qin Zhang and Zheng Xi were examples.

Mencius in Modern Perspectives

The second type is restrained, principled, and scrupulous. They try to preserve their purity. They do not bother nor infringe on others. They abide by propriety rigorously. They are also reserved and conservative.

The above characters are good types. Confucius and Mencius detested the third type: spineless people. They have no principles at all and are hypocrites. To them, there is no right or wrong. They do and say whatever fits their purpose and the circumstance. Their words are flowery and full of rhetoric, and their manners are suave and smooth. They can fit into all circles and are regarded by many to be nice and pleasant. They usually play the roles of mediators, arbitrators, pacifiers, modulators, or leaders. They are usually mistaken by many to be a team player and good leader, but, in fact, they just drift with the current and fly with the wind.

Modern Perspective:

Nowadays, there are too many people of the third type.

Section 38

孟子曰 由堯 舜至於湯 五百有餘歲。若禹 皋陶 則見而知之。若湯 則聞而知之。由湯至於文王 五百有餘歲。若伊尹 萊朱 則見而知之。若文王 則聞而知之。由文王至於孔子 五百有餘歲。若太公望 散宜生 則見而知之。若孔子 則聞而知之。由孔子而來 至於今 百有餘歲。去聖人之世 若此其未遠也。近聖人之居 若此其甚也。然而無有乎爾 則亦無有乎爾。

Mencius said, "It was over 500 years from Yao and Shun to Tang. Men like Yu and Gao Yao saw Yao and Shun and so knew the

Chapter 14: Utmost Dedication (2)

doctrines of these saints, whereas Tang heard and learned their doctrines indirectly. It was over 500 years from Tang to King Wen. Men like Yi Yin and Lai Zhu saw King Tang and knew his doctrine, whereas King Wen heard and learned it indirectly. It was over 500 years from King Wen to Confucius. Men like Tai Gong Wan and San Yi Sheng saw King Wen and knew his doctrine, whereas Confucius heard and learned it indirectly. It was a little over 100 years from Confucius till now. The time since the death of the saint is not too long, and the distance from his residence to here is not too far. Yet, there is still nobody who can match him. Well then, there is still nobody who can match him!"

Annotation:

Yao, Shun and King Tang were early saintly kings.

Yu was another saintly king.

Gao Yao (皋陶) was the earliest Chief Justice in China during the era of Shun. His name stood for the best judge.

The story of Yi Yin (伊尹) is narrated in Section 3 of Endnotes. He was the famous prime minister of King Tang.

Lai Zhu (萊朱) was another prime minister of King Tang.

The story of Tai Gong Wan (太公望, also known as Jiang Zi Ya, 姜子牙, circa 1156–1017 BC) is narrated in Section 7 of Endnotes.

San Yi Sheng (散宜生) was another important minister of King Wen of Zhou (周文王).

Commentary:

Mencius lamented in the last section of his book that he was not as great as ancient saints and sages. This showed his modesty.

Endnotes

1. Story of Yan Ying

Yan Ying (晏嬰, also known as Yan Zhong 晏仲, Yan Zi 晏子, circa 578–500 BC) was born in modern-day Gaomi county, Shandong province. He was a meritorious prime minister during the reigns of Qi Ling Gong (齊靈公, Duke Ling of Qi), Qi Zhuang Gong (齊莊公, Duke Zhuang of Qi), and Qi Jing Gong (齊景公, Duke Jing of Qi). Confucius met Yan Ying in the state of Qi and gave him high credit. The following incidents provide examples of Yan Ying's wisdom and Ren virtue:

Duke Jing had a beloved thoroughbred. He assigned a stableman to take good care of the horse. However, it died suddenly of a disease unknown to the stableman. The sorrowful and upset Duke Jing ordered to kill the stableman by mutilation, which was a cruel punishment. While the stableman was arrested by guards, Yan Ying, who was standing by Duke Jing, stepped forward, stopped the guards, and said to Duke Jing in front of other ministers, "Your Majesty, there is a step-by-step procedure of how to dismember a person. Do we know the standard procedure taught by our ancient saintly kings, Yao and Shun? Which part of the body should be cut off first?" Duke Jing was shocked and embarrassed by the question because everybody knew that the saintly kings, Yao and Shun, would never punish their people cruelly. Realizing that the order of a cruel punishment would ruin his reputation, Duke Jing rescinded the order of dismemberment, and ordered to imprison the stableman and kill him later by a more humane way. Yan Ying stepped forward again and said respectfully to duke Jing, "Let me announce his offenses before he is punished." Yan Ying then confronted the stableman in the center of the hall and spoke aloud, "You have committed three serious offenses. First, you were careless in taking care of the horse and let it die of disease. It is equivalent to killing the horse. Therefore, you deserve to be killed. Second, you have deprived our king of his beloved belongings. Therefore, you deserve to be killed. Third, you have caused our king to ruin his reputation by killing a servant because of the death of a horse. Therefore, you deserve to be killed." Duke Jing was embarrassed to hear this verdict. He realized that these verdicts were ridiculous. None of them was a crime punishable by death. He felt ashamed to order a capital punishment against a trivial matter. Duke Jing then ordered to release the stableman. This was an example of how Yan Ying applied his wisdom to pursue the Ren principle (see the Commentary in Section 3 of Chapter 2).

In another incident, Duke Jing wore a warm mink coat in a snowy morning. He met Yan Ying and said, "Although it has been snowing for three days, I don't feel cold at all." Yan Ying said, "I heard about the behavior of ancient saintly kings. Although they ate well daily, they could feel the hunger of starving people. Although they had warm clothes, they could feel the cold suffered by poor people. Although they lived in comfort, they could appreciate the hardship of laborers. Your Majesty, why don't you feel cold?" Duke Jing replied, "You are right. I know what to do then." Duke Jing then started to give food, warm clothes, and shelter to poor people in his state.

Yan Ying lived in an old run-down house. Duke Jing told Yan Ying, "Your dilapidated house does not match your status as a prime minister. Let me build a grand house for you." Yan Ying rejected the offer, saying, "This is a legacy of my ancestors. I am satisfied with it. By the way, since it is inside the market, I can easily do shopping." Duke Jing then switched the topic of conversation and said, "Since you live in the market, you must be familiar with prices of goods." Yan Ying replied, "Yes." Duke Jing then asked, "Can you tell me which goods have risen in price and which have fallen?" Yan Ying replied, "Prosthetic legs have risen in price, and shoes have fallen in price." Duke Jing was stunned and embarrassed by Yan Ying's answer. For many years, Duke Jing had imposed severe punishments on his people. One of the punishments was the dismembering of legs. Yan Ying subtly mentioned this exaggeration by saying that since too many legs had been chopped off, people did not need to wear shoes anymore. Instead, they needed more prosthetic legs. Duke Jing realized his mistake and immediately stopped the imposition of severe punishments.

Duke Jing later sent Yan Ying on a diplomatic mission. While Yan Ying was on his trip, Duke Jing quickly demolished Yan Ying's old house and houses in the neighborhood and relocated Yan Ying's neighbors. Duke Jing also built a grand house for Yan Ying. After Yan Ying returned home, he demolished the grand new house and replaced it with his old house. He also rebuilt houses for his neighbors and invited them back. He told the returning neighbors, "It is not the house that will give us auspicious fortune. It is the company of good neighbors that will be an auspice."

Yan Ying was also witty, as illustrated by the following well-known incident:

Yan Ying was sent as an envoy to the state of Chu (楚). Since Yan Ying was short, officials in the state of Chu looked down on him and tried to humiliate him. They asked Yan Ying to pass through a short gate instead of the normal tall gate to the city. Yan Ying refused to enter the city through the short gate, saying, "If my mission is to visit a country of dogs, I do not mind entering through a dog's gate. Now, I am visiting the big state of Chu. It is inappropriate to enter it through a dog's gate." The embarrassed guard then reluctantly opened the normal gate for Yan Ying. When the king of Chu met Yan Ying, the king noticed Yan Ying's shortness and asked in a humiliating tone, "Is there no worthy person in your country? Why did your king send you to see me?" Yan Ying answered, "In the capital of my state of Qi, there are so many people that, if they raise their sleeves simultaneously, the Sun can be blocked, and if they shed their sweat simultaneously, they can produce a rainfall. People there need to walk shoulder-to-shoulder and toe-to-toe. Why do you think that we do not have enough people?" The king of Chu then asked, "Why do they send you here, then?" Yan Ying answered, "The way my state assigns envoys is simple. We assign high caliber officials to great countries. We assign mediocre officials to lesser countries. We assign low quality officials to visit worthless countries. Among my colleagues, I am of the lowest quality."

2. Mo Zi

Mo Zi (墨子, circa 470–391 BC, also known as Mo Di, 墨翟) was a prominent philosopher and a native of the state of Lu (魯國人) during the Warring States Period. He was the founder of the Mohist school of philosophy, which advocated universal and indiscriminative love (兼愛), non-offensive warfare (非攻), and other teachings.

The ancestor of Mo Zi was a member of the royal family of the monarch in the Shang Dynasty. Over many decades, the social status of his ancestors declined, and his father was reduced to be a common peasant. The young Mo Di had been a shepherd boy, a carpenter, and a mechanic. He later studied classics and philosophy under the Confucian school. However, he later criticized Confucianism for its over-emphasis on Zhou Li and extravagant funeral practices. He also criticized Confucians for their lack of respect for gods and spirits, divinity, and divine providence. He then founded a new school of thought, the Mohist school. The Confucian political philosophy tended to be teachings from the point of view of the ruling class and upper echelon of the society and accepted the reality of a monarchial political system in the Zhou Dynasty as given. Mo Zi's new school of political philosophy was based on the point of view of the proletariat. Although Confucians also thought that the people were the ultimate owner and master of the nation, Mo Zi went one step further, degraded the role of the monarch, and objected to the succession of the monarchy by inheritance. To Mo Zi, a competent and meritorious ruler of a country needed to be elected or selected from the grassroots. Mo Zi wanted to revert to ancient social structure during the Yao, Shun, Yu, and Xia Dynasties.

Mo Zi was once a minister of the state of Song (宋), but his tenor did not last long. He then traveled to many states to preach his philosophy. He succeeded in averting an invasion of the state of Cheng (鄭) by the state of Lu (魯), and another invasion of the state of Song (宋) by the state of Chu (楚). The king of the states of Chu planned to hire Mo Zi and enfeoff territories of a few hundred square miles to Mo Zi, who turned down the offer because the king was not serious about his doctrines.

Since Mo Zi's philosophy appealed to the grassroots, his school of thought became popular among common people. The Mohist school had many followers, who later formed an influential group against oppression by warring feudal lords. This group later developed into an organization of chivalrous bandits and warriors called Mohists led by a head called Ju Zi (矩子). The members of the Mohist organization abided by a strict code of conduct: selflessness, fraternity, loyalty, righteousness, bravery, and frugality according to the teachings of Mo Zi.

After Mo Zi died, the Mohist organization broke up into three competing branches, and their influence declined because monarchs felt threatened by reactionary Mohists. By the end of the Warring States Period, the Mohists receded to the state of Qin (秦) only, and by the beginning of the Han Dynasty (漢), they were banned by the Emperor of the Han Dynasty, who endorsed Confucianism.

The philosophy of Mo Zi can be summarized into ten topics:

(1) Indiscriminative love (兼愛)
(2) Against offensive warfare (非攻)
(3) Meritocracy (尚賢)
(4) Consensus and unity (尚同)
(5) Frugality (節用)
(6) Against extravagant funerals (節葬)
(7) Censorship of music (非樂)
(8) Objection to the belief of fate (非命)
(9) Respect of divine providence (天志)
(10) Belief in the existence of gods and spirits and respect of them (明鬼).

Mo Zi's concept of indiscriminative love originated from the Confucian concept of Ren. Both schools advocated that a person with Ren virtue would desire to do good to and to eliminate evil from the world. However, the two concepts had a fundamental difference. Mo Zi proposed that everyone should love other people as himself or herself, and this love should be indiscriminately applied, irrespective of their relationship, affinity, and affiliation with him or her. Benefiting others means benefiting oneself and hurting others means hurting oneself. Every person and every country should try to find win-win solutions to resolve conflicts. This philosophy is extremely idealistic and impractical although it has a noble and altruistic intention. Mo Zi thought that under such ideal, there would be no more conflicts, struggles, and wars, and the society will be peaceful. However, Confucians discredited this philosophy by claiming that, under Mo Zi's philosophy, one will not distinguish one's parents from the parents of another person, one's children from children of another person, one's spouse from the spouse of another person, one's brother from the brother of another person, one's clan from another clan, one's country from another country, and so on. To Confucians, this means that the concepts of parent, children, sibling, spouse, clan, relative, and country and all social relationships are irrelevant and nullified, and therefore, the society will be chaotic. Confucians then argue that such a philosophy will lead to a social structure of animals, not of human beings. This was why Mencius criticized Mohists as animals.

Mo Zi was against the invasion of another country without a solidly righteous reason. However, he endorsed the building of strong defense against invaders.

Mo Zi thought that governments should be run by competent and meritorious people, who should be selected, appointed (or even elected) irrespective of their background and social status. He even suggested that the choice of a ruler should be based on his competence and merits and not on nepotism and inheritance. He stressed that government officials should not remain powerful and revered forever and lowly people should not be stuck in the low class forever. These ideas on governance and social mobility were quite revolutionary in his time. Although Confucians also preached the appointment of competent and meritorious people to government offices by the ruler, they were not as advanced as Mohists in this regard. Confucians interpreted Mo Zi's ideas as rebellious to the sovereign since Mo Zi suggested that even the ruler should be chosen from a pool of competent and meritorious persons. During the ancient times of Yao, Shun, and Yu, the choice of a ruler was indeed based on his competency and merit, and not on inheritance. Mo Zi was brave enough to point this out. Yet, Confucians dared not go against the prevailing political establishment in their times, and pragmatically took the aristocratic structure as given and hoped to educate and convert the ruling class with their doctrines of Ren, Yi, and Li.

Mo Zi stressed the importance of consensus and unity in a government. Subordinates should agree with the boss and should not join gangs to oppose the boss. When the boss has made a hidden mistake or is negligent, his subordinates should help the boss to rectify his mistake. The boss should try to eliminate the grievances of subordinates. When a subordinate has done a good job, the boss should be aware of his contribution and award him. On the other hand, when a person has committed a crime, the boss should punish him. If a king follows this way to foster consensus and unity, he can then rely on the ears, eyes, mouths, hands, and minds of his staff to get things done.

Mo Zi endorsed frugality. He required his followers to live on simple necessities of life. He thought that extravagance and wastes were the main causes of the depletion of the coffers of a country.

Mo Zi considered that traditional practices of funerals were wasteful and unnecessary. The deceased should be buried in thrifty ways. Although Confucius also emphasized that the key element of a funeral ceremony was the mourning rather than the ritual, Confucians treat funeral and memorable vigils seriously. Mencius criticized the doctrine of frugality when applied to the administration of a funeral (see the discussion in Section 5 of Chapter 5).

Mo Zi considered that music was non-essential and did not help to cultivate virtues in a person and to promote a good culture in society. On the contrary, Confucius loved classical music and considered good music as an important means to promote a good culture in the society.

Mo Zi encouraged his followers to take their fates in their own hands. On the other hand, Confucius exclaimed a few times that he could not avoid his fate.

Although both Mo Zi and Confucians considered it necessary to observe and follow divine providence, Mo Zi went one step further. He wrote that whoever did not obey the will of Tian (Sky) would be punished, and whoever was obedient will be rewarded. Such punishment or rewards were real and unavoidable. Confucians do not go that far. They believe that Tian only helps those who help themselves.

Both Mo Zi and Confucians acknowledged the existence of gods and spirits. However, Mo Zi encouraged his disciples to know them. On the other hand, Confucius suggested that one should respect them but stay away from them.

3. Story of Yi Yin

Yu (禹, circa 2237–2139 BC) founded the Xia Dynasty (夏朝, circa 2184–1600 BC) in about 2184 BC. After about 500 years of the dynasty, the 16th successor to the throne was Emperor Jie of Xia (夏桀). His birthname was Lu Gui (履癸). He was an extraordinarily talented person. In addition to being a superb scholar, he was a great fighter with unusual physical strength. He could kill a tiger with his bare hands. However, he was the first tyrant in Chinese history. Years before Jie became Emperor, the Xia Dynasty had already declined substantially. Many feudal states had stopped paying tributes to the central government. Foreign tribes intruded into territories at the border. Class struggles were rampant, and wealth disparity was immense.

When Emperor Jie came to power, he hired and trusted many crooked ministers and got rid of many meritorious officials. Evil confidants taught Emperor Jie how to blackmail, rip off, torture, and terrorize people. As a result, the economy tanked, and the treasury coffer was depleted. To make up for the deficit, Emperor Jie started to invade many smaller states and tribes to rob their land and wealth.

In the 33rd year of his reign, Emperor Jie invaded a tribe, You Shi Shi (有施氏), in the northeast of China (around modern-day Shandong Province). Unable to defend itself, this small tribe surrendered. They presented a large amount of wealth, precious goods, and many beautiful women as slaves and concubines to Emperor Jie. Among these women was Mo Xi (妹喜, also known as Mei Xi). This young girl was so beautiful and charming that the lascivious Emperor Jie was immediately enchanted by her. Having obtained such rare trophy, Emperor Jie agreed to withdraw his army.

Mo Xi told Emperor Jie that she was a foster daughter of the leader of the You Shi Shi tribe. She had admired the greatness of Emperor Jie for a long time and wanted to be his concubine. Emperor Jie made her the queen the next day.

Emperor Jie ordered the construction of a new, gorgeous palace especially for her. This palace had a tower so tall that it rose above the clouds and looked slanting from afar. This tower was called the Slanting Palace. Inside the palace was a grand bedroom, decorated with jade and ivory panels, and ornamented with gems. This room was called the Jade Terrace.

To quell her nostalgic sentiment, Emperor Jie organized troupes of thousands of beautiful dancers and musicians to perform her native music and dances. Emperor Jie ordered his servants to hang roasted meat on trees in the courtyard of the Slanting Palace. The amount of meat was so much that the courtyard was called the Meat Forest. Emperor Jie also ordered his architects to build a large pond to contain wine. This pond was so large that one could row a boat in it. Whenever Emperor Jie and Mo Xi came to the Slanting Palace, they were served with an abundance of gourmet food and entertained by dancers and musicians. After the gang was tired from dancing, they picked and ate meat from trees, jumped into the wine pond, and then drank wine until they got drunk.

Mo Xi had three weird amusements. She was amused by the sight of people who were drunk and drowned in the wine pond. She liked to wear hats made for men, and she was also amused by the sound of shredding and tearing up silk cloth. To please her, Emperor Jie brought in daily a hundred rolls of silk cloths and ordered his servants to tear up silk cloth in front of her. In ancient times, a roll of silk cloth cost more than the annual income of a common person.

Some meritorious ministers advised Emperor Jie to refrain from decadent extravagance. They were all tortured and killed. When Emperor Jie heard that his people hated him, his regarded the report as a rumor, saying, "This is just slander. I owned the whole country, like the sky owns the Sun. When the Sun in the sky vanishes, my country will vanish. Oh Sun, when will you vanish? I would like to vanish with you!"

Some historians have advanced a theory that Mo Xi did all these monstrous acts to revenge on the Xia Dynasty for the destruction of her motherland and native tribe.

Yi Yin (伊尹, circa 1649–1549 BC) was born in the era under the terrible reign of Emperor Jie. His real name at birth was unknown. The first word, Yi (伊), was derived from the Yi River (伊水), which ran through the village where he was born. The second word, *Yin* (尹), meant a government official. Some historians thought that this meant a prime minister, whereas some others considered it to refer to a low-level official. Therefore, his name referred to the government official who came from the Yi River.

Endnotes

His father was also unknown. There was a mystic folklore about Yi Yin's birth. His pregnant mother was a slave who was hired to pick mulberry tree leaves to feed silkworms. One evening, she dreamed of a god telling her, "Water will gush out under the big rock in the front yard of your home. Run toward east. Don't look back." The next morning, she noticed water gushing out under the rock. She immediately told her neighbors to escape. After she had run towards the east for a short distance, she became worried about her other relatives and friends, and looked back. By that time, the entire village was already flooded. Since she disobeyed the god's advice, she was drowned and became a hollow mulberry tree. After the flood had receded the next day, another slave woman discovered a newborn baby under a mulberry tree at the place where she was drowned. A slave woman brought the baby to the king of the tribe, You Shen Shi (有莘氏). This slave woman was the wife of the chef for the King of You Shen Shi. The king then ordered the couple to raise the baby, who was Yi Yin.

Yi Yin grew up in a slave family and therefore adopted the status of a slave. (Note: the status of a slave was for life, unless reprieved by a royal edict). However, being a slave did not deter his ambition and determination to learn. He learned the art of cooking from his foster father and perfected it. He also learned literature, classics, politics, military principles, and philosophy by himself. He was indoctrinated by political philosophies of ancient saintly kings, such as Yao (堯), Shun (舜), and Yu (禹). When he was a teenager, he was already a valuable servant in the royal family. In addition to being a chef for the royal family, he was also the private tutor of princes and princesses.

After a while, Yi Yin was not satisfied with his role as a chef only. He had an ambition to improve the messy country under the Xia Dynasty. Through his expert cooking art, he had the opportunity to befriend the King of You Shen Shi. Yi Yin tried to explain the philosophy of good governance of a country with analogies of culinary art. He tried to convince the king to rebel against Emperor Jie of Xia. However, the king was disinterested, partly because his state was too small, and Emperor Jie was a distant relative.

After a few years, the disappointed Yi Yin resigned from the post of the royal chef and told King of You Shen Shi that he wanted to become a peasant. The king approved his resignation. Before he became a peasant, Yi Yin's first stop was the palace of Emperor Jie of Xia. He became a slave chef in the palace where he was acclaimed for his culinary skills. Because of his skills, he had the opportunity to approach and befriend Emperor Jie and Mo Xi. Yi Yin tried to subtly educate Emperor Jie on the principle of good governance. However, Emperor Jie turned a deaf ear to Yi Yin's good advice. The disappointed Yi Yin left the palace and returned to a village in You Shen Shi and made a living as a peasant. While he was a peasant in the field, Yi Yin also preached his political ideology and philosophy to other peasants. His reputation spread gradually.

In the meantime, King Tang (湯) of the state of Shang (商) was ambitious to build his state. He was eager to recruit talented staff into his government and had heard Yi Yin's name. The curious King Tang then visited You Shen Shi informally. To find out how good Yi Yin was, he went covertly to the village where Yi Yin resided.

King Tang passed by the field in the village at noon on a hot summer day. He took a rest under a tree where many peasants were gathering and chatting. He saw a young man heading toward the group. This young man had an unusual appearance, bright eyes, and a strong and agile body. He carried a new plough, a yellow ox, and another black ox. As the young man passed the group, all peasants in the group waved their hands to the young man and yelled, "Come here, take a rest. We have reserved a space for you under this tree."

King Tang was impressed of the popularity of this young man and thought that he must be highly respected by his friends.

This young man sat next to King Tang, who broke the ice and asked, "Why do you put a sheet of sheepskin on top of the oxen?"

The young man replied, "You look very bright and educated. You can figure out the reason without my explanation."

King Tang said, "Excuse me for my stupid question. Can you please explain?"

The young man replied, "I use two oxen to pull a plough. If I beat one ox, it will step forward faster than the other ox, which will be pulled and feel uncomfortable. This is because my beating force is applied unevenly to the oxen. I place the sheet of sheep-skin on the oxen to spread the beating impact, so that the oxen step forward in tandem. In this way, the oxen will feel more comfortable."

King Tang said, "Good answer. I now understand that a good command comes from a smart commander, not from the beating. May I ask which ox is better, the yellow or the black one?"

The young man replied, "Both of them are good. The yellow ox has more strength, and the black ox walks faster." The young man then stepped away from the oxen and signaled King Tang to join him. The young man then spoke softly, "In fact, the yellow ox is better. I do not want the black ox to feel jealous. Therefore, I said both were as good."

King Tang was surprised and impressed with the answer of the young man. After the young man had left the group, King Tang asked the other peasants who this young man was. Other peasants said, "You don't know him? He is Yi Yin, our respectable sage!" Realizing that this young man had unusual wisdom and virtue, King Tang decided to visit the home of this man on the next day.

On the next day, King Tang visited the home of Yi Yin. After disclosing his identity, King Tang expressed his interest in hiring Yi

Yin, who instantaneously rejected the offer, saying, "I am just a simple peasant. I am not qualified to take a big official responsibility. By the way, my (foster) mother is already in her eighties. I need to take care of her. If I take your offer, I need to do my job wholeheartedly. I also need to fulfill my filial responsibility too. Filial piety is my top priority." Yi Yin's answer impressed King Tank further. Yi Yin was a person of superior integrity.

In the spring of next year, King Tang heard that Yi Yin's mother had impaired vision. King Tang personally traveled from his capital to Yi Yin's village and brought precious herbal medicine to cure Yi Yin's mother. For days, King Tang stayed in the shabby house of Yi Yin, where King Tang personally boiled medicine for Yi Yin's mother. King Tang stayed in the house for many days until Yi Yin's mother recovered.

A year later, Yi Yin's mother died of brain disease. King Tang arranged an elaborate funeral for her and personally attended the funeral. By then, Yi Yin was moved with King Tang's sincerity and agreed to work for him. However, Yi Yin told King Tang that he needed to observe the traditional three-year mourning period for his mother. He agreed to join King Tang after the mourning period was over.

Three years later, Yi Yin invited all his neighbors to a ceremony to officially welcome King Tang and to celebrate Yi Yin's new appointment as an official of the state of Shang. On the day of the ceremony, King Tang came with his ministers. However, King Tang did not announce any official appointment.

Yi Yin was deeply disappointed. On the next day, he asked an envoy of King Tang as to why no appointment was announced. The envoy replied that it was not the right time for Yi Yin to join the state of Shang. After further questioning, the envoy disclosed that the King of You Shen Shi did not agree to Yi Yin's joining the state

Endnotes

of Shang. Furthermore, King Tang had already made a marriage proposal to the daughter of King of You Shen Shi. Before the envoy left, he hinted to Yi Yin that, in the marriage proposal, King Tang had included a condition that the princess needed to bring her own servants and chefs to the palace in the state of Shang.

In fact, King Tang was interested in hiring Yi Yin. However, since Yi Yin had a slave status in the state of You Shen Shi, Yi Yin needed to obtain the approval from the King of You Shen Shi to join the state of Shang. Since the King of You Shen Shi objected to the release of Yi Yin, King Tang found a way to overcome the obstacle. Incidentally, the King of You Shen Shi was eager to marry off his teenage daughter to a good husband, and King Tang also liked the princess. Therefore, King Tang made a marriage proposal to the princess and tactfully included a condition that the princess must bring her own chef. Since Yi Yin had been her private tutor, mentor, and family chef, the King of You She Shi should welcome the idea of sending Yi Yin to the state of Shang to accompany and take care of his daughter.

Upon hearing the hint, Yi Yin went to see the King of You Shen Shi and proposed to join the group of servants to accompany the princess. Since the King of You Shen Shi was worried that his daughter was not used to food in another country, he agreed to send Yi Yin as a private chef of the princess.

This gave Yi Yin a great opportunity to join King Tang. After Yi Yin had arrived at the palace of King Tang, he expected to receive an official appointment from King Tang. However, the appointment did not come for months. Yi Yin still had to work in the kitchen. In fact, King Tang wanted to further observe Yi Yin to make sure that he was not an imposter, hypocrite, or just a theorist.

The impatient and frustrated Yi Yin devised a tactic to approach King Tang. One evening, King Tang ate dinner with his wife and other family members. The dishes for that dinner were surprisingly unpalatable. The upset King Tang then summoned the chef who cooked those disgusting dishes. It was Yi Yin who deliberately prepared those dishes. Having a great opportunity to approach King Tank, Yi Yin hurriedly carried all the cooking pots, utensils, ingredients, and spices to the royal dining hall. Yi Yin told the royal family the reason why previous dinners were delicious and why the last dishes were unpalatable. Step by step, Yi Yin demonstrated his culinary art. At the same time, he used his cooking steps as analogies for running a good government. For example, Yi Yin said, "You should not put too much or too little salt in the food. You just need to put an appropriate amount of salt. It is like running a government. You should not rule it too tightly or too loosely. You need to apply the appropriate level of control. Like cooking, some steps need to be taken prior to other steps. You need to sort out the priorities." King Tang was impressed with Yi Yin's demonstration and lecture and agreed with Yi Yin's political ideology.

Since that dinner, King Tang discussed with Yi Yin daily on governance and politics. King Tang was convinced that he had recruited the right aide. King Tang then appointed Yi Yin as one of the two prime ministers of the state. As a result, Yi Yin's status was elevated from a slave to a nobleman.

In ancient China, it was extremely important to worship Tian (Sky), Earth, and ancestors. The tribe, Ge (葛), lived next to the state of Shang. Ge Bo (葛伯), the leader of Ge, did not organize worship ceremonies. King Tang sent his envoy to reprimand Ge Bo, who responded, "My tribe is poor. We cannot afford to sacrifice an animal for the worship." King Tang then provided cows and lambs for Ge Bo's ceremonies. Instead of sacrificing these animals on the altar, Ge Bo ate them. King Tang then sent his envoy to reprimand Ge Bo, who responded, "My tribe does not have enough grain to eat.

Why should we waste these animals for the sacrifice to the gods?" King Tang then sent his own peasants to work for the Ge tribe and donated food to their elderly and poor people. Ge Bo intercepted the delegates on their way, stole the food, and killed the boy carrying the food. In response to Ge Bo's barbaric act, King Tang invaded Ge and killed Ge Bo. King Tang's invasion of Ge did not upset Emperor Jie significantly.

Yi Yin volunteered to be the envoy to be stationed in the capital of Xia so that he could collect more reliable intelligence on the Xia government. King Tang then prepared a large amount of tribute in the forms of gold, jewelry, cattle, silk, native produce, and a group of attractive women as gifts to Emperor Jie. After Yi Yin had presented these gifts, Emperor Jie asked Yi Yin, "Why did King Tang invade Ge?" Yi Yin replied, "We did that for the sake of your Majesty. Ge Bo had committed many crimes against laws laid down by you. We punished Ge Bo to maintain your power so that other feudal lords would learn to obey your order." Emperor Jie was then satisfied with Yi Yin's flowery answer. Yi Yin then asked Emperor Jie, "King Tang has assigned me to serve in your government. I am now at your disposal." Emperor Jie said, "You just hang around until I have found a meaningful role for you."

Therefore, Yi Yin stayed in the palace for three years waiting for an assignment from Emperor Jie. In the meantime, Yi Yin met Mo Xi, an old acquaintance. She had grown older a little and looked unhappy and disgruntled. Yi Yin successfully recruited her to spy on Emperor Jie and the government of Xia. Historians have advanced two theories as to why Mo Xi agreed to become a spy for King Tang. One theory hypothesized that Mo Xi, from the very beginning of her marriage to Emperor Jie, had planned to revenge on the Xia Dynasty for the destruction of her motherland and native tribe. She did all monstrous acts for many years since her marriage to ruin Emperor Jie. Therefore, she was glad to cooperate with Yi Yin. Another theory hypothesized that Emperor Jie brought back two beautiful and young girls, Wan (琬) and Yan (琰), from the tribe Min Shan Shi (岷山氏) after his conquest over the tribe. Since these two girls were more attractive and younger than Mo Xi, they had become new favorites of Emperor Jie. The estranged and jealous Mo Xi wanted to revenge Emperor Jie.

The recruitment of Mo Xi as a spy was a great achievement for Yi Yin during the three-year stay in the capital of Xia. Emperor Jie had, thus far, not assigned any role for Yi Yin, who then resigned and returned to state of Shang.

Yi Yin then told King Tang, "Emperor Jie is extremely decadent, and the Xia government was corrupt and messy. However, now is not the right time to revolt against Emperor Jie because the Xia Dynasty still had strong support from some feudal lords. We need to continue to build our strength covertly and wait for the right opportunity to revolt."

A few years passed by, and the Xia Dynasty continued to deteriorate. More feudal lords joined the camp of King Tang. Only three states, the state of Wei (韋, in modern-day Henan Province in China), the state of Gu (顧, in modern-day Shandong Province in China), and the state of Kun Wu (昆吾, in modern-day Henan Province in China) were die-hard supporters of the Xia Dynasty. While King Tang was preparing to invade the state of Wei, Emperor Jie heard about King Tang's plan. The Emperor then summoned King Tang to justify the invasion. Since King Tang was only a feudal lord in the Xia Dynasty, he had to comply with the summons. Upon King Tang's arrival at the royal court, he was immediately imprisoned by Emperor Jie.

Yi Yin immediately assembled a huge gift package, which included precious antiques, jewelry, gold, silver, jade, and many beautiful women to be presented to Emperor Jie to beg for the pardon of King Tang. Upon receipt of this gift, Emperor Jie was gratified and agreed to release King Tang.

The imprisonment of King Tang alerted the other feudal lords. Threatened by the tyranny of Emperor Jie, many feudal lords then joined the state of Shang to revolt against the Xia Dynasty. After hundreds of feudal lords had joined the alliance, King Tang decided to act. Yi Yin suggested to conquer the state of Wei first, followed by the state of Gu and the state of Kun Wu. In a short time, King Tang conquered all three states.

Yi Yin then suggested to King Tang to stop paying tribute to the Xia Dynasty to test Emperor Jie's reaction. The enraged Emperor Jie then raised an army from nine loyal tribes to punish King Tang. Emperor Jie's act inadvertently revealed the identity of Emperor Jie's supporters and the size of his alliance. To avoid immediate confrontation with Emperor Jie, Yi Yin suggested resuming the payment of tribute to the Xia Dynasty to buy time for the preparation for the final rebellion.

In one year, King Tang's alliance was ready to launch an attack on Emperor Jie. After many defections, Emperor Jie's army was overwhelmed by a big margin by King Tang's alliance. In a short time, the Xia Dynasty was toppled. Emperor Jie managed to escape to the wilderness. King Tang then founded the Shang Dynasty (商朝) in approximately 1600 BC.

Emperor Tang died in 1587 BC. Yi Yin became the prime minister and the guardian-teacher to the subsequent three successors to the throne. The fourth emperor was the young Emperor Tai Jia (太甲), who was a spoiled kid. He ignored the rules and laws laid down by his grandfather Emperor Tang. To teach Tai Jia a lesson, Yi Yin confined Tai Jia to a cottage next to the tomb of Emperor Tang. Tai Jia was asked to study books on governance and politics written by Yi Yin. Tai Jia was not allowed to leave the cottage until he repented. After three years, Tai Jia repented and wrote a confession of his past misbehaviors. Convinced that Tai Jia had sincerely repented, Yi Yin then welcomed Tai Jia back to the throne. Tai Jia later became one of the best rulers of the Shang Dynasty.

Yi Yin died in about 1549 BC at 100 years of age. He wrote many books on philosophy, politics, governance, and culinary art. His works inspired many philosophers in later centuries, such as Laozi (老子) and Confucius.

4. Story of Bai Li Xi

The following story is excerpted from *Shi Ji* (史記, *Records of the Grand Historian*) written by Sima Qian (司馬遷, 145–86 BC):

The family name of Bai Li Xi (百里奚, circa 725–621 BC) was Bai Li. Xi was his first name. He was a poor scholar during the Spring-Autumn Period. His good wife appreciated his rare talents and immense knowledge. She encouraged him to leave his poor village, Nan Yang, and look for an official job abroad. On the day of his departure, their family was almost void of food. His wife killed the only egg-laying chicken of the family to give him a good meal before his journey. However, since they had no firewood to cook the food, she took off the shutter bar of the door as firewood and burned it.

Xi spent the next few years roaming many states in the hope of finding an official job. He traveled to the states of Song and Qi but could not find work because he lacked a sufficient network. After spending all his pocket money, he had to beg for food and shelter for years in the state of Qi. In the meantime, war broke out and his wife and son left Nan Yang to become refugees. She therefore lost touch with Bai Li Xi for decades.

Endnotes

In the state of Qi, Xi was fortunate to meet a native of Qi, Jian Shu (蹇叔), who appreciated Xi because they had the same political vision. Xi and Jian Shu became good friends, and Jian Shu provided food and shelter for Xi. Later, Xi had an opportunity to find an official job in the state of Qi. Jian Shu dissuaded Xi from getting that job because the king's political status was shaky. It so happened that a coup occurred in the state of Qi soon afterwards and the king and many of his officials were killed. Xi was fortunate to have avoided that crisis. Xi then went to the capital of the Zhou Dynasty. Prince Tui (頹) of the Zhou Emperor loved oxen as pets. Since Xi had expertise in rearing oxen, he hoped to impress Prince Tui with his skill and find a job under Tui. However, Jian Shu dissuaded Xi again from working for Prince Tui. It also happened that a struggle for succession to the throne ensued and Prince Tui and all his aides were killed. Xi was lucky again to have avoided another disaster. Xi later got an offer from the king of the state of Yu (虞). Jian Shu again dissuaded Xi from taking this job again because Jian Shu thought that the king of Yu was unworthy. Having been unemployed for a long time, Xi was too eager to get that job and a good salary. He ignored Jian Shu's advice and became an official of the state of Yu.

The state of Jin (晉國) planned to invade the state of Guo (虢國), a neighbor and ally of the state of Yu. The army of the state of Jin needed to pass through the state of Yu to reach the state of Guo. The king of Jin gave many pieces of top-quality jade produced in Chui Ji (垂棘) and many thoroughbreds as presents to the king of Yu and asked for his permission to give way to the army of Jin. The king of Yu was a greedy person and intended to agree to the deal. Bai Li Xi objected to it for two reasons: (1) the state of Guo was a close ally, and the relationship between Guo and Yu was like lips and teeth; if the lips were gone, the teeth would be exposed and chilly, and (2) the state of Jin would conquer the state of Yu after the fall of the state of Guo. On the contrary, another minister, Gong Zhi Qi (宮之奇), said, "Passing so many valuable gifts is like throwing jewels away. Only stupid fools would do so." As a result, the king of the state of Yu agreed to give way to the army of Jin. In a short time, the state of Guo was conquered. Immediately after the conquest, the army of Jin turned around and invaded the state of Yu.

The state of Yu was conquered by the state of Jin. The king of Yu and all his officials, including Bai Li Xi, became captives. The king of Jin appreciated the competency of Xi and invited him to serve the state of Jin. Since Xi turned down the offer, he became a slave. In the meantime, Qin Mu Gong (秦穆公, also known as Duke Mu of the state of Qin) was about to marry the princess of the state of Jin. The king of Jin then sent Bai Li Xi as a slave servant to accompany the princess to the state of Qin. Xi detested such a humiliating arrangement and escaped to the state of Chu. He was later caught by guards at the border of the state of Chu.

Not knowing the background of Bai Li Xi, the king of the state of Chu made Xi a slave in charge of raising cattle. Qin Mu Gong had a great ambition to improve and expand his state. He heard about Bai Li Xi's talents and competency, and wanted to hire Xi by making him a big offer. An advisor of Qin Mu Gong said, "King Cheng of Chu must not be aware of the rare talent of Bai Li Xi. Otherwise, he would not have given Xi a lowly job of raising cattle. If we offer a large sum to the king of Chu to redeem Bai Li Xi from slavery, we will then alert the king of Chu about Xi's talents. We should just offer the prevailing market price of a slave, which is just five sheets of ram skin. This will then avoid the suspicion of the king of Chu." Therefore, Bai Li Xi was sold as a slave for five sheets of ram skin.

Qin Mu Gong personally received Bai Li Xi at the border of the state of Qin. Upon his arrival, Xi told Qin, saying, "I was an official of a fallen state. I do not deserve to be your official." Qin Mu Gong said, "It was the fault of the king of Yu, and not yours." Qin Mu Gong personally released Xi's bondage. The two then held a meeting for three days and nights, in which they spoke about governance and geopolitics. At the end of the meeting, Qin Mu Gong was so impressed with Xi that Qin Mu Gong immediately appointed Xi as his prime minister. At that time, Xi was already 70 years old. Xi then recommended his good friend Jian Shu to Qin Mu Gong, who also appointed Jian Shu as another minister.

In his role as the prime minister of Qin, Bai Li Xi was ardently devoted to his job, magnanimous to the people of Qin, and dedicated to re-building the civilization, economy, and army of Qin. He led a modest lifestyle and attended to the needs of the poor. He also made peace treaties with neighboring states. In a short time, the state of Qin lived in great peace and prosperity, and thus became a major hegemon. Qin Mu Gong also became a respectable and dominant leader among other feudal lords.

During one banquet inside the house of the prime minister, guests were entertained by singers and dancers. One old woman came into the banquet hall and begged to sing a song to the prime minister. That old woman was a cleaning lady in the laundry room. Looking at the pitiful eyes of that woman, Bai Li Xi gave her permission to sing a song. She then sang the following verse in a soft, touching, and sad tone:

"Bai Li Xi, worthy of five sheets of skin. On the farewell day, I cooked a chicken and burned the door shutter. You are now rich and noble. You have forgotten me.

Bai Li Xi, Bai Li Xi, your mother is already dead, buried in the south brook, her body in a jar, cremated with wood, pounded into ash."

Bai Li Xi walked to her side and enquired about the source of these words. To his surprise, she was his old wife. They had been separated for many decades. After Bai Li Xi's departure from home, she also left the village with her son and became a refugee roaming and begging from place to place. She had suffered terribly for many decades. She heard that Bai Li Xi had become the prime minister of the state of Qin. She then walked a thousand miles to look for her old husband (note: it was a heroic and almost impossible feat thousands of years ago). When she arrived at the capital of the state of Qin and the doorsteps of the estate of the prime minister, the guards beat her up and kicked her away repeatedly because of her dreadful appearance in rags. They thought that she must have gone insane to claim that she was the wife of the prime minister. At last, she sold herself as a slave to work in the house of the prime minister. She was then assigned to be a cleaning lady in the laundry department.

Bai Li Xi felt extremely regretful and apologetic. The two hugged and could not stop from crying. He immediately announced her to be his good old wife.

When Qin Mu Gong heard the story of this great lady, he sent her valuable gifts to her and congratulated her on her reunion with her husband.

When Bia Li Xi died, all men and women of the state of Qin wept, children stopped singing their folk songs, and farmers stopped pestling the grains.

This story is popular in Chinese operas and folklores.

5. Story of Bo Yi and Shu Qi

The following story is an excerpt from *Shi Ji* (史記, *Records of the Grand Historian*), written by Sima Qian (司馬遷, 145–86 BC):

During the Shang Dynasty (商朝, 1766–1046 BC), Bo Yi (伯

夷) and Shu Qi (叔齊) were two princes of the last duke of the feudal state of Gu Zhu (孤竹國). Bo Yi was the eldest brother, and Shu Qi was the youngest. Before their father died, Shu Qi was nominated to be his successor. Shu Qi abdicated his throne to his eldest brother, Bo Yi, and stressed that the eldest son should be the successor to the throne according to tradition. Bo Yi refused to accept out of the respect for his father's wishes, and both eventually renounced the throne and migrated to the territory of the state of Zhou (周). In the meantime, another brother was enthroned.

Later, Bo Yi and Shu Qi heard that King Wen of Zhou was a benevolent and magnanimous ruler. They planned to work for King Wen. However, King Wen died when they arrived at the state of Zhou. On the road, they met King Wu of Zhou (周武王), who was carrying the memorial tablet of his father on his way to invade the Shang Dynasty. Both Bo Yi and Shu Qi knelt in front of King Wu's chariot and begged King Wu not to invade the Shang Dynasty. They held up the chariot of King Wu and said, "You are waging a war before the burial of your father. Are you filial? You are trying to kill your emperor. Do you have Ren virtue?" Soldiers of King Wu tried to kill Bo Yi and Shu Qi but the chief commander of King Wu's army, Jiang Zi Ya (姜子牙), said, "They are righteous guys. Don't kill them." Therefore, Bo Yi and Shu Qi were let go.

King Wu eventually conquered the Shang Dynasty and founded the Zhou Dynasty (周朝). Bo Yi and Shu Qi refused to be subjects of the Zhou Dynasty and eat its food. They moved to the mountains and ate wild grass and fern leaves for food. They eventually starved to death. Before their death, they wrote a song, which included the following lyrics: "We went to the mountain, Shou Yang. We ate wild grass for food. He fights violence with violence. There is no end of his sin. The ancient saints are dead. We cannot find refuge in them. Alas, our deaths are near. Our lives are withering." The two ancient characters were regarded by Confucius to be model Jun Zis who had the Ren virtue.

6. Story of Qi Huan Gong and Guan Zhong

The Duke Xi of the state of Qi (齊僖公), a descendant of Jiang Zi Ya, died in 698 BC during the Spring-Autumn Period of China. He had three sons, Jiang Zhu Er (姜諸兒), Jiang Jiu (姜纠), and Jiang Xiao Bai (姜小白). The succession to the throne went to the eldest son, Jiang Zhu Er, who was later called Duke Xiang of Qi (齊襄公). Notoriously decadent and cruel, he committed incest by marrying his own half-sister after killing her husband, and his government was in a mess.

Having watched in horror the tyrannical acts of their elder brother, Jiang Jiu and Jiang Xiao Bai escaped to the state of Lu and the state of Ju, respectively. Duke Xiang of Qi was overthrown and killed by his cousin, Gongsun Wu Zhi (公孫無知). Two years later, Gongsun Wu Zhi was, in turn, killed by officials of Qi in a coup.

Jiang Jiu had a private tutor, Guan Zhong (管仲, 725–645 BC). Jiang Xiao Bai had a private tutor, Bao Shu Ya (鮑叔牙, circa 723–644 BC). Guan Zhong and Bao Shu Ya were good friends since childhood. Guan Zhong grew up in a poor family while Bao Shu Ya was born with a silver spoon in his mouth. Guan Zhong was brighter than Bao Shu Ya. They vowed that no matter which prince would become the successor to the throne, they would work for the same master.

Having heard the news that Gongsun Wu Zhi was killed and the throne was vacant, the two princes hurried home to grab the throne. Jiang Jiu was accompanied by Guan Zhong, and Jiang Xiao Bai was accompanied by Bao Shu Ya. By coincidence, the four persons met on the road to the capital of Qi. Guan Zhong was a good archer.

Endnotes

From a distance, he shot an arrow at Jiang Xiao Bai. The arrow hit Xiao Bai, who instantly fell on the ground and vomited blood. Believing that Jiang Xiao Bai was dead, Jiang Jiu and Guan Zhong slowed down their journey to the capital.

In fact, the arrow did not kill Jiang Xiao Bao; it only hit his belt. The smart Jiang Xiao Bao feigned to be killed by deliberately falling onto the ground and biting his tongue. The blood in his mouth was from his bitten tongue. After Jiang Jiu and Guan Zhong were out of sight, Jiang Xiao Bai sped up his journey to the capital and arrived there earlier than his brother.

When Jiang Jiu and Guan Zhong arrived at the capital, the throne was already taken by their opponent, Jiang Xiao Bai, who became the Duke Huan of Qi (齊桓公, also known as Qi Huan Gong). The incidence of the antagonistic encounter with Guan Zhong was still on Duke Huan of Qi's mind. He wanted to revenge and kill Guan Zhong. However, Bao Shu Ya dissuaded him, saying, "If you have the ambition to rebuild the state of Qi to greatness, I have the caliber to help you. However, if you have the ambition to conquer and rule the entire empire, only Guan Zhong has the caliber. For your own sake, you should treasure an extraordinarily talented person rather than killing him." Being a magnanimous person, Duke Huan of Qi agreed to pardon Guan Zhong.

Guan Zhong then became a strategic advisor of the government of Qi. However, Duke Huan did not trust him yet. Against the advice of Guan Zhong, Duke Huan of Qi waged a war against the small state of Lu (魯國). The disappointed Guan Zhong resigned from his job and stayed home writing books. As predicted by Guan Zhong, the Qi army was defeated badly by general Cao Sui (曹劌) of the state of Lu.

Recognizing his mistake of ignoring Guan Zhong, Duke Huan of Qi thought of recalling Guan Zhong but hesitated for losing face.

Bao Shu Ya showed to Duke Huan of Qi books on military principles, governance, law and order, agricultural science, political philosophy, people management, and so on written by Guan Zhong after his retirement. Duke Huan of Qi immediately realized that he would have missed a genius. Duke Huan of Qi invited Guan Zhong to the Golden Terrace in the palace, officially apologized, and appointed Guan Zhong to be the prime minister.

Duke Huan of Qi had an ambition to become the leader of all hegemons. Many small states supported Duke Huan of Qi. However, the neighboring state of Lu refused to join the alliance because of previous military confrontations with the state of Qi. Guan Zhong devised an ingenious plan to subdue the state of Lu. The state of Qi produced one kind of silk cloth called the "Qi Wan," whereas the state of Lu produced another kind of white silk cloth called the "Lu Gao." Guan Zhong asked Duke Huan of Qi and all government officials to stop wearing clothes made of Qi Wan and instead switch to wearing clothes made of Lu Gao. In a short time, the citizens in Qi all imitated the Duke of Huan and other government officials, and Lu Gao became trendy in the state of Qi. In addition, the government of Qi bought tens of thousands of rolls of Lu Gao from the state of Lu at an elevated price of three gold ounces per ten rolls. At such a lucrative price, peasants of Lu swamped to produce large quantities of Lu Gao and abandoned other crops. Factories in the state of Lu switched to weaving silk cloth made of Lu Gao and abandoned other products. In a few years, the citizens of the state of Lu became wealthy in terms of the amount of gold they earned. Duke Zhong of Lu was also happy with the tax revenue of his state, which benefited from the increase in exports of Lu Gao. However, since the farmland had become barren and the factories of other basic consumer goods were closed, the state of Lu had to rely on imports of food and basic consumer goods. Guan Zhong then declared a trade sanction against the state of Lu. Imports of Lu Gao into the state of Qi and exports of food and other consumer goods from the state of Qi to the state of Lu were prohibited. Farmers and factories of Lu Gao in the state of Lu were then stuck with a huge inventory of unsold Lu Gao, and mass bankruptcies and unemployment ensued. In addition, the shortage of food in the state of Lu led to huge inflation in the price of food and resulted in widespread starvation in the state of Lu. Duke Zhong of Lu had no choice but to beg Duke Huan of Qi for help and to agree to sign a treaty to support the state of Qi as the leader of all hegemons.

With similar ingenious stratagems of Guan Zhong, Duke Huan of Qi overcame resistance from many non-alliance states and became the leader of all hegemons in the Spring-Autumn period. In the 35th year of the reign of Duke Huan, he organized a large assembly of feudal lords at Kui Qui (葵丘 in modern-day Henan Province). Although Duke Huan was the de facto ruler of the Zhou empire, he still pledged loyalty to the emperor of the Zhou Dynasty and demanded the same from other allied feudal lords. Although historians and Confucians regarded Guan Zhong to be the best prime minister of that period, Mencius still criticized Duke Huan for his grab of power from the emperor of Zhou.

Guan Zhong was deeply thankful for Bao Shu Ya. Guan Zhong said, "In the past, I had given strategic advice to Bao Shu Ya. It sometimes turned out that my advice ruined him. He still excused my mistakes as bad luck. When my bosses fired me, Bao Shu Ya did not consider me to be incompetent. When I was hesitant to fight a war, Bao Shu Ya did not consider me to be a coward. He knew that I need to consider the well-being of my mother. After Jiang Jiu failed in his struggle against Jiang Xiao Bai, I was imprisoned. It was Bao Shu Ya who saved me from imprisonment and recommended a job for me. He knew that I had an extraordinary caliber. My parents gave birth to me, and nobody but Bao Shu Ya knows me."

When Guan Zhong was on his death bed, Duke Huan of Qi asked whether Bao Shu Ya was competent enough to be the prime minister. Guan Zhong said, "Bao Shu Ya is extremely upright and strict. Such character is excellent for self-control but could be over critical on people. You know, there is no fish in a clear pond!" Bao Shu Ya heard about this comment and laughed, "Guan Zhong considers truth more important than friendship in official matters. That is why I respect him so much."

7. Story of Jiang Zi Ya

Jiang Zi Ya (姜子牙, circa 1156–1017 BC) was born in a poor family. The Great Yu of the Xia Dynasty once enfeoffed the territory Lu (吕) to an ancestor of Jiang Zi Ya. The descendants of the ancestor grew to the tribe of Lu. Another ancestor was later enfeoffed the territory of Shen (申), whose inhabitants had the surname of Jiang (姜). Therefore, Jiang Zi Ya got his family name as Jiang. He was also called Lu Shang (吕尚) because he was born to the tribe Lu. After many centuries, only a few descendants retained their status as noblemen, whereas most had become common peasants. Therefore, Jiang Zi Ya's parents were common peasants.

When he was young, Jiang Zi Ya had been a butcher, a bartender, owner of a restaurant and bar, and a small businessman. He could barely make a living from all his trades. He had also been a junior official in the government of the Shang Dynasty (商朝). Disgusted with the corruption of the Shang government, he resigned shortly after. His wife divorced him because of his poverty and lack of future. Although he lived a hermit-like life until he was 70, he did not give up his aspiration to serve the country in a leadership role.

He diligently and relentlessly studied all subjects related to military affairs, politics, governance, philosophy, economics, classics, and so on. He kept waiting for an opportunity to be hired by a good leader until he was 72.

Jiang Zi Ya spent his spare time fishing on the riverside where he lived. He had a peculiar way of fishing. He used a short fishing rod and a short rope. Attached to the rope was a straight piece of bamboo stick, which was supposed to be a "hook." There was no fishing bait attached to the stick. The "hook" was a few feet above water. Neighbors who passed by laughed at him, saying, "You are wasting your time. Even if you sit here for hours, days, or hundreds of years, you will not catch one fish!" Jiang Zi Ya replied, "Yes, common people try to catch small fish. I try to catch big fishes, which are kings and emperors. I want fishes to bite my hook voluntarily without baits" (this has since become a famous idiom in the Chinese language, "Only the willing will be caught (願者上鉤)").

In the meantime, the state of Zhou (周) in the western part of the country had emerged in prominence in that region. It had a meritorious and benevolent ruler, Ji Chang (姬昌), who was called Earl Wen of Zhou and later, King Wen of Zhou (周文王). He remembered an ancient prophecy that his state would become an empire with the help of a great man. On one summer day, before he planned to take part in a hunting game, he sought a verdict from an oracle. The verdict said, "You will get an invaluable trophy today. It will not be a dragon, tiger, bear, or any wild animal. It will be a great man."

Earl Wen passed by the riverside while he was hunting on horseback and saw Jiang Zi Ya fishing without hook and bait. The curious Earl Wen then sat by the side of Jiang Zi Ya and asked about the peculiar method of fishing. Jiang Zi Ya noticed that Earl Wen was a prominent nobleman from his attire and thoroughbred. Jiang Zi Ya immediately used fishing as an analogy of ruling a country and fighting a war. His started with the theme that a ruler needs to get support from his people. If people like him, they will join, support, and die for him, without even asking. Earl Wen was impressed with Jiang Zi Ya's sermon and listened for hours. Earl Wen realized that he had met a sage—the "great man" in the ancient prophecy. Before sunset, Earl Wen bowed to Jiang Zi Ya and begged, "Could you be my tutor and foster father?" Earl Wen pulled close the thoroughbred and helped Jiang Zi Ya get on the horse. Earl Wen then walked the horse as if he was a bodyguard of Jiang Zi Ya.

Jiang Zi Ya then became the top strategic advisor to Earl Wen. With the assistance of Jiang Zi Ya, the state of Zhou grew in prominence and reach. Earl Wen then declared himself the King of Zhou and started a revolution against the Shang Dynasty. After King Wen died, Jiang Zi Ya assisted King Wu of Zhou (周武王) to fight against the Shang Dynasty under Emperor Zhou (紂王). Jiang Zi Ya was the chief commander of an army in the Battle of Mu Ye, in which Emperor Zhou was defeated.

After Emperor Wu of Zhou had founded the Zhou Dynasty, he enfeoffed the state of Qi to Jiang Zi Ya. The Duke Huan of Qi, who was the top hegemon in the Spring-Autumn period, was a descendant of Jiang Zi Ya.

After Jiang Zi Ya had become a nobleman and a prominent minister of the Zhou Dynasty, the ex-wife of Jiang Zi Ya begged to re-unite with Jiang Zi Ya. She was rejected by Jiang Zi Ya by a witty tactic. Jiang Zi Ya poured a cup of water onto the ground and asked her to re-collect water on the ground into the cup. If she could put the water back into the cup, she would be allowed to return home. Of course, she could not. This was the origin of the common idiom in the Chinese language, "It is impossible to re-collect poured water from a toppled cup (覆水難收)."

Jiang Zi Ya wrote the first book on military principles in ancient China and many texts on politics and government.

8. Story of Fu Yue

Fu Yue (傅說, circa 1335–1246 BC) was a great politician, militarist, and structural engineer in the Shang Dynasty (商朝). He was regarded by later generations as a saint. Confucius and Zhuang Zi (莊子) gave him high regard. He was the prime minister of Emperor Wu Ding (武丁, circa 1250–1192 BC), and a major contributor to the renaissance of the Shang Dynasty. His name at birth was unknown. Emperor Wu gave him the family name, Fu, meaning "assistance to the emperor." The personal name of Yue (happiness) was also given to him by the emperor to mean that the emperor was happy to have him as a prime minister.

There were two versions about the early part of his life. One version described him as a hermit living in Fu Rock (傅岩, in modern-day Shaanxi Province) at the border between the states of Yu (虞) and Gu (虢) near the North Sea. According to the description of the chapter about Fu Yue in the *Book of Classic History* (尚書·說命), there was a major road between the two states, and this road was bordering the rivers. To prevent the flood onto the road, local lords sent their slaves to build mud levees to retain the water. Fu Yue voluntarily joined the slaves and provided food to them. He later invented a new method to construct retention walls. Instead of piling up mud by hand, he recommended to first construct a hollow frame with wood planks, then ram the mud into the frame, and finally, pound the mud hard with big poles and hammers. After the mud had dried up and solidified, the entire structure was then carried to the riverbank and installed. This method not only saved time but also built more solid walls. His reputation spread because of this invention.

The second version, according to the *Annals of Spring-Autumn*, described him as a prisoner and a slave after being punished by some local lords because his invention threatened the lords' status. He was then forced to work as a slave in the project of building levees.

When Wu Ding was young, the Shang Dynasty had declined substantially. After he was enthroned, he desired to revive the country. During the three-year period of mourning for the death of his father, he did not talk to anyone. His ministers were worried that he had a mental problem. In fact, he grieved for the lack of talented ministers to help him. He told his minister that he was not competent and virtuous enough and did not want to commit to an erroneous policy. Therefore, he was silent during the previous years, thinking about how to rule the country well. According to the first chapter about the life of Fu Yue in the *Book of Classic History*, Wu Ding woke up one morning screaming in ecstasy and told his ministers that he had a dream. In the dream, Tien (Sky) told him that he would find a great sage who would help him rebuild his country and speak for him. Wu Ding then asked artists to draw the picture of the man in his dream. He then sent his staff to look all over the country for the person in the picture. They finally found Fu Yue in Fu Rock who looked identical to the man in the picture. Wu Ding met Fu Yue and said, "Can you counsel me day and night. Help me cultivate my virtue. To me, you are like a millstone to metallic utensils, a boat and ore in the river, and rain during a drought. Let the spring in your heart nourish my heart. If the medicine is not strong enough, a disease will not be cured. If one walks on bare feet, they will be hurt. I hope you can rectify me so that I can follow the teachings of my ancestors, be a great emperor, and bring peace to my people." Fu Yue said, "To cut a straight piece of wood, one needs to draw a straight line with a string. To become a great king, one needs to listen to good counselors. Without a doubt, I pledge to be your good counselor."

Another legend narrated that the officer in charge of the search for Fu Yue went to Fu Rock and identified Fu Yue to be the person in the picture. The officer brought Fu Yue to Wu Ding, who then described his dream and asked Fu Yue, "Tien (Sky) has bestowed you to me. Is it true?" Fu Yue replied, "Yes, I also had the same dream. In that dream, you held my hand and bowed." Wu Ding was exalted and immediate made Fu Yue his prime minister.

Some later scholars considered this story to be fictitious and made up by Wu Ding. They thought that Wu Ding once traveled around the country and met Fu Yue in Fu Rock. After many conversations together, they became good friends. Wu Ding greatly respected the talent and virtue of Fu Yue, and wanted to hire him as the prime minister. However, since Fu Yue was a slave, it was difficult to convince other ministers to accept Fu Yue as their leader. In the time of Shang Dynasty, people were superstitious. They worshipped gods and spirits and strongly believed in divine providence. Therefore, Wu Ding devised the story of his dream to bestow power to Fu Yue as if he were sent by Tien (Sky).

Fu Yue then assisted Wu Ding to rebuild the country and achieved great success.

In the *Book of Classic History,* the second chapter about the life of Fu Yue recorded some recommendations of Fu Yue to Wu Ding. These included: (1) the emperor should work for the people, not for his own wealth and pleasure, (2) the ruler should be fair and just, (3) an order issued rashly would bring shame and resistance, (4) more military spending would induce more wars, (5) glamorous garments and decorations were for awarding officials and would hurt the image of the emperor, (6) officials should be appointed based on capability and not on heritage, and official posts should not be inherited, (7) nobility titles should not be granted to wicked people but meritorious people instead, (8) one should think thoroughly before taking actions, but should not miss good opportunities, (9) boasting would miss good opportunities, (10) boasting about one's successes would lead to failures, and (11) the emperor should not feel ashamed to acknowledge and correct his mistakes. The most salient and frequently quoted saying by Fu Yue was: "Knowledge is easy, but practice is really difficult", or "It is easy to know these principles but difficult to put them into practice."

Fu Yue was one of the early and great political philosophers in Chinese history. A temple in his honor is still standing in Fu Rock in modern-day Shaanxi Province.

9. Story of Jiao Ge

Jiao Ge (膠鬲) was a national of the Shang Dynasty during the reign of Emperor Zhou (紂王). He started off as a hawker selling fish and sea salt and lived in poverty when he was young. However, through his business acumen, he gradually amassed a fortune and became the richest person in the country.

Near the end of Shang Dynasty, the empire was ruled by a brutal tyrant, Emperor Zhou (紂). He had a notoriously decadent and extravagant lifestyle. He spent a fortune on his grand pavilion, called the Deer Terrace (鹿台), on which he indulged in debauchery with beautiful and bewitching concubines, including the malicious Da Ji (妲己). He drank from ponds of wine and ate from forests of meat.

He ruled by brutality and terror. He invented a cruel method of torturing dissidents by tying them onto red-hot iron pillars. His concubine, Da Ji, was amused when she saw victims being fried to death by this cruel method. Emperor Zhou carried out this torture repeatedly to please Da Ji. His uncle and private tutor, Bi Gan (比干), once advised Zhou to stop his brutality. Bi Gan wrote that being a counsel of the Emperor, he had the responsibility to advise the emperor. He would rather die than keep his mouth shut. The enraged Zhou said to his other ministers, "I heard that a virtuous person's heart has seven holes. Let us verify whether Bi Gan's heart has seven holes." Zhu then ordered to cut out Bi Gan's heart alive to show to other ministers that Bi Gan's heart did not have seven holes.

Because of his tyranny, Emperor Zhou lost support of his people, including close relatives and good ministers. For example, Ji Zi (箕子) was another uncle of Emperor Zhou and his private tutor. Ji Zi repeatedly advised Zhou to stop his tyranny but failed to change him. Ji Zi then faked madness. He was imprisoned and enslaved by Emperor Zhou. Wei Zi Qi (微子啓) was Emperor Zhou's elder brother and a viscount. Wei disagreed with Emperor Zhou on his brutality, quit the royal court, and later became a turncoat.

Emperor Zhou was also a warmonger. He expanded his empire by invading many tribes in the east and southeast and captured hundreds of thousands of slaves from his conquests. However, years of invasion depleted the treasury coffers.

The state of Zhou (周) in western China was populated by a tribe in the Wei River valley. Because of fertile land, favorable climate, and a prudent government, this state emerged in prominence in that region. They had a meritorious and benevolent ruler, Ji Chang (姬昌), who was also called Earl Wen of Zhou. He fostered a culture of humaneness, reverence for the elderly, kindness to youth, and respect of knowledge and competency. He implemented policies to protect the underclass and peasants, focused on economic development, and introduced free trade. He ran a clean and lean government. He also promoted morality in society. He set a good example by his virtuous behaviors. The state of Zhou prospered as a result, and its people were happy. Many neighboring tribes joined the state or became its allies. During an official visit by Earl Wen to pay homage to Emperor Zhou of Shang, Emperor Zhou trapped, arrested, and imprisoned Earl Wen. When Earl Wen of Zhou was still a prisoner, he met Jiao Ge. When the treasury coffer of the Shang Empire was depleted due to years of war, Earl Wen suggested that Emperor Zhou borrow money from Jiao Ge. Because of his special role as a lender, Jiao Ge rose to prominence in the Shang government. Jiao Ge detested the tyranny of Emperor Zhou but kept his feelings secret. Jiao Ge believed that Earl Wen had the potential to overthrow Emperor Zhou and agreed to work for Earl Wen as a spy in the Shang government.

After Earl Wen returned home, he planned to overthrow the Shang Dynasty. He started to build an alliance with other feudal lords and states. They later called him King Wen of Zhou and supported him as their leader. King Wen of Zhou (周文王, 1152–1056 BC) died at the age of 97. His son, Ji Fa (姬發), also called King Wu of Zhou (周武王), was the successor. King Wu of Zhou formed an alliance to overthrow Emperor Zhou in 1048 BC. King Wu had two competent and virtuous assistants—his younger brother, the Zhou Gong (周公), as his prime minister, and Jiang Zi Ya (姜子牙, 1156–1017 BC, also known as Lu Shang, 呂尚, Jiang Tai Gong, 姜太公), as his strategic advisor and chief commander of army (see Section 7 of Endnote above).

When Emperor Zhou heard about King Wu's plan, he sent an envoy consisting of Jiao Ge, Wei Zi Qi, Bo Yi, and Shu Qi to the state of Zhou. Duke Dan of Zhou met with them and offered a high place to Jiao Ge in the future government and offered Wei Zi Qi the throne of the state of Shang and the right to worship ancestors of Shang after Emperor Zhou was overthrown. Both Jiao Ge and Wei Zi Qi agreed to be spies for the King Wu, but Bo Yi and Shu Qi refused. Later, when King Wu's army was advancing toward the capital, Chao Ge (朝歌), the capital of the Shang Dynasty, Emperor Zhou sent Jiao Ge to find out when King Wu's army would arrive. Jiao Ge met King Wu, who told Jiao Ge that the army of the alliance would arrive at Chao Ge in 15 days. Jiao Ge then reported his finding to Emperor Zhou.

The march to Chao Ge was interrupted by heavy rain and hazardous roads. Generals of King Wu asked him to pause until bad weather was over. King Wu told them, "We have to move on to reach Chao Ge by the deadline. If not, Jiao Ge will be killed by Emperor Zhou for reporting a false intelligence."

When Emperor Zhou heard about the approach of the army of King Wu, in haste, Emperor Zhou gathered a large army predominantly comprising of slaves who had been captured during previous conquests. When the two armies confronted each other at Mu Ye (牧野), many of Shang's soldiers, who were slaves and had no loyalty to the Shang Dynasty, turned back and fled. As regular soldiers and officers at the back of the Shang army tried to stop the desertion, the slaves turned against the regular officers of the Shang army and joined King Wu's army. Back in Chao Ge, Wei Zi Qi, and Jiao Ge staged a coup and captured all officials and generals who were loyal to Emperor Zhou. The desperate and horrified Emperor Zhou then escaped to Chao Ge, where he was pursued everywhere. He finally committed suicide by setting himself on fire on the Deer Terrace.

10. Story of Sun Shu Ao

Sun Shu Ao (孫叔敖, circa 630–593 BC) was the prime minister of the state of Chu (楚) during the regime of King Zhuang of Chu (楚莊王) in the Spring-Autumn Period. He was noted for water and flood management. His family name was originally Mi (芈), and the name of his clan was Wei (蔿). His father Wei Jia (蔿賈) was the Chief Commander of Army of the state of Chu. Wei Jia was involved in a political struggle and killed. His wife and son escaped the persecution and hid in the shore of the Wei River (淮河). Being escapees, Sun Shu Ao and his mother were destitute and needed to depend on financial support from friends. The family changed their names to Sun (孫) to avoid being recognized by enemies. Shu Ao (叔敖) was a personal name.

When Sun Shu Ao was young, he was kind-hearted. One day, while playing in the mountain, Sun Shu Ao saw a snake with two heads. He was frightened because superstitious villagers at that time believed that it was an extremely bad omen to meet a two-headed snake and one would die in a few days after seeing it. He killed the snake with a piece of stone and buried it in the ground. He went home in tears and told his mother, "I saw a two-headed snake today and I will soon die." His mother asked, "What did you do to it? Where is it now?" He replied, "I killed it. I later buried it so that nobody will see it again. Although I am going to die, I do not want other people to die." His mother told him, "Don't worry, son. Since you are so kind-hearted and care about other people, Tien (Sky) will bless you and you will not die." When Sun Shu Ao was growing up, he continued to develop his Ren virtue. He set his goal to help all people in the country.

At that time, flood control and water irrigation in the region round the Wei River were major problems for residents. After Sun Shu Ao has grown up, he participated in civil engineering projects to control and manage water by donating money and volunteering. He later became a project leader and successfully re-directed the water from the tributary Qi Si (期思) to irrigate the fields in Yu Lou (雩婁). The project solved major environmental and agricultural problems for the people in the region. Sun Shun Ao then became famous.

The prevailing prime minister Yu Qiu (虞邱) of the state of Chu heard about the achievement and competency of Sun Shu Ao. He recommended Sun Shu Ao to King Zhuang of Chu as the candidate for the next prime minister. King Zhuang then met Sun Shu Ao at the shore of a lake near the Wei River when Sun Shu Ao was vacationing there. After days of acquaintance with Sun Shu Ao, King Zhuang was convinced of Sun's capability and virtue and appointed Sun as his prime minister.

In three years, the state of Chu prospered and became one of the five hegemons during the Spring-Autumn period.

Although Sun received large awards from King Zhuang for great performance, Sun led a frugal life. He gave away most of his income to the poor and to water management projects. One day, Sun met an old sage, who told him, "I heard that there are three kinds of good fortune and three kinds of misfortune." Sun asked, "Can you please enlighten me?" The old man said, "Being in a high position will draw jealousy. Having great power will threaten your king and provoke his fear. Getting a large salary will invite grievance." Sun replied, "These do not apply to me. The higher my position is, the humbler I am. The more power I have, the more careful I am. The more salary I receive, the more I give to charity. Can I avoid these misfortunes by my behavior?" The old man said, "Good! Even Yao and Shun cannot do so."

During the banquet to celebrate the appointment of Sun Shu Ao to be the prime minister, an old man came, dressed in a white coarse cloth and hat as if he were joining a mourning vigil for the dead. Sun Shu Ao received the old man and said to him, "All my guests join this party to celebrate my appointment. Yet, you come here to mourn my death. Do you have anything to teach me?" The old man said,

Mencius in Modern Perspectives

"If you are arrogant in your top position, your people will leave you. If you abuse your power, you king will hate you. If you ask for endless raises of salary, misfortunes will come." Sun Shu Ao said, "Thank you for your advice. I will remember it." The old man said, "The higher is your position, the humbler you should be. The greater is your power and responsibility, the more careful you should be. The more salary you receive, the more you should resist greed." Sun Shu Ao replied, "I will remember your advice."

Sun Shu Ao died at the age of 38, but his achievement in water management projects has benefited people for millennia. Although he was the prime minister when he died, his family and descendants were poor because he gave away all his wealth to the poor. His family could not afford a decent coffin for him and his son needed to wear coarse cloth for the rest of his life.

References

1. Raymond K. Li, *Confucius Analects, A New Translation with Annotations and Commentaries,* (Bloomington, Indiana, iUniverse, 2020).

2. Raymond K. Li, *Sun Tzu's Military Principles*, *Applications to Business and Daily Life*, (Amazon Kindle Books, 2020).

Index

Of each pair of numbers associated with each item on the following list, the first number refers to the chapter, and the second number refers to the section in which the item appears.

Ai Gong (哀公) 3-2, 7-14, 12-8, 13-22, 14-38

Bai Gui (白圭) 12-10, 12-11
Bai Li Xi (百里奚) 9-9, 12-6, 12-15, Endnotes-4
Bao Shu Ya (鮑叔牙) 4-2, Endnotes-6
Bao Si (褒姒) 11-6
Battle of Gui Ling (桂陵) Introduction-2, 1-1, 1-5, 14-1
Battle of Ma Ling (馬陵) Introduction-2, 1-1, 1-5, 14-1
Bei Gong Yao (北宮黝) 3-2
Bi (費) 10-3
Bi Gan (比干) 2-3, 3-1, 11-6, Endnotes-9
Bi Hui Gong (費惠公, Duke Hui of Bi) 10-3
Bi Ying (畢郢) 8-1
Bi Zhan (畢戰) 5-3
Bin (邠) 2-15
Bo Fu (伯服) 11-6
Bo Yi (伯夷) 3-2, 3-9, 6-10, 7-13, 10-1, 12-6, 13-22, 13-42, 14-15, Endnotes-5
Book of Poetry (詩經) Introduction-4, 1-2, 1-7, 2-3, 2-5, 3-3, 3-4, 5-3, 5-4, 6-1, 6-9, 7-1, 7-2, 7-4, 7-7, 7-9, 8-21, 9-2, 9-4, 10-7, 11-6, 11-17, 12-3, 13-32, 14-19

Cai (蔡) 4-9, 8-21, 14-18

Index

Cai Shu (蔡叔) 4-9
Cao Jiao (曹交) Introduction-3, 12-2
Cao Sui (曹劌) Endnotes-6
Chang Xi (長息) 9-1, 10-3
Chao Ge (朝歌) 2-3, Endnotes-9
Chao Wu (朝儛) 2-4
Chen (陳) 14-18
Chen Dai (陳代) 6-1
Chen Jia (陳賈) 4-9
Chen Liang (陳良) 5-4
Chen Qin (陳臻, Chen Zi, 陳子) 4-3, 4-10, 12-14, 14-23
Chen Xiang (陳相) 5-4
Chen Xin (陳信) 5-4
Chen Zhong Zi (陳仲子) 6-10, 13-34
Cheng (鄭) 1-7, 8-24, 14-37, Endnotes-2
Cheng Gan (成覸) 5-1
Chong (崇) 4-14
Chong Yu (充虞) 4-7, 4-13
Chu (楚) 1-1, 1-5, 1-7, 2-6, 2-13, 5-1, 5-4, 6-5, 6-6, 8-21, 12-4, 12-15, Endnotes-1, Endnotes-2, Endnotes-4, Endnotes-10
Chu Zi (儲子) 8-32
Chui Ji (垂棘) 9-9, Endnotes-4
Chun Shen Jun (春申君) 7-6
Chun Yu Kun (淳于髡) 7-17, 12-6
Compassion (惻隱之心) 3-6
Cui Zhu (崔杼) 1-7

Da Ji (妲己) 2-3, 6-5, Endnotes-9
Dai Bu Sheng (戴不勝) 6-6
Dai Ying Zhi (戴盈之) 6-8
Dan Zhu (丹朱) 9-6

633

Dao (道) Introduction-4, 3-2, 3-4, 4-1, 5-1, 9-7, 11-16, 12-2, 13-5, 13-9, 13-13, 13-24, 13-26, 13-41, 13-42, 14-9, 14-16, 14-24, 14-32, 14-33

Declaration of Revolt (湯誓) 1-2

Deer Terrace (鹿台) 2-3, Endnotes-9

Di (狄) 2-11, 2-15

Die Ze (垤澤) 13-36

Doctrine of the Mean (中庸之道) Introduction-1, Introduction-3, Introduction-4, 2-5, 3-9, 4-2, 4-11, 8-7, 10-6, 12-6, 13-7, 14-37

Dong Guo (東郭) 4-2

Duan Gan Mu (段干木) 6-7

Duke Jing of Qi (齊景公, Qi Jing Gong) 2-4, 2-16, 5-1, 6-1, 9-8, 12-6, Endnotes-1

Duke Ping of Lu (魯平公, Lu Ping Gong) Introduction-3, 2-16

Duke Wen of Teng (滕文公, Teng Wen Gong) 2-13, 2-14, 2-15, 4-6, 5-1, 5-2, 5-3, 5-4, 13-43

Duke Xi of Qi (齊僖公) Endnotes-6

Eastern Zhou Dynasty (東周) Introduction-2, 1-1, 8-21

Emperor Jie of Xia Dynasty (夏桀) Introduction-2, 1-2, 2-3, 2-8, 3-2, 3-3, 6-5, 7-9, 9-6, 9-7, 12-2, 12-6, 12-9, 12-10, 13-21, Endnotes-3

Emperor Ku (嚳) 14-14

Emperor Li of Zhou (周厲王) 11-6

Emperor Ping of Zhou (周平王) 8-21, 12-3

Emperor Tai Jia (太甲) 3-4, 7-8, 9-6, 13-31, Endnotes-3

Emperor Wu Ding (武丁) Endnotes-8

Emperor Xin (帝辛) Introduction-2, 2-3, 3-3, 6-5

Emperor Yan (炎帝) Introduction-2, 3-8, 5-4, 12-2

Emperor You of Zhou (周幽王) 11-6, 12-3

Index

Emperor Zhou of Shang (紂王) Introduction-2, 1-7, 2-3, 2-4, 2-8, 3-1, 3-3, 4-9, 6-5, 6-9, 7-9, 7-13, 8-21, 9-6, 10-1, 11-6, 12-15, 13-22, 14-3, Endnotes-7, Endnotes-9
Emperor Zhuan Xu (顓頊) Introduction-2, 14-14

Fan (范) 13-36
Fan Li (范蠡) 2-3, 8-25
Fang Shu (方叔) 8-21
Fei Lian (飛廉) 6-9
Feng Fu (馮婦) 14-23
Four Virtuous Beginnings (四端) Introduction-4, 3-6, 11-6, 13-1
Fu Rock (傅岩) Endnotes-8
Fu Xia (負夏) 8-1
Fu Yue (傅說) 12-15, Endnotes-8

Gan (干) 8-21
Gao Yao (皋陶) 5-4, 13-35, 14-38
Gao Zi (告子) 3-2, 11-1
Gao Zi (高子) 4-12, 14-21, 14-22
Ge (葛) 2-3, 2-11, Endnotes-3
Ge Bo (葛伯) 2-3, Endnotes-3
Gong Du Zi (公都子) 4-5, 6-9, 8-30, 11-5, 11-6, 11-15, 13-43
Gong Hang Zi (公行子) 8-27
Gong Liu (公劉) 2-5
Gong Ming Gao (公明高) 9-1
Gong Ming Yi (公明儀) 5-1, 6-3, 6-9, 8-24
Gong Shu Zi (公輸子, Lu Ban, 魯班) 7-1
Gong Sun Chou (公孫丑) Introduction-1, Introduction-3, Introduction-4, 3-1, 3-2, 4-2, 4-6, 4-14, 6-7, 7-18, 12-3, 12-13, 13-31, 13-32, 13-39, 13-41, 14-1, 14-36
Gong Sun Yan (公孫衍) 6-2

Gong Yi Zi (公儀子) 12-6
Gong Zhi Qi (宮之奇) 9-9, Endnotes-4
Gongsun Wu Zhi (公孫無知) Endnotes-6
Good Fortune (福) 13-3
Great families (巨室) 7-6
Great Manifesto (太誓) 6-5
Great Valor (大勇) Introduction-3, 3-2, 6-1, 8-23, 10-7
Gu (虢) Endnotes-8
Gu (顧) Endnotes-3
Gu Sou (瞽瞍) 7-28, 9-2, 9-4, 11-6, 11-7, 13-35
Gu Zhu (孤竹國) 6-10, 7-13, Endnotes-5
Guan Shu (管叔) 4-9
Guan Zhong (管仲, Guan Yi Wu, 管夷吾) 3-1, 4-2, 12-7, 12-15, Endnotes-6
Gui Ling (桂陵) 1-1
Guiguzi (鬼谷子) 6-2
Gun (鯀) 9-3
Guo (虢國) 9-9, Endnotes-4

Hai Tang (亥唐) 10-3
Han (漢水) 5-4
Han (韓) Introduction-1, Introduction-2, Introduction-3, 1-1, 1-3, 1-5, 6-3, 13-11, 14-1
Han Dan (邯鄲) 1-1
Hao Jing (鎬京) 1-1, 8-21
Hao Sheng Bu Hai (浩生不害) 14-25
Happiness (樂) 13-3
History Book of the Warring State Period (戰國策) 8-20
Hou Ji (后稷) 5-4, 8-29, 14-14
Hu He (胡齕) 1-7
Hua Zhou (華周) 12-6

Index

Huai (淮水) 5-4
Huan Dou (驩兜) 9-3
Huan Tui (桓魋) 9-8
Huang Di (黃帝, Yellow Emperor) Introduction-2, 3-8, 5-4, 12-2
Huo Shu (霍叔) 4-9
Hymn of Lu (魯頌) 5-4

Ji (濟水) 5-4
Ji Chang (姬昌) 2-3, 6-5, Endnotes-7, Endnotes-9
Ji Fa (姬發) 2-3, 6-5, 7-7, 8-20, 10-4, Endnotes-9
Ji Huan Zi (季桓子) 10-4
Ji Kang Zi (季康子) 7-14
Ji Ren (季任) 12-5
Ji Sun Si (季孫氏) 6-7
Ji Wu Zi (季武子) 14-37
Ji Zi (箕子) 2-3, 3-1, 7-14, 11-5, 12-5, Endnotes-9
Jian Shu (蹇叔) Endnotes-4
Jiang Jiu (姜纠) Endnotes-6
Jiang Xiao Bai (姜小白) Endnotes-6
Jiang Yuan (姜原) 14-14
Jiang Zhu Er (姜諸兒) Endnotes-6
Jiang Zi Ya (姜子牙, Jiang Tai Gong, 姜太公) 1-7, 2-3, 2-4, 3-1, 7-13, 7-14, 12-5, 12-8, 13-22, Endnotes-5, Endnotes-9
Jiang Zi Ya (姜子牙, Lu Shang, 呂尚) Endnotes-7
Jiang Zi Ya (姜子牙, Tai Gong Wan, 太公望) 14-38
Jiao Ge (膠鬲) 3-1, 12-15, Endnotes-9
Jiao Xun (焦循) 8-26
Jin (晉) Introduction-2, 1-1, 1-5, 4-2, 6-1, 6-3, 6-7, 8-21, 9-9, 10-3, 11-17, 14-23, Endnotes-4
Jin Ping Gong (晉平公, Duke Ping of Jin) 10-3
Jin Wen Gong (晉文公, Duke Wen of Jin) 1-7, 12-7, 13-30

Jing Chou (景丑) 4-2
Jing Chun (景春) 6-2
Ju Long (句龍) 14-14
Ju Zi (矩子) Endnotes-2
Jun Zi (君子) 2-3, 12-3

Kai Feng (凱風) 12-3
King Cheng of Zhou (周成王) 4-9
King Fu Chai (夫差) 2-3, 8-25
King Gou Jian (勾踐) 2-3, 8-25
King Hui of Liang (梁惠王) Introduction-3, 1-1, 1-3, 1-4, 1-5, 14-1
King Kuai of Yan (燕王噲, Zi Kuai, 子噲) 4-8, 14-11
King Ping (周平王) Introduction-2, 1-1, 8-21, 12-3
King Tai (Gu Gong Tan Fu, 古公亶父) 2-5, 2-14, 2-15
King Tang of Shang (商湯) 1-2, 2-3, 2-8, 2-11, 3-2, 3-3, 3-4, 4-2, 4-12, 6-5, 7-8, 7-9, 8-20, 9-6, 9-7, 12-2, 12-6, 12-7, 13-30, 13-31, 14-4, 14-33, 14-38, Endnotes-3
King Wei of Qi (齊威王) 1-1
King Wen of Zhou (周文王) 2-3, 3-3, 5-1, 5-3, 6-5, 8-21, 11-6, 13-22, 14-19, Endnotes-7, Endnotes-9
King Wu of Zhou (周武王) Introduction-2, 1-7, 2-3, 2-4, 2-8, 2-10, 3-1, 3-2, 3-3, 4-9, 5-1, 5-3, 6-5, 6-9, 6-10, 7-7, 7-9, 7-13, 7-14, 8-20, 8-21, 10-1, 11-6, 12-8, 13-22, 13-30, 14-3, Endnotes-5, Endnotes-7, Endnotes-9
King Xiang of Liang (梁襄王, King Xiang of Wei) 1-6
King Xuan of Qi (齊宣王) Introduction-3, 1-7, 2-1, 2-2, 2-3, 2-4, 2-5, 2-6, 2-7, 2-8, 2-9, 2-10, 2-11, 4-3, 4-4, 7-17, 8-3, 10-9, 11-9, 12-5, 12-6, 13-33, 13-37, 13-39, 14-23
King Yan (宋王偃) 6-5
King You of Zhou (周幽王) 1-1, 8-21

Index

King Zhao of Yan (燕昭王) 4-8
King Zhuang of Chu (楚莊王) 12-7, 12-15, 13-30, Endnotes-10
Kong Ju Xin (孔距心) 4-4
Kuang Zhang (匡章) 6-10, 8-30
Kui Qui (葵丘) Endnotes-6
Kun Wu (昆吾) Endnotes-3

Lai Zhu (萊朱) 14-38
Lang Xie (琅邪) 2-4
Laozi (老子) Endnotes-3
Li Ji (禮記) 6-3
Li Lou (離婁) 7-1
Liao (繚) 8-21
Ling Qiu (靈丘) 4-5
Ling Zi (陵子) 6-10, 13-34
Listening Discerningly (知言) 3-2
Liu Xia Hui (柳下惠) 3-9, 10-1, 12-6, 13-28, 14-15
Long Zi (龍子) 5-3, 11-7
Lu (律) 7-1, 14-22
Lu (魯) Introduction-1, Introduction-2, Introduction-3, 1-1, 2-12, 12-16, 3-9, 4-7, 4-11, 5-2, 5-4, 5-5, 6-7, 6-9, 7-6, 7-14, 8-21, 8-31, 10-1, 10-3, 10-4, 10-6, 10-7, 12-6, 12-8, 12-13, 13-24, 13-36, 14-17, 14-25, Endnotes-2, Endnotes-6
Lu Ding Gong (魯定公, Duke Ding of Lu) 12-6
Lu Gui (履癸) 1-2, Endnotes-3
Lu Mao Shou (鹿毛壽) 4-8
Lu Mu Gong (魯穆公, Duke Mu of Lu, 魯缪公) 4-11, 10-6, 12-6
Luo (濼水) 5-4
Luo Yang (洛陽) Introduction-2, 1-1, 8-21
Luo Yi (雒邑) Introduction-2, 1-1, 8-21

639

Ma Ling (馬陵) Introduction-2, 1-1, 1-5, 14-1
Magnanimous Spirit and Character (浩然之氣) 3-2
Meng Ben (孟賁) 3-2
Meng Chang Jun (孟嘗君) 7-6
Meng Ji Zi (孟季子) 11-5
Meng Jiang Nu (孟姜女) 12-6
Meng Shi She (孟施舍) 3-2
Meng Xian Zi (孟獻子) 10-3
Meng Zhong Zi (孟仲子) 4-2
Mi (芈) Endnotes-10
Mi Zi (彌子) 9-8
Mian Ju (縣駒) 12-6
Min Shan Shi (岷山氏) Endnotes-3
Min Zi Qian (閔子騫) 3-2
Ming Tiao (鳴條) 8-1
Mo (貉) 12-10
Mo Qi (貉稽) 14-19
Mo Xi (妹喜, Mei Xi) Endnotes-3
Mo Zi (墨子, Mo Di, 墨翟) Introduction-1, 5-5, 6-9, 11-5, 13-26, 13-27, 13-45, 14-26, Endnotes-2
Mountain Chong (崇山) 9-3
Mountain Qi (箕山) 9-6
Mountain Yu (羽山) 9-3
Mu Pi (牧皮) 14-37
Mu Ye (牧野) 2-3, 6-5, 14-3, Endnotes-9
Mu Zhong (牧仲) 10-3

Pang Juan (龐涓) Introduction-1, 1-1, 14-1
Pang Meng (逢蒙) 8-24
Peng Cheng Kuo (盆成括) 14-29
Peng Geng (彭更) 6-4

Index

Ping Lu (平陸) Introduction-3, 4-4, 12-5
Ping Yuan Jun (平原君) 7-6
Prince Chu Jiu (杵臼) 1-7
Prince Dian (王子墊) 13-33
Prince Guang (光) 1-7
Prince Ping (太子平) 4-8
Prince Shen (申) 14-1
Prince Tui (頹) Endnotes-4

Qi (啟) 9-6
Qi (齊) Introduction-1, Introduction-2, Introduction-3, Introduction-4, 1-5, 1-7, 2-1, 2-4, 2-6, 2-10, 2-11, 2-13, 2-14, 3-1, 3-2, 4-2, 4-3, 4-4, 4-5, 4-6, 4-7, 4-8, 4-9, 4-10, 4-11, 4-12, 4-13, 4-14, 5-1, 6-1, 6-2, 6-5, 6-6, 6-9, 6-10, 7-7, 7-17, 7-24, 7-25, 8-21, 8-23, 8-27, 8-30, 8-31, 8-32, 8-33, 9-4, 9-8, 9-9, 10-1, 10-4, 12-5, 12-6, 12-8, 12-15, 13-33, 13-34, 13-36, 13-39, 14-17, 14-23, 14-29, Endnotes-1, Endnotes-2, Endnotes-4, Endnotes-6, Endnotes-7
Qi Huan (瘠環) 9-8
Qi Huan Gong (齊桓公, Duke Huan of Qi) 1-7, 4-2, 7-17, 11-7, 12-7, 12-15, 13-30, Endnotes-6
Qi Jing Gong (齊景公, Duke Jing of Qi) 2-4, 5-1, 6-1, 9-8, 12-6, Endnotes-1
Qi Liang (杞梁) 12-6
Qi Ling Gong (齊靈公, Duke Ling of Qi) 1-7, Endnotes-1
Qi Si (期思) Endnotes-10
Qi Wa (蚔蛙) 4-5
Qi Zhou (岐周) 8-1
Qi Zhuang Gong (齊莊公, Duke Zhuang of Qi) Endnotes-1
Qin (秦) Introduction-1, 1-1, 1-5, 4-8, 6-2, 6-9, 8-21, 9-9, 12-4, 12-15, Endnotes-2, Endnotes-4

641

Qin Mu Gong (秦穆公, Duke Mu of Qin) 9-9, 12-6, 12-7, 12-15, 13-30, Endnotes-4
Qin Zhang (琴張, Zi Zhang, 子张) 14-37
Que (缺) 8-21
Queen Shen (申后) 11-6

Ran Niu (冉牛, Bo Niu, 伯牛, Ran Bo Niu, 冉伯牛) 3-2
Ran You (然友) 5-2
Ren (任) 12-1, 12-5
Resolute, Undaunted, Incorruptible Heart (不動心) 3-2
River Cang Lang (滄浪) 7-8
River Han (漢水) 7-8
Ru (汝水) 5-4
Ryo (呂) 7-1, 14-22

San Mei (三苗) 9-3
San Wei (三危) 9-3
San Yi Sheng (散宜生) 14-38
Shang Dynasty (商朝) Introduction-2, 1-2, 1-7, 2-3, 2-4, 2-8, 2-11, 3-1, 3-2, 3-3, 3-4, 4-2, 4-9, 4-12, 5-3, 6-5, 6-9, 6-10, 7-7, 7-8, 7-9, 7-13, 8-20, 9-6, 12-7, 12-15, 13-21, 13-22, 13-30, 13-31, 13-39, 14-3, 14-4, 14-33, Endnotes-2, Endnotes-3, Endnotes-5, Endnotes-7, Endnotes-8, Endnotes-9
Shao Gong Shi (召公奭) 4-8
She (社) 14-14
She Ji (社稷) 14-14
Shen Nong (神農) 5-4
Shen Tong (沈同) 4-8
Shen Xiang (申詳) 4-11
Shen You Xing (沈猶行) 8-31

Index

Shen Zi (慎子, Shen Gu Li, 慎滑釐) 12-8
Shi Ji (史記, Records of the Grand Historian) Introduction-1, 1-5, 2-4, 12-10, 14-14, Endnotes-4, Endnotes-5
Shi Kuang (師曠) 7-1, 11-7
Shi Qiu (石丘) 12-4
Shi Zi (時子) 4-10
Shu Qi (叔齊) 3-2, 3-9, 6-10, 7-13, Endnotes-5, Endnotes-9
Shun (舜) Introduction-2, Introduction-4, 3-8, 4-8, 5-1, 5-4, 6-4, 7-2, 7-26, 7-28, 8-1, 8-19, 8-28, 9-1, 9-2, 9-3, 9-4, 9-5, 9-6, 9-7, 9-9, 10-3, 10-6, 11-7, 12-2, 12-3, 12-7, 12-10, 12-11, 12-15, 13-16, 13-20, 13-25, 13-30, 13-35, 13-46, 14-6, 14-24, 14-33, 14-38, Endnotes-3, Endnotes-10
Si (泗水) 5-4
Si Cheng Zhen Zi (司城貞子) 9-8
Si Ma Niu (司馬牛) 9-8
Sima Qian (司馬遷) Introduction-1, 1-5, 2-4, 14-14, Endnotes-4, Endnotes-5
Song (宋) 1-1, 4-3, 5-1, 6-5, 9-8, Endnotes-2
Song Guo Jian (宋勾踐) 13-9
Song Keng (宋牼) 12-4
Song Xiang Gong (宋襄公, Duke Xiang of Song) 12-7, 13-30
Su Dai (蘇代) 4-8
Su Qin (蘇秦) Introduction-1, 6-2
Sun Bin (孫臏) Introduction-1, 1-1, 14-1
Sun Shi (孫奭) 8-26
Sun Shu Ao (孫叔敖) 12-15, Endnotes-10

Tai Ding (太丁) 9-6
Tai Jia (太甲) 3-4, 7-8, 9-6, 13-31, Endnotes-2
Tai Shan (太山) 13-24
Tang (棠) 14-23

643

Tao Ying (桃應) 13-35
Teng (滕) Introduction-3, 2-13, 4-6, 5-1, 5-2, 5-3, 5-4, 6-5, 13-43, 14-30
Teng Ding Gong (滕定公, Duke Ding of Teng) 5-2
Teng Geng (滕更) 13-43
Teng Wen Gong (滕文公, Duke Wen of Teng) Introduction-3, 2-13, 4-6, 5-1, 5-2, 5-3, 5-4, 13-43
The Book of Classic History (書, Shu Jing, 書經) Introduction-4, 2-3, 2-11, 5-1, 6-5, 6-9, 9-4, 10-4, 12-5, Endnotes-8
The Book of Poetry (詩經) Introduction-4, 1-2, 1-7, 2-3, 2-5, 3-3, 3-4, 5-3, 5-4, 6-1, 6-9, 7-1, 7-2, 7-4, 7-7, 7-9, 8-21, 9-2, 9-4, 10-7, 11-6, 11-17, 12-3, 13-32, 14-19
The Book of Rites (禮記) 4-2
Tian (Sky, 天) Introduction-4, 1-1, 1-2, 2-3, 3-2, 3-5, 3-7, 4-3, 4-7, 4-8, 4-13, 5-4, 7-1, 7-7, 7-28, 8-21, 8-25, 9-1, 9-5, 9-6, 9-7, 10-1, 10-4, 11-6, 11-15, 11-16, 13-1, 13-2, 13-4, 13-5, 13-19, 13-20, 14-1, 14-14, Endnotes-2, Endnotes-3
Tian Ji (田忌) 1-1, 14-1
Tong (桐) 13-31

Wai Bing (外丙) 9-6
Wan (琬) Endnotes-3
Wan Zhang (萬章) Introduction-1, 3-2, 6-5, 9-1, 9-2, 9-3, 9-5, 9-6, 9-7, 9-8, 9-9, 10-3, 10-4, 10-6, 10-7, 10-8, 14-37
Wang Bao (王豹) 12-6
Wang Liang (王良) 6-1
Wang Zi Ao (王子敖, Wang Huan, 王驩) 4-6, 7-24, 7-25, 8-27
Wei (蒍) Endnotes-10
Wei (韋) Endnotes-3
Wei (魏) Introduction-1, Introduction-2, 1-1, 1-5, 3-2, 5-4, 6-3, 6-5, 13-11, Endnotes-3

Index

Wei Jia (蒍賈) Endnotes-10
Wei Zhong Yan (微仲衍) 3-1
Wei Zi Qi (微子啓) 2-3, 3-1, 11-6, Endnotes-9
West Earl (西伯) 7-13
Western Zhou Dynasty (西周) Introduction-2, 1-1, 8-21, 11-6, 12-3
Wey (衛) 8-31, 9-8, 14-18
Wey Ling Gong (衛靈公, Duke Ling of Wey) 9-8, 10-4
Wey Xiao Gong (衛孝公) 10-4
Wu (吳) 1-1
Wu (武) 8-21
Wu Cheng (武城) 8-31
Wu Cheng (武成)
Wu Geng (武庚) 4-9
Wu Huo (烏獲) 12-2
Wu Ling (於陵) 6-10
Wu Lu Zi (屋廬子) 12-1, 12-5

Xi (奚) 6-1
Xi Shi (西施) 8-25
Xia Dynasty (夏朝) Introduction-2, 1-2, 2-3, 2-4, 2-8, 2-11, 3-2, 3-3, 5-3, 5-4, 6-5, 7-2, 7-9, 7-13, 8-20, 8-29, 9-6, 10-4, 12-2, 12-7, 12-9, 12-10, 12-11, 13-20, 14-14, Endnotes-3, Endnotes-7
Xian Qiu Meng (咸丘蒙) 9-4
Xiang (庠) 5-3
Xiang (襄) 8-21
Xiang (象) 7-28, 9-2, 11-6
Xiao (校) 5-3
Xiao Pan (小弁) 12-3
Xiao Ren (小人) 2-3

645

Xie (契) 5-4
Xie Liu (泄柳) 4-11, 6-7
Xin Ling Jun (信陵君) 7-6
Xiu (休) 4-14
Xu (序) 5-3
Xu Bi (徐辟) 5-5
Xu Xing (許行) 5-4
Xu You (許由) 4-8
Xue (學) 5-3
Xue (薛) Introduction-3, 2-14, 4-3, 6-5
Xue Ju Zhou (薛居州) 6-6
Xun Yu (獯鬻) 2-3

Yan (燕) Introduction-3, 1-1, 2-10, 2-11, 4-8, 4-9, 4-10, 4-11
Yan (琰) Endnotes-3
Yan Chou You (顏讎由) 9-8
Yan Hui (顏回, Yan Yuan, 顏淵) Introduction-4, 3-2, 5-1, 5-2, 8-29, 13-1, 13-21
Yan Ying (晏嬰, Yan Zhong, 晏仲, Yan Zi, 晏子) 2-4, 3-1, 12-6, Endnotes-1
Yang (陽) 8-21
Yang Cheng (陽城) 9-6
Yang Huo (陽貨, Yang Hu, 陽虎) 5-3, 6-7, 10-4, 12-16
Yang Zhu (楊朱, Yang Zi) 6-9, 6-10, 13-26, 13-34, 14-26
Yangtze River (長江) 5-4
Yao (堯) Introduction-2, Introduction-4, 3-2, 3-8, 4-2, 5-1, 5-4, 6-4, 6-9, 7-1, 7-2, 7-28, 8-18, 8-29, 9-1, 9-2, 9-3, 9-4, 9-5, 9-6, 9-7, 10-1, 10-3, 10-4, 10-6, 11-6, 11-20, 12-2, 12-7, 12-8, 12-10, 13-19, 13-30, 13-35, 13-41, 13-46, 14-6, 14-14, 14-33, 14-37, 14-38, Endnotes-1, Endnotes-2, Endnotes-3
Yi (夷) 2-11

Index

Yi (益) 5-4, 9-6
Yi (羿, Hou Yi, 后羿) 8-24, 11-20, 13-41
Yi Qi (弈秋) 11-9
Yi Ya (易牙) 11-7
Yi Yin (伊尹) 3-2, 3-4, 4-2, 7-8, 9-6, 9-7, 10-1, 12-6, 13-31, 14-38, Endnotes-3
Yi You (宜臼) 11-6, 12-3
Yi Zi (夷子) 5-5
Yin (嚚) 7-28
Yin Dynasty (殷朝) 3-3, 4-9, 5-3
Yin Gong Tuo (尹公之他) 8-24
Yin Shi (尹士) 4-12
Ying (嬴) 4-7
Yong Ju (癰疽) 9-8
You Bei (有庳) 9-3
You Ruo (有若, You Zi, 有子) 3-2, 5-4
You Shen Shi (有莘氏) Endnotes-3
You Shi Shi (有施氏) Endnotes-3
You Zhou (幽州) 9-3
Yu (禹) Introduction-2, Introduction-2, Introduction-3, 1-2, 2-3, 3-2, 3-8, 5-4, 6-5, 7-9, 8-20, 8-29, 12-2, 12-7, 12-11, Endnotes-2, Endnotes-3, Endnotes-7
Yu (虞) 9-9, Endnotes-4, Endnotes-8
Yu Gong Zhi (庾公之斯) 8-24
Yu Lou (零婁) Endnotes-10
Yu Qiu (虞邱) Endnotes-10
Yuan Si (原思, Yuan Xian, 原憲, Zi Si, 子思) 8-31
Yue (嶽) 6-6
Yue (越) 1-1, 8-25
Yue Zheng Qiu (樂正裘) 10-3
Yue Zheng Zi (樂正子) 2-16, 7-24, 7-25, 12-13, 14-25

647

Yun Han of the Book of Poetry (詩經:大雅, 雲漢篇) 9-4

Zai Wo (宰我, Zai Yu, 宰予) 3-2
Zang Can (臧倉) 2-16
Zhang Yi (張儀) 6-2
Zhao (趙) 1-1, 1-5, 6-3, 14-1
Zhao Jian Zi (趙簡, Zhao Yang, 趙鞅) 6-1
Zhao Meng (趙孟) 11-17
Zhao Qi (趙岐) 8-26
Zheng Xi (曾晳, Zheng Dian, 曾點) 3-1, 7-19, 14-36, 14-37
Zheng Yuan (曾元) 7-19
Zheng Zi (曾子, Zheng Shen, 曾參) Introduction-4, 2-12, 3-1, 3-2, 4-2, 5-1, 5-2, 5-4, 6-3, 6-7, 7-19, 7-24, 8-31, 9-1, 12-13, 14-25, 14-36, 14-37
Zhi (摯) 8-21
Zhong Ren (仲壬) 9-6
Zhong Zi (陳仲子, Cheng Zhong Zi) 13-34
Zhou (周) 6-10
Zhou (晝) 4-11, 4-12
Zhou Dynasty (周朝) Introduction-2, Introduction-4, 1-1, 2-3, 3-1, 3-2, 3-3, 4-7, 4-8, 4-9, 4-12, 4-13, 5-1, 5-3, 6-2, 6-3, 6-9, 6-10, 7-7, 7-9, 7-13, 7-14, 8-20, 8-21, 9-4, 9-6, 10-1, 10-2, 10-4, 10-7, 11-6, 12-3, 12-7, 12-8, 13-30, 14-2, 14-3, 14-14, 14-33, Endnotes-2, Endnotes-4, Endnotes-5, Endnotes-6, Endnotes-7
Zhou Gong (周公, Duke Dan of Zhou, 周公旦) Introduction-4, 4-7, 4-9, 5-1, 6-9, 7-14, 8-20, 8-21, 9-6, 12-8, Endnotes-9
Zhou Li (周禮) Introduction-4, 4-7, 12-5, 13-39, Endnotes-2
Zhou Xiao (周霄) 6-3
Zhu Feng (諸馮) 8-1
Zhu Xi (朱熹) 8-26

Index

Zhuan Fu (轉附) 2-4

Zhuang (莊) 6-6

Zhuang Bao (莊暴) 2-1

Zi Chan (子產, Gong Sun Qiao, 公孫僑) 8-2, 9-2

Zi Du (子都) 11-7

Zi Gong (子貢, Duan Mu Ci, 端木賜) 3-2

Zi Lu (子路, Zhong You, 仲由) Introduction-4, 3-1, 3-2, 3-8, 6-7, 9-8, 14-18

Zi Mo (子莫) 13-26

Zi Sang Hu (子桑户) 14-37

Zi Si (子思) Introduction-1, Introduction-3, 4-11, 8-31, 10-3, 10-6, 10-7, 12-6

Zi Xia (子夏) 3-2, 5-4

Zi You (子有, Ran You, 冉有, Ran Qiu, 冉求) 5-4, 7-14, 8-23

Zi You (子游, Yan Yan, 言偃) 3-2, 4-11

Zi Zhang (子張) 3-2, 4-11, 5-4

Zi Zhi (子之) 4-8

Zi Zhuo Ru (子濯孺子) 8-24

Zou (鄒) Introduction-1, Introduction-3, 2-12, 5-2, 12-2, 12-5

Zou Mu Gong (鄒穆公, Duke Mu of Zou) 2-12

www.ingramcontent.com/pod-product-compliance
Lightning Source LLC
Chambersburg PA
CBHW082102250426
43661CB00079B/2546